T0336676

Migrating Legacy Applications:

Challenges in Service Oriented Architecture and Cloud Computing Environments

Anca Daniela Ionita
University "Politehnica" of Bucharest, Romania

Marin Litoiu
York University, Canada

Grace Lewis
Carnegie Mellon Software Engineering Institute, USA

Information Science
REFERENCE

Managing Director:	Lindsay Johnston
Editorial Director:	Joel Gamon
Book Production Manager:	Jennifer Romanchak
Publishing Systems Analyst:	Adrienne Freeland
Development Editor:	Monica Speca
Assistant Acquisitions Editor:	Kayla Wolfe
Typesetter:	Erin O'Dea
Cover Design:	Nick Newcomer

Published in the United States of America by
Information Science Reference (an imprint of IGI Global)
701 E. Chocolate Avenue
Hershey PA 17033
Tel: 717-533-8845
Fax: 717-533-8661
E-mail: cust@igi-global.com
Web site: http://www.igi-global.com

Copyright © 2013 by IGI Global. All rights reserved. No part of this publication may be reproduced, stored or distributed in any form or by any means, electronic or mechanical, including photocopying, without written permission from the publisher. Product or company names used in this set are for identification purposes only. Inclusion of the names of the products or companies does not indicate a claim of ownership by IGI Global of the trademark or registered trademark.

Library of Congress Cataloging-in-Publication Data

Migrating legacy applications: challenges in service oriented architecture and cloud computing environments / Anca Daniela Ionita, Marin Litoiu, and Grace Lewis, editors.
    p. cm.
 Includes bibliographical references and index.
 ISBN 978-1-4666-2488-7 (hardcover) -- ISBN 978-1-4666-2489-4 (ebook) -- ISBN 978-1-4666-2490-0 (print & perpetual access) 1. Systems migration. 2. Service-oriented architecture (Computer science) 3. Cloud computing. 4. Software maintenance--Management. I. Ionita, Anca Daniela, 1966- II. Litoiu, Marin. III. Lewis, Grace A.
 QA76.9.S9M45 2012
 004.67'82--dc23
                    2012026466

British Cataloguing in Publication Data
A Cataloguing in Publication record for this book is available from the British Library.

All work contributed to this book is new, previously-unpublished material. The views expressed in this book are those of the authors, but not necessarily of the publisher.

Editorial Advisory Board

Dan Ionescu, *University of Ottawa, Canada*
Gabriel Iszlai, *IBM Canada, Canada*
Philippe Lalanda, *University of Grenoble, France*
Hanan Lutfiyya, *University of Western Ontario, Canada*
Michele Missikof, *LEKS-IASI CNR, Italy*
Liam O'Brien, *CSIRO, Australia*
Massimiliano Di Penta, *University of Sannio, Italy*
Jerry Rolia, *Hewlett Packard Labs, UK*
Dennis Smith, *CMU Software Engineering Institute, USA*
Eleni Stroulia, *University of Alberta, Canada*
Nicolae Tapus, *University Politehnica of Bucharest, Romania*
Robert Woitsch, *BOC Asset Management GmbH, Austria*

List of Reviewers

Juncal Alonso, *TECNALIA, Spain*
Michael Athanasopoulos, *National Technical University of Athens, Greece*
Jose Delgado, *Instituto Superior Tecnico, Portugal*
Marisa Escalante, *TECNALIA, Spain*
Michael Gebhart, *Gebhart Quality Analysis (QA) 82, Germany*
Nicklas Holmberg, *Lunds University, Sweden*
Yanguo Jing, *London Metropolitan University, UK*
Ravi Khadka, *Utrecht University, The Netherlands*
Parastoo Mohagheghi, *SINTEF, Norway*
Leire Orue-Echevarria, *TECNALIA, Spain*
Dana Petcu, *West University of Timisoara, Romania*
Eric Richardson, *Chemical Abstracts Service, USA*
Juan Manuel Rodriguez, *ISISTAN, Argentina*
Eric Simon, *University of Grenoble, France*
Andreas Winter, *Carl von Ossietzky University, Germany*

Table of Contents

Section 1
Introduction

Section 2
Migrating to SOA Environments

Section 3
Migrating to Cloud Environments

Section 4
Migrating to Service-Oriented Systems:
Frontier Approaches

Detailed Table of Contents

Section 1
Introduction

This first chapter provides basic guidelines for understanding the migration to Service-Oriented Architecture and Cloud Computing environments, with references to book chapters where these issues are explored in detail. It analyzes the general context that led to the co-existence of three important needs: changing existing software, preserving legacy, and implementing a gradual migration. It also points out important aspects of migration for three types of targets: SOA, cloud environments, and service-oriented systems in general.

Section 2
Migrating to SOA Environments

This section contains literature reviews, research roadmaps, technical solutions, strategies, and practical experiences regarding the migration of legacy applications to SOA environments.

Even if service-oriented architecture represents a validated solution for integrating and leveraging legacy applications, the expectations related to it are sometimes unrealistic, and current research is not focused enough on the primary issues. Therefore, the first chapter of this section presents the research agenda for the maintenance and evolution of service-oriented systems, including tools, techniques, environments, multilingual issues, process reengineering, transition patterns, and runtime monitoring.

Chapter 3

Ravi Khadka, Utrecht University, The Netherlands
Amir Saeidi, Utrecht University, The Netherlands
Andrei Idu, Utrecht University, The Netherlands
Jurriaan Hage, Utrecht University, The Netherlands
Slinger Jansen, Utrecht University, The Netherlands

Taking into account the significant research results reported in the scientific literature during the last decade, the authors present a historical overview of approaches for migrating legacy applications to SOA systems, which bring advantages of portability, decoupling, and a high level of abstraction. Many details of this review are described, starting with its information sources and its strategies, and continuing with the evaluation criteria and the results that led to identification of best practices and open research issues.

Chapter 4

Harry M. Sneed, ANECON GmbH, Austria

While service-oriented architecture is able to support new business processes and the advantages that come with it, users would like to take advantage of the existing large volumes of legacy code and wrap it as Web services to avoid the high costs of developing from scratch. The chapter analyzes both business and technical issues regarding legacy reuse and modernization, inspired from real-life situations. It introduces selection criteria, transformation methods, tools, and lessons learned in three migration projects.

Chapter 5

Michael Gebhart, Gebhart Quality Analysis (QA) 82, Germany

Based on models of existing legacy systems and their business processes, it is possible to identify and specify the services required for migrating to SOA environments. This chapter uses Service-oriented architecture Modeling Language (SoaML) for describing service interfaces and components. It follows a rigorous approach for creating services, starting from analyzing the requirements and identifying services, and getting into details regarding message and data types.

Chapter 6

Juan M. Rodriguez, Universidad Nacional del Centro de la Provincia de Buenos Aires, Argentina
Marco Crasso, Universidad Nacional del Centro de la Provincia de Buenos Aires, Argentina
Cristian Mateos, Universidad Nacional del Centro de la Provincia de Buenos Aires, Argentina
Alejandro Zunino, Universidad Nacional del Centro de la Provincia de Buenos Aires, Argentina
Marcelo Campo, Universidad Nacional del Centro de la Provincia de Buenos Aires, Argentina
Gonzalo Salvatierra, Universidad Nacional del Centro de la Provincia de Buenos Aires, Argentina

Many business and government applications are still written in COBOL; meanwhile, the current trend is to adopt service-oriented and Web technologies for integrating large, distributed systems. Given this challenge, migration becomes the right answer, but there is more than one option. This chapter analyzes the performance and assesses the cost implications of three approaches applied for modernizing a government agency: a direct one, wrapping legacy code; an indirect one, redesigning and re-implementing Web services; and a third one, trying to combine the advantages of the first two.

Chapter 7

Andreas Fuhr, University of Koblenz-Landau, Germany

Andreas Winter, Carl von Ossietzky University, Germany

Uwe Erdmenger, pro et con GmbH, Germany

Tassilo Horn, University of Koblenz-Landau, Germany

Uwe Kaiser, pro et con GmbH, Germany

Volker Riediger, University of Koblenz-Landau, Germany

Werner Teppe, Amadeus Germany GmbH, Germany

It is clear that benefits can be obtained by adopting new technologies and, at the same time, by preserving the software assets validated by practice. Several state-of-the-art methods for reaching this objective are analyzed in the first part of this chapter. Among them, one outlines the horseshoe model, enriched by applying Model-Driven Engineering. This model is used for defining a complete migration process, which takes into account the entire life cycle, followed by presenting a customizable tool suite built for this purpose.

Section 3
Migrating to Cloud Environments

This section presents strategies, solutions, and experiments for migrating existing applications and data to Cloud environments, taking full advantage of the virtualization, scalability, and elasticity potential.

Chapter 8

Leire Orue-Echevarria, TECNALIA, Spain

Juncal Alonso, TECNALIA, Spain

Marisa Escalante, TECNALIA, Spain

Gorka Benguria, TECNALIA, Spain

The transition from off-the-shelf software to Software as a Service entails many business and technical challenges concerning security, scalability, and multi-tenancy, which cannot be solved by classical methods applied for migration to SOA environments. As a consequence, the first chapter of this book section comparatively analyzes the SOA architectural model and the SaaS delivery / business model. The chapter introduces a global strategy for migrating legacy applications to Software as a Service, which takes into account, besides technical issues, business-related phases such as evaluation and decision-making.

Chapter 9

Shreyansh Bhatt, DA-IICT, India

Sanjay Chaudhary, DA-IICT, India

Minal Bhise, DA-IICT, India

Migrating applications to environments that offer on-demand services also involves migrating data storages, which have to adopt technologies capable of supporting and accessing much larger volumes of data. As a response to this need, the authors provide algorithms for transforming legacy data, based on defining mappings between underlying source data schemas and the target data model, and passing through an RDF/RDFS intermediate model. Such algorithms are demonstrated and evaluated in the chapter.

Besides defining strategies and algorithms, best practices can often be discovered through empirical studies. Applying this principle, the authors of this chapter migrated a Web-based system to the Cloud, adopting two different platforms, Hadoop and HBase. They performed a quantitative analysis of the data storage performance and of the development effort. Criteria for selecting between these alternative solutions are discussed.

An application domain where Cloud environment potential still awaits to be valued is social networking, which undertakes a continuous progression and has to respond to new requirements. An example is sharing online content with colleagues and friends, for which existing products cannot offer enough scalability and synchronization capabilities. The chapter deals with this challenge by performing a gradual migration, first to a cluster of virtualized servers, then to a multi-server application in the Cloud, and finally to a geographically-distributed multi-cloud application.

Section 4
Migrating to Service-Oriented Systems:
Frontier Approaches

This section looks at the vision of service-orientation beyond SOA and Cloud, providing an insight on their connections with REST (Representational State Transfer) architectures and Service-Oriented Computing in general.

In distributed systems, interoperability is generally approached by concentrating on one of the following two concerns: behavior and state. The former is addressed in Service Oriented Architecture, while the latter is the focus of the Representational State Transfer (REST) architectural style. This chapter attempts reconciliation between the two concerns, presenting a model that relates resources, services, and processes. It introduces a hierarchy of architectural styles, and presents a structural service style that combines characteristics inherited from SOA and REST.

Chapter 13

Michael Athanasopoulos, National Technical University of Athens, Greece

Kostas Kontogiannis, National Technical University of Athens, Greece

Chris Brealey, IBM Canada, Canada

This chapter approaches a different kind of migration—adaptation of existing service-oriented systems to the REST style for increasing the potential of scalability and loose coupling. It describes a full adaptation framework that contains: a procedure-oriented API specification, adaptation configuration metadata, the RESTful Service Model, and the Dynamic Behavior Model, together with their generation processes, an intra-service protocol, and various policies.

Chapter 14

Eric Simon, Laboratoire Informatique de Grenoble, France

Jacky Estublier, Laboratoire Informatique de Grenoble, France

Migration, as part of system evolution, is based on administration-related actions. If only functionalities are of concern, it is possible to integrate heterogeneous artifacts as services. However, if integration includes application management, like in Cloud Computing, a consistent management of the artifact life cycle is required. A metamodel-based run-time platform is presented in this chapter for supporting such management, which considers multiple life cycle concerns, such as packaging, deployment, and selection.

Foreword

A service system is a system of systems that depends on distributed control, cooperation, cascade effects, orchestration, and other emergent behaviours as primary compositional mechanisms to achieve its purpose. A service system's purpose, structure, and number of components are increasingly unbounded in their development, use, and evolution. Service systems support the development of Web-scale service-based applications that are characterised by unbounded numbers and combinations of software-intensive, geographically dispersed, and globally available services.

Service-based applications are qualitatively different from traditional large-scale applications. They are typically realized by creating alliances between service providers, each offering services to be used or syndicated within other external services. They usually comprise aggregations of end-to-end processes that cross organizational borders and can deliver full or partial service application solutions on the Web.

Service development is continuously in flux. The pace of development has accelerated greatly due to the advanced requirements of service systems and the increasing complexity of application architectures (e.g., heterogeneous, virtualised, and increasingly cloud-based). The standardization of core Internet services (often called software or application, platform, infrastructure-as-a service) in conjunction with the advent of cloud technologies offers new possibilities for developing Web-scale service-based applications because of their flexibility and "on-demand" nature.

The foundation of Cloud Computing is the delivery of dynamically scalable and often virtualized resources that are provided as a service over the Internet to multiple external clients, while its focus is on the user experience. The essence is to decouple the delivery of computing services from their underlying technology. At its core, Cloud Computing is a service delivery model designed to help organizations procure and consume service-based solutions as needed, based on some metering and pricing scheme. It allows organizations to move costs from capital expenditures to operating expenditures while allowing them to become more flexible and service oriented. It is therefore obvious that both Cloud Computing and SOA share concepts of service orientation.

When we compare SOA with Cloud Computing solutions, we notice that SOA is a conceptual software architecture pattern, while the cloud can be viewed as a target deployment platform for that architecture pattern. In particular, Cloud Computing provides the ability to leverage on-demand new computing resources and platforms that SOA applications require but an organization does not own. In fact, we observe that Cloud Computing and SOA have important overlapping concerns and common considerations. The combination of Cloud Computing and SOA facilitates service deployment and collaboration with partners over the Web to deliver global SOA solutions to multiple clients across multiple geographic locations. Overall, we see different types of service providers (commercial, public, or community organized) that need to be considered when designing these Web-scale service-based applications.

It is precisely the nexus of service-oriented and Cloud Computing approaches and the migration of legacy applications to these environments that is being explored in this book. An important characteristic of service orientation is that it enables application developers to dynamically grow application portfolios by creating compound SOA-application solutions that inter-mix internally existing organizational software assets with external services that possibly reside in remote locations. So far, the development of service-based applications is still far from being fully achieved. It is mainly based on ad hoc and haphazard techniques. No effective, easy-to-use, focused methodological support is provided to assist in coping with many of the intricacies of flexible service provisioning. I am especially aware of the need to build this area on strong practical foundations. This book provides just such a foundation for software engineers, application developers, and enterprise architects.

You have picked up the right book for just about any topic you wish to learn about in legacy migration to modern computing environments and platforms. The editors of this book have brought together insights, best practices, and a variety of research approaches that address all aspects of legacy migration to service-oriented and Cloud Computing environments, including business drivers. They show how migration to service-oriented and Cloud Computing environments fits in the broader context of modern software application development.

This book covers an impressive number of topics and presents a wealth of research ideas, techniques, practical experiments, use cases, and strategies in relation to modern service provisioning that will excite any researcher (or practitioner) wishing to understand legacy migration to service-oriented and Cloud Computing systems. Important topics that are covered in this book include: re-engineering and wrapping techniques, integration, leverage and evolution of legacy systems, model-driven software migration and development, data migration to cloud environments, examining the trade-off between development/re-design effort, and performance/scalability improvements for cloud application development, collaborative cloud application development, and adaptation of existing service-oriented systems to a RESTful architecture. The book chapters are organized in three logical parts: Migrating to SOA Environments, Migrating to Cloud Environments, and, Frontier Approaches to Service-Oriented Systems.

It is pleasant to see that diverse and complex topics relating to legacy migration and service provisioning are explained in an eloquent manner and include important references to help the interested reader find out more information about these topics. All in all, this is an inspiring book and an invaluable source of knowledge for advanced students and researchers working in or wishing to know more about this exciting field.

I commend the editors and the authors of this book on the breadth and depth of their work and for producing a well thought out and eminently readable book on such a complicated topic.

Michael P. Papazoglou
European Research Institute in Service Science, The Netherlands

Michael P. Papazoglou *holds the Chair of Computer Science at Tilburg University. He is also the Executive Director of the European Research Institute in Service Science (ERISS) and the Scientific Director of the EC's Network of Excellence, S-Cube. He is also an Honorary Professor at the University of Trento in Italy, and Professorial Fellow at the Universities Lyon 1 (France), Univ. of New South Wales, and RMIT Melbourne (Australia), Universidad Rey Juan Carlos, Madrid, and Universitat Politècnica de Catalunya, Barcelona (Spain). He has acted as an Advisor to the EU in matters relating to the Internet of Services and as a reviewer of national research programs for numerous countries in Europe, for the Middle East and Asia, for the NSF* *and NSERC in North America, and the ARC in Australia. His research interests lie in the areas of service-oriented computing, Web services, business processes, distributed computing systems, large scale data sharing, and manufacturing execution systems and processes. He has published 22 books, monographs, and international conference proceedings, and well over 250 journal and international conference papers. He serves on several committees around the globe and is frequently invited to give invited talks and tutorials on service-oriented computing in international conferences. He is the editor-in-charge of the MIT Press book series on Information Systems as well as the founder and editor-in-charge of the new Springer-Verlag book series on Service Science.*

Preface

Future software development in a global environment, based on service provision, discovery, and composition, will be substantially influenced by two important areas: Service Oriented Architecture (SOA)—with a strong background in research communities—and Cloud Computing—with its Software as a Service component and mainly promoted by industrial players.

Generally, scientific literature that presents principles, methods, and tools for engineering service-oriented systems assumes that these systems are developed from scratch, even if this is rarely the state of practice. Because of economic and social constraints, preserving legacy systems is a necessity. Moreover, the adoption of newly developed systems for service provisioning may be costly in terms of money, time, and human resources. Therefore, experience has proved that a gradual transition is more efficient, and a well-conducted migration can have beneficial effects on the evolution of an organization.

Service Oriented Architecture (SOA) enables a system to respond easily to new requirements, and to assimilate new business services and new service providers while the business is developing. Services may be created for processing data, streamlining and reusing functionality incorporated in legacy systems, and integrating activities performed by multiple businesses or government partners. The SOA architecture supports a wide distribution of the deployed software artifacts. Agility and extensibility are increased with the use of services discovered at design time, or even runtime with the use of semantic technologies. SOA is meant to reduce system maintenance efforts and to prevent current and future integration problems via loose coupling between service providers and consumers implied by the composition of reusable and replaceable services.

Cloud Computing is emerging as a new computational model in which software is hosted, run, and managed in large server farms and data centers and provided as a service over the Web. Users of cloud services are exonerated from software licensing, installation, and maintenance, which would be necessary if the software was executed on their own computers. The dream of providing computing as a utility has been made easier by two emerging technologies: virtualization and Software as a Service (SaaS). Depending on the content of the service, a cloud can also offer Infrastructure as a Service (IaaS)—raw computing services such as CPU and storage, and Platform as a Service (PaaS)—COTS products, tools, and middleware for developing and deploying applications.

Migration to SOA and cloud environments can be challenging. From a SOA perspective, the challenges come from the nature of the legacy systems being migrated, as well as the characteristics of the SOA environment targeted for migration. Legacy system challenges include poor separation of concerns, tool availability, architectural mismatch, operational mismatch, and dependencies on commercial products. SOA environment characteristics can also create challenges for migration, including size of the service consumer community, internal vs. external service consumers, open vs. closed SOA infrastructure technologies, and legacy system operations. From a cloud perspective, the challenges include technology mismatch, calculating cost/benefit analysis, security, data privacy, and legal issues. However, the challenges in both cases have to be evaluated against the opportunities of system modernization, potential for serving a larger number of users, scalability, and systems interoperability and integration.

Chapter 1 of this book, "Introduction to the Migration from Legacy Applications to Service Provisioning," analyzes the global context that led to the major change in the ownership paradigm—the shift towards provisioning and consuming services—and to the need to make changes, yet preserve legacy, so to migrate applications gradually towards service orientation. The chapter offers a background for understanding the solutions, the research challenges, and the experiments presented in this book, pointing out some landmarks of migration to SOA environments, specifics of cloud environments, and an opening towards other approaches based on services. Hints for navigating through the book chapters are also provided.

After that, the book is organized in three more sections: Section 2, "Migrating to SOA Environments," Section 3, "Migrating to Cloud Environments," and Section 3, "Migrating to Service-Oriented Systems: Frontier Approaches."

MIGRATING TO SOA ENVIRONMENTS

This section contains literature reviews, research roadmaps, technical solutions, strategies, and practical experiences regarding the migration of legacy applications to SOA environments.

Chapter 2, "Research Challenges in the Maintenance and Evolution of Service-Oriented Systems," presents the research agenda of the domain, including current approaches, as well as challenges, gaps, and needs for future work. Five important topics are identified and analyzed: (1) tools, techniques, and environments to support maintenance activities; (2) multilanguage system analysis and maintenance; (3) reengineering processes for migration to SOA environments; (4) transition patterns for service-oriented systems; and (5) runtime monitoring of service-oriented systems. Chapter 3, "Legacy to SOA Evolution: A Systematic Literature Review" offers a historical overview of migration of business-critical legacy applications to SOA systems, based on platform- and language-independent interfaces and abstraction of underlying logic. The chapter describes the review protocol, including research question, data sources, search strategy, study selection strategy, data extraction, and data synthesis. It also presents the evaluation framework, followed by a discussion on findings, best practices, and open research issues. Chapter 4, "Reengineering and Wrapping Legacy Modules for Reuse as Web Services: Motivation, Method, Tools, and Case Studies," starts with an analysis of business and technical reasons for reusing legacy code and migrating to SOA environments. It focuses on transforming legacy modules into Web services, introducing selection criteria, and transformation methods and tools, followed by outlining the lessons learned in three modernization projects. Chapter 5, "Service Identification and Specification with SoaML," maps service design elements onto SoaML and describes the necessary steps for creating services: (1) requirements analysis – including data models, use cases, and business processes; (2) service identification – for fulfilling the necessary functionalities and aligning with business and with legacy systems; and (3) specification of service interfaces, messages types, and data types. Chapter 6, "The SOA Frontier: Experiences with Three Migration Approaches," deals with the set of registered Web Services that represent the frontier between consumer and provider. It presents three migration approaches that were applied for modernizing a government agency system written in COBOL: (1) wrapping for developing Web services; (2) redesign and reimplementation; and (3) an optimized combination. The assessment of cost and time required for performing refactoring and the discussion on service interface quality represent important contributions of this chapter. Chapter 7, "Model-Driven Software Migration: Process Model, Tool Support, and Application," analyzes the state-of-the-art regarding migration methods and selects one derived from the horseshoe model and enriched by extensively applying model-driven engineering. It introduces a four-phase process composed of preparation, conceptualization, migration, and transition, and presents a customizable tool suite supporting the migration.

MIGRATING TO CLOUD ENVIRONMENTS

This section presents strategies, solutions, and experiments for migrating existing applications and data to cloud environments, taking full advantage of the virtualization, scalability, and elasticity potential.

Chapter 8, "Moving to SaaS: Building a Migration Strategy from Concept to Deployment," analyzes the parallel between SOA as an architectural model, and Software as a Service as a delivery or business model. It questions the efficiency of applying approaches for migration to SOA to migration to SaaS, outlining shortcomings related to quality of service, security, configurability, scalability, and multi-tenancy. The chapter proposes a global migration strategy, from business to technology, with a first phase dedicated to evaluation and decision-making, and a second phase for implementation and service provisioning, ending with the presentation of a practical use case. Chapter 9, "Migration of Data between Cloud and Non-Cloud Datastores," considers the need to migrate legacy data, which accompanies application migration and also involves a transformation of the underlying schemas. It proposes an approach based on an RDF/RDFS intermediate model, with detailed mapping algorithms and their proofs, plus performance evaluation. Chapter 10, "Migrating a Legacy Web-Based Document-Analysis Application to Hadoop and HBase: An Experience Report," considers a lexical-analysis tool implemented in Ruby with SOAP4R Libraries as the source of migration, and two potential target solutions for data storage. The solutions are compared with respect to the development effort (e.g. lines of code and conceptual difficulty) and the method of performance (e.g. time required to construct indices and number of operations per minute achieved for representative services). It discusses criteria for selecting between solutions based on this comparison. Chapter 11, "Geographically-Distributed Cloud-Based Collaborative Applications," describes a triple transformation, first to a logical server as a cluster of virtualized servers, then to a multi-server application in cloud, and finally to a multi-cloud application with geographically distributed clusters in order to improve end-to-end latency.

MIGRATING TO SERVICE–ORIENTED SYSTEMS: FRONTIER APPROACHES

This section looks at the vision of service-orientation beyond SOA and Cloud, providing an insight on their connections with REST architectures and Service–Oriented Computing in general.

Chapter 12, "Bridging the SOA and REST Architectural Styles," introduces a hierarchy of architectural styles, and presents a structural service style that combines the constraints and the complementary characteristics inherited from Service-Oriented Architecture and Representational State Transfer (REST) styles. Chapter 13, "Considerations of Adapting Service-Offering Components to RESTful Architectures," considers the case of migrating legacy SOA applications to REST architectures, and defines a full adaptation framework accompanied by a process model. Chapter 14, "Model-Driven Integration of Heterogeneous Software Artifacts in Service–Oriented Computing," introduces a parallel between integrating legacy artifacts in Cloud Computing environments and integrating devices in Ubiquitous Computing environments using service-orientation principles such as separation between provider and consumer parts. Because the migration of a legacy application may represent a complex endeavor, there is also the possibility to reuse existent software artifacts and integrate them in a redefined service-oriented system. The approach aims to manage these reused legacy artifacts, proposing a platform that would allow their integration regardless of their original type, equally supporting iPOJO, WS-Spring, and UPnP, and having the possibility of extending to any service-oriented, component-based and service-oriented component-based systems.

TARGET AUDIENCE

The book assumes that its readers have a background in software engineering and basic knowledge of Service-Oriented Computing.

Areas of Interest

The goal of this book was to provide an opportunity for closer collaboration between the SOA and Cloud Computing communities and for identifying potential solutions to the challenges raised by current business environment dynamics. In addition, the goal was to offer an insight into related research originating from other approaches concerned with the migration of legacy data and applications to new, emerging technologies for comparing the experience gained in creating services, architectures, models, and methods.

Types of Professionals

Service-oriented systems bring together a large variety of stakeholders, including technical and managerial staff; in addition, educational programs at all levels are concerned with this topic in response to a growing occupational sector. This book targets professionals involved in developing, maintaining, or studying software based on services, including researchers, practitioners, as well as PhD students and university professors whose research areas pertain to services science.

Technical Levels

The main purpose of the book is to grasp the most advanced principles and techniques of migration to service provisioning by presenting state-of-the art strategies, roadmaps, methods, tools, and real-life and academic experiments. However, it is also important to cover all technical levels, from introductory to expert, so that each reader can navigate through the book to discover the large number and scale of issues related to reusing and migrating legacy systems and obtain answers appropriate for his or her particular expertise.

CONCLUSION

The endeavor of editing this book revealed that research on migrating legacy applications to SOA and Cloud environments is spread all over the world, both in academic and industrial organizations. This topic is often blended with reengineering and maintenance, but it emerges as a distinct, up-to-date concern, which has its own agenda, and whose future growth can be definitely foreseen. We hope this book will awake or meet your already existing interest in the achievements, best practices, and challenges of modernizing existing information systems by converting them to a service-provisioning paradigm.

Anca Daniela Ionita
University "Politehnica" of Bucharest, Romania

Marin Litoiu
York University, Canada

Grace Lewis
Carnegie Mellon Software Engineering Institute, USA

Section 1
Introduction

Chapter 1
Introduction to the Migration from Legacy Applications to Service Provisioning

Anca Daniela Ionita
University "Politehnica" of Bucharest, Romania

ABSTRACT

Despite the clear advantages of Service Oriented Architecture (SOA) and Cloud Computing environments, enterprises are strongly chained to their business tradition; they cannot easily give up to their legacy because they have made significant investments in the form of money, people, regulations, and technology. They see the advantages of migrating to a service provisioning architecture for adapting to new technology and business models, and for facing globalization challenges and change of ownership paradigms. At the same time, they realize that migration to SOA and Cloud Computing environments is a complex endeavor, requiring business reanalysis, code reengineering, automatic transformations, architectural changes, new strategies, well-defined methods, and, last but not least, assessment of economical impacts.

This chapter presents the fundamental ideas related to migrating legacy applications to service-oriented systems, and provides an overview of the available approaches that are presented in this book. The goal is to provide a "big picture" while also analyzing each chapter and indicating the way it covers several essential concerns, such as state-of-the-art, methods, standards, tools, business perspective, practical experiments, strategies, and roadmaps.

INTRODUCTION

Nowadays, the business landscape is profoundly influenced by changing ownership paradigms. On one hand, the complexity of software applications has continuously increased mainly due to incorporation of advanced technologies; this

phenomenon has critically required a "divide et impera" approach, leading to a wide distribution of resources, activities, artifacts, and projects. This distribution can be seen from several points of view:

- **Technical:** With the rise of the distributed processing era in 1990 (Greenfield, 2004);

DOI: 10.4018/978-1-4666-2488-7.ch001

Copyright © 2013, IGI Global. Copying or distributing in print or electronic forms without written permission of IGI Global is prohibited.

- **Managerial:** With the proliferation of multi-partner projects, or by outsourcing part of product development and services to third-parties;
- **Geographical:** Working with and for people worldwide, and relocating certain activities of business processes.

The degree of globalization continues to increase and has gone through three important stages (O'Brian, 2008):

- **International:** With foreign subsidiaries based on local information systems;
- **Global:** Including worldwide operations;
- **Transnational:** With central information systems supported by the Internet.

One can see that, apart from decomposing—sustained by the first part of the Latin maxim "divide"—there is an increasing need of the second part: "impera." This is expressed as new approaches and trends for sharing resources, connecting people, offering support for collaborative work, or managing software artifacts.

In this context, ownership is also much more distributed than before, requiring better specification of agreements between partners; interoperability support represents a priority for technical stakeholders. One way of dealing with these challenges is a shift towards service provisioning, based on advanced Information Technology (IT) infrastructures, platforms and software, as well as on a holistic approach that involves specialists from economy, engineering, social sciences, and arts (Donofrio, 2010). This trend is also influenced by an increase in the workforce in the service sector, which is valid for countries with various levels of development (Sporer, 2007).

However, enterprises are not in a hurry to give up to their legacy and abruptly switch to service-oriented systems. The main reason is economic because business processes cannot be suddenly modified and introduction of new technology has its costs. Therefore, it is more and more clear that

the transition towards completely new systems is rarely an option. Except for startups, it becomes vital for enterprises to reuse their legacy systems as application front-ends and back-ends. It is also important to do it in a gradual manner. Indeed, there are quick solutions for moving applications to run on Cloud infrastructures (Varia, 2010), but this is only possible under certain conditions: statelessness and decoupling from external agents. It is difficult to conform to the latter and, at the same time, stay aligned with current trends. Generally, the move towards service provisioning requires supplementary work for wrapping or completely reengineering existent code; buying new services, platforms or infrastructures; reanalyzing business requirements; and conducting a forward-engineering process with the constraint of reusing as much as possible.

This chapter introduces the background of migrating legacy applications in the larger context of software maintenance and reuse. After that, it presents an overview of approaches for migrating to Service-Oriented Architecture, Cloud Computing environments, and related service-oriented approaches. Finally, it analyzes several concerns regarding migration to service provisioning and indicates the book chapters where these concerns are covered in detail.

BACKGROUND

Why Do We Need to Make Changes?

As previously stated, software has to enable business operations in an environment characterized by globalization, increased competition, and mobility. This requires enterprises to rapidly adapt to changes in the business environment. However, the monolithic and highly coupled nature of many applications precludes them from responding to new functional and non-functional requirements. For attracting new customers and supporting a rapid growth, often based on mergers and acquisitions, the information systems used by enterprises should be able to adapt to new rules, regulations and policies; changes in operating conditions; and redesign of business processes. Therefore, maintenance continues to represent an important challenge, as discussed in detail in Chapter 2.

Software dynamics are still subject to Lehman laws (Lehman, 1997), including:

- "Continuous change" of requirements, environments and business rules;
- "Increasing complexity" of software systems;
- "Self regulation" determined by the domain specificity and the end-user community;
- "Organizational stability," judged as the transparency of the global, distributed management style;
- "Conservation of familiarity" needed by traditional users;
- "Continuing growth" of the back-end system; and
- "Declining quality" in the absence of proactive measures.

Why Do We Need to Preserve Legacy?

The development of completely new systems, adapted to the current trends, would involve complex development cycles, high costs, plus the need to maintain the old system during this endeavor. This represents an effort that cannot be supported by those who have already invested in their information systems and have trained personnel to work with them.

The need to preserve legacy contains multiple aspects that are common to the advantages of reuse: taking advantage of software that has been extensively tested in real life, reducing risk, preserving domain knowledge, and speeding up the process for reaching current business objectives. It often represents low-scale reuse, performed for creating a new version that is ready for reusing at a larger scale. Service orientation is considered among the most important reuse techniques, along with

libraries, program generators, configuration tools, product lines, or component based development (Sommerville, 2006).

Moreover, in order to create reusable entities out of existent assets, and preserve part of the legacy, it is often necessary to restructure the system. The need for reengineering for legacy migration is outlined in Chapter 4, and the differences between reengineering and migration are further analyzed in Chapter 7.

Why Do We Need to Migrate?

Software maintenance can have four possible goals:

- Corrective,
- Adaptive,
- Preventive, and
- Perfective (Lientz, 1980).

The first one concerns typical life cycles and does not relate to our concerns. However, all the other three are valid for transforming a monolithic legacy system into a service-oriented one because they concern the adaptation to a new environment—new infrastructure, platforms, or business rules. It can be considered as a method for preventing maintainability problems, which often involves radical changes such as reconsidering the software architecture. Last but not least, even if functionality or quality improvements are not explicitly planed, this kind of maintenance has a very clear goal of modernization, and many non-functional properties are changed.

According to the staged model of software lifecycle (Bennet, 2000), after the initial development, maintenance is composed of three phases:

- **Evolution:** When adaptation and correction are done without restructuring or substantial changes;
- **Servicing:** When patches and wrappers are introduced with the inevitable effect of damaging the architectural integrity;

- **Phase-out:** When it is only possible to work around for preserving the application in use.

The question is what place legacy migration has in such a lifecycle. Taking into account the versioned staged model (Bennet, 2000), one can create a new version for keeping the software in the beneficial stage of evolution, which can be accomplished by migrating the application to a service-oriented system. The new architecture can be preserved for a longer time and future changes can be delegated to lately bounded services, often replaceable and supplied by third parties. This can be done by adopting a SOA framework or a Cloud Computing environment, offering software, platforms or infrastructure as a service.

MIGRATION TO SERVICE PROVISIONING

A Framework for Migrating to SOA Environments

SOA is capable of solving problems of integrating software supported by heterogeneous platforms and of using various data formats, based on loose coupling between the assembled parts. The main reason is that a client is not directly connected to a service provider, but rather discovers the services that serve its needs and can then choose among similar offers, based on functions, semantics, and other properties such as Quality of Service (QoS), monitored during the system operation. A client can connect to its provider at runtime, and can also switch to another one dynamically. Besides, these services can be composed inside an application, using one of the following approaches:

- Orchestration, performed from a higher level of abstraction, generally by executing processes, or

- Choreography between business processes representing different parties (Peltz, 2003).

Building a service-oriented system, and gaining its benefits, is not a simple task. The "Cold Turkey" strategy, based on a sudden withdrawal of the legacy application and its replacement with a new one based on service provisioning, may disrupt business processes. Migration to services responds better to iterative, incremental approaches, as the alternative called "Chicken Little," which proposes to use gateways between the legacy parts and the new ones. These strategies are generic for migrating legacy information systems and were defined in the DARWIN project (Brodie, 1998).

Another important landmark for migration is the "Horseshoe Model," introduced for integrating software architecture and reengineering (Kazman, 1998). The three sides of the horseshoe are represented by the recovery of the legacy architecture, its transformation, and development based on the desired architecture. This model is described in Chapter 2, in a larger context of reengineering processes for migration to SOA environments, where various derived models are also discussed. An updated version, where the upper level is an enterprise model, was used for defining eight families of SOA migration, based on a systematic literature review (Razavian, 2010). Winter proposes another version of the horseshoe model, based on metamodeling (Winter, 2007), which is also adopted and applied in the process model described in Chapter 7.

Generalizing these approaches, one can conclude that the reverse engineering side is concerned with legacy system analysis, followed by restructuring and separation of reusable code, and ending with creating a model of the existent system (see Figure 1). The transformations may be conducted according to diverse strategies and methods, and with various tools, for producing a model of the service-oriented system. The forward-engineering side performs identification of service candidates and their specification, followed by implementation based on reusing legacy assets. Besides these reengineering concerns, one has to add elements that are specific to the SOA architecture, such as service registry and service discovery modules. If the architecture is more advanced, one can also take into account elements for service composition, run-time monitoring, security, and autonomic capabilities for service management (Papazoglou, 2007).

Figure 1 shows a mapping of the book chapters to the Horseshoe Model of migration, as follows:

- **Chapter 2:** Overviews these topics with a focus on identification of research areas;
- **Chapter 3:** Covers all these topics as well, presenting a systematic literature review on migration to SOA environments;
- **Chapter 4:** Covers the lower and the upper parts of the horseshoe; the model is not explicit, but it provides many practical details about analysis, separation of reusable code, and service identification and implementation;

- **Chapter 5:** Provides insight into service identification and specification, based on the SoaML standard modeling language;
- **Chapter 6:** Describes real life experiments of migration using three different methods, covering analysis and implementation topics and assessing the transformation effects;
- **Chapter 7:** Has a global coverage because it proposes a comprehensive migration process based on Model-Driven Engineering.

Specifics for Migrating to Cloud Environments

There are several aspects that separate migration to Cloud environments from migration to SOA environments:

- Cloud Computing intrinsically implies specific requirements such as virtualization, elasticity, reliability (Jeffery, 2010).
- Generally, Cloud Computing applications are intended to operate on a large scale; the number of users is not possible to predict

Figure 1. Mapping of the book chapters on the horseshoe model of migration

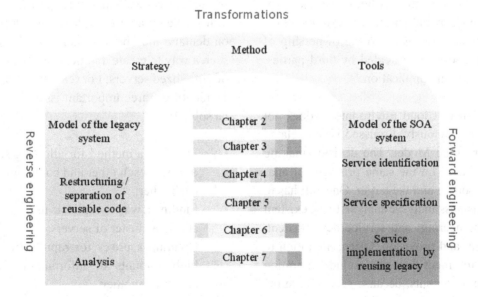

and therefore there is a need for elasticity and horizontal and vertical scalability.

- End-users can belong to different third parties that should work as if the software/platform/infrastructure is their own, creating the illusion of ownership for the employees belonging to a given tenant. This creates the need for multitenant architectures (Mietzner, 2009), as explained in detail in Chapter 8.
- Cloud solutions are more dependent on their specific provider and inter-Cloud interoperability is not a state of practice. There is ongoing research for decoupling application development from their deployment and execution environments, and using services offered by external Cloud providers (Petcu, 2011).
- Specific Service Level Agreements (SLAs) are necessary due to the flexibility of the delivery model and of the inherent variability in cloud; they have to be self-created and negotiated, based on a flexible pricing model, and the performance should be monitorable for technical adaptations and legal purposes (Chauhan, 2011).
- However, Cloud Computing does not propose a particular architecture but rather a delivery mode that pushes the service provisioning paradigm to an extreme. One might not only give up the ownership of certain services provided by third parties, but the entire application.

Migration to Cloud Environments does not exclude the previously discussed issues related to the Horseshoe Model. The decision-making process is based on the same principle of analyzing the source and the target. One still has to perform business analysis; analysis of the existent code; reengineering; and service development, deployment, and provision. Often, migration to Cloud environment does not exclude migration to SOA environments, because services are the main composition elements that require a mature architecture for being managed so that system coupling does not get out of control.

Before starting migration, alternative solutions for selecting new Cloud platforms have to be carefully evaluated with respect to business needs. For example, as shown in Chapter 10, the Apache Hadoop Distributed File System (HDFS) is good for "write-once-read-many" workloads, while HBase—a NoSQL database based on Google's BigTable—is better for random "read-write" operations. Apart from the platform, an important issue is also data migration, which generally constitutes an important legacy of the enterprise. An indirect transformation method can be applied, consisting of mapping the source database format (generally a relational one) to a standard intermediate format, and then mapping this to the target, schema free, document-oriented database, capable of handling large amounts of unstructured data assuring elasticity. An approach based on an RDF (Resource Description Framework) intermediate data model in explained in Chapter 9.

Even if Cloud Computing does not promote a particular architecture, migration to Cloud environments may also require major changes to the system architecture in order to take full advantage of scalability, virtualization, and autonomy. For instance, given a client-server application, a solution for being able to scale up and down based on demand may be to modularize the server in such a way to create a logical server as a cluster of virtualized servers. For realizing this, Chapter 11 identifies three important issues that have to be solved:

- Defining a method for allowing servers to discover each other and communicate with each other;
- Finding a way to replicate user information across a cluster of servers;
- Creating a proxy for rapidly transmitting high amounts of information from one server to another.

Apart from that, one has to add generic components specific to Software as a Service (SaaS), dedicated for billing, monitoring, security, and, eventually, an Application Programming Interface (API) for different Cloud providers.

From Legacy to Related Service-Oriented Approaches

The world has become service-driven—service sectors are continuously growing and they need to be supported by appropriate technology, methodologies, and policies. This has created an emergence of service-specific paradigms to cover all aspects of services:

- **Service Science (Spohrer, 2007):** As an integration of service-related areas such as management, marketing, operations, engineering, computing, human resource management, and economics;
- **Internet of Services (Cardoso, 2009):** As a business model and appropriate technologies for using the Internet as a means for delivering and consuming services at a large scale, in a similar way to its current usage for the World Wide Web;
- **Service-Oriented Computing (SOC) (Papazoglou, 2008):** As a manner of rapidly developing massive distributed applications, by composing services available over the network.

Some parallels between SOC and Cloud Computing are presented in Chapter 14, which proposes a platform for administration of new and legacy software artifacts. This chapter does not address the complete migration of an application, but rather the migration of its parts to reusable services. Migration of the application as a whole may have no efficiency, so an intermediate situation—between exposing the entire application in a service-oriented environment and rewriting it completely—would be to reuse some of its legacy components as services, which is also considered in SMART (Service-Oriented Migration and Reuse Technique), where criteria for assessing the candidates' reuse capabilities and a migration strategy are clearly defined (Lewis, 2008).

Another parallel can be made between the SOA and REST (Representational State Transfer) architectural styles, which are both commonly for interoperability in distributed systems. The former is oriented towards behavior, while the latter towards state and resources (see details in Chapter 12). The combination of them can be beneficial for dealing with Cloud Computing challenges. This opens a new migration trend—the adaptation of existing services to RESTful ones. An adaptation framework based on Model-Driven Engineering (MDE) for reengineering and horizontal transformations, followed by Service Component Architecture (SCA) for forward engineering, is presented in Chapter 13.

MIGRATION CONCERNS

Migration complexity leads to a need to analyze it theoretically, to perform research experiments, and to learn lessons from the best practices. Therefore, it has to be treated from multiple points of view to be able to capture the entire picture. Seven main concerns were identified within this book: the knowledge of the existing state-of-the art, the importance of choosing an optimal strategy, following a well-defined migration method, the availability of tools to support the entire migration life cycle, conformance to standards, lessons learned from practice, and pre- and post-migration business analysis.

State-of-the-Art

Migration to SOA environments is currently marked by well-defined methods, strategies and standards, plus a clearly drawn research roadmap; tools are generally borrowed from reengineering and model transformations. Migration to Cloud environments has inherited part of the knowledge gained from the experience of migration to SOA environments, but it clearly needs specific methods and tools for introducing architectural modules that enable virtualization and elasticity to leverage the application performance.

Strategy

The strategies intend to guide decisions that are made during the entire migration life cycle, starting with the analysis of motivation and potential benefits, and ending with the direct or gradual replacement of the legacy system. They may integrate points of view of the multiple stakeholders involved, including economists, project managers, software engineers, and experts in the application domain.

Methods

Migration methods are based on raising the level of abstraction, adapting conceptual aspects for supporting service orientation, then developing the new application based on the co-existence of services originated from the legacy code and new services, developed in-house or delivered by third parties.

Tools

Migration can be a very laborious task, which has triggered the development of tools that automate, or at least assist, certain steps of migration methods. Because service provision includes aspects of engineering and management, the landscape includes code reengineering tools, model transformers, modeling editors, code generators, configuration systems, and decision support environments.

Standards

Interoperability of SOA solutions has been a distinct focus of research and industrial communities. Many standards have been defined for service modeling, description, discovery, and orchestration. Important organizations that support some of these standards include the Object Management Group (OMG) and Organization for the Advancement of Structured Information Standards (OASIS). Cloud environments are currently more focused on individual producers, but migration can still take advantage of existing standards related to services. Interoperability between Clouds, even if far from reaching its maturity, has attracted activities of multiple organizations, like Distributed Management Task Force (DMTF), Open Cloud Consortium (OCC), The Open Group, etc.

Practice

There are two types of practical experiments: (1) academic case studies for assessing new methods and tools, and for creating a comparison framework; and (2) real-life projects that have to deal with their limited time and cost resources and outline new challenges for researchers. This book presents experiments from both categories for migration to SOA and Cloud environments.

Business

Business is the main driver for all migration efforts; it imposes non-functional requirements for software development and constraints for project management. A realistic estimation of the Return Of Investment (ROI) to create a well-founded business case are essential for choosing the right strategies, methods and tools. Alignment between business and IT concerns represents one of the current challenges.

Table 1 shows which of these migration concerns are addressed in each of the book chapters for benefit of the readers.

Table 1. Mapping of book chapters to migration concerns

Chapter No.	Chapter Title	State-of-the-art	Strategy	Methods	Tools	Standards	Practice	Business
1	Introduction to the Migration from Legacy Applications to Service Provisioning	Y	Y					Y
2	Research Challenges in the Maintenance and Evolution of Service-Oriented Systems	Y	Y					
3	Legacy to SOA Evolution: A Systematic Literature Review	Y		Y				
4	Reengineering and Wrapping Legacy Modules for Reuse as Web Services (Motivation, Method, Tools, and Case Studies)		Y	Y	Y		Y	Y
5	Service Identification and Specification with SoaML			Y		Y		Y
6	The SOA Frontier: Experiences with 3 Migration Approaches	Y		Y	Y	Y	Y	
7	Model-Driven Software-Migration: Process Model, Tool Support, and Application	Y		Y	Y		Y	Y
8	Moving to SaaS: Building a Migration Strategy from Concept to Deployment	Y	Y				Y	Y
9	Migration of Data between Cloud and Non-Cloud Datastore			Y			Y	
10	Migrating a Legacy Web-Based Document-Analysis Application to Hadoop and HBase: An Experience Report	Y		Y	Y		Y	Y
11	Geographically Distributed Cloud Based Collaborative Application	Y		Y			Y	
12	Bridging the SOA and REST Architectural Styles	Y	Y					
13	Considerations of Adapting Service-Offering Components to RESTful Architectures	Y	Y	Y		Y		Y
14	Model Driven Integration of Non-Homogeneous Software Artifacts in Service Oriented Computing			Y	Y		Y	

CONCLUSION

Migration of legacy applications to service provisioning environments relies on mature software engineering disciplines in areas such as maintenance, reengineering, and reuse to take advantage of their methods and tools. However, specific challenges remain, some of them related to the service foundation and others specific to the approach (SOA or Cloud Computing). Even if traditional models prove to be useful, this research and practice area has to define its own strategies, methods, tools, for supporting the entire life cycle, and for keeping a constant alignment with business needs.

REFERENCES

Bennett, K. H., & Rajlich, V. T. (2000). Software maintenance and evolution: A roadmap. In A. Finkelstein (Ed.), *Proceedings of the Conference on the Future of Software Engineering*, (pp. 3-22). ACM Press.

Brodie, M. L., & Stonebraker, M. (1998). *Migrating legacy systems: Gateways, interfaces & the incremental approach*. San Francisco, CA: Morgan Kaufmann Publishers Inc.

Cardoso, J., Voigt, K., & Winkler, M. (2009). Service engineering for the internet of services. *Lecture Notes in Business Information Processing*, *19*, 15–27. doi:10.1007/978-3-642-00670-8_2

Cervantes, H., & Hall, R. (2004). Autonomous adaptation to dynamic availability using a service-oriented component model. In *Proceedings of the 26th International Conference on Software Engineering*, (pp. 614-623). Washington, DC: IEEE Computer Society Press.

Chauhan, T., Chaudhary, S., Kumar, V., & Bhise, M. (2011). Service level agreement parameter matching in cloud computing. In *Proceedings of the World Congress on Information and Communication Technologies (WICT)*, (pp. 564-570). WICT.

Donofrio, N., Sanchez, C., & Spohrer, J. (2010). Collaborative innovation and service systems: Implications for institutions and disciplines. In Grasso, D., & Burkins, M. (Eds.), *Holistic Engineering Education*. Berlin, Germany: Springer.

Fielding, R. T. (2000). *Architectural styles and the design of network-based software architectures*. (Ph.D. Dissertation). University of California. Irvine, CA.

Greenfield, J., & Short, K. (2004). *Software factories: Assembling applications with pattern, models, frameworks, and tools*. New York, NY: Wiley Publishing.

Jeffery, K., & Neidecker-Lutz, B. (2010). *The future of cloud computing: Opportunities for European cloud computing beyond 2010*. Geneva, Switzerland: European Commission, Information Society and Media.

Kazman, R., Woods, S., & Carrière, J. (1998). Requirements for integrating software architecture and reengineering models: CORUM II. In *Proceedings of the Firth Working Conference on Reverse En-gineering (WCRE)*, (pp. 154-163). Washington, DC: IEEE Computer Society Press.

Lehman, M. M. (1996). Laws of software evolution revisited. In C. Montangero (Ed.), *Proceedings of the 5th European Workshop on Software Process Technology (EWSPT 1996)*, (pp. 108-124). London, UK: Springer-Verlag.

Lewis, G., Morris, E., Simanta, S., & Smith, D. (2008). *SMART: Analyzing the reuse potential of legacy components in a service-oriented architecture environment*. Technical Note CMU/SEI-2008-TN-008. Retrieved from http://www.sei.cmu.edu/library/abstracts/reports/08tn008.cfm

Lientz, B. P., & Swanson, E. B. (1980). *Software maintenance management: A study of the maintenance of computer application software in 487 data processing organizations*. Reading, MA: Addison-Wesley.

Mietzner, R., Metzger, A., Leymann, F., & Pohl, K. (2009). Variability modeling to support customization and deployment of multi-tenant-aware software as a service applications. In *Proceedings of the ICSE Workshop on Principles of Engineering Service Oriented Systems (PESOS)*, (pp. 18-25). Washington, DC: IEEE Computer Society Press.

O'Brian, J. A., & Marakas, G. M. (2008). *Management information systems*. Columbus, OH: McGraw-Hill.

Papazoglou, M. P., Traverso, P., Dustdar, S., & Leymann, F. (2007). Service-oriented computing: State of the art and research challenges. *IEEE Computer*, *40*(11), 38–45. doi:10.1109/MC.2007.400

Papazoglou, M. P., Traverso, P., Dustdar, S., & Leymann, F. (2008). Service-oriented computing: A research roadmap. *International Journal of Cooperative Information Systems*, *17*(2), 223–255. doi:10.1142/S0218843008001816

Peltz, C. (2003). Web services orchestration: A review of emerging technologies, tools, and standards. *Hewlett Packard, Co.* Retrieved March 23, 2012, from http://itee.uq.edu.au/~infs3204/interesting_websites/WSOrchestration.pdf

Petcu, D., Craciun, C., Neagul, M., Rak, M., & Lazcanotegui Larrarte, I. (2011). Building an Interoperability API for sky computing. In *Proceedings of the International Conference on High Performance Computing and Simulation (HPCS)*, (pp. 405-411). HPCS.

Razavian, M., & Lago, P. (2010). A frame of reference for SOA migration. *Lecture Notes in Computer Science, 6481*, 150–162. doi:10.1007/978-3-642-17694-4_13

Sommerville, J. (2006). *Software engineering* (8th ed.). Reading, MA: Addison-Wesley.

Spohrer, J., Maglio, P. P., Bailey, J., & Gruhl, D. (2007). Steps toward a science of service systems. *IEEE Computer, 40*(1), 71–77. doi:10.1109/MC.2007.33

Varia, J. (2010). *Amazon web services - Migrating your existing applications to the AWS cloud.* Retrieved March 23, 2012, from http://media.amazonwebservices.com/CloudMigration-main.pdf

Winter, A., & Ziemann, J. (2007). Model-based migration to service-oriented architectures: A project outline. In H. M. Sneed (Ed.), *CSMR 2007 Workshop on a "Research Agenda for Service-Oriented Architecture Maintenance"*, (pp. 107–110). Amsterdam, The Netherlands: Vrije Universiteit Amsterdam.

KEY TERMS AND DEFINITIONS

Cloud Computing: It characterizes infrastructures, platforms and software based on a delivery paradigm that distinguish them from the classical ownership, and assumes that any of them can be considered to be a service offered on demand.

Legacy Application: It defines a software system that has been traditionally used within an enterprise and represents one of its important assets, with a strong influence on its business processes, human resources, and clients.

Service: In the context of this book, a service is considered to be an autonomous piece of software designed for being reused and delivered remotely, based on loose coupling between its provider and its consumer.

Service-Oriented Architecture: It defines an architectural style formed of three basic elements: a service provider that hosts, publishes, and delivers services; a service registry that contains standard descriptions of the published services; a client that is able to discover services from the registry for the need of its application, and to communicate with their providers for consuming them.

Software Maintenance: The life cycle for application development does not end with delivery of a product to customers. In order to keep the product on the market for a long time, a producer has to perform appropriate changes, which can range from bug corrections to improvements and adaptations.

Software Migration: Unlike "big-bang" modernization, software migration is based on reusing existing legacy assets and on a gradual, incremental path from the old information systems and working styles to the new ones that require adapting to modern technologies and business environments.

Software Reengineering: It represents the modification of existing code for creating a new application with different functional or non-functional requirements.

Software Reuse: Despite continuous changes in the environment, there are elements that are immutable or valid for a long time because one has made a huge investment in their implementation. It is critical to preserve these elements and reduce the time and cost of future development, even if it concerns maintaining an existing application or creating a new one.

Section 2
Migrating to SOA Environments

Chapter 2
Research Challenges in the Maintenance and Evolution of Service–Oriented Systems

GraceA. Lewis
Carnegie Mellon Software Engineering Institute, USA

Dennis B. Smith
Carnegie Mellon Software Engineering Institute, USA

ABSTRACT

Service-Oriented Architecture (SOA) is a viable option for systems development, systems integration, and leverage of legacy systems. Despite its positive contributions and potential, SOA has been subjected to significant hype and inflated expectations, and past research efforts in this area have been unfocused. As a result, there is a strong need for systematic and unbiased research. Based on a synthesis of two leading efforts, this chapter presents a framework of research challenges for service orientation and focuses on the topics related to the migration and evolution of service-oriented systems. The chapter reviews current progress as well as gaps in addressing challenges that are derived from the framework.

INTRODUCTION AND BACKGROUND

Service-Oriented Architecture (SOA) is a way of designing, developing, deploying, and managing systems characterized by coarse-grained services that represent reusable business functionality. Service consumers compose applications or systems using the functionality provided by these services through well-documented, standard interfaces. However, getting the benefits from SOA projects requires the implementation of enterprise-wide business, operations, and engineering plans.

The term SOA has often been misunderstood, and it has been associated with considerable hype and inflated expectations. As long ago as 2003, a Gartner Group report stated that "Attempted SOA will cause great successes and great failures of software projects. Understanding its role and meaning, beyond the simplistic hype, is the imperative for every enterprise software architect"

DOI: 10.4018/978-1-4666-2488-7.ch002

Copyright © 2013, IGI Global. Copying or distributing in print or electronic forms without written permission of IGI Global is prohibited.

(Natis, 2003). While service orientation has the potential to provide agility, adaptability, and legacy leverage, its mixed record of success suggests that there are significant challenges that need to be addressed.

Nevertheless, current research efforts have evolved in a number of uncoordinated directions. This research community has gone through a substantial growth spurt, and there is a need to better channel these research efforts, identify critical research challenges, and establish priorities for addressing these challenges.

Because many SOA projects begin by exposing legacy assets, successful migration of legacy systems to SOA environments represents a crucial aspect of these projects. Using existing research agenda frameworks as a starting point, this chapter identifies key challenges and reviews progress and gaps in current research related to the maintenance and evolution of service-oriented systems.

EXISTING RESEARCH ON DEVELOPING AN SOA RESEARCH AGENDA

The two most prominent contributions toward developing an SOA research agenda are:

- The EU Framework documented in the work of Papazoglou and colleagues (Papazoglou, Traverso, Dustdar, & Leyman, 2007; Papazoglou, Traverso, Dustdar, Leyman, & Kramer, 2006) that was originally developed at a Dagstuhl seminar on service-oriented computing and then expanded into the European Network of Excellence in Software Services and Systems (S-Cube). This project funded a series of research studies based on the framework and initiated the PESOS (Principles of Engineering Service-Oriented Systems) series of workshops at the International Conference on Software Engineering (ICSE).

- An SOA research agenda developed by the Carnegie Mellon University Software Engineering Institute (SEI) (Kontogiannis, et al., 2007; Kontogiannis, Lewis, & Smith, 2008; Lewis, Smith, & Kontogiannis, 2010). The SEI project developed its taxonomy through an international group of researchers. The taxonomy and research challenges were elaborated through the results of the SDSOA (Systems Development in SOA Environments) workshops at ICSE, the SOAM (SOA Maintenance and Evolution) workshops at the European Conference on Software Maintenance and Reengineering (CSMR), the Maintenance and Evolution of Service-Oriented and Cloud-Based Systems (MESOCA)[1] workshops at the International Conference on Software Maintenance (ICSM), and the PESOS workshops at ICSE.

EU Framework

Papazoglou and colleagues developed an SOA research roadmap as a follow-up to a Dagstuhl workshop on service orientation (Papazoglou, et al., 2006, 2007). This roadmap was motivated by the practical importance of service orientation as well as the fact that research activities were fragmented and uneven and needed a focus. Results of the follow-up S-Cube project are reported in Papazoglou, Pohl, Parkin, and Metzger (2010) as well as on the S-Cube Web site.[2] While the S-Cube project was funded as an EU Framework Programme, it has been influential in the broader SOA research community, and many of the cited references in this chapter make reference to S-Cube literature.

The roadmap identifies three technical foundation levels, plus a crosscutting service-oriented design and development level that relies on the three technical foundation planes. It characterizes the state of the art associated with each level as well as "grand challenges."

The three technical levels of the roadmap, together with grand challenges associated with each level, are:

1. Service foundations, which use middleware and architectural concepts for service publication, discovery, selection, and binding. These foundations are most commonly implemented by different types of Enterprise Service Buses (ESBs). Grand challenges are:
    a. Dynamically reconfigurable runtime architectures,
    b. Dynamic connectivity capabilities,
    c. Topic- and content-based routing capabilities,
    d. End-to-end security solutions,
    e. Infrastructure support for application integration,
    f. Infrastructure support for data integration,
    g. Infrastructure support for process integration, and
    h. Service discovery.
2. Service composition, which enables coordination, conformance, and transactions. This level includes orchestration standards and processes. Grand challenges are:
    a. Composability analysis operators for replaceability, compatibility, and conformance, including:
        i.   Typing/syntactic conformance,
        ii. Behavioral conformance, and
        iii. Semantic conformance.
    b. Autonomic composition of services,
    c. Quality-of-Service (QoS)-aware service composition, and
    d. Business-driven automated composition.
3. Service management, which performs measurement, state management, load balancing, and change management. Service management includes such approaches as Web Services Distributed Management (WSDM),

Management Using Web Services (MUWS), and Management of Web Services (MOWS). Grand challenges are:
    a. Self-configuring services,
    b. Self-healing services,
    c. Self-optimizing services, and
    d. Self-protecting services.

In addition to the three technical levels, a service design and development level (also called services engineering) focuses on the business processes that utilize services to support the development of distributed application with the technical foundations. It integrates the technologies of the three technical levels with the business goals and rules for a specific organization. This level also addresses the fact that standard development methods, such as object orientation and component-based development, do not adequately address services. Its grand challenges include:

*   Design principles for engineering service applications,
*   Associating a services-design methodology with standard software development and business process modeling techniques,
*   Flexible gap analysis techniques, and
*   Service governance.

The sum of the grand challenges represents a community-wide research agenda.

SEI SOA Research Agenda

Based on a similar motivation to focus diverse research efforts, the SEI developed and evolved the SOA Research Agenda (Kontogiannis, et al., 2007; Kontogiannis, et al., 2008; Lewis, Chapin, Kontogiannis, & Smith, 2010; Lewis, Kontogiannis, & Smith, 2011; Lewis, et al., 2010). Its core was a taxonomy of research areas that identified research topics to support strategic service-oriented systems development and evolution. This taxonomy was updated on an annual basis through a series of workshops and input from emerging literature.

In addition to the taxonomy of research topics, this effort also developed an organizational SOA strategic framework and a high-level service-oriented systems development life cycle to support the SOA strategic framework. To keep the focus on research challenges, we limit the discussion in this chapter to the taxonomy.[3]

The taxonomy, shown in Figure 1, is divided into decision areas of business, engineering, operations, and crosscutting topics. Each decision area has a set of topics (such as process and life cycle, requirements, and service selection under engineering). The research topics include areas for which new, different, or additional research is needed. Figure 1 illustrates the major topics under each decision area.

The 27 research topics have a total of 114 detailed research areas. Because this book focuses on migration to service-oriented and cloud-based environments, Figure 2 shows the detailed research areas of the Maintenance and Evolution topic.

RESEARCH CHALLENGES FOR MAINTENANCE AND EVOLUTION OF SERVICE-ORIENTED SYSTEMS

The EU Framework and SEI SOA Research Agenda described briefly in the previous section both made important contributions toward defining a set of needed research directions. In this chapter, we use the detailed research areas from Figure 2 as discussion areas:

- Tools, Techniques, and Environments to Support Maintenance Activities
- Multilanguage System Analysis and Maintenance
- Reengineering Processes for Migration to SOA Environments

- Transition Patterns for Service-Oriented Systems
- Runtime Monitoring of Service-Oriented System Evolution

The grand challenges from the EU Framework provide additional specification, especially in the area of Runtime Monitoring of Service-Oriented System Evolution, for which the framework and the subsequent EU S-Cube project are particularly strong on self-monitoring and self-adaptation.

Each area contains rationale; current research; and challenges, gaps, and needs for future research.

Topic 1: Tools, Techniques, and Environments to Support Maintenance Activities

Rationale

The complexity of the maintenance process in an SOA environment continues to increase, especially as implementations become more complex and systems are integrated with external service consumers and service providers. This complexity affects maintenance activities in the following ways:

- Impact analysis activities for service providers have to consider a potentially unknown set of service consumers, unless there are mechanisms for tracking service consumers in the SOA infrastructure.
- Impact analysis for service implementation code has to consider direct calls to service implementation code as well as calls via service interfaces.
- Configuration management becomes more complex, starting from the decision of what to put under configuration management: service interfaces, service test instances, configuration files, infrastructure services, and business processes.

Figure 1. SOA research taxonomy

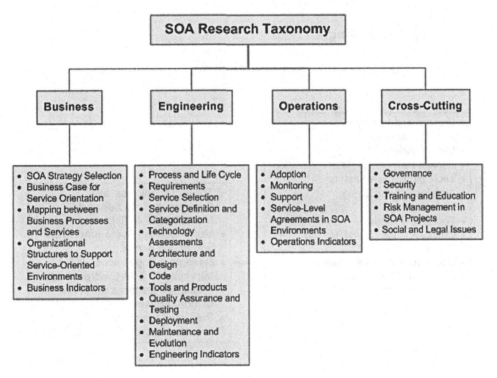

Release cycles between services and consumers, services and infrastructure, and consumers and infrastructure ideally should be coordinated, which may not be possible when these are external to the organization.

In addition, maintenance is challenging as increasing numbers of services are shared among multiple business processes or consumers. It is necessary to ask these questions:

- Who is responsible for the maintenance of a shared service?
- What happens when multiple business units have different requirements for the same service?
- How is a service evolved in the context of the multiple business processes that use it?

Current Research

Current research has focused on the following areas:

- **Root cause analysis:** Zawawy, Mylopoulos, and Mankovski (2010) have developed an approach for root cause analysis in SOA environments to cut down on the manual effort required to resolve problems in enterprise SOA applications. Because these applications tend to have complex interactions in heterogeneous environments, determining the cause of problems can be time consuming and error prone. This method and tool enables developers to analyze log data files against annotated goal trees derived from requirements to enable determination of the root causes of problems.

Figure 2. Detailed research areas for the maintenance and evolution of service-oriented systems

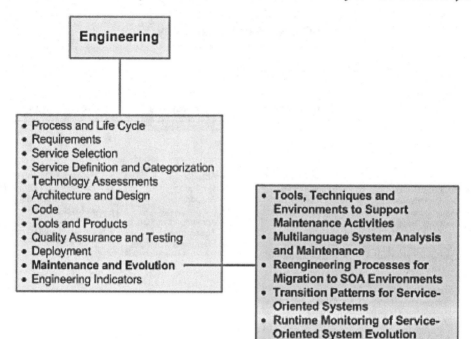

- **Change impact analysis:** This is an active area of research at different levels. A top-down approach focuses on the impact of changes to business processes all the way down to the source code to identify affected system components (Den Haan, 2009; Ravichandar, Nanjangud, Narendra, & Ponnalagu, 2008; Xiao, Guo, & Zou, 2007). A bottom-up approach focuses on the impact of changes to a service—or its implementation—on the business processes and other consumers of the service (Zhang, Arsanjani, Allam, Lu, & Chee, 2007). Multiple Integrated Development Environments (IDEs) integrate impact analysis, but the usual assumption is that there is control and full access to all system elements, which is not always the case.
- **Change management and version control:** This area has received significant attention from the research and vendor community.

  ○ Version management has been the subject of a number of research studies. Peltz and Anagol-Subbarao (2004) recognized that versioning is more difficult in an SOA environment because more distributed sets of components are not under the control of developers. They proposed Web service facades as a design strategy for Web service upgrades to map interfaces to business processes rather than objects. This enables continued support for earlier versions, and it avoids the need to manage very fine-grained services that are more prone to change. Fang et al. (2007) designed and developed a prototype in Eclipse of a version-aware Web service client model. This model included a flexible architecture to enable selection of an appropriate version by a client. Flurry (2008) proposed a model for understanding how changes in service-oriented systems are instantiated through services. The model is represented in a service registry to enable governance rules for controlling change. The registry notifies relevant stakeholders about change, using an ESB to minimize the impact of change. Laskey (2008) uses the OASIS SOA reference model to identify versioning considerations, especially the versioning of services and service descriptions. Lublinsky (2007) presents guidelines for new versions of services as well as for versioning of the infrastructure.

○ Patterns represent a potential source for technical and business needs for services versioning. Bechara (2008) identifies patterns (such as the consumer binding pattern, layer of indirection pattern, and adapter pattern) that may be useful for versioning of services, together with preliminary guidelines for their use. Robinson (2006) provides evidence that the consumer-driven contract pattern can specify consumer expectations and focus the evolution of services on key business functionality that consumers require.

○ Erl et al. (2009) have a set of principles and patterns for Web service contract design and versioning. Of specific relevance is the proposal to apply the concurrent contracts pattern to Web services in order to provide a single body of service logic for a number of potential Web service contracts.

○ Two vendor approaches address the problem of service versioning. Brown and Ellis (2004) have developed a set of best practices from IBM experiences with Web service versioning

based on unique namespaces and version-aware repositories. Recognizing the risk of the lack of standards-based guidance for service versioning, Evdemon (2005) provides a set of design principles from Microsoft that supports message versioning and contract versioning.

• **Backward compatibility:** Becker, Pruyne, Singhal, Milojicic, and Lopes (2011) propose a method to automatically determine when two service descriptions are backward compatible. This method has the goals of enabling (a) service developers to assess the impact of proposed changes, (b) proper versioning requirements for client implementations to minimize runtime incompatibilities, and (c) the validation of exchanged messages.

• **Extensions to standards:** Juric and Šaša (2010) propose Business Process Execution Language (BPEL) extensions to support versioning of processes and partner links. The extensions would apply to development, deployment, and runtime. Šaša and Juric (2010) propose extensions to the Web Service Definition Language (WSDL) to address service-level and operation-level versioning, service endpoint mapping, and version sequencing. These extensions are meant to represent a solution for service- and process-level versioning at development, deployment, and runtime.

• **Maintenance processes:** SOA life cycles, such as the one proposed by IBM and others, include maintenance in the postdeployment management phase of an iterative life cycle (High, Kinder, & Graham, 2005). In this model, SOA life-cycle maintenance is part of the "Manage" step, and it involves routine maintenance; administering and securing applications, resources, and users; and projecting needs and capacity for future growth. Mittal (2005) recommends the use of a robust development methodology the first time the service-oriented system is rolled out and the use of lighter methodologies to support ongoing maintenance.

- **Change management governance:** The relationship between change management and SOA is being addressed at the governance level, where it extends beyond physical system components to organizational components (Berry, 2009; Mynampati, 2008). Lhotka (2005) focuses on the distinction between syntactic and semantic agreements. Syntactic agreements focus on the service interface, while semantic agreements focus on the specific actions that take place upon service execution. The article introduces the term covenant as opposed to contract in order to allow multiple interfaces, depending on different QoS requirements.

- **Organizational structures and roles:** Kajko-Mattsson, Lewis, and Smith (2007, 2008) propose a framework for roles that are required for evolving and maintaining service-oriented systems. The framework was based on a questionnaire that was piloted at SAS Airlines. It identifies roles that are required for service-oriented systems, such as front-end support roles (business process support), back-end support roles (service developer, business process manager), business process teams, traditional back-end support, SOA strategy and governance, SOA design and quality management, and SOA development and evolution.

Challenges, Gaps, and Needs for Future Research

Over the past 15 years, the software reengineering community has investigated and developed a wide range of methods and tools to support the analysis, comprehension, and maintenance of legacy systems. However, the development of specialized methods and tools to support the maintenance and evolution of large service-oriented systems is in the early stages. Current efforts often assume that maintenance activities for service-oriented systems are not that different from traditional systems. This may derive from the fact that many current service-oriented systems are deployed for internal integration, where there is still some control over the use of services and their evolution.

The emergence of the market for third-party services and the deployment of more service-oriented systems that cross organizational boundaries will require changes to current maintenance practices. From an engineering perspective, processes to support the incremental evolution of service-oriented systems, configuration management, impact analysis, and versioning in this environment are challenges. From a business perspective, the organizational structures and roles to support maintenance of service-oriented systems as well as models to support the development and maintenance of shared services are areas of much needed research.

Changes that do not require modifications to the service interface will potentially have no impact on service consumers. However, a change in underlying technology may have a negative effect on QoS, even if the interface remains the same. Changes that do require modifications to the service interface can have a potentially large impact on service consumers. Important research issues are related to maintenance of multiple interfaces, impact analysis techniques for service consumers and providers, change notification mechanisms for service consumers, and proper use of extensibility mechanisms in messaging technologies (e.g., Simple Object Access Protocol [SOAP] extensibility mechanisms).

Service-oriented systems can be deployed over a wide geographic area and on a set of different server computers. Owners of the service-oriented system may not have control over some of the services used. Despite the fact that robust techniques for configuration management in centralized systems are available, there are open issues with respect to managing change in distributed code bases and code repositories, especially when third-party services are involved. Furthermore, there may be additional requirements for the configuration management of large service-oriented systems. As a result, an open research issue is the development of a unified model for managing and controlling change in such systems.

Topic 2: Multilanguage System Analysis and Maintenance

Rationale

One of the benefits associated with service orientation, and especially Web Service implementations, is true platform independence. Even though standard interfaces are exposed, the underlying service implementation could be written in almost any language. While this is a significant benefit, it makes looking at the system as a whole difficult. In addition, as we discuss below, mapping between data types of different languages can create unexpected challenges.

Current Research

The reengineering community has been working on the issue of multilanguage analysis for a number of years to assist in analysis and migration of multilanguage systems (Deruelle, Melab, Boune, & Basson, 2001). Most work in this area is based on parsing of source code to create common higher level representations that can then be analyzed using tools. Some of the problems with multilanguage analysis are related to the mapping of data types between different languages.

In a Web Services environment, the multilanguage problem is often alleviated because XML Schema data types are used at the service interface level. There has been some work in using string

analysis to understand Web Services, given that messages are XML-based collections of strings (Martin & Xie, 2006). There are many instances of using ESBs as a mechanism for providing integration between applications with heterogeneous languages. Sward and Whitacre (2008) reported on a prototype using an open source Mule 1.4 ESB configuration. This study demonstrated communication between SOAP and Representational State Transfer (REST) Web services written in both Java and Ada.

However, Lu, Zou, Xiong, Lin, and Zha (2009) point to problems in invoking Web services from clients that are written in different languages. This article attributes the problem to complex data structures in the service interface; the use of additional information, such as WS-Security headers; and missing language features. As a result, the effort to migrate to and evolve a multilanguage SOA environment can be more difficult than it initially appears. Lu and colleagues propose the Invocation Complexity of Multi-Language Clients (ICMOC), which collects data on the service interface, message content, and language features. They then develop metrics and decision rules for engineering difficulty. The multilanguage difficulties need to be addressed particularly in developing security and privacy protections for different credential types and formats in a heterogeneous environment. Dushin and Newcomer (2007) propose a data structure for storing and propagating user credentials as well as the trust relationships between credential instances.

Sneed (2011) proposes converting special data types to ASCII before migration to services. Once the data types are converted to a common ASCII format, the databases can then be converted using a data conversion utility. The chapter presents the results of a case study of a Customer Information Control System (CICS) conversion for a Swiss bank. Examples show how packed and other data fields are identified by the utility, commented out, and converted to ASCII.

Challenges, Gaps, and Needs for Future Research

Because the SOA architecture style focuses on interfaces, and it does achieve significant interoperability between heterogeneous languages, this area has not had as many research studies as other areas. However, as Lu et al. (2009) point out, the problem is far from solved. Most research in this area is limited to small projects and a small number of languages, which is a problem for an environment that promotes platform independence. Additional research needs to be performed to address mapping of different data types, idiosyncrasies between language versions, and security concerns.

In the case of third-party service providers, access to source code is probably not possible. If so, an important area of research is the identification of the type of information that service providers would need to expose to service consumers—in interfaces or service registries/repositories—that wish to do code analysis, as well as tools and techniques to support the process.

Topic 3: Reengineering Processes for Migration to SOA Environments

Rationale

Because it has characteristics of loose coupling, published interfaces, and a standard communication model, service orientation enables existing legacy systems to expose their functionality as services, presumably without making significant changes to the legacy systems. Migration of legacy assets to service environments has been achieved within a number of domains, including banking, electronic payment, and development tools, showing that the promise is beginning to be fulfilled. While migration can have significant value, any specific migration requires the strategic identification and extraction of services from legacy code, including a concrete analysis of the feasibility, risk, and cost involved.

Current Research

The overall conceptual model for reengineering is the "SOA-Migration Horseshoe," such as the one proposed by Winter and Ziemann (2007). This approach derives from a more general reengineering model proposed by Carriere, Kazman, and Woods (1998). The horseshoe model integrates software reengineering techniques with business process modeling and applies reverse engineering techniques to extract a Legacy Enterprise Model from the legacy code. Then, it applies enterprise modeling techniques to create a Consolidated Enterprise Model from which services are identified using forward engineering techniques. Finally, legacy code is mapped to services via wrapping or transformation. This model, illustrated in Figure 3, can serve as a conceptual framework for analyzing existing approaches.

Razavian and Lago (2010a, 2010b) did a systematic review of the SOA migration literature using the approach recommended by Kitchenham (2004). They developed an SOA Migration Framework (SOA-MF) based on the horseshoe model with three major types of activities:

1. Reverse engineering to recover lost abstractions and determine the legacy components that can be migrated,
2. Transformation of legacy abstractions to service-based abstractions, and
3. Forward engineering to the target system based on transformed abstractions as well as new requirements.

The study then identified eight different types (families) of SOA migration approaches and mapped these to the SOA-MF. Razavian and Lago identified two main goals of existing research on SOA migration:

1. Migration for modernization, where the focus is how to adapt the legacy systems to the SOA environment, and

2.   Migration to new service-based systems.

Legacy Code Analysis

A substantial amount of previous work has focused on techniques in the "bottom portion" of the horseshoe for exposing legacy functionality as services, mainly Web Services (Chawla & Peddinti, 2007). Tools to support this type of migration are available as language libraries and/or integrated into common IDEs such as the Eclipse Web Tool Platform and the .NET Windows Communication Foundation, or as part of infrastructure products such as Apache Axis2 (Apache Software Foundation, 2009; Eclipse Foundation, 2009; Microsoft Corporation, 2009).

In the context of Web Services, Aversano, Di Penta, and Palumbo (2007) propose to combine information retrieval tracing with structural match-ing of the target WSDL with existing methods. Their approach performs library schema extraction and then feature extraction to build a WSDL document from the legacy code. Then, it compares the generated WSDL document with the target WSDL document using structural matching.

Sneed (2006) reports on an approach, supported by a set of tools, for salvaging legacy code, wrapping the salvaged code, and making the code available as a Web service. In the salvaging step, he proposes a technique for extracting services based on identifying business rules that produce a desired result. Sneed applied this approach to a legacy life insurance system with 20 million lines of COBOL code. Canfora, Fasolino, Frattolillo, and Tramontana (2008) propose an approach for exposing interactive functionality of legacy systems as Web Services using black-box reverse engineering techniques on user interfaces.

Figure 3. SOA-migration horseshoe

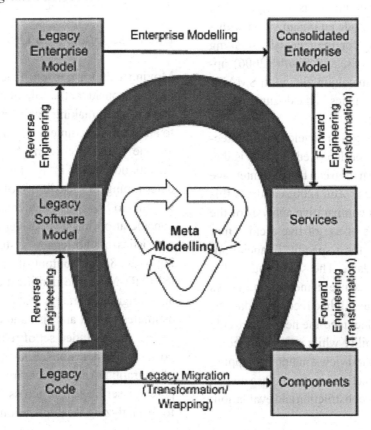

Khadka, Reijnders, Saeidi, Jansen, and Hage (2011) propose the serviceFi method, which combines an analysis of migration feasibility with supporting technology. This approach reuses method fragments from existing service-oriented development methods and extracts legacy code through slicing.

Architecture Reconstruction and Patterns

Moving up the left side of the horseshoe, an additional set of studies focuses on recovery of architecture assets and architecture patterns in developing higher-level abstractions for migration toward an SOA environment. Kazman and Carriere (1999) introduced the approach of architecture reconstruction to recover as-is architecture assets from a system that has inadequate architecture documentation and to enable proceeding to forward engineering from the architecture assets. O'Brien, Smith, and Lewis (2005) proposed the use of architecture reconstruction to identify dependencies between components for migration to services and thus provide an organization with a better understanding for their decision-making process. Lewis, Morris, and Smith (2006) applied this approach in conjunction with SMART to make up for deficiencies in the documentation of the existing system.

One of the challenges in developing architecture documentation for deployed systems is that architecture reconstruction can be labor intensive and costly. Gorton and Zhu (2005) address this challenge through a comparative analysis of the capabilities and ease of use of five architecture reconstruction tools for a specific financial application coded in Java. The study found that these tools can produce useful metrics and views within about three days. It had recommendations for these tools that included the need to provide high levels of flexibility while supporting commonly used architectural views, maintain mapping levels between abstraction levels, and use design metrics for guiding reconstruction and evaluation.

Arcelli, Tosi, and Zanoni (2008) expanded the architecture reconstruction view and proposed the use of design pattern detection in the migration to SOA environments. They proposed several classic design patterns including Façade, Bridge, Mediator, and Abstract Factory for SOA migration. They point out the similarity, for example, between the orchestration process in a service-oriented system and the Mediator pattern in which services may be controlled by a mediator, such as a BPEL processor.

In analyzing the potential for the migration of a large number of legacy COBOL applications to services, Van Geet and Demeyer (2007) focus on the architectural challenge of identifying dependencies between programs. They present a lightweight technique using Perl scripts for visualizing functional dependencies and data dependencies. This type of visualization plus corresponding metrics provide an early estimate of dependencies and the corresponding level of difficulty of separating programs into services.

Business Goals and Drivers

Moving to the top portion of the horseshoe, a body of work considers the role of business goals and drivers when making decisions about migration to an SOA environment.

The SOA Migration, Adoption and Reuse Technique (SMART)[4] is a family of methods for determining the feasibility of migrating legacy systems to SOA environments, which takes into consideration business drivers as well as characteristics of the legacy system (Lewis, et al., 2006, 2008). The output of the original method (SMART-MP) is the identification of a pilot project and a migration strategy that includes preliminary estimates of cost and risk and a list of migration issues. An expanded set of related methods supports making decisions about the initial feasibility of migrating to an SOA environment, identifying potential services from across the enterprise portfolio, analyzing the implications of migrating to a specific target SOA environment, and developing a complete service-oriented system.

Zhang, Yang, Zhou, and Zhong (2010) propose a user-oriented migration model. This model initially performs a domain analysis and an analysis of the legacy systems. It inputs a set of user priorities and develops a migration strategy based on these priorities.

Most major vendors offer services for the migration of legacy assets to SOA environments. IBM's Service-Oriented Modeling and Analysis (SOMA) focuses on full system development but has some portions that address legacy reuse. The purpose of the Existing Asset Analysis activity in the Identification phase is "to identify such assets as systems, packages, and legacy functionality that are capable of supporting the realization of services that meet business needs (Arsanjani, et al., 2008, p. 388).

Fuhr, Winter, Gimnich, and Horn (2009) have extended SOMA for model-driven migration to SOA environments.

Cetin et al. (2007) propose a mashup-based[5] approach for migration of legacy systems to service-oriented computing environments. The interesting aspect about this work is the inclusion of presentation services, which is not typical. The approach is a combination of top-down, starting from business requirements, and bottom-up, looking at legacy code. Business requirements are mapped to services and integrated through a mashup server, which then eliminates the need for developing specific applications to access the services.

Model Transformation

Tran, Zdun, and Dustdar (2011) address the problem that at the upper end of the horseshoe, technical process languages such as BPEL are not easily understood by nontechnical stakeholders, who may develop alternative process descriptions using notations such as Business Process Modeling Notation (BPMN). This chapter describes a method called the View-Based Modeling Frame-

work that automates the integration of models at different levels of abstraction.

The SOAMIG project in Germany has been developing a comprehensive, model-driven migration process that is supported by analysis and transformation tools. Winter and colleagues (2011) report on two case studies: a language migration from COBOL to Java Web services and an architecture migration from a monolithic Java client to a service-oriented JavaEE Web application.

Challenges, Gaps, and Needs for Future Research

The ideal reengineering process would be one that implements the full SOA-Migration Horseshoe. The problem, as shown under Current Research, is that most techniques and tools implement portions of the horseshoe but not the full horseshoe. An important area of research would be the development of concrete processes that implement the horseshoe and tools (or suites of tools) to support the process. The automation of this process would be a very complex task that is worth investigating.

In addition, most researchers recognize that mining legacy code for services that have business value continues to represent a significant challenge. Research needs in this area include:

- Tools and techniques for analyzing large source code bases to discover code that is of business value;
- Metrics for "wrapability" and business value to determine reusability (Sneed, 2007); and
- Application of feature extraction techniques to service identification, given that services usually correspond to features (Sneed, 2007).

Topic 4: Transition Patterns for Service-Oriented Systems

Rationale

One of the potential advantages of SOA adoption is that it enables incremental system modernization. A number of technical migration strategies can be used, such as wrapping, integration of legacy components into the SOA infrastructure, and development from scratch. These strategies are not mutually exclusive, and there may be a sequence in using them. For example, legacy system components can be initially wrapped using Web Services technology and replaced with newer components incrementally. As long as the interfaces remain stable, service consumers have to be modified only once to initially access the new services. However, this means that throughout the life cycle of the project there will be a mix of migrated legacy components, legacy components waiting to be migrated, and legacy components that will not be migrated. Legacy components include application front ends, business logic, data logic, and actual data. A major challenge for incremental migration is to minimize the throwaway cost and effort to support intermediate system states. In addition to technical feasibility, the economic feasibility as well as users' background and expectations need to be considered. The research that is reviewed below takes into account these nontechnical needs as well.

Current Research

There is active academic and industrial work related to incremental modernization and enterprise transformation by migrating legacy systems to SOA environments.

Classic reengineering decision models provide decision rules on whether to do low-level maintenance, low-priority reengineering, replacement, or modernization based on a weighting of technical quality and business value (Seacord, Plakosh, & Lewis, 2003). Once an overall strategy is deter-

mined, a set of transition decisions need to be made. These have been most starkly described as "Chicken Little" or "cold turkey" strategies, depending on whether the transition is incremental or total (Brodie & Stonebraker, 1995).

Incremental models for transition to SOA environments have been proposed by Ahmad and Pohl (2010) as well as Marchetto and Ricca (2009). Ahmad presents a layered framework to support an incremental transformation of SOA elements (atomic and composite services) at different levels of abstraction (structure, design, and architecture). The goal is to enable service architecture evolution at the different abstraction levels independent of specific implementation details. Marchetto and Ricca introduce an incremental tools-based approach for transforming Java applications to equivalent Web service–based applications. In each migration step, a specific piece of functionality is migrated to a Web service and tested. Specific migration problems of wrapping, deployment, and testing are discussed.

Umar and Zordan (2009) present a strategic and technical decision model specifically for service-oriented systems. This model identifies two basic strategies:

1. **Integration:** black-box methods in which the underlying application is not touched, and
2. **Migration:** decomposition of applications into reusable services.

Integration is further decomposed into "partial" (point to point) and "full" (communication is handled by an ESB) integration. It is then further decomposed into "gradual" migration and "complete" (or sudden) replacement. The article presents a set of decision criteria and cost-benefit tradeoffs for determining which strategies, architectural decisions, and operational approaches to take.

Almonaies, Cordy, and Dean (2010) offer a framework that organizations can use for making choices between many of the alternative modernization approaches that were described in the previous section. The framework is based on a matrix of modernization category (replacement, redevelopment, wrapping, or migration) and comparison criteria (modernization strategy, legacy system type, degree of complexity, analysis depth, process adaptability, tool support, degree of coverage, and validation maturity). This enables an organization to choose an appropriate strategy based on its goals and available resources.

A number of techniques, tools, and consulting services are available to help organizations migrate legacy systems to SOA environments. Architectural reconstruction and program analysis techniques, discussed earlier, could be used to isolate "chunks" of code. This enables discovering dependencies between components and discovering the impact of migrating alternative sets of legacy components. Erl (2009) has developed several design patterns that can be used when legacy system components are part of service-oriented systems, such as service façade, service data replication, legacy wrapper, and file gateway.

Nasr, Gross, and Van Deursen (2011) address the mixed record of migration to SOA projects and analyze lessons learned from two recent case studies. The first example was the migration of a large heterogeneous set of systems in the transport domain to an SOA environment. The second example was a government system that managed the life cycle of smart identification cards. In both cases, initial phases of the project were successful, though full implementation had not yet been completed. Best practices abstracted from these studies included:

1. The necessity of a phased approach (rather than a big-bang approach) for implementation;
2. Recognition that organizational structure and ownership need to be addressed up front and can become contentious issues;
3. The need for a central coordinating body to set priorities on different views and expectations of consuming and providing systems;

4. The necessity of gaining the buy-in and establishing coordination of stakeholders from a diverse set of groups;
5. The importance of educating the user about the SOA concept and how it differs from more traditional development approaches;
6. The need for investing sufficient resources in the technical feasibility of the system, and the identification and analysis of potential services, with a recognition that a number of applications may not be mature enough to expose services;
7. The need to focus on both an effective infrastructure and exposing services, rather than a primary focus on one or the other; and
8. The importance of a layered approach to separate core functionality from new services.

These findings are consistent with those in a case study by Credit Suisse (Worms, 2011). The Credit Suisse case study is significant because of its scale as well as the fact that it has been under way since 1998. Worms highlighted the challenges, lessons learned, and future directions. The initial goals for the SOA implementation were to create greater efficiency for their mainframe applications and to make reusable business data and functionality available across the organization. Over the years, they have established an enterprise architecture that drives all systems decisions. As of 2010, there were 1,200 deployed services.

Challenges reported by Credit Suisse in the maintenance and evolution of their SOA implementation include:

- Managing complexity due mainly to size.
- Finding the proper IT architecture governance and structure. This includes making decisions about appropriate business processes that are candidates for services; mapping between business processes, applications, and components; and determining the most effective IT infrastructure.

- Anticipating future trends. For example, one of their goals is to go from monolithic to loosely coupled components/subdomains with interfaces along the borders of subdomains instead of direct access between consumers and components.
- Managing and federating multiple integration infrastructures—service, messaging, file transfer, and portal infrastructures.
- Making SOA scale for more than 1,000 services. They created an in-house Interface Management System that provides a service catalog, design tool, governance enforcement, life-cycle management, and code generation.
- Adapting the software engineering life cycle models for SOA. An example is the creation of an Interface Engineering Process that includes early generation of test cases, generation of mocks for testing and support, preparation of test environments, and compilation of test reports.
- Testing and versioning of interfaces. Credit Suisse had to establish clear criteria for what constitutes a major and a minor version, as well as testing processes for major and minor versions for the service provider and the service consumer.
- Migration from regional and national services with single backend platforms to global services with broadly distributed backend platforms.

Challenges, Gaps, and Needs for Future Research

The body of research and commercial approaches on transition patterns for service-oriented systems continues to grow. Most of these approaches have started with strategic decision making that leads to technical decisions. They generally move beyond the assumption that the legacy systems will simply be wrapped and integrated into a service-oriented system and remain relatively stable. They have

explicit decision points and analyses that focus on incremental versus sudden transitions, as well as strategies for wrapping legacy assets versus developing new services. The research and commercial perspectives need to be integrated, and objective case studies, such as the ones reported by Nasr and colleagues (2011) and Worms (2011), need to be factored into decision making more effectively.

In addition, existing studies have not accounted for such factors as making decisions about the right number of increments to minimize the throwaway costs attributed to temporary infrastructure, such as gateways and ETL (Extract, Transform, Load) tools. Current research has also not covered tools and temporary code that deal with mismatches and changes to legacy code waiting to be modernized (e.g., adding code to invoke a service knowing that it will be modernized in a future increment).

Lewis et al. (2011) introduce the concept of Total Modernization Cost and identify some initial directions for addressing this topic.

Topic 5: Runtime Monitoring of Service-Oriented System Evolution

Rationale

In a service-oriented environment, it is difficult to monitor the satisfaction of requirements, reference architectures, Service-Level Agreements (SLAs), and business goals while business processes and services change dynamically. This is exacerbated because the execution environment of service-oriented systems is only partially known at design time. This situation can be addressed by pushing design decisions to runtime and enabling the system to reason about its state and environment. As a result, service-oriented systems have been incorporating self-adaptation and self-management mechanisms into their design.

Given the strong links between business strategy and SOA, runtime monitoring is a best practice to verify if business goals are being met. Current

SOA infrastructures provide the capabilities to define metrics and collect data. The real challenge is to define the most relevant data to measure and monitor and to determine the adaptation strategies to execute when certain conditions are met.

Current Research

The vision for monitoring and adapting service-oriented systems was articulated by Di Nitto, Ghezzi, Metzger, Papazoglou, and Pohl (2008), who cited service-oriented computing as having the promise of creating dynamic and agile business processes to span organizations and platforms by assembling components into a loosely coupled network of services.

SOA governance provides the ability to ensure that the independent efforts (in design, development, deployment, and operations of a service) come together to meet the enterprise SOA requirements (Gupta, 2010). Autonomic monitoring of SOA governance can perform regression tests and V&V (Verification and Validation) operations dynamically to observe satisfaction of requirements and to monitor compliance and conformance.

The evolution toward monitoring and self-adaptation requires changes to the classic software life cycle, especially with regard to requirements, an extended operations phase, and continuous quality assurance. Metzger, Sammodi, Pohl, and Rzepka (2010) point out that because of incomplete knowledge about interacting parties and context, a service-oriented system cannot be completely specified in advance and more decisions need to be made at runtime. Müller (2010) asserts that as monitoring becomes more critical, there needs to be an evolution from satisfaction of requirements through traditional top-down engineering toward the satisfaction of requirements by complex, decentralized systems. The introduction of uncertainty requires a new set of trade-offs between flexibility and assurance. This leads to the questions of how much uncertainty can be afforded, what are the costs, and what benefits can be gained. A cornerstone of the capability of monitoring and adapting systems is the insertion of control loops that collect data and process it through a built-in controller according to a set of decision rules. The system makes the adaptation, records its strategy, and informs relevant stakeholders (Müller, Pezzè, & Shaw, 2008; Salehie & Tahvildari, 2009). De Nitto et al. (2008) recognize that the operations phase assumes greater importance as service-oriented systems become increasingly oriented toward monitoring and identifying the need for adaptation. Quality assurance is monitored continuously because of the addition and evolution of

Figure 4. S-cube SOA life cycle

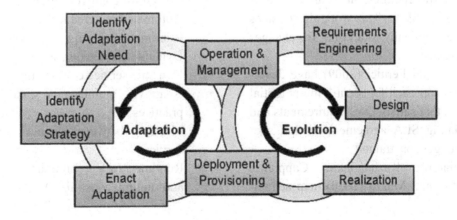

services, especially services that come from third parties (Bianculli, Ghezzi, & Pautasso, 2009).

These changes have resulted in a refined life cycle that the S-Cube project has developed for self-adaptive service-oriented systems (Metzger, et al., 2010). Metzger and colleagues describe this life cycle as consisting of two incremental loops for development and adaptation, as shown in Figure 4.

1. The development and evolution loop (right side of Figure 4) addresses the classical development and deployment life-cycle phases, including requirements, design, construction, operations, and management.
2. The operation and adaptation loop (left side of Figure 4) extends the classical life cycle by explicitly defining phases for addressing changes and adaptations during the operation of service-oriented applications.

Research that is contributing to insights in monitoring and adaptation of service-oriented systems includes the following:

- Villegas and Müller (2011) provide an early report on work that is developing a feature-based model to represent relevant context and monitoring requirements, an adaptive control-based reference architecture to implement dynamic context monitoring infrastructures, and runtime renegotiation of SLAs. This work also updates SLAs dynamically to account for changes in context.
- Comuzzi and Pernici (2009) have developed an approach for identifying potential services that satisfy QoS requirements and negotiating SLA agreements within specific budget constraints.
- Bucchiarone, Kazhamiakin, Cappiello, Di Nitto, and Mazza (2010) map adapta-

tion triggers to adaptation strategies. For example, the trigger "changes in service functionality" may have adaptation strategies that include service substitution, re-execution, and renegotiation.

- Mahbub and Zisman (2009) identify replacement policies to support dynamic changes in service-oriented systems. These replacement policies are used in a service discovery framework to support proactive identification of services in parallel with the execution of the system.
- Espinha (2011) reports on the use of tags to trace requests for Web services, enable analysis of flows and patterns, and facilitate testing for scalability.
- Solomon and Litoiu (2011) have added a feedback evolution loop to standard BPMN and BPEL models. The proposed approach creates a simulation model that matches the real system in order to create trust in the results of what-if scenario analyses.

Challenges, Gaps, and Needs for Future Research

The area of runtime monitoring and adaptation represents a frontier for future research. Lewis, Chapin, and colleagues (2010) identified the following research challenges that are relevant for monitoring and adaptation:

- Design for context awareness
- Automated governance
- Runtime monitoring
- Dynamic service discovery
- Dynamic service composition
- Adaptive maintenance and evolution practices
- Mapping between business process and services
- Runtime V&V (compliance with design and runtime constraints)

The S-Cube project has sponsored significant work in this area. While current work has focused on adaptation based on monitoring that is detected after a fault has occurred (reactive adaptation), Hielscher, Kazhamiakin, Metzger, and Pistore (2008) argue that proactive adaptation is required to conduct continuous online testing and predict potential problems before their occurrence. This enables replacing a service before it is invoked and the system fails to meet its QoS requirements (Papazoglou, Pohl, Parkin, & Metzger, 2010). Metzger et al. (2010) also identify the need to protect against "false positives" in proactive adaptation. This would involve analyzing past monitoring data to recalculate assumptions about the execution of the full set of services that will be invoked.

CONCLUSION

The most common form of SOA implementation is related to enterprise-wide IT systems in which applications interact with standard Web services in a traditional request-response pattern, predominantly to access data that resides in legacy systems. For these types of systems, the research challenges predominantly cover business, operations, and crosscutting concerns. As third-party services become the new business model, there needs to be support for SLAs, runtime monitoring, end-to-end testing involving third parties, pricing models for third-party services, and service usability from a design and an adoption perspective. In addition, non-vendor studies and experiments are needed to produce more concrete guidance, rather than additional basic research. Some examples of these areas are SOA governance, business case for SOA adoption, return on investment for SOA adoption, and development processes and practices for service-oriented systems development.

However, if SOA is to be used in advanced ways, such as for dynamic service discovery and composition, real-time applications, and multi-organizational implementations, then significant research challenges need to be addressed in such areas as design for context awareness, service usability, federation, automated governance and runtime monitoring, and adaptation. For maintenance and evolution of service-oriented systems, in the short term, maintenance and evolution practices will have to evolve and adapt to support this dynamic and changing environment.

There are other topics, such as semantics, on which there is significant academic research but no support from industry to test ideas in real scenarios. There needs to be more collaborative research between industry and academia to create real practices. In addition, there need to be more objective studies of large industrial cases, such as the Credit Suisse example, to provide validation for research findings; to identify challenges of scalability, performance, security, and reliability in real-world settings; and to provide the capability of analyzing trends and experiences across organizations.

REFERENCES

Ahmad, A., & Pohl, K. (2010). Pattern-based customizable transformations for style-based service architecture evolution. In *Proceedings of the 2010 International Conference on Computer Information Systems and Industrial Management Applications (CISIM)*, (pp. 371–376). Washington, DC: IEEE Computer Society Press.

Almonaies, A., Cordy, J., & Dean, T. (2010). Legacy system evolution toward service-oriented architecture. In G. Lewis, F. Ricca, U. Steffens, & A. Winter (Eds.), *SOAME 2010: IEEE International Workshop on SOA Migration and Evolution*, (pp. 53–62). Washington, DC: IEEE Computer Society Press.

Apache Software Foundation. (2009). *Apache Axis2*. Retrieved October 6, 2011, from http://ws.apache.org/axis2

Arcelli, F., Tosi, C., & Zanoni, M. (2008). Can design pattern detection be useful for legacy system migration towards SOA? In K. Kontogiannis, G. A. Lewis, D. B. Smith, & M. Litoiu (Eds.), *SDSOA 2008: Proceedings of the 2nd International Workshop on Systems Development in SOA Environments,* (pp. 63–68). Washington, DC: IEEE Computer Society Press.

Arsanjani, A., Ghosh, S., Allam, A., Abdollah, T., Ganapathy, S., & Holley, K. (2008). SOMA: A method for developing service-oriented solutions. *IBM Systems Journal, 47,* 377–396. doi:10.1147/sj.473.0377

Aversano, L., Di Penta, M., & Palumbo, C. (2007). *Identifying services from legacy code: An integrated approach*. Paper presented at the Working Session on Maintenance and Evolution of SOA-Based Systems (MESOA 2007), ICSM 2007: 23rd IEEE International Conference on Software Maintenance. Paris, France.

Bechara, G. (2008). *Web services versioning*. Retrieved October 6, 2011, from http://www.oracle.com/technetwork/articles/web-services-versioning-094384.html

Becker, K., Pruyne, J., Singhal, S., Milojicic, D., & Lopes, A. (2011). Automatic determination of compatibility in evolving services. *International Journal of Web Services Research, 8*(1), 21–40. doi:10.4018/jwsr.2011010102

Berry, D. (2009). *Avoid disaster, embrace people-processes like change management*. Retrieved October 6, 2011, from http://blogs.oracle.com/governance/2009/06/avoid_disaster_embrace_peoplep_1.html

Bianculli, D., Ghezzi, C., & Pautasso, C. (2009). Embedding continuous lifelong verification in service life cycles. In E. Di Nitto & S. Dustdar (Eds.), *PESOS '09: Proceedings of the 2009 ICSE Workshop on Principles of Engineering Service Oriented Systems,* (pp. 99–102). New York, NY: Association for Computing Machinery.

Brodie, M., & Stonebraker, M. (1995). *Migrating legacy systems*. San Francisco, CA: Morgan Kaufman.

Brown, K., & Ellis, M. (2004). Best practices for web services versioning: Keep your web services current with WSDL and UDDI. *IBM DeveloperWorks*. Retrieved October 6, 2011, from http://www-128.ibm.com/developerworks/webservices/library/ws-version

Bucchiarone, A., Kazhamiakin, R., Cappiello, C., Di Nitto, E., & Mazza, V. (2010). A context-driven adaptation process for service-based applications. *PESOS '10: Proceedings of the Second International Workshop on Principles of Engineering Service-Oriented Systems,* (pp. 50–56). New York, NY: Association for Computing Machinery.

Canfora, G., Fasolino, A., Frattolillo, G., & Tramontana, P. (2008). A wrapping approach for migrating legacy system interactive functionalities to service oriented architectures. *Journal of Systems and Software, 81,* 463–480. doi:10.1016/j.jss.2007.06.006

Carriere, J., Kazman, R., & Woods, S. (1998). Requirements for integrating software architecture and reengineering models: CORUM II. In M. Blaha, A. Quilici, & C. F'erhoef (Eds.), *WCRE 1998: Proceedings of the Working Conference on Reverse Engineering,* (pp. 154–163). New York, NY: Association for Computing Machinery.

Cetin, S., Altintas, N. I., Oguztuzun, H., Dogru, A., Tufekci, O., & Suloglu, S. (2007). Legacy migration to service-oriented computing with mashups. In S. Dascalu, P. Dini, S. Morasca, T. Ohta, & A. Oboler (Eds.), *ICSEA 2007: Proceedings of the Second International Conference on Software Engineering Advances*. Washington, DC: IEEE Computer Society Press.

Chawla, M., & Peddinti, V. (2007). Exposing SOA enabled C apps as web services. *SOA World Magazine*. Retrieved October 6, 2011, from http://webservices.sys-con.com/read/314105.htm

Comuzzi, M., & Pernici, B. (2009). A framework for QoS-based web service contracting. *ACM Transactions on the Web, 3*(3).

Den Haan, J. (2009). *A framework for model-driven SOA*. Retrieved October 6, 2011, from http://www.theenterprisearchitect.eu/archive/2009/06/03/a-framework-for-model-driven-soa

Deruelle, L., Melab, N., Boune, M., & Basson, H. (2001). Analysis and manipulation of distributed multi-language software code. In *Proceedings of the First IEEE International Workshop on Source Code Analysis and Manipulation,* (pp. 43–54). Washington, DC: IEEE Computer Society Press.

Di Nitto, E., Ghezzi, C., Metzger, A., Papazoglou, M., & Pohl, K. (2008). A journey to highly dynamic, self-adaptive service-based applications. *Automated Software Engineering, 15,* 313–341. doi:10.1007/s10515-008-0032-x

Dushin, F., & Newcomer, E. (2007). Handling multiple credentials in a heterogeneous SOA environment. *Security and Privacy, 5*(5), 80–82. doi:10.1109/MSP.2007.110

Eclipse Foundation. (2009). *Web tools platform (WTP) project*. Retrieved October 6, 2011, from http://www.eclipse.org/webtools

Erl, T. (2009). *SOA design patterns*. Upper Saddle River, NJ: Prentice Hall.

Erl, T., Karmarkar, A., Walmsley, P., Haas, H., Umit, Y., & Liu, C. K. (2009). *Web service contract design and versioning for SOA*. Upper Saddle River, NJ: Prentice Hall.

Espinha, E. (2011). Understanding service-oriented systems using dynamic analysis. In D. Smith & G. Lewis (Eds.), *Proceedings of the 2011 International Workshop on the Maintenance and Evolution of Service-Oriented and Cloud-Based Systems (MESOCA)*. Washington, DC: IEEE Computer Society Press.

Evdemon, J. (2005). *Principles of service design: Service versioning*. Redmond, WA: Microsoft Corporation. Retrieved October 6, 2011, from http://msdn2.microsoft.com/en-us/library/ms954726.aspx

Fang, R., Lam, L., Fong, L., Frank, D., Vignola, C., Chen, Y., et al. (2007). A version-aware approach for web service directory. In F. Leymann & M.-C. Shan (Eds.), *Proceedings of 2007 IEEE International Conference on Web Services,* (pp. 406–413). Washington, DC: IEEE Computer Society Press.

Flurry, G. (2008). Service versioning in SOA. *IBM DeveloperWorks*. Retrieved October 6, 2011, from http://www.ibm.com/developerworks/websphere/techjournal/0810_col_flurry/0810_col_flurry.html

Fuhr, A., Gimnich, R., Horn, T., & Winter, A. (2009). Extending SOMA for model-driven software migration into SOA. *Softwaretechnik-Trends, 29*(2).

Gorton, I., & Zhu, L. (2005). Tool support for just-in-time architecture reconstruction and evaluation: An experience report. In G.-C. Roman, W. Griswold, & B. Nuseibeh (Eds.), *ICSE 2005: Proceedings of the 27th International Conference on Software Engineering,* (pp. 514–523). New York, NY: Association for Computing Machinery.

Gupta, P. (2010). *Characterizing policies that govern service-oriented systems.* (Unpublished Master's Thesis). University of Victoria. Victoria, Canada.

Hielscher, J., Kazhamiakin, R., Metzger, A., & Pistore, M. A. (2008). A framework for proactive self-adaptation of service-based applications based on online testing. *Lecture Notes in Computer Science, 5377,* 10–13. doi:10.1007/978-3-540-89897-9_11

High, R., Kinder, S., & Graham, S. (2005). *IBM's SOA foundation: An architectural introduction and overview.* Retrieved October 6, 2011, from http://download.boulder.ibm.com/ibmdl/pub/software/dw/webservices/ws-soa-whitepaper.pdf

Juric, M. B., & Šaša, A. (2010). Version management of BPEL processes in SOA. In *Proceedings of the 2010 IEEE Sixth World Congress on Services,* (pp. 146-147). New York, NY: Association for Computing Machinery.

Kajko-Mattsson, M., Lewis, G., & Smith, D. (2007). A framework for roles for development, evolution and maintenance of SOA-based systems. In *Proceedings of the International Workshop on Systems Development in SOA Environments.* New York, NY: Association for Computing Machinery.

Kajko-Mattsson, M., Lewis, G., & Smith, D. (2008). Evolution and maintenance of SOA-based systems at SAS. In *Proceedings of the 41st Hawaii International Conference on System Sciences.* New York, NY: Association for Computing Machinery.

Kazman, R., & Carriere, J. (1999). Playing detective: Reconstructing software architecture from available evidence. *Automated Software Engineering, 6*(2), 106–138. doi:10.1023/A:1008781513258

Khadka, R., Reijnders, G., Saeidi, A., Jansen, S., & Hage, J. (2011). A method engineering based legacy to SOA migration method. In A. Marcus, J. R. Cordy, & P. Tonella (Eds.), *Proceedings of the 27th International Conference on Software Maintenance (ICSM),* (pp. 163–172). Washington, DC: IEEE Computer Society Press.

Kitchenham, B. (2004). *Procedures for performing systematic reviews.* NICTA Tech. Rep. 0400011T.1. Keele, UK: Keele University and National ICT Australia.

Kontogiannis, K., Lewis, G., Litoiu, M., Müller, H., Schuster, S., Smith, D., et al. (2007). The landscape of service-oriented systems: A research perspective. In *Proceedings of the International Workshop on Systems Development in SOA Environments: ICSE Workshops 2007.* New York, NY: Association for Computing Machinery.

Kontogiannis, K., Lewis, G. A., & Smith, D. B. (2008). A research agenda for service-oriented architecture. In *Proceedings of the Second International Workshop on Systems Development in SOA Environments,* (pp. 1–6). New York, NY: Association for Computing Machinery.

Laskey, K. (2008). Considerations for SOA versioning. In *Proceedings of 12th Enterprise Distributed Object Computing Conference Workshops,* (pp. 333–337). New York, NY: Association for Computing Machinery.

Lewis, G., Morris, E. J., Smith, D. B., & Simanta, S. (2008). *SMART: Analyzing the reuse potential of legacy components in a service-oriented architecture environment.* Pittsburgh, PA: Carnegie Mellon University.

Lewis, G. A., Chapin, N., Kontogiannis, K., & Smith, D. B. (Eds.). (2010). *Proceedings of the third international workshop on a research agenda for maintenance and evolution of service-oriented systems (MESOA 2009).* Pittsburgh, PA: Carnegie Mellon University.

Lewis, G. A., Kontogiannis, K., & Smith, D. B. (Eds.). (2011). *Proceedings of the Fourth International Workshop on a Research Agenda for Maintenance and Evolution of Service-Oriented Systems (MESOA 2010)*. Pittsburgh, PA: Carnegie Mellon University.

Lewis, G. A., Morris, E. J., & Smith, D. B. (2006). Analyzing the reuse potential of migrating legacy components to a service-oriented architecture. In G. Visaggio, G. A. Di Lucca, & N. Gold (Eds.), *Proceedings of the 10th European Conference on Software Maintenance and Reengineering (CSMR 2006),* (pp. 15–23). Washington, DC: IEEE Computer Society Press.

Lewis, G. A., Smith, D. B., & Kontogiannis, K. (2010). *A research agenda for service-oriented architecture (SOA): Maintenance and evolution of service-oriented systems*. Pittsburgh, PA: Carnegie Mellon University.

Lhotka, R. A. (2005). SOA versioning covenant. *SearchWinDevelopment.com*. Retrieved October 6, 2011, from http://searchwindevelopment.techtarget.com/tip/0,289483,sid8_gci1277472,00.html

Lu, X., Zou, Y., Xiong, F., Lin, J., & Zha, L. (2009). ICOMC: Invocation complexity of multilanguage clients for classified Web services and its impact on large scale SOA applications. In K. Nakano & S. Olariu (Eds.), *Proceedings of the 2009 International Conference on Parallel and Distributed Computing, Applications and Technologies,* (pp. 186–194). Washington, DC: IEEE Computer Society Press.

Lublinsky, B. (2007). Versioning in SOA. *Architect Journal, 11*. Retrieved October 6, 2011, from http://msdn2.microsoft.com/en-us/arcjournal/bb491124.aspx

Mahbub, K., & Zisman, A. (2009). Replacement policies for service-based systems. In A. Dan, F. Gittler, & F. Toumani (Eds.), *ICSOC/ServiceWave 2009: Proceedings of the 2009 International Conference on Service Oriented Computing,* (pp. 345–357). New York, NY: Association for Computing Machinery.

Marchetto, A., & Ricca, F. (2009). From objects to services: Toward a tool supported stepwise approach. *International Journal on Software Tools for Technology Transfer, 11*, 427–440. doi:10.1007/s10009-009-0123-4

Martin, E., & Xie, T. (2006). Understanding software application interfaces via string analysis. In L. J. Osterweil, D. Rombach, & M. L. Soffa (Eds.), *ICSE 2006: Proceedings of the 28th International Conference on Software Engineering,* (pp. 901–904). New York, NY: Association for Computing Machinery.

Metzger, A., Sammodi, O., Pohl, K., & Rzepka, M. (2010). Towards proactive adaptation with confidence: Augmenting service monitoring with online testing. In R. de Lemos & M. Pezzè (Eds.), *Proceedings of the 2010 ICSE Workshop on Software Engineering for Self-Adaptive and Self-Monitoring Systems,* (pp. 20–28). New York, NY: Association for Computing Machinery.

Microsoft Corporation. (2009). *Windows communication foundation*. Retrieved October 6, 2011, from http://msdn.microsoft.com/en-us/netframework/aa663324.aspx

Mittal, K. (2005). Build your SOA, part 1: Maturity and methodology. *IBM DeveloperWorks*. Retrieved October 6, 2011, from http://www-128.ibm.com/developerworks/webservices/library/ws-soa-method1.html

Müller, H. (2010). *Perspectives on SOA control science*. Paper presented at the Fourth International Workshop on a Research Agenda for Maintenance and Evolution of Service-Oriented Systems (MESOA 2010). Timisoara, Romania.

Müller, H. A., Pezzè, M., & Shaw, M. (2008). Visibility of control in adaptive systems. In K. Sullivan & R. Kazman (Eds.), *ULSSIS 2008: Proceedings of the Second International Workshop on Ultra-Large-Scale Software-Intensive Systems,* (pp. 23–26). New York, NY: Association for Computing Machinery.

Mynampati, P. (2008). SOA governance: Examples of service life cycle management processes. *IBM DeveloperWorks.* Retrieved October 6, 2011, from http://www.ibm.com/developerworks/webservices/library/ws-soa-governance/index.html

Nasr, K., Gross, H., & Van Deursen, A. (2011). Realizing service migration in industry—Lessons learned. *Journal of Software Maintenance and Evolution, 21*(2), 113–141.

Natis, Y. (2003). *Service-oriented architecture scenario.* Stamford, CT: Gartner Group.

O'Brien, L., Smith, D. B., & Lewis, G. A. (2005). Supporting migration to services using software architecture reconstruction. In Kontogiannis, K., Zou, Y., & Di Penta, M. (Eds.), *Proceedings of Software Technology and Engineering Practice 2005* (pp. 81–91). Washington, DC: IEEE Computer Society Press. doi:10.1109/STEP.2005.29

Papazoglou, M., Pohl, K., Parkin, M., & Metzger, A. (2010). *Service research challenges and solutions for the future Internet: Towards mechanisms and methods for engineering, managing, and adapting service-based systems.* New York, NY: Springer.

Papazoglou, M., Pohl, K., Parkin, M., Metzger, A., & van den Heuvel, W.-J. (2010). The s-cube research vision. In Papazoglou, M., Pohl, K., Parkin, M., & Metzger, A. (Eds.), *Service Research Challenges and Solutions for the Future Internet: Towards Mechanisms and Methods for Engineering, Managing, and Adapting Service-Based Systems* (pp. 1–26). New York, NY: Springer.

Papazoglou, M., Traverso, P., Dustdar, S., & Leyman, F. (2007). Service oriented computing: State of the art and research challenges. *Computer, 40*(11), 38–45. doi:10.1109/MC.2007.400

Papazoglou, M., Traverso, P., Dustdar, S., Leyman, F., & Kramer, B. (2006). Service-oriented computing: Research roadmap. In F. Curbera, B. J. Kramer, & M. P. Papazoglou (Eds.), *Dagstuhl Seminar Proceedings: Vol. 5462: Service Oriented Computing (SOC).* Schloss Dagstuhl, Germany: Internationales Begegnungs und Forschungszentrum für Informatik. Retrieved October 6, 2011 from http://drops.dagstuhl.de/volltexte/2006/524/pdf/05462.SWM.Paper.524.pdf

Peltz, C., & Anagol-Subbarao, A. (2004). Design strategies for web services versioning: Adapting to the needs of the business. *Web Services Journal, 4.* Retrieved October 6, 2011, from http://webservices.sys-con.com/read/44356.htm

Ravichandar, R., Nanjangud, C., Narendra, K., & Ponnalagu, D. (2008). Morpheus: Semantics-based incremental change propagation in SOA-based solutions. In W. Chou, P. Hofmann, & M. Devarakonda (Eds.), *Proceedings of the IEEE International Conference on Services Computing,* (pp. 193–201). Washington, DC: IEEE Computer Society Press.

Razavian, M., & Lago, P. (2010a). A frame of reference for SOA migration. *Lecture Notes in Computer Science, 6481,* 150–162. doi:10.1007/978-3-642-17694-4_13

Razavian, M., & Lago, P. (2010b). *Towards a conceptual framework for legacy to SOA migration.* Paper presented at the Fifth International Workshop on Engineering Service-Oriented Applications (WESOA 2009). Stockholm, Sweden.

Robinson, I. (2006). Consumer-driven contracts: A service evolution pattern. *MartinFowler.com.* Retrieved October 6, 2011, from http://www.martinfowler.com/articles/consumerDrivenContracts.html

Salehie, M., & Tahvildari, L. (2009). Self-adaptive software: Landscape and research challenges. *ACM Transactions on Autonomous and Adaptive Systems, 4*(2).

Šaša, A., & Juric, M. (2010). Version management of service interfaces in SOA. In S. S. Yau, E. Geig, M.-C. Shan, & P. Hung (Eds.), *Proceedings of the 2010 Sixth World Congress on Services,* (pp. 150–151). Washington, DC: IEEE Computer Society Press.

Seacord, R. C., Plakosh, D., & Lewis, G. A. (2003). *Modernizing legacy systems.* Boston, MA: Addison-Wesley.

Sneed, H. (2006). Integrating legacy software into a service oriented architecture. In G. Visaggio, G. A. Di Lucca, & N. Gold (Eds.), *Proceedings of the 10th European Conference on Software Maintenance and Reengineering (CSMR 2006),* (pp. 3–14). Washington, DC: IEEE Computer Society Press.

Sneed, H. (2007). *Migrating to web services: A research framework.* Paper presented at the International Workshop on SOA Maintenance Evolution (SOAM 2007), 11th European Conference on Software Maintenance and Reengineering (CSMR 2007). Amsterdam, The Netherlands.

Sneed, H. (2011). SOA integration as an alternative to source migration. In G. A. Lewis, D. B. Smith, & K. Kontogiannis (Eds.), *Proceedings of the Fourth International Workshop on a Research Agenda for Maintenance and Evolution of Service-Oriented Systems (MESOA 2010),* (pp. 41–48). Pittsburgh, PA: Carnegie Mellon University.

Solomon, A., & Litoiu, M. (2011). Using simulation models to evolve business processes. In G. A. Lewis, D. B. Smith, & K. Kontogiannis (Eds.), *Proceedings of the Fourth International Workshop on a Research Agenda for Maintenance and Evolution of Service-Oriented Systems (MESOA 2010),* (pp. 9–21). Pittsburgh, PA: Carnegie Mellon University.

Sward, R. E., & Whitacre, K. J. (2008). A multi-language service-oriented architecture using an enterprise service bus. In M. B. Feldman & L. C. Baird (Eds.), *SIGAda 2008: Proceedings of the 2008 ACM Annual International Conference on SIGAda,* (pp. 85–90). New York, NY: Association for Computing Machinery.

Tran, H., Zdun, U., & Dustdar, S. (2011). VbTrace: Using view-based and model-driven development to support traceability in process-driven SOAs. *Software & Systems Modeling, 10*(1), 5–29. doi:10.1007/s10270-009-0137-0

Umar, A., & Zordan, A. (2009). Reengineering for service oriented architectures: A strategic decision model for integration versus migration. *Journal of Systems and Software, 82,* 448–462. doi:10.1016/j.jss.2008.07.047

Van Geet, J., & Demeyer, S. (2007). Lightweight visualizations of COBOL code for supporting migration to SOA. *Electronic Communications of the EASST, 8.*

Villegas, N. M., & Müller, H. A. (2011). Context-driven adaptive monitoring for supporting SOA governance. In G. A. Lewis, D. B. Smith, & K. Kontogiannis (Eds.), *Proceedings of the Fourth International Workshop on a Research Agenda for Maintenance and Evolution of Service-Oriented Systems (MESOA 2010),* (pp. 111–133). Pittsburgh, PA: Carnegie Mellon University.

Wikipedia. (2011). *Mashup (web application hybrid).* Retrieved October 6, 2011, from http://en.wikipedia.org/wiki/Mashup_%28web_application_hybrid%29

Winter, A., & Ziemann, J. (2007). *Model-based migration to service-oriented architectures*. Paper presented at the International Workshop on SOA Maintenance Evolution (SOAM 2007), 11th European Conference on Software Maintenance and Reengineering (CSMR 2007). Amsterdam, The Netherlands.

Winter, A., Zillmann, C., Fuhr, A., Horn, T., Riediger, V., Herget, A., et al. (2011). The SO-AMIG process model in industrial applications. In T. Mens, Y. Kanellopoulos, & A. Winter (Eds.), *Proceedings of the 15th European Conference on Software Maintenance and Reengineering*, (pp. 339-342). Washington, DC: IEEE Computer Society Press.

Worms, K. (2011). *Challenges for maintenance and evolution of service-oriented systems at credit Suisse*. Paper presented at the Fourth International Workshop on a Research Agenda for Maintenance and Evolution of Service-Oriented Systems (ME-SOA 2010). Timisoara, Romania.

Xiao, H., Guo, J., & Zou, Y. (2007). Supporting change impact analysis for service oriented business applications. In *Proceedings of the International Workshop on Systems Development in SOA Environments (SDSOA 2007), ICSE Workshops 2007*. Washington, DC: IEEE Computer Society Press.

Zawawy, H., Mylopoulos, J., & Mankovski, S. (2011). Requirements-driven framework for root cause analysis in SOA environments. In G. A. Lewis, D. B. Smith, & K. Kontogiannis (Eds.), *Proceedings of the Fourth International Workshop on a Research Agenda for Maintenance and Evolution of Service-Oriented Systems (MESOA 2010)*, (pp. 22–40). Pittsburgh, PA: Carnegie Mellon University.

Zhang, L., Arsanjani, A., Allam, A., Lu, D., & Chee, Y. (2007). Variation-oriented analysis for SOA solution design. In E. Feig & H. T. Kung (Eds.), *Proceedings of the 2007 IEEE International Conference on Services Computing (SCC 2007)*, (pp. 560–568). Washington, DC: IEEE Computer Society Press.

Zhang, Z., Yang, H., Zhou, D., & Zhong, S. (2010). A SOA based approach to user-oriented system migration. In G. Min & T. El-Ghazawi (Eds.), *Proceedings of the 2010 IEEE 10th International Conference on Computer and Information Technology (CIT)*, (pp. 1486–1491). Washington, DC: IEEE Computer Society Press.

KEY TERMS AND DEFINITIONS

Legacy System: System that exists in an organization and continues to be used either because it meets desired capabilities or because the cost replacing or redesigning the system despite its poor quality or technology obsolescence is too high.

Legacy System Migration: The process of converting a legacy system and all its assets —e e.g., code, data, processes — from one platform to another.

Research Agenda: The identification of the fully -relevant research that needs to take place to advance a personal career or field of study.

Service-Oriented Architecture: Way of designing, developing, deployingdeploying, and managing systems in which (1) services provide coarse-grained, discoverable, reusable functionality via well-defined standardized interfaces and (2) developers use these services as part of their applications.

Service-Oriented Systems: Systems that are implemented using the SOA paradigm.

Software Evolution: The study and management of the process of making changes to software over time.

Software Maintenance: The activity of modifying software after it has deployed in order to maintain its usefulness.

Software Modernization: Evolution of a legacy system, or elements of the system, when conventional evolutionary practices, such as maintenance and enhancement, can no longer achieve the desired system properties.

ENDNOTES

[1.] The MESOCA workshops evolved from the ICSM workshops on Maintenance and Evolution of Service-Oriented Systems (MESOA).

[2.] See http://www.s-cube-network.eu for more information.

[3.] Lewis, et al. (2010) have further information on the strategic framework and life cycle.

[4.] The initial version of SMART (Lewis, et al., 2006) was focused on one specific technique for making decisions about changes required for migrating legacy components to an SOA environment. This specific technique was referred to as the "Service Migration and Reuse Technique." It has been broadened to a family of approaches to accommodate different starting points to SOA adoption. The broader family of methods is now referred to as the SOA Migration, Adoption, and Reuse Technique.

[5.] A mashup is an application that combines data from more than one source into a single view.

Chapter 3
Legacy to SOA Evolution:
A Systematic Literature Review

Ravi Khadka
Utrecht University, The Netherlands

Andrei Idu
Utrecht University, The Netherlands

Amir Saeidi
Utrecht University, The Netherlands

Jurriaan Hage
Utrecht University, The Netherlands

Slinger Jansen
Utrecht University, The Netherlands

ABSTRACT

Enterprises depend on business-critical systems that have been developed over the last three decades or more, also known as legacy systems. They have several well-known disadvantages (e.g., inflexible, domain unspecific, and hard to maintain), and this is recognized by both vendors and customers of these software systems. Both vendors and customers of these systems are well aware that better and more flexible customer specific solutions can be created following the service-oriented paradigm. Hence, momentum is growing within enterprises to evolve legacy systems towards Service-Oriented Architecture (SOA). The evolution to SOA is favored because of various advantages including well established sets of open standards, platform and language independent interfaces, clear separation of service interface and implementation, and loose-coupling among services.

In the last decade, there have been significant developments in legacy to SOA evolution, and that has resulted in a large research body of which there exists no comprehensive overview. This chapter provides a historic overview, focusing on the methods and techniques used in legacy to SOA evolution. The authors conducted a systematic literature review to collect legacy to SOA evolution approaches reported from 2000 to August 2011. To this end, 121 primary studies were found and evaluated using an evaluation framework, which was developed from three evolution and modernization methods widely used in the software re-engineering domain. The evaluation constitutes the inventory of current research approaches and methods and techniques used in legacy to SOA evolution. The result of the SLR also identifies current research issues in legacy to SOA evolution and provides future research directions to address those research issues.

DOI: 10.4018/978-1-4666-2488-7.ch003

Copyright © 2013, IGI Global. Copying or distributing in print or electronic forms without written permission of IGI Global is prohibited.

INTRODUCTION

Recently, many enterprises have focused on increasing their business flexibility and achieving cross-enterprise collaboration to remain competitive in the market, and to meet their business objectives. Enterprises are especially challenged by constant changes in the business environment and changes in the supporting Information Technology (IT) infrastructures that hinder the overall success of enterprises (van Sinderen, 2008). Furthermore, most enterprises still rely on so called legacy system- software developed over the previous decades using 3GL programming languages like COBOL, RGP, PL/I, C, C++. Despite the well-known disadvantages, such as being inflexible and hard to maintain, legacy systems are still vitally important to the enterprises as they support complex core business processes; they cannot simply be removed as they implement and store critical business logic. Unsurprisingly, the knowledge contained in these systems is of high value to an enterprise. On the other hand, proper documentation, skilled manpower, and resources to evolve these legacy systems are scarce. Therefore, momentum is growing to evolve and reuse those legacy systems within new technological environments—Service-Oriented Architecture (SOA) being the most promising one (Bisbal, Lawless, Wu, & Grimson, 1999; Lewis, Morris, O'Brien, Smith, & Wrage, 2005).

SOA has emerged as an architectural style that enables the reuse of existing legacy assets within a new paradigm that facilitates loose coupling, abstraction of underlying logic, flexibility, reusability and discoverability (Papazoglou, 2008). The evolution from legacy to SOA can be beneficial from both economical and technical perspectives. From an economical perspective, legacy to SOA evolution fosters change management including intra-organizational changes, and changes in enterprises (Khadka, Sapkota, Pires, Sinderen, & Jansen, 2011; Papazoglou, Traverso, Dustdar, & Leymann, 2007). From a technical perspective,

seamless enterprise collaboration through service composition (Khadka & Sapkota, 2010) and reduction in maintenance cost are claimed as long term benefits (Papazoglou, et al., 2007; Schelp & Aier, 2009). Motivated by these benefits, there has been significant research in legacy to SOA evolution. However, there is no systematic overview of legacy to SOA evolution, particularly focusing on the techniques, methods and approaches used to evolve legacy systems to a SOA environment. In the systematic literature review conducted by Razavian (Razavian & Lago, 2010), an overview of SOA migration families is reported. It focuses on classifying the SOA migration approaches into eight distinct families. The classification is inspired by the reengineering horseshoe method (Bergey, Smith, Weiderman, & Woods, 1999) rather than giving a historical overview of SOA migration methods. Also, a brief overview of legacy to SOA evolution is reported by Almonaies (Almonaies, Cordy, & Dean, 2010) that divides the legacy to SOA evolution approaches into four categories: replacement, redevelopment, wrapping and migration. The legacy to SOA evolution approaches reported in this research were not based on any systematic literature review process, so a complete, historical overview of the legacy to SOA evolution approaches is still lacking.

In this chapter, we provide a Systematic Literature Review (SLR) of the existing literature of legacy to SOA evolution. We provide a historical overview of the legacy to SOA evolution approaches reported in academia. We focus on identifying techniques, methods and approaches that are relevant to legacy to SOA evolution or that facilitate the legacy to SOA evolution process. In order to provide such a historical overview, we have developed an evaluation framework inspired by three software evolution frameworks reported in literature. The evaluation framework consists of six distinct phases and each phase has its own evaluation criteria to evaluate any legacy to SOA evolution approach reported in academia.

The main contributions of this research are as following:

1. A historical overview of legacy to SOA evolution.
2. A legacy to SOA evolution process framework.
3. An inventory of methods and techniques used in various phases of legacy to SOA evolution.
4. A series of research issues and recommendations for future research directions.

We argue that our evaluation framework enables a more comprehensive understanding of legacy to SOA evolution allowing us to recognize the contributions made so far, opportunities for combining approaches and identifying open issues and research challenges that still exist in legacy to SOA evolution. We believe that such an overview will benefit academic researchers and industrial practitioners. The academic researchers can contribute on identified research issues to foster the legacy to SOA evolution, whereas the industrial practitioners can adopt various methods and techniques that are reported in research in real world industrial practices.

The chapter is structured as follows: Section 2 provides the details of our research method; Section 3 presents the evaluation framework; Section 4 discusses the overview of the primary studies; Section 5 elaborates the findings of our SLR; Section 6 discusses the findings and best practices in legacy to SOA evolution; Section 7 describes the threats to validity; and in Section 8, we present the conclusions of our research and possible future research directions.

RESEARCH METHOD

We have adopted the procedures of conducting a systematic review process based on the guidelines proposed by Kitchenham (2004). A systematic review consists of a review protocol that details the rationale of the survey, research objectives, search strategy, selection criteria, data extraction, synthesis, and analysis of the extracted data and interpretation of the findings. Such a review process is typically appropriate in our research since it summarizes the existing contributions, identifies the gaps in the current research and avenues for further research, and provides a background to position new research activities in a research framework.

Review Protocol

A review protocol is a plan that specifies the procedures to be undertaken prior to the execution of a systematic review. Such a review protocol describes how to conduct the search, select relevant studies and selection criteria, and the analysis of the extracted data. A review protocol is composed of the following: research question, data sources, search strategy, study selection strategy, data extraction, and data synthesis. The first four define the scope and motivation of the research while the last two describe how the results are concluded from the data.

Research Question

In order to achieve our objective of creating an overview of legacy to SOA evolution approaches, we have formulated the following research questions:

1. How can a legacy to SOA evolution method be systematically defined?
2. What methods and techniques are used to facilitate such a systematic legacy to SOA evolution method?
3. What are the existing research issues and what should be the future research agenda in legacy to SOA evolution?

Data Sources

For our research, we have included the following eight electronic libraries/indexing sources as data sources: ACM Digital Library, CiteseerX, IEEE Xplore, ISI Web of Knowledge, ScienceDirect, Scopus, SpringerLink, and Wiley Inter Science Journal Finder.

Search Strategy

We have constructed a search string using SOA, legacy, and migration as main keywords, and have included synonyms and related terms. The search string is then constructed using Boolean "AND" to connect the three keywords and Boolean "OR" to allow synonyms and word class variants of each keyword. The resulting search string is depicted in Listing 1.

The search string was executed in the digital libraries/indexing services to titles, abstracts and metadata- assuming that these provide a concise summary of the work. Besides the search string, the range of study dates also has to be defined in the search strategy. We decided to choose 2000 as the starting year for the search strategy because SOAP (Box, et al., 2000) was first submitted to W3C in 2000.

Study Selection

It is likely that some of the results (study data) of a search might contain the keywords but are irrelevant to our research. For instance, a study data with the title "An evaluation of legacy systems and grid service systems of health-care domain: An initial step towards transformation to cloud-based system" is included in the result of the initial selection. In order to exclude such irrelevant studies, study selection is performed such that the study data is assessed to determine the actual relevance. A set of inclusion and exclusion criteria based on the scope of research and the quality of the studies were determined by us. The inclusion and exclusion criteria are given in Table 1.

The study selection not only eliminates irrelevant studies, but also ensures the quality of the study and the scoping of the research. For instance, inclusion criterion I1 and exclusion criterion E4 ensure that the study data meet the standards of peer-reviewed scientific papers. Inclusion criteria I2, I3, and exclusion criteria E1, E2, and E3 scope the research in accordance with the research objective/motivation.

Data Extraction

We extracted the study selection in a spreadsheet including the following details: title, authors, publication year, publication form (journal/conference/workshop/book chapter), name, and abstract. We conducted the first selection round based on the "title and abstract" of the study. The study was categorized as follows:

1. Relevant (study inside the scope of the research),
2. Irrelevant (study outside the scope of the research), and
3. Moderate (unable to decide the relevancy of the paper).

Listing 1. Search string

(SOA **OR** "Service-Oriented" **OR** "Service-Based" **OR** "Service-Centric" **OR** "Service-Engineering" **OR** "SOSE" **OR** "Web service" **OR** "service-oriented computing") **AND** (Monolith **OR** "legacy code" **OR** "Legacy system" **OR** "existing system" **OR** "legacy component" **OR** "legacy software" **OR** "monolithic system" **OR** "existing software" **OR** "pre-existing software" **OR** "legacy information system" **OR** "legacy program" **OR** "pre-existing assets") **AND** (migration **OR** evolution **OR** modernisation **OR** reengineering **OR** re-engineering **OR** reuse **OR** "service identification" **OR** "candidate service identification" **OR** "service extraction" **OR** bridging **OR** reconstruction **OR** modernization **OR** decomposing **OR** "incubating services" **OR** integrating **OR** redesigning **OR** "Service mining" **OR** migrating **OR** transformation)

Table 1. Inclusion and exclusion criteria for study selection

Inclusion Criteria	Exclusion Criteria
I1. A study in the form of a scientific peer-reviewed paper. **Motivation**: A scientific paper guarantees a certain level of quality through a peer review process and contains a substantial amount of content.	**E1**. A study that is not about legacy to SOA evolution. **Rationale**: Our objective is to study legacy to SOA evolution, so we exclude any other legacy modernization. For example, legacy modernization to object-orientation, cloud computing or grid services will be excluded.
I2. A study that is focused on legacy to SOA evolution. **Motivation**: We are interested in legacy to SOA evolution, which implies that any study targeting legacy to SOA evolution should be included.	**E2**. A study that is related to challenges and issues while modernizing legacy systems to SOA. **Rationale**: We focus on a specific solution to legacy to SOA evolution. We exclude papers with an objective of presenting challenges, issues, and future directions to legacy to SOA evolution.
I3. The objective of the study is to present/propose a solution(s) to legacy to SOA evolution. **Motivation**: We are interested in a specific solution to legacy to SOA modernization. A solution could be a complete evolution process/method or solution enabling legacy to SOA evolution.	**E3**. A study that has other objective(s) than providing a solution(s) to legacy to SOA evolution. **Rationale**: We exclude papers with a main objective other than proposing a solution to legacy to SOA evolution. For instance, we exclude papers with an objective of presenting challenges, issues, future directions to legacy to SOA evolution and comparing the modernization techniques of legacy to SOA evolution.
	E4. The Study is reported in another language than English. **Rationale**: We exclude the papers that are written in languages other than English, since English is the common language for reporting in most of the international venues of computer science

For each irrelevant and moderate study, explicit reasons were provided in the spreadsheet. The moderate category was decided by repeating the review by a reviewer other than the initial reviewer and by discussing the paper with the team. The final outcome is the collection of relevant studies, which we refer to as the primary studies.

Data Synthesis

The primary studies were evaluated against the evaluation framework presented in Section 3 and various findings are reported in Section 4 and Section 5.

We conducted a review process adhering to the review protocol. Initially, we had 8493 hits when we ran the search query over the electronic libraries/indexing sources. Those 8493 articles were analyzed by five researchers to determine the relevancy based on title and abstract, which left 269 articles. These articles were then evaluated based on inclusion and exclusion criteria, which resulted in 121 primary studies. The details of the review process can be found in Idu, Khadka,

Figure 1. The review process with number of studies

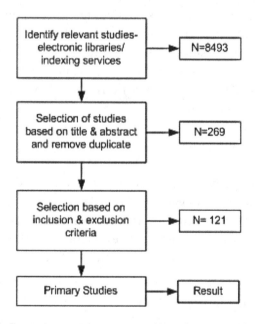

Saeidi, Jansen, and Hage (2012). Figure 1 depicts the review process.

EVALUATION FRAMEWORK FOR LEGACY TO SOA EVOLUTION

To develop an evaluation framework for legacy to SOA evolution, we needed to identify the phases that are typically related to evolution/modernization of legacy systems. Based on a high number of citations (popularity), availability of documentation, and completeness of the legacy evolution/modernization process, the following methods from software re-engineering domain were used to identify the phases for our evaluation framework: the butterfly method (Wu, et al., 1997), the Renaissance method (Warren & Ransom, 2002), and the Architecture-Driven Modernization (ADM) (Khusidman & Ulrich, 2007). The main reason for using these evolution/modernization methods is that the software re-engineering domain has been extensively researched and widely practiced in industries, as compared to SOA evolution methods. In particular, we want to reuse the concepts from those methods in the development of a new method for legacy to SOA evolution. Method engineering (Brinkkemper, 1996) allows us to reuse existing concepts from existing methods to construct new methods. Hence, we use method engineering and reuse the concepts from the three above-mentioned legacy evolution/modernization methods. We argue that reusing the methods and practices from existing standards/methods saves time and reduces the adoption problem (i.e., it is easier to adapt to the existing methods/practices than learning new methods). Due to limitations of space, we do not provide the details of the construction of the evaluation framework in this chapter. The details are reported in Idu et al. (2012). One can argue that there are sufficient relevant legacy to SOA evolution methods that could have been used to develop the evaluation framework. Most of the legacy to SOA evolution methods reported in literature, either focus on developing supporting technology (i.e., implementation techniques to expose legacy systems in SOA) or planning the legacy to SOA evolution (i.e., determining the feasibility of evolution) (Razavian & Lago, 2010). However, a legacy to SOA evolution requires the consolidation of both, developing supporting technology and planning the legacy to SOA evolution (De Lucia, Francese, Scanniello, & Tortora, 2008; Khadka, Reijnders, Saeidi, Jansen, & Hage, 2011). In our approach, we aim at developing such a framework that combines both aspects (i.e., planning legacy to SOA evolution and implementation). Furthermore, we aim at assessing those existing legacy to SOA evolution methods using our developed evaluation method rather than using them to develop a new method.

From the three methods, we have identified phases that are common to all of them. For instance, legacy system understanding, target system understanding, evolution feasibility determination, and implementation of evolution are common phases in the above-mentioned methods. To make our evaluation framework more relevant to the SOA domain and to reflect the intent of legacy to SOA evolution, we further analyzed and identified some phases from the following service-oriented development methods: Service-Oriented Design and Development Methodology (SODDM) (Papazoglou & Van Den Heuvel, 2006), Web Service Implementation Methodology (WSIM) (Lee, Chan, & Lee, 2006), and Service-Oriented Modeling and Architecture (SOMA) (Arsanjani, et al., 2004). The details of the identification of the phases are detailed by Reijnders et al. (Reijnders, Khadka, Jansen, & Hage, 2011) using the method engineering approach. From these service-oriented development methods, we have added candidate service identification and deployment and provisioning phases to our evaluation framework. Finally, our evaluation framework includes six phases divided over two generic stages. The evaluation framework and the phases are depicted in Figure 2. The evolution planning addresses the question "what to do?" and "is evolution feasible in the given context?" The evolution implementation & management addresses the question "how to do it?" and "what techniques can be used to perform

Figure 2. The evaluation framework

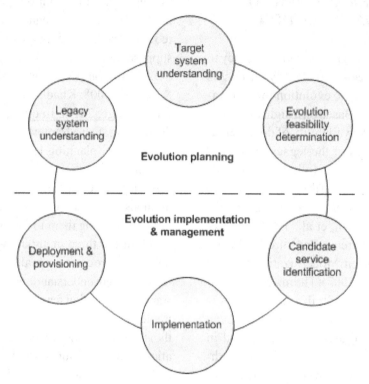

the evolution?" In the following subsections, we explain the phases of our evaluation framework.

Legacy System Understanding

Understanding the legacy system and its as-is situation are crucial to the success of any evolution (Seacord, Plakosh, & Lewis, 2003). This includes a detailed analysis of the legacy system and various techniques can be used. For instance, reverse engineering, program understanding, architectural recovery can be used, often with tool support to generate system artifacts. Legacy system understanding often includes analyzing the development history, interviewing the developers (if any) and current users to come to an understanding of the architecture of the legacy system. In our evaluation framework, we have defined evaluation criteria to investigate if any legacy to SOA evolution method includes legacy system understanding and to what extent this phase is discussed.

Target System Understanding

The target system understanding phase facilitates the representation of the desired architecture of the to-be SOA. This phase describes the target SOA environment, which includes activities like defining major components/functionalities of SOA environment, specific technologies and standards to be used, state of targeted SOA, and availability of existing similar services to reuse. In our evaluation framework, we have defined evaluation criteria to determine whether a legacy to SOA evolution method includes target system understanding for the desired SOA system and to what extent this phase is discussed.

Evolution Feasibility Determination

The legacy system understanding and the target system understanding phases provide better understanding of the as-is and to-be situations, respectively. Based on this understanding, the feasibility of the evolution has to be determined and is done in the evolution feasibility determination phase. The feasibility assessments are carried out at a technical, economical, and organizational level. The technical assessment includes measuring the code complexity of the legacy system in terms of cohesion, coupling, reusability and abstraction (Reddy, Dubey, Lakshmanan, Sukumaran, & Sisodia, 2009). Economical assessment includes determining economic feasibility of the evolution, for instance by using the cost-benefit analysis, as suggested by Sneed (1995a). Upon analyzing the technical and economical feasibility, the organization approves the evolution project by also considering whether its business goals are met by the intended SOA system. In our evaluation framework, we have defined evaluation criteria to determine whether a legacy to SOA evolution method includes evolution feasibility and if so, how is it performed.

Candidate Service Identification

Legacy systems are subjected to evolutionary development and bug fixing in the source code often by people who did not develop it. This typically leads to much redundancy in the code. Furthermore, poor documentation and lack of appropriate resources (e.g. developers, architects) make the understanding of source code a hard task. In such a scenario, identifying the potential services and service-rich areas in a legacy code is definitely a challenging task (Khadka, 2011). The candidate service identification phase aims at locating the service-rich areas. Various techniques can be used for this purpose. For instance, architectural reconstruction, feature location, design pattern recovery, cluster analysis techniques, concept analysis, source code visualization can be used to identify the service-rich areas in a large body of legacy code. In our evaluation framework, we have defined evaluation criteria to investigate if

any legacy to SOA evolution method includes techniques to identify potential candidate services.

Implementation

The implementation phase is concerned with the technical evolution of the whole legacy system to the target system using various techniques, often supported by the tools. For instance, wrapping, program slicing, concept slicing, graph transformation, code translation, model-driven program transformation, screen scraping, code query technology, graph transformation can be used to extract/ leverage the legacy code as services. In our evaluation framework, we have defined evaluation criteria to investigate if a legacy to SOA evolution method includes any techniques to extract/ leverage legacy code as services.

Deployment and Provisioning

The deployment and provisioning phase is concerned with deployment and management of the services after extraction of the legacy code. Upon extraction, services are deployed in the service infrastructure. Service provisioning typically includes the after-deployment activities such as publishing, versioning of services, metering and billing of the usage of the services (Khadka, Saeidi, Jansen, Hage, & Helms, 2011). In our evaluation framework, we have defined evaluation criteria to determine whether a legacy to SOA evolution method includes deployment and provisioning.

Based on the identified phases, we have derived the list of evaluation criteria given in Table 2: the first column presents the stages within an evolution, the second column lists the identified phases of our evaluation framework, the third column presents the evaluation question as evaluation criterion for each phase, and the final column gives possible answers for each evaluation question. The answers can be of three types: Yes/No- to indicate whether the given criterion is met, narrative- to answer an open question, and

Table 2. The evaluation criteria based on the evaluation framework

Stage	Phase	Evaluation question	Answer
Evolution planning	Legacy system understanding	Does the solution include legacy system understanding?	Yes/No
		Which technique(s) is used for legacy system understanding?	Narrative
		To what extent are those techniques used?	Scale
		Is there any tool support for legacy system understanding?	Yes/No
	Target system understanding	Does the solution include target system understanding?	Yes/No
		What criteria/factors are included for target system understanding?	Narrative
		To what extent are those criteria/factors used?	Scale
	Evolution feasibility determination	Does the solution include evolution feasibility assessment?	Yes/No
		What technique(s) is used for evolution feasibility assessment?	Narrative
Evolution implementation & management	Candidate service identification	Does the solution include candidate service identification?	Yes/No
		What technique(s) is used for identifying candidate services?	Narrative
		Is there tool support for candidate service identification?	Yes/No
	Implementation	Does the solution provide any implementation technique for evolution?	Yes/No
		What technique(s) is used for implementation?	Narrative
		Is there tool support for the implementation?	Yes/No
	Deployment and provisioning	Does the solution provide deployment and provisioning of the services?	Yes/No
Case study		What empirical evidence (industrial/experiment) is provided?	Narrative
		In which language is the legacy system developed?	Narrative

scale- to quantify the degree of support for any criterion. The judgment of scale is presented in Appendix B.

OVERVIEW OF THE PRIMARY STUDIES

In total, we found 121 publications as our primary after evaluating against the inclusion and exclusion criteria. Figure 3 shows the distribution of primary studies published per year along with the trend-line. The positive slope of the trend-line not only indicates an increasing amount of research being carried out in legacy to SOA evolution domain, but also reflects the increase of legacy to SOA evolution approaches along with the maturity of SOA paradigm- SOA being used as architectural style after SOAP (Box, et al., 2000) was first submitted to W3C in 2000. We cannot be certain that we have covered all studies with a publication date in 2011, since studies may not have been indexed yet at the time. This is one of the possible reasons for the sharp decrease in publication in 2011.

Figure 4 presents the distribution of the primary studies across venues from which at least two articles were selected. It is very interesting to notice that the largest amount of research is reported at venues related to system maintenance, evolution and re-engineering such as CSMR, ICSM, WSE rather than core service-oriented computing venues such as SCC, ECOWS, ICSOC. This implies legacy to SOA evolution is often seen as a solution to maintenance/evolution problems of (legacy) software systems. Also, the frequency of publication in journals is also relatively low as compared to conferences or workshops, which is not surprising in such a young field. Note that we have not included the venues with less than two occurrences.

Figure 3. Distribution of the primary studies published per year

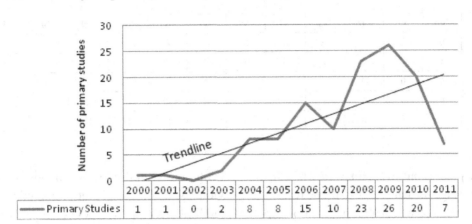

Figure 4. Summary of primary studies across different venues

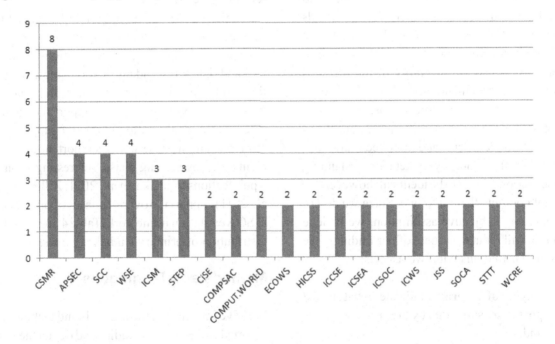

Table 3 presents the distribution of the primary studies according to the kind of source. The result shows that conferences are the most widely used method of dissemination for legacy to SOA evolution approaches. The journal papers for legacy to SOA evolution approaches score quite low as compared with the conference papers.

RESULTS

The result of our SLR is based on the evaluation criteria described in Table 2. Using our evaluation criteria, we evaluated 121 publications. Due to limitations of space, we have not included the full result of our complete evaluation in this chapter. Appendix A depicts an evaluation of a small number of articles. For the complete evalu-

Table 3. Summary of primary studies according to the sources

Source/year	'00	'01	'02	'03	'04	'05	'06	'07	'08	'09	'10	'11	Total
Book	0	0	0	0	0	0	0	0	1	2	0	1	4
Conference	1	1	0	1	6	4	13	9	12	17	17	4	85
Journal	0	0	0	0	1	0	2	1	7	5	2	2	20
Workshop	0	0	0	1	1	4	0	0	3	2	1	0	12
Total	1	1	0	2	8	8	15	10	23	26	20	7	121

ation result, please consult Khadka et al. (Khadka, Saeidi, Idu, Hage, & Jansen, 2012). The result is primarily focused on whether the publication supports the phases of our evaluation framework, what methods and technologies are used (if supported), and whether any tool support for methods and techniques is discussed. Furthermore, the details of empirical evidence (case study) reported in each publication are also presented. In our evaluation, we created the inventory of the methods and techniques as mentioned in the publication. We did not conduct any subjective assumption for categorization. For instance, in many publications "architectural recovery" and "architectural reconstruction" of the legacy system understanding phase are considered to be identical; however, we did not combine them into one. Since we do not conduct any subjective assumption, we believe that this will reduce biasness of our findings. We present our findings with two aspects:

1. **Degree of coverage:** Indicates what stages/phases are supported by the primary studies and,
2. **Methods and techniques used:** Inventory of what methods and techniques are generally in practice in each phase.

Degree of Coverage

Out of 121 publications, 12 publications have full coverage of the evolution planning stage, i.e., 12 publications support the legacy system understanding, target system understanding and

evolution feasibility determination phases. Individually, under the evolution planning stage, 66 publications support legacy system understanding, 43 publications support target system understanding and 20 publications support an evolution feasibility determination phase.

Similarly, 15 publications out of 121 have full coverage of the evolution implementation and management stage, i.e., 15 publications support the candidate service identification, implementation, and deployment and provisioning phases. Individually, 59 publications support the candidate service identification phase, 97 support the implementation phase and 22 support the deployment and provisioning phase. Interestingly, only 2 publications (Khadka, et al., 2011; Zillmann, et al., 2011) support the overall phases of our legacy to SOA evolution framework. Table 4 presents the distribution of primary studies per phase.

Methods and Techniques

We have inventoried the methods and techniques reported in the primary studies and depict them as in bar chart accordingly, one for each of the phase of our evaluation framework. Note that in most of the phases the information was Not Available (N/A) and that the results presented in the bar charts do not include N/A.

Figure 5 depicts the methods and techniques that are used for the legacy system understanding phase. Reverse engineering technique is by far the most widely used technique. Documentation and Interviewing are the second and third most

Table 4. Distribution of primary studies per phase

Legacy to SOA evolution 2					
Evolution Planning 12			Evolution Implementation and Management 15		
Legacy System Understanding 66	Target System Understanding 43	Evolution Feasibility Determination 20	Candidate Service Identification 59	Implementation 97	Deployment and Provisioning 22

Figure 5. Distribution of methods and techniques used for legacy system understanding

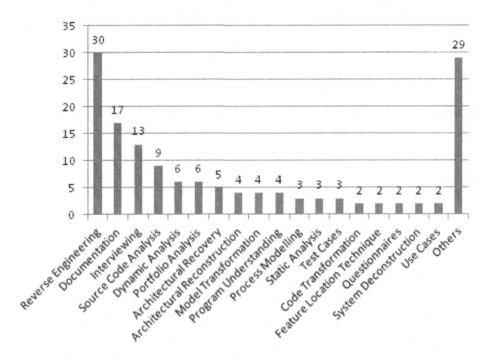

used techniques followed by mostly source code analysis or architectural reconstruction techniques. Based on the Scale criteria (-, +, ++, +++), 22 papers extensively discussed legacy system understanding with +++, 18 papers with ++, and 20 papers with +. In most of the cases, multiple methods and techniques were used for legacy system understanding. An interesting observation is that most of the methods and techniques used for legacy system understanding are technical in nature such as reverse engineering, architectural recovery, program understanding. Manual techniques like documentation and interviewing

are less common than in-depth descriptions of technical methods. One of the reasons for using methods and techniques of such technical nature is that legacy resources like documentation and developers are scarce- a widely identified problem in legacy evolution (Bennett, 1995; Bisbal, et al., 1999). Furthermore, only 26/121 papers discuss tool support for legacy system understanding. In most of the papers, multiple techniques are combined for legacy system understanding.

Figure 6 depicts the methods and techniques that are used for target system understanding. Here selection of a specific architecture is most

Figure 6. Distribution of methods and techniques used for target system understanding

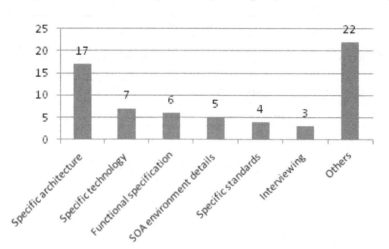

Figure 7. Distribution of methods and techniques used for evolution feasibility determination

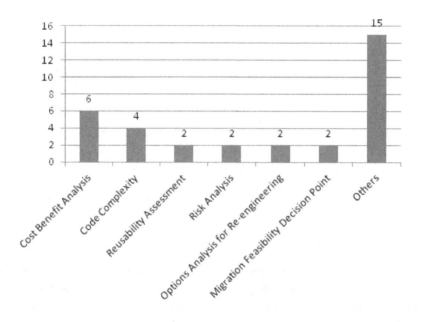

widely used. It is interesting to note that almost all of the instances in the chart are techniques that actually represent the technological aspect of target system, while only Interviewing refers to the process (i.e., organizational) perspective. Only 13/121 papers extensively discusses the target system understanding with +++, 12/121 papers with ++, and 12/121 papers with +.

The methods and techniques that are used for the evolution feasibility determination phase are shown in Figure 7. Here Cost-Benefit Analysis (CBA) is widely used, followed by Code complexity. While CBA technique is primarily an economically oriented analysis, the other most used techniques, Code complexity and Reusability assessment, refer to a technical analysis. The details of CBA are presented by Sneed (1995a) and Umar et al. (Umar & Zordan, 2009) and the details of Code complexity is explained by Sneed (2009). The concept of Option Analysis for Re-engineering (OAR) is proposed by Bergey (2001); it has been used in SMART (Balasubramaniam, Lewis, Morris, Simanta, & Smith, 2008; Lewis, et al., 2005).

Figure 8 depicts the methods and techniques that are used for the candidate service identification phase. Manual identification is most commonly used. It is also noteworthy that none of the other techniques are widely used, leading to 51 distinct techniques encountered in the primary studies other than Manual. It is interesting to note that candidate service identification has also been separately researched to foster legacy to SOA evolution.

Alahmari et al. (Alahmari, Zaluska, & De Roure, 2010) propose model-driven architecture based service identification using a SOA meta-model to identify services in legacy code. Aversano et al. (Aversano, Cerulo, & Palumbo, 2008) combined information retrieval techniques with a similarity based metric to identify potential services in legacy systems. In Chen, Zhang, Li, Kang, and Yang (2009), the authors propose an ontology based approach in which an ontology stores knowledge of both the application domain and the legacy code. Later, formal concept analysis and relational concept analysis are used to identify the candidate services. The authors in Nakamura, Igaki, Kimura, and Matsumoto (2009) generate data flow diagrams from the legacy code using reverse engineering techniques to aid candidate service identification. The authors of Zhang, Liu, and Yang (2005) use clustering technique to analyze the architectural information and identify the related modules as potential candidate services.

The methods and techniques that are used in the implementation phase are presented in Figure 9. Wrapping is by far the most widely used. Considering the big difference between Wrapping and the other techniques used, we believe that most

of the legacy to SOA evolution techniques do not focus on altering existing legacy code bases. In addition, wrapping is a fast, less risky, economical, and easy solution although the legacy system remains monolithic. The result of our evaluation shows that techniques like model transformation, program slicing, and code transformations are much less frequently used. From Table 4, we find that 97 out of 121 papers support the Implementation phase. In our evaluation, we also found out that 74 papers out of these 97 papers (i.e., papers supporting the implementation phase) also have tool support for implementation. Furthermore, 22 publications support the deployment and provisioning phase.

Figure 10 depicts the distribution of empirical studies conducted to validate the proposed legacy to SOA evolution in the primary studies. The majority of primary studies presented case studies, which were performed at an Industrial level. Interesting to note is the fact that there was a small number of studies that presented both Experimental and Industrial case studies, thus covering a wider applicability of validation. Among the industrial case studies, C++ and COBOL based legacy systems are most common: four cases for each. In the experimental case studies, Java-based systems were widely used (sixteen in all), followed by COBOL (four systems).

DISCUSSION

Based on the SLR, we present our findings and best practices, and open research issues and agenda in the following paragraphs.

Findings and Best Practices

The evolution planning stage of the evaluation framework (see Figure 2) addresses the feasibility of evolution from business and technical perspectives. The evolution planning focuses on justifying whether the legacy system is economically and

Figure 8. Distribution of method and techniques used for candidate service identification

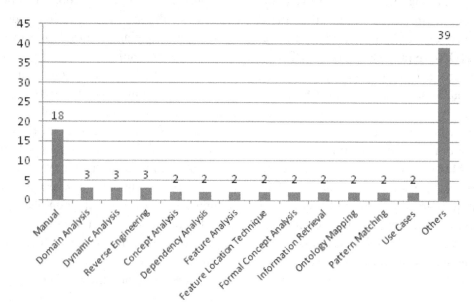

Figure 9. Distribution of method and techniques used for implementation

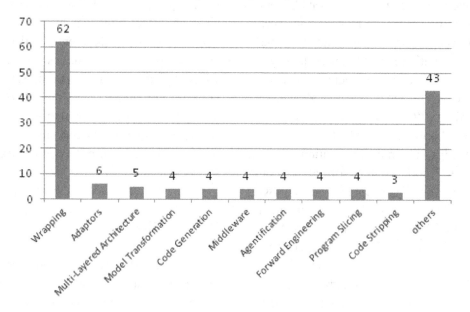

technically suitable for evolution. To a large extent, the success and failure of an evolution project depends on proper planning (Sneed, 1995a). In the context of legacy to SOA evolution, evolution planning becomes more complicated as various technical factors of the legacy systems should be

well understood. Such technical factors include complexity metrics (Sneed, 1995b) and coupling and cohesion metrics for reusability (Gui & Scott, 2006; Perepletchikov, Ryan, Frampton, & Tari, 2007). In the case of legacy systems, obtaining such information is a challenging task, particularly

Figure 10. Distribution of case study performed

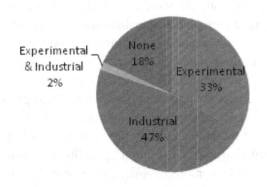

due to the unavailability of resources and documentation. Other important factors include cost estimation for evolution and economic feasibility to determine the profitability of evolution. The economic feasibility should take into account the current expense of maintaining the legacy system and the costs predicted for maintaining the target system after evolution. Hence, evolution planning should also consider the architecture and standards of the target system.

Within evolution planning, legacy system understanding has been extensively investigated, primarily with reverse engineering techniques. The two major categories under reverse engineering in legacy system understanding are program understanding and architectural reconstruction. Program understanding (Corbi, 1989) is defined as the process of acquiring knowledge about a computer program and is extensively used for software maintenance, software evolution and software re-engineering. Corbi (1989) identifies three actions that can be used to understand a program: read about the program (e.g., documentation), read the program itself (e.g., read source code) and run the program (e.g., watch execution, get trace data, etc.). All these three actions have been used in legacy to SOA evolution under various related topics, such as documentation, source code analysis, static analysis and dynamic analysis. Most of the articles state that program understanding or source code analysis techniques are used to understand

the legacy codes. However, only few articles explain such program understanding techniques in detail. Source code analysis techniques have been presented well by Zhang (Zhang, Yang, & Chu, 2006); static analysis in Zillmann et al. (2011) using Flow Graph Manipulator (FGM) and dynamic analysis using JGrabLab/GReQL in Zillmann et al. (2011) and TGraph in Fuhr, Horn, Riediger, and Winter (2011). Architectural reconstruction is a process in which the architecture representations of a software system are obtained from the existing source code (Kazman, O'Brien, & Verhoef, 2001) and is widely used in the software reengineering domain. Similarly, the use of architectural reconstruction has been also been reported in legacy to SOA evolution approaches. Cuadrado et al. (2008) used the QUE-es Architecture Recovery (QAR) workflow to reconstruct the architecture of legacy systems using Jude, Omondo UML studio and Eclipse Test and Performance Tools Platform (TPTP) tool. Lewis et al. (2006) and O'Brien et al. (O'Brien, Smith, & Lewis, 2005) used the ARMIN tool to reconstruct the architecture of the DoD Command and Control (C2) legacy application such that various undocumented dependencies in the source code were identified. Li and Tahvildari (2008) used the Extracting Business Services (E-BUS) toolkit to reconstruct the architecture of various Java-based systems. Similarly, Zhang et al. (2005) uses architecture recovery to obtain design and architectural information that are used as input for service identification. Our evaluation indicates that architectural reconstruction has been used more often with tool support than program understanding. In addition, in most of the cases both program understanding and architectural reconstruction have been employed. Feature location techniques (Chen, Li, Yang, Wang, & Chu, 2005; van Geet & Demeyer, 2010; Vemuri, 2008) have also been reported in understanding legacy systems.

The target system understanding phase intends to choose the architecture and related SOA technologies of the future system, which eventually plays an important role in the quality of the future SOA system. Lewis (2005) argues that the characteristics of the target system will temper decisions about whether legacy components can be reused. Basically, target system understanding can be viewed from two perspectives: functional characteristics and technical characteristics of the target system. The functional characteristics include the potential functionalities to-be evolved from the legacy code. This process is referred to as service design. It also defines to what level of granularity the services are to be defined and, accordingly, the orchestration of the services has to be managed to support business processes. Various functional and non-functional properties should also be considered, such as maintainability, interoperability, responsiveness, performance, security, and availability. The technical characteristics of the target environment include service technology (SOAP or REST-based), messaging technologies, communication protocols, service description languages, and service discovery mechanisms. Despite the importance, target system understanding is not described in detail in most of the articles. Rather, the articles just state that target architecture or target system is an important aspect. However, the functional characteristics of target system understanding has been well explored in SOAMIG (Fuhr, et al., 2011; Zillmann, et al., 2011) and SMART (Lewis, Morris, & Smith, 2006; Lewis, Morris, Smith, & O'Brien, 2005). The SOAMIG method describes the importance of service design, which is the result of forward engineering (design of the target architecture and the orchestration of services) and reverse engineering (potential functionalities as services from legacy system understanding). The SMART method focuses on designing the target system based on the potential functionalities as services and to assess them with the stakeholders by taking into account of various functional and non-functional characteristics of the target system. From the technical characteristics perspective, Cuadrado et al. (Cuadrado, García, Duenas, &

Parada, 2008) provide a clear explanation of using the OSGi specification and service platform. The authors consider maintainability and interoperability as important criteria of the target system and accordingly use OSGi specifications to support those non-functional characteristics.

One of the important phases from the organizational perspective is evolution feasibility determination that determines the go or no-go of the evolution project. Evolution feasibility determination focuses on an economical and technical assessment of the legacy system and the target system along with the business goals that the organization wants to achieve through evolution. The evolution feasibility determination phase uses the finding of the legacy system understanding (e.g., code complexity, cohesion and coupling metrics, etc) and the findings of the target system understanding (e.g., non-functional characteristics, selection of service technology, orchestration design, etc) to determine the technical and economical feasibility. The best practices in the evolution feasibility determination phase include the cost-benefit analysis proposed by Sneed (1995a) for re-engineering projects and serves as a good starting point. This CBA model has been widely followed in legacy to SOA evolution (Khadka, et al., 2011; Sneed, 2008, 2009). Umar and Zordan (2009) extended the CBA model to include the integration costs which facilitates the strategic decision making in legacy to SOA evolution. The SMART method uses Options Analysis for Re-engineering (OAR) (Smith, O'Brien, & Bergey, 2002) to determine the so called migration feasibility decision point. Based on the SMART method and a decision framework by Erradi (Erradi, Anand, & Kulkarni, 2006), Salama and Aly (2008) present a decision making tool for the selection of the legacy to SOA modernization strategies, which also considers evolution feasibility.

Based on the outcome of the evolution planning, the next step is to decide how to implement the evolution and what techniques are favorable for implementation. It has been widely recognized that legacy evolution is not purely a technical problem, but involves business engineering as well (Ziemann, Leyking, Kahl, & Werth, 2006). The main challenges are how to identify business functionality as a potential service, how to evolve such business functionality as a service and finally, how to maintain and monitor the service once it is deployed. Based on these three requirements, we have identified three phases under evolution implementation and deployment stage.

Identifying service-rich areas in a huge chunk of legacy code has been a challenging task in legacy to SOA evolution. Our survey has revealed that techniques applied to locate service-rich areas can be broadly classified into two: modeling the business requirements (top-down) approach and legacy code to business functionalities (bottom-up) approach. In modeling the business requirement approach, the core business process is designed from the functionalities identified from the legacy system understanding and then the process is subdivided until that can be mapped to functionalities in legacy system. In most of such approaches, BPMN is used to model the business process (Alahmari, Roure, & Zaluska, 2010; Fuhr, et al., 2011; Li, Anming, Naiyue, Jianbin, & Zhong, 2009; Ricca & Marchetto, 2009; Zillmann, et al., 2011). The legacy code to business functionalities approach utilizes legacy code as starting point to discover existing business knowledge within legacy systems. Various techniques have been used, such as information retrieval (Aversano, et al., 2008), concept analysis (Zhang, et al., 2006), cluster analysis (Zhang & Yang, 2004), business rule recovery (Marchetto & Ricca, 2008) and pattern matching and discovery (Guzman, Polo, & Piattini, 2007; Jiang & Stroulia, 2004; Zhang, Zhou, Yang, & Zhong, 2010).

Based on the findings of the Implementation phase, the legacy to SOA evolution can be either categorized as legacy system integration or legacy system migration. Legacy system integration is an approach in which the legacy codes is not substantially modified and is used from

within a new environment. The legacy systems typically remain in their original environment. Generally, techniques like wrapping, adaptors and middleware based approaches fall into the integration category, which is the predominant implementation technique as far we have seen in legacy to SOA migration (cf Figure 9). Integration is claimed to be a fast, less risky, economical and easy solution but the legacy system remains as it is (Almonaies, et al., 2010; Umar & Zordan, 2009). Wrapping based legacy to SOA evolution are reported by Sneed (2008, 2009) in which the author has developed various tools to support the evolution; Ricca and Marchetto (2009) used wrapping to evolve ATM functionality to SOA; Zhang et al. (2008) used wrapping to evolve GUI-based legacy systems to SOA. On the other hand, the legacy system migration approach is one in which the legacy code is transformed, internally modified, or reused in a new environment. Umar and Zordan (2009) define migration as "an internal restructuring and modification of legacy systems into target systems." The migration technique is claimed to be costly, time consuming but in the long run the organization can gradually replace the existing legacy system. Various techniques have been used to migration legacy systems to SOA (program slicing [Bao, Yin, He, Ge, & Chen, 2010; Chen, et al., 2009; Khadka, et al., 2011; Marchetto & Ricca, 2008; Zhang, et al., 2006]; model transformation techniques [Chen, Yang, Qiao, & Chu, 2006; Fuhr, et al., 2011; Hoyer, et al., 2009]). The distinction between integration and migration is discussed by Umar et al. (Umar & Zordan, 2009) in detail with respective benefits and drawbacks.

In the deployment and provisioning phase, the evolved services have to be deployed and activities are required to manage and control the behavior of services during usage. In the context of legacy to SOA evolution, activities such as testing, versioning and monitoring are important. Service testing has been a research challenge in the SOA domain due to the dynamic binding (Canfora & Di Penta,

2006) and the fact that the source code of services might not reside within a single organization (Lewis, Smith, Chapin, & Kontogiannis, 2009). Service testing in the context of legacy to SOA evolution is even more complicated because the exposed service after evolution should perform correctly when compared to the legacy system. Some legacy to SOA evolution approaches also address the testing of exposed services (Fuhr, et al., 2011; Khadka, et al., 2011; Marchetto & Ricca, 2008; Sneed, 2008; Zillmann, et al., 2011). Due to changing business requirements, services need to evolve and this leads to multiple versions of an exposed service (Fang, et al., 2007; Khadka, et al., 2011). Service versioning is inevitable in legacy to SOA evolution as well, particularly, in legacy system integration approaches. In legacy system integration, the legacy code is exposed through interfaces, without making any changes to the original code. Later, changes made to legacy code after evolution have to be reflected in the service interfaces as well and this creates multiple versions of the original service. In addition, service monitoring for non-functional attributes becomes important while the exposed services are in use. Service versioning and service monitoring has not received much attention in legacy to SOA evolution.

An increasing number of articles from 2000 to 2011 on legacy to SOA evolution suggests that the hype is gaining momentum in academia and is still in maturing stage. It is also interesting to see that almost half of the results of the research are evaluated in an industrial context (see Figure 10). Some good examples of such research include: the SMART (Lewis, et al., 2005) which has been evaluated in migrating the Department of Defense Mission Status System and Command and Control system, the SOAMIG process model (Fuhr, et al., 2011; Zillmann, et al., 2011) in Amadeus Germany's RAIL-system, the wrapping method (Sneed, 2008, 2009) for a COBOL-based insurance system, the migration of Java-based legacy application to SOA (Bhallamudi & Tilley,

2011), the feature analysis method for migrating a COBOL-based telecommunication systems (Millham, 2010), and a case study of adopting SOA in the transportation sector (Nasr, Gross, & Deursen, 2010).

Research Issues and Agenda

Several research issues still persist in legacy to SOA evolution. In the following subsection, we present research topics based on the results of our evaluation.

Legacy to SOA Evolution as a Process

Legacy to SOA evolution is a complex process, which is influenced by technical, economical and organizational factors. So, any legacy to SOA evolution requires a structured process model that can address these technical, economical and organizational factors. The need of such a structured process model has been also argued by various researchers (Kontogiannis, et al., 2007; Lewis, et al., 2009). Such a structured evolution process should include a legacy system assessment to recover knowledge, the standards and architecture of the target system, technical & economical feasibility, a risk analysis, candidate service identification, and the implementation and maintenance of the system after evolution. Our evaluation framework (see Figure 2) addresses these requirements as it covers all the aspects necessary to support any legacy to SOA evolution project. One interesting finding of our SLR is that only two articles (Khadka, et al., 2011; Zillmann, et al., 2011) cover all aspects of legacy to SOA evolution as identified by our evaluation framework.

Automation of the Legacy to SOA Evolution Process

Upon establishing a legacy to SOA evolution process model, the next challenge is the automation of such legacy to SOA evolution process through the development of tools and techniques. As identified by various researchers, e.g., Kontogiannis, et al. (2007), Lewis et al. (2009), and Nasr et al. (2010), one of the major issues of legacy to SOA evolution is tool support for the various phases. In fact such automation would be expensive and needs a huge effort due to variation in legacy systems. As can be seen from our SLR finding, various tools and techniques have already been successfully developed and used in legacy to SOA evolution. Establishing the suitability of those tools and techniques following a legacy system assessment (technical qualities of legacy code) in the various phases is an interesting and challenging future research topic. Another issue that is worth investigating is "Can legacy to SOA evolution be carried out in language independent manner?" A potential research direction to address this issue could be model-driven legacy to SOA evolution. We are currently involved in an ongoing research project (Servicifi, 2010) that aims at generating a model of the legacy code and identifying patterns to locate service-rich areas. Such patterns are then employed in tandem with a code-query based program slicer after which the sliced out functionality can be exposed as a service. There have been other initiatives in the model-driven legacy to SOA evolution as well (ADM, 2010; Fleurey, Breton, Baudry, Nicolas, & Jézéquel, 2007; Fuhr, et al., 2011; REMICS, 2012).

After-Evolution Experience Reporting

Legacy to SOA evolution is not just about the successful technical transformation of an existing state to a new state. Most reports about the legacy to SOA evolution claim successful evolution because it was technically and economically feasible and the desired target state of SOA has been achieved (Nasr, et al., 2010). However, this "successful" evolution does not really indicate that the enterprise has achieved its business goals. Answers to various questions still remain unclear after such a "successful" evolution. Did the legacy to SOA evolution deliver the promised benefits such as increased flexibility, enhanced maintainability, and reduced costs? In many legacy to SOA evolution projects, there were explicit requirements of the enterprise (e.g., Cuadrado et al., 2008) aimed at increased usability and interoperability. Does the evolution to SOA successfully meet such requirements? As identified by Sneed (Sneed, 2006) one of the issues after evolution is performance. Such issues are still to be investigated in sufficient detail through experimental analysis.

Determining the Decomposability of Legacy Systems

One of the fundamental issues, pointed out by Brodie and Stonebraker (1998), is that the evolution of legacy system depends on its decomposability. The less decomposable a system is, the more difficult evolution will be. However, there are still no explicit factors that determine the decomposability of a legacy system. Sneed (2006, 2009) provides requirements in terms of code properties for determining the suitability of legacy code for wrapping. Similar requirements should also be investigated to determine the decomposability of a legacy system based on the legacy code and complexity. Determining the decomposability of the legacy code facilitates the evolution feasibility process and thus enables choosing the right evolution strategy (i.e., wrapping, replacement, redevelopment, migration) (Almonaies, et al., 2010).

Evolution from Organizational Perspective

The SLR reveals that legacy to SOA evolution is primarily seen as a technical challenge, focused on finding an efficient solution for evolution. However, legacy to SOA evolution also introduces various organizational challenges such as ownership of services, responsibility of maintaining and monitoring of services and resistance from the current IT staffs to change. One of the peculiar challenges includes the adoption problem

(Khadka, et al., 2011; Mahmood, 2007) in which the existing users of legacy systems may fear that their expertise may become redundant due to the introduction of SOA. Such organizational issues should also be properly investigated and considered in legacy to SOA evolution.

THREATS TO VALIDITY

In our SLR, various subjective measurements have been involved. For instance, the selection of primary studies and data extraction process of review protocol and the scale measurement in the evaluation framework itself have subjective measurements. Such subjective measurements can bias the overall result of the findings. Hence, we justify the validity of the results by discussing the possible threats to our result and the countermeasures that we have taken to minimize them. Our literature survey is subjected to the following three types of threats: threats to construct validity, threats to internal validity, and threats to external validity.

Construct validity concerns with "to what extent the inferences can be made correctly." In our research, construct validity refers to the consistent understanding between the study designers and executors. In our review, the review process was designed by one researcher and executed by a group of researchers. Since, the review process was designed by a single researcher there is a chance of misinterpretation of the theoretical concepts by other executors. One potential area of such misinterpretation is the selection of the search keywords. In order to avoid such misinterpretation, we have included possible synonyms and even related terms for each keyword and had them reviewed by all five researchers. Further, we have followed specific guidelines to conduct the systematic literature review, which also enhances the consistent understanding among the researchers. The other potential area of subjective misinterpretation is the scale measurement in the evaluation framework. For such subjective

interpretation, we provide a clear explanation of the judgment scale (see Appendix B).

Internal validity refers to the extent to which the design and execution of the study are likely to prevent systematic errors. In our research, internal validity refers to the elimination of bias. In our review, the involvement of five researchers in the study selection and evaluation process minimizes the threats to internal validity. Furthermore, in each round of study selection the distribution of the studies were done in such a way that each researcher obtains a different set of studies. We have introduced three categories of studies "relevant," "irrelevant," and "moderate." For each moderate study, the next categorization is done by a researcher other than the one who categorized the study as "moderate." Another potential area of bias is the categorization of the studies into "relevant," "irrelevant" and "moderate." Such a threat is mitigated by clearly specifying the inclusion and exclusion criteria (see Table 1). Furthermore, the data selection (initial selection, secondary selection, and primary study) process was distributed among five researchers rather than one researcher. This step also reduces the possibility of bias.

External validity refers to the generalizability of the results of the study. The scope of our study is restricted purely to the academic domain and in particular peer-reviewed scientific papers. We are aware of the fact that legacy to SOA evolution approaches also originate in industry, and may not have been reported upon academically. Due to feasibility issues and to maintain the quality of the research, we did not include such industry-based legacy to SOA evolution approaches.

CONCLUSION AND FUTURE RESEARCH

In this chapter, we have reported on a systematic literature review on legacy to SOA evolution. We have collected 121 relevant papers, published in between 2000 and August 2010, and evaluated them. In order to evaluate those relevant papers, we have described an evaluation framework for legacy to SOA evolution consisting of six phases, categorized over two stages. The proposed evaluation framework is designed by analyzing common phases from three major frameworks related to evolution/modernization of legacy systems, taken from the domain of software engineering. Based on our legacy to SOA evolution framework, we defined evaluation criteria against which all 121 papers were evaluated.

The resulting overview of the evaluation has created an inventory of historical contributions to the evolution of legacy to SOA, and a list of methods and techniques that are widely practiced. Due to limitations of space, only a snapshot of the result of evaluation can be presented in Appendix A. Particularly, the methods and techniques according to the phases of our evaluation framework have provided insights into existing practices in the legacy to SOA evolution process. In summary, the work described in this chapter offers the following contributions:

1. A historical overview of legacy to SOA evolution approaches.
2. A systematic evaluation framework for legacy to SOA evolution.
3. An inventory of methods and techniques used in legacy to SOA evolution.
4. An overview of research issues and future research directions.

We believe that the contributions of this work will benefit researcher on addressing the identified research issues. On the other hand, the inventory of methods and techniques successfully used in academic research can be used by legacy to SOA evolution practitioners in real world industrial practices.

We have identified several possible improvements of our research as well. One of the enhancements of the current evaluation process includes double checking the evaluation result. In the presented evaluation, the primary articles were divided among five researchers and then evaluated. As an enhancement, we aim at double checking each evaluation result by at least one other researcher. This will surely reduce bias (i.e., no subjective categorization are made) and lead to a more accurate finding. In our evaluation, we reported what was reported in the article. For instance, "architectural recovery" and "architectural reconstruction" techniques can be considered to be the same and both of them again can be considered to fall under the heading of "reverse engineering." In our evaluation, we have not made use of such subjective assumptions. In the future, we aim at refining the results of our evaluation with attribute generalization (Cornelissen, Zaidman, van Deursen, Moonen, & Koschke, 2009): a technique to generalize the values of the finding into common and related category. Furthermore, we also aim at evaluating the proposed evaluation framework with case studies and enhance it accordingly. Currently, our research is only focused on the legacy to SOA evolution reported in academia. In future, we aim to also provide similar insights into the legacy to SOA evolution approaches practiced in industry.

REFERENCES

ADM. (2010). *Architecture-driven modernization*. Retrieved March 26, 2012, from http://adm.omg.org/

Alahmari, S., Roure, D. D., & Zaluska, E. (2010). A model-driven architecture approach to the efficient identification of services on service-oriented enterprise architecture. In *Proceedings of the 2010 14th IEEE International Enterprise Distributed Object Computing Conference Workshops*. IEEE Press.

Alahmari, S., Zaluska, E., & De Roure, D. (2010). A service identification framework for legacy system migration into SOA. In *Proceedings of the 2010 IEEE International Conference on Services Computing*. IEEE Press.

Almonaies, A. A., Cordy, J. R., & Dean, T. R. (2010). *Legacy system evolution towards service-oriented architecture*. Paper presented at the Interrnational Workshop on SOA Migration and Evolution (SOAME 2010). Madrid, Spain.

Arsanjani, A., Ghosh, S., Allam, A., Abdollah, T., Ganapathy, S., & Holley, K. (2004). SOMA: A method for developing service-oriented solutions. *IBM Systems Journal*, *47*(3), 377–396. doi:10.1147/sj.473.0377

Aversano, L., Cerulo, L., & Palumbo, C. (2008). Mining candidate web services from legacy code. In *Proceedings of the 10th International Symposium on Web Site Evolution, 2008 (WSE 2008)*. IEEE.

Balasubramaniam, S., Lewis, G. A., Morris, E., Simanta, S., & Smith, D. (2008). *SMART: Application of a method for migration of legacy systems to SOA environments*. Paper presented at the 6th International Conference on Service-Oriented Computing. Berlin, Heidelberg.

Bao, L., Yin, C., He, W., Ge, J., & Chen, P. (2010). Extracting reusable services from legacy object-oriented systems. In *Proceedings of the IEEE International Conference on Software Maintenance (ICSM 2010)*. IEEE Press.

Bennett, K. (1995). Legacy systems: Coping with success. *IEEE Software*, *12*(1), 19–23. doi:10.1109/52.363157

Bergey, J. (2001). *Options analysis for reengineering (OAR): A method for mining legacy assets*. DTIC.

Bergey, J., Smith, D., Weiderman, N., & Woods, S. (1999). *Options analysis for reengineering (OAR): Issues and conceptual approach. No. CMU/SEI-99-TN-014*. SEI.

Bhallamudi, P., & Tilley, S. (2011). SOA migration case studies and lessons learned. In *Proceedings of the IEEE International Systems Conference (SysCon 2011)*. IEEE Press.

Bisbal, J., Lawless, D., Wu, B., & Grimson, J. (1999). Legacy information systems: Issues and directions. *IEEE Software*, *16*(5), 103–111. doi:10.1109/52.795108

Box, D., Ehnebuske, D., Kakivaya, G., Layman, A., Mendelsohn, N., Nielsen, H. F., et al. (2000). *Simple object access protocol (SOAP) 1.1*. Paper presented at the World Wide Web Consortium. New York, NY.

Brinkkemper, S. (1996). Method engineering: Engineering of information systems development methods and tools. *Information and Software Technology*, *38*(4), 275–280. doi:10.1016/0950-5849(95)01059-9

Brodie, M. L., & Stonebraker, M. (1998). *Migrating legacy systems: gateways, interfaces & the incremental approach*. San Francisco, CA: Morgan Kaufmann Publishers Inc.

Canfora, G., & Di Penta, M. (2006). Testing services and service-centric systems: Challenges and opportunities. *IT Professional*, *8*(2), 10–17. doi:10.1109/MITP.2006.51

Canfora, G., Fasolino, A. R., Frattolillo, G., & Tramontana, P. (2008). A wrapping approach for migrating legacy system interactive functionalities to service oriented architectures. *Journal of Systems and Software*, *81*, 463–480. doi:10.1016/j.jss.2007.06.006

Chen, F., Li, S., Yang, H., Wang, C. H., & Chu, C.-C. W. (2005). Feature analysis for service-oriented reengineering. In *Proceedings of the 12th Asia-Pacific Software Engineering Conference*. IEEE.

Chen, F., Yang, H., Qiao, B., & Chu, W. C. (2006). A formal model driven approach to dependable software evolution. In *Proceedings of the 30th Annual International Computer Software and Applications Conference*. IEEE.

Chen, F., Zhang, Z., Li, J., Kang, J., & Yang, H. (2009). *Service identification via ontology mapping*. Paper presented at the 33rd Annual IEEE International Computer Software and Applications Conference (COMPSAC 2009). Seattle. WA.

Corbi, T. A. (1989). Program understanding: Challenge for the 1990s. *IBM Systems Journal, 28*(2), 294–306. doi:10.1147/sj.282.0294

Cornelissen, B., Zaidman, A., van Deursen, A., Moonen, L., & Koschke, R. (2009). A systematic survey of program comprehension through dynamic analysis. *IEEE Transactions on Software Engineering, 35*(5), 684–702. doi:10.1109/TSE.2009.28

Cuadrado, F., García, B., Duenas, J., & Parada, H. A. (2008). A case study on software evolution towards service-oriented architecture. In *Proceedings of the 22nd International Conference on Advanced Information Networking and Applications - Workshops*. IEEE.

De Lucia, A., Francese, R., Scanniello, G., & Tortora, G. (2008). Developing legacy system migration methods and tools for technology transfer. *Software, Practice & Experience, 38*(13), 1333–1364. doi:10.1002/spe.870

Del Castillo, R. P., García-Rodríguez, I., & Caballero, I. (2009). PRECISO: A reengineering process and a tool for database modernisation through web services. In *Proceedings of the 2009 ACM Symposium on Applied Computing*. ACM Press.

Erradi, A., Anand, S., & Kulkarni, N. (2006). Evaluation of strategies for integrating legacy applications as services in a service oriented architecture. In *Proceedings of the IEEE International Conference on Services Computing (SCC 2006)*. IEEE Press.

Fang, R., Lam, L., Fong, L., Frank, D., Vignola, C., Chen, Y., et al. (2007). *A version-aware approach for web service directory*. Paper presented at the IEEE International Conference on Web Services. Salt Lake City, UT.

Fleurey, F., Breton, E., Baudry, B., Nicolas, A., & Jézéquel, J.-M. (2007). Model-driven engineering for software migration in a large industrial context. In Engels, G., Opdyke, B., Schmidt, D., & Weil, F. (Eds.), *Model Driven Engineering Languages and Systems* (*Vol. 4735*, pp. 482–497). Berlin, Germany: Springer. doi:10.1007/978-3-540-75209-7_33

Fuhr, A., Horn, T., Riediger, V., & Winter, A. (2011). Model-driven software migration into service-oriented architectures. *Computer Science - Research and Development*. Retrieved from http://www.se.uni-oldenburg.de/documents/fuhr+2011.pdf

Gui, G., & Scott, P. D. (2006). Coupling and cohesion measures for evaluation of component reusability. In *Proceedings of the 2006 International Workshop on Mining Software Repositories*. IEEE.

Guzman, I., Polo, M., & Piattini, M. (2007). An ADM approach to reengineer relational databases towards web services. In *Proceedings of the 14th Working Conference on Reverse Engineering (WCRE 2007)*. IEEE.

Hoyer, P., Gebhart, M., Pansa, I., Link, S., Dikanski, A., & Abeck, S. (2009). A model-driven development approach for service-oriented integration scenarios. In *Proceedings of the 2009 Computation World: Future Computing, Service Computation, Cognitive, Adaptive, Content, Patterns*. IEEE.

Idu, A., Khadka, R., Saeidi, A., Jansen, S., & Hage, J. (2012). *Technical report on performing a systematic literature review*. Retrieved March 26, 2012, from http://servicifi.files.wordpress. com/2012/01/technical_report_drft.pdf

Jiang, Y., & Stroulia, E. (2004). Towards reengineering web sites to web-services providers. In *Proceedings of the 8th European Conference on Software Maintenance and Reengineering (CSMR 2004)*. IEEE.

Kazman, R., O'Brien, L., & Verhoef, C. (2001). *Architecture reconstruction guidelines*. DTIC.

Khadka, R. (2011). Service identification strategies in legacy-to-SOA migration. In *Proceedings of the Doctoral Consortium of the 26th International Conference on Software Maintenance (ICSM 2011)*. IEEE.

Khadka, R., Reijnders, G., Saeidi, A., Jansen, S., & Hage, J. (2011). A method engineering based legacy to SOA migration method. In *Proceedings of the 27th IEEE International Conference on Software Maintenance (ICSM 2011)*. IEEE Press.

Khadka, R., Saeidi, A., Idu, A., Hage, J., & Jansen, S. (2012). *Legacy to SOA evolution: Evaluation results. No. UU-CS-2012-006*. Utrecht, The Netherlands: Utrecht University.

Khadka, R., Saeidi, A., Jansen, S., Hage, J., & Helms, R. (2011). *An evaluation of service frameworks for the manangement of service ecosystems*. Paper presented at the 15th Pacific Asia Conference on Information System (PACIS 2011). Brisbane, Australia.

Khadka, R., & Sapkota, B. (2010). An evaluation of dynamic web service composition approaches. In *Proceedings of the 4th International Workshop on Architectures, Concepts and Technologies for Service Oriented Computing (ACT4SOC 2010)*. SciTePress.

Khadka, R., Sapkota, B., Pires, L. F., Sinderen, M., & Jansen, S. (2011). *Model-driven development of service compositions for enterprise interoperability*. Paper presented at the 3rd International IFIP Working Conference on Enterprise Interoperability (IWEI 2011). Retrieved from http://dx.doi. org/10.1007/978-3-642-19680-5_15

Khusidman, V., & Ulrich, W. (2007). *Architecture-driven modernization: Transforming the enterprise draft* (*Vol. 5*). OMG.

Kitchenham, B. A. (2004). *Procedures for performing systematic reviews. Technical Report*. Staffordshire, UK: Keele University.

Kontogiannis, K., Lewis, G. A., Smith, D. B., Litoiu, M., Muller, H., Schuster, S., et al. (2007). *The landscape of service-oriented systems: A research perspective*. Paper presented at the International workshop on Systems Development in SOA Environments (SDSOA 2007). Minneapolis, MN.

Lee, S. P., Chan, L. P., & Lee, E. W. (2006). Web services implementation methodology for SOA application. In *Proceedings of the IEEE International Conference on Industrial Informatics*. IEEE Press.

Lewis, G., Morris, E., O'Brien, L., Smith, D., & Wrage, L. (2005). *SMART: The service-oriented migration and reuse technique. No. CMU/SEI-2005-TN-029*. Software Engineering Institute.

Lewis, G., Morris, E., & Smith, D. (2006). Analyzing the reuse potential of migrating legacy components to a service-oriented architecture. In *Proceedings of the 10th European Conference on Software Maintenance and Reengineering (CMSR 2006)*. IEEE.

Lewis, G., Morris, E., Smith, D., & O'Brien, L. (2005). Service-oriented migration and reuse technique (SMART). In *Proceedings of the 13th IEEE International Workshop on Software Technology and Engineering Practice*. IEEE Press.

Lewis, G., Smith, D., Chapin, N., & Kontogiannis, K. (2009). *MESOA 2009: 3rd International workshop on maintenance and evolution of service-oriented systems*. No. 1424448972. SEI.

Li, S., & Tahvildari, L. (2008). E-BUS: A toolkit for extracting business services from java software systems. In *Proceedings of the Companion of the 30th International Conference on Software Engineering*. IEEE Press.

Li, Z., Anming, X., Naiyue, Z., Jianbin, H., & Zhong, C. (2009). A SOA modernization method based on tollgate model. In *Proceedings of the 2009 International Symposium on Information Engineering and Electronic Commerce*. IEEE.

Mahmood, Z. (2007). The promise and limitations of service oriented architecture. *International Journal of Computers, 1*(3), 74–78.

Marchetto, A., & Ricca, F. (2008). Transforming a java application in an equivalent web-services based application: Toward a tool supported stepwise approach. In *Proceedings of the 10th International Symposium on Web Site Evolution (WSE 2008)*. IEEE.

Millham, R. (2010). Migration of a legacy procedural system to service-oriented computing using feature analysis. In *Proceedings of the 2010 International Conference on Complex, Intelligent and Software Intensive Systems*. IEEE.

Nakamura, M., Igaki, H., Kimura, T., & Matsumoto, K.-I. (2009). Extracting service candidates from procedural programs based on process dependency analysis. In *Proceedings of the IEEE Asia-Pacific Services Computing Conference*. IEEE Press.

Nasr, K. A., Gross, H.-G., & Deursen, A. V. (2010). Adopting and evaluating service oriented architecture in industry. In *Proceedings of the 2010 14th European Conference on Software Maintenance and Reengineering*. IEEE.

O'Brien, L., Smith, D., & Lewis, G. (2005). *Supporting migration to services using software architecture reconstruction*. Paper presented at the 13th IEEE International Workshop on Software Technology and Engineering Practice (STEP 2005). Budapest, Hungary.

Papazoglou, M. (2008). *Web services: Principles and technology*. Reading, MA: Addison-Wesley.

Papazoglou, M., Traverso, P., Dustdar, S., & Leymann, F. (2007). Service-oriented computing: State of the art and research challenges. *Computer, 40*(11), 38–45. doi:10.1109/MC.2007.400

Papazoglou, M., & Van Den Heuvel, W. J. (2006). Service-oriented design and development methodology. *International Journal of Web Engineering and Technology, 2*(4), 412–442. doi:10.1504/IJWET.2006.010423

Perepletchikov, M., Ryan, C., Frampton, K., & Tari, Z. (2007). Coupling metrics for predicting maintainability in service-oriented designs. In *Proceedings of the 18th Australian Software Engineering Conference (ASWEC 2007)*. IEEE.

Razavian, M., & Lago, P. (2010). A frame of reference for SOA migration. In Di Nitto, E., & Yahyapour, R. (Eds.), *Towards a Service-Based Internet (Vol. 6481*, pp. 150–162). Berlin, Germany: Springer. doi:10.1007/978-3-642-17694-4_13

Reddy, V. K., Dubey, A., Lakshmanan, S., Sukumaran, S., & Sisodia, R. (2009). Evaluating legacy assets in the context of migration to SOA. *Software Quality Journal, 17*(1), 51–63. doi:10.1007/s11219-008-9055-6

Reijnders, G., Khadka, R., Jansen, S., & Hage, J. (2011). *Developing a legacy to SOA migration method. No. UU-CS-2011-008.* Utrecht, The Netherlands: Utrecht University.

REMICS. (2012). *Reuse and migration of legacy applications to interoperable cloud services.* Retrieved from http://www.remics.eu/

Ricca, F., & Marchetto, A. (2009). A quick and dirty meet-in-the-middle approach for migrating to SOA. In *Proceedings of the Joint International and Annual ERCIM Workshops on Principles of Software Evolution (IWPSE) and Software Evolution (Evol) Workshops.* ACM.

Salama, R., & Aly, S. G. (2008). *A decision making tool for the selection of service oriented-based legacy systems modernization strategies.* Paper presented at the The International Conference on Software Engineering Research and Practice. Las Vegas, NV.

Schelp, J., & Aier, S. (2009). SOA and EA-sustainable contributions for increasing corporate agility. In *Proceedings of the 42nd Hawaii International Conference on System Sciences.* IEEE.

Seacord, R. C., Plakosh, D., & Lewis, G. A. (2003). *Modernizing legacy systems: Software technologies, engineering processes, and business practices.* Reading, MA: Addison-Wesley Professional.

Servicifi. (2010). *ServiciFi: Decomposing monolithic software systems in the finiancial domain.* Retrieved March 26, 2012, from http://servicifi.org/

Smith, D., O'Brien, L., & Bergey, J. (2002). Using the options analysis for reengineering (OAR) method for mining components for a product line. In *Proceedings of the Software Product Lines.* Springer.

Sneed, H. M. (1995a). Planning the reengineering of legacy systems. *IEEE Software, 12*(1), 24–34. doi:10.1109/52.363168

Sneed, H. M. (1995b). Understanding software through numbers: A metric based approach to program comprehension. *Journal of Software Maintenance: Research and Practice, 7*(6), 405–419. doi:10.1002/smr.4360070604

Sneed, H. M. (2006). Integrating legacy software into a service oriented architecture. In *Proceedings of the 10th European Conference on Software Maintenance and Reengineering.* IEEE.

Sneed, H. M. (2008). COB2WEB: A toolset for migrating to web services. In *Proceedings of the 10th International Symposium on Web Site Evolution (WSE 2008).* IEEE.

Sneed, H. M. (2009). A pilot project for migrating COBOL code to web services. *International Journal on Software Tools for Technology Transfer, 11*(6), 441–451. doi:10.1007/s10009-009-0128-z

Umar, A., & Zordan, A. (2009). Reengineering for service oriented architectures: A strategic decision model for integration versus migration. *Journal of Systems and Software, 82*(3), 448–462. doi:10.1016/j.jss.2008.07.047

van Geet, J., & Demeyer, S. (2010). Reverse engineering on the mainframe: Lessons learned from in vivo research. *IEEE Software, 27*(4), 30–36. doi:10.1109/MS.2010.65

van Sinderen, M. (2008). Challenges and solutions in enterprise computing. *Enterprise Information System, 2*(4), 341–346. doi:10.1080/17517570802442063

Vemuri, P. (2008). IEEE TENCON - 2008 Modernizing a legacy system to SOA - Feature analysis approach. In *Proceedings of the TENCON 2008 - 2008 IEEE Region 10 Conference.* IEEE Press.

Warren, I., & Ransom, J. (2002). Renaissance: A method to support software system evolution. In *Proceedings of the 26th Annual International Computer Software and Applications Conference.* IEEE.

Wu, B., Lawless, D., Bisbal, J., Grimson, J., Wade, V., O'Sullivan, D., et al. (1997). Legacy systems migration - A method and its tool-kit framework. In *Proceedings of the Joint 1997 Asia Pacific Software Engineering Conference and International Computer Science Conference*. IEEE.

Zhang, Z., Liu, R., & Yang, H. (2005). Service identification and packaging in service oriented reengineering. In *Proceedings of the 7th International Conference on Software Engineering and Knowledge Engineering (SEKE)*. World Scientific Pub.

Zhang, Z., & Yang, H. (2004). Incubating services in legacy systems for architectural migration. In *Proceedings of the 11th Asia-Pacific Software Engineering Conference*. IEEE.

Zhang, Z., Yang, H., & Chu, W. C. (2006). Extracting reusable object-oriented legacy code segments with combined formal concept analysis and slicing techniques for service integration. In *Proceedings of the 6th International Conference on Quality Software*. IEEE.

Zhang, Z., Yang, H., Zhou, D., & Zhong, S. (2010). A SOA based approach to user-oriented system migration. In *Proceedings of the 2010 10th IEEE International Conference on Computer and Information Technology (CIT 2010)*. IEEE Press.

Zhang, Z., Zhou, D.-D., Yang, H.-J., & Zhong, S.-C. (2010). A service composition approach based on sequence mining for migrating e-learning legacy system to SOA. *International Journal of Automatic Computing, 7*, 584–595. doi:10.1007/s11633-010-0544-2

Ziemann, J., Leyking, K., Kahl, T., & Werth, D. (2006). SOA development based on enterprise models and existing IT systems. In Cunningham, P. (Ed.), *Exploiting the Knowledge Economy: Issues, Applications and Case Studies*. Amesterdam, The Netherlands: IOS Press.

Zillmann, C., Winter, A., Herget, A., Teppe, W., Theurer, M., Fuhr, A., et al. (2011). The SOAMIG process model in industrial applications. In *Proceedings of the 15th European Conference on Software Maintenance and Reengineering (CSMR 2011)*. IEEE.

KEY TERMS AND DEFINITIONS

Candidate Service Identification: Candidate service identification refers to a process of locating service-rich areas in a legacy code.

Legacy Evolution: Legacy evolution is a gradual process of performing structural changes to legacy systems such that they comply with new technological and organizational requirements.

Legacy System: Legacy system is an old application program written using outdated techniques and programming languages such as COBOL, RGP, PL/I, but it continues to do useful work.

Legacy System Understanding: Legacy system understanding refers to as-is analysis of the existing legacy systems and thus enabling in better understanding of technical and functional characteristics of the legacy systems.

Service: A service in SOA is defined as a self-contained, platform-agonistic computational element that supports rapid, low-cost and composition of loosely-coupledloosely coupled software applications.

Service-Oriented Architecture (SOA): SOA is an architectural style that enables the reuse of existing legacy assets within a new paradigm that facilitates loose coupling, abstraction of underlying logic, flexibility, reusabilityreusability, and discoverability.

Systematic Literature Review (SLR): SLR is a systematic approach that aims at providing an exhaustive summary of literature relevant to a research question.

APPENDIX A

Table 5. An overview of primary studies w.r.t the evaluation criteria

Reference	Evolution Planning								
	Legacy System Understanding				Target System Understanding			Evolution Feasibility Determination	
	Y/N	Technique	Scale	Tool supp.	Y/N	Technique	Scale	Y/N	Technique
(Salama & Aly, 2008)	Y	Source Code Analysis	+	Y	N	N/A	-	Y	Filtration, Organizational Assessment, Cost Benefit Analysis
(Khadka, Reijnders, et al., 2011)	Y	Technical Analysis, Functional Analysis, Documentation, Interviewing	+++	N	Y	Service Requirements Identification	-	Y	Cost Benefit Analysis
(Sneed, 2009)	N	N/A	-	N	N	N/A	-	Y	Code Complexity, Reusability Assessment
(Zhang, Yang, Zhou, & Zhong, 2010)	Y	Reverse Engineering, Domain Analysis	++	N	Y	Domain Business Logical Model	++	N	N/A
(Canfora, Fasolino, Frattolillo, & Tramontana, 2008)	Y	Reverse Engineering, Static Analysis, Dynamic Analysis	++	N	N	N/A	-	N	N/A
(Lewis, et al., 2006)	Y	Documentation, Interviewing, Interviewing, Source Code Analysis, Architectural Reconstruction	+++	Y	Y	SOA Environment Details, Functional Specification	+++	Y	Code Complexity, Dependency Analysis, Risk Analysis, Cost Benefit Analysis
(Sneed, 2008)	N	N/A	-	N	N	N/A	-	Y	Code Complexity, Reusability Assessment
(Erradi, et al., 2006)	Y	Portfolio Analysis, Interviewing, Source Code Analysis	+++	Y	Y	Decision Making Criteria	+++	Y	Multi Criteria Decision Making
(Zhang, et al., 2006)	Y	Source Code Analysis	+++	N	N	N/A	-	Y	Options Analysis for Re-engineering
(Vemuri, 2008)	Y	Test Cases, Feature Analysis	+++	N	N	N/A	-	Y	Return of Investment
(Sneed, 2006)	N	N/A	-	N	N	N/A	-	N	N/A
(Fuhr, et al., 2011)	Y	Code Parsing, Model Transformation	++	Y	N	N/A	-	N	N/A
(Del Castillo, García-Rodríguez, & Caballero, 2009)	Y	Interviewing, Database Model Recovery	-	N	Y	Interviewing	-	N	N/A
(Umar & Zordan, 2009)	Y	Strategic Analysis	++	N	N	N/A	-	Y	Strategic Analysis, Architecture Analysis, Cost Benefit Analysis
(Lewis, Morris, Smith, et al., 2005)	Y	Interviewing, Documentation	++	N	Y	Interviewing, Reference Models, SOA Environment Details	++	Y	Cost Benefit Analysis, Code Complexity
(O'Brien, et al., 2005)	Y	Architectural Reconstruction, Program Understanding	+++	Y	Y	Interviewing, Documentation, Requirements	+++	Y	Options Analysis for Re-engineering
(Zillmann, et al., 2011)	Y	Reverse Engineering, Documentation, Test Cases, Static Analysis, Dynamic Analysis	+++	N	Y	Specific Architecture Selection	-	Y	Technical Feasibility

continued on following page

Table 5. Continued

Evolution Implementation and Management						Deploy & Provisioning	Case Study	
Candidate Service Identification			Implementation					
Y/N	Technique	Tool supp.	Y/N	Technique	Tool supp.		Exp./Ind.	Language
N	N/A	N	N	N/A	N	N	N/A	N/A
Y	Concept Analysis	N	Y	Concept Slicing	Y	Y	Ind., Exp.	COBOL, C++
Y	Manual	N	Y	Code Stripping, Wrapping	Y	N	Exp.	Cobol
Y	Matching Algorithm	N	Y	Wrapping, Code Modification, Re-development	N	N	Exp.	Java
Y	Business Value, Technical Quality Assessment, Use Cases	N	Y	Wrapping, Finite State Automaton Specification	N	Y	Ind.	N/A
Y	Manual	N	N	N/A	N	N	Ind.	C++
Y	Manual	N	Y	Code Stripping, Wrapping	Y	N	Ind.	COBOL
N	N/A	N	N	N/A	N	N	Ind.	N/A
Y	Formal Concept Analysis	Y	Y	Program Slicing, Wrapping	N	N	Exp.	Java
Y	Feature Analysis	N	Y	Wrapping, Rewriting, Refactoring, COTS, Declarative Rule Engine	N	N	Ind.	N/A
Y	Business Rule and Value Analysis	N	Y	Code Stripping, Wrapping	Y	N	Ind.	COBOL
Y	Graph Query	Y	Y	Graph Transformation	Y	N	Exp.	Java
Y	Model Driven Pattern Matching	Y	Y	Model Driven Program Transformation	Y	Y	Ind.	.NET
N	N/A	N	N	N/A	N	N	Ind.	N/A
Y	Manual	N	N	N/A	N	N	Ind.	C++
N	N/A	N	N	N/A	N	N	Ind.	C++
Y	Business Process Mapping	N	Y	Code Transformation	Y	Y	Ind.	Java

APPENDIX B

Table 6. The judgment scale to assess the support of techniques and method used

Scale point	Scale Definition	Representation
No support	The specified technique is not mentioned.	-
Implicitly discussed	The specified technique is mentioned.	+
Explicitly discussed	The specified technique is mentioned and discussed but no detailed information is given.	++
Explicitly discussed with evidence of use	The specified technique is mentioned, discussed and there is empirical evidence of its usability.	+++

Chapter 4
Reengineering and Wrapping Legacy Modules for Reuse as Web Services:
Motivation, Method, Tools, and Case Studies

Harry M. Sneed
ANECON GmbH, Austria

ABSTRACT

In almost every IT-user shop where a mainframe computer is still in operation, there are hundreds if not thousands of legacy code modules with several million lines of code. Most of them are written in COBOL, but also many in PL/I and 4GL languages like Natural and PowerBuilder. Some are running online in dialog mode while others run in batch mode as background jobs. Many of these users would now like to migrate to a service-oriented architecture using the mainframe as a hub where a wide assortment of Web services are available to the client business units to be built into their new business processes. However, they are inhibited in doing so by the high costs of such a migration. The biggest costs lie in developing the Web services from scratch or adapting those that can be found on the market.

These high costs could be avoided if the user were able to reuse the software he already has. Most of the elementary business functions required by the new business processes already exist inside the old legacy modules. If they could be extracted and reused, the user would save the costs of having to develop them. However, their current architecture prohibits their reuse. They have no clearly defined interface, they are dependent on an old teleprocessing monitor or batch framework; they are intertwined with the other modules around them and their data is more often incompatible with the data types used for interacting with Web services. That means the modules have to be reengineered before being reused.

This chapter deals with how this reengineering can be done. The goal is to make modular, flexible, and independent Web services from the monolithic, rigid, and dependent legacy modules. The methods used to achieve this goal are static analysis, code restructuring, code stripping, code transformation, and code

DOI: 10.4018/978-1-4666-2488-7.ch004

Copyright © 2013, IGI Global. Copying or distributing in print or electronic forms without written permission of IGI Global is prohibited.

wrapping. The legacy code can be either left in a procedural form in the original language or translated to an object-oriented architecture in the Java language. The result is in both cases an independent, wrapped service with a standard WSDL interface and a separate database access shell. All of the steps of the migration process are supported by automated tools. The wrapped services are available to all applications capable of sending and receiving SOAP messages. The automated process described here has been successfully applied in three industrial migration projects. The experience gained in those projects is discussed at the end of the chapter.

INTRODUCTION

There are many reasons for users to want to migrate to a service-oriented architecture. There are both business and technical reasons. The business reasons are among others:

- To become faster and more flexible in responding to user requirements,
- To give the users a wide range selection of ready-made services,
- To unify common business functionality,
- To cut the costs of maintaining an oversized software base.

In short, the business goal is to provide more business functionality in shorter time with fewer costs.

The technical reasons for migrating are among other:

- To reduce the complexity of the existing IT-landscape,
- To eliminate the many redundancies associated with a silo-type software architecture,
- To reduce the amount of software which has to be maintained,
- To unify the diverse software solutions in a common architectural mode.

In short, the technical goal is to simplify and unify the user's software base, thus reducing the costs of maintaining it.

The Case for Reusing Legacy Modules as Web Services

In moving from traditional silo type architectures of loosely coupled application systems to a service-oriented architecture, users have a number of options (Sneed, 2007). One is to purchase a standard set of Web services from a software vendor and to adapt their business processes to them. This requires them to give up much of their local rules and specific business logic. They can customize the overall processes, but they have to accept the detailed data and algorithms provided by the vendor. A variation of this option is to use the standard Web services on demand, thus avoiding the costs of owing them. Cloud services promise to be a cheap and readily accessible. They can be incorporated into the user business processes and integrated with the existing components. From an economic point of view this is a tempting solution, but it does not alter the fact that the user has to adapt his way of working to fit these off-the-shelf solutions (Yau & Ho, 2011).

A second option is to take over Web services from the open source community and to modify them to fit his needs. This give him the possibility of inserting his own rules and detailed logic, but it requires him to have specialists who can work with the open source. If such specialists are not available, this approach can become very expensive depending on the degree of change. Besides, it is error prone. Any alteration of the open source can lead to a chain of errors, which if the developers are not familiar with the source, will be difficult to correct. It appears to be cheap, but in the long run this could turn out to be the most costly solution.

A third option for users is to develop their own Web services. To do that the user must start with an analysis of his requirements and identify each and every Web service he will need in his planned business processes. Once he has identified them, he can begin to develop them, for instance by an agile development process. This can be viewed as a top-down approach, starting with the concept of what is required and proceeding down to the level of the elementary services, which may be implemented as a set of interrelated classes. In this way, he can model a hierarchy of services having abstract logical services with virtual interfaces at the top and a series of real codes services, i.e. code components, at the bottom. Each elementary service can be implemented to fit exactly to the role it should play in the orchestra of services (Smith & Lewis, 2007).

This approach appears to be very enticing—producing a set of customized services to fit exactly to the requirements of the user, but it can become very expensive. Experience at the early pioneers of SOA like the German Post and the Swiss Credit bank has shown that this path to a service-oriented architecture can take many years and cost several million dollars. The Swiss Credit bank required over 10 years and more than 400 person years to get their SOA operational. While the new software is under development, the old systems have to be maintained and this too drives up the costs. Not only does it increase costs, but it also drains off personnel. Key persons familiar with the logic of the old systems have to remain with them and are not available to help in the construction of the Web services. Their knowledge is not available where it would be needed, unless they can be replaced. The Swiss Credit Bank brought in an Indian software house to take over the maintenance of the existing applications to allow their developers to work on the new SOA solution (Worms, 2010).

In any case developing the services from scratch not only requires time and money but also the knowledge of key personnel familiar with the business. It is a major undertaking, recommendable only to those organizations large enough to sustain it. For small and middle-sized enterprises, developing their own services is definitely not the way to go. The developing and testing of a customized service costs at least five times more than using a ready-made solution.

A fourth option is to reuse the existing legacy systems or, at least, parts of them as the building stones of the new SOA architecture. The advantage of this approach is that it is quicker and cheaper. The wrapping of a module requires no more than one person day. The testing can take another 3 person days, making it all together 4 person days for a module of circa 1000 statements or 1500 lines of code. To develop such a service would require at least 20 person days with a productivity of 50 statements per person day. That implies a relationship of 1:5. Not only is the legacy module more readily available, but it retains the old business logic and allows the old developers to accompany their components over into the new world. It is easier for them to maintain the existing systems while working on the new services if both of them have the same components. Another big advantage is that the old components have been tested over the years in production, whereas new Web services have to be tested from scratch in a simulated test environment, before they can be integrated and tested as a service (see Figure 1).

The disadvantage of this reuse option is of course that the software remains in its old language, e.g. COBOL, PL/1, C, or whatever. So the user is obligated to keep the old development environment as well as the old developers. Their knowledge is essential to maintaining the Web services. For instance, if the legacy software is in COBOL, then the user would require a COBOL development workbench and COBOL programmers to test and maintain the services. If the additional Web services are to be written in Java, he needs to sustain two development environments, one for the reused services and one for the newly development services. At some time in the future he could convert the COBOL code over into Java, but this too incurs costs and makes the COBOL developers obsolete. Reusing old code in a modern SOA architecture may also cause performance problems, especially if a lot of data has to be converted, but these problems are really much less than what most people believe. The real problem is that of finding personnel capable of dealing with the legacy software carried over into the SOA architecture. If this problem can be solved then there is no real argument against the reuse of legacy components as Web services since Web services are autonomous and it should no matter in what language they are written. As will be pointed out later, the data should all be put into the same format as to be independent of the programming language. Then the implementation language is no longer an issue (Zdun, 2002).

Economic Arguments for Reusing Legacy Code

The case for reusing existing software modules as Web services can easily be made on the basis of economic arguments. We take for example a billing service. This service should be invoked with the customer and the order data as request inputs. It is up to the service to access the billing data. The output should be a bill to the customer.

To program this service from scratch would require a detailed requirement specification with the billing rules, some sort of design model with UML diagrams, several Java classes, and a set of test cases to test it. Even if it only amounts to 50 Function-Points and contains some 1500 Java statements, it will still take at least two months to develop it and another month to test it. So we are speaking here of at least three person months.

The same billing service could be taken from an existing COBOL program and automatically converted into a Web service with a standard WSDL interface in less than a day. It may require several additional days to adapt the logic to the new requirements, but this should not exceed a week. Another two weeks in needed to test the interfaces. The core logic will have already been tested. In the end, the reuse option costs less than one person or 1/3 of the costs of developing the service new. Clearly, the reuse of the existing software is more economical.

If an enterprise needs 500 such services and can take 400 from existing code then it will save the money equivalent of 800 person months. Besides there is also time. To develop and test 500 services of this size would require 1500 person months or 150 person years. That amount of effort will take at least three calendar years. The reuse option would only need a year and a half even if 20% of the services are developed new. This demonstrates the fact that building up a SOA architecture from existing code modules can be 1/3 cheaper and take less than ½ the time required to develop all of the services required from scratch (Nadico, 2007). Besides that reuse is economical, it also has an advantage in personnel continuity. The same persons who have been maintaining the code before the migration can continue to maintain it after the migration. There is no need for them to learn a new language. If the code was in COBOL it remains in COBOL and the maintenance personnel can make full use of their COBOL knowledge even though the code is running in a SOA environment. This has an added economic benefit in that the maintenance personnel do not have to be retrained. That too is a significant saving. It is true that the user remains dependent on the same old staff, but it may be the lesser of two evils. The only way to escape the personnel dependency trap is to buy standard services or to use Web services in the cloud, but then the user becomes dependent on the service provider. Dependency is the price for using software at all. Either the user organization is dependent on internal personnel who use that dependency to their own personal advantage or it is dependent on external providers who use that dependency to improve their business position.

Figure 1. Reusing existing software to build up a SOA

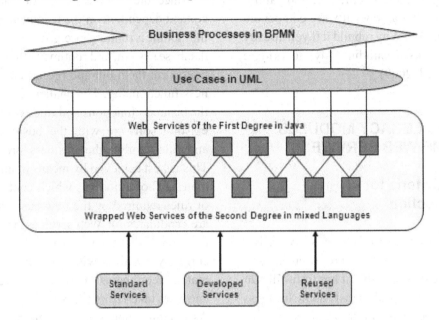

Technical Arguments for Reusing Legacy Code

There are also technical reasons for wanting to reuse existing software in a service-oriented architecture. The development of new software, whether it be conventional, procedural or object-oriented components or Web services is error prone. According to a study made by the U.S. Software Engineering Institute there are 11 to 15 errors per 1000 code lines of Web application software after it is released (Laird & Brennan, 2006]. Removing an error once the software is in production costs up to 2.5 days of personnel effort (Boehm, et al., 2004). Thus, a significant amount of time and effort is spent on removing errors in newly written Web services. This effort can be avoided by reusing ripened software.

Removing errors causes patches to be made which derivate from the original logic of the code. With each such patch, the code quality deteriorates and the code complexity increases. After a number of such patches the code is no longer changeable and has to be refactored. Thus, it may

take months before a new Web service is stable. Software must evolve to become useful (Belady & Lehman, 1975).

The existing code components have evolved over the years. Their errors have been exposed by testing and usage. There may still be some hidden errors but the majority of the errors will have been removed, in particular those that disturb the users. Therefore, we can assume that existing legacy components are basically error free. They have been fine-tuned to the problem they are intended to solve and solve this problem in an acceptable, if not optimal, manner. Otherwise, they would not have survived so long (Reiss, 2006).

The evolution of software is much like the evolution of living creatures according to Darwin. Only the fittest survive. Those software components which have survived through years of productive use can be considered to be fit. They have evolved to perform that task which the user expects. On the other hand, the user has accepted their behavior and their results and has accommodated himself to them. The stability of ripened software is a major reason for wanting to reuse it rather than going through the long and painful process of evolving a new software component from the beginning. Why rebuild it if you already have it and it works. Rebuilding only causes more problems (Sneed, 2000).

SELECTING LEGACY MODULES TO BECOME WEB SERVICES

Business Criteria for Module Selection

Not every existing piece of legacy software is a candidate for a Web service. There are business as well as technical criteria that it has to fulfill. On the business side, it should satisfy some business function required by a current business process, or which could be required by some future business process. Most likely it already fulfills the first criteria; otherwise it would not still be in operation. The question is whether that business process will be carried over into the new service-oriented architecture. If not, the functions used only by that process will not be needed.

The question of playing a role in some future business process is not so easy to answer. For that, the projected future business processes have to be modeled and their elementary functions, or steps, identified. Each of those steps has to be described and compared with a description of the current legacy modules. This presupposes that the current software systems are modeled and their modules defined in terms of their functionality. This leads to an association, i.e. matching problem. A business process performs one or more elementary business functions governed by one or more business rules. A legacy software system can contain hundreds of modules, each of which can perform several business functions based on one or more business rules. Thus, a module is a collection of functions and rules, some of which are of a technical nature and others of a business nature.

Since the technical functions are primarily context dependent on the technical environment the module is running in, e.g. transaction-monitor, database system, and runtime system, it is important to cut them out and preserve only the business functionality. The challenge is to associate the business functions and rules contained in the existing software with the business functions and rules within the business process model. This is best achieved by means of an association matrix. Those modules which contain functions or rules required by the new business processes are candidates for Web services. Therefore, it is necessary to list out all functions or business rules currently contained within legacy modules and to match them against a list of business functions and rules taken from the business process model. Associating functions by name and description alone may prove difficult since the semantics of the two descriptions will seldom be the same. The key to associating functions is by their outputs. A function has the purpose of producing a single result value on a set of result values in accordance with the equation

$$x = f(y)$$

where x is one or more output values and y is one or more input variables. The names of data variables are more precise than the names of functions, which in legacy software often have no meaning at all. The names of data in legacy code may be abbreviated and terse but it is still possible to understand them. Possibly they can be translated into longer, more meaningful names with the aid of a data dictionary. This way the name "DayofWeek" might be derived from the abbreviated name WDAY. The naming of data variables is one of the biggest obstacles to reusing old code, but changing the names is labor intensive and error prone, so it is often better to leave them as they are.

Functions from the code are best matched to functions from the business model by associating the names of their results. If the two result sets are similar in name, type and number, then the two functions are probably the same. The exceptions will be clones. The matching functions should be joined together in the function association matrix (see Figure 2).

Business functions and rules may be fully or only partly fulfilled in a particular module. A module may, on the other hand, fully or partly implement one or more functions. If a module contains at least one function, which matches to the requirements of the new business process, it becomes a candidate for wrapping. Then one can proceed with the next step and that is to check if that module is technically reusable.

Technical Criteria for Module Selection

Even if an old module contains functions, which fulfill the new requirements, it may still not be technically feasible to reuse it. There are several technical reasons why a code module may not be reusable:

- Because it is too intertwined with the other modules around it, i.e. it has a too high degree of coupling,
- Because it uses external data that will not be available to the new Web service,
- Because it has too many data inputs from too many different sources, i.e. it has a high fan-in rate,
- Because the quality of the code is so bad that it is not worth reusing it.

If any of these situations exit, it will not be possible to reuse the module without a major restructuring operation. However, this is exactly what wrapping wants to avoid. The goal of a wrapping project is to reuse existing code with a minimum of change. If this goal cannot be reached, it is better to try something else. That is why it is necessary to first check the reusability of a module before starting to wrap it. To determine if the reuse of a module is feasible, the module has to be measured, in particular in terms of modularity, reusability, and flexibility (Sneed, 1998).

Modularity is measured here in terms of coupling. Coupling is the number of calls or branches to other modules relative to the number of state-

Figure 2. Function association matrix

Association of Business Functions and Rules to existing Modules

Modules	Implemented Business Functions / Rules								
	Func1	Func2	Func3	Func4	Func5	Func6	Rule7	Rule8	Rule9
Module_A	partly					partly			
Module_B		full		partly					partly
Module_C						full			
Module_D	partly		full	partly					
Module_E					full			full	
Module_F						partly			partly
Module_G				partly					

ments in the module under analysis. If the degree of coupling exceeds a given limit, the module is not a candidate for reuse. It is too dependent on its environment.

Reusability is the ease with which a module can be extracted from its current environment. It is measured according to a reusability index. Reusability is decreased by the use of a global data, by direct access to a common database and by branches out of the scope of the module. It can be computed as the inverse of the number, of dependencies relative to the number of statements.

Flexibility is the degree to which the module is free of hard-coded data. There should be no numeric constants or literal texts contained within the procedural statements. If there are too many, the code is too inflexible to be reused so here the metric is the number of statements.

Together with other quality characteristics such as readability, testability, and portability, these features make up what we refer to as the inherent quality of code. If any of these negative features are present, the module is not a candidate for reuse. It may still possible to reengineer the module to make it more reusable, but there are limits to that. You cannot make a racing horse out of a donkey, meaning there are limits to reengineering. If a module was conceived by a blithering idiot, which many programmers were, especially at the time the legacy software was originally produced, there is no way to convert the original concept into a viable solution. If a module is not feasible for reuse, it is better to leave it out. In the end only a few modules may be left to be considered for wrapping. If there are too few it may be better to abandon the wrapping approach altogether and try something else. The quality of the old code is a decisive factor in deciding whether to reuse it or not. For that reason, it is imperative to measure it.

Measuring the Candidate Modules

In order to assess the technical suitability of a legacy module it has to be measured and for

that a tool is needed. The tool should measure not only complexity and quality, but also the size of the candidate module. Size is measured in terms of lines of code, number of statements, weighted number of processed data variables—Data-Points—and weighted number of inputs and outputs—Function-Points.

Measuring Module Complexity

Module complexity of procedural code can be measured in terms of eight complexity metrics:

- Chapin's data complexity (Chapin, 1977)
- Elshof's data flow complexity (Elshof, 1976)
- Card's data access complexity (Card & Agresti, 1988)
- Henry's interface complexity (Henry, 1981)
- McCabe's control flow complexity (McCabe, 1976)
- McClure's decisional complexity (McClure, 1981)
- Sneed's branching complexity (Sneed & Merey, 1985)
- Halstead's language complexity (Halstead, 1977)

The weighted sum of these metrics is a good indicator of program complexity (Sneed, 1995). Complexity in software is a question of the relation between software elements and their relationships to one another. The more relationships there are relative to the number of elements, the higher the complexity. The Chapin metric is measuring the relationship of output and conditional data to input data. The Elshof metric is measuring the number of data references relative to the number of referenced data. The Card metric is measuring the number of data accesses relative to the number of data stores. The Henry metric is measuring the relation of module interactions to the number of modules, i.e. their fan-in and fan-out rate. The

McCabe metric is measuring the relation between edges and nodes of a graph. The McClure metric is measuring the decisional density, i.e. the number of decisional nodes relative to the number of action nodes. The Sneed metric is measuring the number of branches to other procedures relative to the number of procedural blocks. The Halstead metric is measuring the relation between operands and operators on the one side and references to them on the other. There are, of course, many other metrics which could be applied but these suffice to give an impression of the complexity of a procedural module.

To give an overall impression of the degree of complexity the various complexity measurements should be normalized to a rational scale, i.e. expressed as a coefficient on a scale of 0 to 1 with 0.5 being the median complexity. Being over 0.5 indicates that this aspect of the program is overly complex. Being under 0.5 indicates that the complexity is not a problem. By inverting the scale for quality originally proposed in the

ISO-9126 standard for product assessment, 0 to 0.4 indicates low complexity, 0.4 to 0.6 indicates average complexity, 0.6 to 0.8 indicates high complexity and over 0.8 indicates that the code is overly complex (ISO, 1993) (See Figure 3).

The following complexity measures represent the average complexities of a COBOL application system by the name of BESSY for paying the salaries at the German foreign office. They indicate that the data flow and data access complexities were very high as a result of the many dependencies on the underlying data bases. The control flow complexity was also high because of the many GOTO branches within the code. Interface complexity was low since there are few direct interactions between programs. They were linked via the databases. The language complexity was low because the same operators and operators were used over and over again. Halstead compares the number of different operands and operators defined with the frequency of their reference. COBOL programs have as a rule a low

Figure 3. Assessing the reusability of existing programs

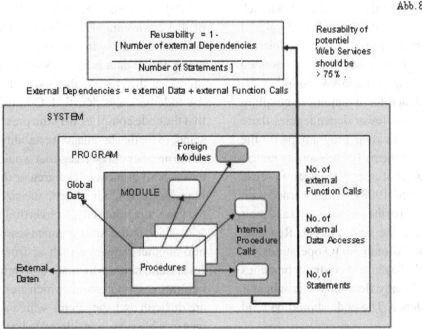

language volume because they are so long. Decisional complexity was also low because the business rules applied were relative simple and the code was not deeply nested. This can be considered a typical complexity profile of a legacy business application system originating in the 1980s (Sneed & Nyary, 1999).

- DATA COMPLEXITY 0.524
- DATA FLOW COMPLEXITY 0.768
- DATA ACCESS COMPLEXITY 0.718
- INTERFACE COMPLEXITY 0.125
- CONTROL FLOW COMPLEXITY 0.678
- DECISIONAL COMPLEXITY 0.362
- BRANCHING COMPLEXITY 0.578
- LANGUAGE COMPLEXITY 0.215
- AVERAGE PROGRAM COMPLEXITY 0.518

Measuring Module Quality

Module quality is measured in terms of the quality characteristics modularity, portability, reusability, convertibility, flexibility, testability, conformity, and maintainability. Judging the quality of a software system depends very much on the goals one is striving for as pointed out by Basili and Rombach (1994). Of particular importance for the sake of reuse as a Web service are the qualities modularity, reusability and flexibility. Modularity is defined in terms of high cohesion and low coupling. Of particular importance for wrapping is coupling (Stevens, 1974). The fewer dependencies there are between the individual program parts, the easier it is to extract them. The reusability metric has been the subject of a special paper on reuse measurement (Sneed, 1998). It is concerned with the self-containment of the program parts and their independence from the environment. Reusable code blocks should contain no IO operations, no references to global data, and no direct branches into other blocks. Finally, flexibility is an indicator of data independence. The code should be void

of context dependent, hard coded data to allow it to be used in a different context.

The quality of legacy procedural code can be measured in terms of eight quality metrics:

- Modularity (Sarkar & Rama, 2007)
- Portability (Card & Glass, 1991)
- Flexibility (Drake, 1996)
- Conformity (Kemmerer & Paulk, 2009)
- Testability (Hutcheson, 2003)
- Convertibility (Sneed, 1991)
- Reusability (Li, 1997)
- Maintainability (Oman, et al., 1994)

Modularity is measured in terms of the granularity of the modules and their degree of interdependence. The greater their size is and the higher their dependency on other modules the less modular they are. Portability implies that the modules can be easily ported from one environment to another, which means that they have few dependencies on the environment. If a legacy module contains for example many connections to a particular database and teleprocessing environment like CICS or IMS, then it is not portable. The software cited below was operating in an ADABAS environment, but used only few features of that environment. Flexibility is the degree to which the code is independent of the data it is using. If that data is hard-coded in constants and literals in the statements as was the case below the code becomes petrified. Conformity implies that the code complies with the prevailing coding standard for that language. Testability is a measure of the number of test cases that would be required to reach all branches. The greater the number of branches there are relative to the size of the code, the lower the testability. Convertibility is the ease with which individual statements can be converted into another language such as from COBOL to Java. Statements which are convertible on a 1:1 basis are easy, statements which are converted 1:n are difficult and statements which are converted on a m:n basis are considered to be very difficult.

Reusability is the ease with which the code or portions thereof can be reused in another context such as a Web service. It is measured in terms of the data and procedural dependencies. Maintainability is a compound metric—the maintainability index—which combines different complexity metrics with selected quality metrics which effect maintenance effort.

As with the complexity metrics, these metrics are converted to a common scale, in this case a ration scale from 0 to 1 with 1 denoting maximum possible fulfillment, 0 denoting the lowest acceptable fulfillment and 0.5 representing the median quality. There is a justified criticism of the ratio scale, but for measuring the relations of various quantities it is the most practical means and also the one best understood by managers, who must make decisions based on the numbers they have (Erdogmus, 2008).

The following quality measures were taken from the same BESSY system of the German foreign office as the complexity metrics. The audit of the code was conducted prior to a reengineering project back in 1999 (Sneed & Nyary, 1999). They indicate that this code was highly inflexible because of the wide use of hard coded data. A good part of the data including salary levels was embedded in the code. The reusability was low because of the many interconnections between code blocks via GOTO branches. Almost every third statement in the code was a GOTO. On top of that, the modules used a big block of global data. Modularity and testability were also below average as a result of the large size of the code blocks and the many GOTOs between them. On the positive side, convertibility was high because most of the statements used were of a very simple nature and could be readily converted.

- MODULARITY 0.498
- PORTABILITY 0.668
- FLEXIBILITY 0.100
- CONFORMITY 0.774
- TESTABILITY 0.498

- CONVERTIBILITY 0.821
- REUSABILITY 0.150
- MAINTAINABILITY 0.464
- AVERAGE PROGRAM QUALITY 0.448

In the sample shown, the quality of the programs was too low to justify wrapping them. They first had to be reengineered. The GOTOs had to be reduced to a tolerable degree and the hard coded literals and constants had to be moved out to resource tables. Only after bringing up the quality to above 0.6 and pushing down the complexity below 0.5 could these legacy modules be considered for wrapping. Fortunately, the restructuring was highly automated so that the costs for reaching these goals remained low. This example shows that measurement of the code is essential in deciding which modules to wrap, as they are, which modules to first reengineer before wrapping and which not to bother with. The costs of wrapping is very much dependent on the size of the programs, their data access and interface complexity as well as on their modularity, reusability and flexibility. All too often code is wrapped for reuse, which should have been discarded.

THE LEGACY MODULE TRANSFORMATION PROCESS

Once the legacy modules have been selected, they are transformed to Web services in a eight step process with the steps:

1. Reformat and cleanse the code.
2. Convert numeric data to ASCII character format.
3. Refactor the module interfaces.
4. Restructure the control logic.
5. Strip unwanted code.
6. Transform module code.
7. Wrap the module.
8. Test the wrapped service (see Figure 4).

Figure 4. Code transformation process

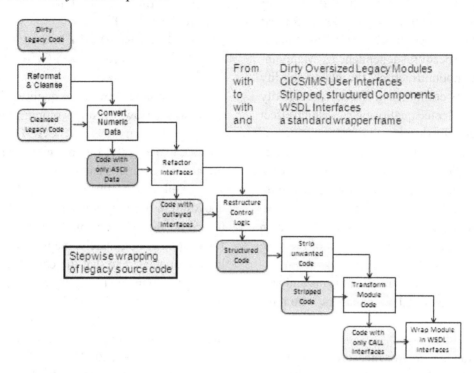

Reformat and Cleanse the Code

The first step in transforming a legacy module over into a Web service is to reformat and clean up the code. Old code in languages like COBOL, PL/I and C can become very unreadable (Buse & Weimer, 2010). It is not always indented and there are often several statements on the same line. It also abounds with literal texts and numeric constants, i.e. hard-coded data. In principle, this could all be carried over into the wrapped Web service, but eventually the code should be cleaned up, so it is better to do that at the start. As a minimum, nested statements should be indented, lines cut up into one statement per line, comment blocks inserted and hard-coded texts removed to a resource table. There is now a large body of literature on code refactoring and tools to support it (Seacord, Plakosh, & Lewis, 2003). It may be recommendable to submit the code to be wrapped to a refactoring process before commencing with the wrapping, but it is not a prerequisite to wrapping, since this would increase the costs and extend the time required. One should not forget that the motivation for wrapping is to reuse existing functionality with a minimum of time and cost. Getting involved in a major refactoring operation would be against those principles. If the wrapped code is subjected to a high degree of change, then it can always be improved later. The maxim of wrapping is to change as little as possible (Pinker, et al., 2002).

Convert Numeric Data to ASCII Character Format

One of the greatest sources of errors is incompatible data types and improper casting. Machine specific data types like bit and packed-decimal are also not portable to other platforms. Numeric data types are difficult to convert and cause problems with the alignment of records. There is really no justification for storing data in numeric form, since it can be converted to a numeric data type when it is computed. Above all one must consider that Web service messages are in ASCII character format. The data values should be readable. If the data is in binary format within the Web service it will have to be converted each time a request is received and converted back each time a response is sent. It is better to convert the numeric data within the Web service. Of course this costs CPU time on the server, but this time is insignificant compared to the costs of communication. This is really something that should be done when wrapping (Sneed, 2010).

Refactor the Module Interfaces

Legacy modules can have many interfaces to their environment. On the front side, they receive input messages from the teleprocessing monitor and forward output messages back to it. On the back side, they retrieve data objects from a database and insert, delete and update data objects in the database. Very often, the database access statements in the IBM database language DLI or SQL are scattered throughout the code. This reduces portability and should be corrected. It is recommended to factor out the teleprocessing and database access operations into an access shell and to invoke them there from the main line logic. This refactoring also enhances maintainability since all interactions with the framework are centralized.

Restructure the Control Logic

Despite all of the efforts to promote structured programming in the 1970s and 80s most practicing programmers never got the message. They continued to work with GOTO's to guide their flow of control. Of course if the legacy code contains too many GOTOs it is probably not worth reusing it. However, if there is a limited number, they can be dealt with. The GOTOs can be replaced by label variables and a controller inserted to invoke the target procedures. The important thing is that procedures are not directly linked by GOTO branches, otherwise they cannot be reused independently of

one another. Since this restructuring can be done automatically, there is no extra cost.

Strip Unwanted Code

Code stripping is a technique used to select given paths through a module by blending out all of the data and statements not used. It was originally used for testing purposes. The idea was to test one path through a program at a time and not to be concerned with the rest. The code was submitted to an automatic slicing machine, which left the slice selected as it was, while commenting out the rest. Then the module was compiled and tested for that one path. This was then repeated for each path until all control paths had been tested. This technique was refined and used in a European research project—TRUST—for testing embedded, real time software, where it was not possible to instrument the code (Puhr & Sneed, 1989). However, the technique can be applied to business systems as well to isolate strips of code to be extracted without taking over the full code. In this way, individual functions can be stripped out of the existing code mass for reuse.

In the context of wrapping, the technique of code stripping is used to generate multiple instances of the same module. Each instance can be a separate Web service. An instance corresponds to a particular business rule. In the past, for efficiency reasons, programs were written to fulfill several business rules at one time. This led to the intertwining of business functions with one another. This, among other things, is one of the main deterrents to reusing existing programs as Web services, since a Web service should correspond to one and only one business rule, so that the sequence and combination of business rules can be determined in the business process, which uses the services. This is after all, one of the major goals of a service-oriented architecture (Boldyreff, 2004). Business processes should be able to arbitrarily combine individual Web services to meet different requirements.

By selecting particular paths through the control logic, the responsible developer can cause individual functions or business rules to be cut out of the original legacy module and to become separate modules, to be wrapped and used as Web services. One of the primary goals of a service-oriented architecture is, after all, flexibility and flexibility can only be achieved by combining small units of code with a single purpose and not using gigantic, multipurpose programs. It is like building a house with bricks as opposed to building with ready-made slabs. Building a house with ready-made slabs means you have to fit the house to the slabs. The slabs dictate the architecture of the house. To avoid that in software, it is necessary to cut up the monolithic code blocks into smaller, single purpose units of code, i.e. bricks, before wrapping them. This is what code stripping is intended to accomplish.

To perform the selection of code strips to be reused as Web services it is necessary that the person selecting the paths is familiar with the legacy language and also familiar with the business process. Either this person is the developer responsible for the code working alone or it is the responsible developer working together with a wrapping expert. This is not something that a wrapping expert can solve alone. He must understand the role of the legacy module within the current business process.

Transform Module Code

In transforming the code, the objective is to change as least as possible. Only that is changed which is required to receive Web service requests and to dispatch responses. There are three types of legacy modules and each one has to be transformed in a different way. The three types are:

- Online modules
- Batch modules and
- Subroutine modules

Online modules have a message interface to the teleprocessing monitor with which they receive and send maps. Normally this is some kind of macro like Exec CICS or Exec DLI. This macro has to be replaced by a call statement, which calls the wrapper. In the case of a receive macro, it is called to deliver the next input message. In the case of a send macro, it is called to dispatch the next response. Other special macros for communicating with the teleprocessing monitor are replaced by corresponding statements in the host language. The database access operations should be left as they are.

Batch modules are driven by one or more parameter files. The parameter files identify what input files are to be read in order to create other files, to generate reports or to update a database. To convert them to Web services, the input parameters have to be replaced by Web requests. Here the "read" statements for the parameters are replaced by calls to the wrapper to deliver the Web request containing the parameters for the batch job. The rest of the code can be left as it is.

Subroutine modules are called from super-ordinate modules to perform a given function. They already have an entry with a set of input arguments and a set of output results. The task of the transformation is to replace the "entry" and "return" statements. The entry statements—there may be more than one—are replaced by calls to the wrapper to deliver the data from the next Web service request. The return statements are replaced by calls to the wrapper to pick up the data from the result parameters to create a Web service response. This is the simplest transformation, but if there are many entries and many exits there will be many statements to be replaced (Gannon, 2010).

Wrap the Module

The last step in the transformation process is to generate a WSDL interface and a wrapper for each wrapped Web service. The WSDL interface is created from a standard template and from the interface definitions of the legacy code. If a map is the source of the input data then the map fields will be the arguments of the requests and the results of the responses. The WSDL will be generated from the map description. If a parameter file is the source of the input data then the records will be the message parts of the Web request. The response is only a return code to confirm the completion of the batch run or to indicate an error condition. If a parameter list is the input, e.g. a Linkage Section in COBOL, then the parameter fields become the input arguments. The final result is in any case a complete and correct Web service interface definition.

That interface definition is then used to generate a wrapper component. This component should be in the language of the wrapped service to ensure compatibility. It will have two sub components. The one subcomponent is to accept the next Web service request and to convert the data of the request over into the interface data of the wrapped service by matching the WSDL schema description to the target language interface description. The other subcomponent is to take the data in the output interface of the wrapped service and to create a Web service response from it on the basis of the WSDL interface description. The end results are an executable wrapper component and a WSDL interface definition to be used by the client components when invoking this particular Web service (Sneed, 2006).

Test the Wrapped Service

After the transformation process has been completed, the wrapped Web service has to be tested. Compared to the wrapping, which is highly automated, testing is a long and tedious job. There is no guarantee that the wrapped legacy code will behave in the same way as a service as it did as part of a batch or online transaction. There can be data type and data conversion as well as logical and timing errors. To uncover them the Web service has to be tested with a wide range of parameters.

The difficulty lies in creating the many different Web requests. In a wrapping project for PLI programs on the mainframe it took up to three days to test a service that only took one day to wrap. The old test data which had been used to test the old IMS transaction was not directly reusable to test the new Web service. The content was the same, but it had to be totally restructured and put in the form of a WSDL interface. This required the development of yet another tool. Even then, the data had to be distributed across many requests. At the moment, the test problem is still open but there are already a number of tools for testing Web services (Zhu, 2006).

TOOLS FOR THE TRANSFORMATION PROCESS

There should be a tool for automating every step in the source transformation process:

- A static analyzer for analyzing, checking and measuring the code
- A code cleaner for reformatting and cleaning up the code
- A data converter for converting the numeric data to ASCII character data
- An interface refactorer for factoring out the interfaces
- Code restructurer for restructuring the control logic
- Code stripper for stripping out the unused paths
- Code transformer for transforming the code
- Code wrapper for wrapping the modules (See Figure 5)

Analyzing the Code with the Tool SoftAudit

To check and measure the candidate modules for reuse as Web services, a static analyzer tool

Figure 5. Code transformation tools

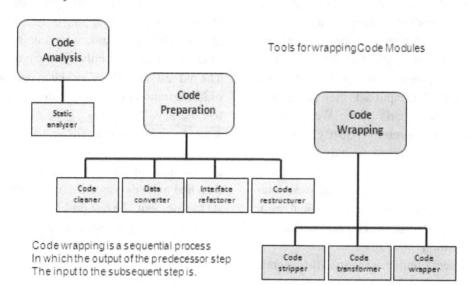

is required. This tool should, on the one hand, be able to compare the source code against a set of coding rules for enforcing reuse. On the other hand, it should be capable of measuring the size, complexity and quality of the candidate code. Such a tool is the tool SoftAudit for auditing source code. SoftAudit has a user interface which allows the user to set certain rules to be checked, rules such as no GOTOs and no hard-wired data. If these rules are violated, they are listed out in a deficiency report. At the end of this report the rate of conformance is computed. If it is too low, i.e. below 60%, then the source should not be reused.

In measuring the source code SoftAudit counts several size metrics, statements, control nodes, used data elements, call connections, GOTO branches, files, database accesses, etc. From these entity and relationship counts eight complexity metrics are computed, metrics like data flow complexity, control flow complexity, interface complexity, language complexity etc. Parallel to these complexity metrics eight quality metrics like modularity, reusability, testability and portability, are computed. All of the metrics are collected together in a module metrics report. The modules are also ranked based on their reusability.

With the help of these reports the user can decide which modules are good candidates for Web services, which could become Web services if they are improved and which are out of the question.

Reformatting and Cleansing the Code with the Reformer of SoftRedo

The tool for reformatting and cleansing code is the reformer component of SoftRedo. In reformatting the source code it splits code lines in which there are more than one statement per line and creates a line per statement. If a line exceeds 100 characters, it is cut into two lines. This not only makes it easier to analyze and read the code, but it also helps to close the gap between the number of statements and the number of lines of code. In addition, SoftRedo indents nested code, i.e. code included in code blocks, loops and if conditions. This indentation makes the code more readable. Many of the older source texts were created with an old unreliable editor. Special characters may be represented with a non-standard code and blank characters, carriage control and line end markers may be missing. It is here that the source text is cleaned up for further processing. Since not only the program code but also the macros, copies, includes and header files can be poorly formatted with multiple data definitions on a single line, these sources should also be reformatted.

With the code of PL/I and C++ programs comments that are in the same lines as the code are taken out and put in a separate line proceeding the line where they were originally located. This is done to make it possible to distinguish between code lines and comment lines, as is the case in COBOL. It also makes it easier to reengineer and to convert the code into another language.

It is, of course, difficult to assign meaningful names to symbolic constants after the fact but SoftRedo can at least remove the hard-wired data from the procedural statements replacing them with generated symbolic constant names. The symbolic constants are collected together either in a separate copy or include member or in a resource header file. These new source member files are added to the source library where the original source is located. There they can be included in the original source code at compile time. This makes it possible to change constants and text literal independently of the procedural code. It is even possible for non-programming staff to edit them, thus reducing the costs of change. Afterwards a text editor can scan through the code and replace the generated names with the speaking ones.

With this feature, external resource files, i.e. text or code tables, can be created which are exchangeable. This can be important when it comes to the localization of code, e.g. replacing German texts with English texts or changing numeric codes like postal codes. Such an evolution can be achieved without going into the actual source code. One need only alter the tables or resource files.

Converting the Numeric Data with the Data Converter of SoftRedo

To make the data inside the wrapped modules compatible with the incoming XML data and to make the code portable to any machine, the numeric data types should be converted to ASCII character format. This is a function of the data conversion component of SoftRedo. It scans through the source and converts the numeric data types like Binary, Packed-Decimal and Floating into character strings. Bit fields are converted to characters. Should these numeric fields be part of a data structure then the structure is lengthened. If the length of the structure is contained in a variable, that length variable has to be adjusted. If the structure in which the converted fields are contained is redefined then the redefining field will be automatically padded to match the length of the redefined field. In either case, a comment is inserted in the data definition to give the programmer the length of the new extended data structure. Overlay data structures using redefinition is one of the worst features of legacy programs. Removing them is one of the most important functions in reengineering.

Should the user want to retest the adapted programs in their old environment, he will have to adjust the record lengths of the files according to the new lengths. This will require a data conversion. Therefore, it is better to convert the data types to a standard character format before wrapping the programs or porting them to another platform. Usually the migration to SOA is connected with a data migration, so here two problems can be solved with the same solution.

In C and C++ it is not data types which are removed but environment specific macros such as EXEC CICS and EXEC SQL. They may also be user-defined macros. The macros are placed into comments so as not to affect the compilation. It is up to the user to replace them by equivalent macros for the new environment. The goal here is to produce a portable version of the code.

Factoring Out the Interfaces with the Interface Refactorer of SoftRedo

Programs which mix the technical I-O and database access operations with the business logic code are neither portable nor reusable since their business logic is totally dependent on a particular user interface and database driver. It is not possible to reuse them in another environment, which uses another database system or another teleprocessing monitor. This is a particularly strong handicap when it comes to wrapping the code for reuse in a SOA environment, since only those code units can be reused, i.e. wrapped, which are independent of the technical environment. With many old applications, this is less than half of the code. For this reason, it is essential to separate the interactions with the environment from the functional operations.

To overcome this handicap, SoftRedo relocates all such environment dependent operations such as file operations, database access operations and user dialog operations into separate code blocks of an access shell, either in PL/I internal procedures, in COBOL sections or in C++ dedicated IO-functions. Each and every such operation becomes a performable function, which is then invoked from the location where it previously was. In this way, the business rule logic becomes free of dependencies on the environment. If there are many such IO and access operations, e.g. opens, writes, reads, closes, EXEC-CICS, EXEC-DLI, EXEC-ADABAS, send, receive, etc., this comes to a major code revision. SoftRedo is able to make this revision automatically in that it relocates all such interactions with the environment to an I/O/Access shell, replacing them by standard procedure calls. By separating the business logic from the input/output and access logic, the portability and reusability of the code is vastly improved.

Restructuring the Control Flow Logic with the Code Restructurer of SoftRedo

To remove any GOTO branches within the wrapped code a restructuring tool is needed. There were many such tools produced in the past using different algorithms to restructure the control flow. The safest and most reliable solution is to replace the branches with a label variable in the code. This label variable points to the next block of code to be executed. The GOTO statements are placed in comments so that the programmers may see where they are. In their place, a label variable is set to the label to which the GOTO jumps. All of the following statements up to the end of that code block are then masked by a nested if. In the end, there are no more branches out of the individual code blocks. In PLI the code blocks are internal procedures, in COBOL paragraphs, in C++ functions. The GOTOs can be removed optionally by the tool SoftRedo. If they are local within the strip of code to be wrapped, they can remain. However, if they connect control paths, which are intended to be wrapped separately, they must be removed. Should the code have to be converted into an object-oriented language without GOTO statements, then the prerequisites for such a conversion are fulfilled here.

Restructuring the code not only makes the code easier to wrap, but also makes it easier to maintain. A Code Restructurer helps to fulfill both goals. Experience has shown that it is much better to clean up the code before wrapping it than after. Wrapping problematic code only carries the problems over into the new environment.

Stripping the Code with the Code Stripper of SoftWrap

If it is not feasible to reuse a program as a whole, it is necessary to strip the code. Readers may not be aware of the fact that legacy programs, particularly on the mainframe, can become terribly big. It is not unusual to find COBOL or PL/I programs with more than 5000 lines of code. These programs combine many business functions, which may be carried out at the same time, but are not really related. When it comes to migrating them to Web services it is better to wrap them separately. The tool SoftWrap will do this, but it requires some human interaction. The user must mark which results he wishes to obtain from the program. For this he is given a view of the output data in the Data Division. For online programs this output data is normally to be found in the data structure corresponding to the map of the user interface. In AS400 programs this is the screen section. For CICS programs, it is the Basic Map Service data definition. For IMS programs, it is the Message Format Service map together with the map attribute bytes. By means of data slicing, the tool locates all the procedures, e.g. COBOL paragraphs, required to produces those results selected by the user. These include not only the procedures or blocks of code where the map fields are set, but also those procedures, which produce intermediate results used by the procedures that set the map fields. At the other end of the data flow are those procedures, which receive and check the input maps. Very often output map fields are set from database contents. Therefore, those paragraphs, which access the database, have to be included. What is left of the procedural code is placed in comments.

The result of the tool is a partial program consisting of selected code blocks and a data area containing only those data structures processed by the selected paragraphs. It most cases this amounted to less than 1/3 of the original code. This is then compiled as a separate stand-alone module to be reused as a Web service.

Transforming the Code with the Code Transformer of SoftWrap

Once the stripped versions of the existing legacy modules are available and compiled, the next step is to transform them to a Web service. The tool for this purpose is a code transformer like SoftWrap. SoftWrap processes a stripped module to replace the terminal input/output operations with calls to a wrapper module and to move the input/output data from the Linkage section to the Working-Storage section. In the case of IMS the input maps are received via a call to the IMS transaction monitor:

- CALL 'CBLTDLI' USING PARAM-NR, IO-PCB, INPUT-MAP.

The same type of call is used to send the output map to the terminal.

- CALL 'CBLTDLI' USING PARAM-NR, IO-PCB, OUTPUT-MAP.

SoftWrap simply places the original call in comments and inserts another call to the generated wrapper module behind it.

- CALL 'CBL2WSDL' USING PARAM-NR, IO-PCB, INPUT-MAP.

In the case of CICS programs the CICS EXEC SEND and RECEIVE macros are replaced by calls to the wrapper with the map buffer serving to exchange the data. In batch programs, the READ statements are replaced by calls, and in subroutines, the entries are altered to receive a message while the exits are altered to return a message.

The data in the Linkage-Section of CICS programs is moved to the Working-Storage Section as CICS programs are actually subprograms of the CICS TP-Monitor. In the case of IMS-DC the opposite is true. The COBOL program is the main program and the IMS-DC monitor is implemented as a subprogram to handle the data flow to and from the user terminal. Therefore, IMS-DC programs are much easier to wrap. It is only a question of replacing the IMS-DC calls with calls to the wrapper. With CodeWrap the author has transformed both COBOL and PL/I modules as well as IBM-Assembler modules in batch as well as in online modus (Sneed & Majnar, 1998).

Wrapping the Legacy Module with the Code Linker of SoftWrap

The final step of the legacy code transformation process is to connect the wrapped components to the Internet via the available middleware, e.g. Web-

Sphere. This is where the CodeLink component of the tool SoftWrap comes into play. CodeLink generates two wrapper modules to be linked to the wrapped program. The input to the generation is the source code of the altered legacy module. Based on the declarations of the input parameters, CodeLink creates a WSDL schema for the Web service request and at the same time generates a wrapper module for translating that request into the input parameters of the server program. In a second run, CodeLink creates another WDSL schema for the Web service response while, at the same time, generating another wrapper module for transferring the output parameters of the server program into the WSDL response.

The four results of CodeLink are the two WSDL schemas—one for the Web service request and the other for the Web service response—plus the two wrapper modules—one for handling the inputs and the other for handling the outputs. The two wrapper modules are generated from a template modified and enhanced by the parameter data taken from server program source. The two WSDL schemas are generated from the program interface definitions within the legacy code. This technique has been applied already in several migration projects (Aversano, 2001). Since everything is generated automatically, it goes very fast and is much more reliable than if the wrappers were to be coded by hand.

It is very important for the transformation process to be fully automated since this is the only way to keep costs down and to make wrapping a viable alternative. Otherwise, it would be too expensive and error prone.

EXPERIENCE WITH LEGACY CODE REUSE AS WEB SERVICES

The approach to reusing legacy code described has its roots in the in the field of software migration. During the past twenty years, the author has participated in several large-scale migration projects

helping IT users to move their legacy systems into a more modern technical environment. In the 1990s the target environment was a client/server architecture. Users ported their applications from a mainframe to distributed computer networks. This often involved downsizing and restructuring the user software before converting it to another language. In particular new data access shells were introduced and the user interfaces exchanged. As early as 1996, the author suggested using wrapping technology to wrap legacy modules behind a standard CORBA interface for reuse as server components (Sneed, 1996). After the year 2000, IT users began to move to Web applications. The challenge here was to wrap existing components as Web services, which could be accessed by clients of the Web network. Since 2005, many user organizations are considering moving their IT operations to a Service-Oriented Architecture—SOA (Winter, 2011). This is, of course, a relatively big step and has to be considered well. Users need a very long lead-time to prepare it. Part of that preparation is the execution of pilot projects to test various alternatives for that transition. One such alternative is the reuse of existing legacy software components as Web services. It cannot be stated that this approach is already widespread, but there are cases where it has been used successfully. The author has participated in several such migration projects, three of which will be briefly outlined here.

Wrapping Mainframe COBOL Programs at the Deutsche Bank

The first real test of the approach described here was at the German Bank Savings and Loan Division in the year 2000. The goal of this division was to make its COBOL/CICS application for maintaining the savings and loan accounts accessible to the users via the Internet. At the time of this project, this legacy system had been in operation for almost 20 years. Only recently the IMS databases had been replaced by DB2 relational databases by inserting an access shell named HIREL from Tata Consultancy between the COBOL programs and their data. This was done to make the data available to other more recent applications. This extension however added to the amount of code to be maintained. The system included 990 CICS online programs, 593 batch programs, 183 subprograms, 437 CICS maps, i.e. user interfaces, 194 relational database tables and circa 500 VSAM files with over 4 Million lines of COBOL code. In view of the size and complexity of the system, it was decided not to redevelop it but to wrap it. In this way the old maintenance team could be kept on the job. They only needed to become familiar with the new Web service interfaces. A new and younger team was created to develop the Web server running in a Unix environment as well as the Web clients running on the PC workstations of the end users. Thus, the new Web architecture was to be a three-tier J2EE architecture with Web clients on the PC, Web server on the intermediate Unix platform and the database server with all of the old batch applications running on the IBM mainframe. BEA WebLogic was the middleware product used to connect the Web clients with the Web server while MQ-Series from IBM was used to connect the J2EE server with the mainframe CICS transactions. The product used to create the new Web interfaces to the CICS-COBOL programs was a product named XML4COBOL from Mass High Tech, a German company from Stuttgart (see Figure 6).

The task of the author was to prepare the CO-BOL sources for wrapping. The programs had to be restructured and new Linkage Section interfaces generated to replace the previous CICS Map interfaces. This work required more than a year for the 990 online programs, since the reengineering tools were still under development and had to be tested in practice. Nonetheless, the project was in the end a success even if it required altogether three years to finish. A team of 7 developers developed the Java software for the frontend while the author worked together with a team of

5 COBOL programmers to wrap the backend online programs. The batch programs were left as they were. The wrapping of the mainframe programs was highly automated so the greater portion of the time spent on the backend was devoted to testing the transactions. A test driver was developed to simulate the messages coming in from MQ-Series and to catch the outgoing responses. In this way, the test of the backend could be made independently of the frontend development. Still the testing remained tedious as the least little change to the interfaces of the legacy programs had side effects which had to be dealt with. After three years, the wrapped versions of the COBOL programs could go into production together with the Java Web server and the users were able to access the system via the Internet (Sneed, 2003).

Wrapping a COBOL System for a Debt Collection Company

The second major application of the techniques described here was reported on by the author at the 8th European Conference on Software Maintenance and Reengineering—CSMR—in 2005. The stepwise integration of the existing COBOL components into a new Web-based architecture was part of a larger migration project, which included the conversion of Forté programs over into Java. The goal of that project was to incrementally migrate the existing debt collection applications over a period of five years. InFoScore, a German incasso company located in Baden-Baden, had already began with the reimplementation of their debt collection systems in the late 1990s. These systems were based on a large debtor's database with some 11 million entries. The database Informix was maintained in a Unix environment with both Sun and HP hardware. For the COBOL applications, the data had to be copied over into Index-Sequential files to be processed. Over top of the database were diverse application systems for billing, for letter processing, for call services

Figure 6. Wrapping COBOL programs on the IBM mainframe

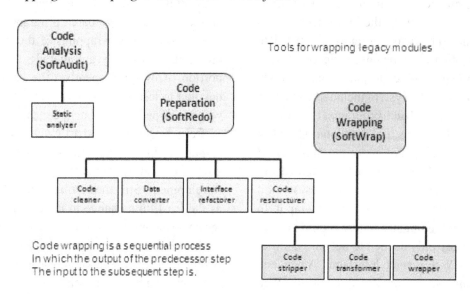

and for providing credit information. These original systems encompassing more than 800.000 statements had originally been implemented in COBOL-74 on a Unisys mainframe and later ported to a HP Unix platform. They were being maintained and continually further developed by a staff of only 14 programmers. There were at the time of this project still 800 to 1000 change requests per annum so that the system was still growing at a rate of 9% annually.

The first attempt to replace these systems by redevelopment was a failure. The goal was to replace all of the existing systems within a three-year period, starting with a new requirement analysis, and proceeding to an object-oriented design and a new implementation in the 4GL language Forté from Sun. As it turned out, it was extremely difficult to replicate the old business logic in the new programming language. It was too intertwined with the features of the old architecture. After seven years only 60% of the functionality of the old applications had been reimplemented in Forté. When Sun then cancelled its support for UDS-Forté, the project was stopped leaving 40% of the code still in COBOL. The attempt to reimplement the entire functionality of the legacy systems in a

single project was too much for the company to handle even with the support of several external software houses. At one time more than 40 persons were working on the project, so this resulted in a tremendous loss to the otherwise healthy middle size business. Not only that, but the user was obliged now to maintain two IT-worlds in parallel. The COBOL applications remained on the HP platform, whereas the new Forté applications were running on a SUN platform. There were also two separate maintenance groups, one for the COBOL and one for the Forté, working next to one another. The end users were obliged to switch back and forth between the two systems depending on what transaction they were performing.

The second attempt proved to be a more viable solution. Instead of trying to redevelop all of the applications from scratch, the company adapted an incremental strategy and began migrating one subsystem at a time. The systems first had to be split up into subsystems with no more than 50.000 statements apiece. The subsystems interacted with one another via a common database, a common user interface and by XML import/export files. The data was converted to an Oracle database for use by both the Java and the COBOL programs.

The COBOL programs were reengineered to access that database directly. The important thing was that all systems had a common user interface so the end users were no longer forced to switch back and forth between systems. Thus, a preliminary project had to be made to implement the new interfaces. This way, each subsystem could be dealt with in a separate project. The Forté subsystems were sent to India to be converted to Java, the remaining COBOL subsystems were left in COBOL and wrapped by the Hungarian company of the author and some with the most outstanding requirements were rewritten in Java by the developers in Germany. The integration and system testing took place at the daughter company of the InfoScore in Ireland. Therefore, this was a good example of a globally distributed reengineering project.

The new architecture for the applications was J2EE with a Java Script user interface and a Java objects data access shell. This development of the common user interface and a common database access shell was done first as a prerequisite to migrating the individual subsystems. The next step was to wrap all of the old COBOL applications between the common front end and back end layers. This was done by inserting XML compatible interfaces into the COBOL code to replace the previous map interfaces and to insert an access shell for the new Oracle database. This was done automatically with the help of the SoftWrap tools. For the batch programs, a new entry interface had to be inserted with the control parameters coming from the Java client. The Forté applications were converted to native Java and connected to the user via the Java Script GUIs and to the database via the Java Objects access shell. In the meantime, the production went on by running the unconverted subsystems in the old environment parallel to the converted components in the new environment. This could be achieved smoothly because the user interface level and the database access level were the same for both (see Figure 7).

It took more than three years to integrate all of the wrapped and converted applications into the new environment, but in the end, all applica-

Figure 7. Incremental migration project

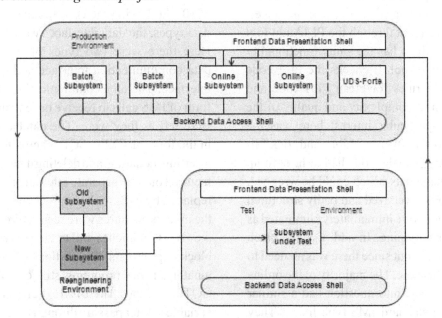

Integrating wrapped COBOL modules into a J2E Framework

tions were running under the same user interface with the same data basis. The work could then begin on the conversion of the remaining COBOL applications to Java, but there was no longer any time pressure to make this, since the COBOL was already running in a Java environment (Sneed, 2005).

A Pilot Project for Wrapping PL/I Programs on an IBM Mainframe

The third case study concerns the wrapping of selected PL/I programs as Web services on the main frame. The programs were selected from a home loan company in the German state of Baden-Wuerttemburg. The goal of the project was to test if the programs could be wrapped and if so what it would cost. This was seen as a pilot project for a planned migration to a service-oriented architecture. The programs were online transactions running under the IMS teleprocessing monitor and using the database system DB2. They had been in operation for over 20 years.

The first step was to analyze the entire PL/I library consisting of 22,839 sources of which there were 8654 PL/I programs. The rest include members for defining data structures and interfaces. The sources were put through the PLIAudit tool of the author, which has the same functionality as the COBAudit tool. It checks the PL/I code against a set of rules for clean PL/I code and measures the size, complexity and quality of the programs. Of particular interest here was the modularity, portability, reusability and, flexibility of the code, since the code had to be split up into reusable segments which could be wrapped. There were some oversized and badly structured programs, which were immediately eliminated as candidates for wrapping. In addition, the batch programs were left out since there was no need to wrap them at this time. The majority of the online programs that came into question had a similar structure and a standard IMS type frame. They were basically of two types—update and query

programs. The query programs received a map from the 3270 terminal with the match codes of the data desired, selected the requested columns from the rows affected and displayed the data back on the screen. If the selected data was too much the screen had to be scrolled. Much of the code in the query programs was devoted to this scrolling. The update programs received a MFS—Message Format Service—map from the 3270 terminal, edited the content, retrieved the master data from the DB2 relational tables, updated the columns of the rows in the selected tables and returned a message to the user what had been changed. The business rules were mostly embedded in the update code of the main procedures. Some business rules were contained in separate sub procedures called by the main procedure (Bender, 2008).

The next step was to restructure the online programs with the tool PLIRedo. The source code was first reformatted and the literal constant texts extracted and put into constant tables. Then all of the numeric data types—binary, packed, and bit—were converted to zoned decimal types in character format. That action and the justification thereof is described in the proceedings of the MESOA workshop of September 2010 (Sneed, 2010). Following the conversion of the numeric data types, the data interfaces were factored out. Here there were two types of interfaces—the data communication interface and the database interface. The data communication interfaces in form of IMS calls to receive or send the next map were left as they were. The database interfaces in the form of EXEC SQL macros for selecting, inserting, updating, and deleting data records were factored out into separate internal procedures and replaced by calls to those procedures. After that, the main procedures were restructured to remove the GOTO branches and to chop oversized code blocks up into smaller portions of code. Unfortunately, these programs still contained many GOTO branches. These had to be replaced by label variables. After passing through the restructuring engine, the PL/I code was quite different. Each external procedure contained a series of internal procedures invoked by the control loop at the top depending on the value of the next label variable until an exit statement was reached.

Only after the restructuring of all the online programs, were the programs selected for wrapping. There were two programs of each type selected, two query programs, two update programs, and two business rule procedures, altogether six. The selection was based on the suitability of those programs for wrapping, i.e. on their size, complexity, and quality. The two sub procedures remained as they were, but the four main procedures were stripped to remove code not related to the core business function. This amounted to circa 40% of the total code, code that was mainly directed toward handling the IMS maps, checking and setting the Program Control Blocks—PCBs—and checking and setting the control information of the map fields. When reusing mainframe programs running under a teleprocessing monitor like IMS-DC or CICS, stripping is absolutely necessary to remove these dependencies on the old environment. These housekeeping functions have no role in the new Web service, which is receiving its data from the WSDL interface.

After stripping, the six selected modules were put through the tool PLIWrap to replace the IMS-DC calls by calls to the wrapper. The parameter lists were altered to leave out the PCB blocks and to include a function code. Other calls to the wrapper were inserted before each return statement to ensure that the Web service request could be closed properly. This was the least of the code alterations. Following that, the programs were submitted to PLILink, which generated for each program a WSDL schema and a PLI sub module for converting the data from the Web service request to the PLI input parameters and for converting the PLI output parameters to the Web service response. Then each wrapped module was linked together with the common controller and with its own spe-

Figure 8. Wrapping PL/I programs under WebSphere

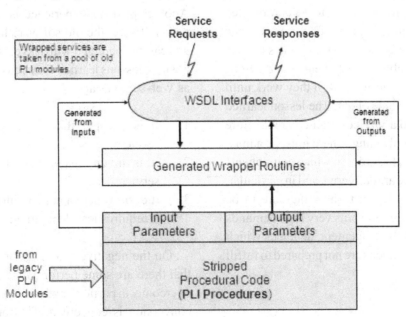

Stripping out and wrapping PLI procedures

cific wrapper subroutine. On the mainframe, the controller ran under the IBM Websphere monitor which activated a new transaction each time a new request came in. Based on the transaction code, the controller invoked the desired Web service and it called its wrapper subroutine to read in the request inputs (see Figure 8).

The purpose of this pilot project was to demonstrate the feasibility of wrapping PLI modules on the mainframe. This purpose was accomplished with a minimum of costs. After the tools had been debugged, the PLI code could be stripped, wrapped, and linked within a half day. Therefore, this was not the problem. The problem came up in testing the new Web services. Since the interfaces had been changed, it was not possible to reuse the old tests, which were made on the 3270 terminal. New tests had to be set up which could be dispatched from a client work station and for this client components were required which were not yet available. Therefore, the test had to be postponed. This situation is typical of a migration to SOA. There are many dependencies between the various activities. The development of the client business processes has to be coordinated with the development of the Web services. If the Web services are created first, there has to be a test driver available to test them immediately, otherwise one will never know if they work until they are used by some client. The lesson learned is that moving to a service-oriented architecture requires through planning. There must be a master plan to govern the order in which components of the architecture are delivered, and in particular, there must be a plan as to how they are to be tested. A SOA migration puts very high demands on the responsible management, demands which many user organizations are not prepared to fulfill (Sneed, 2009).

LESSONS LEARNED IN REUSING LEGACY MODULES AS WEB SERVICES

The lessons learned so far in reusing legacy code to create Web services are partly positive and partly negative. On the positive side, experience has shown that it is quick and inexpensive provided it can be automated. Also on the positive side is the fact that the existing maintenance team can go on maintaining the same old code, even though it is running in another environment. There is no need for them to be replaced by younger programmers or for them to have to learn a new language. This is particularly important in Europe where personnel continuity is a business goal. It is expected to keep programmers employed until they are close to retirement, which depending on the country is when they are 60 to 70 years old. Programmers who started as COBOL programmers will remain COBOL programmers until they retire. Therefore, it is opportune to keep COBOL programs. Otherwise, the employer is obliged to find other jobs for them, which may not be easy. Another positive experience is that, relative to new software, the old software has fewer errors and can be debugged with less cost. Thus, the four positive lessons learned from reusing legacy code as Web services are:

1. It is cheaper than developing new Web services.
2. It is much faster than developing new services.
3. It ensures personnel continuity.
4. It requires less debugging.

On the negative side, experience shows that that there are some performance problems to be overcome, in particular when a lot of runtime data conversion is concerned. This problem can be reduced by converting all numeric data to ASCII character code, but the performance penalty is pushed on to the compiler which still has to convert the numeric variables prior to each arithmetic operation and restore them to their original format after each such operation. Another negative factor is maintenance. The wrapped code still has to be maintained. Of course, it can be restructured as was demonstrated here, but if the naming is bad and the commentary lacking, it will remain difficult for new programmers to understand. One is obliged to keep on the old programmers. Finally, there is the problem of retesting. Even though the code may have been changed only slightly, it still has to be retested in the new environment. If the wrapping itself is automated, then the costs of retesting will appear prohibitive to the user managers. Whereas a legacy module could be restructured and wrapped to become a Web service within a half day, it took 3 to 5 days to test the Web service for all possible usages. This was the reason for the last pilot project to be stopped. In summary the major negative lessons are:

1. Reusing legacy code causes performance problems.
2. Reused code is difficult to maintain.
3. Reused legacy code requires programmers that are familiar with the legacy language.
4. Reused legacy code has to be retested as if it were new.

FUTURE WORK REQUIRED

To make the reuse of legacy modules as Web services a more viable alternative, work in two areas is required. First, the techniques of restructuring and refactoring the old code have to be improved to make that code more maintainable. In particular, ways of assigning meaningful names and inserting useful comments have to be found. It is bad enough for younger programmers that the code is in an ancient language that they are

not familiar with. It is even worse if that code is incomprehensible to them.

Secondly, work must go into the automated testing of Web services. Independently of whether the services are wrapped or not, they have to be tested thoroughly and that costs a big effort, unless the test is automated. It should be possible to automatically generate representative Web service requests based on the Web service interface definition and to automatically validate Web service responses against the service level agreement. These are important topics for future research. The author himself is working on such a tool and hopes to make it available within the next year.

CONCLUSION

This chapter has outlined the reasons for wanting to migrate to a service-oriented architecture. There are both technical and business reasons. One alternative of making that migration is to reuse existing code modules as Web services. For that, they have to be stripped and wrapped. A tool supported process for achieving that was presented and the tools described. The chapter then cited three case studies in which this approach was applied. These case studies unveiled the advantages and disadvantages of following this approach. In the end, it is up to the user management to decide which way to go. They can restrict themselves to using standard Web services offered on the market. This way the vendor would have the responsibility for ensuring that the services function properly. A variation of this approach is to take the services from the open source community, but then the user has the responsibility for testing and maintaining them. A third option is for the user to develop the Web services new and to maintain them for himself. This option is costly and full of risks. A fourth option and the one presented here is to reuse existing software to build up the required services. The advantages and disadvantages of this approach have been covered. A fifth and final option is to combine the other four. This is the option most likely to be selected by most user organizations.

REFERENCES

Aversano, L., Canfora, G., & Cimitile, A. (2001). *Migrating legacy systems to the web – An experience report*. Paper presented at 5th European Conference on Software Maintenance and Reengineering (CSMR 2001). Lisbon, Portugal.

Basili, V., Rombach, H.-D., & Caldiera, C. (1994). Goal question metric paradigm. In *Encyclopedia of Software Engineering* (*Vol. 1*, pp. 528–551). New York, NY: John Wiley.

Belady, L., & Lehman, M. (1975). The evolution dynamics of large programs. *IBM Systems Journal, 3,* 11.

Bender, M., Lörnker, A., & van der Vekens, A. (2008). Evolution of a PL/I application towards SOA. *ObjectSpectrum, 18*(5), 54–63.

Boehm, B., Huang, L., Apurva, J., & Madachy, R. (2004). The ROI of software dependability. *IEEE Software Magazine, 21*(3), 54–61.

Boldyreff, C., Lavery, J., & Allison, C. (2004). Modelling the evolution of legacy systems to web-based systems. *International Journal of Software Maintenance and Evolution, 16*(2), 5–22. doi:10.1002/smr.282

Buse, R., & Weimer, W. (2010). Learning a metric for readability. *IEEE Transactions on Software Engineering, 36*(4), 546–558. doi:10.1109/TSE.2009.70

Card, D., & Agresti, W. (1988). Measuring software design complexity. *Journal of Systems and Software, 8,* 185. doi:10.1016/0164-1212(88)90021-0

Card, D., & Glass, R. (1991). *Measuring software design quality*. Englewood Cliffs, NJ: Prentice-Hall.

Chapin, N. (1977). *A measure of software complexity*. Paper presented at 3rd National Computing Conference. Dallas, TX.

Drake, T. (1996). Measuring software quality – A case study. *IEEE Computer Magazine, 29*(11), 78–87.

Elshof, J. (1976). An analysis of commercial PL/I programs. *IEEE Transactions on Software Engineering, 2*(1), 306.

Erdogmus, H. (2008). The infamous ratio measure. *IEEE Software, 25*(3), 4–7. doi:10.1109/MS.2008.81

Gannon, G., Zhu, H., & Mudian, S. (2010). *On-the-fly wrapping of web services to support dynamic integration*. Paper presented at 17th Working Conference on Reverse Engineering (WCRE 2010). Boston, MA.

Halstead, M. (1977). *Elements of software science*. Amsterdam, The Netherlands: North-Holland.

Hutcheson, M. (2003). *Software testing fundamentals – Fundamental metrics for software testing*. New York, NY: John Wiley & Sons.

ISO. (1993). *Software product evaluation*. Geneva, Switzerland: ISO/IEC Standards Office.

Kemmerer, C., & Paulk, M. (2009). The impact of design and code reviews on software quality. *IEEE Transactions on Software Engineering, 35*(4), 534–550. doi:10.1109/TSE.2009.27

Laird, B., & Brennan, C. (2006). *Software measurement and estimation – A practical approach*. New York, NY: John Wiley & Sons. doi:10.1002/0471792535

Li, W. (1997). An empirical study of software reuse in reconstructive maintenance. *Journal of Software Maintenance, 9*(2), 69. doi:10.1002/(SICI)1096-908X(199703)9:2<69::AID-SMR147>3.0.CO;2-5

McCabe, T. (1976). A complexity measure. *IEEE Transactions on Software Engineering, 2*(4), 308–319. doi:10.1109/TSE.1976.233837

McClure, C. (1981). *Managing software development and maintenance*. New York, NY: Van Nostrand.

Nadico, O. (2007). SOA transformation of legacy applications. *ObjectSpectrum, 17*(5), 18–21.

Oman, P., Coleman, D., Ash, D., & Lowther, B. (1994). Using metrics to evaluate software system maintainability. *IEEE Computer Magazine, 27*(8), 44.

Pinker, E., Seidmann, A., & Foster, R. (2002). Strategies for transitioning old economy firms to e-business. *Communications of the ACM, 45*(5), 77–90. doi:10.1145/506218.506219

Puhr, P., & Sneed, H. (1989). *Code stripping as a means of instrumenting embedded systems. EU ESPRIT Project 1258 – Report-1258-3*. Liverpool, UK: EU ESPRIT.

Reiss, S. (2006). Incremental maintenance of software artifacts. *IEEE Transactions on Software Engineering, 32*(9), 682. doi:10.1109/TSE.2006.91

Sarkar, S., & Rama, G. (2007). API-based and information: Theoretic metrics for measuring the quality of software modularization. *IEEE Transactions on Software Engineering, 33*(1), 14–32. doi:10.1109/TSE.2007.256942

Seacord, R., Plakosh, D., & Lewis, G. (2003). *Modernizing legacy systems*. Boston, MA: Addison-Wesley.

Smith, D., & Lewis, G. (2007). *Standards for service-oriented systems*. Paper presented at the 11th European Conference on Software Maintenance and Reengineering (CSMR 2010). Amsterdam, The Netherlands.

Sneed, H. (1991). Economics of software reengineering. *International Journal of Software Maintenance, 3*(3), 129.

Sneed, H. (1995). Understanding software through numbers. *International Journal of Software Maintenance, 7*(6), 405–427. doi:10.1002/smr.4360070604

Sneed, H. (1996). *Encapsulating legacy software for reuse in client/server systems*. Paper presented at Working Conference on Software Reverse Engineering (WCRE 1996). Monterey, CA.

Sneed, H. (1998). Measuring reusability of legacy software systems. *International Journal of Software Process, 4*(1), 43–54.

Sneed, H. (2000). Encapsulation of legacy software – A technique for reusing legacy software components. In Verhoef (Ed.), *Annals of Software Engineering,* (vol 9, pp. 113-132). Amsterdam, The Netherlands: Baltzer.

Sneed, H. (2005). *An incremental approach to system replacement and integration*. Paper presented at 9th European Conference on Software Maintenance and Reengineering (CSMR 2005). Manchester, UK.

Sneed, H. (2006). *Integrating legacy software into a service-oriented architecture*. Paper presented at 10th European Conference on Software Maintenance and Reengineering. Bari, Italy.

Sneed, H. (2007). *Migrating to web services – A research framework*. Paper presented at 11th European Conference on Software Maintenance and Reengineering. Amsterdam, The Netherlands.

Sneed, H. (2009). A pilot project for migrating COBOL code to web services. *International Journal of Software Tools Technology Transfer, 1*(2), 103–129.

Sneed, H. (2010). *SOA integration as an alternative to source migration*. Paper presented at SOAME Workshop. Timisoara, Romania.

Sneed, H., & Majnar, R. (1998). *A case study in software wrapping*. Paper presented at International Conference on Software Maintenance (ICSM 1998). Washington, DC.

Sneed, H., & Merey, A. (1985). Automated software quality assurance. *IEEE Transactions on Software Engineering, 11*(9), 909–916. doi:10.1109/TSE.1985.232548

Sneed, H., & Nyary, E. (1999). *Salvaging an ancient legacy system at the German foreign office*. Paper presented at the International Conference on Software Maintenance (ICSM 1999). Oxford, UK.

Sneed, H., & Sneed, S. (2003). *Web-basierte systemintegration*. Wiesbaden, Germany: Vieweg Verlag. doi:10.1007/978-3-322-89822-7

Stevens, W., Myers, G., & Constantine, L. (1974). Structured design complexity. *IBM Systems Journal, 13*(2), 115–138. doi:10.1147/sj.132.0115

Winter, A., & Zillmann, C. (2011). *The SOAMIG process model in industrial applications*. Paper presented at 15th European Conference on Software Maintenance and Reengineering. Oldenburg, Germany.

Wurms, K. (2010). *Experience of a Swiss bank in migrating to SOA*. Paper presented at 25th International Conference on Software Maintenance (ICSM 2010). Timisoara, Romania.

Zdun, U. (2002). *Reengineering to the web – A reference architecture*. Paper presented at 6th European Conference on Software Maintenance and Reengineering (CSMR 2002). Budapest, Hungary.

ADDITIONAL READING

Bodhuim, T., Guardabasco, E., & Tortorella, M. (2003). *Migration of non-decomposable systems to the web using screen proxies*. Paper presented at 10th Working Conference on Reverse Engineering. Victoria, Canada.

Canfora, G., Fasolino, H., & Frattolillo, G. (2006). *Migrating interactive legacy system to web services*. Paper presented at 10th European Conference on Software Maintenance and Reengineering. Bari, Italy.

Garlan, D., Allan, R., & Ockerbloom, J. (1995). Architectural mismatch – Why is reuse so hard. *IEEE Software Magazine, 12*(6), 26–36.

Hasselbring, W., Conrad, S., Koschel, A., & Tritsch, R. (2006). *Enterprise application integration*. Heidelberg, Germany: Elsevier Spectrum Akademischer Verlag.

Horowitz, E. (1998). Migrating software to the world wide web. *IEEE Software Magazine, 15*(3), 18–26.

Keyes, J. (1998). *Data casting – How to stream data over the internet*. New York, NY: McGraw-Hill.

Krafzig, D., Banke, K., & Schama, D. (2004). *Enterprise SOA*. Upper Saddle River, NJ: Prentice-Hall.

Seacord, R., Plakosh, D., & Lewis, G. (2003). *Modernizing legacy systems*. Boston, MA: Addison-Wesley.

Sneed, H. (2003). Business reengineering in the age of the internet. In *Encyclopedia of Software Engineering* (*Vol. 9*). Amsterdam, The Netherlands: North-Holland.

Stroulia, E., & El-Ramly, P. (2002). *From legacy to web through interaction modelling*. Paper presented at 18th International Conference on Software Maintenance. Montreal, Canada.

Yau, S., & Ho, G. (2011). Software engineering meets services and cloud computing. *IEEE Computer Magazine, 44*(10), 47–58.

Zhu, H. (2006). A framework for service-oriented testing of web services. In *Proceedings of the 30th Annual International Computer and Application Conference*, (Vol. 2, pp. 145-150). IEEE.

KEY TERMS AND DEFINITIONS

Legacy Code: Code of a system that has been developed before the last technology upgrade.

Modules: Separately compilable units of code which can be linked together to build an executable component.

Refactoring: Splitting existing code blocks into smaller units and flattening them by taking out blocks of deeply nested statements.

Rengineering: Restructuring, refactoring, renovating.

Renovating: Removing hard-coded data, relocating interfaces with the environment reform and converting data types.

Restructuring: Reordering the static sequence of existing code blocks and removing all direct links between them.

Reusing: Transplanting existing code of an old system into a new system.

Stripping: Removing all code not belonging to the function to be reused.

Web Services: Standard software functions that can be accessed via the WWW.

Wrapping: Encapsulation of existing code behind an access shell.

Chapter 5
Service Identification and Specification with SoaML

Michael Gebhart
Gebhart Quality Analysis (QA) 82, Germany

ABSTRACT

This chapter focuses on the identification and specification of services based on prior modeled business processes and legacy systems. The resulting service interfaces and service components formalized by using the Service oriented architecture Modeling Language (SoaML) describe the integration of legacy systems into a service-oriented application landscape. The legacy systems provide services for integration purposes and represent the implementations of service components. Additionally, the resulting architecture allows functionality of legacy systems to be replaced with functionality provided by external cloud services. According to model-driven development concepts, the formalized service interfaces and service components as part of the service designs can be used to automatically derive service interface descriptions using the Web Services Description Language (WSDL). These descriptions enable the technical integration of legacy systems. If necessary, service implementations based on the Service Component Architecture (SCA) and the Business Process Execution Language (BPEL) can be generated.

INTRODUCTION

Nowadays, companies organize their Information Technology (IT) by means of services. This means that systems within the application landscape provide and require services business aligned and supporting certain business processes. In order to reuse existing legacy systems and their capabilities, their integration into such a service-oriented application landscape is targeted. This integration requires a determination and realization of required

services that constitute the gateways to existing functionality. These services can be provided by the legacy systems in order to enable their integration or these services can be required by the systems in order to invoke remotely provided functionality, for example, cloud services as part of a public cloud (Chang, Abu-Amara, & Sanford, 2010, p. 46). In this case, these external services are embedded into an internal service-oriented application landscape.

Before services are realized, their detailed planning is necessary. This means that before

DOI: 10.4018/978-1-4666-2488-7.ch005

Copyright © 2013, IGI Global. Copying or distributing in print or electronic forms without written permission of IGI Global is prohibited.

performing the implementation phase they must be methodically identified and specified as part of a systematic design phase. The final service designs are formalized using common and widespread modeling languages. This enables the usage of modeling tools and an analysis and revision of the services already during the design phase, which reduces effort and costs.

The following chapter introduces a methodology for the systematic identification and specification of services that enable the integration of legacy systems into a service-oriented application landscape in order to integrate already implemented functionality and thereby increase its reuse. For this purpose, the methodology combines a derivation of services that support prior defined business requirements with a subsequent revision that considers functionality provided by legacy systems.

Since the systematic identification of services expects a clear understanding of the underlying business requirements, this chapter also introduces artifacts that are created during the requirements analysis phase and their formalization using common, standardized, and wide-spread modeling languages, such as the Unified Modeling Language (UML) (Object Management Group, 2010) and the Business Process Model and Notation (BPMN) (OMG, 2011). Afterwards, the identification and subsequently the specification of services are described. Also during these phases, the modeling of resulting artifacts is considered. In this context, the Service oriented architecture Modeling Language (SoaML) (OMG, 2009) is applied as it is a standardized metamodel and UML profile for modeling service-oriented architectures. It has been created out of a request for proposal (OMG, 2006) and gains increasing vendor and tool support. The usage of these common and wide-spread languages enables the application of existing development tools and the integration of this methodology into existing tool chains.

The chapter concludes with an outlook into the implementation phase based on the prior specified services. In this context, the transformation of the created artifacts into service implementations using the Web Services Description Language (WSDL) (World Wide Web Consortium, 2007b), Service Component Architecture (SCA) (Open Service Oriented Architecture, 2009), and Business Process Execution Language (BPEL) (Organization for the Advancement of Structured Information Standards, 2007) is outlined. This embeds the methodology into a model-driven development scope as introduced by Stahl, Voelter, Bettin, and Stockfleth (2006) and applied in Hoyer, Gebhart, Pansa, Link, Dikanski, and Abeck (2009, 2010).

BACKGROUND

This section gives a brief introduction into the foundations that constitute the basis for the contribution of this chapter. Elementary terms, such as service-oriented architectures or cloud computing, are taken for well known. Only divergences or aspects that are considered as important are repeated. Instead, this section focuses on the specifics of this contribution, such as service designs and their formalization using SoaML. The definitions of these terms are taken from existing work and enhanced with additional aspects if necessary.

Service Design

The design of services constitutes an elementary task when establishing a service-oriented architecture and integrating existing systems. The result of this design phase is a set of so-called service designs with each of them concretely specifying one certain service. The elements of a service design can be derived by considering development processes for services as they are introduced in existing work.

According to Erl (2006, 2008), within the here-mentioned service-oriented design phase especially the service interfaces are created. The elements of a service interface are oriented towards the specification of WSDL and explained in Erl

(2009). A service interface is comprised of provided operations, message types, used data types, a specification of participating roles, an interaction protocol, and operations the service consumer has to provide in order to receive callbacks. For modeling the service interfaces Erl chooses his own notation.

That a service design consists of these elements is confirmed by the Rational Unified Process for Service-Oriented Modeling and Architecture (RUP/SOMA) introduced by the Internal Business Machines (IBM) Corporation (2006) and Arsanjani and Allam (2006). This development process includes a phase meant for the specification of services too, called service specification phase. It consists of a creation of the service interfaces and so-called service components that comprise the internal logic of the service, such as the composition in case of a composed service. For modeling service designs, IBM chooses UML and their proprietary UML profile for software services (Johnston, 2005). In newer work, there is also SoaML as language applied (Amsden, 2010).

A similar understanding of service designs can also be found in Papazoglou (2003, p. 3). He confirms that "the fundamental logical view of a service in the basic SOA is that it is a service interface and implementation."

Summarized, a service design consists of a service interface and a service component for a certain service. The service interface describes provided operations, required operations in order to receive callbacks, the participating roles, the interaction protocol, and message and data types. The service component represents the realizing component of the service. It includes provided and required services and specifies the internal behavior representing the composition in case of a composed service.

Modeling Service Designs

Since SoaML as emerging standard for modeling service-oriented architectures is increasingly applied, in this chapter it is chosen as modeling language for service designs. SoaML provides all elements necessary for modeling of service designs according to the understanding introduced above. Its applicability for service designs has been demonstrated by Gebhart and Abeck (2011b) and Amsden (2010). Table 1 maps the elements of a service design onto elements in SoaML as introduced by Gebhart and Abeck (2011b) and Gebhart (2011) including adaptations to SoaML in version 1.0 beta2.

Based on this mapping, Figure 1 illustrates a service interface in SoaML. It provides two operations and requires one operation to be provided by the service consumer. Furthermore, the interaction protocol is specified, which determines the order the operations have to be called for receiving a valid result.

Service Candidate

According to the development processes introduced by Erl (2006), IBM Corporation (2006), or Gebhart and Abeck (2011b), prior to the service designs so-called service candidates are created. They represent preliminary services that due to their abstractness consist of operation candidates also known as capability candidates (Erl, 2008, p. 523). The service candidates are directly derived from functional requirements and include all functionality necessary for supporting the business. The architect has to decide, whether a certain candidate is expected to be completely new specified, or whether there is an existing service that has been specified in the past. In this case an again specification is not required. Additionally to the grouping of operation candidates to service candidates, also the dependencies are determined. A dependency states that a service candidate requires another service candidate for fulfilling one or more of its operation candidates.

The creation of service candidates can be found in different phases within existing development processes. For example, in Erl (2006), the phase that results in service candidates is called service-oriented analysis phase and it is performed prior to

Table 1. Mapping of service design elements onto SoaML

Service Design Element	Element in SoaML
Service Interface	ServiceInterface (UML class that is stereotyped with "ServiceInterface")
Provided Operation	Operation within an interface that is realized by the ServiceInterface element
Realized Operation	Operation within an interface that is associated with the ServiceInterface by using a Usage Dependency in UML
Role	Property within the ServiceInterface that is typed by the interface that contains the provided operations or by the interface that contains the required operations
Interaction Protocol	A behavior, such as an UML Activity
Service Component	Participant (UML component that is stereotyped with "Participant")
Provided Service	Service (UML Port that is stereotyped with "Service")
Required Service	Request (UML Port that is stereotyped with "Request")
Internal Behavior	UML Activity that is added as OwnedBehavior to the Participant

the service-oriented design phase. IBM classifies the creation of service candidates under the service identification phase distinct from the service specification phase that creates service designs.

In this chapter, also the terms service identification and service specification including their introduced distinction are chosen. These two phases constitute sub-phases to the superior service design phase.

Modeling Service Candidates

Similar to final specifications of services called service designs, the service candidates can be modeled using SoaML. Table 2 maps the elements of a service candidate onto elements in SoaML as introduced by Gebhart and Abeck (2011b). Here, especially the modeling element of a Capability is used, which represents a group of abstract capabilities. In Erl (2008) the term capability candidate as alternative for an operation candidate is introduced, which shows the similarity between a service candidate and a Capability element in SoaML.

According to this mapping, Figure 2 shows a set of three service candidates in SoaML, with one service candidate requiring two other ones in order to fulfill its functionality.

SERVICE IDENTIFICATION AND SPECIFICATION

The following section introduces the necessary steps for creating final service designs from prior acquired requirements. These service designs take existing legacy systems into account and enable their integration into a service-oriented application landscape.

Issues, Controversies, Problems

As introduced in the previous section, the so-called service design phase can be refined into the following steps: First, the required services have to be broadly identified. For this purpose, only a description of capabilities, their grouping to preliminary services, and the dependencies between these groups are necessary. During this step, the resulting service descriptions are called service candidates. The term candidate implies that this service is only a proposal for a required service that has to be further specified if an adequate service does not already exist. In this case, final service designs are specified in the service specification phase. Each service design consists of one service interface and one service component, which can represent a composition of other service compo-

Figure 1. Service interface in SoaML

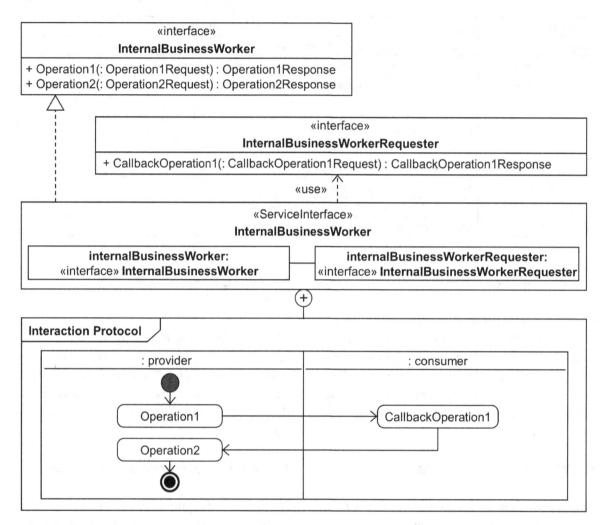

nents. The service interface describes operations that are provided by the service and the ones to be offered by the service consumer in order to receive callbacks. Furthermore, the participating roles and the interaction protocol are formalized. The service component determines provided and required services and the internal logic for instance by means of a service composition performed when a certain service operation is called.

Besides the functional requirements, both in the service identification and service specification phase also non-functional requirements, such as existing legacy systems, have to be considered as

they can heavily impact on the service designs. For example, in case when the desired service includes operations with functionality that cannot be provided by only one legacy system, the service has to be broken down into more detailed services that can be composed to the desired one. Similarly, if necessary the data types of a service have to be mapped onto available data types, both in respect of their granularity and the used terms and their semantics. As this abstract modeling within the design phase allows a detailed planning according to present circumstances prior to the implementation phase, the consideration of

Table 2. Mapping of service candidate elements onto SoaML

Service Candidate Element	Element in SoaML
Service Candidate	Capability (UML class that is stereotyped with "Capability")
Operation Candidate	Operation within an Capability element
Dependency	Usage Dependency between Capability elements

legacy systems during the design phase helps to reduce costs and effort.

Work in the context of service design methodologies, such as the processes introduced by Erl (2006, 2008), IBM (2006), and Krafzig, Banke, and Slama (2005) provide detailed information about the necessary steps to create services. Even though they mention non-functional requirements, such as quality attributes or legacy systems, as important, they do not exactly describe, how these requirements should be taken into account. Gebhart (2011) and Gebhart and Abeck (2011b) illustrate a design process considering quality attributes as non-functional requirements. However, legacy systems are not considered. Canfora, Fasolino, Frattolillo, and Tramontana (2006) provide an approach for migrating interactive legacy systems to Web services. The created services enable the access to existing functionality in case when the legacy system cannot be modified. If a modification is possible, approaches introduced by Sneed (2006), Zhang and Yang (2004), and Alahmari, Zaluska, and De Roure (2010) for re-engineering the existing systems in a service-oriented manner can be chosen. The advantages and disadvantages of these migration strategies are listed in Almonaies, Cordy, and Dean (2010). Even though all approaches support the integration of legacy systems into a service-oriented application landscape, the resulting services are not aligned with the entire service-oriented architecture. Furthermore, mostly the services are not explicitly designed using widespread modeling languages as part of a detailed planning phase.

Thus, a service design methodology for a systematic creation of service designs is required that considers both the fulfillment of functional requirements and the integration of legacy systems as well. The designed services have to be aligned with the entire architecture and common and widespread modeling languages should be used to increase practical applicability and to enable a detailed planning phase. For this purpose, work introduced by Gebhart and Abeck (2011b) is enhanced as it provides a holistic approach by taking the entire service-oriented architecture into account, using wide-spread modeling languages, and allowing the consideration of various non-functional requirements. Other approaches focusing on the re-engineering of legacy systems or the creation of wrapper services can be applied for the realization of resulting service designs. This enables the classification of this work under an entire service design process and enriches the service design process with further realization strategies.

Service Design Process

The following section introduces the methodology for identifying and specifying services. It bases on the quality-oriented service design process as presented by Gebhart and Abeck (2011b) combining a systematic derivation of artifacts with subsequent revisions that consider non-functional requirements. The consideration of quality attributes as non-functional requirements, such as lose coupling or autonomy, is described in Gebhart, Baumgartner, Oehlert, Blersch, and Abeck (2010) and Gebhart and Abeck (2011a). The application of this design process for the creation of a service-oriented system that considers certain quality attributes is exemplarily demonstrated in Gebhart, Sejdovic, and Abeck (2011). The following design process extends this approach with legacy systems that have to be taken into account. Figure 3 illustrates the service design process.

The methodology starts with modeled requirements. They include a description of functional and non-functional requirements. Former are formalized by means of business use cases that are expected to be supported by IT and underlying business processes. Non-functional requirements are constituted by a domain model that determines the used terminology, quality attributes that have to be considered, and legacy systems expected to be integrated into the service-oriented application landscape. Besides the domain model that supports the requirements analysis, this chapter especially focuses on legacy systems as non-functional requirements. A simultaneous regard of both legacy systems and other non-functional requirements, such as quality attributes, is supported too. However, a prioritization of conflicting non-functional aspects might be necessary.

Within the service design phase, in a first step, the functional requirements are used to systematically derive service candidates. These service candidates represent proposals for services that enable the functional fulfillment of the requirements in a service-oriented manner. Afterwards, the non-functional requirements are taken into account. This means, that the identified and for-

malized service candidates are correlated with functionality provided by legacy systems in order to map required functionality onto available one. The correlation of the derived service candidates with existing legacy systems may result in a revision of these service candidates. In the next step, these will be transformed into service designs. As introduced in the Background chapter, each service design consists of a service interface describing the provided functionality and a service component that realizes the provided functionality. Also during the service specification, the non-functional requirements i.e., the legacy systems are considered. For example, automatically derived data types and message types are revised in order to correlate with information kept within legacy systems. In addition, wrapper components may be added to the service component in order to enable the provision of a desired service interface. As a result, final service designs are created that enable an embedding of these legacy systems into a service-oriented application landscape. The following sections describe the steps of the service design process in detail.

Besides the domain independence of the methodology, which allows a wide application, this approach applies common and standardized languages, such as the Unified Modeling Language (UML), the Business Process Model and Notation

Figure 2. Service candidates in SoaML

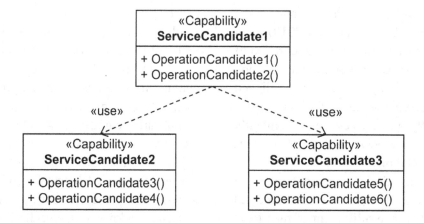

Figure 3. Service design process considering legacy systems

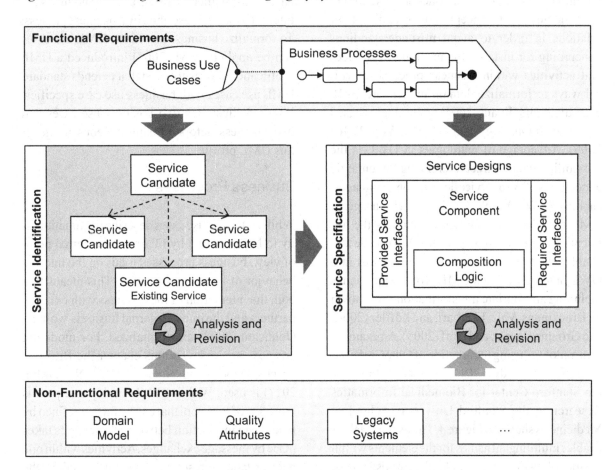

(BPMN) and the Service oriented architecture Modeling Language (SoaML) within the entire process. This supports a wide application of this methodology and enables the tool support required for practical usage.

Requirements Analysis

Since the modeled requirements constitute the basis for the determination of service designs, this section introduces the artifacts to be created in advance. The requirements can be divided into two central parts: the functional requirements that describe functionality to be supported and non-functional requirements that result in revisions of service candidates and service designs. The functional requirements are comprised of formalized business use cases and realizing business processes. The non-functional requirements are represented by formalized legacy systems that are expected to be integrated. In addition, a domain model is part of the non-functional requirements. It determines a terminology the designed services are supposed to be aligned with. Even though it is not necessary for the integration of legacy system, it is important for acquiring functional requirements as it helps to understand concepts within business use cases and business processes.

Domain Model

The domain model describes the terminology of the considered domain. It is especially used for determining the names of services, their operations, and data types. In addition, it supports the acquisition of functional requirements as it assists the understanding of used concepts. The model consolidates used concepts and specifies their relations in order to avoid misunderstandings concerning for instance the meaning of services and activities within business processes. Typical ways to formalize domain models are UML class diagrams (Evans, 2004) or ontologies based on the Web Ontology Language (OWL) (W3C, 2009). Advantage of ontologies in OWL is the possibility of their direct referencing by semantic annotations of Web service descriptions languages, such as SAWSDL (W3C, 2007a). The usage of UML for semantic annotations requires the application of an ontology specific UML profile that enables the transformation of UML classes into OWL ontologies. Such UML profile approaches including appropriate transformations are shown by Brockmans, Volz, Eberhart, and Löffler (2004) and Grønmo, Jaeger, and Hoff (2005). An example of an ontology using the notation of OntoGraf used in Protégé (Horridge, 2011), a tool developed by the Stanford Center for Biomedical Informatics Research at the Stanford University School of Medicine, is shown in Figure 4. The usage of labels enables multilingual names for the elements within the model. In this case, besides the English terms, the translation in German is provided.

Business Use Cases

Business use cases represent the parts of the business that are expected to be supported by IT. A business use case is invoked by external partners, so-called business actors, and hides the internal behavior described by a business process. To formalize business use cases, UML use cases can be applied. IBM (2007) introduced a UML profile including a notation that extends standard UML use cases with business use case specifics. Figure 5 illustrates two business use cases and two business actors by simultaneous usage of this UML profile.

Business Processes

Whilst business use cases describe the functionality to be supported by IT from an external point of view, business processes focus on the internal behavior of business use cases. This means that both the interaction of the business with external partners and the one of internal business workers (Johnston, 2004) are formalized. For modeling business processes, in this chapter the Business Process Model and Notation (BPMN) (OMG, 2011) is used. Within BPMN each participant is represented by a pool that can be further refined by lanes. The interaction between participants takes place by message exchanges. Activities within one pool or lane represent actions performed by the participant on its own. The names of elements, such as activities, messages, and participants, are expected to follow the terms specified within the domain model. To improve the reuse of existing services, the activities within the pools or lanes are expected to be aligned with available operations of services regarding their granularity and names.

Figure 4. Formalized domain model

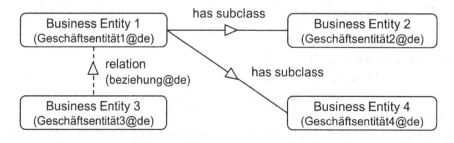

In order to find appropriate services for certain activities, the similarity between Web services and requirements has to be assessed. Wang and Stroulia (2003) introduce a methodology for this purpose. Likewise, Spanoudakis, and Zisman (2010) provide a methodology that enables the discovery of services that provide required functionality. As the business processes are expected to completely describe the functional requirements, further methodologies in the context of requirements engineering, such as work introduced by Zachos, Maiden, and Howells-Morris (2008) and Zachos, Maiden, Zhu, and Jones (2007), can be applied. Their work supports the identification of possibly appropriate functionality in order to increase the completeness of defined requirements. Figure 6 illustrates a business process in BPMN. In this scenario, an external business actor is invoking an operation of the considered business, in particular an operation of an internal business worker. In order to fulfill its functionality, the internal business worker invokes an operation of an external service provider. Later on, this operation will be part of an external cloud service provided for instance by a public cloud that has to be integrated into an internal service-oriented application landscape.

Legacy Systems

Legacy systems constitute the non-functional requirements that are expected to be considered in this chapter. They provide functionality that should be reused when realizing the functional requirements described by business use cases and business processes. This means that the created service designs possibly have to be revised, so that already existing functionality can be adequately integrated or legacy systems can be adapted for using services provided by external partners, such as cloud services.

Similar to the distinction of service candidates as preliminary services and service designs that specify services in detail, legacy systems can be described on two levels of abstraction. The first level, the more abstract one, is represented by system use case and illustrated by UML use case diagrams. Since system use cases describe system boundaries, they are especially necessary for the revision of service candidates. Furthermore, system use cases specify functionality of legacy systems on the same level of abstraction as operation candidates within service candidates. This is confirmed by the circumstance that activities within the business processes transferred into operation candidates within the service candidates are further refined and realized by system use cases (IBM, 2006). Further information about the relevant legacy systems, such as concrete operations or data types, is not required during the identification phase.

The more detailed level of abstraction is formalized by means of service designs for each legacy system in case of service interfaces availability that enables the access to provided functionality. During the service identification, the information about available service interfaces is important in order to map required functionality onto existing functionality. If there is no exact matching, the considered service candidate has to be broken down into more detailed and legacy system specific service candidates.

Additionally, UML component diagrams and UML class diagrams that describe the legacy systems in detail i.e., their internal components can

Figure 5. Formalized business use cases

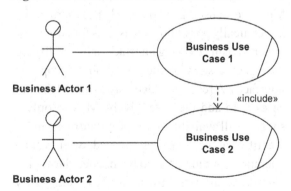

Figure 6. Formalized business process

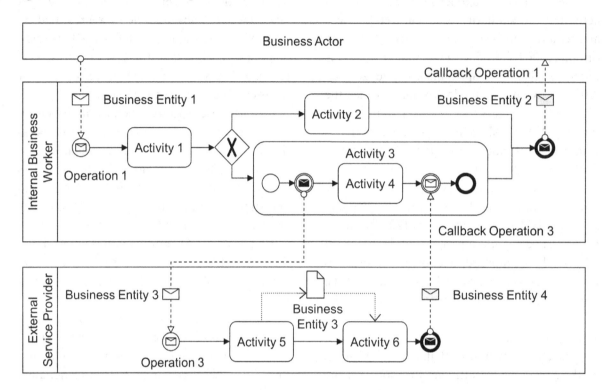

be created. This information is necessary during the revision of service designs, especially service components. If necessary, wrapper components are added to the service components i.e., the legacy systems that map available operations and data types onto required ones as described by the externally visible service interfaces.

In order to reduce costs and effort, only those use cases of a certain legacy system should be modeled that are known as relevant, i.e., that have to be integrated to fulfill functional requirements. Moreover, a use case should only be regarded if it is technically possible to access this functionality, either by using existing interface or by modifying the legacy system in order to provide appropriate interfaces. A recommended way to model the use cases is to add them iteratively. Mostly, only a subset of all available and appropriate ones can be identified at the beginning. Instead, whenever an operation candidate has to be mapped during the identification or specification phase, the legacy

systems are analyzed and use cases affecting functionality of the considered operation candidate are extracted. If only the source code without any knowledge about the internal functionality is available, source code analysis as introduced by Reiss (2009) can be performed.

Service Identification

The service identification phase as part of the superior service design phase leverages the prior modeled requirements in order to identify adequate services. The resulting services represent candidates for the subsequent service specification phase. This is why the services as a result of the service identification phase are named service candidates.

The service identification consists of two essential steps: the systematic derivation and the subsequent analysis and revision. The former considers the functional requirements and ensures that the resulting services provide required capabilities. The subsequent analysis and revision involves non-functional requirements, such as quality attributes and—as focused in this chapter—legacy systems. Systematically derived service candidates are revised according to these aspects. As a result, the service identification phase delivers service candidates that fulfill both functional requirements and additional, non-functional requirements i.e., in this case consider legacy systems that are expected to be integrated. The following sections describe these steps in detail.

Derivation of Service Candidates

The first step, the derivation of service candidates, bases on functional requirements modeled in the initial requirements analysis phase. It ensures that the resulting service candidates fulfill required functionality and are business aligned. For this purpose, the artifacts modeled in the requirements analysis phase are systematically transformed into artifacts of the service design phase, namely into elements of service candidates. Based on the functional requirements introduced in the Requirements Analysis Section and their formalizations, this section illustrates the transformations that have to be performed.

For service candidates modeled business processes are to be considered as they describe the internal behavior of business use cases that are expected to be supported by IT. Services enable the interaction of various participants, such as business partners or their IT systems. Thus, for the derivation of service candidates especially the interactions between the participants modeled in the business processes are to be considered. These interactions are formalized by message exchanges between pools. Accordingly, in a first step, each pool within the business process models is transformed into a service candidate, and operations called by a participant are represented by an operation candidate as part of the respective service candidate. Dependencies between service

candidates are derived from the interaction between according participants i.e., the pools. Figure 7 illustrates this systematic derivation.

If also internal activities within the pools are appropriate to be provided as service, the derivation of service candidates can be recursively continued. This means that for each lane further service candidates used by the superior one representing the entire pool are created. As operation candidates, the activities within the according lane are added. This increases the flexibility of the architecture, as it allows the reuse of internal functionality and supports its later replacement with other services, such as external cloud services. In addition, some technical constraints may require the outsourcing of internal functionality. For example, if the executable business process is expected to be implemented with BPEL, the single activities have to be available as Web service operations. The recursive continuation of the derivation of service candidates is described in Gebhart (2011) and Gebhart and Abeck (2011b). For simplicity, in this chapter the derivation ends with the transforming of pools into service candidates.

Consideration of Legacy Systems

Subsequent to the systematic derivation of service candidates, analysis and revision—if by the results of the analysis required—are performed. This means that the derived service candidates are examined for their alignment with existing legacy systems that are supposed to be integrated. If the service candidates do not optimally consider these systems, they are revised. However, the service candidates themselves are not changed as they are in this form aligned with the business. Instead, they are revised by breaking them down into more fine-grained service candidates that can be composed to the desired one. The service candidates should only be changed if they violate desired quality attributes, such as loose coupling, and thus do not support the objectives of a service-oriented

Figure 7. Derivation of service candidates

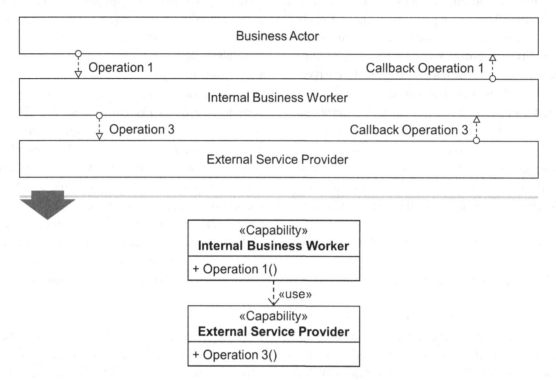

application landscape (Gebhart, Baumgartner, & Abeck, 2010). In some cases, the consideration of quality attributes even supports the integration of legacy system. For example, there exist quality attributes that ensure clear responsibilities concerning business entities (Gebhart & Abeck, 2009, 2011a). Thus, a service candidate that manages more than one independent business entities may be divided into several service candidates responsible for only one certain business entity. This exactly maps to existing legacy systems that manage only one particular business entity.

To align the services candidates and consequently the final services with legacy systems, the provided operation candidates that represent their capabilities have to be brought into line with functionality provided by legacy systems. For this purpose, the modeled use cases of the legacy systems and the according diagrams can be leveraged as they describe which functionality is provided by which system. As mentioned before, the use cases that were created during the

requirements analysis should be seen as an initial set. When new operation candidates have to be mapped, the legacy systems are analyzed and all use cases describing functionality relevant for the considered operation candidates are extracted. Afterwards, the operation candidates have to be correlated with the use cases, whereas the following cases of matching can occur:

- The operation candidates of a service candidate require functionality that is part of the use cases within one use case diagram.

This case represents the circumstance that there is only functionality of one certain legacy system to be reused. If this legacy system can be changed and thus adapted to the needs of the service candidate, there is no further revision necessary. However, if the legacy system cannot be modified and only existing service interfaces of the legacy system can be used that do not exactly match to the service candidate, the service candidate has to be broken down into additional service candidates that represent the existing and required service interfaces. Figure 8 illustrates this case.

If one of the operation candidates requires business logic that is not part of this certain legacy system, it will be implemented later. If the legacy system can be modified, this logic will be added directly to the legacy system. Otherwise, the logic will be part of the new service component that uses the existing service interfaces of the legacy system and realizes the operations defined in the service candidate.

- The operation candidates of a service candidate require functionality that is part of the use cases within several use case diagrams.

In this case, the operation candidates require functionality of several legacy systems. In order to provide a service that combines this functionality, for each legacy system an additional service that enables accessing its capabilities is necessary. If service interfaces that provide the required functionality exist, these service interfaces are integrated as service candidates. Otherwise, new service candidates are created with operation candidates taken from the activities within the according business process. If additional logic, such as business logic or composition logic, is required, it will be part of the new service component that implements the superior service candidate. Figure 9 illustrates this case.

In every case, when breaking down a service candidate into legacy system specific ones, already existing usage dependencies to other service candidates that represent internal services or external services, such as cloud services, have to be rethought. If a service candidate has been revised and new service candidates for legacy systems have been created, the other subordinate service candidates have to be rearranged under one of the new service candidates if they represent functionality of a legacy system that has to be replaced and this legacy system can be modified.

In this case, the legacy system can be adapted and internal functionality will be replaced by capabilities of existing services. An example is illustrated in Figure 9. Otherwise, necessary functionality of the legacy system will be exposed and combined with functionality of other services. This means that instead of the original functionality, all subordinate functionality is provided as operation candidate in order to enable a new composition of functionality provided by legacy systems with capabilities of other services. This results in a replacement of a certain component of the legacy system without modifying it. Figure 10 illustrates both approaches to replace existing functionality.

If a service candidate has been broken down into legacy system specific ones, these services should be considered as private in a later service repository. This means, whilst the original service candidate is public and thus available to service consumers, due to their usage of legacy specifics in respect of operations and data types the legacy system specific service candidates should be exclusively used by this superior service candidate.

These analysis and revision steps are iteratively repeated until there is no revision performed and thus there is no service candidate modified or a new one created. An example for an iterative continuation is the refinement of service candidates created as part of Case 2 according to existing interfaces as introduced in Case 1. In addition, even though this chapter does not focus on further non-functional requirements, such as quality attributes, they have to be kept in mind for all service candidates including the private ones when performing the analysis and revision steps. This means that depending on the modifiability, further non-functional requirements are to consider. In case of conflicting non-functional requirements, an appropriate prioritization is necessary.

Service Specification

This phase targets the detailed specification of prior determined service candidates and results in a service design for each service candidate. Since service candidates, as their name implies, represent only preliminary services, first, those service candidates that have to be newly specified are to determine. For already existing services, implementation artifacts, such as data types based on XML Schema Definitions (XSD) as well as Web service descriptions using the Web Service Description Language (WSDL), have to be transformed into service design elements, such as service interfaces, messages types, and data types. This enables the integration of existing services into the design phase for the other new services. Examples for such transformations are given by Gebhart (2011) and Grønmo, Skogan, Solheim, and Oldevik (2004). When the services that have to be newly created are determined, the service specification phase can be performed.

Derivation of Service Designs

Similarly, to the identification phase, the specification phase starts with a systematic derivation of service designs from service candidates and artifacts of the requirements analysis phase. For this purpose, for each service candidate a service interface is created. The operation candidates are transferred into operations within a new interface that is realized by the service interface. If an operation sends a callback to the service consumer, adequate callback operations are added to an interface used by the service interface. Whether an operation sends a callback can be determined by means of the business process. Furthermore, the service interface is enhanced by an interaction protocol and participating roles. For roles, standardized identifiers, such as consumer and

Figure 8. Matching with use cases of one legacy system

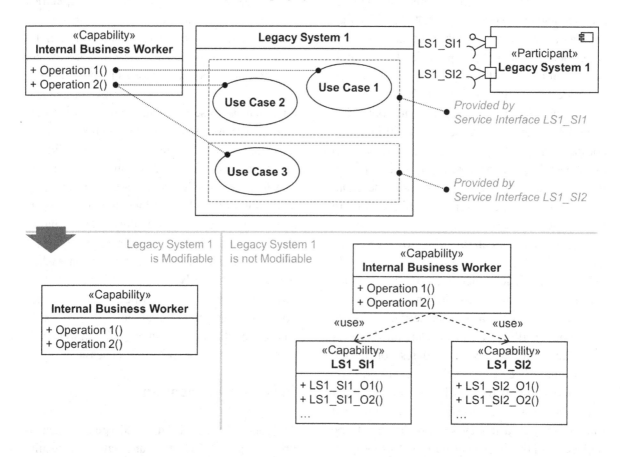

Figure 9. Matching with use cases of several legacy systems

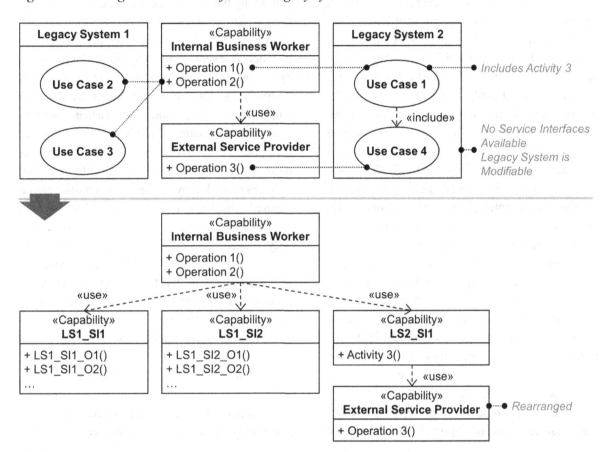

provider, can be used. The interaction protocol can be derived from the business process too, equally message and data types that are specified within the according message exchanges. The used terms for elements, such as operations, roles, message types, and data types should follow common naming conventions. Also in order to reduce misunderstandings and increase the discoverability by using functional names the terms of the domain model should be applied (Erl, 2009; Gebhart & Abeck, 2011a). Figure 1 illustrates a service interface that has been systematically derived from a service candidate and the business process according to the rules introduced by Gebhart (2011) and Gebhart and Abeck (2011b).

Additionally to the service interface, a service component is created. It contains one service point that is typed by the service interface and one request point for each service candidate associated

by means of a usage dependency. Furthermore, the internal behavior is described by an UML Activity that can be derived from the business process. Figure 11 illustrates the derivation of a service component. More detailed information about the derivation of the service interface and the service component is provided by Gebhart (2011) and Gebhart and Abeck (2011b).

Consideration of Legacy Systems

In the subsequent analysis and revision, the alignment of derived service designs with legacy systems is ensured. Since during the identification phase the operations were already grouped to services that consider legacy systems, within the specification phase especially the service design specifics, such as additional details within service interfaces and the service components and their internal behavior, are revised. When a legacy system has to be enhanced with services that have to follow the internals of the legacy system, as it is not modifiable, the automatically derived service interfaces have to be revised according to the internal constraints. For example, the names of operations and the used data types have to be brought into line with the considered legacy system. On the other hand, when a service is meant to be provided by a modifiable legacy system, necessary internal components that realize required transformations have to be added to the legacy system. In addition, components for new business logic are to align appropriately. Thus, in this phase, software service engineering specifics (Van den Heuvel, Zimmermann, Leymann, Lago, Schieferdecker, Zdun, & Avgeriou, 2009) may fade into the background. Instead, more general software engineering aspects that enable the internal design of a service component by means of traditional software components, such as wrapper components, may be relevant.

Besides the integration of legacy systems into a service-oriented application landscape by enhancing them with necessary services, this approach also enables a systematic refactoring of legacy systems in a service-oriented manner. For instance, if several service candidates contain only operation candidates as part of the same legacy system, these services will be transferred into the current legacy system and result in a legacy system structured by means of services. This simplifies the reuse of internal functionality and the replacement with other services, such as external cloud services provided by for instance a public cloud. Figure 12 illustrates a service-oriented refactoring.

The depicted legacy system provides functionality of several depending service candidates. As a result of this methodology, the legacy system is modified in a way that the desired functionality is provided and the external service provider is embedded. Additionally, the internals are refactored in a service-oriented way.

Outlook into Service Implementation

Subsequently to the service identification and specification phase, the service designs are expect-

Figure 10. Replacing existing functionality

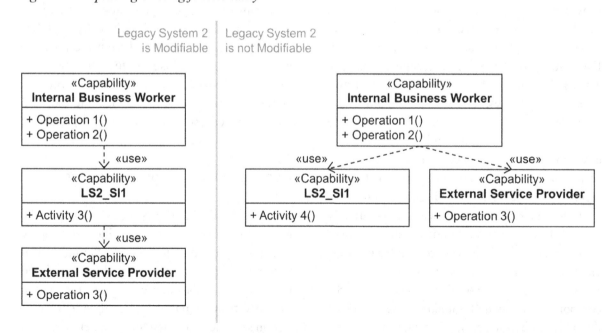

Figure 11. Derivation of service components

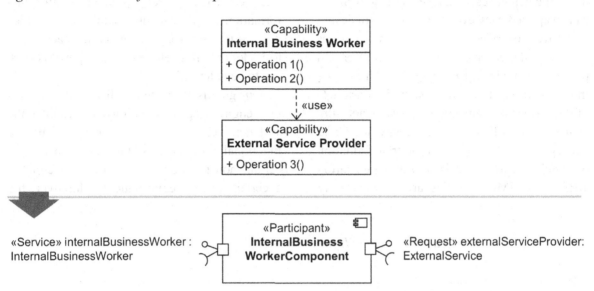

ed to be implemented. For this purpose, the service design artifacts can be transformed into artifacts of the implementation phase. For example, service interfaces, especially the interface that contains provided operations can be transferred into a WSDL service interface description as introduced by Grønmo et al. (2004) and into XSD data types (Sparx Systems, 2010). The service components can be used to derive a component model based on SCA and the internal behavior of the service component, presumed it is a composition of services, can be mapped onto a composition using BPEL as introduced by IBM (2012). As alternative to BPEL, also the BPMN business process can be enriched with details in order to create an executable BPMN process. If a semantic annotation is desired, these annotations can be derived from the relation of used terms to the domain model. If the domain model is formalized using UML class diagrams, it first has to be transformed into an ontology using OWL. Afterwards, the WSDL service interface description can be enriched by means of annotations using SAWSDL.

In order to re-engineer legacy systems according to the designed services or to realize the internal logic of wrapper services, existing approaches can be applied: Sneed (2006), Zhang and Yang

(2004), and Alahmari, Zaluska, and De Roure (2010) illustrate service-oriented re-engineering methodologies for legacy systems. These can be chosen in case when the considered system is modifiable. Otherwise, the migration approach for interactive legacy systems introduced by Canfora, Fasolino, Frattolillo, and Tramontana (2006) can be applied.

FUTURE RESEARCH DIRECTIONS

Based on the contribution of this chapter and previous work, nowadays our software service engineering methodology enables the systematic creation of service designs that fulfill functional requirements and consider both quality attributes and legacy systems as non-functional requirements. In the future, the methodology is supposed to be enriched with further non-functional requirements that may influence the design of services. Examples for further requirements are available programming languages and runtime environments. Additionally, an appropriate methodology for prioritizing conflicting requirements has to be elaborated, which helps to find best compromises. Due to the usage of common and widespread modeling languages, already existing tool chains can be applied. However, the provision of design hints to revise service candidates or service designs according the criteria given in this chapter and previous work is still missing. In addition, the transformation of service designs into artifacts of the service implementation phase is not fully available in tools nowadays. Mostly, tools and conceptual work focuses on the transformation of standard UML models into implementation artifacts. SoaML specifics are only partially

regarded. Thus, in order to enable a full transformation of all elements contained by service designs into service implementations according to model-driven development principles this work has to be extended.

Our goal is to create a holistic software service engineering methodology that enables the systematic creation of service designs fulfilling functional requirements, but also considering certain non-functional requirements present in a certain project environment. Moreover, the

Figure 12. Service-oriented refactoring of legacy systems

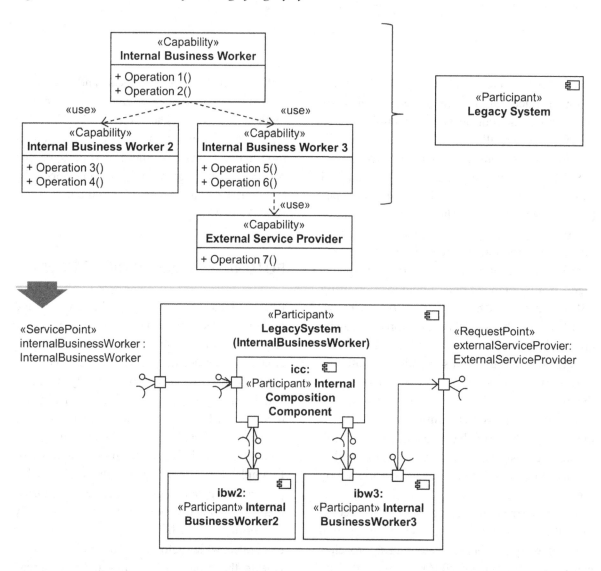

methodology contains transformations that enable a derivation of service implementation artifacts from service designs based on SoaML.

CONCLUSION

This chapter described the systematic creation of service designs that both fulfill functional requirements in terms of business use cases and business processes and consider legacy systems as non-functional requirements. For this purpose, the necessary steps to systematically derive service candidates and service designs and to revise these artifacts were introduced. The consideration of legacy systems results in service designs that allow the integration of legacy systems into a service-oriented application landscape. This enables the achievement of two central advantages: On the one hand, existing functionality provided by legacy systems is integrated and thus reused. On the other hand, legacy systems can be adapted for the purpose of simplifying the replacement of functionality that has been implemented and provided by its own with external functionality, such as cloud services. Finally, an outlook into the service implementation phase and the transformation of service designs into service implementation artifacts was given.

REFERENCES

W3C. (2007a). *Semantic annotations for WSDL and XML schema.* Retrieved September 28, 2011, from http://www.w3.org/TR/sawsdl/

W3C. (2007b). *Web services description language (WSDL) version 2.0 part 1: Core language.* Retrieved September 28, 2011, from http://www.w3.org/TR/wsdl20/

W3C. (2009). *OWL 2 web ontology language.* Retrieved September 28, 2011, from http://www.w3.org/TR/2009/REC-owl2-overview-20091027/

Alahmari, S., Zaluska, E., & De Roure, D. (2010). A service identification framework for legacy system migration into SOA. In *Proceedings of the Seventh International Conference on Services Computing (SCC) 2010,* (pp. 614-617). SCC.

Almonaies, A., Cordy, J. R., & Dean, T. R. (2010). Legacy system evolution towards service-oriented architecture. In *Proceedings of the International Workshop on SOA Migration and Evolution (SOAME) 2010,* (pp. 53-62). SOAME.

Amsden, J. (2010). Modeling with SoaML, the service-oriented architecture modeling language: Part 1 service identification. *IBM DeveloperWorks,* Retrieved September 28, 2011, from http://www.ibm.com/developerworks/rational/library/09/modelingwithsoaml-1/index.html

Arsanjani, A., & Allam, A. (2006). Service-oriented modeling and architecture for realization of an SOA. In *Proceedings of the 2006 IEEE International Conference on Services Computing (SCC) 2006,* (p. 521). IEEE Press.

Brockmans, S., Volz, R., Eberhart, A., & Löffler, P. (2004). Visual modeling of OWL DL ontologies using UML. In S. A. McIlraith, D. Plexousakis, & F. van Harmelen (Eds.), *Proceedings of the Third International Semantic Web Conference (ISWC) 2004,* (pp. 198-213). ISWC.

Canfora, G., Fasolino, A. R., Frattolillo, G., & Tramontana, P. (2006). Migrating interactive legacy systems to web services. In *Proceedings of the 10th European Conference on Software Maintenance and Reengineering (CSMR) 2006,* (pp. 27-36). CSMR.

Chang, W. Y., Abu-Amara, H., & Sanford, J. (2010). *Transforming enterprise cloud services*. Dordrecht, The Netherlands: Springer. doi:10.1007/978-90-481-9846-7

Erl, T. (2006). *Service-oriented architecture – Concepts, technology, and design*. Boston, MA: Prentice Hall.

Erl, T. (2008). *SOA – Principles of service design*. Boston, MA: Prentice Hall.

Erl, T. (2009). *Web service contract design and versioning for SOA*. Boston, MA: Prentice Hall.

Evans, E. (2004). *Domain-driven design: Tackling complexity in the heart of software*. Boston, MA: Addison-Wesley Professional.

Gebhart, M. Baumgartner, & Abeck, S. (2010). Supporting service design decisions. In J. Hall, H. Kaindl, L. Lavazza, G. Buchgeher, & O. Takaki (Eds.), *Proceedings of the Fifth International Conference on Software Engineering Advances (ICSEA) 2010*, (pp. 76-81). ICSEA.

Gebhart, M. (2011). *Qualitätsorientierter entwurf von anwendungsdiensten*. Karlsruhe, Germany: KIT Scientific Publishing.

Gebhart, M., & Abeck, S. (2009). Rule-based service modeling. In K. Boness, J. M. Fernandes, J. G. Hall, R. J. Machado, & R. Oberhauser (Eds.), *Proceedings of the Fourth International Conference on Software Engineering Advances (ICSEA) 2009*, (pp. 271-276). ICSEA.

Gebhart, M., & Abeck, S. (2011a). Metrics for evaluating service designs based on SoaML. *International Journal on Advances in Software*, *4*(1-2), 61–75.

Gebhart, M., & Abeck, S. (2011b). Quality-oriented design of services. *International Journal on Advances in Software*, *4*(1-2), 144–157.

Gebhart, M., Baumgartner, M., Oehlert, S., Blersch, M., & Abeck, S. (2010). Evaluation of service designs based on SoaML. In J. Hall, H. Kaindl, L. Lavazza, G. Buchgeher, & O. Takaki (Eds.), *Proceedings of the Fifth International Conference on Software Engineering Advances (ICSEA) 2010*, (pp. 7-13). ICSEA.

Gebhart, M., Sejdovic, S., & Abeck, S. (2011). Case study for a quality-oriented service design process. In L. Lavazza, L. Fernandez-Sanz, O. Panchenko, & T. Kanstrén (Eds.), *Proceedings of the Sixth International Conference on Software Engineering Advances (ICSEA) 2011*, (pp. 92-97). ICSEA. Retrieved from http://www.thinkmind.org/

Grønmo, R., Jaeger, M. C., & Hoff, H. (2005). Transformations between UML and OWL-S. In A. Hartman & D. Kreische (Eds.), *Proceedings of the First European Conference on Model Driven Architecture – Foundations and Applications (ECMDA-FA) 2005*, (pp. 269-283). ECMDA-FA.

Grønmo, R., Skogan, D., Solheim, I., & Oldevik, J. (2004). Model-driven web services development. In S. Yuan & J. Li (Eds.), *Proceedings of the 2004 IEEE International Conference on e-Technology, e-Commerce and e-Service (EEE) 2004*, (pp. 42-45). IEEE Press.

Horridge, M. (2011). A practical guide to building OWL ontologies using Protégé 4 and CO-ODE tools. Retrieved September 28, 2011, from http://owl.cs.manchester.ac.uk/tutorials/protegeowl-tutorial/resources/ProtegeOWLTutorialP4_v1_3.pdf

Hoyer, P., Gebhart, M., Pansa, I., Dikanski, A., & Abeck, S. (2010). Service-oriented integration using a model-driven approach. *International Journal on Advances in Software*, *3*(1-2), 304–317.

Hoyer, P., Gebhart, M., Pansa, I., Link, S., Dikanski, A., & Abeck, S. (2009). A model-driven development approach for service-oriented integration scenarios. In P. Dini, W. Gentzsch, P. Geraci, P. Lorenz, & K. Singh (Eds.), *Proceedings of the Computation World 2009*, (pp. 353-358). Computation World.

IBM. (2006). IBM RUP for service-oriented modeling and architecture V2.4. *IBM DeveloperWorks*. Retrieved September 28, 2011, from http://www.ibm.com/developerworks/rational/downloads/06/rmc_soma/

IBM. (2012). *Interpretation of UML elements by UML-to-BPEL transformations*. Retrieved September 28, 2011, from http://publib.boulder.ibm.com/infocenter/rsahelp/v7r0m0/index.jsp?topic=/com.ibm.xtools.transform.uml2.bpel.doc/topics/rubpelmap.html

Johnston, S. (2004). Rational UML profile for business modeling. *IBM DeveloperWorks*. Retrieved September 28, 2011, from http://www.ibm.com/developerworks/rational/library/5167.html

Johnston, S. (2005). UML 2.0 profile for software services. *IBM DeveloperWorks*. Retrieved September 28, 2011, from http://www.ibm.com/developerworks/rational/library/05/419_soa/

Krafzig, D., Banke, K., & Slama, D. (2005). *Enterprise SOA: Service oriented architecture best practices*. Boston, MA: Prentice Hall.

OASIS. (2007). *Web services business process execution language (BPEL), version 2.0*. Retrieved September 28, 2011, from http://docs.oasis-open.org/wsbpel/2.0/wsbpel-v2.0.html

OMG. (2006). *UML profile and metamodel for services (UPMS), request for proposal*. Retrieved September 28, 2011, from http://www.omg.org/cgi-bin/doc?soa/06-09-09.pdf

OMG. (2009). *Service oriented architecture modeling language (SoaML) – Specification for the UML profile and metamodel for services (UPMS), version 1.0 beta2*. Retrieved September 28, 2011, from http://www.omg.org/spec/SoaML/1.0/Beta2/PDF

OMG. (2010). *OMG unified modeling language (OMG UML), superstructure, version 2.3*. Retrieved September 28, 2011, from http://www.omg.org/spec/UML/2.3/Superstructure/PDF/

OMG. (2011). *Business process model and notation (BPMN), version 2.0*. Retrieved September 28, 2011, from http://www.omg.org/spec/BPMN/2.0/PDF

OSOA. (2009). *Service component architecture (SCA), SCA assembly model specification, version 1.0*. Retrieved September 28, 2011, from http://www.osoa.org/download/attachments/35/SCA_AssemblyModel_V100.pdf?version=1

Papazoglou, M. P. (2003). Service-oriented computing – Concepts, characteristics and directions. In T. Catarci, M. Mecella, J. Mylopoulos, & M. E. Orlowsk (Eds.), *Proceedings of the Fourth International Conference on Web Information Systems Engineering (WISE) 2003*, (pp. 3-12). WISE.

Reiss, S. P. (2009). Semantics-based code search. In *Proceedings of the 31st International Conference on Software Engineering (ICSE) 2009*, (pp. 243-253). ICSE.

Sneed, H. M. (2006). Integrating legacy software into a service oriented architecture. In *Proceedings of the 10th European Conference on Software Maintenance and Reengineering (CSMR) 2006*, (pp. 4-14). CSMR.

Spanoudakis, G., & Zisman, A. (2010). Discovering services during service-based system design using UML. *IEEE Transactions on Software Engineering*, 36(3), 371–389. doi:10.1109/TSE.2009.88

Sparx Systems. (2010). *XML schema generation.* Retrieved September 28, 2011, from http://www.sparxsystems.com.au/resources/xml_schema_generation.html

Stahl, T., Voelter, M., Bettin, J., & Stockfleth, B. (2006). *Model-driven software development: Technology, engineering, management.* Hoboken, NJ: John Wiley & Sons.

Van den Bos, G., Knapp, S., & Doe, J. (2001). Role of reference elements in the selection of resources by psychology undergraduates. [from http://jbr.org/articles.html]. *Journal of Bibliographic Research, 5,* 117–123. Retrieved October 13, 2001

Van den Heuvel, W., Zimmermann, O., Leymann, F., Lago, P., Schieferdecker, I., Zdun, U., & Avgeriou, P. (2009). Software service engineering: Tenets and challenges. In *Proceedings of the 2009 ICSE Workshop on Principles of Engineering Service Oriented Systems (PESOS) 2009,* (pp. 26-33). ICSE.

Wang, Y., & Stroulia, E. (2003). Semantic structure matching for assessing web-service similarity. In *Proceedings of the 1st International Conference on Service Oriented Computing (ICSOC) 2003,* (pp. 194-207). ICSOC.

Zachos, K., Maiden, N. A. M., & Howells-Morris, R. (2008). Discovering web services to improve requirements specifications: Does it help? In B. Paech & C. Rolland (Eds.), *Proceedings of the 14th International Working Conference on Requirements Engineering: Foundation for Software Quality (REFSQ) 2008,* (pp. 168-182). REFSQ.

Zachos, K., Maiden, N. A. M., Zhu, X., & Jones, S. (2007). Discovering web services to specify more complete system requirements. In J. Krogstie, A. L. Opdahl, & G. Sindre (Eds.), *Proceedings of the 19th International Conference on Advanced Information Systems Engineering (CAiSE) 2007,* (pp. 142-157). CAiSE.

Zhang, Z., & Yang, H. (2004). Incubating services in legacy systems for architectural migration. In *Proceedings of the 11th Asia-Pacific Software Engineering Conference (APSEC) 2004,* (pp. 196-203). APSEC.

ADDITIONAL READING

Allen, P. (2006). *Service orientation – Winning strategies and best practices.* Cambridge, UK: Cambridge University Press. doi:10.1017/CBO9780511541186

Almeida, J. P., Van Sinderen, M., Pires, L. F., & Quartel, D. (2003). A systematic approach to platform-independent design based on the service concept. In *Proceedings of the Seventh IEEE International Enterprise Distributed Object Computing Conference (EDOC) 2003,* (pp. 112-123). IEEE Press.

Bézivin, J., Hammoudi, S., Lopes, D., & Jouault, F. (2004). Applying MDA approach for web service platform. In *Proceedings of the 8th IEEE International Enterprise Distributed Object Computing Conference (EDOC) 2004,* (pp. 58-70). IEEE Press.

Erl, T. (2009b). *SOA design patterns.* Boston, MA: Prentice Hall.

Erradi, A., Anand, S., & Kulkarni, N. (2006). SOAF – An architectural framework for service definition and realization. In *Proceedings of the 2006 IEEE International Conference on Services Computing (SCC) 2006,* (pp. 151-158). IEEE Press.

Jansen, A., & Bosch, J. (2005). Software architecture as a set of architectural design decisions. In *Proceedings of the Fifth Working IEEE/IFIP Conference on Software Architecture (WICSA) 2005,* (pp. 109-120). IEEE Press.

Krafzig, D., Banke, K., & Slama, D. (2005). *Enterprise SOA – Service-oriented architecture best practices*. Upper Saddle River, NJ: Pearson Education.

Kroll, P., & Kruchten, P. (2007). *The rational unified process made easy – A practitioner's guide to the RUP*. Boston, MA: Addison-Wesley.

Maiden, N. (2012). Exactly how are requirements written? *IEEE Software, 29*(1), 26–27. doi:10.1109/MS.2012.6

Rahmani, A. T., Rafe, V., Sedighian, S., & Abbaspour, A. (2006). An MDA-based modeling and design of service oriented architecture. *Lecture Notes in Computer Science, 3993*, 578–585. doi:10.1007/11758532_76

Sawyer, P., & Maiden, N. A. M. (2009). How to use web services in your requirements process. *IEEE Software, 28*(1), 76–78. doi:10.1109/MS.2009.11

Stojanovic, Z., Dahanayake, A., & Sol, H. (2004). Modeling and design of service-oriented architecture. In *Proceedings of the 2004 IEEE International Conference on Systems, Man & Cybernetics 2004,* (pp. 4147-4152). IEEE Press.

Wang, Y., & Stroulia, E. (2003). Flexible interface matching for web-service discovery. In *Proceedings of the Fourth International Conference on Web Information Systems Engineering (WISE) 2003,* (pp. 147-156). WISE.

Zachos, K., & Maiden, N. A. M. (2008). Inventing requirements from software: An empirical investigation with web services. In *Proceedings of 16th IEEE International Requirements Engineering Conference (RE) 2008,* (pp. 145-154). IEEE Press.

KEY TERMS AND DEFINITIONS

Cloud Service: Service provided by an external cloud provider that can be integrated into an internal service-oriented architecture in order to implement new or replace existing functionality.

Legacy System: Existing system within an organization that keeps business logic that is expected to be reused, thus integrated into a service-oriented application landscape.

Service Candidate: Preliminary service that contains a set of operation candidates that represent preliminary operations.

Service Design: Specification of the service interface and service component for a certain service.

Service Design Phase: Performed on basis of functional and non-functional requirements and results in service designs for each service.

Service Identification: Sub-phase of the service design phase that focuses on the identification of required services and results in a set of service candidates.

Service Implementation: Phase that is performed after the service design phase and results in implemented services that realize certain functionality.

Service Specification: Sub-phase of the service design phase that addresses the concrete specification of prior determined service candidates.

Chapter 6
The SOA Frontier:
Experiences with Three Migration Approaches

Juan M. Rodriguez
*Universidad Nacional del Centro de la
Provincia de Buenos Aires, Argentina*

Alejandro Zunino
*Universidad Nacional del Centro de la
Provincia de Buenos Aires, Argentina*

Marco Crasso
*Universidad Nacional del Centro de la
Provincia de Buenos Aires, Argentina*

Marcelo Campo
*Universidad Nacional del Centro de la
Provincia de Buenos Aires, Argentina*

Cristian Mateos
*Universidad Nacional del Centro de la
Provincia de Buenos Aires, Argentina*

Gonzalo Salvatierra
*Universidad Nacional del Centro de la
Provincia de Buenos Aires, Argentina*

ABSTRACT

Service Oriented Architecture (SOA) and Web Services are the current trend to integrate large and distributed systems, which is a common situation in both the business and government worlds. However, within these worlds, systems are commonly written in COBOL because they were developed several decades ago. Therefore, migration of COBOL systems into service-oriented architectures becomes a necessity. Two main approaches are used to migrate COBOL systems to SOA systems: direct and indirect migration. Direct migration implies wrapping the current COBOL routines of a system with a software layer developed under a newer platform that can be used to offer Web Services. In contrast, indirect migration requires re-designing and re-implementing the COBOL routines' functionality using a newer platform as well. In this chapter, the authors propose a novel migration approach, which takes the best of the two previous approaches. To assess the advantages and disadvantages of these approaches, this chapter presents a case study from a government agency COBOL system that has been migrated to a Web services-based system using the three approaches. As a result of having these migration attempts, the authors present the trade-off between direct and indirect migration, the resulting service interfaces quality, and the migration costs. These results also show that this new migration approach offers a good balance to the above trade-off, which makes the approach applicable to similar COBOL migration scenarios.

DOI: 10.4018/978-1-4666-2488-7.ch006

Copyright © 2013, IGI Global. Copying or distributing in print or electronic forms without written permission of IGI Global is prohibited.

INTRODUCTION

Information systems were adopted by enterprises several decades ago, and they have been used ever since. As a result, operationally, most enterprises rely on old, out-of-date systems. These systems are known as legacy systems. Well-known examples of this kind of systems are COBOL systems because, according to Gartner consulting[1], there are over 200 billion lines of operative COBOL still running worldwide. Furthermore, since enterprises' goals and context vary, in time these systems have suffered modifications to be kept suitable for the enterprises. For example, nowadays it is impossible to conceive a bank that does not offer Home Banking services, yet most bank systems were originally written in COBOL. Therefore, it is common to find a 50 year old technology, such as COBOL, working alongside with the most modern technologies (Lewis, et al., 2011), like .Net, AJAX, or JEE, in the same enterprise. As a result of this situation, enterprises have to face high costs for maintaining their systems. This is mainly because these systems usually run on mainframes that must be rented. In addition, there is the necessity of hiring developers specialized in old technologies for updating the system functionality, which is both expensive and rather difficult.

Taking these facts into consideration, many enterprises opt for modernizing their legacy systems using a newer technology. This process is called migration. Currently, a common target paradigm for migrating legacy systems is SOA (Service-Oriented Architecture) (Bichler & Lin, 2006; Ionita, et al., 2008). In SOA, systems are built using independent functionalities called services that can be invoked remotely. Services are offered as platform-agnostic functionalities that can be used by any system inside or outside their owner organization. To ensure platform independence, Web Services technologies are the commonest way of implementing SOA systems since the former relies on well-known Internet protocols, such as SOAP and HTTP (Erickson & Siau, 2008). Therefore, migrating legacy systems to Web Services technologies is a fairly common practice. However, there is no standard recipe to effectively migrate legacy systems to SOA.

Recent literature (Li, et al., 2007) proposes that a legacy system can be migrated by following two approaches. The first approach, called direct migration, consists in wrapping a legacy system with a software layer that exposes the original system programs as Web Services. This approach is known to be cheap and fast, but it has the disadvantage that the legacy system is not replaced by a new one. Instead, the enterprise obtains two systems to maintain: a legacy system, and its newly-built SOA layer. On the other hand, the approach called indirect migration is based on re-implementing the legacy system using a modern platform. This approach is expensive and time consuming because not only the system should be reimplemented and re-tested, but also in some cases, the business logic embodied in the legacy system should be reverse-engineered. This happens because system documentation could have been lost or not kept up-to-date. The result of an indirect migration is not only an improved version of the system, but also updated documentation for future reference.

From the SOA point of view, an important difference between direct migration and indirect migration is the quality of the SOA frontier that is the set of Web Services exposed to potential consumers as a result of migrating a legacy system. The SOA frontier quality is a very important factor for the success of a SOA system (Blake & Nowlan, 2008; Beaton, et al., 2008; Rodriguez, et al., 2010b) because, as Figure 1 depicts, SOA frontier is used for both service registries and consumer. Service registries use the SOA frontier for indexing services and, then, allowing service consumers to search for them. In contrast, service consumers need the SOA frontier to understand and invoke the services. In addition, a SOA system success can be measure by how many service consumers it has. This is however ignored by most enterprises as direct migration is by nature the least expensive and fastest way of deriving a SOA frontier from a legacy system, but such a SOA frontier commonly is a mere "Internet-ready" representation of original system program interfaces, which were not designed with SOA best design practices or even conceived for being used by third-parties as Web Services essentially are. Instead, a SOA frontier design is commonly benefited by the re-implementation of original system programs during indirect migration.

To obtain a better trade-off between cost and SOA frontier quality, we have developed a new migration approach with similar quality than the one obtained using indirect migration, but based on direct migration. Our approach, called assisted migration, takes a legacy system migrated using direct migration and performs an analysis of possible refactoring actions to increase the SOA frontier quality. Although this approach does not remove the legacy system, we think that the obtained SOA frontier can be used as a starting point for re-implementing it. Therefore, such a SOA frontier smoothes system replacement because it does not change when the legacy system is replaced by the new one.

For evaluating the viability of assisted migration, we used a case study involving a COBOL system in which direct migration and indirect migration were applied. This system is owned by the biggest Argentinean government agency, and manages data related to almost the entire Argentinean population. The system was firstly migrated using the direct migration approach because of strict deadlines. Since the SOA frontier quality of the first migration was not suitable for new developments, the agency decided to perform a second migration. In this case, the indirect migration approach was used to improve the SOA frontier quality. Having these two migration attempts, we applied the assisted migration approach by feeding it with the direct migration version of the original system. Then, we compared the three obtained SOA frontiers in terms of cost, time, and quality. According to this analysis, our approach produces a SOA frontier nearly as good as that the indirect migration, but at a cost similar to that of direct migration.

The rest of this work is organized as follows. The next section discusses related works on migrating legacy system to SOA. This section also presents the case study. The following section outlines the traditional migration approaches,

Figure 1. SOA frontier importance

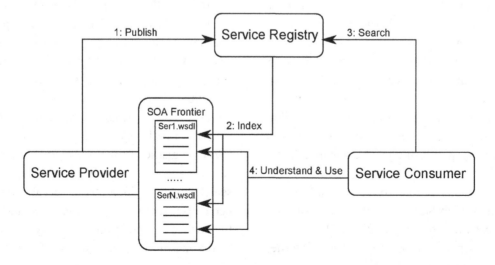

namely direct and indirect migration. This section also explains why both methods have been applied to the same system, and discusses the cost difference between the direct migration and indirect migration attempts. Within this section is a description of the proposed approach to reduce SOA frontier definition costs and a discussion of the effects of using each approach in terms of SOA frontier quality. The last section concludes this chapter, and outlines future research opportunities.

BACKGROUND

Migration of mainframe legacy systems to newer platforms has been receiving lots of attention, as organizations have to shift to distributed and Web-enabled software solutions. Different approaches have been explored, ranging from wrapping existing systems with Web-enabled software layers, to 1-to-1 automatic conversion approaches for converting programs in COBOL to 4GL. Therefore, current literature presents many related experience reports.

Because migration has been a problem since the first enterprise systems started to become obsolete, there is plenty of work on this topic. For instance, researchers have developed several methodologies for migrating system from their original technology to newer technologies, such as Cold Turkey, Chicken Little (Brodie & Stonebrake, 1993), and Renaissance (Battaglia, et al., 1998). Yet, these methodologies do not explicitly address how to migrate systems to SOA. To solve this issue, researchers have developed Service-Oriented Migration and Reuse Technique (SMART) for selecting migration strategies, but there is a lack of tools for assisting developers to apply it (Lewis, et al., 2005). In addition, SMART does not take into account SOA frontier quality as a main concern in this kind of migration.

Another COBOL to SOA migration methodology is SOAMIG (Zillmann, et al., 2011) that, in contrast with SMART, provides both a migration methodology and tools. The migration methodology consists of four phases and each of these phases might be carried out in several iterations. The main idea behind SOAMIG is to transform the original system into a SOA oriented one using several translation tools. For instance, it proposes to use a tool that translates COBOL code to Java code, which is easier to expose as Web Service. However, this approach might negatively impact on the quality of the SOA frontier because COBOL code was designed using out-of-date design criteria, and this kind of tools do not redesign the system. In addition, COBOL impose some length limitations to routine names and comments that might be probably translated to the SOA frontier, which might also represent a quality issue for the SOA frontier.

In this context, migrating legacy systems to SOA, while achieving high-quality service interfaces instead of just "webizing" the systems is an incipient research topic. Harry Sneed has been simultaneously researching on automatically converting COBOL programs to Web Services (Sneed, 2009) and measuring service interfaces quality (Sneed, 2010). In Sneed (2009), the author presents a tool for identifying COBOL programs that may be servified. The tool bases on gathering code metrics from the source to determine program complexity, and then suggests whether programs should be wrapped or re-engineered. As such, programs complexity drives the selection of the migration strategy. As reported in Sneed (2009), Sneed plans to inspect resulting service interfaces using a metric suite of his own, which comprises 25 quantity, 4 size, 5 complexity and 5 quality metrics.

In Alahmari et al. (2010), the authors present a framework and guidelines for migrating a legacy system to SOA, which aims at defining a SOA frontier having only the "optimal" services and with an appropriate level of granularity. The framework consists of three stages. The first stage is for modeling the legacy system main components and their interactions using UML. At the second stage, service operations and services processes are identified. The third stage is for aggregating identified service elements, according to a pre-defined taxonomy of service types (e.g. CRUD Services, Infrastructure services, Utility services, and Business services). During the second and third stages, software analysts are assisted via clustering techniques, which automatically group together similar service operations and services of the same type.

This work presents a comparison of applying different migration approaches. Two of them together with their pros and cons are well known within the community, while the other is a new approach that aims at obtaining the pros of both previous migrations without their cons. The following section discusses the case study used for this analysis.

Case Study

The case under study in this work consists of a data-centric system composed of several subsystems for maintaining data records related to individuals including complete personal information, relationships, work background, received benefits, and so forth. The system is written in COBOL, runs on an IBM mainframe, and accesses a DB2 database with around 0.8 PetaBytes. On the other hand, there are some COBOL programs accessing historic data through VSAM (Virtual Storage Access Method), a storage and data access method featured by a number of IBM mainframe operating systems. Moreover, some of the COBOL programs are only accessed through an intra-net via 3270 terminal applications, while other programs are grouped in CICS (Customer Information Control System) transactions and consumed by Web applications. CICS is a transaction manager designed for rapid, high-volume processing, which allows organizing a set of programs as an atomic task. In this case, these programs consist of business logic and database accesses, mostly input validations and queries, respectively.

For the sake of illustration, a brief overview of only 6 transactions is shown in Table 1, which indicates the number of non-commented source code lines[2], the number of SQL queries performed, and the number of lines and files associated with a transaction. When a program P1 calls a program P2, or imports a Communication Area (COMMAREA) definition C, or includes an SQL definition S, it is said that P1 is associated with P2, or C, or S, respectively. On average, each transaction had 18 files, comprised 1803 lines of code, and performed 6 SQL SELECT statements.

EMPLOYED MIGRATION APPROACHES

The system described in the previous section has been migrated to a SOA system by employing two different migration approaches. Clearly, this is an uncommon situation in practice; however, each migration attempt has reasonable reasons behind them.

The first migration attempt was originated by the need for providing Web access to the legacy system functionality with critic time deadlines and no more resources than the agency's IT department resources present at the moment. In other words, the system needed to be rapidly migrated by permanent staff and using the software development tools which the agency had licenses for use them. One year after, the agency IT members outsourced the second migration attempt to a recognized group of researchers with remarkable antecedents in SOC, Web Services, and Web Services interface design. The reason to do this was that the project managers responsible for building the Web applications found the resulting SOA frontier from the first migration attempt extremely hard to be understood and consequently reused. The next subsections explain each migration attempt in detail. Finally, we have applied a third migration in the context of a research project in which the agency was not involved.

Table 1. Characteristics of most important system transactions according to the mainframe load in terms of executed calls during January 2010

Transaction	SQL	COMMAREA(s)		Include(s)	
# of lines	# of queries	# of lines	# of files	# of lines	# of files
265	2	518	7	683	6
416	2	1114	6	141	5
537	3	10	2	800	29
1088	10	820	4	580	16
543	10	820	4	411	10
705	10	956	6	411	10

Direct Migration

Methodologically, the IT department members followed a wrapping strategy (Almonaies, et al., 2010) that comprised 4 steps for each migrated transaction:

1. Automatically creating a COM+ object including a method with the inputs/outputs defined in the associated COMMAREA, which forwards invocations to the underlying transaction. This was done by using a tool called COMTI Builder (Leinecker, 2000).
2. Automatically wrapping the COM+ object with a C# class having only one method that invokes this object by using Visual Studio.
3. Manually including specific annotations in the C# code to deploy it and use the framework-level services of the .NET platform for generating the WSDL document and handling SOAP requests.
4. Testing the communication between the final Web Service and its associated transaction. This was performed by means of a free tool called soapUI (http://www.soapui.org).

To clarify these 4 steps, a word about the employed technologies and tools is needed. A COMMAREA is a fixed region in the RAM of the mainframe that is used to pass data from an application to a transaction. Conceptually, a COMMAREA is similar to a C++ struct with (nested) fields specified by using native COBOL data-types. COMTI (Component Object Model Transaction Integrator) is a technology that allows a transaction to be wrapped with a COM+ (Component Object Model Plus) object. The tool named COMTI Builder receives a COMMAREA as input to automatically derive a Type Library (TLB), which is accessible from any component of the .NET framework as a COM+ object afterwards. COM+ is an extension to COM that adds a new set of functions to introspect components at run-time. Finally, the tool listed in 4 receives one or more WSDL documents and automatically generates a client for the associated service(s), which allows the generation of test suites.

Basically, each step, but step 4, adds a software layer to the original transactions. In this context, the Wrapper Design Pattern is central to the employed steps, since wrapping consists in implementing a software component interface by reusing existing components, which can be any of a batch program, an on-line transaction, a program, a module, or even just a simple block of code. Wrappers not only implement the interface that newly developed objects use to access the wrapped systems, but are also responsible for passing input/output parameters to the encapsulated components. Then, from the inner to the outer part of a final service, by following the described steps the associated transaction was first wrapped with a COMTI object, which in turn was wrapped by a COM+ object, which finally was wrapped by a C# class that in the end was offered as a Web Service. To do this, implementation classes were deployed as .NET ASP 2.0 Web Service Applications, which used the framework-level services provided by the .NET platform for generating the corresponding WSDL document and handling SOAP requests. As the reader can see, the SOA frontier was automatically derived from the C# code, which means that WSDL documents were not made by human developers but they were automatically generated by the .NET platform. This WSDL document construction method is known as code-first (Mateos, et al., 2010).

Indirect Migration

Methodologically, the whole indirect migration attempt basically implied five steps:

1. Manually defining potential WSDL documents basing on the knowledge the agency had on the interface and functionality of the original transactions. For each service operation, a brief explanation using WSDL documentation elements was included.
2. Exhaustively revising the legacy source code.
3. Manually refining the WSDL documents defined during step 1 by basing on opportunities to abstract and reuse parameter data-type definitions, group functionally related transactions into one cohesive service, improve textual comments and remove duplicated transactions, which were detected at step 2. For data-type definitions, we followed best practices for naming type elements and constraining their ranges.
4. Supplying the WSDL documents defined at step 3 with implementations using .NET.
5. Testing the migrated services with the help of the agency IT department.

During the step 1, three specialists on Web Services technologies designed preliminary WSDL documents, based on the knowledge the agency had on the functionality of the transactions, to

sketch the desired SOA frontier together. This step comprised daily meetings not only between the specialists and the project managers in charge of the original COBOL programs, but also between the specialists and the project managers responsible for developing client applications that would consume the resulting migrated Web Services. Unlike the code-first approach, in which service interfaces are derived from their implementations, the three specialists used contract-first, which encourages designers to first derive the technical contract of a service using WSDL, and then supply an implementation for it. Usually, this approach leads to WSDL documents that better reflect the business services of an organization, but it is not commonly used in industry since it requires WSDL specialists (Ordiales Coscia, et al., 2011). This step might be carried out by defining service interfaces in C# and then using code-first for generating WSDL documents, especially when analysts with little WSDL skills are available.

The step 2 involved revising the transactions code with the help of documents specifying functionality and diagrams illustrating the dependencies between the various transactions to obtain an overview of them. This was done to output a high-level analysis of the involved business logic, since the existing COBOL to some extent conditioned the functionality that could be offered by the resulting services. The target transactions comprised 261688 lines of CICS/COBOL code (600 files). Six software analysts exhaustively revised each transaction and its associated files under the supervision of the specialists during three months. This allowed the external work team to obtain a big picture of the existing transactions.

The step 3 consisted in refining the WSDL documents obtained in the step 5 by basing on the output of the step 2. Broadly, the three specialists abstracted and reused parameter data-type definitions, grouped functionally related transactions into one cohesive service, improved textual comments and names, and removed duplicated transactions. For data-type definitions, the specialists followed best practices for naming type elements and constraining their ranges. From this thorough analysis, potential interfaces were derived for the target services and a preliminary XSD schema document subsuming the entities implicitly conveyed in the original COMMAREA definitions. Conceptually, this represented a meet-in-the-middle approach to service migration that allowed the specialists to iteratively build the final service interfaces based on the desired business services, which impact on the implementation of services, as well as the interfaces derived from the existing CICS/COBOL code, which to some extent condition the functionality that can be exposed by the resulting software services.

The step 4 was re-implementing the services and began once the WSDL documents were defined. Two more people were incorporated in the project for implementing the services using the .NET ASP 2.0 Web Service Application template as required by the agency. Hence, the 3 specialists trained 8 software developers in Visual Studio 2008, C# and a data mapper, called MyBatis[3]. This library frees developers from coding typical conversions between database-specific datatypes and programming language-specific ones. MyBatis connects to DB2 mainframe databases using IBM's DB2Connect[4], an infrastructure for connecting Web, Windows, UNIX, Linux, and mobile applications to z/OS and mainframe back-end data. It is worth noting that to bind the defined WSDL documents with their .NET implementations, the specialists had to extend the ASP 2.0 "httpModules" support. Concretely, the three specialists developed a custom module that returns a manually specified WSDL document to applications, instead of generating it from source code, which is the default behavior of .NET.

The step 5 was to test the resulting services with assistance of the agency IT department. Basically, each new Web Service was compared to its CICS/COBOL counterpart(s) to verify that with the same input the same output was obtained. If some inconsistency between the new services and the old CICS/COBOL system was detected, the services were revised and re-tested. This step was repeated until the agency IT department had the confidence that the new SOA-based system was as good as the old system from both a functional and non-functional point of view.

Costs Comparison of the Direct and Indirect Migration Attempts

As reported by the agency's IT department, it took 1 day to train a developer on the direct migration method and the three tools employed, namely COMTI Builder, Visual Studio, and soapUI[5]. Then, trained developers migrated one transaction per hour, mostly because all the steps but one (step 3) were tool-supported and automatic. Since the agency had the respective software licenses for COMTI Builder and Visual Studio tools beforehand, choosing them was a harmless decision from an economical viewpoint.

Regarding the costs of the indirect migration attempt, monetarily, it cost the agency 320000 US dollars. Table 2 details the human resources involved in the second attempt of the project. All in all, it took one year plus one month for 6 software analysts, 2 more developers incorporated at step 4, and 3 specialists to migrate 32 priority transactions. It is worth noting that no commercial

Table 2. Required manpower over months of the indirect migration attempt

Step	People	Role	Time (in months)
1	3	WSDL specialists	1
2	6	Software analysts	3
3	3	WSDL specialists	1
4	8	Software developers	6
5	8	Software developers	2

Table 3. Costs comparison for the migration of 32 transactions during direct and indirect attempts

Resources	First attempt: direct migration	Second attempt: indirect migration
Developers	1	8
Specialists	0	3
Time	5 days	13 months
Money	u$s 3000 (*)	u$s 320000

(*) This was the average monthly salary in Argentine for a senior .NET Developer at the time of the bottom-up migration attempt.

tools were needed, apart from the IDE for which the agency already had licenses.

Table 3 presents an illustrative comparison of the resources needed by each migration attempt. The first migration attempt succeeded in delivering Web Services within a short period of time and without expending lots of resources, by employing a direct migration approach with wrapping. As shown in the second column of the Table, with the associated methods and tool-set, it only took 5 days and 1 senior developer to migrate 32 CICS/COBOL transactions. It is worth noting that the first attempt was inexpensive since no software licenses had to be bought, and no developers had to be hired, i.e. a regular member of the IT department performed the first migration attempt. However, this could be not the case for many enterprises and therefore there may be costs associated to buying the necessary tool-set and hiring external manpower when performing a direct migration with wrapping. In contrast, an indirect migration attempt with re-engineering was much more expensive and required more time to be completed. In particular, 8 junior developers (undergraduate UNICEN students), 3 Web Services specialists (UNICEN researchers with a PhD. and several publications in the Web Service area), 13 months and 320000 US dollars for re-engineering the same 32 transactions were required. For this attempt, external specialists and

developers were hired, whose salaries have been included in this cost.

Assisted Migration: Software-Assisted SOA Frontier Definition

From the previous section, it is clear that the indirect migration approach demanded much more resources than its direct counterpart. Indeed, as shown in Table 2, near a half of the time demanded by the indirect attempt was for defining service interfaces. Concretely, the output of steps 1, 2, and 3 of the indirect migration method employed, was the WSDL documents of the SOA frontier, and these steps took 5 months. Regarding needed people, the mentioned three steps required 3 WSDL experts and 6 software developers more than the direct migration attempt. Therefore, we have explored the hypothesis that, to some extent, some of the tasks performed for defining the SOA frontier could be automated, improving migration efficiency.

Basically, we propose a fast and cheap approach to imitate the tasks performed at some of the steps of the employed indirect migration approach. These tasks include exhaustively analyzing the legacy source code (step 2), and supplying software analysts with guidelines for manually refining the WSDL documents of the SOA frontier (step 3). The step 1, in which interviews were conducted, was left out of the scope of this approach. Thus, the input of this approach was the SOA frontier of the direct migration attempt, instead of those WSDL documents that were sketched together during the meetings of the indirect attempt.

The proposed approach can be iteratively executed for generating a refined SOA frontier at each iteration. The main idea is to iteratively improve the defined service interfaces, by removing those WSDL anti-patterns present in them. A WSDL anti-pattern is a recurrent practice that hinders Web Services chances of being discovered and understood by third-parties. In (Rodriguez, et al., 2010c) the authors present a catalog of WSDL anti-patterns and describe each of them in a general way by including a description of the underlying problem, its solution, and an illustrative example. Then, the catalog of anti-patterns can be used to compare two WSDL-modeled SOA frontiers. Specifically, one could account anti-pattern occurrences within a given set of service interfaces because the fewer the occurrences are, the better the resulting WSDL documents are in terms of discoverability and understandability.

Figure 2 depicts the proposed steps. Mainly, these steps can be organized in two groups, automatic and manual. First, our approach starts by automatically detecting potential WSDL anti-patterns root causes within the SOA frontier given as input its WSDL documents plus their underlying implementation ("Anti-patterns root causes detection" step). Then, a course of actions to improve the SOA frontier is generated ("OO refactorings suggestion" step). The manual step "OO refactorings application" takes place when the software analysts in charge of migration apply the suggested refactoring actions. Accordingly, software analysts obtain a new SOA frontier and fed it to the anti-patterns root causes detection step. Notice that although this approach uses as input the COBOL code and the SOA frontier generated by the direct migration, the proposed refactorings are intended to be applied on the SOA frontier and the SOA-enabled wrapper, i.e. the COBOL wrapping software layer and the WSDL documents. Hence, the resulting SOA frontier can be deployed over the legacy system without disrupting its normal operation. The next subsections describe both groups of steps.

In the following two sections, we describe how the automatic steps of the assisted migration are performed. In the next subsection, we present how the WSDL anti-patterns root causes are detected. In the following subsection, we outline how OO refactorings are suggested. Finally, in last subsection, we describe how much takes to perform these steps, which are automatic. How to apply OO refactorings is not described through this section because it is out of this chapter scope and there is plenty of literature on that topic (Fowler, 1999).

Anti-Patterns Root Causes Detection

One of the lessons learned from past migration experiences is that manually revising legacy system source code is a cumbersome endeavor. However, such an exhaustive code revision is crucial not only because the legacy system implementation conditions the functionality that can be exposed by the resulting SOA frontier, but also to detect service interfaces improvement opportunities. Thus, the anti-pattern root causes detection step is performed automatically. To do this, by basing on the work published in Rodriguez et al. (2010b), we have defined and implemented the ten heuristics summarized in Table 4. Broadly, a defined heuristic receives the implementation in CICS/COBOL of a migrated transaction or its associated WSDL document. Then, a heuristic outputs whether specific anti-patterns root causes are present in the given input or not. Actually, in

Figure 2. Software-assisted SOA frontier definition steps

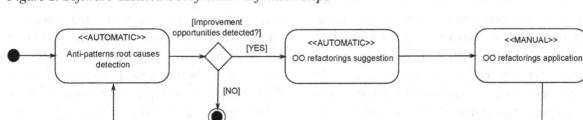

most cases a heuristic output does not provide enough evidence of anti-patterns root causes existences by itself. Therefore, some heuristics have been combined as follows:

- 8 and 9 → Remove redundant operations
- 4 → Improve error handling definitions
- 3 or 5 or 6 or 7 → Improve business object definitions
- 8 → Expose shared programs as services
- 1 and 2 → Improve names and comments
- 10 → Improve service operations cohesion

where several heuristic ids (see column Id from Table 4) are logically combined within rules antecedents and WSDL document improvement opportunities are rules consequents.

It is worth noting that we will refer to WSDL document improvement opportunity, on analogy with removing particular WSDL anti-patterns root causes. For instance, the first rule is for detecting the opportunity to remove redundant operations, which may be the origin of at least two anti-patterns, namely Redundant Port-types and Redundant Data Model (Rodriguez, et al., 2010c). When processing COBOL code, this rule is fired when two or more programs share the same dependencies (heuristic 8) but also the parameters of one program subsume the parameters of the other program (heuristic 9).

Most heuristics have been adapted from (Rodriguez, et al., 2010b), whereas heuristics 6, 7, 8, 9, and 10 were inspired by the migration attempt. Thus, heuristics 6 to 10 will be further explained next. With regard to "Looking for data-types with inconsistent names and types" (id 6), the heuristic analyzes names and data-types of service operations parameters to look for known relationships between names and types. Given a parameter, the heuristic splits the parameter name by basing on classic programmers' naming conventions, such as Camel Casing and Hungarian notation. Each name token is compared to a list of keywords with which a data-type is commonly associated. For example, the token "birthday" is commonly as-

sociated with the XSD built-in xsd:date data-type, but the token "number" with xsd:int data-type. Therefore, the heuristic in turn checks whether at least one name token is wrongly associated with the parameter data-type.

The heuristic to "Detect not used parameters" (id 7) receives the COBOL source code of a migrated program and checks whether every parameter of the program output COMMAREA is associated with the programming language assignation statement, i.e. the COBOL MOVE reserved word. In other words, given a COBOL program, the heuristic retrieves its output COMMAREA, then gets every parameter from within it, even parameters grouped by COBOL records, and finally looks for MOVE statements having the declared parameter. One limitation of this heuristic is that the search for MOVE statements is only performed in the main COBOL program, whereas copied or included programs are left aside, and those parameters that are assigned by the execution of an SQL statement are ignored by this heuristic.

The heuristic to "Look for shared dependencies among two service implementations" (id 8) receives two COBOL programs as input. For each program builds a list of external COBOL programs, copies, and includes, which are called from the main program, and finally checks whether the intersection of both lists is empty or not. In order to determine external programs calls, the heuristic looks for the CALL reserved word.

With regard to "Look for data-types that subsumes other data-types" heuristic (id 9), this receives a WSDL document as input and detects the inclusion of one or more parameters of a service operation in the operations of another service. To do this, parameter names and data-types are compared. For comparing names classic text preprocessing techniques are applied, namely split combined words, remove stop-words, and reduce them to stems. For comparing data-types the heuristic employs the algorithm named Redundant Data Model, which is presented in Rodriguez et al. (2010b).

Table 4. Heuristics for detecting WSDL anti-patterns root causes

Id	Description	Input	Output
1	Look for comments in WSDL <documentation> elements	WSDL document	**true**: if at least one operation lacks documentation **false**: otherwise
2	Search inappropriate names for services, port-types, operations and arguments	WSDL document	**true**: when the length of a name token is lower than 3 characters (e.g. "c_person," token "c" has 1 character), or when token refers to a technology (e.g. "PeopleDetailsSOAP"), or when an operation name contains two or more verbs or an argument name contains a verb **false**: otherwise
3	Detect operations that receive or return too many parameters	WSDL document	**true**: when at least one operation input/output has more than P paremeters **false**: otherwise
4	Look for error information being exchanged as output data	WSDL document	**true**: when an output message part has any of the tokens: "error," "errors," "fault," "faults," "fail," "fails," "exception, "exceptions, "overflow," "mistake," "misplay" **false**:otherwise
5	Look for redundant data-type definitions	WSDL document	**true**: when at least two XSD data-types are syntacticly identical **false**: otherwise
6	Look for data-types with inconsistent names and types	WSDL document	**true**: when the name of a parameter denotes a quantity but it is not associated with a numerical data-type (e.g. numberOfChildren:String) **false**: otherwise
7	Detect not used parameters	COBOL source code	**true**: when at least one parameter is not associated with a COBOL MOVE statement **false**: otherwise
8	Look for shared dependencies among two service implementations	COBOL source code	A list of COBOL programs that are copied, or included, or called from two or more service implementations. The list is empty when no shared dependencies are found **true**: when the list is not empty **false**: otherwise
9	Look for data-types that subsumes other data-types	WSDL document	**true**: when an XSD complex data-type contains another complex XSD data-type, or a list of parameters subsumes another list of parameters **false**: otherwise
10	Detect semantically similar services and operations	WSDL document	**true**: when a vectorial representation of the names and associated documentation of two services or operations, are near in a vector space model **false**: otherwise

The tenth heuristic, namely "Detect semantically similar services and operations," is based on measuring the similarity among textual information of a pair of services or operations. This heuristic exploits textual information present in WSDL names and documentation elements. Textual similarity is assessed by representing associated textual information as a collection of terms and in turn as a vector in a multi-dimensional space. For each term, there is a dimension in the space, and the respective vector component takes as value the term frequency. Finally, looking for similar operations reduces to looking for near vectors in the space by comparing the cosine of the angle among them (Stroulia & Wang, 2005).

Object-Oriented Refactorings Suggestion

Until now, this section focused on the first part of the proposed approach, which is intended to reproduce the task of exhaustively looking for SOA frontier improvement opportunities within a legacy source code. Once we have all the evidence gathered by the heuristics, the second part of the proposed approach consists of providing practical guidelines to remove the potential anti-patterns root causes detected. These guidelines consist of a sequence of steps that should be revised and potentially applied by the development team in charge of the migration attempt. It is worth noting that the proposed guidelines are not meant to be automatic, mostly due to the fact that there is not a unique approach to build a SOA frontier and in turn improve or modify it, which makes the automation of these proposed guidelines non-deterministic.

The cornerstone of the proposed guidelines is that classic Object-Oriented (OO) refactorings can be employed to remove anti-patterns root causes from a SOA frontier. The rationale behind this is that services are described as OO interfaces exchanging messages, whereas operation data-types are described using XSD, which provides some operators for expressing encapsulation and inheritance. Then, we have organized a sub-set of Fowler et al.'s catalog of OO refactorings (Fowler, 1999), in order to provide a sequence of refactorings that should be performed for removing each anti-pattern root cause. This work bases on Fowler et al.'s catalog since it is well-known by the software community and most IDEs provide automatic support for many of the associated refactorings.

The proposed guidelines associate a SOA frontier improvement opportunity with one or more logical combinations of traditional OO refactorings (see Table 5). The first column of the Table presents SOA frontier improvement opportunities, while the second column describes which OO refactorings from (Fowler, 1999) should be applied. As shown in the second column, the OO refactorings are arranged in sequences of refactoring combinations. Combining two refactorings by "?" means that software developers may choose among them, i.e. they should apply only one refactoring from the set. Instead, using "?" means that the corresponding refactorings should be applied in that strict order. Moreover, in the cases of "Improve business objects definition" and "Improve service operations cohesion," the associated refactorings comprise more than one step. This means that at each individual step developers should analyze and apply the associated refactorings combinations as explained.

Regarding how to apply OO refactorings, it depends on how the WSDL documents of the SOA frontier have been built. Broadly, as mentioned earlier, there are two main approaches to build WSDL documents, namely code-first and contract-first. Code-first refers to automatically extracting service interfaces from their underlying implementation. For instance, let us suppose a Java class named CalculatorService that has one method signature sum(int i0, int i1):int. Then, its code-first WSDL document will have a port-type named CalculatorService with one operation sum related to an input message for exchanging two integers and an output message that conveys another integer. Here, the CalculatorService class represents the outermost component of the service implementation. On the other hand, when following the contract-first approach, developers should first define service interfaces using WSDL and then supplying implementations for them in their preferred programming language.

Then, when the WSDL documents of a SOA frontier have been implemented under code-first, the proposed guidelines should be applied on the outermost components of the services implementation. Instead, when contract-first has been followed, the proposed OO refactorings should be applied on the WSDL documents. For instance, to remove redundant operations from a code-first Web Service, developers should apply the "Extract Method" or the "Extract Class" refactorings on the underlying class that implements the service. In case of a contract-first Web Service, by extracting an operation or a port-type from the WSDL document of the service, developers apply the "Extract Method" or the "Extract Class" refactorings, respectively. When contract-first is used, developers should also update service implementations for each modified WSDL document.

Table 5. Association between SOA frontier refactorings and Fowler et al.'s refactorings

SOA Frontier Refactoring	Object-Oriented Refactoring
Remove redundant operations	1: Extract Method ∨ Extract Class
Improve error handling definition	1: Replace Error Code With Exception
	1: Convert Procedural Design to Object ∧ Replace Conditional with Polymorphism
	2: Inline Class
Improve business objects definition	3: Extract Class ∧ Extract Subclass ∧ Extract Superclass ∧ Collapse Hierarchy
	4: Remove Control Flag ∧ Remove Parameter
	5: Replace Type Code with Class ∧ Replace Type Code with Subclasses
Expose shared programs as services	1: Extract Method ∨ Extract Class
Improve names and comments	1: Rename Method ∨ Preserve Whole Object ∨ Introduce Parameter Object ∨ Replace Parameter with Explicit Methods
Improve service operations cohesion	1: Inline Class ∧ Rename Method
	2: Move Method ∨ Move Class

Empirically Assessing Time Demanded for Executing Heuristics and Performing OO Refactorings

We hypothesized that automatizing some steps of the indirect migration attempt could reduce the time demanded for executing heuristics and performing OO refactorings. We have empirically assessed the time demanded by each heuristic for analyzing the legacy system under study. The experiments have been run on a notebook with a 2.8 GHz QuadCore Intel Core i7 720QM processor, 6 Gb DDR3 RAM, running Windows 7 on a 64 bits architecture. To mitigate noise introduced by underlying software layers and hardware elements, each heuristic has been executed 20 times and the demanded time was measured per execution. Then, the heuristic executions times have been averaged. Table 6 summarizes the average time required for each automatic operation. Briefly, the average execution time of a heuristic was 9585.78 milliseconds (ms), being 55815.15 ms (less than one minute) the biggest achieved response time, i.e. the "Detect semantically similar services and operations" was the most expensive heuristic in terms of response time.

Furthermore, we have assessed the time demanded for manually applying the OO refactorings proposed by the approach on the SOA frontier resulted from the direct migration attempt. To do this, one software analyst with full knowledge about the system under study was supplied with the list of OO refactorings produced by the approach. It took two full days to apply the proposed OO refactorings. It is worth noting that OO refactorings have been applied at the interface level, i.e. underlying implementations have not been accommodated to interface changes. The reason to do that was that we only want to generate a new SOA frontier and then compare it with the ones generated by the previous two migration attempts. Therefore, modifying interfaces implementation, which would require a huge development and testing effort, will not contribute to verifying the aforementioned hypothesis. All in all, to have an approximation of what the total cost of migrating the system under study with this approach would be, let assume that the cost for supplying the refactored SOA frontier with implementations will be near to the cost of step 4 plus step 5 of the indirect approach. Returning to Table 2, the first three rows can be condensed in one row with one software analyst, who must known

Table 6. Average operation time

Operation	Time
Look for comments in WSDL <documentation> elements	56.55 ms
Search inappropriate names for services, port-types, operations and arguments	39460.25 ms
Detect operations that receive or return too many parameters	58.7 ms
Look for error information being exchanged as output data	57.75 ms
Look for redundant data-type definitions	60.9 ms
Look for data-types with inconsistent names and types	93.45 ms
Detect unused parameters	56.45 ms
Look for shared dependencies among two service implementations	82.95 ms
Look for data-types that subsumes other data-types	115.70 ms
Detect semantically similar services and operations	55815.15 ms

the system in order to promptly apply OO refactorings suggested, and 2 days.

To sum up, the migration approach described in this section aims at automatically reproducing some of the steps of the indirect migration approach, so that their inherent costs are mitigated, and at the same time, a SOA frontier with an acceptable quality is obtained. In this sense, the next section provides empirical evidence on the service frontier quality achieved by the three approaches to legacy software migration to SOA described so far, namely direct migration, indirect migration, and our software-assisted migration.

Service Interface Quality Comparison

After migrating a system, the resulting service interface quality might be affected by several factors related to the migration methodology, and the original system design. While direct migration interfaces heavily depend on the original system design, indirect migration interfaces might be independent of it because indirect migration means re-implementing the old system with new technologies and design criteria. Despite having better results in terms of SOA frontier, indirect migration is known to be costly, and time consuming. The assisted migration approach then tries to

balance the trade-off between cost and interfaces quality, hence this section presents evidence that assisted migration produces much better service interfaces than direct migration at a fraction of the indirect migration cost.

The evaluation relies not only on a quantitative analysis of Lines Of Code (LOC), lines of comments, and offered operations, but also on a well-established set of quality metrics for WSDL-based interfaces (Rodriguez, et al., 2010c). The advantage of the quantitative analysis is that they are accepted as providers of evidence about system quality in general. Moreover, the advantage over other set of metrics is that they are WSDL document oriented; thereby, they are suitable for comparing SOA frontiers quality. These metrics are based on a catalog of common bad practices found in public WSDL documents. These bad practices, which are presented in the well-known anti-pattern form, jeopardize Web Service discoverability, understandability, and legibility. We have used anti-pattern occurrences as a quality indicator because the fewer the occurrences are, the better the WSDL documents are. In addition, we have analyzed business object definitions reuse by counting repeated data-type definitions across WSDL documents, and the use of XSD files to define shared data-types. Notice that other typical non-functional requirements (Litoiu, 2004), such as performance, reliability or scalability, have intentionally not been considered since we were interested in WSDL document quality after migration. It is worth noting that though the metrics were gathered from the case study presented in Case Study section, the examples used through this section are general because of our confidentiality agreement with the agency.

The comparison methodology consisted of gathering the aforementioned metrics from the SOA frontiers that resulted from each migration attempt. In this sense, three data sets of WSDL documents were obtained, namely:

- **Direct Migration:** The WSDL documents that resulted from the first attempt of the project. As such, the associated services were obtained by using direct migration and implementing wrappers to the transactions, and by using the default tool-set provided by Visual Studio 2008 that supports code-first generation of service interfaces from C# code.
- **Indirect Migration:** The WSDL documents obtained from the approach followed during the second attempt of the project, i.e. indirect migration and at the same time the contract-first WSDL generation method.
- **Software-Assisted SOA Frontier Definition (or Assisted Migration for short):** The WSDL documents obtained

after automatically detecting improvement opportunities on the direct migration dataset, and in turn applying the associated suggested guidelines.

The next subsections present the quantitative metrics comparison results, the qualitative comparison and the data-model reuse analysis, respectively.

Quantitative Analysis

Firstly, there was a significant difference in the number of WSDL document generated by each approach. As Table 7 shows, Direct Migration data set comprised 32 WSDL documents, which means one WSDL document per migrated transaction. In contrast, Indirect Migration and Assisted Migration data sets had respectively 7 WSDL documents + 1 XSD file, and 16 WSDL documents + 1 XSD file. The first advantage observed in the Indirect Migration and Assisted Migration data sets over Direct Migration data-set was the XSD file used for sharing common data-type definitions across the WSDL documents. In addition, having less WSDL documents means that several operations were in the same WSDL document. This happened because the WSDL documents belonging to Indirect Migration and Assisted Migration data-sets were designed to define functional related operations in the same WSDL document,

Table 7. Classical metrics

Approach	WSDL documents	Offered operations	LOC per file	LOC per operation	Comments per file	% Comments
Direct Migration	32 WSDL documents	39	157.25	129	0.00	0.00%
Indirect Migration	7 WSDL documents + 1 XSD file	45	495.5	88	30.25	6.10%
Assisted Migration	16 WSDL documents + 1 XSD file	41	235.35	97	15.41	6.54%

which is a well-known design principle (Yourdon & Constantine, 1979).

Secondly, the number of offered operations was: 39, 45, and 41 for Direct Migration, Indirect Migration, and Assisted Migration data-sets. Although originally there were 32 transactions to migrate, Direct Migration resulted in 39 operations because one specific transaction was divided into 8 operations. This transaction used a large registry of possible search parameters plus a control couple to select which parameters upon a particular search represents the desired input, ignoring the rest of them. During the first migration attempt, this transaction was wrapped with 8 operations with more descriptive names, and each of them end up calling the same COBOL routine with a different control couple.

On the other hand, the second and third attempts further divided the CICS/COBOL transactions into more operations. There were two main reasons for this, namely disaggregating functionality and making public common functionality. Disaggregating functionality means that some transactions, which returned almost 100 output parameters, had various purposes, thus they were mapped to several purpose-specific service operations. The second reason was that several transactions internally call the same COBOL routines, which might be useful for potential service consumers. In consequence, what used to be COBOL internal routines now are also part of the SOA frontier offered by the agency.

The resulting average LOC per file, and per operation were also a difference among the data sets. Although Indirect Migration data set had more LOC per file than the other two data sets, it also resulted in less files. However, the number of LOC per operation of the Indirect Migration data set was the lowest. Interestingly, the Assisted Migration presented a slightly higher number of LOC per operation than the Indirect Migration data set. In contrast, the number of LOC resulted from applying the first migration attempt was

more than twice as much as the LOC generated by other approaches. This means that a service consumer must read more code to understand what an operation does and how to call it. Basically, this makes using the WSDL documents of the Direct Migration data set harder than using the WSDL documents from both Indirect Migration and Assisted Migration data sets.

Table 7 also points out the difference in the number of comment lines of WSDL and XSD code per document. Firstly, WSDL documents belonging to the Direct Migration data-set had no comments because the tools are unable to correctly pass COBOL comments on to COM+ wrappers, and then to WSDL documents. Besides, developers that used these tools did not bother about placing comments manually, which is consistent with the findings reported by previous studies (Fan & Kambhampati, 2005; Rodriguez, et al., 2010b). In contrast, Indirect Migration and Assisted Migration WSDL documents had 30.25 and 16 lines of comments per file, respectively. Despite having more comment lines per file, the percentage of comment lines in Indirect Migration WSDL documents were slightly lower that the percentage of comment lines in Assisted Migration WSDL documents.

Anti-Pattern Assessment

Web Service discoverability anti-patterns were inferred from real-life WSDL document data sets (Rodriguez, et al., 2010a). These anti-patterns encompass bad practices that affect the ability of a service consumer to understand what a service does, and how to use it. Therefore, these anti-patterns' occurrences can be used to evaluate how good a SOA frontier is. Hence, we used the anti-patterns to measure the quality of the WSDL document generated by the different migration approaches. In particular, we found the following anti-patterns in at least one of the WSDL documents in the three data sets:

- **Inappropriate or lacking comments (Fan & Kambhampati, 2005):** Some operations within a WSDL have no comments or the comments do not effectively describe their associated elements (messages, operations).
- **Ambiguous names (Blake & Nowlan, 2008):** Some WSDL operation or message names do not accurately represent their intended semantics.
- **Redundant port-types:** A port-type is repeated within the WSDL document, usually in the form of one port-type instance per binding type (e.g. HTTP, HTTPS, or SOAP).
- **Enclosed data model:** The data model in XSD describing input and output datatypes is defined within the WSDL document instead of being defined in a separate file, which makes data-type reuse across several Web Services very difficult. The exception of this rule occurs when it is known before-hand that data-types are not going to be reused. In this case, including data-type definitions within WSDL documents allows constructing self-contained contracts, so it is said that the contract does not suffer from the anti-pattern.
- **Undercover fault information within standard messages (Beaton, et al., 2008):** Error information is returned using output messages rather than Fault messages.
- **Redundant data models:** A data-type is defined more than once in the same WSDL document.
- **Low cohesive operations in the same port-type:** Occurs in Web Services that place operations for checking the availability of the service and operations related to its main functionality into a single port-type. An example of this bad practice is to include operations such as "isAlive," "getVersion" and "ping" in a port-type, though the port-type has been designed for pro-

viding operations of a particular problem domain.

Table 8 summarizes the results of the anti-patterns analysis. When an anti-pattern affected a portion of the WSDL documents in a data-set, we analyzed which is the difference between these WSDL documents and the rest of the WSDL documents in the same data-set. Hence, the inner cells present under which circumstances the WSDL documents were affected by a particular anti-pattern. Since there are anti-patterns whose detection is inherently more subjective (e.g. "Inappropriate or lacking comments" and "Ambiguous names") (Rodriguez, et al., 2010b), we performed a peer-review methodology after finishing their individual measurements to prevent biases.

Achieved results show that the WSDL documents of the Direct Migration data set were affected by more anti-patterns than those of the Assisted Migration data set, while no anti-pattern affected WSDL documents in the Indirect Migration data set. The first two rows describe anti-patterns that impact on services comments and names (Crasso, et al., 2010). It is reasonable to expect that these anti-patterns affected the WSDL documents of the Direct Migration data set since all information included in them was derived from code written in CICS/COBOL, which does not offer a standard way to indicate from which portions and scope of a code existing comments can be extracted and reused. At the same time, names in CICS/COBOL have associated length restrictions (e.g. up to 4 characters in some CICS and/or COBOL flavors), names in the resulting WSDL documents were too short and difficult to be read. In contrast, these anti-patterns affected WSDL documents in Assisted Migration data set only when the original CICS/COBOL is designed using control couples. This is because properly naming and commenting this kind of couples is known to be a complex task (Yourdon & Constantine, 1979).

Table 8. Anti-patterns in the three WSDL data sets

Anti-pattern/Data-set	Direct Migration	Indirect Migration	Assisted Migration
Inappropriate or lacking Comments	**Always**	Never	When the original transactions use control couples
Ambiguous names	**Always**	Never	When the original transactions use control couples
Redundant port-types	When supporting several protocols	Never	**Never**
Enclosed data model	**Always**	Never	**Never**
Undercover fault information within standard messages	**Always**	Never	**Never**
Redundant data models	When two operations use the same data-type	Never	**Never**
Low cohesive operations in the same port-type	**Never**	Never	When several related transactions use a non related operation, such as formatting routines

The third row describes an anti-pattern that ties abstract service interfaces to concrete implementations, hindering black-box reuse (Crasso, et al., 2010). We observed that this anti-pattern was caused by the tools employed for generating WSDL documents during the first migration attempt. By default, the employed tool produces redundant port-types. To avoid this anti-pattern, developers should provide C# service implementation with rarely used annotations. Likewise, the fourth row describes an anti-pattern that is generated by many code-first tools, which force data models to be included within the generated WSDL documents, and could not be avoided within the Direct Migration WSDL documents. In contrast, neither the Indirect Migration nor the Assisted Migration data sets were affected by these anti-patterns.

The anti-pattern described in the fifth row of the table deals with errors being transferred as part of output messages, which for the Direct Migration data-set resulted from the original transactions that used the same COMMAREA for returning both output and error information. In contrast, the WSDL documents of the Indirect Migration data set and the Assisted Migration data set had a proper designed error handling mechanism based on standard WSDL fault messages.

The anti-pattern described in the sixth row is related to bad data model designs. Redundant data models usually arise from limitations or bad use of the tools employed to generate WSDL documents. Therefore, this anti-pattern only affected Direct Migration WSDL documents. Although there were not repeated data-types at the WSDL document level, the Assisted Migration data set had repeated data-types at a global level, i.e. when taking into account the data-types in all the documents. For instance, the error type, which consists of a fault code, string (brief description), actor, and description, was repeated in all the Assisted Migration WSDL documents. This is because this data-type was derived several times from the different sub-systems. Finally, this did not happen when using indirect migration because the WSDL document designers had a big picture of the system. We further analyze resulting datatypes in the next section.

The last anti-pattern stands for having no semantically related operations within a porttype. This anti-pattern did not affected WSDL documents generated through direct migration or indirect migration. The Direct Migration data set was not affected because each WSDL document included only one operation, while the Indirect Migration WSDL documents were specifically

Table 9. Data-type definition: detailed view

Data Model characteristics	Direct Migration	Indirect Migration	Assisted Migration
Defined data-types	182	235	191
Average definitions per data-type	1.29	1.0	1.13
Unique data-types	141 (77%)	235 (100%)	169 (88%)

designed to group related operations. However, the assisted migration approach uses an automatic process to select which operations go to a port-type. In our case study, we found that when several related operations used the same unrelated routines, such as text-formatting routines, the Assisted Migration approach suggested that these routines were also a candidate operation for that service. This resulted in services that had port-types with several related operation, and one or two unrelated operations.

Although the assisted migration has a step to eliminate WSDL document anti-pattern causes, some of the generated WSDL documents were affected by some anti-patterns. This might be for two reasons, the first one is that the assisted migration is an iterative process and we only performed one iteration. The second reason is that the OO refactorings are not enough to remove all the anti-pattern causes. For instance, the enclosed data model anti-pattern usually results from the tool used for generating WSDL documents, when this tool does not support separating the XSD definitions in another file, regardless how the source code implementing the associated service is refactored. In both cases, further research is needed to fully assess the capabilities of the assisted migration.

Data Model Analysis

Data model management is crucial in data-centric software systems such as the one under study. Therefore, we further analyzed the data-types produced by each migration approach. Table 9 shows metrics that depict the data-types definitions

obtained using the different migration approaches. This table has a special focus on which percentage of the data-type are defined more than once, which is undesirable because it hinders data-type definitions reuse. The first clear difference was the number of data-types defined. The Direct Migration data set contained 182 different data-types and 73% of them were defined only once. Since the associated WSDL documents did not share data-type definitions, many of the types were duplicated across different WSDL documents. In contrast, all the 235 unique data-types were defined for the WSDL documents of the Indirect Migration data set. Among this set, 104 data-types represented business objects, including 39 defined as simple types (mostly enumerations) and 65 defined as complex types, whereas 131 were elements used for compliance with Web Service Interoperability standards (WS-I)[6]. Finally, 196 data-types were defined in the Assisted Migration data set. From these 191 data-types, 116 definitions were business objects (34 simple types + 82 complex types), while 75 definitions were elements used for WS-I compliance reasons.

The WS-I defines rules for making Web Services interoperable between different platforms. One of these rules is that message parts always should use XSD elements, although according to the Web Service specification message parts might use XSD elements or XSD types. For example, Listing 1 shows a data-type defined using a complex type, and the element shown in Listing 2 wraps the complex type.

Regarding to data-type repetitions, the Direct Migration data set included 182 data-types definitions of which 133 where unique. This means that

Listing 1. Complex type definition example

```
<xsd:complexType name="Cuil">
<xsd:sequence>
<!-- Preffix -->
<xsd:element name="prefijo" type="tns:CuilPrefijo"/>
<!-- Identity document -->
<xsd:element ref="tns:Documento"/>
<!-- Control (validation) digit -->
<xsd:element name="digitoControl" type="tns:CuilDigito"/>
</xsd:sequence>
</xsd:complexType>
```

Listing 2. Wrapper element definition example

```
<xsd:element name="cuil" type="ns:Cuil"/>
```

27% of the definitions were not necessary and could be substituted by other data-type definitions. In contrast, the Indirect Migration data set comprised 235 data-types—all of them were unique—meaning that the data-types were well defined and correctly shared across the associated WSDL documents. Finally, the Assisted Migration data set had 191 data-types, and 169 of them were unique. Therefore, Assisted Migration generated WSDL documents almost as good as the the ones generated by the indirect migration. To sum up, the Direct Migration, Indirect Migration and the Assisted Migration data sets had 1.36, 1, and 1.13 data-type definitions per effective data-type.

The fact that the WSDL documents of the Indirect Migration data-set had fewer data-type definitions for representing business objects (104) than the others (i.e. 182 for the Direct Migration WSDL documents and 116 for the Assisted Migration WSDL documents), indicates a better level of data model reutilization and a proper utilization of the XSD complex and element constructors to be WS-I compliant. However, notice that the Assisted Migration and the Indirect Migration data-sets almost included the same number of business objects.

Finally, we studied how the different services belonging to Indirect Migration and Assisted Migration data sets reused the data-types. We intentionally left out the services generated by the direct migration because they did not share data-types among individual services. Figure 3 depicts a graph in which services and data-types are nodes, and each edge represents a use relationship between a service and a data-type. An evident feature in both graphs is that there was a data-type that is used by most of the services. This data-type is CUIL, which is the main identifier for a person. The main difference between the graphs is that the one belonging to the Indirect Migration is a weakly connected graph without "islands," while the Assisted Migration graph is a disconnected graph. This happened because the assisted migration is not as good as exhaustively detecting candidate reusable data-types by hand. Despite of this, only 2 services were not connected to the biggest graph, which means that the ability of assisted migration to detect data-type reuse is fairly good.

FUTURE RESEARCH DIRECTIONS

We are at present extending our work in several directions. First, we are refining the heuristics of our tool so as to make them more accurate. Second, we are planning to enforce our findings by using other legacy systems. As a starting point, we will use an RM-COBOL system that comprises 319 programs and 201828 lines of code. Third, we will investigate whether our ideas hold for legacy systems written in other languages, such as in C or Java. Lastly, even when we found that using direct migration certainly has incidence in service quality at the service frontier level, intuitively many WSDL anti-patterns might be actually introduced by the tools employed to build the corresponding WSDL documents. Indeed, recently, we have shown that there is a statistical correlation between the WSDL anti-patterns present in a SOA frontier depending on the code-first WSDL generation tool being employed (Ordiales Coscia, et al., 2011). We

Figure 3. Data-type reuse comparison

Indirect migration data-type reuse

Assisted migration data-type reuse

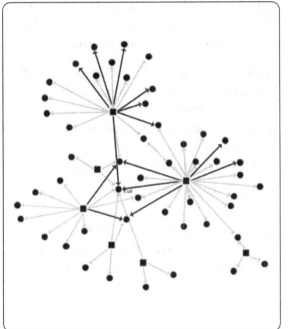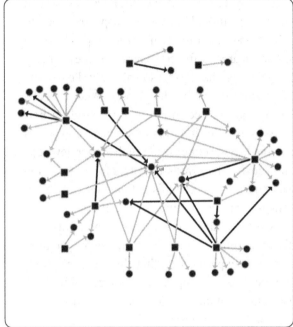

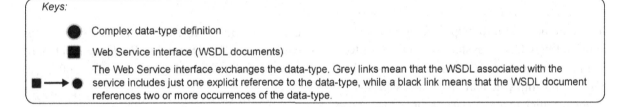

Keys:

● Complex data-type definition

■ Web Service interface (WSDL documents)

The Web Service interface exchanges the data-type. Grey links mean that the WSDL associated with the service includes just one explicit reference to the data-type, while a black link means that the WSDL document references two or more occurrences of the data-type.

are therefore planning to extend this analysis to other languages and therefore WSDL construction tools. Our utmost aim is to determine how much WSDL anti-patterns occurrences are explained by the approach to migration itself, and how much of them depend on the WSDL tools used.

Another research direction is taking into account other design service quality metrics (e.g. Gebhart & Abeck, 2011) for improving the results of applying the assisted migration. These metrics might be used for assisting developers to make decisions when they are performing the manual part of the assisted migration. For instance, these metrics can be used to identify real services from a list of candidate services.

CONCLUSION

Nowadays, organizations are more and more faced with the need of modernizing their legacy systems to newer platforms. Particularly, current legacy systems are mostly written in COBOL, whereas the target paradigm for migrating these systems is commonly SOA (Service-Oriented Architecture) due to its widely recognized benefits in terms interoperability and reusability. A question that arises is, however, which is the best way to painlessly moving from a legacy system to exploit the advantages of SOA, since migration is in general an arduous endeavor for any organization.

In this chapter, through a real-world case study involving the migration of an old CICS/COBOL system to SOA and .NET, we have shown that the traditional "fast and cheap" approach to migration—i.e. direct migration—produced a not-so-clear SOA frontier. Therefore, the resulting services were hard to reason about and consume by client application developers. Alternatively, through an indirect migration approach, a better SOA frontier in terms of service quality was obtained, at the expense of much higher development costs. The common ground for comparison was basically an established catalog of WSDL anti-patterns (Rodriguez, et al., 2010c) that are known to hinder service understandability and discoverability. All in all, an interesting finding from this experience is that there is a relationship between the approach to migration to SOA used and the number of anti-patterns found in the resulting SOA frontiers.

Motivated by the high costs of indirectly migrating that system by hand, we also proposed a semi-automatic tool to help development teams in migrating COBOL systems to SOA. Our tool comprises a number of heuristics that detect bad design and implementation practices in legacy systems, which in turn serve as a mean to propose early code refactorings so that the final SOA frontier is free from as much WSDL anti-patterns occurrences as possible. To evaluate the approach, we used the CICS/COBOL system mentioned above. In the end, results were encouraging, since migration costs were dramatically reduced and service quality was very acceptable and close to that of indirect migration.

REFERENCES

Alahmari, S., Zaluska, E., & Roure, D. D. (2010). A service identification framework for legacy system migration into SOA. In *Proceedings of the IEEE International Conference on Services Computing*, (pp. 614–617). IEEE Computer Society.

Almonaies, A., Cordy, J., & Dean, T. (2010). Legacy system evolution towards service-oriented architecture. In *Proceedings of the International Workshop on SOA Migration and Evolution (SOME)*, (pp. 53-62). Madrid, Spain: OFFIS.

Battaglia, M., Savoia, G., & Favaro, J. (1998). Renaissance: A method to migrate from legacy to immortal software systems. In *Proceedings of the 2nd Euromicro Conference on Software Maintenance and Reengineering (CSMR 1998)*, (p. 197). Washington, DC: IEEE Computer Society.

Beaton, J., Jeong, S. Y., Xie, Y., Jack, J., & Myers, B. A. (2008). Usability challenges for enterprise service-oriented architecture APIs. In *Proceedings of the IEEE Symposium on Visual Languages and Human-Centric Computing (VL/HCC)*, (pp. 193–196): IEEE Computer Society.

Bichler, M., & Lin, K.-J. (2006). Service-oriented computing. *Computer*, *39*(3), 99–101. doi:10.1109/MC.2006.102

Blake, M. B., & Nowlan, M. F. (2008). Taming web services from the wild. *IEEE Internet Computing*, *12*(5), 62–69. doi:10.1109/MIC.2008.112

Brodie, M. L., & Stonebrake, M. (1993). *DARWIN: On the incremental migration of legacy information system. Technical Report*. Berkeley, CA: University of California.

Crasso, M., Rodriguez, J. M., Zunino, A., & Campo, M. (2010). Revising WSDL documents: Why and how. *IEEE Internet Computing*, *14*(5), 30–38. doi:10.1109/MIC.2010.81

Erickson, J., & Siau, K. (2008). Web service, service-oriented computing, and service-oriented architecture: Separating hype from reality. *Journal of Database Management*, *19*(3), 42–54. doi:10.4018/jdm.2008070103

Fan, J., & Kambhampati, S. (2005). A snapshot of public web services. *SIGMOD Record*, *34*(1), 24–32. doi:10.1145/1058150.1058156

Fowler, M. (1999). *Refactorings in alphabetical order*. Retrieved March 23, 2012, from http://www.refactoring.com/catalog/index.html

Gebhart, M., & Abeck, S. (2011). Metrics for evaluating service designs based on SoaML. *International Journal on Advances in Software*, *4*, 61–75.

Ionita, A. D., Catapano, A., Giuroiu, S., & Florea, M. (2008). Service oriented system for business cooperation. In *Proceedings of the 2nd International Workshop on Systems Development in SOA Environments, SDSOA 2008*, (pp. 13–18). New York, NY: ACM Press.

Leinecker, R. C. (2000). *Com+ unleashed*. Sams.

Lewis, G., Morris, E., Simanta, S., & Smith, D. (2011). Service orientation and systems of systems. *IEEE Software*, *28*(1), 58–63. doi:10.1109/MS.2011.15

Lewis, G., Morris, E., & Smith, D. (2005). Migration of legacy components to service-oriented architectures. *Journal of Software Technology*, *8*, 14–23.

Li, S.-H., Huang, S.-M., Yen, D. C., & Chang, C.-C. (2007). Migrating legacy information systems to web services architecture. *Journal of Database Management*, *18*(4), 1–25. doi:10.4018/jdm.2007100101

Litoiu, M. (2004). Migrating to web services: A performance engineering approach. *Journal of Software Maintenance and Evolution: Research and Practice*, *16*(1-2), 51–70. doi:10.1002/smr.285

Mateos, C., Crasso, M., Zunino, A., & Campo, M. (2010). Separation of concerns in service-oriented applications based on pervasive design patterns. In *Proceedings of Web Technology Track (WT) - 25th ACM Symposium on Applied Computing (SAC 2010)*, (pp. 2509-2513). Sierre, Switzerland: ACM Press.

Ordiales Coscia, J. L., Mateos, C., Crasso, M., & Zunino, A. (2011). Avoiding wsdl bad practices in code-first web services. In *Proceedings of the 12th Argentine Symposium on Software Engineering (ASSE2011)*, (pp. 1–12). ASSE.

Rodriguez, J. M., Crasso, M., Mateos, C., Zunino, A., & Campo, M. (2010a). The EasySOC project: A rich catalog of best practices for developing web service applications. In *Proceedings of Jornadas Chilenas de Computación (JCC) - INFONOR 2010* (pp. 33–42). Antofagasta, Chile: SCC. doi:10.1109/SCCC.2010.12

Rodriguez, J. M., Crasso, M., Zunino, A., & Campo, M. (2010b). Automatically detecting opportunities for web service descriptions improvement. In *Proceedings of the 10th IFIP WG 6.11 Conference on e-Business, e-Services, and e-Society (I3E 2010)*, (vol 432, pp. 139-150). Buenos Aires, Argentina: Springer.

Rodriguez, J. M., Crasso, M., Zunino, A., & Campo, M. (2010c). Improving web service descriptions for effective service discovery. *Science of Computer Programming*, *75*(11), 1001–1021. doi:10.1016/j.scico.2010.01.002

Sneed, H. (2009). A pilot project for migrating COBOL code to web services. *International Journal on Software Tools for Technology Transfer*, *11*, 441–451. doi:10.1007/s10009-009-0128-z

Sneed, H. (2010). Measuring web service interfaces. In *Proceedings of the 12th IEEE International Symposium on Web Systems Evolution*, (pp. 111–115). IEEE Press.

Stroulia, E., & Wang, Y. (2005). Structural and semantic matching for assessing web service similarity. *International Journal of Cooperative Information Systems*, *14*(4), 407–438. doi:10.1142/S0218843005001213

Yourdon, E., & Constantine, L. L. (1979). *Structured design: Fundamentals of a discipline of computer program and systems design*. Upper Saddle River, NJ: Prentice-Hall, Inc.

Zillmann, C., Winter, A., Herget, A., Teppe, W., Theurer, M., & Fuhr, A. … Zimmermann, Y. (2011). The soamig process model in industrial applications. In *Proceedings of the 2011 15th European Conference on Software Maintenance and Reengineering, CSMR 2011,* (pp. 339–342). Washington, DC: IEEE Computer Society.

ADDITIONAL READING

Adams, B., Schutter, K. D., Zaidman, A., Demeyer, S., Tromp, H., & Meuter, W. D. (2009). Using aspect orientation in legacy environments for reverse engineering using dynamic analysis: An industrial experience report. *Journal of Systems and Software, 82*(4), 668–684. doi:10.1016/j.jss.2008.09.031

Alahmari, S., Zaluska, E., & Roure, D. D. (2010). A service identification framework for legacy system migration into SOA. In *Proceedings of the International Conference on Services Computing,* (pp. 614-617). IEEE Computer Society.

Aversano, L., Canfora, G., Cimitile, A., & de Lucia, A. (2001). Migrating legacy systems to the web: An experience report. In *Proceedings of the Fifth European Conference on Software Maintenance and Reengineering, CSMR 2001* (p. 148). Washington, DC: IEEE Computer Society.

Balasubramaniam, S., Lewis, G. A., Morris, E., Simanta, S., & Smith, D. B. (2009). Challenges for assuring quality of service in a service-oriented environment. In *Proceedings of the 2009 ICSE Workshop on Principles of Engineering Service Oriented Systems, PESOS 2009,* (pp. 103-106). Washington, DC: IEEE Computer Society.

Baski, D., & Misra, S. (2011). Metrics suite for maintainability of extensible markup language web services. *IET Software, 5*(3), 320–341. doi:10.1049/iet-sen.2010.0089

Beaton, J., Jeong, S. Y., Xie, Y., Jack, J., & Myers, B. A. (2008). Usability challenges for enterprise service-oriented architecture APIs. In *Proceedings of the IEEE Symposium on Visual Languages and Human-Centric Computing (VL/HCC),* (pp. 193-196). IEEE Computer Society.

Canfora, G., Fasolino, A. R., Frattolillo, G., & Tramontana, P. (2008). A wrapping approach for migrating legacy system interactive functionalities to service oriented architectures. *Journal of Systems and Software, 81*(4), 463–480. doi:10.1016/j.jss.2007.06.006

Channabasavaiah, K., Holley, K., Services, I. G., Tuggle, E. M., & Group, I. S. (2004). *Migrating to a service-oriented architecture. Technical Report.* New York, NY: IBM.

Chung, S., Davalos, S., An, J. B. C., & Iwahara, K. (2008). Legacy to web migration: service-oriented software reengineering methodology. *International Journal of Services Sciences, 1,* 333–365. doi:10.1504/IJSSCI.2008.021769

Flores, A., Cechich, A., Zunino, A., & Usaola, M. (2010). Testing-based selection method for integrability on service-oriented applications. In *Proceedings of the Fifth International Conference on Software Engineering Advances (ICSEA),* (pp. 373-379). ICSEA.

Gao, S. S., Sperberg-McQueen, C. M., & Thompson, H. S. (2009). *XML schema definition language (XSD) 1.1 part 1: Structures*. Retrieved from http://www.w3.org/TR/xmlschema11-1

Geet, J. V., & Demeyer, S. (2007). Lightweight visualisations of COBOL code for supporting migration to SOA. *ECEASST, 8,* 80–87.

Geet, J. V., & Demeyer, S. (2010). Reverse engineering on the mainframe: Lessons learned from "in vivo" research. *IEEE Software*, *27*, 30–36. doi:10.1109/MS.2010.65

Gudgin, M., Hadley, M., Mendelsohn, N., Moreau, J.-J., Nielsen, H. F., Karmarkar, A., & Lafon, Y. (2007). *SOAP version 1.2 part 1: Messaging framework*. Technical Report. W3C Consortium.

Lewis, G., Morris, E., Simanta, S., & Smith, D. (2011). Service orientation and systems of systems. *IEEE Software*, *28*(1), 58–63. doi:10.1109/MS.2011.15

Mateos, C., Crasso, M., Zunino, A., & Coscia, J. L. O. (2011). Detecting WSDL bad practices in code-first web services. *International Journal of Web and Grid Services*, *7*(4), 357–387. doi:10.1504/IJWGS.2011.044710

Oracle. (2009). *Mainframe rehosting with Oracle Tuxedo: Accelerating cost reduction and application modernization*. Technical Report. Oracle.

Page. (2012). *N. P. S. C.* Retrieved from http://code.google.com/p/naca/

Papazoglou, M. P., & Heuvel, W.-J. (2007). Service oriented architectures: Approaches, technologies and research issues. *The VLDB Journal*, *16*, 389–415. doi:10.1007/s00778-007-0044-3

Pórez-Castillo, R., de Guzmán, I. G.-R., & Piattini, M. (2011). Knowledge discovery metamodel-iso/iec 19506: A standard to modernize legacy systems. *Computer Standards & Interfaces*, *33*(6), 519–532. doi:10.1016/j.csi.2011.02.007

Rodriguez, J. M., Crasso, M., Mateos, C., Zunino, A., & Campo, M. (2012). Bottom-up and top-down COBOL system migration to Web Services: An experience report. *IEEE Internet Computing*, *99*.

Sneed, H. (2009). A pilot project for migrating COBOL code to web services. *International Journal on Software Tools for Technology Transfer*, *11*, 441–451. doi:10.1007/s10009-009-0128-z

Sneed, H. (2010). Measuring web service interfaces. In *Proceedings of the 12th IEEE International Symposium on Web Systems Evolution*, (pp. 111 -115). IEEE Press.

Torchiano, M., Penta, M. D., Ricca, F., Lucia, A. D., & Lanubile, F. (2011). Migration of information systems in the Italian industry: A state of the practice survey. *Information and Software Technology*, *53*(1), 71–86. doi:10.1016/j.infsof.2010.08.002

Van Engelen, R. A., & Gallivan, K. A. (2002). The gsoap toolkit for web services and peer-to-peer computing networks. In *Proceedings of the 2nd IEEE/ACM International Symposium on Cluster Computing and the Grid*, (pp. 128-135). IEEE Computer Society.

KEY TERMS AND DEFINITIONS

Code-First: A method for automatically deriving services interfaces from the implementation of these services.

Contract-First: A method for manually defining services interfaces.

Direct Migration: An 1-to-1 approach to migrate main parts of a legacy system.

Indirect Migration: An approach to migrate main parts of a legacy system by re-engineering them.

Legacy System Migration: The process of modernizing a legacy software system using newer technologies or computing paradigms.

Service Interface Design: The act of logically arrange and describe the functionality provided by a service.

Services-Oriented Architecture: A software architecture in which main components are loosely-coupled services.

Web Services: Technologies for materializing a services-oriented architecture using the Internet.

ENDNOTES

1. http://www.gartner.com

2. SLOC metric for COBOL source code was calculated using the SLOCCount utility available at http://www.dwheeler.com/sloc-count, which does not count commented lines.

3. MyBatis: http://www.mybatis.org/dotnet.html

4. IBM's DB2Connect: http://www-01.ibm.com/software/data/db2/db2connect/

5. Professional and paid versions of the two first tools were used, whereas a standard and free version of soapUI was employed.

6. Basic Profile Version 1.1: http://www.ws-i.org/Profiles/BasicProfile-1.1.html

Chapter 7
Model–Driven Software Migration:
Process Model, Tool Support, and Application

Andreas Fuhr
University of Koblenz-Landau, Germany

Tassilo Horn
University of Koblenz-Landau, Germany

Andreas Winter
Carl von Ossietzky University, Germany

Uwe Kaiser
pro et con GmbH, Germany

Uwe Erdmenger
pro et con GmbH, Germany

Volker Riediger
University of Koblenz-Landau, Germany

Werner Teppe
Amadeus Germany GmbH, Germany

ABSTRACT

Established software systems usually represent important assets, which are worth preserving in new software structures, to combine already proven functionality with the benefits of new technologies. The SOAMIG project is aimed at developing an adaptable migration process model with an accompanying tool support based on model-driven technologies. This process model, which combines reverse and forward engineering techniques, was applied in two different case studies on migrating a monolithic software system to service-oriented architecture and to a transformation-based language migration from COBOL to Java.

INTRODUCTION

Most commercially built information systems are based on traditional technologies preventing them from unfolding their full potential in future software development. Service-Oriented Archi-tectures (SOA) (Arsanjani, et al., 2008; Gold, Knight, Mohan, & Munro, 2004) provide a modern and promising approach to increase flexibility in software adaptation, maintenance and evolution by referring to the underlying business processes to be supported by the software systems. Necessary functionality is specified by services which

DOI: 10.4018/978-1-4666-2488-7.ch007

Copyright © 2013, IGI Global. Copying or distributing in print or electronic forms without written permission of IGI Global is prohibited.

are implemented by loosely coupled components that can easily be rearranged to fulfill changing user needs.

Current software systems, already established and time-proven, are not implemented in a service-oriented manner. These legacy systems usually provide software functionality by monolithic and deeply interwoven modules. Without significant reengineering, these systems will not benefit from Service-oriented Architectures. Referring to the staged model for the software life cycle (Rajlich & Bennett, 2000), appropriate techniques are requested to keep them in evolution instead of passing them to service or replacing them.

Software migration, i.e., transferring existing software systems to a new environment, provides elaborated methods and techniques allowing already established software systems to benefit from the advantages of new technologies. Migration does not change the functionality of the original systems; it only changes their embedding in appropriate environments. Although migration activities use the same technologies as reengineering activities, migration and reengineering have to be distinguished from each other. Whereas reengineering focuses on improving software quality, migration only focuses on conserving legacy systems in new environments (Sneed, Wolf, & Heilmann, 2010). Migrating legacy systems to SOA, as depicted in this section, allows the reuse of already established and proven software assets and their integration with newly created services, including their further evolution (Fuhr, Horn, Riediger, & Winter, 2011). Orchestrating migrated and newly realized service components to support new business processes is done in additional projects; the migration only enables the reuse of legacy functionality in a new service-oriented embedding. Migration to a new environment is not viewed as activity to improve code quality. This allows clearly separating migration, i.e., transformation, tasks from reengineering, i.e., quality improvement, tasks. Nevertheless, migration projects should be framed by reengineering

projects to improve the legacy's quality prior to (pre-renovation) and the migrated system's quality after migration (post-renovation).

Migrating to SOA addresses architecture migration, which describes essentially reworking the software structure. Here, software assets have to be identified and abstracted to services supporting business processes. Furthermore, code has to be reorganized in new service components implementing the extracted services. These migrations deal with various aspects of software systems: data and databases, code and users and system interfaces are affected during migration. Occasionally, migration to SOA comes with language migration where—next to structural adaptations—programming languages like COBOL to Java are changed as well.

Migrating software systems requires a deliberated process taking into account the different aspects of migration projects. This process has to be supported by an adequate migration tool support. Empirical studies in the METAMORPHOS project (de Lucia & Tortora, 2010) impressively demonstrated the increase of productivity in migration projects by using tailored migration tool suites instead of traditional software development frameworks. SOAMIG's objective was to define such a process and to present and evaluate a corresponding tool chain. Here, the main purpose was to show its applicability. Discussion, assessment, and improvement of migration and reengineering efforts were not part of the SOAMIG project. The improvement of maintenance efforts based on appropriate methodology and tooling is described elsewhere (see e.g. Borchers, 1997; de Lucia & Tortora, 2010).

Current process models in software development are primarily focused on the initial development of software systems. More modern, iterative and agile approaches like Unified Process (Kruchten, 2003), Extreme Programming (Beck & Andres, 2004) or SCRUM (Schwaber, 2004) view maintenance and migration activities only as additional iterations. These process models do not consider reverse engineering activities like comprehending programs, identifying and evaluating reusable software assets and legacy conversion. Hence, there is also no significant tool support given for migration activities. Furthermore, migration projects have to deal with legacy and target architecture, including their interdependencies. Particularly in SOA migration, these architectures have to be aligned to business processes (Fuhr, et al., 2011; de Lucia, Francese, Scanniello, & Tortora, 2008). In the same vein, approaches for developing Service-oriented Architectures only focus on its initial creation. Here, e.g., SOMA (Arsanjani, et al., 2008) presents an expandable approach, which was partially completed to include migration support by using model-driven techniques (Fuhr, et al., 2011). Khadka et al. (2011) merge SOA development processes and extend them by feasibility analysis techniques. The V-Model XT (IABG, 2009) provides a specialized project type merging enhancement and migration. Here, legacy analyses and the definition of a migration strategy are considered, but migration in V-Model XT only focuses on data migration.

Specialized migration approaches only address certain facets of migration projects. Accordingly, tool support is—if presented—also restricted to these facets. The Chicken Little approach (Brodie & Stonebraker, 1995) defines an incremental process for migration of software systems in contrast to Cold-Turkey approaches, where migrations are performed and delivered at one go. Chicken Little focuses on long-lasting migration projects and is based on running legacy and migrated systems in parallel by using appropriate gateways and wrappers, which might lead to additional complexity of migration projects. Fleurey et al. (2007) present a general model-driven migration approach not focused on migration to SOA. Like the V-Model XT, the Butterfly approach (Wu, et al., 1997) focuses on data migration. The reengineering factory approach by Jens Borchers (1997) targets the coordination of outsourced migration projects and SMART (Lewis & Smith, 2008) assists in planning migration projects. A conceptual framework to SOA migration similar to Winter and Ziemann (2007) is being developed in the SAPIENSA project (Razavian & Lago, 2010; Razavian, Nguyen, Lago, & van den Heuvel, 2010). Both view legacy and target systems on code, architecture, and business process/requirements level and pursue a model-based migration strategy. Oldevik et al. (2011) present a model-driven SOA migration approach lacking a specialized tool support for reverse engineering activities. The ReMIP (Reference Migration Process) (Gipp & Winter, 2007; Sneed, et al., 2010) introduces a general and adaptable process model for software migration. The migration process presented in Section 2 substantiates the ReMIP, complements appropriate tool support and shows its application in industrial case studies (see Sections 3-5).

The SOAMIG project aimed at providing a general and adaptable migration process model including a customizable tool suite supporting the migration process. In particular, SOAMIG supports architecture migration to Service-oriented Architectures and language migration. In contrast to wrapping-based migrations which hamper further evolution of the migrated systems, SOAMIG considers transformation-based language migration. Transformation-based language migration converts legacy systems completely into a new (language) environment, without keeping the legacy in its original form and adding more complexity by further different languages. The SOAMIG project consortium consisted of industrial and academic technology providers, research institutes and industrial application providers, which allowed practical validation of the SOAMIG process in two different migrations (Zillmann, et al., 2011). The SOAMIG project was partly funded by the German Federal Ministry of Education and Research program for small and medium size enterprises (Grant no. 01IS09017A-D).

The SOAMIG approach follows a model-based manner (Winter & Ziemann, 2007) with respect to the SEI horseshoe model (Kazman, Woods,

& Carrière, 1998). On code level, on platform specific model level (architecture) and on conceptual level (requirements), software artifacts of the legacy and target system are represented by appropriate models (Figure 1). In the case of Service-oriented Architectures, a target system's architecture refers to a typical SOA-layered architecture consisting of enterprise service layer, business process layer and view layer with their corresponding implementations on code level. Target system requirements models represent the business processes.

In SOA, the target systems architecture strongly refers to the supported business processes. Thus, the target architecture in a SOA migration is (partially) predefined by the given processes and the according service specifications. Depending on further individual economic and technical constraints of the migration project, target architecture design requires adaptations

when orchestrating the system. In a transformation-based migration, realization of the required service components exploits the legacy code.

Reverse engineering activities are used to derive higher-level abstractions of a legacy's source or to verify if already existing or newly recovered documentation fits the existing implementation. In a SOA migration, this information is used to identify both: the services to be supported by the target systems analysis model and their implementation in the legacy code. In the target system, these extracts of the legacy code will be transformed to service components originating from the target's requirements model by classical forward engineering steps. To provide integrated analysis on all levels of abstraction in legacy and target systems, a common repository is used which conforms to an integrated metamodel covering all relevant modeling notations including programming languages.

Figure 1. SOAMIG horseshoe model

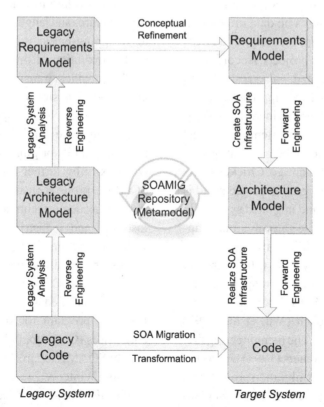

The remainder of this chapter is organized as follows. Section 2 presents the iterative and adaptable SOAMIG process model and introduces the main phases and relevant activities in software migration projects. A generic tool suite supporting this process and synchronizing all reverse engineering and migration technologies by a common repository is shown in Section 3. Practical experiences with the SOAMIG process and its corresponding tool suite are presented in Sections 4 and 5. Section 4 shows its application in the RAIL case study which deals with architecture migration from a monolithic Java system to SOA. A language migration is presented in Section 5. Here, a COBOL system that already partially follows a service-oriented thinking is migrated to a Java implementation to allow future software evolution in a more modern language environment. Section 6 concludes the introduction of SOAMIG.

THE SOAMIG PROCESS MODEL

Migrating legacy systems, in particular towards Service-oriented Architectures, is a complex task requiring a structured approach. The SOAMIG process model has been developed by industrial practitioners and researchers to structure software migration projects (Zillmann, et al., 2011). In this section, the SOAMIG process is described.

During the life-cycle of a migration project, four different phases are distinguished in the SOAMIG process: Preparation, Conceptualization, Migration and Transition (Figure 2).

Each phase collates various disciplines (see Section 2.2) highlighting activities during each phase. In the following, the four phases and their disciplines are presented.

Four Phases of the SOAMIG Process

The SOAMIG Process is divided into four phases—Preparation, Conceptualization, Migration, and Transition—defining important organizational steps during a migration project.

The Preparation phase deals with setting up the project and with preparing legacy systems for migration by optionally renovating them. The current status of legacy systems may prohibit migration efforts. Therefore, legacy code has to be reengineered in Pre-Renovation, by using common technologies to improve the quality of the legacy and to allow smoother migration. During the Project Set Up, organizational aspects of the project are managed. This discipline includes activities like defining project goals, work packages

Figure 2. Four phases of the SOAMIG process and their disciplines

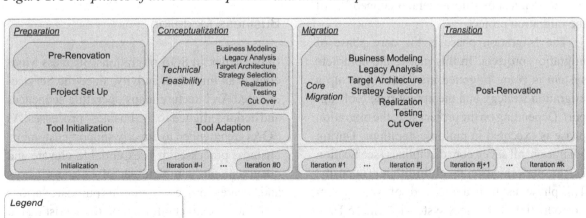

and schedules or managing resources. Migration projects require a high level of automation by appropriate tool sets. During Tool Initialization, new tools are developed and already existing tools are prepared. Detailed tool adaptation with respect to current project needs is a key activity in migration projects; it is addressed during the Conceptualization phase. The Preparation phase results in a clearly differentiated legacy system ready for migration, a sufficient migration plan and an initial migration tool suite.

The Conceptualization phase deals with checking the feasibility of the migration project by migrating an exemplary part of the system (technical cut-through). During the Technical Feasibility discipline, the core disciplines of the SOAMIG process (see Section 2.2) are being performed. Borchers (1997) already showed that 70-75% of migration activities are independent from concrete project needs allowing a broad automation by eligible migration factories. A key factor for successful and efficient migration projects is the project-specific adaptation of the migration factory to provide almost full automation. These necessary Tool Adaptations are being done in parallel to assessing the technical feasibility by migrating selected small but representative subsets of the legacy system. The Conceptualization phase concludes with a tailored and validated tool suite allowing mostly automatic migration. In addition, it shows the general practicability of the migration project.

The Migration phase is the core phase of migration projects. In this phase, the complete system is being migrated after having set up a migration strategy and the appropriate tool support. Depending on the project size, the migration phase is executed in multiple iterations. During Migration, all seven core disciplines (see Section 2.2) are performed iteratively in different intensity. This phase results in a migrated software system in production. The legacy system is turned off and archived to allow backtracking to former decisions based on the legacy, if required.

Finally, during the Transition phase, quality improvement of the migrated system is performed to clean up the migrated code. A Post-Renovation might be necessary as some migration techniques may reduce future maintainability of the system. Therefore, it could be necessary to reengineer the migrated system—e.g., by refactorings—to enhance software quality again. The transition phase results in a migrated and improved software system.

Core Disciplines of the SOAMIG Process

During Conceptualization and Migration, the seven SOAMIG core disciplines are performed to migrate (parts of) the legacy system. Figure 3 shows the seven core disciplines of the SOAMIG process. In the SOAMIG approach, all disciplines exchange artifacts with an integrated repository that stores all relevant information in an integrated model. The disciplines can be brought into a loose, logical order by reading Figure 3 clockwise starting from the top (Business Modeling). In real projects, however, the order may change to reflect dynamic project needs.

A general description of each core discipline as well as a more detailed description of the associated activities of each discipline is given in the following sections.

Business Modeling

In particular, in SOA migrations Business Modeling is an important activity, since the Service-oriented Architecture maps operating sequences and actions aligned to the business processes. As SOAs are intended to directly support customers' business processes, it is essential to elevate and document the complete set of business actors and business processes. For this purpose, various activities to extract information from existing but not necessarily manifested business knowledge have to be performed:

Figure 3. Seven SOAMIG core disciplines (Winter & Ziemann, 2007)

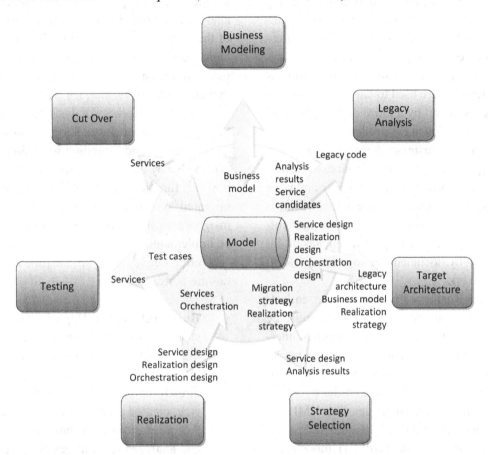

- **Analyze Legacy Business Model:** If available, legacy business models are analyzed. Without doubt, legacy business models are useful to identify business processes. However, if these models are deprecated and do not fit reality anymore, they can become distracting and might lead to incorrect business models. Therefore, actuality of legacy business models must be confirmed, e.g., by comparing concrete system behavior with documented business processes.
- **Analyze Legacy Test Cases:** If available, legacy test cases and test case documentations are analyzed. They are promising sources to identify business processes. Test cases in acceptance tests typically define user task scenarios and therefore describe how the system is being used. Business processes can be extracted from these scenarios.
- **Analyze Legacy Documentation:** If available, other types of legacy documentation are analyzed. Various types of legacy documentation are suited for collecting business processes, e.g.:
  ◦ User documentation of the system,
  ◦ Training material for the system,
  ◦ General guidelines for employees about how to do their job right.

Analyzing this documentation can reveal additional business processes, keeping in account the usual obsolescence of this kind of information.

- **Discover Legacy Functionality:** Using the legacy system to discover functionality may be suited to identify what business processes are supported by the software. The results are documented in workflow models that are used to enrich the business process model by a more detailed view on the steps of business processes.

- **Interview Business Actors:** In addition to (possibly) existing business models and test cases, business processes must be gathered by analyzing the actual business operations. Business operations are collected by interviewing different stakeholders and by documenting how they perform their work.

- **Model Business Processes:** After collecting all business processes, they must be modeled in one common machine-understandable format. The final business model will contain information on which activities are performed in what order by which actor. Modeling languages like UML 2.0 activity diagrams or Business Process Modeling Notation (BPMN) models are suited to design the business model. The business processes are enriched by the workflow model and build a detailed view on the workflow of the business processes by that.

In addition, this discipline includes the initialization of the integrated repository. Metamodels to describe the business modeling language are needed and the business model is parsed into the integrated repository.

Legacy Analysis

Legacy Analysis deals with exploring and understanding the legacy system. In order to understand the legacy, all available information like user or technical documentation, legacy test cases, legacy architecture description or legacy source code are analyzed (Teppe, 2010). As abstract descriptions of the system are often unavailable or outdated, legacy source code must be processed to extract useful information. For this purpose, static and dynamic analysis techniques are used.

In addition, Legacy Analysis deals with identifying service candidates. Service candidates are discovered by understanding what functionality is provided by the legacy system and by defining how this functionality should be provided by the migrated system as services. In addition, first insights are gained as to how these services could be implemented by reusing legacy code.

During Legacy Analysis, the following activities are performed.

- **Build Integrated Repository:** The first step is to extend the integrated repository that is used to store all necessary data as model. In SOA migrations, the repository already contains the business model that was created during Business Modeling. According to the information to be stored and analyzed (e.g., legacy code, legacy architecture or legacy test cases), metamodels describing the information are necessary. Parsers and extractors are needed to store all information into the integrated repository.

- **Analyze Legacy Code:** Static analysis helps extracting useful information from the integrated repository by querying the models. According to the project's needs, various static analysis techniques can be used to explore and comprehend the legacy system. Dynamic aspects also have to be included into the analysis to get a more complete understanding of the legacy system. Therefore, dynamic analysis techniques adapted to the requested information are used to enhance the understanding of the legacy system.

- **Analyze Workflow Model:** The workflows captured during Business Modeling document what business functionality is supported by the legacy system. This information can be used to identify service candidates that will later provide the same functionality. In particular, service candidates will be discovered by mapping business processes and workflows to program traces determined during dynamically analyzing the legacy code (see Section 4.2.2).

- **Reverse-Engineer Legacy Architecture:** Static and dynamic analysis techniques are used to reverse-engineer a complete architectural description of the legacy system. If necessary, the legacy architecture description can be modeled explicitly in this step. Together with the ideal target architecture, the legacy architecture spans the solution space to define the target design.

- **Identify Service Candidates:** The most important step in SOA migrations is to use the previously derived understanding of the legacy system to identify service candidates. Service candidates encapsulate functionality provided by the legacy system that may be required to be published as a service in the migrated system. For each service candidate, an initial specification of the service is created and trace links to the source of identification are drawn.

Service candidates can be identified by top-down approaches, bottom-up approaches or a combination of both (Arsanjani, et al., 2008). Top-down approaches like the ones described in Fareghzadeh (2008) and Kim, Kim, and Park (2008) analyze the business domain (e.g., business processes or business goals) to identify what services are required to support them. Bottom-up approaches like the ones described in Zhang, Liu, and Yang (2005) and Zhang and Yang (2004) analyze the legacy system to identify what functionality it provides and how this functionality could be encapsulated into service implementa-

tions. A combination of top-down and bottom-up paradigms leads to so-called meet-in-the middle approaches like the ones described in Alahmari, Zaluska, and de Roure (2010), Fuhr, Horn, and Riediger (2011b), and Ricca and Marchetto (2009). Here, information about the business domain is linked with information about the legacy system to identify service candidates.

The adequate technique for identifying service candidates depends on the migration project itself. Therefore, appropriate techniques should be selected and applied in this phase of the SOAMIG process according to the project.

Target Design

The target architecture is the architecture of the resulting software system. Finding a best suited target architecture has to deal with the legacy architecture and the required software support in its ideal target environment. Zillmann et al. (2010) introduce an iterative method for defining target architectures. The target architecture is iteratively approximated, starting from a technically ideal architecture and taking into account specific requirements from the legacy architecture to allow an economic migration. In a SOA migration, the target architecture consists of the service design, the realization design, and the orchestration design. The service design describes the interfaces of the required services. The realization design describes how to implement the services and the orchestration design specifies how to orchestrate them to support the business processes. The target architecture in language migration projects usually reflects the legacy architecture, if feasible with the new language. To ease both, the migration itself and later evolution of the resulting systems, runtime layers may be added.

During the Target Architecture discipline, the following activities are performed.

- **Analyze Business Processes (Top-Down Approach):** In a SOA migration starting with the business or rather the business processes means to define a target architecture, which matches perfectly the business needs and considers the new architecture paradigm SOA. Next to the architecture paradigm and the business needs, the new target architecture has to consider the existing legacy system and the (automated) migration from the legacy system to the new target system. The architectural hypotheses set up by defining the ideal target architecture have to be evaluated. If implementing these design hypotheses is too costly, the ideal architecture has to be converged to the legacy architecture, potentially losing benefits of the ideal target architecture.

- **Analyze Legacy System (Bottom-Up Approach):** Knowledge about the legacy system can also help to identify target architecture requirements. Hypotheses generated by analyzing the legacy system can also be used for iteratively creating the target architectures. Change requests for changing the target architecture definition are also created for hypotheses originating from legacy system analyses. The hypotheses have to be evaluated by experts.
- **Define Service Design:** Results of business process analysis and legacy system analysis support the definition of interfaces of services candidates, which have been identified during the Legacy Analysis discipline. The service design describes the interfaces of the services in the target architecture.
- **Define Realization Design:** The realization design describes how to implement the service interfaces defined in the previous activity. The realization design is mainly influenced by the realization strategy decision (see Section 2.2.4) about how to implement the services.
- **Define Orchestration Design:** The orchestration design defines how services are orchestrated to support the business processes. Message exchange between ser-

vices is modeled as well as the distribution of services and their access.

- **Restructure Legacy System:** If an architectural hypothesis from the top-down or bottom-up procedure cannot be implemented, the target architecture does not always need to be redesigned. Sometimes it is sensible to restructure the legacy system to enable migration to the target structure wanted. The legacy system has to be restructured to meet the requirements for (automated) transformation. This could be done for example by code restructuring or refactoring tasks.

Strategy Selection

During Strategy Selection, two main decisions are made:

1. How to perform the migration, and
2. How to realize each service.

These decisions are supported by analyzing the legacy system and are based on the project's specific needs. In this discipline, the following activities are performed.

- **Select Transition Strategy:** The first decision to be made is how to migrate the legacy system. This includes deciding what parts of the system should be migrated in the current iteration of the project. Possibilities are (Brodie & Stonebraker, 1995):
  - Migrate the complete system (Big Bang).
  - Migrate only parts of the system in multiple iterations (Chicken Little).

The migration strategy selected decides how the migrated system is deployed to the customer's environment. Migrating the complete system enforces a Big Bang cut over, that is, the legacy system is completely shut down while the migrated system is powered up as a whole. Migrating only parts of the system leads to a co-existence of old and new parts in the customer's environment (Sneed, et al., 2010). Migration to Service-oriented Architectures can be viewed as Chicken Little migration, where each migrated service builds a new increment and the SOA infrastructure serves as gateway structure.

- **Select Realization Strategy:** The second decision is about how the parts of the legacy system should be migrated. This decision can be divided into three strategy decisions about project realization, package realization and service realization.
- **Project Realization Strategy:** Decides how the overall project should be migrated. This strategy is a general strategy that should be followed where possible. However, if necessary, single packages or services can be migrated in a different way.
- **Package Realization Strategy:** Decides how each package or layer of the legacy system is migrated. In addition to the architecture migration towards a SOA, this includes finding strategies for additional aspects of the migration like hardware migration, system environment migration or development environment migration (Gimnich & Winter, 2005). For each package, strategies about how to migrate user interfaces (e.g., graphical user interfaces), data and the program code are needed.
- **Service Realization Strategy:** Finally decides how each service is implemented. As services should be loosely coupled components hiding their implementation to the environment, each service can be implemented in a different way without influencing its environment. Strategies for service realizations are (Wahli, et al., 2007):
  - ○ **Reimplementation:** The service functionality is created from scratch, based on functionality provided by the legacy system.
  - ○ **Wrapping:** A wrapper provides an interface to the new system and accesses legacy functionality directly.
  - ○ **Transformation:** Legacy code is transformed into a new technology to implement a service.
  - ○ **Buying:** Third party software or services are bought and provided as service to the migrated system.

Selecting one of these strategies for each service depends on the quality of the legacy code and the future use of the migrated code. Reimplementation leads to a new and contemporary implementation, but comes with the risks of all new implementations. Wrapping leads to fast results, but hampers future evolution by adding additional layers in different languages. Transformation results in services in contemporary language environments, but requires elaborated automatic converters. And buying relocates responsibility, but results in new dependencies. SOAMIG primarily focuses on transformation-based migration.

The realization strategies are fed back into the Target Architecture discipline and influence the target design there. The transition strategies are input to the Cut Over discipline and influence how to switch from legacy system to migrated system.

Realization

During Realization, services are implemented according to the realization design selected during Strategy Selection (see Section 2.2.4). During Realization, the following activities are performed.

- **Realize Service Design:** In SOA migrations the first step is to create the "external view" on the service. The external view includes the interface definitions (e.g., as WSDL specification) as well as the service description and service level agreements. Model-driven techniques can be used to transform the service design into the service interface specification.

- **Realize Business Functionality:** During this step, the "service stub" (the external view) is filled with business functionality. According to the realization strategy chosen during Strategy Selection (see Section 2.2.4), business functionality can be implemented by reimplementation, wrapping and transformation (Wahli, et al., 2007), if the legacy has to be preserved.

After implementing the business functionality, business functionality as well as external view are combined to the final service implementation. In addition, unit tests are performed to ensure the correct implementation of the services.

- **Realize Orchestration Design:** After implementing all services, they are orchestrated to establish the overall migrated system. Orchestration of migrated services to support new business processes is not part of a migration project, but is made possible by migrating the underlying services.

Testing

Testing deals with estimating the correctness of the overall system (system test) and with checking if the new system still behaves like the legacy system (regression tests). Unit tests are not covered in this phase anymore. Instead, they have already been performed during Realization (see Section 2.2.5). During Testing, the following activities are performed.

- **Perform System Tests:** System tests check if the overall system works together without failures. In SOAs, this includes testing the orchestration and composition

of services, the correct handling of messages or compliance with the service-level agreements.

- **Perform Regression Tests:** Regression tests ensure that the migrated system still behaves like the legacy system (as reminder: migrations aim at changing the technology without affecting the functionality).

- **Perform Performance Tests:** Performance tests check if the migrated system behaves like defined by quality criteria. This means for example that memory and CPU consumption are below defined values.

- **Perform Stress Tests:** Stress tests evaluate if the migrated system works correctly when receiving a high amount of messages in parallel or in a short time period. These tests can be executed best by test drivers or by a replay tool.

- **Perform Acceptance Tests:** Finally, the system is tested by the customer. All aspects of the system are tested (including e.g., the design of user interfaces). It is the customer's decision, whether the migrated system fulfills all requirements.

Cut Over

The Cut Over discipline concludes the core migration. During this phase, the migrated system is deployed at the customer's site while the legacy system is turned out. The Cut Over strategy depends on the transition strategy, chosen during Strategy Selection (see Section 2.2.4). In addition, the migrated system is monitored to ensure that it behaves as expected. During Cut Over, the following activities are performed.

- **Create Fallback:** As the migrated system might fail in the customer's environment, the environment with the legacy system should be backed-up before the new system is deployed. If the migrated system fails or does not behave as expected, the environment is set back to this fallback (rollback).

Depending on the system architecture it could be necessary to log (record) all messages or transactions produced by the new system and to replay those to the legacy system after a fallback scenario to avoid loss of data. E.g., this is necessary after rolling back a database.

Furthermore, a point-of-no-return may be defined. After the new system passes this point, no rollback will be executed. All error situations have to be handled and solved by staying on the new environment. This can be necessary when too much data has been changed and no inverse transactions are possible.

- **Turn Out Legacy System:** After having successfully migrated the legacy system or parts of it, these artifacts are obsolete. The legacy system can be turned out according to the transition strategy in one of the following ways:
  ○ Shutting down the whole system at once (Big Bang strategy),
  ○ Shutting down only parts of the legacy system (iterative cut over).
- **Clean Up Legacy System:** After shutting down the legacy system, all remains of the legacy system have to be cleaned up. Failing to do so might lead to bugs that are hardly to detect. If required, the legacy assets have to be archived to allow future backtracking to former decisions based on the legacy. This also includes the legacy data.
- **Deploy Migrated System:** While shutting down (parts of) the legacy system, the lost functionality must be provided by the migrated system. Therefore, the migrated system (or parts thereof) is deployed to the customer's site.

The previous sections have introduced the main phases and disciplines of the SOAMIG process model as well as the activities to be performed in general during software migrations. The SOAMIG process has to be viewed generically in the sense, that it has to be adapted to certain software migration needs defined by each project. Depending on the projects aims, various disciplines, or activities become more or less important. After shortly introducing a generic, model-based tool suite in Section 3, the applicability of the SOAMIG process and the required tailoring of its disciplines and activities are shown in Section 4 and 5.

THE SOAMIG TOOL SUITE

Applying the SOAMIG process to migration projects requires comprehensive tool support streamlined to the process. In this section, the SOAMIG tool suite supporting the process is described (Fuhr, Horn, & Riediger, 2011a).

Generic Tool Suite

As part of the SOAMIG project, the generic tool suite shown in Figure 4 has been developed to support SOA migration projects.

In migration projects, the legacy system represents the starting point of every migration activity. Depending on the project, the legacy system provides various artifacts. At least, the source code of the legacy system has to be available for transformation-based migrations. Additional artifacts like business process models, requirements, or architectural descriptions might provide further information on the legacy. Using various extractor tools, the legacy artifacts are parsed into the integrated SOAMIG repository. The SOAMIG repository stores all legacy artifacts as models and conforms to one integrated metamodel describing the abstract syntax of its constituents (requirements, business processes, code, archi-

Figure 4. Generic tool suite supporting the SOAMIG process

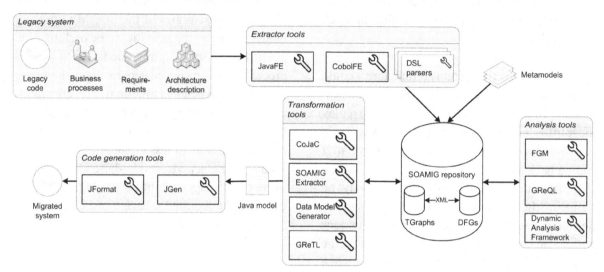

tectural documents, etc.). Analysis tools are used to explore the legacy artifacts in order to understand the legacy system and to extract useful information. Transformation tools are applied to generate new models from legacy artifacts. For example, service interfaces, data models, or even service implementations may be generated. In addition, these models may be combined to form implementation artifacts realizing the migrated system. Code generation tools can be used to generate executable source code from these models, representing the migrated system. In the following, the components of the tool suite are explained in more detail.

Legacy Artifacts

The main source for migrating software systems is the legacy code. Usually the legacy code consists of code in appropriate programming languages, data definitions, and user interface description, complemented by additional information stored in various forms like XML files. Further information on the legacy system like architecture or requirements will help to decide on migration alternatives. As motivated in Figure 1, migration

projects benefit from analyzing legacy systems as to code, architecture and requirements level. Migrating software systems to Service-oriented Architectures is based on an elaborated analysis model describing the business processes. Here both, business processes supported by the legacy as well as business processes strived for in the target system, provide valuable information for SOA migration. The SOAMIG tool suite supports storing and analyzing all relevant sources in an integrated manner.

Whereas code usually is available, architecture, requirements and business processes of the legacy system have to be reverse-engineered or at least it must be validated if they still fit the existing implementation. Business processes supported by the target architecture and their mappings to legacy business processes together with their links to legacy architecture and code provide a significant foundation to decide on legacy assets to be migrated to the new system.

Repository Technology

To be able to store, to analyze, and to transform legacy artifacts, these must be made available to the tool suite. For this purpose, all artifacts are stored in an integrated repository. Repositories provide functionality to store artifacts in a structured way, to query them efficiently, to extract information, and to transform them. Integrated repositories store all artifacts in a connected manner, supporting inter-artifact querying and transformation.

Additionally, the SOAMIG repository integrates two different repository technologies used by the tool suite. According to their special purpose, the tools of the tool suite use two different data storage technologies. For comprehensive analyses, the overall integrated repository is stored as TGraph, a very expressive kind of graphs (Ebert, Riediger, & Winter, 2008). All legacy artifacts are represented by TGraphs and graphs are connected where possible (e.g., legacy methods accessed during execution of business processes are mapped to the process). Source code artifacts are also stored as specialized syntax and Data Flow Graphs (DFGs). Some high-performance tools of the tool suite access these specialized DFGs directly. In order to provide tool interoperability while preserving optimal performance, the SOAMIG repository synchronizes the TGraphs and the DFGs automatically. Synchronization between both data storage paradigms is realized via an XML exchange format. In the following, TGraphs and supporting TGraph technology are introduced.

The TGraph repository is called JGraLab. It can be obtained for free from (Institute for Software Technology, 2012). For querying TGraphs, there is the Graph Repository Query Language (GReQL) and for transformations on TGraphs, there is the Graph Repository Transformation Language (GReTL). In SOAMIG, the integrated metamodel describing the types and relationships of the different kinds of relevant artifacts consists of a package modeling the abstract syntax of the programming languages Java and COBOL, a package containing a subset of UML's activity diagrams for modeling business processes, a package containing elements

for modeling system architecture and some more. From such a metamodel, an object-oriented API is generated which can be used to access, traverse and modify graphs conforming to this metamodel. So beside the generic tools GReQL and GReTL, several special-purpose tools have been developed that directly access the integrated repository by means of the generated API, such as the SOAMIG Extractor (Fuhr, et al., 2011a).

Extractor Tools

In order to convert legacy artifacts into models to be stored in the integrated repository, a set of fact extraction tools has been developed.

The Java Frontend (JavaFE) is a language frontend developed by pro et con, able to parse Java source files up to version 6 (Zimmermann, Uhlig, & Kaiser, 2010). The parser component was generated using pro et con's parser generator BTRACC2 (Erdmenger, 2009). The Java Frontend extracts pro et con DFGs which are synchronized into TGraphs conforming to a Java 6 metamodel.

For parsing COBOL source code, the Cobol Frontend (CobolFE) has been developed by pro et con (Erdmenger & Uhlig, 2011). Like for JavaFE, the parser component of CobolFE was generated by BTRACC2. CobolFE currently supports COBOL 85 and IBM Enterprise COBOL. From legacy source code, CobolFE generates DFGs which are synchronized into TGraphs. Here, the graphs conform to a COBOL metamodel.

Additional legacy artifacts are parsed by Domain-Specific Language (DSL) parsers. As part of the SOAMIG project, business processes have been modeled as UML 2.0 activity diagrams. These diagrams can be created using UML modeling tools that support exporting UML models as XMI files (like IBM's Rational Software Architect). The XMI files of the activity diagrams are processed by a DSL parser for UML activity diagrams and stored as TGraphs conforming to a UML 2.0 activity diagram metamodel.

In the SOAMIG RAIL case study (see Section 4), the control flow between masks in its GUI was programmed with a kind of finite automaton in mind, enforced by a strict set of coding conventions. A transformation has been developed that turns this implicit automaton explicit by means of a simplified UML 2.0 state machine diagram, which is subsequently integrated in the SOAMIG repository, too.

Furthermore, there is an XML message repository defining the structure of the messages exchanged by client and server of the legacy application. To represent the XML message repository, the XML files were parsed using a project-specific parser into a TGraph conforming to a project-specific metamodel for the message repository. This metamodel has been derived from the message repository DTD by transforming the DTD into a grUML diagram. The grUML diagram was refactored manually and exported into a TGraph schema file.

Analysis Tools

For comprehensive analysis of the models, various analysis tools have been developed.

The Flow Graph Manipulator (FGM) developed by pro et con is a tool supporting static program comprehension activities in reverse engineering projects (Beier & Uhlig, 2009). FGM is able to analyze COBOL, Java or NATURAL source code. In addition, embedded languages like SQL, DL/I or CICS are analyzable, too. FGM provides functionality for fine-grained analysis of source code centric information, like data flow or control flow of complex applications. In addition, FGM supports redocumentation of legacy architectures by analyzing dependencies within the entire system. As example for COBOL, information about calls includes or data usage structures are provided. In addition to these analytic capabilities, FGM can compute various metrics and statistics, e.g., for giving hints about the maintainability of a software system.

Static analysis on the overall integrated repository is supported by the Graph Repository Query Language (GReQL) developed by the Institute for Software Technology. GReQL can be used to extract any kind of static information from the integrated repository. Examples for possible applications are the computation of static dependencies in source code or any relationship that can be expressed by means of regular path expressions. Furthermore, the Graph Repository Transformation Language (GReTL) developed by the Institute for Software Technology is built upon GReQL (Ebert & Bildhauer, 2010). The transformation that generated state machines from source code discussed earlier was implemented as a GReTL transformation.

As static analysis may not be sufficient for a comprehensive understanding of legacy systems, the Dynamic Analysis Framework was developed to enhance analysis capabilities. The Dynamic Analysis Framework is able to track the execution of legacy code during business processes. As result, business process steps are mapped to source code that is executed while performing each step. Here, the focus of the RAIL case study was set on identifying legacy code for implementing services. Therefore, service candidates were derived from the business process model manually. Finally, the mapping between business processes and legacy code was used to extract legacy code that is able to implement the service candidates (Fuhr, et al., 2011).

In recent research, this approach has been extended by data mining techniques to support service identification and implementation (Fuhr, et al., 2011b). The approach combines business process modeling with dynamic analysis and clustering techniques to identify service implementations in legacy code. In addition, the clustering groups atomic business processes, giving hints at identifying service candidates. However, this approach has not been applied during the SOAMIG case studies.

Transformation Tools

To transform the legacy system towards a Service-oriented Architecture, a set of transformation tools has been developed.

The COBOL-to-Java Converter (CoJaC) is a language transformation tool developed by pro et con to migrate COBOL source code into Java source code, preserving its semantics (Erdmenger & Uhlig, 2011). CoJaC uses the Cobol Frontend to parse COBOL source files. The COBOL model is then transformed into a Java model using pro et con's Cobol2Java Transformator engine. Cobol2Java consists of general and project-specific transformation rules providing the required transformation capabilities. In further steps, the Java model can be post-processed or unparsed into executable Java code (see next section about code generation tools).

To support one of the most important steps in SOA migration projects, namely the implementation of services by reusing legacy code, the SOAMIG Extractor tool has been developed. This represents a graphical user interface helping developers to identify and extract legacy code that can be reused to implement SOA services. For this purpose, the tool allows selecting all methods that have been executed during a business process. This code might be useful for implementing a service supporting this business process. When selecting a method, all accessed fields and all called methods are selected as well. To give the user a more fine-grained control, the Java syntax graphs in the integrated repository backing this tool can be modified in terms of a few refactoring operations, whose main intent it is to cut down as many dependencies as possible. Using this tool, a software engineer tries to identify and select the legacy code that is able to implement (parts of) a new service in the target architecture. Thereby he uses refactoring operations to keep unwanted dependencies at a minimum. When satisfied, the SOAMIG Extractor exports the slice of the legacy system that contains only the selected classes, methods and fields in the project's XML-based exchange format.

In the migrated SOA system, services exchange information by using messages. The structure of these messages can be derived from legacy data structures. In the RAIL case study, messages between legacy client and server system were specified by an XML message repository. The Data Model Generator (DMG) was developed to transform these legacy data structures into message-ready data structures. For this purpose, the Data Model Generator transforms messages of the legacy XML message repository into Java classes containing fields, getters, and setters. These Java classes are ready to be encapsulated in SOA messages.

The graph-based transformation language GReTL (Horn & Ebert, 2011) was used to extract the control flow of the user interface. In the legacy system, the possible transitions between different user interface masks were designed in terms of a finite state machine including triggers (e.g., clicks on different buttons) and guards (e.g., some checkbox item is enabled). Those were encoded in plain Java using a set of coding conventions. These conventions could be exploited to transform the abstract Java syntax graph to a UML 2.0 state machine model, in order to make the UI control flow explicit. From this project task, a simplified version was derived and submitted as a case for the Transformation Tool Contest 2011 (Horn, 2011a, 2011b) and the GReTL solution was voted the best solution for this case.

Code Generation Tools

As all migration actions are performed on the repository, the results are reflected in the models. Therefore, the models must be unparsed back into artifacts usable in the migrated system. As most important unparsers, two tools generating Java source code have been developed by pro et con (Zimmermann, et al., 2010).

JGen is a code generator unparsing Java models (e.g., migrated COBOL code, services or data models) into executable Java 6 source code. In this step, the Java source code is formatted only in a basic way.

To improve Java formatting, the tool JFormat has been developed. JFormat is based on the Eclipse Java code formatting functionality. It is customizable to project-specific needs. JFormat is used to format the code that was generated by JGen.

RAIL CASE STUDY

The SOAMIG process model and the SOAMIG tool suite were evaluated on two case studies. The first one, the RAIL case study, aimed to migrate Amadeus Germany's RAIL system into a Service-oriented Architecture. RAIL is part of the Amadeus Selling Platform (ASPL), a system that provides travel management capabilities to travel agencies. Features of the ASPL are for example the seamless booking of flights, train tickets, hotels and car rentals. RAIL focuses on selling all products that allow traveling by Deutsche Bahn (the German national railroad).

RAIL is based on a client-server architecture implemented in Java. It is linked to multiple services of Amadeus Germany and its business partners. The RAIL client contains most of the business functionality (fat client with 229,228 LOC). Each time a new version of RAIL is released, the client must be deployed to all customers. This is very inflexible and results in high cost. For this reason, Amadeus decided to migrate the legacy client-server system to a Service-oriented Architecture. This approach allows moving legacy business functionality from the fat client to services which will be deployed on a server. The client will become more lightweight and will be responsible for accessing the business functionality only.

Goal of the RAIL case study was the evaluation and adaption of the SOAMIG process and the SOAMIG tool suite. From a customer's view, the RAIL study was restricted to estimate risks and chances of migrating ASPL. The remaining

section describes the case study streamlined to the SOAMIG process. Because of focusing on evaluating the SOAMIG approach, only the first two phases of the SOAMIG process were executed. The migration of the complete RAIL system as well as post-renovation is subject to future projects.

RAIL: Preparation Phase

During Preparation, the project was initialized. In the following, the results of the three Preparation disciplines are described.

- **Pre-Renovation:** Because of the tight schedule and the restricted scope, the RAIL system was not renovated in advance. However, experiences with the project revealed that pre-renovation is an important step for future SOA migration projects. The RAIL case study illustrated that high coupling between presentation code and business code complicates the extraction of services. Therefore, reengineering of RAIL to separate these concerns would have been useful for the remaining project.

- **Project Set Up:** This discipline covers many organizational tasks like defining work packages, creating a schedule and planning resources. In addition, because of RAIL being part of a research project with four partners in different locations, one important aspect in Project Set Up was establishing reliable communication and teamwork facilities. As example, one common repository was deployed, a wiki was created, and a mailing list was initialized.

- **Tool Initialization:** Some of the tools presented in the tool suite section already existed before the project. The Institute for Software Technology contributed the tools GReQL, GReTL, and JGraLab. pro et con contributed the Java Frontend (JavaFE) and the Flow Graph Manipulator (FGM). During Tool Initialization, these tools had to be extended and to be integrated into one seamless tool suite.

In addition, missing capabilities not covered by the existing tools were identified and tools providing the required functionality were developed. During Tool Initialization, pro et con developed the Java Generator, the Java Formatter (JFormat) and the Data Model Generator. The Institute for Software Technology developed the Dynamic Analysis Framework and the SOAMIG Extractor.

Figure 5 shows the generic SOAMIG tool suite (see Section 3) adapted to the RAIL project. Capabilities for handling COBOL (CobolFE and CoJaC) have been excluded, as they were not needed in the project context. RAIL furthermore requires special sources to lead the migration process. Next to the Java code representing the legacy system, a substantial message repository exists, defining message formats to exchange data with an external Deutsche Bahn system. The performance of legacy RAIL system is optimized by various state machines controlling various operational sequences that are partially stored in XML files. During former migration, this data is used to define new data structures and to decide on associated code fragments. Service-oriented Architectures are strongly depended on the supported business processes. So business processes, mainly derived from interviews with software developers and document analysis, build an important foundation for defining and detailing the target architecture.

RAIL: Conceptualization Phase

During Conceptualization, one core business process of RAIL was used to evaluate the SOAMIG process and tool suite: "Ticket mit Fahrplan" (ticket with timetable, TwT). During TwT, a ticket for the German railroad bound to specific train connections is sold. As this is one of the most representative processes in RAIL, it was used to check the suitability of the approach.

In the following, the results of the migration activities are presented, streamlined to the seven core disciplines of the SOAMIG process.

Business Modeling

As SOAs are strongly related to business processes, Business Modeling is one of the most important disciplines in the SOAMIG process. For RAIL, no documentation of business processes was available. Thus, the business processes were redocumented by interviewing RAIL stakeholders. The business processes were modeled as UML 2.0 activity diagrams. The resulting business process model was stored in the integrated SOAMIG repository.

Legacy Analysis

Due to missing documentation, Legacy Analysis had to focus on analyzing the legacy source code of RAIL. The source code was parsed into the SOAMIG repository using JavaFE. To get an overview about the system, the source code model was analyzed with the Flow Graph Manipulator tool. In addition, the query language GReQL was used to extract additional information about dependencies of the legacy system. These first analyses revealed that the GUI masks of RAIL were controlled by one central state machine hidden in the Java code of the legacy system. A GReTL transformation was used to transform the state machine source code into UML 2.0 state diagrams to make this automaton explicit.

Comparing the state machine model to the business process model showed a high degree of similarity between both models. GUI masks were mapped to steps of the business processes. Analyzing this mapping highlighted one potential problem for migration to SOA: while the business process was modeled in a linear fashion, the GUI allowed jumping between all masks at any time. To provide this flexibility, all required data was

Figure 5. SOAMIG tool suite adapted to the RAIL project

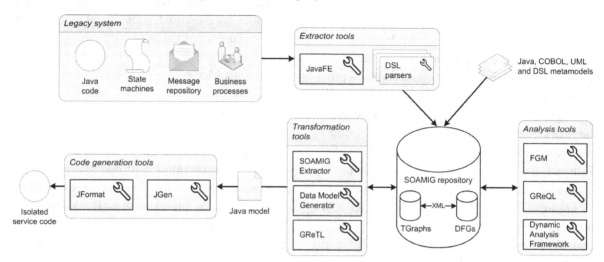

held available in the fat client. This would not be possible in a service-oriented system.

One of the main goals of RAIL was to explore the possibilities of detecting legacy code able to implement services for the migrated SOA system. As services are tightly related to business processes, the relationship between services and processes was exploited. For this purpose, a Dynamic Analysis Framework was developed at the Institute for Software Technology. This framework allows tracing which code is being executed during each step of a business process. This is accomplished in a two-folded way. First, a user can log which step of a business process he is currently executing on the legacy system. In parallel, he operates the legacy system to accomplish the business process step. Second, the legacy system is instrumented (e.g., using AspectJ) so it logs all code executions while it is operated by the user. This results in a mapping between the business process step and the legacy code that was executed during that step. After some post-processing and filtering, the trace links between process and code are stored in the SOAMIG repository. The information can later be used to identify legacy code that might be suited to implement a service supporting the business process.

Target Design

The Target Architecture discipline deals with defining the architecture of the to-be migrated SOA system. Using the iterative architecture design technique described in Section 2.2.3, a three-tier target architecture was defined by OFFIS. On top, the View Layer deals with interacting with the user. The Business Process Layer implements the TwT business process and manages the orchestration of services. At the bottom, the Enterprise Service Bus Layer manages the deployment and message interaction of services.

Services were realized in Java by reusing legacy code embedded in the JAX-WS framework (Java.net, 2011b) to provide service interfaces. The services as well as the Enterprise Service Bus components were deployed on a Tomcat application server.

Business processes were realized using Spring Web Flow (Springsource.org, 2011). Spring Web Flow allows defining service orchestration and manages the interaction with the graphical user interface. On the View Layer the legacy user interface was reimplemented with Java Server Faces (JSF) (Oracle, 2011) and RichFaces (Jboss. org, 2011). The Business Process Layer as well as the View Layer were deployed on a Tomcat application server, too. With this architecture, view and business logic were fully decoupled. Amadeus would now be able to distribute new versions of their software by simply updating the central application. Clients can use ordinary Web browsers to access all functionality.

Strategy Selection

The overall migration strategy was influenced by the explorative nature of the research project. For scientific interest, it was decided to automatically transform legacy code into the new system wherever possible. However, analyses showed that an automatic migration of the legacy graphical user interface was not feasible. Therefore, the GUI was reimplemented.

In addition, the data model was found to be optimized on the GUI instead of business entities. As the GUI would not be transformed to the new system, the data model would not exactly match the GUI anymore. Hence, the data model should not be converted one-on-one into the new system. So it was decided to reimplement the data model and to support the reimplementation by semi-automatic transformation of messages that were sent to and received by the Germany Railroad partner system.

Realization of services was planned to be iterative. In each iteration new services were added. In addition, the degree of automation was increased.

Realization

In the first iteration, one small service was implemented manually. This first migration step was performed to learn how the migration of legacy code into a service could be automated. For this purpose, all manual steps were recorded. This manual migration laid the base for developing the SOAMIG Extractor tool that supports the extraction of legacy code for implementing services. The SOAMIG Extractor visualizes legacy code

in different views like package view or generalization hierarchy view. Various reengineering operations like moving methods to other classes or removing parts of a generalization hierarchy are supported. In the SOAMIG Extractor, packages, classes, or methods that should be used to implement a service can be selected. The Extractor automatically resolves all dependencies of the selected items and selects them, too. In addition to manually selecting items, the Extractor exploits the mapping of business processes to code. So, all methods that had been called during a business process step could be selected automatically. After all packages, classes, and methods required to implement a service have been selected, the items are serialized into an XML file. This file was subsequently processed by the Java Generator JGen and the Java Formatter JFormat to generate executable Java code. This code was afterwards used to implement the services.

In multiple iterations, all services required for the TwT business process were implemented using this tool-supported semi-automatic approach. Experiences made during each iteration were used to adapt and extend the tools.

In addition to the services, the data model for the target architecture was implemented in this discipline. Based on messages exchanged between RAIL and the German Railroad partner system, the Data Model Generator was used to automatically generate the new data model. As additional input, results from dynamic analysis were used to identify which parts of the messages have really been used in the RAIL system.

Orchestration of services was realized by mapping the business process to the target architecture. In addition, the graphical user interface was reimplemented in this phase.

Testing

After having migrated legacy code into a service-oriented system, it is necessary to test if the new system provides the same functionality as the legacy system. In addition, it must be checked if the system meets performance expectations. As the testing discipline was outside of RAIL's project scope, these tests were not performed as sophisticated, automated tests. However, tests were performed manually. The correctness of each service was verified by unit tests (JUnit). The interaction of services, the Enterprise Service Bus, the business process layer and the view layer was assured by manual integration and system tests. In addition, developers of the legacy system ensured that the service-oriented system did behave like the legacy system (manual regression and acceptance tests).

Cut Over

The Cut Over discipline was not included in the project scope, either. Therefore, the migrated system was only deployed on the test system. In the future, however, Amadeus is planning to deploy the system on their productive system. For the transition, the new client will first be deployed to one single customer. Iteratively, the new system will then be introduced to all other customers step by step. This is a standard procedure at Amadeus Germany when deploying new software.

Conclusion of the RAIL Project

The RAIL case study focused on an architectural migration of the legacy Java client-server system into a Service-oriented Architecture. During the RAIL case study, one exemplary business process was migrated into a SOA. As part of this migration, services were designed to support the business process. They were implemented by re-using legacy code. All services were orchestrated and a general SOA environment was developed (Enterprise Service Bus, Business Process Layer).

As lessons learned, the RAIL case study showed the importance of the Pre-Renovation discipline. As view concerns and business logic were tightly related in the legacy system, cutting out

legacy code ready to implement the services was hard to achieve. A reengineering phase to reduce this coupling in advance to the main project might have made the extraction of legacy code easier.

The disciplines Testing and Cut Over were not subject to the case study anymore. However, the services were tested in a productive-like test environment. After migrating the remaining parts of RAIL, successful deployment of the migrated system will be possible.

LCOBOL CASE STUDY

Legacy COBOL (LCOBOL) is a system for user and access management and part of a large production control system. LCOBOL is implemented in Microfocus COBOL and distributed on UNIX platforms. The LCOBOL system is composed of server and batch programs.

Once started, server programs are constantly running, providing services via a middleware. The services are accessed by sending messages to the server program. Messages are sent by user masks or by other COBOL programs (server programs or batch programs). They contain the input data required by the service. After receiving a message, the server program processes the data and sends an answer message back to the requester. The requester has to wait until receipt of this answer before he can continue his work. Batch programs are independent programs started and controlled by JCL scripts (Job Control Language scripts; here Perl).

LCOBOL is composed of 24 server programs, 4 batch programs, 11 subprograms, 216 copybooks, 912 SQL include files. Overall, LCOBOL has about 81,600 lines of code (including blank lines and comment lines). Persistent data is stored in a relational database containing eight tables.

The LCOBOL case study's goal was the automatic transformation of the COBOL server programs into Java Web services running on an application server, so it rather addresses a language than an architecture migration. Language migration will become an important key asset in migration projects if the migrated systems have to be released from legacy language parts to completely provide further development in more modern programming languages. Those activities are necessary when programmers for the legacy languages are no longer available or too expensive, so that wrapping does not constitute a cost-effective alternative in a long term view. The remaining section describes how the SOAMIG process was applied in the LCOBOL case study for language migration.

LCOBOL: Preparation Phase

The Preparation phase in LCOBOL mostly addressed the adaptation of the SOAMIG tool suite to the specific needs of the language migration. Further set up activities were performed as well.

- **Pre-Renovation:** Because of the tight project schedule, no pre-renovation was performed in LCOBOL.
- **Project Set Up:** LCOBOL being part of the SOAMIG project, organizational aspects had already been handled as part of the RAIL case study (see Section 4).
- **Tool Initialization:** For LCOBOL, the main focus was on the language migration from COBOL to Java. During Tool Initialization, pro et con developed the COBOL Frontend (CobolFE) and the Cobol2Java Transformator. Together with already existing tools, the COBOL-to-Java Converter (CoJaC) was assembled.

Figure 6 shows the generic SOAMIG tool suite (see Section 3) trimmed down to the project needs of LCOBOL. As this project focused on the language migration part of an overall migration, the tool suite has been adapted to only contain the tools needed for this language migration. All other tools (e.g., analysis tools or SOA-specific transformation tools) have been excluded from the project-specific LCOBOL tool suite.

The Cobol2Java Transformator works on abstract syntax graphs, i.e., it receives the abstract COBOL syntax graph generated by the CobolFE. For any COBOL statement, the transformator has a rule creating an equivalent Java statement, again in terms of its abstract syntax. The complete Java syntax graph generated by the transformator for a single COBOL program is then serialized back to Java source code by JGen. Finally, the code is formatted according to customizable coding conventions by JFormat.

LCOBOL: Conceptualization Phase

The LCOBOL case study focused on migrating legacy COBOL programs into Java classes able to implement services. Therefore, the SOAMIG process was tailored to the project needs. Architectural considerations were touched exemplarily only. In the following, the activities of the LCOBOL case study are described, streamline to the SOAMIG process.

Business Modeling

In LCOBOL, business processes are realized by the control flow between user masks. These masks define which tasks have to be executed in what order. Therefore, the masks were used to derive the business process model for the LCOBOL case study. As only few masks existed, the business process model was created manually.

Legacy Analysis

The legacy COBOL system was analyzed using pro et con's Flow Graph Manipulator. This first analysis aimed at understanding the structure of the legacy system. In addition, dependencies between all components and interfaces of the components

Figure 6. SOAMIG tool suite adapted to the LCOBOL project

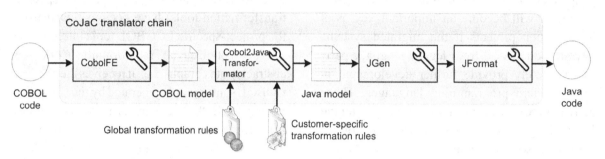

were analyzed. As an important result, legacy analysis revealed that a strict mapping between user masks and server programs existed in most cases. Therefore, one server program could be migrated into one service supporting the business process that was represented by a given user mask. This already SOA-like architecture alignment made it feasible to concentrate on the language migration and achieve a very high degree of automation.

Target Design

A one-to-one mapping between COBOL and Java statements is often not feasible. Although being possible, enforcing such a one-to-one migration might lead to migrated code that is much more complex to maintain than the legacy code. For this reason, a runtime system layer emulating some COBOL features and the COBOL type system was introduced. As a result, the migrated Java system feels quite common to the original COBOL developers, while for Java developers it appears as a usual Java system using some framework. Over the time, the runtime system may be replaced with more idiomatic Java constructs and types, but this can happen incrementally.

As the LCOBOL case study focused on the language migration part of a migration to SOA, the remaining considerations about architecture (e.g., business process modeling or service orchestration) were not targeted in this case study. However, an interface layer between legacy user masks and migrated services was designed to allow communication between both layers.

Strategy Selection

With its focus on enabling legacy code to implement services, the Realization Strategy was most interesting in this discipline. Here it was decided to introduce the runtime system layer that emulates important COBOL functionality in Java. For example, when defining numeric variables in COBOL, the maximum number of digits is given. Many calculations rely on, e.g., the overflow semantics of these types. This mechanism is emulated in Java using a special class for migrated COBOL numbers and a method for initializing numeric variables as instances of this class.

Realization

During Realization, the legacy COBOL code was transformed into Java. The COBOL-to-Java Converter (CoJaC, see Section 3) was used to transform the COBOL server programs into Java classes. Each server program supports a specific part of the business process. Therefore, each transformed server program implements a service in the target system. After generating the Java classes implementing the business functionality of the services, the service interface is created. For this purpose, the tool JAX-B (Java.net, 2011a) was used. Following a bottom-up approach, the Java code is annotated to define what parts realize a service and what methods are service operations. Service operations represent the interface of the service. Finally, JAX-WS was used to generate the WSDL service specification. Messages between services are exchanged using the Simple Object Access Protocol (SOAP).

Realizing the View Layer (i.e., migrating the legacy COBOL user masks), the Business Process Layer (i.e., orchestrating the services), and the Enterprise Service Bus Layer (i.e., handling the message exchange of the services) was not part of the LCOBOL language migration. However, these tasks can be performed similarly to the RAIL case study.

Because the legacy user interface was not migrated, an interface was implemented to allow communication between legacy user masks and migrated services. This interface receives outgoing calls of the user masks (in COBOL, all parameters are handed over via one single character array). It selects the right service and generates a SOAP message to access the functionality. Answering messages from the services are received, translated back into a character array, and handed back to the user masks.

Testing

Language migration requires ensuring that the migrated system behaves semantically identical to the legacy system. A migrated program which is syntactically correct and semantically equivalent to the legacy program has been transformed correctly.

To ensure correct transformations in LCOBOL, various tests were performed. First, single COBOL statements were tested based on the COBOL 1985 ANSI standard. For each type of COBOL statement or definition, a set of test cases was created covering any syntactic and semantic variations of a construct. All test cases of all constructs were included in a test suite. Based on this test suite,

each tool of the language migration was verified. The Cobol Frontend as well as the translator were tested to correctly parse COBOL code and to transform it into Java code. That Java code was verified to be syntactically correct by compiling it. Correctness of semantics was tested by comparing the results of the legacy COBOL constructs with those of the migrated Java constructs.

In advance to these single statement tests, complete legacy LCOBOL programs were transformed and tested on their syntactic and semantic correctness. Finally, sample programs from the Internet were evaluated as well, in order to enlarge the set of supported COBOL constructs. Sample programs were retrieved from two COBOL source Web sites (Cobug.com, 2011; University of Limerick, 2011).

Cut Over

During Cut Over, the migrated services were deployed on a Tomcat application server. In addition, the user mask interface was installed. The user masks were adapted to send their calls to this interface instead of to the legacy COBOL server programs.

LCOBOL: Migration Phase

During the LCOBOL case study, more than 80% of the LCOBOL system were migrated automatically by using the CoJaC translator chain. For the remainder, a manual adaption of the transformed code was needed. The resulting classes were deployed with its showcase user interface to demonstrate the successful migration for the COBOL functionality to Java.

LCOBOL: Transition Phase

The LCOBOL case study basically addressed the core part of a language migration, so post-renovation activities are currently subject to further research. In particular, more experience is requested on future maintainability of the resulting code.

Conclusions of the LCOBOL Project

The LCOBOL case study focused on the language migration from COBOL to Java. It aimed at providing Java code that can be deployed as service. During the LCOBOL case study, COBOL server programs were migrated to semantically equivalent services. For this case study, 80 to 90 percent of the language transformation efforts were automatable.

In future projects, the COBOL-to-Java Converter (CoJaC) will be extended to be able to handle additional COBOL dialects.

CONCLUSION

The previous sections introduced the iterative and generic SOAMIG process model for software migration. The process model is generic in the sense that it covers techniques from forward and reverse engineering which are adequately adaptable to fulfill the individual needs of a migration project. Together with its tool suite, the SOAMIG process model follows a model-driven approach. All techniques are founded on a common and integrated repository representing legacy and target systems on all levels of abstraction, including code, architecture, and analysis models.

The SOAMIG process model was applied in two industrial case studies. These case studies showed its applicability for an architecture migration and a language migration. The RAIL case study showed the application to a monolithic and highly optimized JAVA system, which was migrated to a Service-oriented Architecture. Here, general functionality was identified and extracted from the legacy system. Whereas the functionality could be migrated to the Enterprise

Service Bus Layer (mostly) automatically, user interfaces were reimplemented. In the TwT case, the orchestration was also done manually. This also shows how extracted and migrated legacy assets can be reused in new orchestrations in a Service-oriented Architecture.

To make functionality not developed in contemporary programming languages available to Service-oriented Architectures, the SOAMIG process model was applied to a language migration in the LCOBOL case study. Here, already service-like implementations in COBOL were migrated to Java-services. In contrast to more common wrapping of COBOL sources, the transformation-based approach avoids layers of different programming languages and alleviates further evolution of the migrated software system.

These practical experiences showed in general that software migrations to SOA can successfully be based on model-driven technologies, provided that an integrated and harmonized tool support is given. Future activities have to apply the SOAMIG technologies to huge industrial-scale migrations.

REFERENCES

Alahmari, S., Zaluska, E., & de Roure, D. (2010). A service identification framework for legacy system migration into SOA. In *Proceedings of the 2010 IEEE International Conference on Services Computing (SCC)*, (pp. 614–617). Washington, DC: IEEE Computer Society Press.

Arsanjani, A., Ghosh, S., Allam, A., Abdollah, T., Ganapathy, S., & Holley, K. (2008). SOMA: A method for developing service-oriented solutions. *IBM Systems Journal*, *47*(3), 377–396. doi:10.1147/sj.473.0377

Beck, K., & Andres, C. (2004). *Extreme programming explained: Embrace change* (2nd ed.). Reading, MA: Addison-Wesley.

Beier, A., & Uhlig, D. (2009). Flow graph manipulator (FGM) - Reverse engineering tool für komplexe softwaresysteme. *Softwaretechnik-Trends, 29*(2), 39–40.

Borchers, J. (1997). Erfahrungen mit dem einsatz einer reengineering factory in einem großen umstellungsprojekt. *HMD - Praxis der Wirtschaftsinformatik, 34*(194), 77–94.

Brodie, M. L., & Stonebraker, M. (1995). *Migrating legacy systems: Gateways, interfaces and the incremental approach*. San Francisco, CA: Morgan Kaufmann.

Cobug.com. (2011). *COBOL user groups*. Retrieved March 19, 2012, from http://www.cobug.com/

de Lucia, A., Francese, R., Scanniello, G., & Tortora, G. (2008). Developing legacy system migration methods and tools for technology transfer. *Software, Practice & Experience, 38*(13), 1333–1364. doi:10.1002/spe.870

de Lucia, A., & Tortora, G. (2010). *Metamorphos: Methods and tools for migrating software systems towards web and service oriented architectures: Experimental evaluation, usability and technology transfer*. Catanzaro, Italy: Rubbettino.

Ebert, J., & Bildhauer, D. (2010). Reverse engineering using graph queries. *Lecture Notes in Computer Science, 5765*.

Ebert, J., Riediger, V., & Winter, A. (2008). Graph technology in reverse engineering: The TGraph approach. In R. Gimnich, U. Kaiser, J. Quante, & A. Winter (Eds.), *Proceedings of the 10th Workshop Software Reengineering (WSR)*, (pp. 67–81). Bonn, Germany: Gesellschaft für Informatik.

Erdmenger, U. (2009). Der parsergenerator BTRACC2. *Softwaretechnik-Trends, 29*(2), 34–35.

Erdmenger, U., & Uhlig, D. (2011). Ein translator für die COBOL-java-migration. *Softwaretechnik-Trends, 31*(2), 10–11.

Fareghzadeh, N. (2008). Service identification approach to SOA development. *World Academy of Science. Engineering and Technology, 21*, 258–266.

Fleurey, F., Breton, E., Baudry, B., Nicolas, A., & Jézéquel, J.-M. (2007). Model-driven engineering for software migration in a large industrial context. *Lecture Notes in Computer Science, 4735*, 482–497. doi:10.1007/978-3-540-75209-7_33

Fuhr, A., Horn, T., & Riediger, V. (2011a). An integrated tool suite for model-driven software migration towards service-oriented architectures. *Softwaretechnik-Trends, 31*(2), 8–9.

Fuhr, A., Horn, T., & Riediger, V. (2011b). Using dynamic analysis and clustering for implementing services by reusing legacy code. In M. Pinzger, D. Poshyvanyk, & J. Buckley (Eds.), *Proceedings of the 18th Working Conference on Reverse Engineering (WCRE)*, (pp. 275–279). Washington, DC: IEEE Computer Society Press.

Fuhr, A., Horn, T., Riediger, V., & Winter, A. (2011). Model-driven software migration into service-oriented architectures. *Computer Science - Research and Development*. Retrieved from http://www.se.uni-oldenburg.de/documents/fuhr+2011.pdf

Gimnich, R., & Winter, A. (2005). Workflows der software-migration. *Softwaretechnik-Trends, 25*(2), 22–24.

Gipp, T., & Winter, A. (2007). Applying the ReMiP to web site migration. In S. Huang & M. Di Penta (Eds.), *Proceedings of the Ninth IEEE International Symposium on Web Site Evolution (WSE)*, (pp. 9–13). Washington, DC: IEEE Computer Society Press.

Gold, N., Knight, C., Mohan, A., & Munro, M. (2004). Understanding service-oriented software. *IEEE Software*, *21*(2), 71–77. doi:10.1109/MS.2004.1270766

Horn, T. (2011a). Program understanding: A reengineering case for the transformation tool contest. In P. van Gorp, S. Mazanek, & L. Rose (Eds.), *Electronic Proceedings in Theoretical Computer Science: Proceedings of the Fifth Transformation Tool Contest (TTC)*, (pp. 17–21). Open Publishing Association.

Horn, T. (2011b). Solving the TTC 2011 reengineering case with GReTL. In P. van Gorp, S. Mazanek, & L. Rose (Eds.), *Electronic Proceedings in Theoretical Computer Science: Proceedings of the Fifth Transformation Tool Contest (TTC)*, (pp. 131–135). Open Publishing Association.

Horn, T., & Ebert, J. (2011). The GReTL transformation language. *Lecture Notes in Computer Science*, *6707*, 183–197. doi:10.1007/978-3-642-21732-6_13

IABG. (2009). *V-model XT, version 1.3*. Retrieved March 19, 2012, from http://v-modell.iabg.de/dmdocuments/V-Modell-XT-Gesamt-Englisch-V1.3.pdf

Institute for Software Technology. (2012). *JGraLab*. Retrieved March 19, 2012, from http://jgralab.uni-koblenz.de

Java.net. (2011a). *JAXB reference implementation*. Retrieved March 19, 2012, from http://jaxb.java.net/

Java.net. (2011b). *JAX-WS reference implementation*. Retrieved March 19, 2012, from http://jax-ws.java.net/

Jboss.org. (2011). *RichFaces project page*. Retrieved March 19, 2012, from http://www.jboss.org/richfaces

Kazman, R., Woods, S., & Carrière, J. (1998). Requirements for integrating software architecture and reengineering models: CORUM II. In *Proceedings of the Fifth Working Conference on Reverse Engineering (WCRE)*, (pp. 154-163). Washington, DC: IEEE Computer Society Press.

Khadka, R., Reijnders, G., Saeidi, A., Jansen, S., & Hage, J. (2011). A method engineering based legacy to SOA migration method. In *Proceedings of the 27th IEEE International Conference on Software Maintenance (ICSM)*, (pp. 163–172). Washington, DC: IEEE Computer Society Press.

Kim, S., Kim, M., & Park, S. (2008). Service identification using goal and scenario in service oriented architecture. In *Proceedings of the 15th Asia-Pacific Software Engineering Conference (APSEC)*, (pp. 419–426). Washington, DC: IEEE Computer Society Press.

Kruchten, P. (2003). *The rational unified process: An introduction* (3rd ed.). Reading, MA: Addison-Wesley.

Lewis, G. A., & Smith, D. B. (2008). SMART tool demonstration. In K. Kontogiannis, C. Tjortjis, & A. Winter (Eds.), *Proceedings of the 12th European Conference on Software Maintenance and Reengineering*, (pp. 332–334). Washington, DC: IEEE Computer Society Press.

Oldevik, J., Olsen, G. K., Brönner, U., & Bodsberg, N. R. (2011). Model-driven migration of scientific legacy systems to service-oriented architectures. In A. Fuhr, V. Riediger, W. Hasselbring, M. Bruntink, & K. Kontogiannis (Eds.), *CEUR Workshop Proceedings: Joint Proceedings of the First International Workshop on Model-Driven Software Migration (MDSM 2011) and Fifth International Workshop on Software Quality and Maintainability (SQM 2011)*, (pp. 4–7). CEUR-WS.org.

Oracle. (2011). *JavaServer faces technology*. Retrieved March 19, 2012, from http://java.sun.com/j2ee/javaserverfaces/

Rajlich, V. T., & Bennett, K. H. (2000). A staged model for the software life cycle. *IEEE Computer*, *33*(7), 66–71. doi:10.1109/2.869374

Razavian, M., & Lago, P. (2010). Towards a conceptual framework for legacy to SOA migration. *Lecture Notes in Computer Science*, *6275*, 445–455. doi:10.1007/978-3-642-16132-2_42

Razavian, M., Nguyen, D. K., Lago, P., & van den Heuvel, W.-J. (2010). The SAPIENSA approach for service-enabling pre-existing legacy assets. In G. A. Lewis, F. Ricca, M. Postina, U. Steffens, & A. Winter (Eds.), *Proceedings of the International Workshop on SOA Migration and Evolution (SOAME)*, (pp. 21–30). Oldenburg, Germany: OFFIS.

Ricca, F., & Marchetto, A. (2009). A "quick and dirty" meet-in-the-middle approach for migrating to SOA. In *Proceedings of the Joint International and Annual ERCIM Workshops on Principles of Software Evolution (IWPSE) and Software Evolution (Evol) Workshops*, (pp. 73–78). New York, NY: ACM Press.

Schwaber, K. (2004). *Agile project management with scrum*. Redmond, WA: Microsoft Press.

Sneed, H. M., Wolf, E., & Heilmann, H. (2010). *Softwaremigration in der praxis: Übertragung alter softwaresysteme in eine moderne umgebung*. Heidelberg, Germany: Dpunkt.

Springsource.org. (2011). *Spring web flow 2*. Retrieved March 19, 2012, from http://www.springsource.org/webflow

Teppe, W. (2010). Wiedergewinnung von informationen über legacy-systeme in reengineering-projekten. *Softwaretechnik-Trends*, *30*(2), 68–69.

University of Limerick. (2011). *CSIS - Department of computer science and information systems*. Retrieved March 19, 2012, from http://www.csis.ul.ie/

Wahli, U., Ackerman, L., Di Bari, A., Hodgkinson, G., Kesterton, A., Olson, L., & Portier, B. (2007). *Building SOA solutions using the rational SDP. IBM Redbooks: SG24-7356-00*. Armonk, NY: IBM International Technical Support Organization.

Winter, A., & Ziemann, J. (2007). Model-based migration to service-oriented architectures: A project outline. In H. M. Sneed (Ed.), *CSMR 2007 Workshop on a "Research Agenda for Service-Oriented Architecture Maintenance"*, (pp. 107–110). Amsterdam, The Netherlands: Vrije Universiteit Amsterdam.

Wu, B., Lawless, D., Bisbal, J., Richardson, R., Grimson, J., Wade, V., & O'Sullivan, D. (1997). The butterfly methodology: A gateway-free approach for migrating legacy information systems. In *Proceedings of the Third IEEE International Conference on Engineering of Complex Computer Systems (ICECCS)*, (pp. 200–205). Washington, DC: IEEE Computer Society Press.

Zhang, Z., Liu, R., & Yang, H. (2005). Service identification and packaging in service oriented reengineering. In W. C. Chu, N. J. Juzgado, & W. E. Wong (Eds.), *Proceedings of the 7th International Conference on Software Engineering and Knowledge Engineering (SEKE)*, (pp. 241-249). Skokie, IL: Knowledge Systems Institute.

Zhang, Z., & Yang, H. (2004). Incubating services in legacy systems for architectural migration. In *Proceedings of the 11th Asia-Pacific Software Engineering Conference (APSEC)*, (pp. 196–203). Washington, DC: IEEE Computer Society Press.

Zillmann, C., Erdmenger, U., Fuhr, A., Herget, A., & Horn, T. … Kaiser, U. (2011). The SOAMIG process model in industrial applications. In T. Mens, Y. Kanellopoulos, & A. Winter (Eds.), *Proceedings of the 15th European Conference on Software Maintenance and Reengineering (CSMR)*, (pp. 339–342). Washington, DC: IEEE Computer Society Press.

Zillmann, C., Gringel, P., & Winter, A. (2010). Iterative zielarchitekturdefinition in SOAMIG. *Softwaretechnik-Trends, 30*(2), 72–73.

Zimmermann, Y., Uhlig, D., & Kaiser, U. (2010). Tool- und schnittstellenarchitektur für eine SOA-migration. *Softwaretechnik-Trends, 30*(2), 66–67.

ADDITIONAL READING

Arsanjani, A., Ghosh, S., Allam, A., Abdollah, T., Ganapathy, S., & Holley, K. (2008). SOMA: A method for developing service-oriented solutions. *IBM Systems Journal, 47*(3), 377–396. doi:10.1147/sj.473.0377

Beck, K., & Andres, C. (2004). *Extreme programming explained: Embrace change* (2nd ed.). Reading, MA: Addison-Wesley.

Beier, A., & Uhlig, D. (2009). Flow graph manipulator (FGM) - Reverse engineering tool für komplexe softwaresysteme. *Softwaretechnik-Trends, 29*(2), 39–40.

Bildhauer, D., & Ebert, J. (2008). Querying software abstraction graphs. In M. Verbaere, M. W. Godfrey, & T. Girba (Eds.), *Proceedings of the Working Session on Query Technologies and Applications for Program Comprehension (QTAPC)*. QTAPC.

Brodie, M. L., & Stonebraker, M. (1995). *Migrating legacy systems: Gateways, interfaces and the incremental approach*. San Francisco, CA: Morgan Kaufmann.

Daigneau, R. (2011). *Service design patterns: Fundamental design solutions for SOAP/WSDL and RESTful web services*. Upper Saddle River, NJ: Addison-Wesley.

de Lucia, A., & Tortora, G. (2010). *Metamorphos: Methods and tools for migrating software systems towards web and service oriented architectures: Experimental evaluation, usability and technology transfer*. Catanzaro, Italy: Rubbettino.

Ebert, J., & Bildhauer, D. (2010). Reverse engineering using graph queries. *Lecture Notes in Computer Science, 5765*.

Ebert, J., Riediger, V., & Winter, A. (2008). Graph technology in reverse engineering: The TGraph approach. In R. Gimnich, U. Kaiser, J. Quante, & A. Winter (Eds.), *Proceedings of the 10th Workshop Software Reengineering (WSR)*, (pp. 67–81). Bonn, Germany: Gesellschaft für Informatik.

Erdmenger, U. (2009). Der parsergenerator BTRACC2. *Softwaretechnik-Trends, 29*(2), 34–35.

Erdmenger, U., & Uhlig, D. (2011). Ein translator für die COBOL-Java-migration. *Softwaretechnik-Trends, 31*(2), 10–11.

Fuhr, A., Horn, T., & Riediger, V. (2011). Using dynamic analysis and clustering for implementing services by reusing legacy code. In M. Pinzger, D. Poshyvanyk, & J. Buckley (Eds.), *Proceedings of the 18th Working Conference on Reverse Engineering (WCRE)*, (pp. 275–279). Washington, DC: IEEE Computer Society Press.

Fuhr, A., Horn, T., & Riediger, V. (2011). An integrated tool suite for model-driven software migration towards service-oriented architectures. *Softwaretechnik-Trends, 31*(2), 8–9.

Horn, T. (2011). Program understanding: A reengineering case for the transformation tool contest. In P. van Gorp, S. Mazanek, & L. Rose (Eds.), *Electronic Proceedings in Theoretical Computer Science: Proceedings of the Fifth Transformation Tool Contest (TTC)*, (pp. 17–21). Open Publishing Association.

Horn, T. (2011). Solving the TTC 2011 reengineering case with GReTL. In P. van Gorp, S. Mazanek, & L. Rose (Eds.), *Electronic Proceedings in Theoretical Computer Science: Proceedings of the Fifth Transformation Tool Contest (TTC),* (pp. 131–135). Open Publishing Association.

Horn, T., & Ebert, J. (2011). The GReTL transformation language. *Lecture Notes in Computer Science, 6707,* 183–197. doi:10.1007/978-3-642-21732-6_13

IABG. (2009). *V-model XT, version 1.3.* Retrieved March 19, 2012, from http://v-modell.iabg.de/dmdocuments/V-Modell-XT-Gesamt-Englisch-V1.3.pdf

Khadka, R., Reijnders, G., Saeidi, A., Jansen, S., & Hage, J. (2011). A method engineering based legacy to SOA migration method. In *Proceedings of the 27th IEEE International Conference on Software Maintenance (ICSM),* (pp. 163–172). Washington, DC: IEEE Computer Society Press.

Kruchten, P. (2003). *The rational unified process: An introduction* (3rd ed.). Reading, MA: Addison-Wesley.

Papazoglou, M. P., & van den Heuvel, W.-J. (2007). Service-oriented architectures: Approaches, technologies and research issues. *The VLDB Journal, 16*(3), 389–415. doi:10.1007/s00778-007-0044-3

Rajlich, V. T., & Bennett, K. H. (2000). A staged model for the software life cycle. *IEEE Computer, 33*(7), 66–71. doi:10.1109/2.869374

Razavian, M., & Lago, P. (2010). Towards a conceptual framework for legacy to SOA migration. *Lecture Notes in Computer Science, 6275,* 445–455. doi:10.1007/978-3-642-16132-2_42

Razavian, M., Nguyen, D. K., Lago, P., & van den Heuvel, W.-J. (2010). The SAPIENSA approach for service-enabling pre-existing legacy assets. In G. A. Lewis, F. Ricca, M. Postina, U. Steffens, & A. Winter (Eds.), *Proceedings of the International Workshop on SOA Migration and Evolution (SOAME),* (pp. 21–30). Oldenburg, Germany: OFFIS.

Rosen, M. (2008). *Applied SOA: Service-oriented architecture and design strategies.* Indianapolis, IN: Wiley.

Schwaber, K. (2004). *Agile project management with scrum.* Redmond, WA: Microsoft Press.

Sneed, H. M., Wolf, E., & Heilmann, H. (2010). *Softwaremigration in der praxis: Übertragung alter softwaresysteme in eine moderne umgebung.* Heidelberg, Germany: Dpunkt.

Velmurugan, K., & Maluk Mohamed, M. A. (2010). A model driven approach for migrating from legacy software systems to web services. In *Proceedings of the First Indian Workshop on Reverse Engineering (IWRE),* (pp. 97–101). IWRE.

Wahli, U., Ackerman, L., Di Bari, A., Hodgkinson, G., Kesterton, A., Olson, L., & Portier, B. (2007). *Building SOA solutions using the rational SDP. IBM Redbooks: SG24-7356-00.* Armonk, NY: IBM International Technical Support Organization.

Wu, B., Lawless, D., Bisbal, J., Richardson, R., Grimson, J., Wade, V., & O'Sullivan, D. (1997). The butterfly methodology: A gateway-free approach for migrating legacy information systems. In *Proceedings of the Third IEEE International Conference on Engineering of Complex Computer Systems (ICECCS),* (pp. 200–205). Washington, DC: IEEE Computer Society Press.

Zillmann, C., Gringel, P., & Winter, A. (2010). Iterative zielarchitekturdefinition in SOAMIG. *Softwaretechnik-Trends*, *30*(2), 72–73.

Zimmermann, Y., Uhlig, D., & Kaiser, U. (2010). Tool- und Schnittstellenarchitektur für eine SOA-Migration. *Softwaretechnik-Trends*, *30*(2), 66–67.

KEYWORDS AND DEFINITIONS

Business Process: A set of related business tasks, people and assets working together in order to produce a specific output.

Legacy System: A software system that offers sufficient value deserving maintenance and preservation to provide its functionality in future applications.

Model-Driven Software Development (MDSM): An approach describing software systems by models of decreasing levels of abstraction.

Service: Encapsulated, reusable and business-aligned software functionality with a well-defined interface specification.

Service-Oriented Architecture (SOA): A software architecture paradigm decomposing software systems into reusable services, streamlining software functionality and business processes.

Service Specification: The well-defined definition of interfaces that a service provides.

Software Migration: Transferring legacy software systems towards new environments without changing their semantics.

TGraph: Typed, attributed, directed, and ordered graph where all nodes and edges are first class citizens.

Section 3
Migrating to Cloud Environments

Chapter 8

Moving to SaaS:
Building a Migration Strategy from Concept to Deployment

Leire Orue-Echevarria
TECNALIA, Spain

Marisa Escalante
TECNALIA, Spain

Juncal Alonso
TECNALIA, Spain

Gorka Benguria
TECNALIA, Spain

ABSTRACT

The new market trends include globalization and service orientation as important drivers that are changing the way in which businesses operate. Companies are requesting flexible applications that can be acquired and executed seamlessly and independently of the location. This situation is progressively pushing businesses from a proprietary system orientation to a service one. Accordingly, more and more traditional software vendors are noticing the need to transform their current business and technology model in order to remain competitive in the market. Software as a Service (SaaS) has been set by these companies as a mandatory way to keep their existing customers while at the same time seizing the chance of acquiring new customers in unexplored markets. However, this transition from Software off-the-shelf to Software as a Service is not trivial as many issues (business, application, and technical) come into play. The real hands-on experience in implementing end-to-end SaaS migration strategies considering both business and technological dimensions of the problem are hardly covered. Hence, there exists a real demand for proven methods to perform the transition from traditional software products to the services concept. Based on this premise, this chapter presents a stepwise procedure and a method to migrate non-SaaS applications to SaaS taking into account not only technical and technological issues and constraints but also those issues related to business models and the monetization of the final solution.

These methods are currently being supported by real-life experiments carried out in different companies based on successful SaaS implementation experiences, a deep understanding of the details, and a proven approach to making SaaS transformation happen in an accurate, secure, and sustainable way.

DOI: 10.4018/978-1-4666-2488-7.ch008

Copyright © 2013, IGI Global. Copying or distributing in print or electronic forms without written permission of IGI Global is prohibited.

INTRODUCTION

Synopsis

The chapter presented here starts with an introduction of the topic and a presentation of the current approaches to migrate legacy applications to SaaS, including the distinction of SOA and SaaS concepts. The authors present which challenges that are facing the companies that wish to migrate to the cloud delivery model. The main body of the chapter is devoted to the technical outline of the proposed solution starting with the establishment of the basis for the migration strategy (analysis of the initial and the target situation and a technical and business feasibility analysis) and proposing a set of methods and technologies for the performance of the migration as well as the provision of the final service.

The chapter rounds off with the presentation of the stated approach validation in eight companies in Spain and a detailed explanation of a real use case extracted from one of those companies. The chapter concludes with the considerations arisen from these first implementations of the solution.

General Objectives and Perspective of the Chapter

The transition from a traditional software development and delivery model to the SaaS world is proving to be not trivial and therefore many changes are needed to be performed in order to accomplish the technical, application and business requirements of SaaS. This triple migration is complicated and an overall systematic and standardized approach is, for the time being, not publicly available. Thus, companies humbly face the decision of which existing technology to migrate to and via which distribution channels to make it available but in any case, without risking the sustainability of their business. This decision requires not only from a method but also from tools that provide meaningful figures that can be used in this decision making process. These tools shall at least cover the calculation of the running costs for SaaS solutions as well as the calculation of the income expected from such offers, while considering also additional and numerous factors, which can be levied only based on the choice of a specific platform.

The innovative aspect of the approach presented in this chapter is that it will lead companies in this re-engineering and architecture modernization effort, by analyzing the source code (i.e. searching for clones, degree of coupling, etc.) as well as the architectural patterns in the application-to-be-migrated. This approach will also provide an analysis on

1. Where the current architecture does not address SaaS architectural requirements,
2. Specific changes needed, as well as
3. Suggestions of existing software components and services.

Interplaying with that, other factors will be taking into account such as business goals and models, costs, effort, impact, ROI, and payback.

BACKGROUND

According to NIST (NIST Cloud Computing, 2011), Cloud computing is a model for enabling convenient, on-demand network access to a shared pool of configurable computing resources (e.g., networks, servers, storage, applications, and services) that can be rapidly provisioned and released with minimal management effort or service provider interaction.

The NIST definition of cloud computing defines three delivery models:

- **Software as a Service (SaaS):** The consumer uses an application, but does not control the operating system, hardware, or network infrastructure on which it is running. Examples: Salesforce.com, Gmail, Google Apps, GotoMeeting, Run My Process.

- **Platform as a Service (PaaS):** The consumer uses a hosting environment for their applications. The consumer controls the applications that run in the environment (and possibly has some control over the hosting environment), but does not control the operating system, hardware or network infrastructure on which they are running. The platform is typically an application framework. Examples: Google App Engine, Microsoft Azure, Salesforce.com.

- **Infrastructure as a Service (IaaS):** The consumer uses "fundamental computing resources" such as processing power, storage, networking components or middleware. The consumer can control the operating system, storage, deployed applications and depending on the specific provider the consumer may control networking components such as firewalls and load balancers, even select the characteristics of the virtual image. Examples: Amazon EC2, Mozy, Nirvana.

Cloud computing refers to both hardware and systems software in the data centres that provide services and the applications delivered as services over the Internet. Those services have long been referred to as Software as a Service (SaaS). In fact, SaaS is a model of software deployment where an application is hosted as a service outside of the customer's site and delivered to customers across the Internet.

A successful SaaS application, unlike any other traditional application, is built as a single instance but multitenant and shared among multiple customers on a common infrastructure (hardware and software). These architectural considerations added to other key functional, scalability, security and support requirements are not addressed in traditional software development, and thus need

to be taken into account while adapting traditional applications architecture to SaaS.

SOA vs. SaaS

SaaS is considered (Mell & Grance, 2011) one of the categories of cloud computing. As explained above, a SaaS application is shared across multiple clients using the "one-to-many" model. The advantage offered for the SaaS end user is that (s)he can avoid installing and maintaining software and can free him/herself from complex software/hardware requirements. The provider of SaaS software, also known as hosted software or on-demand software will take care of the security, availability, and performance of the software because they are in charge of the deployment of the system. Using a multitenant architecture, a single application is delivered to millions of users through Internet browsers. Customers do not require upfront licensing while providers enjoy a lower cost because they are maintaining just one application. Popular SaaS software are Salesforce.com, Workday, Google Apps, and Zogo Office.

SOA is an architectural model in which the solution logic is presented as services (Indika, 2011). By having services as the main method of delivering solutions, SOA strives to be more agile and productive than other existing technology solutions for reusing features from existing components. Besides, SOA makes it possible to access information no accessible by the integration of components in our solutions, such as real time information of stocks or weather. SOA provides support to realize the advantages of service-oriented principles and service-oriented computing. Many different technologies, various products, application programming interfaces, and other various extensions typically make up a SOA implementation.

SOA is a manufacturing model which deals with designing and building software by applying the service oriented computing principles to software solutions, while SaaS is a model for sales and distribution of software applications. In simpler terms, SaaS is a means of delivering software as services over the Internet to its subscribers, while SOA is an architectural model in which the features of a software component are provided as services to other software components. So, SOA (an architectural strategy) and SaaS (a business model) cannot be directly compared. However, to get the maximum benefits of cost reduction and agility, it is highly recommended that enterprises integrate SOA and SaaS together.

The potential of reusing basic services in the SaaS model is no longer restricted to just services running in a defined SOA environment, but the service supplier himself can make use of services from external infrastructures. Theoretically, the SaaS and cloud model allows service developers to completely focus on the subject or domain-specific parts of their software, while profiting from external services by other suppliers to solve all their generics needs such as accounting, billing, or load balancing. However, practice is showing that the utilization of this wide range of offered services is not easy due to several reasons. Nowadays most of the commercial providers of service-infrastructures (e.g. Salesforce.com, Microsoft, or Amazon) offer lots of attractive services, but in order to the most of them, they prompt developers to use also their proprietary development tools, APIs, programming languages and distribution channels. Subsequently these services can be provisioned and executed only in the cloud infrastructure, within which they are also developed.

This approach, which is part of the vendor lock-in strategy, is not convenient to most of the companies, especially small and medium ones that wish to migrate to cloud as it risks their own business sustainability. Additionally, these companies find themselves confronted with other restrictions in the development process such as the obligation of using a certain programming language such as Perl, Python or Ruby. These language restrictions would mean for many companies and especially

Small-Medium Enterprises (SME), the redevelopment their applications right from scratch by using the tool-sets provided by the specific cloud vendor with all the implications that that means.

Nevertheless, these commercial service platforms cannot be ignored, neither as possibility for lowering development costs nor as attractive distribution channels with high visibility in the market. Thus, for technical and business decisions concerning SaaS, it is not only essential to define a technical SOA architecture but also to define, which parts of this SOA can be operated in which, public, hybrid or private, infrastructure to reduce costs while enhancing visibility without drifting in a vendor lock-in.

Migration to SOA Approaches

Transforming legacy applications to services allows systems to remain mostly invariable while exposing functionalities to a large number of customers through well-defined service interfaces. Some migration strategies to SOA, by wrapping components or modules as Web Services may be relatively straightforward but in the long term not efficient. Characteristics such as platform, language, architecture and the target SOA environment play an important role in this complicated task.

There are currently available on literature some approaches to migrate legacy applications to SOA. Even though they attack the problem from different perspectives, they all have some common aspects and some major shortcomings.

The Service-Oriented Migration and Reuse Technique (SMART) (Grace, Lewis, Morris, Smith, & Simanta, 2008) has been developed by SEI at Carnegie Mellon University. SMART process helps organizations to make initial decisions about the feasibility of reusing legacy components as services within an SOA environment. SMART considers the specific interactions that will be required by the target SOA environment and any changes that must be made to the legacy components. To achieve this, SMART gathers information about legacy components, the target SOA environment, and candidate services to be produced. With this information, SMART provides the following outcomes: 1) a preliminary analysis of the viability of migrating legacy components to services, 2) an analysis of the migration strategies available, and 3) preliminary estimates of the costs and risks involved in the migration. SMART is vendor and tool independent, and provides a clear roadmap of the steps to consider in the migration. This approach does not address additional issues on a formal basis like QoS, security, configurability, scalability, and multi-tenancy.

Another approach, the Enterprise Model Driven Migration from legacy to SOA (from now on EMDMA) (Ziemann, Leyking, Kahl, & Dirk, 2006) proposes a business driven legacy-to-SOA migration approach based on "enterprise modelling" to leverage the potential of SOA while considering current enterprise requirements as well as existing (legacy) systems. According to EMDMA, a major contribution of enterprise models for Web Service engineering is the determination of a functional abstraction degree suitable for a flexible business process composition. EMDMA proposes therefore "a procedure to define an adequate granularity of Web Services of an existing legacy system based on a function tree model of the legacy systems." This model represents a hierarchical structure of all functions used within the system. Each node represents a function and its sub-nodes represent sub-functions. From this tree, the task is to select the right functions in the right granularity that has to be converted (i.e. wrapped) into Web Services. Major focus of this approach is put on gaps situated on the conceptual level leaving aside other issues such as functional granularity, security, reliability, QoS.

IBM has also developed its own method to migrate to SOA (Channabasavaiah, Holley, & Tuggle, 2004), known widely as IBM SOMA. Unlike previous approaches that only consider the integration process/service, IBM considers other types of integration such as: Application integration, Integration at the end-user interface, Application connectivity, Process integration, Information integration, and a build to integrate development model. The roadmap of IBM SOMA includes the leveraging of existing assets, the definition of a governance framework, as well as the definition of roles and responsibilities. As for this method, the major drawback is its dependency to the vendor and tools that they offer.

Other tool vendors such as Oracle (Davies, Shaffer, & Demed, 2009), Microsoft (Microsoft Corporation, 2007), or SAP (Enterprise Service-Oriented Architecture, 2012) have also defined their own migration strategies locked to their own products (i.e. Oracle, SAP) or relying heavily on the use of XML technology (Microsoft), limiting scaling possibilities. However, most of these methods proposed by vendors lack of a holistic method to prepare companies to a SOA migration, where both requirements of current legacy systems and business needs have to be taken into account to achieve a successful migration.

BUILDING A GLOBAL MIGRATION STRATEGY: FROM BUSINESS TO TECHNOLOGY

Challenges Addressed

As expressed above, existing approaches and methods for transforming a product based software company into a service based one still present some shortcomings. These shortcomings appear both on technical side, in the way in which they treat interoperability, reliability, QoS, SLA management, scalability, configurability, and multitenancy, basic issues in the development of a SaaS application and on the business issues associated to the business model change usually associated with the service provision.

A deficient management of these shortcomings may end up with high investments from the side of the companies with little security that the product, offered as a service, will be accepted by their current customer spectrum.

Therefore, a new complete procedure model is needed, which helps enterprises improve their technical know-how in order to migrate their software to cloud computing platforms as well as to supply them with methods and principles with respect to developing a SaaS-ready business model. This solution will need to face up with the following identified challenges:

- The transformation of legacy software into SaaS is a complex process where both technical and business aspects have to be considered as part of the same problem.
- Service based software is linked to specific architectural aspects such as multitenancy, monitoring, metering, billing, security, SLA and QoS that have to be taken into consideration.
- The quality of services-based software is especially critical when transforming and maintaining the performance of the legacy application in the new environment.
- The evolution and re-engineering of legacy software is unpredictable, costly, and time-and-resource-consuming, thus, is difficult to calculate the resources needed and the ROI to achieve.
- Software provided as a Service needs to be managed and controlled in the provision phase. Several generic functionalities such as monitoring, billing, accounting, and access control have to be included for each service offered as a Service.
- Currently, the provision of cloud services (namely IaaS and PaaS) is concentrated on a number of large companies. Placing an application on any of these providers usually means automatic vendor-lock in and no interoperability with other cloud providers, especially critical when wishing to

port an application from one provider to another.
- Software off the shelf business model cannot be applied directly without adjustments to the SaaS business model. Changes are required in the business model in order to ensure some degree of success in the service provision.
- SaaS business model may involve the automation of some processes in order to meet the customer expectations over some *de-facto* standard in the interaction with SaaS. For example, online subscription, message based support or configurable mail notifications.
- Redefinition of the pricing model for the product.
- Implications that changing to this new business model has in the company, as new considerations need to be taken into account: creation of SLA's, definition of legal procedures for trust issues, redefinition of roles within the employees, creation of new departments, change in the internal business processes, etc.

Approach

The presented approach tries to face up the aforementioned challenges introducing some innovative points, which are not being tackled in current existing solutions:

- Holistic focus mixing technological challenges and business related aspects.
- Stepwise approximation to the problem enabling the coexistence of both business models (SaaG/SaaS), minimizing failure risks.
- Support in the decision making process with the provision of impact assessment tools.
- Complete technical scope including current needs related to Cloud Computing

challenges such as cloud portability, scalability, and multi-tenancy.

- Application independent SaaS provision ecosystem for the complete management of the service offered including security, billing, monitoring and infrastructure abstraction components.

The envisioned approach is shown in Figure 1. The solution is mainly based on 3 layers:

1. A set of tools to assess the impact, cost, effort needed, ROI and migration implies.
2. Stepwise procedure with tailoring strategies to migrate legacy software to a service oriented paradigm.
3. A SaaS ecosystem to support the implementation and provisioning of Service based software.

Migration Solution

The precedent picture depicts the suggested solution to migrate legacy software to a SaaS business model. This approach is iterative, stepwise and thus, minimizes risks. The phases of the solution are:

Phase 1: Migration Evaluation and Decision Making: This phase comprises as a first step the evaluation of the initial situation of the application to migrate and the establishment of the desired situation to achieve. The evaluation will be performed through a bi-dimensional quadrant where both technical aspects and business aspects are detailed. Following, a set of tools to assess the impact, cost, effort needed, and ROI to move from the initial situation to the final one will be used to help

Figure 1. Migration approach

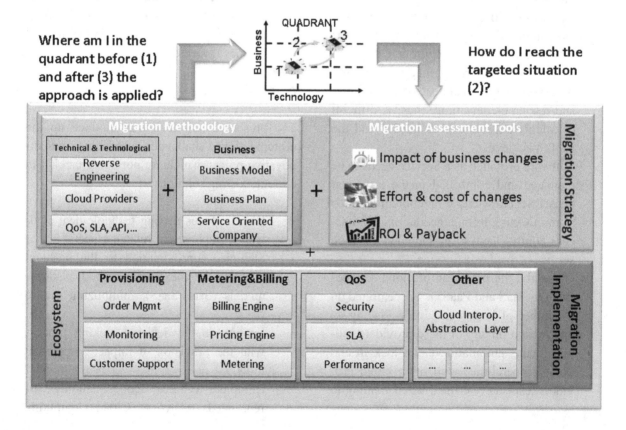

the decision making whether to go ahead with the migration or not.

Phase 2: Migration Implementation and Service Provision: Once the decision has been taken, the solution proposes a methodology to perform. This methodology is supported by a set of tools to automate as much as possible the migration process. Furthermore, an ecosystem of generic components needed to offer software as a service (such us metering and billing components, monitoring, customer support tools, etc.) is provided.

These phases and the associated tools are explained in the following sections.

Phase 1: Migration Evaluation and Decision Making

Phase 1.1: Quadrant

A successful migration must start with the analysis of the product to be migrated, both now ("Analysis of the initial situation") and the desired situation after the migration has taken place ("Analysis of the target situation"), in terms of technology and business. This is especially critical when talking about migration to SaaS, where architecture modernization issues and new business models are so much intertwined.

There are several ways to perform this analysis. In this case, the way selected has been a Quadrant. This Quadrant analyses the information under two axes, one focusing on Technology (architecture, performance, reliability, how coupled the code is, security, data base design, etc) and the other one on Business, namely pricing model, business internal processes and sustainability.

Similar to the evaluation of quality criteria as motivated by the ISO 9126 quality model standard and used in the methodology of the "bidirectional quality model" (Simon, Seng, & Mohaupt, 2006), this approach, the Quadrant, measures several metrics by evaluating questions, checklists and

analyzing features of the existing software. The measured metrics are aggregated to indicators of interest, which define a characteristic used to calculate the maturity of the business model and the maturity of the technology model, both before the migration and after the migration takes place (see Figure 2).

For the time being[1], the maturity of each axis is defined as follows:

- Technology axis
  - (0,0) **Monolithic:** Interface logic, business logic, data logic are in the same machine.
  - (0,0.5) Client-server with a thick client (i.e. VB application), event driven. Code tightly coupled to the interface. DB is in the local network or on a server outside but all the logic remains in the same machine.
  - (0,1) Client-server with a thin client (i.e. j2EE application, 2-n tier), with no usage of Web services. Multiple DB instances.
  - (0,2) Client-server with a thin client such as Mozilla, opera, chrome or Internet explorer (i.e. J2EE application, 2-n tier), with usage of Web services. A unique instance of the DB. Multiple instances of the application.
  - (0,3) Client-server with a thin client, 1 DB instance, 1 DB application, n appearance customizations.
- Business axis
  - (0,0) License (installment), support, updates, upgrades, maintenance are paid under a different fee model than the license. No helpdesk. No SLA. No upgrade protocol and procedures.
  - (0,0.5) Most revenues are obtained from sales of licenses. Even though, there exist some sales (less than 10% of the total amount) that are made in a service form with a flat rate model.

Figure 2. Quadrant

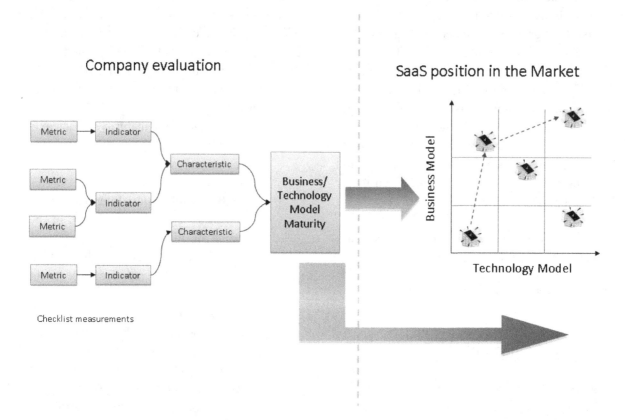

○ (1,0) Most revenues are obtained from sales of licenses. Between 10-20% are from the product sale as service with pay per use, flat rate, hybrid pricing models. SLA is being defined. Upgrade protocol and procedures are being defined.

○ (2,0) More than 60% of the sales are from the product as a service. Helpdesk is institutionalized but not 24x7 and only in certain languages. Existence of SLA, upgrade protocol but upgrades are still seldom, legal department.

○ (3,0) 100% of the sales are from the product as a service. Existence of a 24x7 helpdesk, multilingual, Marketing mostly done through the Internet (social media), SLA, upgrade protocol and procedures, Long Tail.

There are two main outcomes of the application of the quadrant:

1. Where the product is right now, before the migration takes place,
2. Where the company desires the product to be once the migration takes place.

Phase 1.2: Impact Assessment Tools

Once the company is able to visualize both their actual and future situation, it is time to analyze what this gap means in terms of impact in the company (how will the company's processes be affected?, will different commercialization models of the same product be able to cohabit?), in terms of approximate costs (how much will this migration cost the company?), and in terms of ROI and payback (When will the company recover this investment? Which will be the return of this investment?). The solution presented here considers these issues in three additional tools baptized as "Impact Assessment Tools." The main purpose of these tools is to assess and help companies decide whether the migration is feasible for them based on objective numbers and indicators and not on subjective considerations. Besides, these objective numbers are presented in measurement units easily understandable by the management of the company as they are expressed in $, hours, or years.

The main characteristics of these tools include the following:

1. **Impact of business changes:** Tool to measure how the business model of the migrated solution will impact the overall results of the company as a whole, considering a pessimistic situation, an optimistic one and an average one, and will be compared to the situation in which the product would not be migrated.

2. **Effort of changes and required actions to migrate:** This tool analyses code patterns, code clones, how coupled the code is and from there, it calculates how many actions will be required to migrate the code and how much effort they will cost. Monetization of the effort can easily be derived.

3. **Calculation of ROI and payback:** This tool will calculate the return of investment and payback, taken into account as entry parameters how much the migration will cost, and the expected benefits (savings in trips, savings in error correction, savings in development as the target technological environment is one and not many, sales margin, etc).

Phase 2: Migration Implementation and Service Provision

Methodology and Tools

If the company decides that the costs and effort are not feasible and they cannot face them, then they must search for another target situation by making use of the Quadrant. On the other hand, if the company decides positively on the feasibility, then the Improvement (Migration) Approach must be determined and applied. Unlike current existing migration approaches, in the case of migrating towards a service as a service provision model, both architecture modernization and business model need to be taken into account. These are probably the most important challenges that are faced in this step.

Not all companies have the same maturity at technology level and therefore cannot be suggested a "one size fits all" approach or a "big bang approach." In addition, each product is a world and has a different starting point and thus, different requirements. However, most products, when migrating to Cloud, face similar requirements:

- **Architecture:** How to address multitenancy and other architectural needs related to the Cloud Paradigm and what implications they have in the code and in the Data Base.
- Service Level Agreements and QoS considerations
- Security for cloud applications
- Monitoring, i.e. of actions performed by users, usage of resources
- **Billing:** How to bill automatically different users based on their pricing model.
- **Changes in the business processes:** Need to have, for example, a permanent helpdesk, multilingualism, or legal issues.
- Different strategies for different parts of the system. For each component of the new system different decisions have can be made during the feasibility analysis: create

Figure 3. Migration activity areas

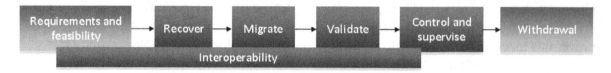

the component by wrapping a existing one, reengineer the component, use the component as is in the legacy, buy a new one from the market, developed from scratch or even subcontract the development.

The Migration Methodology currently implements the activity areas shown in Figure 3.

Step 1: Requirements

The purpose of the requirements activity area is to gather the additional requirements for the migrated system, and to identify the main components of the solution and their implementation strategy. The purpose is not an exhaustive description of all requirements of the objective system, but the description of the requirements that will require develop effort and will be used as a basis for the validation of the system. In this initial requirement elicitation process, it is also not necessary to focus on those requirements that will come up from the systematic analysis of the legacy. This affects mainly the requirements of components that are going to be reengineered.

The main source for the specification of these requirements and the components of the solution is the result of the application of the impact assessment tool. The impact assessment tool evaluates different alternatives for the cloud system implementation having the idea of the system in mind. This activity focuses on the selected alternative and the requirements derived from the idea of the new system.

Step 2: Recover

The purpose of this activity area is recover the knowledge from those legacy components that in the feasibility analysis has been pointed as candidates to be reengineered. The application of recover methods and tools will provide the application model of the legacy application. Moreover, the application of recover methods and tools may provide information on the requirements and even in the testing procedures for the migrated code.

Step 3: Migrate

The purpose of this macro-activity is to define and implement the new system based on the elements identified during the requirement and recover phases. This will include also the definition of the necessary new components to fulfill the past features and the additional requirements.

As stated above, one of the basic requirements of a well-designed SaaS application is the existence of monitoring, security, and billing components. These components need to be fully integrated in the resulting application and the methodology must give companies indications on when and why these components must be used.

These components are generic and independent from the application provided but at the same time they are tightly linked to the software migrated. The separation of the supporting functionalities into different elements will provide a set of reusable components for each application to be migrated, avoiding the necessity of having to develop these components from scratch for each new migrated product. Following, an overview of the components and the functionalities required for each one is provided. This list is not exhaustive but it does show the basic components that a well-designed application must have:

- **Billing Component:** Support for variable prizing plans and for automatic billing, purchase/clients order management and support for credit card payments.
- **Monitoring Component:** Management of different monitoring parameters, SLA shaping and monitoring, and alert generation.
- **Security Component:** Security for Multi-tenant environments, Information security management, and support of different security levels (technical, legal, and business levels).
- **Intercloud API:** Transparent support for different clouds providers.

Step 4: Validation

The purpose of this activity area is to define testing strategy to verify that the generated system implements the requirements identified and verify that the components (including those not reengineered) work properly.

Once all the migration activities are finalized, the validation phase starts. This validation phase includes not only functional validation but also what it is more important, non-functional validation, especially performance, reliability, and security. In the case of cloud computing applications, these three aspects must be stressed on.

Step 5: Supervise

The purpose of this macro-activity is to provide elements to control the performance of the system and to modify that performance.

The last step, control and supervision, allows a company to monitor at all times, the performance of the application once this has been released and provisioned as a service, so it can be improved in performance, reliability, resources used and beware of possible degradation.

Step 6: Interoperability

The purpose of this macro-activity is to provide tools that facilitate the development and monitoring of the features on interoperability areas. This may include the development of new components.

Interoperability is a crosscutting activity to the general methodology that deals with the interoperability issues that affect SaaS along the other activity areas (requirements, recover, migrate, validate, supervise, and withdrawal).

Step 7: Withdrawal

The purpose of this macro-activity is to provide elements to stop the service, with the purpose of finalizing it or with the purpose of moving to another cloud infrastructure.

These activities may be organized in several ways, waterfall, prototyping, or even v-model. The selection of the appropriate life cycle to for the implementation of the migration depends highly on the culture of the enterprise and the characteristics of the migration project. As a general rule an iterative and incremental life cycle is recommended such as those applied in well know methodologies like RUP (rational unified process), Open UP, or the agile methodologies (XP or SCRUM) (see Figure 4).

PRACTICAL USE CASE

The approach presented before is currently being piloted in eight companies in Spain and for the time being, no major shortcomings were encountered. Next, one of the most challenging cases will be presented. For confidentiality reasons, the name of the company and the product have been changed but not the steps taken to migrate their product into the form of service offering.

Value Solutions is a company that develops mostly turnkey software. They recently acquired another company that develops a BPM product named "Management by Processes," which is

Figure 4. Migration lifecycle model

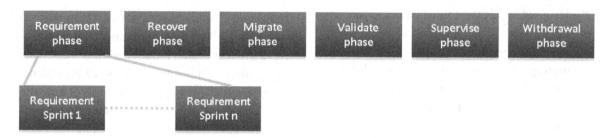

commercialized as a package, with licenses and yearly maintenance fee.

The management of Value Solutions sees great potential in the tool and would like to open new markets, as they are now mainly oriented to the Spanish-speaking one. However, they also know that the product cannot be sold any longer solely as it is now, as the travel expenses incurred by their consultants installing the product at the customer's site would increase exponentially, shall the market get global.

Value Solutions CIO has heard of a new way in which to offer software. It is something that is called "Software as a Service," offered through the Internet or the Cloud, but he really does not know what this means from the technical point of view or from the business point of view. He has read that this way of selling a product offers the company several benefits: development costs decrease, consultants do not have to travel to install the software as it is offered through the Internet, upgrades in the case of severe errors can also be done almost on the fly, having always a working version accessible by all customers, new international markets are easier to reach. So, he proposes, what if the company moved to this way of selling their product? To help the rest of the managers decide, he suggests analysing both the current status of their product and the future one, in terms of architecture and technology but also in terms of business model and the implications that this change would have in the whole company.

The approach presented in this chapter is the one that has been applied at Value Systems. A first step has been the analysis of the current situation of the product "Management by Processes." These are the main facts obtained:

- Technology
  - Source Code in Java, database from a commercial vendor
  - Developed with a proprietary SDK, that it is not updated and improved any more
  - Accessed through a Heavyweight client, based on SWT
  - No security mechanisms
  - Nothing is monitored
  - GUI in Spanish
- Business
  - License fee
  - Maintenance fee
  - Consultants must travel to the customer's site to install, repair and upgrade the software
  - No helpdesk by email or telephone, only by direct contact
  - Market is all Spanish speaking countries

And its position in the Quadrant is shown in Figure 5.

As expressed in the process exposed before, in order to set the migration path, the company must reflect on how they would like to offer their

Figure 5. Value solutions initial position in the quadrant

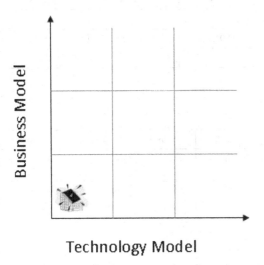

Figure 6. Value solutions desired position in the quadrant

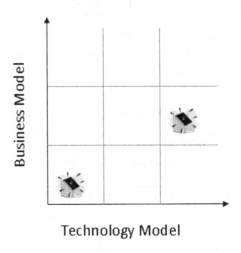

application. Value Solutions has decided the following:

- Highest level of multi-tenancy, where there is one instance of the application and multiple tenants that share the Database, the Operative System, the Middleware and the rest of Hardware Resources
- **Environment:** Java based application, usage of Web services (also aggregated), on Linux, Apache and MySQL
- GUI customized in several languages
- Private Cloud Provider for the infrastructure
- **Pricing Model:** Flat Rate
- Both products (the one offered as a service and the one offered as a package) must cohabit
- Helpdesk by email and telephone at certain times of the day
- Global market (see Figure 6)

Therefore, the desired situation places them in the Quadrant as follows (in colour):

Now that Value Solutions has analysed where their product is at the moment and how they will like to offer their product in the future, it is time to analyse whether this migration is financially feasible and affordable in terms of effort, impact and business sustainability. In order to achieve this data, the next steps are performed:

1. **Analysis of the source code:** Functions and parameters, complexity of the functions, code clones, usage of libraries, dependences with the proprietary development framework, internal components and other external components, analysis of the database queries, interface with other systems.

2. High Level Analysis of the candidate functions or modules that might be exposed as services in an easy manner.

3. Modelling of the application, expressed as UML.

4. Analysis of the Database Schema and Tables.

5. **Analysis of the current economic context of the application:** Actual number of customers, maximum and minimum development and deployment costs in the last five years, benefits, existence of SLA's with customers.

6. Analysis of the company's internal procedures.

7. **Time to market for the new application:** 3 years.

Table 1. ROI and payback calculations

ROI Measures	Year 1	Year 2	Year 3	Year 4	Year 5
Net present value €21.725					
Return on investment	38,4%	57,9%	82,9%	105,7%	127,3%
Payback (in years) 2,62					

Table 2. Cost of changes

Initial Investment	Year 0	Year 1	Year 2	Year 3	Year 4	Year 5
Initial investment (infrastructure acquisition and migration execution)	€39028	€117084	€78056	€0	€0	€0
Implementation costs (maintenance of the infrastructure)	€0	€2400	€2400	€4800	€9600	€9600
Ongoing support costs	€0	€35000	€35000	€35000	€35000	€35000
Training costs (in the new technologies and architecture)	€0	€30000	€15000	€5000	€5000	€5000
Other Costs	€0	€0	€0	€0	€0	€0
Total Costs	€39028	€184484	€130456	€44800	€49600	€49600

The outcome of all these analysis is shown in Table 1.

1. ROI and Payback
2. **Impact of business changes:** High
   a. Two product offerings must cohabit (as a package and as a service).
   b. SLA's must be defined and respected.
   c. A helpdesk must be created and resources assigned.
   d. Personnel must be trained in this new architecture model and programming requirements.
   e. Code is tightly coupled. Exposition of functions as services may not be possible in most cases. The only alternative for most of the application will be and MDA-ADM approach.
   f. Some company internal business processes have to be changed and readapted (i.e. invoicing process).
3. Cost of changes for the next 5 years, with a time to market of 3 years (see Figure 2).

These data allows Value Solutions decide, based on actual numbers, whether they can confront the migration or not. In this case the answer is positive … and the migration will take place!

The steps performed to execute the migration, based on the kind of product, its characteristics and the desired characteristics, can be summarized as follows:

1. Since the service will be offered using the infrastructure installed at the company's premises (through a private Cloud), the first step was to perform a feasibility analysis on which virtualization infrastructure was best to support the application's technical requirements. Once the most adequate infrastructure has been selected, purchase it and install it.
2. Redefine the database schema and tables to make it multitenant compliant. Value Solutions has decided to share instances of the same Database, at database server level. In this case, all tenants share a common database user schema. This solution, although

complicated to implement and optimize, was selected after a careful cost analysis.

3. From the high level analysis of candidate functions/modules to be migrated performed in the feasibility phase, differ the "real" candidates vs. the "fake" ones, that is, those functions that even before the migration is executed, the low level analysis confirms that the overall performance will decrease. In the case of this product, only 10% of the functions can be exposed as service in an easy manner.

4. Model the rest of the code (From Code to KDM to UML to SoaML).

5. Generate automatically the code based on the SoaML profile. Modify and update when necessary, including the particularities of having a multitenant application.

6. Develop new functionalities from scratch.

7. Parameterize the GUI side of the application so it can be easily customised based on customers' and language's requirements.

8. Integrate this code/services with basic components that make a SaaS application well designed namely a security component, a monitoring one, and a billing one. These components were selected among a set of different ones available in open source communities, customized and updated according to the company's needs and product's requirements. For this case, these components were customized as follows:

    a. **Security:** Authentication and access control functionalities including a users' repository implementation with the roles and permissions. Guidelines and procedures on how to deal with the current legislation on data privacy.

    b. **Billing:** Component to support automation of the purchasing and invoicing process. The functionalities were customized to the new business model selected (monthly paid flat rate).

    c. **Monitoring:** Functionalities mostly used depending on the role, event response time, queries performed.

9. Perform validation and verification tests of the whole application with special focus on performance (comparison of current response times with old response times – the company has decided that the product will not be released until these times are similar), stress and load in different situations. Other points of interests: SOA Governance, WS-SLA, security, and of course, functional issues. Most of these tests have been automated in order to be able to execute regression tests each time the product is upgraded.

10. Develop an SLA for the new service. Some of the topics that need to be treated in this SLA are:

    a. Incident Management (Helpdesk levels support, answering times, classification of incidences, …)

    b. Privacy, Trust, and Data Protection

    c. Quality of Service commitments (Availability time, Performance, …)

11. Develop an upgrade protocol and procedure to perform it.

12. Determine the price under which the service will be sold. Input parameters: forecast of average monthly costs (infrastructure maintenance, resilient development costs), estimation of customers (part of this number will come from questionnaires launched to current customers and their interest to migrate to this new delivery model, whilst the other part will be based on a market analysis).

13. Analyse which business process(es) inside the company are affected by shifting to this new offering and under which circumstances. An important consideration is the fact that the product will be offered at least for 5 more years as a good but also as a service. Thus, new business processes need to be created

while others need to be updated to the new situation.

14. Model these processes with "Management by Processes" and prepare them for being executed.

15. Train personnel to understand this business model shift.

Feedback Obtained

All actions expressed above were completely executed, and in this case, quarterly checkpoints were planned in order to identify potential shortcomings, deviations, major risks of not achieving the ideal situation and how far the migration that is taking place is from that ideal situation. Preliminary feedback commented:

- The knowledge of the process and the impact of its application previous to make the migration have been very valuable to actually take the decision and prepare the required resources. This process has shown to be fast and accurate.

- The methodology applied has reduced the migration process as key points were previously identified in the evaluation phase. Supporting tools and techniques such as SOAML have reduced the time required to recode the application by approximately 20%.

- The identification of existing components for generic functionalities (security, billing, and monitoring) has reduced the required resources to develop them and promote the reutilisation of those in following migrations. Until now, these functionalities were ad-hoc developed for each migration. This has been also reported as a weakness, since these components will not be able to be reused in other applications that the company may wish to migrate.

- The development and adaptation of the business model as well as the technical so-

lution established have improved the performance of the migration process.

FUTURE RESEARCH DIRECTIONS

This approach is currently being validated in eight companies in Spain, with different maturity levels, market, and technology. As it is still early to say, for the time being, no major shortcomings were encountered. This indicates that the overall solution is adequate and addresses software evolution problems. However, there is still a lot of work to do and improvements to make. These include:

- **Quadrant:** The set of questions have proved to be valid for the eight cases in which the approach was tested and piloted. However, as the environment was quite controlled in terms of current and target business models and migrated products and technologies, it is clear that if the scope is widened, a new set of questions may arise.

  In addition, due to different time constraints, the analysis of the position of the products in the quadrant was performed manually. The idea is to automate this analysis as much as possible and provide it as a Web service apart from just a spreadsheet.

- **Methodology:** The methodology is currently mainly focused on the technical aspects of the migration, leaving aside some important business aspects in each of the phases of the methodology. Thus, a more cohesive methodology integrating the business aspects needs to be further extended. Additionally, the methodology is not now supported by an integrated tool chain. Instead, companies must move from one tool to the other, which generates a lot of confusion and even discrepancies. Therefore, a next step will be to integrate all these aspects (code analysis, reverse engineering, modeling, SoaML, …) in one toolset with clear and specific user guidelines.

- **Components:** In the case of the components, these research and implementation extensions need to be tackled.
  - The components have been developed and customized following the requirements of the 8 companies participating in the pilots making hard its application in other environments.
  - More components should be added to the ecosystem to fulfill upcoming requirements.

- A benchmarking tool to assess the current and desired company situation around SaaS, including both the technological and business dimension.
- A set of tools to calculate the impacts of core issues involved in the migration process.
- A risk minimized, stepwise procedure with tailoring strategies to migrate legacy software to a service oriented paradigm.
- A catalogue of essential components needed to deploy and provide successful and sustainable service based software.

CONCLUSION

Currently, a large number of companies have identified the SaaS business model as the one to be adopted in the near future for their software products. Nevertheless, the performance of this migration, from a Software off the shelf based company to a SaaS oriented company, is an important challenge to face. Due to the complexity and the implications (at technical, business, and organizational levels) an incorrect transition of business models or technology migration may lead to a fatal situation, even bankruptcy or disappearance or the company.

The theoretical and practical solution presented in this chapter, as well as the envisioned future research directions will bridge the transition towards the new era of Internet of Services providing the Software Industry methods and criteria that will enable important breakthroughs in software engineering methods and architectures, allowing flexible, dynamic, dependable and scalable development, provision, and consumption of advanced Service based Software.

This complete solution includes key features like:

REFERENCES

Channabasavaiah, K., Holley, K., & Tuggle, E. M. (2004). *Migrating to a service-oriented architecture*. Retrieved from ftp://service.boulder.ibm.com/s390/audio/pdfs/G224-7298-00_Final-MigratetoSOA.pdf

Davies, J., Shaffer, D., & Demed, L. (2009). *Oracle SOA suite 11g*. Retrieved from http://www.oracle.com/technetwork/middleware/soasuite/overview/wp-soa-suite-11gr1-2-129551.pdf

Enterprise Service-Oriented Architecture. (2012). *SAP enterprise service-oriented architecture: Adoption program*. Retrieved from http://www.sap.com/platform/soa/adoptionprogram.epx

Grace, A., Lewis, G. A., Morris, E. J., Smith, D. B., & Simanta, S. (2008). *SMART: Analyzing the reuse potential of legacy components in a service-oriented architecture environment*. Technical Note: CMU/SEI 2208-TN-008. Retrieved from http://www.sei.cmu.edu/reports/08tn008.pdf

Indika. (2011). *Differences between SaaS and SOA*. Retrieved from http://www.differencebetween.com/difference-between-saas-and-vs-soa/

Mell, P., & Grance, T. (2011). *The NIST definition of cloud computing*. Retrieved from http://www.nist.gov/itl/cloud/index.cfm

Microsoft Corporation. (2007). *Real world SOA at the edge*. Retrieved from http://download.microsoft.com/download/d/d/e/ddeb427d-dc05-4ab0-b47e-74f0a936d892/Real-World-SOA-At-The-Edge.pdf

Simon, F., Seng, O., & Mohaut, T. (2006). *Code-quality-management*. Heidelberg, Germany: Dpunkt.

Ziemann, J., Leyking, K., Kahl, T., & Dirk, W. (2006). *Enterprise model driven migration from legacy to SOA*. Paper presented at the Software Reengineering and Services Workshop. Passau, Germany.

KEY TERMS AND DEFINITIONS

Evolutionary Software: Similar to software modernization.

Legacy Application Or Legacy Software: Legacy software is an existing software product developed compliant to the specifications of the source framework, while the target software system is a software product, compliant to the specifications of the target framework and resulted as outcome of a migration process. We assume our legacy software (regardless it is already running on a production framework or not) was produced in the context of a source framework different from the target framework subject of migration. By framework we refer, in general, to the complete software infrastructure required to produce and execute a software system, including software development and execution environments (SDKs, Application Containers, data storage, etc.), software specifications and languages, etc. By software, we refer to the complete software sources, not exclusively code, but also data schemas, data sources, artefacts, documentation, etc.

Migration vs. Modernization: In this chapter, we address software migration in general, but also software modernization in particular. For example, depending on the nature of the legacy software product in particular, the migration to the Cloud can be considered as modernization or just migration. In other words, we address in general software migration, regardless the business reasons behind that migration need. That is, here, legacy software is not necessarily obsolete.

Multi Tenancy: It refers to a principle in software architecture where a single instance of the software runs on a single infrastructure, serving multiple client organizations (tenants) and supporting a high consolidation of the resources. Multitenancy is contrasted with a multi-instance architecture where separate software instances (or hardware systems) are set up for different client organizations. There are 3 different levels for creating a multi-tenant environment depending on the types of resources shared among the different tenants: hardware consolidation level, application consolidation level, data base consolidation level.

Payback: The length of time required to recover the cost of an investment.

Software: Migration: It implies that the source (legacy) and target frameworks are different in some essential aspects, which impede the legacy system to be executed on the target framework without accomplishing important changes on the legacy software system. Therefore, this framework mismatching requires applying transformations on the legacy software.

Software Modernization: A particular case of software migration is software modernization, where the target software framework was specified (and created) time after the source software framework was, whereby target specification can be consider much more modern that source specification. In the way around, source software framework can be considered obsolete.

ENDNOTES

1. The current maturity levels of the Technology and Business axis have been established based on the professional experience and SoTA studies from the authors. Nevertheless, the maturity levels will be accordingly updated with new achievements.

Chapter 9
Migration of Data between Cloud and Non-Cloud Datastores

Shreyansh Bhatt
DA-IICT, India

Sanjay Chaudhary
DA-IICT, India

Minal Bhise
DA-IICT, India

ABSTRACT

The on demand services and scalability features of cloud computing have attracted many customers to move their applications into the cloud. Therefore, application, data access, storage, and migration to and from cloud have garnered much recent attention, especially with well-established legacy applications. Cloud service providers are following different standards to host applications and data. In the present chapter, the authors focus on data migration from various datastores to cloud and vice versa. They have discussed various challenges associated with this reciprocal migration and proposed a simple yet powerful model whereby data can be migrated between various datastores, especially cloud datastores. The results show an efficient way to move data from conventional relational databases to Google App Engines and how data residing in the Google App Engines can be stored on relational databases and vice versa. They provide a generalized architecture to store data in any cloud datastore. The authors use RDF/RDFS as an intermediate model in the migration process.

INTRODUCTION

This chapter introduces the data interoperability problem associated with cloud computing. The chapter begins with introduction to various cloud datastores to emphasize how their different data storage schemes affect data interoperability. RDF/RDFS has been used to provide interoperability in Web services (Auer, 2010) and in relational database merging (Nagarajan, 2006); we have used it to provide interoperability in cloud data migration. Mapping algorithms are discussed in detail to facilitate the migration. We have used

DOI: 10.4018/978-1-4666-2488-7.ch009

Copyright © 2013, IGI Global. Copying or distributing in print or electronic forms without written permission of IGI Global is prohibited.

mySQL as non-cloud datastore and the Google App Engine as cloud datastore to show the migration process. We have further proposed the generalized framework for cloud data migration. The main objective of this chapter is to provide a solution to migrate data between datastores with different schema. In other words, we have aimed and achieved data and schema migration.

MAIN FOCUS OF THE CHAPTER

Cloud Datastore

Various cloud datastores and their data storage schemes are discussed. An application running on the cloud requires dealing with a huge amount of data. Applications must be as scalable as the database of application. RDBMS is not suitable for such a requirement, e.g. handling a large amount of unstructured data, providing elastic scalability, etc. Therefore, new document oriented distributed datastores are emerging to cater to these requirements. Moreover, different cloud datastores are following different schemes to store the data. We discuss the data storage scheme of such cloud datastores to elaborate the point.

Apache CouchDB

CouchDB is an open source document-oriented schema free database-management system, accessible using a RESTful JavaScript Object Notation (JSON) API. Couch stands for Cluster of Unreliable Commodity Hardware. It stores data in JASON format. It can include all native datatypes in programming language. It stores data in the form of a document.

CouchDB is schema free, i.e. one document can have fields that another document doesn't have. Documents are the actual representation of data objects. CouchDB stores uniquely named documents with document ID and revision number.

Each document can be made of a number of fields not bound by size and with unique names. Documents can have attachments that can be both text as well as digital. When changes are made, a new version of document called revision is created. It does not have a locking mechanism. Two users can load and edit the same document at same time. It maintains consistency by ensuring updates either work or fail (Bhat, 2010).

It achieves scalability and availability by periodically copying documents between servers. It supports file attachments, which can be in the form of music, images, etc. This feature is not seen in traditional databases. It assigns a universally unique identifier to each and every document. It does not support join. It allows creating arbitrary relations between documents.

Amazon SimpleDB

Items are stored as resources in simpleDB. These resources can have multivalued attributes. These resources can be related to each other, and the relationship between these resources can be visualized as a hierarchical tree structure as shown in Figure 1.

As it is a schema-less storage, an item can have a different set of attributes from other items in the domain. It does not store raw data. Rather, it expands input data and creates indices over multiple dimensions to quickly query that data. It can be used as a flat file store. Individual item name, attribute names, and attribute values can be up to 1024 bytes in length. Amazon simpleDB allows 10GB of storage for each domain with 100 domains per customer account, which provides 1TB of total storage.

Bigtable: Google App Engine Datastore

The most popular way of persisting data in Web applications has been the use of relational databases.

Figure 1. Amazon simpleDB data storage model

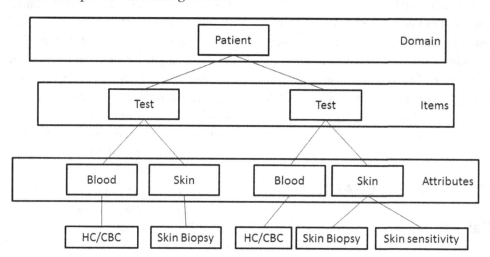

However, setting the focus on high flexibility and scalability, the GAE (Google App Engine) uses a different approach for data persistence, called Bigtable (Chang, 2008). Bigtable is a distributed storage system that is designed to scale to a very large size, i.e. terabytes of data across thousands of commodity servers. Many projects at Google store data in Bigtable, including Google Finance and Google Earth.

Instead of the rows found in a relational database, Bigtable stores data in the form of entities. Entities are always associated with a certain kind (like table in relational database). These entities have properties resembling columns in relational database schema. However, here entities are actually schema-less, i.e. one entity can have a different number and/or different types of properties or columns than other entities of the same kind.

Consider, there are 3 entities in (OR "of") one kind, as shown in Table 1. It is possible that E1 has columns P1, P2. E2 has columns A1, A2, A3. E3 has only one column A1. It is also possible to store multiple values in single cell, i.e. to have multi-valued attributes for an entity. There is a notion of reference key having a similar notion of foreign key in relational databases, but here a child entity can exist independently from parent

Table 1. Kind in bigtable

E1	P1	P2	
E2	A1	A2	A3
E3	A1		

entity, i.e. even if a parent entity is deleted, a child entity can exist in its kind. Each entity has entity key, which is unique among all entity of all applications hosted on Google App Engine. Suppose we have a query that a leader board for the game app would need to retrieve the 10 Player entities with the highest score property values.

This query includes, the kinds of the entities to query, zero or more filters, zero or more sort orders. A query based on property values can only return entities of a single kind. This is the primary purpose of kinds: to determine which entities are considered together as a possible result for a query. GQL is developed to query GAE datastore. Python environment includes rich API for preparing queries using GQL. However, Java environment does not have such API. JDO/JPA can be used to query GAE datastore for Java application.

Cloud Benefits

One of the prime benefits of platform as a service, a cloud service model, is allowing offsite software development. This really cuts out the overhead of managing and updating servers, operating systems, hardware, and installing newer versions of development software. The service provider handles these headaches so the development staff can focus on goals to be met.

Platform as a service provides scalability and a pay as you go pricing model. It allows the customer to focus on the application and the benefits a customer can get from that application rather than worrying about managing application resources (application server, operating system, database, etc.) and infrastructure resources (processor, memory, datacenter, etc.).

One of the companies that benefits from cloud computing is ECMInstitute LLC, in Fredricksburg, Virginia. The company distributes data about content management for large businesses to 1,000 members. Since the application is managed and maintained from a centralized location, maintenance is worry-free.

Programmers from anywhere can collaborate on the same project. This provides businesses the opportunity to hire the best talent without having to worry about expenses, such as travel or relocation. In addition, since version control is built into the design, if something does not work right, the business can go back to the previous version of the software without having to experience downtime.

Migration to Cloud

A recent survey from the International Association of Outsourcing Professionals (IAOP) found two-thirds of outsourcing customers currently do utilize or have plans to implement cloud computing solutions. This fact shows how cloud is becoming favorite among enterprises for cost savings.

In this section, we will assess threats, which are moderating the acceptance of the cloud for organizations. The first question that any customers face after knowing the cloud benefits is, "How can I move my existing application to the cloud?" Cloud service providers have provided answers for such questions, but it raises an issue of lock-in. Let us consider a case study to illustrate this point in detail. We will mainly focus on the data aspect to illustrate integrity and problems of data migration.

An automobile company wants to have their all IT services from one cloud service provider to reduce IT cost. The first issue is how currently running applications can be migrated. Being specific and focusing on the data migration of applications, currently data is hosted using relational schema and the cloud service provider uses a datastore that is not relational. Moving current data to such cloud datastore induces a very costly operation of restructuring the database. As discussed about different cloud datastores in the previous section, cloud datastores are not following a single scheme to store data. Therefore, if the company finds out that another cloud service provider is providing better deal, it has to perform data restructuring again.

Consider a specific scenario of moving relational database to Google App Engine datastore (bigtable) without restructuring data. Bigtable expects data in the form of entities and encourages denormalization of data. Therefore, if data is in a normalized form, it requires more queries to be fired to get a specific result, as queries with join are not supported. Now, the number of queries allowed is limited for application. In other words, the application will suffer.

Data restructuring is imposed by the migration process. It becomes more tedious when restructured data compliant to Bigtable has to be migrated to a different cloud datastore, e.g. Amazon simple db, which is storing data in form of resources. We have come up with a simple yet powerful approach to this problem, i.e. to have a rich representation of data to match requirements of various cloud datastores.

Figure 2. An approach for data migration

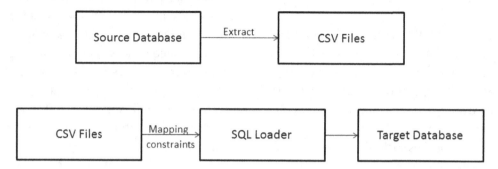

Data Migration Approach

Figure 2 shows one of the approaches for data migration currently used, CSV (Comma Separated Value) files are generated from source database. Using SQL Loader, data in these CSV files is loaded in Target Database.

Database tables are represented in text format. Each record in the table is one line of text file. Each field value is separated by comma (","). Sometimes it is separated by semicolon. Each record is one line terminated by line feed. Source database is represented by CSV file, where the first row contains the column name of the table and then each row contains a value for that column separated by a comma. CSV file contain record in text format. CSV files cannot have information about constraints, e.g. foreign keys.

The data in CSV files can be loaded in target database using SQL loader. However, here constraints must be added before loading data using SQL loader. It may happen that relational schema might have changed in target database as it was in source database. In that case, mapping between source database and target database is required. As shown in figure before loading data in target database, constraints must be added and mapping should be performed manually.

Some tools are available e.g. swissql (swissql, 2010) using which database can be migrated between two platforms e.g. from oracle to post-gresql. So data can be migrated from one database to another using this approach. One important thing should be noted that both source and target databases are following relational schema to store the data.

Proposed Approach for Cloud Data Migration

An approach discussed in the previous section cannot be applied to migrate database to or from cloud datastores, as cloud datastores are not following single scheme to store the data, e.g. migration from relational datastore to Bigtable. Therefore, cloud data migration is data as well as schema migration.

To meet the requirement mentioned above, a model is required, which can describe data and schema in machine process-able form. Such a model must be rich enough so as to describe data from different datastores following different schemes to store the data. Following which data can be restructured and can be stored in cloud datastores, CSV will not suffice for this model, as it can only describe data.

We are looking at RDF/RDFS (Resource Description Framework/Resource Description Framework Schema) model as an option.

Figure 3 shows the proposed approach for data migration using RDF/RDFS which is described in steps:

Figure 3. Cloud data migration approach

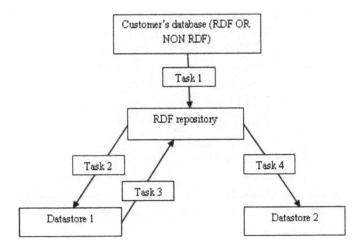

1. Get the data into RDF/RDFS (Task 1 in Figure 3).
2. Map the RDF/RDFS database to the underlying cloud datastore according to the cloud datastore requirements (Task 2 in Figure 3).
3. When a need arises to migrate database, map the database in datastore to RDF/RDFS (Task 3 in Figure 3), then map the RDF/RDFS database to targeted datastore (Task 4 in Figure 3). We need to remember that Task 4, mapping RDF/RDFSdata to cloud datastore, is equivalent to Task 2.

A technique is required to store RDF/RDFS data in cloud datastore not following relational schema. Hence, it becomes important to develop and implement an algorithm that can provide mapping between RDF and cloud datastore. Deciding the mapping between elements of a datastore's schema and RDF will provide an algorithm.

RDF/RDFS as an Intermediate Model

RDF data model is similar to classic conceptual modeling approaches such as Entity Relationship. It is based upon the idea of making statements about resources in the form of subject-predicate-object expressions (W3C Incubator Group, 2009).

These expressions are known as triples in RDF terminology. The subject denotes the resource, and the predicate denotes property of the resource and expresses a relationship between the subject and the object. For example, Mahesh lives in Vadodara, here Mahesh is a subject, "lives in" is a predicate and Vadodara is an object. Each resource is identified by a unique URI (Uniform Resource Identifier). It follows XML and RDF syntax to describe resource.

Example 1 is shown using RDF syntax. Here rdf:Description defines the subject, contact:livesin is a predicate and Vadodara is an object.

Example 1: Mahesh lives in Vadodara

```
<?xml version="1.0"?>
<rdf:RDFxmlns:rdf="http://www.
w3.org/1999/02/22-rdf-syntax-ns#"
 xmlns:contact="http://www.
w3.org/2000/10/swap/pim/contact#">
<rdf:Description rdf:about= "http://
www.w3.org/People/EM/contact#Mahesh">
<contact:staysin> Vadodara </
contact:staysin>
<contact:name> Mahesh </contact:name>
</rdf:Description>
</rdf:RDF>
```

Figure 4. RDF/RDFS example

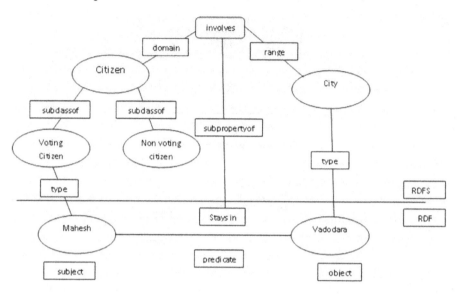

RDF schema describes properties, classes (as a group of resources) and relationship between groups of resources. The members of a class are known as instances of the class. Classes are themselves resources. They are often identified by RDF URI References and may be described using RDF properties. The rdf:type property may be used to state that a resource is an instance of a class.

Figure 4 shows an example by a graph. It can be seen how classes and properties are defined in RDF schema. Mahesh is a type of voting citizen, indicates that resource Mahesh is instance of class voting citizen. Classes and properties are defined in RDF schema. RDF schema follows RDF syntax. For example, voting citizen is subclass of citizen is also a statement where voting citizen is a subject, subclass of is a predicate and citizen is an object.

Use of RDF as Intermediate Model

As discussed previously, a data model is needed to describe data as well as schema, which should be rich enough to describe data available in different cloud datastore. Using RDF/RDFS data and schema can be described, and its rich vocabulary allows describing data available in a different

format. It is a standard model to describe data. Algorithms are developed to transfer or store RDF data on different data store, e.g. Stein (2010) provides a way to store RDF data on Amazon simpleDb, Ramanujam (2009) provides a way to store RDF data to relational database. So this algorithm can be used if we have data available in RDF/RDFS.

Rich representation of schema in owl and data in RDF allows creation of relationships between resources when the data is to be stored on apache couch db. It may happen that data, to be stored in cloud datastore, should be retrieved from different heterogeneous databases. Therefore, data integration is required before storing data into cloud datastore. RDF/RDFS allows semantic data integration to accept data from various heterogeneous data sources. The idea is a data provider extracts data from a data source, converts this data into RDF, and integrates this RDF into the cloud datastore. This procedure for storing data is defined in Haas (2010). Automatic mapping generation from RDF/RDFS to various cloud datastore and vice versa can also become possible. This is discussed in a later section.

Mapping Algorithms

We have considered Google App Engine as the cloud service provider and Google App Engine datastore (Bigtable) as underlying cloud datastore. RDF/RDFS representation of relational database is generated using D2R (Bizer, 2003). We have developed and implemented algorithms for storing RDF/RDFS data into Bigtable and converting data lying in Bigtable to RDF/RDFS.

Google App Engine allows limited numbers of queries to be performed on a database and joins are not supported in queries. Thus, de-normalization of database, to be stored in datastore, is encouraged. Proposed algorithm provides mapping between RDF/RDFS and google app engine datastore.

The proposed algorithm generates entities out of given RDF/RDFS files. These entities can be stored in Google App Engine datastore.

Bulkloader, An open source tool, provided by Google is used to load data in Google App Engine. According to configuration file, it stores data provided in data file. Data can be provided in CSV, XML, or other form (Depending on available connector). CSV file format is chosen to provide data. If CSV file, containing data and configuration (.yaml) file is generated then data can be stored in Google App Engine using Bulkloader (see Figure 5).

In this section, we will look at the algorithms introduced above to facilitate migration process. We will describe whole migration process i.e. from relational database to App Engine datastore and App engine datastore to relational database. Consider a database storing information about student and professor (refer to results section for database).

We will generate RDF/RDFS form of the database using D2R tool. The generated form will be as described in RDF generated by D2R. Now we will apply algorithm 1 on this RDF/RDFS.

Figure 5. Algorithm 1

```
Algorithm 1 findInitialMapping
   INPUT: RDF/RDFS dataset
   OUTPUT: List of Entities
 1: Parse RDF file
 2: for all subject in RDF do
 3:    Make a new entity as Entity
 4:    if subject!=URI then
 5:       assign temporary URI to subject (to process the subject)
 6:    end if
 7:    for all property of subject do
 8:       if property==type then
 9:          set obj = object
10:          if obj==statement then
11:             get subject and parse RDFS for subject
12:             get class hierarchy
13:             set kind=superclass
14:             set entitykey=hierarchy:subject
15:             get predicate and make a new property
16:             get object
17:             set propertyname=predicate
18:             set propertyval=object
19:          else
20:             parse schema file
21:             get class hierarchy for obj
22:             get superclass for obj
23:             set kind=superclass
24:             set entitykey=hierarchy:subject
25:          end if
26:       else
27:          if range==preliminary datatype then
28:             check for same property in list
29:             if property is found then
30:                get property
31:             else
32:                make a new property
33:             end if
34:             set propertyname=property
35:             set propertyval=object
36:             add it to entity's property list
37:          else
38:             set Entity=recurFun(Entity, object)
39:          end if
40:       end if
41:    end for
42: end for
```

RDF/RDFS to Bigtable

Data file and configuration files can be generated from the algorithm described above. At the end of step 5, kind information and entity key information is added in configuration file and after generating each property its information is added in CSV file as well as configuration file.

Algorithm 1 shows how list of entities can be generated from RDF/RDF. map() function returns datatype of Bigtable equivalent to RDF/RDFS. Comment, label, seeAlso, isDefinedby properties are those for which a new property will be created and their value will be stored as they are. Statement, subject, object, predicate represent a statement

Figure 6. Algorithm 2

```
Algorithm 2 recurFun
   INPUT: Entity, Resource
   OUTPUT: Entity
 1: for all property of Resource do
 2:    if range!=priliminary datatype then
 3:       obj—object
 4:       Entity = recurFun(Entity, obj)
 5:    else
 6:       check for same property in list
 7:       if property is found then
 8:          get property
 9:       else
10:          make a new property
11:       end if
12:       set propertyname=property
13:       set propertyval=object
14:       set datatype = map(range)
15:       add it to entity's property list
16:    end if
17: end for
```

Table 2. RDF, bigtable mapping table

RDF/RDFS	Bigtable
Resource	Entity
Class	Kind
Subclassof(Property)	To build Entity key
Comment (Property)	New property
Label (Property)	New property
Domain (Property)	To decide property membership
Range (Property)	To decide datatype
seeAlso (Property)	New property
isDefinedBy (Property)	New property
Literal (Datatype)	Datatype
Type (Property)	To decide instance
Predicate	Property
Statement	New entity and property is created According to subject
Subject	
Object	
Predicate	

Table 3. Datatype mapping table

Datatype (RDF)	Datatype (Bigtable)
Literal	Text string
Text	Text string
Int	Int
Float	Float
Date	Date
Boolean	Bool
Short	Int
Long	Int
Double	float

on which a statement can be made (reification). A new entity is created according to the subject having property = predicate (see Figure 6).

Algorithm 2 is the function recurFun recursively parse the resource referred in any resource's property. Through this function, every entity in bigtable will contain all the information about it, e.g. every student entity will contain all the information about the student as well as any information related to that student.

Table 2 shows how RDF/RDFS elements are mapped to Bigtable elements. Table 3 shows mapping of datatypes from RDF/RDFS to Bigtable.

After applying the discussed algorithm, we will get a configuration file and csv files, which can be accepted by bulkoader to load the data on google app engine. Loading data using bulkloader and data on google cloud is shown in Figure 8 and Figure 9, respectively.

Proof of Algorithm

Hypothesis 1: Each resource belongs to one particular class.

Hypothesis 2: Each resource has a URI.

Hypothesis 3: Range is defined for each property. Consider EDP = set of properties in RDF having range as elementary data type, RiefP = set of properties in RDF which are prop-

Figure 7. Algorithm 3

Algorithm 3 findInitialMapping

INPUT: RDF/RDFS

OUTPUT: List of Entities

```
1:  for all subject in RDF do
2:      Make a new entity
3:      if subject!=URI then
4:          assign temporary URI
5:      end if
6:      for all property of subject do
7:          if property==type then
8:              set obj.value = object
9:              if object==statement then
10:                 call handle_reif(subject)
11:             else
12:                 class.value=obj.value
13:             end if
14:         else
15:             set pred.value=getpredicate
16:             set datatype = map(range)
17:             set obj.value = object
18:             call map(sub,pred,obj,class)
19:             call build_"entity"(sub,pred,obj,class)
20:             call build_"kind"(class,pred,datatype)
21:         end if
22:     end for
23: end for
```

erties of statement to be reified, ResP = set of properties in RDF referring to another resource, S = set of subject, C = set of classes, P = set of properties, R = set of resources, E = set of Entities.

Lemma 1: $\forall S1 \in S$ in RDF, S1 maps to individual entity $E1 \in E$.

Proof: An individual entity is created for each resource in RDF. Therefore, it is true.

Lemma 2: $\forall P1$, $P1 \in P$, P1 maps to a particular property $P1 \in P$ of and entity $E1 \in E$.

Proof: Suppose $\exists P1 \in P$ and P1 does not map to a Property of an entity, Now P = EDP U ReifP U ResP.

$P1 \in EDP \Rightarrow$ a new property created for entity E1 and object value is stored $\Rightarrow P1 \notin EDP$ $\qquad$ (1)

$P1 \in ReifP \Rightarrow$ a new entity E is created for statement and property p is created for $P1 \Rightarrow P1 \notin ReifP$ $\qquad$ (2)

Figure 8. Bulkloader to load users kind

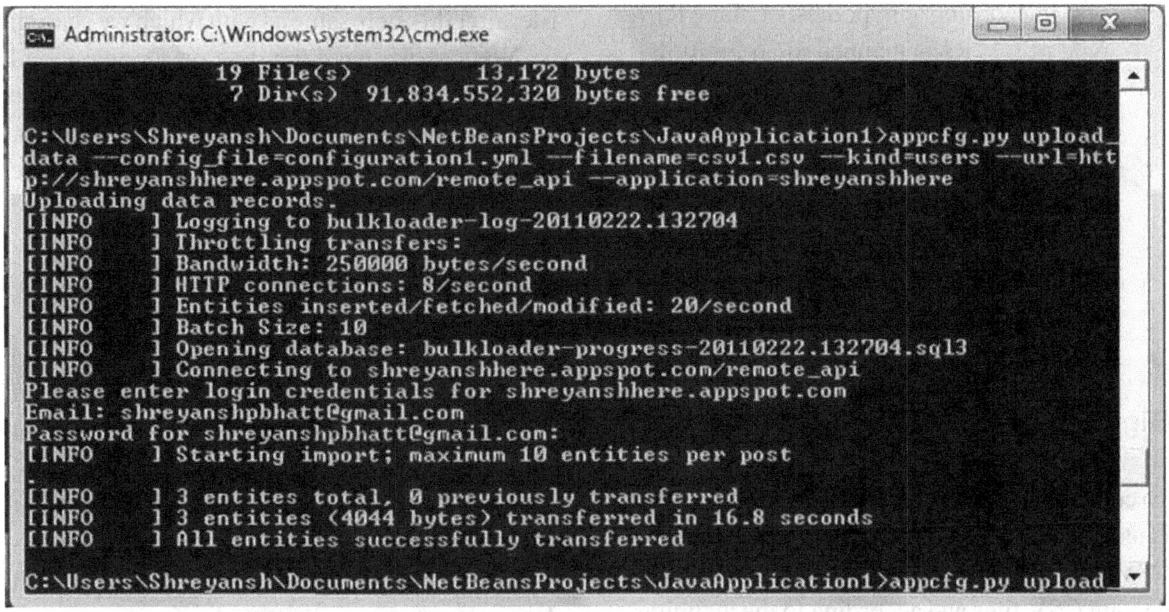

Figure 9. User kind in app engine datastore

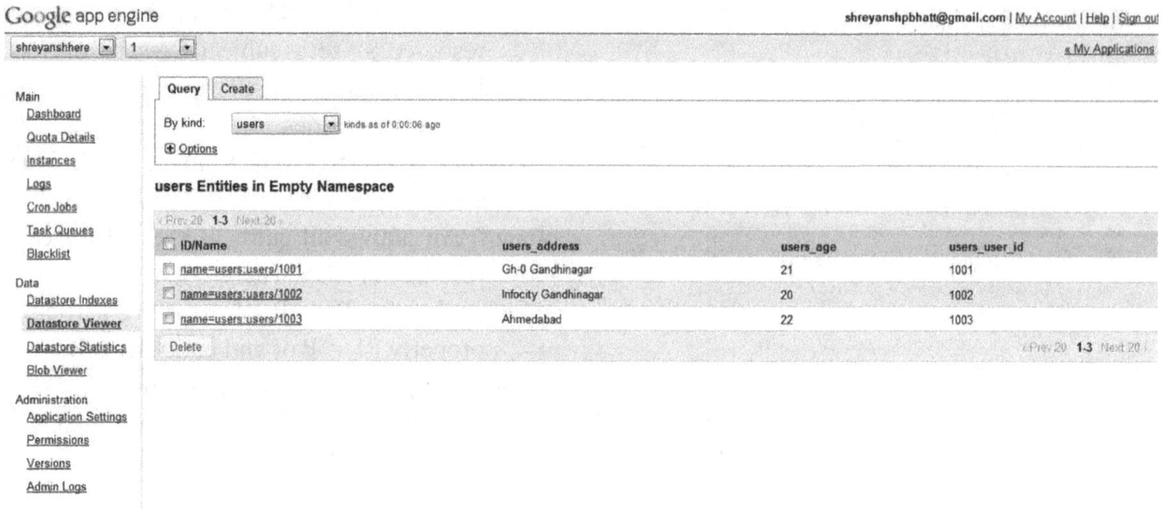

$P1 \in ResP \Rightarrow P1 \in EDP$ or P1 is a key, P1 is a key $\Rightarrow$ property named key is created $\Rightarrow P1 \notin ResP$ (3)

From, (1), (2) and (3) $P1 \notin P$. This is wrong. Hence, $\forall P1, P1 \in P$, P1 maps to a particular property $P1 \in P$ of and entity $E1 \in E$.

Lemma 3: $\forall P1 \in P$ is part of a correct entity.

Proof: $\forall R1 \in R, \exists C1 \in C$ such that R1 is type of C1 according to hypothesis 1. Take R1 is type of C1, R1 is mapped to an Entity E1. And C1 is mapped to a kind $K1 \Rightarrow E1$ lies in kind K1.

Suppose $\exists P1 \in P$, P1 is part of E1.

P1 is wrongly mapped $\Rightarrow$ E1 lies in wrong kind $K1 \Rightarrow R1$ is not type of C1, Which is wrong.

So P1 is not mapped to wrong Entity E1. Hence, $\forall P1 \in P$ is part of a correct entity.

Bigtable to RDF/RDFS Algorithm

To convert data in RDF, Bulkloader (Blein, 2010) is used to download data. Data is downloaded in CSV files. RDF is generated from CSV files by parsing CSV files and according to the mapping, reverse from previous algorithm, i.e. entity (row in CSV file) is converted into subject, property is converted into predicate, and property value is converted into object. The RDF generated out of CSV file will be similar to the RDF from which the data was loaded in Google App Engine. Resources are mapped to correct class in RDFS by looking at the entity key as it contains the class hierarchy. Properties of referred resources are not stored as predicate. Therefore, we will have RDF file, after this step, same as with which we started.

Now, as we have the data on Google cloud and we want to migrate from Google cloud, we will get our data back in csv file using bulkloader. Figure 10 shows generation of RDF using the discussed algorithm.

RDF/RDFS to Relational Database Algorithm

To achieve this task we have developed and implemented an algorithm based on the element and datatype mapping tables, Table 4 and Table 5, respectively. The example can be considered that when a customer wants to move data to a datastore following relational database (e.g. Microsoft Azure datastore).

Figure 10. Generating RDF

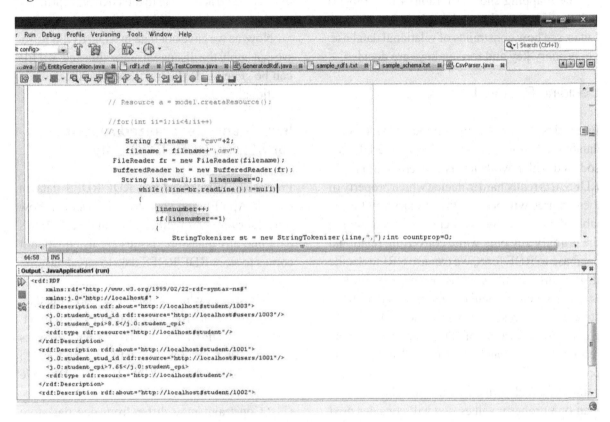

Table 4. Element mapping, RDF to RDB

RDF/RDFS	Relational Database
Resource	Row in a table
Class	Table
Subclassof (Property)	-
Comment (Property)	New property
Label (Property)	New property
Domain (Property)	To decide column membership
Range (Property)	To decide datatype
seeAlso (Property)	New property
isDefinedBy (Property)	New property
Literal (Datatype)	Datatype
Type (Property)	To decide instance
Predicate	Column
Statement	<Not handled in this algorithm>
Subject	
Object	
Predicate	

Table 5. Datatype mapping

Datatype (RDF)	Datatype (Bigtable)
Literal	Varchar
Text	Varchar
Int	Int
Float	Float
Date	Date
Boolean	Bool
Short	Smallint
Long	Bigint
Double	Double

The mapping shown in Table 4 and Table 5 will provide the relational database in .sql form. Let us see how constraints of relational database, i.e. primary key and foreign keys are decided.

Deciding Primary Key

Every class is mapped to a single table in relational database. As the resource has a unique URI associated with it while it was converted into RDF/RDFS, it is really hard to decide which property of the resource will become the primary key for the table. As we had the URI generated according to the primary key only while converting relational database to RDF form, we can use URI to decide it. Resource of the class is parsed, e.g. student is a class and particular student entry as RDF statement is a resource. The value of the URI is compared with values of other properties of same resources. The matched value will indicate the property eligible for primary key. In case of tie, i.e. value extracted from URI being matched to more than one property values, we will consider next resource of the same class to decide primary key.

To get a clear idea of the process, consider the example discussed in RDF introduction section, here URI of the resource is http://www.w3.org/People/EM/contact#Mahesh. We can extract Mahesh from URI and match this value with other properties. As it is matched with property "name," we can have name as primary key. This will provide definite result as D2R considers primary key of the table while generating URI. It goes as a limitation of the algorithm if it needs to be used as standalone algorithm for transforming any RDF/RDFS to relational database.

Deciding Foreign Key

In RDF, property of a resource referring to another resource does not contain the exact value for that property rather contains URI of the resource only. To determine the foreign key, referred resource is extracted and according to the URI value primary key is found which will be the foreign key value.

Now, as we have our data in RDF/RDFS form, we can apply the discussed algorithm and .sql file can be generated which will contain database in relational form.

Issues and Generalized Algorithm for Storing RDF/RDFS Data

Proposed algorithm stores RDF/RDFS data in Google App Engine Datastore. It is shown how this algorithm can facilitate storing RDF/RDFS data into any datastore. Issues are listed when it comes to store RDF/RDFS data to any datastore.

- Format in which a datastore stores the data is different from one datastore to another, e.g. RDF/RDFS to Relational requires creating relationship table as and when required whereas RDF/RDFS to Bigtable does not require the same.
- Constraint may differ from one datastore to another datastore, e.g. foreign key constraint of relational database is different from foreign key constraint of Bigtable.
- Requirements may be different, e.g. Bigtable requires data in denormalize form whereas Relational database requires data in normalize form.
- Data types can be different.
- Mapping of elements can be different, e.g. subject is mapped to entity in Bigtable whereas subject is mapped to individual row in Relational database.

If datatype and element mapping are available then similar algorithm can be used to store RDF/RDFS data into different datastore.

Generalized Algorithm for Storing RDF/RDFS Data

When it comes to mapping RDF/RDFS to any cloud datastore, cloud datastores may differ in following things:

- Mapping of subject, object, predicate elements of RDF/RDFS.
- Datatype mapping.
- Property mapping from RDF/RDFS to cloud datastore, e.g. certain property is converted into a separate table when RDF/RDFS is converted into relational database where this will not be the case in RDF/RDFS to Bigtable.

Therefore, property generation and kind or table creation is separated. Based on that, Algorithm 1 is modified and following algorithm is proposed (see Figure 7).

Build_entity and build_kind functions handles the part which can differ from one datastore to another, e.g. build_"entity" will denormalize the data and build_"row" (function which generated row for relational database) will handle generating relation table between two entities (entity tables).

Structure of variables used is as follow:

- Sub {String value, intpos},
- Pred {String value, int pos},
- Obj {String value, int pos},
- Class {String value, intpos},
- Dataype {String value, int pos}.

Variable pos contain the number of argument at which the build_"row" is accepting the mapped structure, e.g. consider build_"row" function is already available and it follows the signature as shown. Arguments in call of step 6 are arranged

Table 6. Argument name and number of build_entity

Element	Number
Propname	1
Propval	2
Table	3
Datatype	4

Table 7. Argument name and number of build_kind

Element	Number
Table	1
Propname	2
Datatype	3

Table 8. Element mapping table

Element (RDF)	Element (Bigtable)
Class	Kind
Predicate	Property
Object	Propval
Subject (Resource)	Entity

according to the pos. So it is required to arrange the arguments according to the mapping table.

Map function maps the particular RDF/RDFS element with datastore element and populates the pos part of each structure, e.g. Map(sub,pred,obj,class) call will first check table 3.5 to decide mapping of subject, predicate, object, and class, and then it will check Table 6, Table 7 to assign pos to sub, pred, obj, and class. This facilitates building build_entity and build_kind functions independently without worrying of mapping.

Table 3 shows datatype mapping table. These mapping tables, Table 3 and Table 8, can be given as an input and mapping can be performed. We have proposed a way by which these mapping tables can be generated.

Mapping Table Generation

If we can describe RDF/RDFS and cloud datastore in structured and rich manner then matching can be applied between these descriptions and mapping table can be generated out of it. RDF description of RDF/RDFS is provided by W3C. We have described datastore, bigtable for instance, using relationship ontology available at (Obofoundary Ontology, 2010).

Ontology mapping algorithm can be applied between these two ontologies and mapping can be decided based on that. Ontology matching algorithms (Maedche, 2002; Guichiglia, 2003) match two elements in ontology based on the hierarchy in which they lie and the label of nodes. This approach does not help in matching the description we have.

To illustrate this, a part each description is shown below, it is derived that if two properties are matched then their domain and range gets mapped.

A part of RDF description of RDFS is shown in Example 2.

Example 2: Pat of RDF description of RDFS.

```
<rdf:Propertyrdf:about="http://
www.w3.org/1999/02/22-rdf-syntax-
ns#type">
<rdfs:label>type</rdfs:label>
<rdfs:comment>
```

The subject is an instance of a class.

```
</rdfs:comment>
<rdfs:rangerdf:resource="http://www.
w3.org/2000/01/rdf-schema#Class"/>
<rdfs:domainrdf:resource="http://www.
w3.org/2000/01/rdf-schema#Resource"/>
</rdf:Property>
```

A part of owl description of Bigtable is shown below.

```
<rdf:RDFxmlns:x= http://www.obofound-
ry.org/ro/ro.owl>
<owl:classrdf:about="http://entity">
<rdfs:label>entity</rdfs:label>
<x:contained_inrdf:resource="http://
kind"/>
<x:has_partrdf:resource="http://Prop-
erty">
</owl:class>
</rdf:RDF>
```

If property type and contained_in are matched, then entity gets mapped to resource and class gets mapped to kind. To match two properties their description can be considered. The description of both properties suggests that these two properties can be matched.

Our aim is to provide a framework, which will actually reduce the dependency of migration process to the underlying datastore. Additionally, allowing automatic mapping generation really make migration, to completely new datastore, a structured and easy task.

Limitations and Assumptions

Currently we are supporting only data migration from relational database, we are not supporting migration of other aspects e.g. queries, triggers, indexes, etc. to cloud datastore. It is assumed in current migration model that relational database is transformed into RDF/RDFS using D2R, i.e. we have data as well as schema in RDF form. It is assumed that whole database, to be transformed, is processed the same time, i.e. from relational to RDF/RDFS transformation and RDF/RDFS to cloud datastore transformation. In other words, live migration to support very large databases, i.e. processing data by dividing in chunks, is not supported currently. Our results still shows processing of data in Mega Bytes still takes few seconds only on normal machine to get transformed into RDF/RDFS and consequently App Engine datastore

Table 9. Relational database

Table	Property1	Property2	Property3
Users	User_id(p.k.)	Age	Address
Student	Stud_id(fk,pk)	Cpi	
Professor	Prof_id	Area_of_expertise	

Table 10. Generated RDF by D2R

Class	Property1	Property2	Property3
Student	Student_stud_id	Student_cpi	
Users	Users_user_id	Users_age	Users_add
Professor	Professor_prof_id	Professor_area_of_expert	

but allowing live migration will really increase efficiency.

As shown in Table 3, almost all the RDF/RDFS elements, described by W3C are handled as part of algorithm 1 except Container elements. Container elements are helpful in making statement about group of resources, e.g. for a statement R1 teaches C1 where C1 = {CS1, CS2, CS} is a container element. It indicates that resource R1 teaches courses = CS1, CS2, CS3. It can be replaced by R1 teaches CS1, R1 teaches CS2, R1 teaches CS3, which can be parsed by Algorithm 1.

While transformation from RDF/RDFS to relational database reification property, i.e. making statements about statement, of RDF/RDFS is not currently supported. While conducting experiments for different databases we did not encounter occurrence of reification. Supporting it will allow it to be used as a standalone algorithm for storing any RDF/RDFS data to relational datastore.

Results

As discussed earlier, relational database is converted into RDF/RDFS and RDF/RDFS data is stored in Google App Engine datastore. This section elaborates on corresponding results (see Table 9).

Stud_id is a foreign key to user_id of users table. This database is created in MySql and D2R is then used to convert it into RDF (see Table 10).

Generated RDF is parsed by Algorithm 1. It will generate configuration file (.yml) and data file (.csv) corresponding to each class in RDF. Using bulkloader data is loaded in GAE datastore.

Figure 9 shows the data stored in Google App Engine datastore. We created an application on Google App Engine and used the database part. It can be seen that 3 entities are generated for the user kind. Columns show the properties of entity. Next task is to get this stored data in form of csv files, which can be achieved similarly as shown in Figure 8, i.e. using bulkloader.

After getting data in csv file(s), next step is to get data in form of RDF. A java application, representing algorithm discussed in 9, will have the csv file as an input and it'll generate the RDF file out of it. It can be verified that this RDF file will be similar to the one we gave as input to Algorithm 1, i.e. to store data in Google App Engine. Figure 11 shows how .sql file, i.e. relational database, is generated from RDF file using RDF/RDFS to Relational database algorithm discussed earlier.

The generated .sql file can be loaded directly to any relational database e.g. MySql. Similarly, student and professor kinds are loaded into app engine datastore. Figure 10 shows how RDF is

Figure 11. Relational database from RDF/RDFS

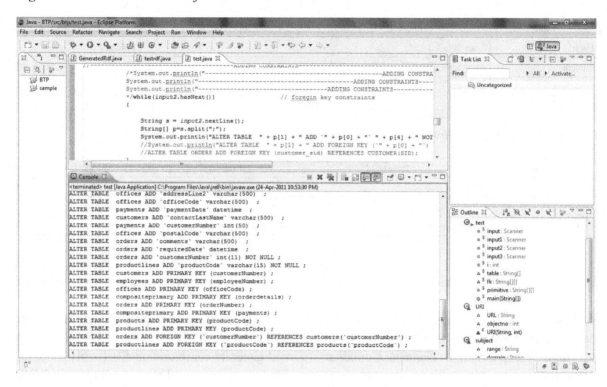

generated from the csv files, which contains the data and generated by bulkloader. Figure 11 shows relational database converted from RDF/RDFS. Experiments are performed to store sample mysql database and Sakila database (Sakila Database, 2010) often used for benchmarking.

Performance Evaluation

- **Amount of manual work needed:** Migration of database requires mapping between source and target datastores, e.g. when a relational database is to be migrated to GAE datastore, mapping and denormalization have to be provided manually which is very difficult for large databases. We have achieved it through mapping algorithms.

Further, in algorithm 3, i.e. storing RDF/RDFS data to any cloud datastore, our design helps in handling RDF/RDFS property transformation (for instance handling denormalization) independently from element mapping. Transformation algorithm works by providing only mapping which can be decided automatically by a good ontology matching algorithm as shown earlier. Still the algorithm requires separate function to be written for property handling for each datastore. It is required as generalization of datastore schema is quite difficult, e.g. properties, datatypes, and data storage scheme of bigtable are quite different than those of relational database.

- **Transformation time:** Focusing on time complexity of algorithm 1, in worst-case scenario, each subject will have all the properties and all the objects for the particular property. So in worst case the complexity will be O (S.P.O) where S = All the subjects in RDF, P = All the properties in RDF, O = All the objects for the particular property. Algorithm took 2 seconds for transforming RDF/RDFS database having 50-60 triples, 6 seconds for transforming database (sample database taken from mysql site) having 9000 triples and 22 seconds for transforming database, a movie database (sakila) often used for benchmarking, having 95000 triples. For same database (in RDF/RDFS form, 10 MB data), it took 13 seconds to convert and store it into relational database (Mysql) where Ramanujam (2009) took 175 seconds to convert 75KB data to relational database. This difference is because we are creating relational schema from RDF schema, which is not a case in Ramanujam (2009). Experiments were performed on the computer having 3 GB of RAM, Intel core 2 duo 2.66 GHz processor.

- **Data transformation efficiency:** GAE datastore stores data in form of schema less entities so converting data into RDF/RDFS and then storing it to GAE datastore will allow taking advantage of RDF/RDFS as RDF/RDFS aims at storing data resource wise. Each resource will contain all the information it needed to have to answer any query after converting RDF/RDFS data into the form of entities using Algorithm 1.

Consider a case where we have database storing information about a film and actor and we want information actors who worked in particular film. For relational schema three tables are generated for this database namely, Film (filmid, name) FilmActor (filmid, actorid), Actor (actorid, actorname). However, this will not be an efficient design for GAE as it can't support queries with joins. Thus, different design is needed which is also pointed out in Slatkin (2009).

Our approach first converts the relational database into RDF/RDFS. So now, RDF/RDFS will have only two classes Film (filmid, name, actorids) and Actor (actorid, actorname). Storing it into GAE datastore using Algorithm 1 will lead to have two kinds in GAE datastore Film and Actor where each film contains all the information including the actors who worked in that film which does not require queries with join.

Related Work

Relational database migration is supported by using CSV as a common intermediate model. AABC Migration Toolkit (2010) allows this migration. As CSV is unable to describe database schema and constraints, similar approach cannot be used for a cloud data migration.

Google App Engine has provided java support. JDO is used as an interface to support database operations. So hibernate ORM can be used to generate relational database from the annotated classes, i.e. to store data, available in GAE, to relational database but reverse is not possible using hibernate.

Oracle 11g, VirtusoRDF, Talis platform provides a way to store RDF/RDFS data but using same approach RDF data cannot be stored on GAE or other cloud datastore efficiently, e.g. Oracle 11g stores RDF data by storing subject, predicate object triples in tables.

Krishna (2009) provides a framework for data migration in cloud. They have tried to address similar issue considering Azure as target cloud datastore which is actually a relational database migration as azure is following relational schema to store the data. We have tried to address the issue in broader way by considering both relational to non-relational data and schema migration.

FUTURE RESEARCH DIRECTIONS

An algorithm for ontology matching will allow generation of Element mapping table and data type mapping generation. When large amount of data is to be stored then mapping from relational to RDF and RDF to cloud datastore can become a bottleneck. To overcome this issue data can be divided in chunks and processed in other words, live migration should be achieved. Query transformation also becomes important in this environment as different datastore are following different ways and standards to query the stored data. Denormalization can be achieved according to the queries that are to be fired on database.

CONCLUSION

Due to benefits of cloud computing, more customers are migrating their applications into cloud. For effective migration of applications, database must be migrated effectively. Unfortunately, cloud service providers are following different standards to host applications and data. There is an urgent need to pay attention on issue related to data migration from various datastore to cloud and vice versa. Various challenges associated with this reciprocal migration are addressed in this chapter to propose a simple and powerful model for data to be migrated between various datastores, especially cloud datastores. Relational database can be stored on Google App Engine using this approach and algorithms. Data can be retrieved from Google App Engine and RDF/RDFS can be generated from the stored data. Database migration from one cloud to another can be achieved using proposed approach. RDF model works as an intermediate model and mapping algorithm provides automation in migration process. Data lock-in issue in cloud computing can also be solved using this migration technique. Proposed framework facilitates automatic mapping generation hence provides a way to store RDF/RDFS data to any cloud datastore. Experimental results showed an efficient way to move data from conventional relational database to Google App Engine and how data residing in Google App engine can be stored on relational database and vice versa. We have provided a generalized architecture to store data in any cloud datastore using RDF/RDFS as an intermediate model in migration process.

REFERENCES

W3C RDB2RDF Incubator Group. (2009). *A survey of current approaches for mapping relational database to RDF*. Retrieved from http://www.w3c.org

Artefactual. (2010). *AABC data migration toolkit*. Retrieved on December 2010, from http://www.artefactual.com/wiki/index.php

Auer, S., et al. (2010). *Use cases and requirements for mapping relational databases to RDF*. Retrieved from http://www.w3c.org

Bhat, U., & Jadhav, S. (2010). Moving towards non-relational databases. *International Journal of Computers and Applications*, *1*, 40–46. doi:10.5120/284-446

Bizer, C. (2003). D2R MAP – A database to RDF mapping language. In *Proceedings of Twelfth International World Wide Web Conference*, (pp. 2-3). IEEE.

Blain, M. (2010). Data migration in app engine. *Google I/O 2010*. Retrieved November 2010 from http://www.google.com/events/io/2010/

Chang, F. (2008). Bigtable: A distributed storage system for structured data. *ACM Transactions on Computer Systems*, *26*(2), 1–26. doi:10.1145/1365815.1365816

Giunchiglia, F., & Svaiko, P. (2003). Semantic matching. *The Knowledge Engineering Review Journal, 18*(3).

Haase, P., Math, T., Schmidt, M., Eberhart, A., & Walther, U. (2010). Semantic technologies for enterprise cloud management. In *Proceeding of the Ninth International Conference on Web Services*. Shanghai, China: IEEE.

Krishna, B., Reddy, E., Jagadamba, K., Krishnamoorthy, S., & Krishna, P. (2009). A unified and scalable data migration service for the cloud environments. In *Proceedings of COMAD*. COMAD.

Maedche, A., & Staab, S. (2002). Measuring similarity between ontologies. In *Proceedings of the International Conference on Knowledge Engineering and Knowledge Management (EKAW)*, (pp. 251–263). EKAW.

MySQL. (2010). *Sakila database for MySql.* Retrieved on December 2010, from http://dev.mysql.com/doc/sakila/en/sakila.html

Nagarajan, M., Verma, K., Sheth, A., Miller, J., & Lathem, J. (2006). Semantic interoperability of web services-challenges and experiences. In *Proceeding of the Fourth IEEE International Conference on Web Services,* (pp. 3-4). Chicago, IL: IEEE Press.

Obofoundry. (2011). *Obofoundary relationship ontology.* Retrieved on January 2011 from http://www.obofoundry.org/ro/

Ramanujam, S., Gupta, A., Khan, L., Seida, S., & Thuraisingham, B. (2009). R2D: A bridge between the semantic web and relational visualization tools. In *Proceedings of the Third International Conference on Semantic Computing,* (pp. 303–311). Berkeley, CA: IEEE.

Slatkin, B. (2009). Building scalable, complex apps on app engine. *Google IO 2009.* Retrieved on January 2011 from http://www.google.com/events/io/2009/sessions/BuildingScalableComplexApps.html

Stein, R., & Zacharias, V. (2010). RDF on cloud number nine. In Proceedings of the Workshop on NeFoRS: New Forms of Reasoning for the Semantic Web: Scalable and Dynamic. IEEE.

Swissql. (2010). *SwiSQL migration solution – Database migration tools.* Retrieved December 2010 from www.swissql.com/dbmigration-tool-ds.pdf

KEY TERMS AND DEFINITIONS

Cloud Computing: Cloud computing is a way to provide computing, data, software as a services rather than as a product.

Cloud Data Migration: It refers to migration of data between cloud or non-cloud environment.

Cloud Datastore: Cloud service providers have built non-conventional non-relational distributed datastores to store large data and cater the requirement of retrieval of quick retrieval of data.

Google App Engine: Google App Engine is a cloud service provided by Google. It provides platform as a service.

Mapping Algorithm: In the context of chapter, it refers to element mapping between two different datastore and allowing data migration based on that.

Mapping Table: In the context of chapter, it refers to how elements of different datastores are associated with each other.

RDF/RDFS: Resource description framework/ Resource description framework schema to describe data in semantically rich form, standardized by w3c.

Chapter 10

Migrating a Legacy Web–Based Document–Analysis Application to Hadoop and HBase:
An Experience Report

Himanshu Vashishtha
University of Alberta, Canada

Michael Smit
University of Alberta, Canada

Eleni Stroulia
University of Alberta, Canada

ABSTRACT

Migrating a legacy application to a more modern computing platform is a recurring software-development activity. This chapter describes the authors' experience with a contemporary rendition of this activity, migrating a Web-based system to a service-oriented application on two different cloud software platforms, Hadoop and HBase. Using the case study as a running example, they review the information needed for a successful migration and examine the trade-offs between development/re-design effort and performance/scalability improvements. The two levels of re-design, towards Hadoop and HBase, require notably different levels of effort, and as the authors found through exercising the migrated applications, they achieve different benefits. The authors found that both redesigns led to substantial benefit in performance improvement, and that expending the additional effort required by the more complex migration resulted in notable improvements in the ability to leverage the benefits of the platform.

DOI: 10.4018/978-1-4666-2488-7.ch010

Copyright © 2013, IGI Global. Copying or distributing in print or electronic forms without written permission of IGI Global is prohibited.

INTRODUCTION

Migrating applications to cloud-computing environments is a software-engineering activity attracting increasing attention, as cloud environments become more accessible and better supported. Such migrations pose questions regarding the changes necessary to the code and to the architecture of the original software system, the effort necessary to perform these changes, and the possible performance improvements to be gained by the migration. The software-development team undertaking a migration-to-the-cloud project needs to address the following questions.

- What types of software (i.e., components and/or libraries) can developers expect when undertaking a migration project?
- What are the modifications typically required in order for the migrated application to better leverage the potential of the target cloud platform? What are the implications of the various platforms to the architectural and detailed design of the software deployed on them?
- Will the particular software application benefit from its migration to a cloud environment? How might one assess the trade-off between the costs of the planned modifications vs. the improvements anticipated of the application post-migration?

The term cloud computing characterizes the perspective of end users, who are offered a service (which could be in the form of a computing platform or infrastructure) while being agnostic about its underlying technology. The implementation details of the service are abstracted away, and it is consumed on a pay-per-use basis, as opposed to being acquired as an asset. In principle, one distinguishes among three different types of cloud-based services. When infrastructure is offered as a service (IaaS), end users are able to procure virtualized hardware. When a software platform is offered as a service (PaaS), end users consume a software platform, i.e., a combination of an operating system, basic tools and libraries. Finally, when a software application is offered as a service (SaaS), end users consume as clients a specific application that is independently deployed and managed. Of course, these offerings can be combined into a stack of service offerings.

All three above scenarios promote improved scalability albeit through different mechanisms. The first scenario eliminates the need for users to acquire, manage and replace hardware, since any number of appropriately configured virtual machines can be easily procured (and abandoned), for example, through Amazon Web Services[1]. The second scenario promises improved scalability with novel tools and computational metaphors, such as those of the Hadoop ecosystem for storing and manipulating "big data." Finally, when a software system is offered as a service, such as SalesForce[2], its consumers are offered state-of-the-art functionality, regularly maintained, and extended, with guaranteed quality, at negotiable costs.

In this chapter, we report on our experience migrating a legacy application, TAPoR, to take advantage of IaaS (using AWS) and PaaS (in two scenarios, Hadoop and HBase). The original version of TAPoR had severe performance limitations and it was the promise of scalability through its migration "to the cloud" that motivated our study. The original application ran on a single machine, in a single thread, within a single process. Taking advantage of the IaaS model, we modified it to incorporate a load-balancing component to distribute incoming requests to multiple identical processes, running on multiple virtual machines (Smit, Nisbet, Stroulia, Iszlai, & Edgar, 2009). This change however did not address the fundamental inability of the application to scale to large documents. To that end, we investigated the advantages of an architectural shift to exploit the advantages of (two variants of) the Hadoop ecosystem as a platform. To summarize, we have performed three types of modification to the original system:

- No architectural changes; deploy the software (with a load balancer) to multiple machines (on Amazon EC2, for instance);
- Rearchitecting towards the MapReduce paradigm; modify the architecture and implementation to make use of the distributed computation features of Hadoop; and
- Rearchitecting to use a NoSQL database; further change the implementation to also make use of the distributed database feature of Hadoop, HBase[3].

Each of these scenarios required an increased level of development effort and a deeper conceptual understanding of the expected use cases of the software (i.e., costs). Each offers varying performance, flexibility, and scalability (i.e., benefits). To investigate the impact of these varied degrees of modification, we identified a set of standard text-analysis tasks and we compared the performance of the original version to the three modified versions on these tasks. We migrated four TAPoR operations to the Hadoop ecosystem, and comparatively evaluated the effort involved in making the transition to the performance benefit achieved. We found that expending additional effort did result in corresponding performance increases; we were not able to find the point at which further effort no longer resulted in appreciable gains. We believe that our results are, to some extent, generalizable to other similar software-migration projects, particularly those related to text analysis, business analytics, search, and similar. The degree to which a shift in functionality is practical and will achieve similar performance benefits will vary.

The rest of the chapter is organized as follows. The next section describes MapReduce as a computational paradigm, its implementation in Hadoop, and HBase, a no-SQL database in the Hadoop family. In "Legacy System Migration to the Hadoop Ecosystem," we describe previous studies of application migration to Hadoop and HBase, and general efforts at cloud migration tasks. "Text Analysis with TAPoR" introduces the legacy application that is the subject of our study. We describe the architectural changes and development tasks for three different approaches to migrating TAPoR to the cloud in "The TAPoR Migration." "Experiments and Results" describes the experiments we set up to evaluate these case study migrations and the lessons we learned from the experience. Finally, we present the conclusions we can draw from our work to date and lay out some ideas for future work.

PLATFORM AS A SERVICE: THE HADOOP ECOSYSTEM

In this section, we discuss the key concepts underlying the computational model supported by the two platforms to which we migrated TAPoR: Hadoop, the open-source implementation of the MapReduce paradigm, and HBase, a no-SQL database relying on HDFS, the Hadoop file system.

MapReduce and Hadoop

The now seminal MapReduce paper (Dean & Ghemawat, 2008) sparked ongoing growth in data analytics using this paradigm. MapReduce is a scalable and straightforward approach to processing large amounts of data (up to petabyte scale) in parallel, on a cluster of commodity machines. It is not a silver bullet for all kinds of big-data problems; rather, it is conceived to specifically address data-parallel workloads. It proposes the design of applications in terms of a map and a reduce function: the map process consumes raw data as key-value pairs and generates intermediary key-value pairs; the reduce process consumes this output and somehow "aggregates" it to produce the final desired output. The map-reduce workflow is shown in Figure 1. The processing of the map phase relies on the data-locality concept, with computation performed at the data nodes (nodes where data resides). The MapReduce paradigm had already been part of functional languages in general (e.g., LISP); however, its usage in data-parallel big-data applications, where individual map tasks can be completed independently, has been a key factor in its popularity. It is being used in large production systems, where multiple terabytes of data are processed on a daily basis. The Apache Hadoop project offers an open-source implementation of MapReduce.

The main advantage of this model is the inherent support for execution in a distributed environment. Using Hadoop, developers do not need to take care of inter-process communication among the nodes. This helps in using this framework on a cluster of commodity machines, possibly virtualized by an IaaS offering, instead of requiring high-end shared-memory machines.

Given the general availability of IaaS offerings, one can easily leverage the potential of the MapReduce paradigm using a utility computing model from a provider such as Amazon, Rackspace, etc. Some providers, including Amazon, offer MapReduce through a Platform as a Service (PaaS) approach, assuming the overhead of setting up a Hadoop system. In this environment, software developers can rather easily develop distributed software on a virtual cluster, by implementing the two functions. Platform libraries take care of the rest, including RPCs, distributing the workload among nodes, using data locality, handling node failures, etc.

One important consideration for MapReduce is that it provides a high throughput when run in a cluster environment. Though there has been some work using it in multi-core shared-memory machines (Chu, et al., 2006; Gordon & Lu, 2011), its real advantage is using it for a distributing-computing application, on a cluster of machines.

Its core features, namely handling node failures and re-running of failed tasks, work on the assumption of using a distributed file system. We discuss the essential features of such file systems in the next section.

Hadoop Distributed File System (HDFS)

MapReduce jobs impose a different set of requirements for reading/storing files as compared to traditional native file systems (POSIX-compliant). Below, we review the main requirements for such a file system.

- A distributed file system should run on inexpensive commodity machines, and it should continuously monitor itself and recover from inconsistencies.
- It should be optimized to store large files, with file sizes in the multiple of gigabytes being the common case.
- It should primarily support two kind of "read" workloads: large streaming reads (up to few MBs) and small random reads (up to few KBs).
- It should support large sequential writes; updates are relatively rare, primarily file appends.
- It should support concurrent updates and reads, as there may be more than one application using the file system.

Google designed and implemented the Google File System (GFS) (Ghemawat, Gobioff, & Leung, 2003) to provide the above functionalities. An open-source implementation, which we used in the work described in this chapter, is the Apache Hadoop Distributed File System (HDFS). The HDFS architecture is based on a single master (Namenode) and multiple workers (Datanodes) nodes. Files are divided in blocks of configurable size, with 64MB being a common block size for

Figure 1. Workflow of the MapReduce paradigm (adapted from Dean & Ghemawat, 2008)

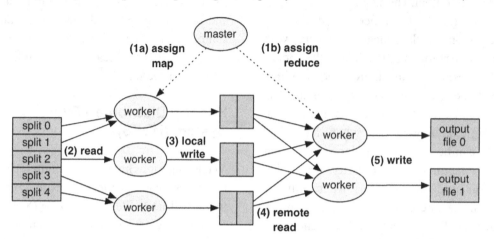

Hadoop. The HDFS Namenode contains the metadata about mapping files to blocks, and blocks to addresses in datanodes; these worker nodes are also sometimes referred to as "chunk servers." A client interacts with the master Namenode only when it has to look for a chunk location (whether reading an existing or, writing to a new chunk); it caches that location thereafter and connects directly to the chunk server without any master Namenode lookup. Thus, the master node never sees the stored data.

The workflows in the file system are such that the interaction between the client and the master Namenode is minimal, to prevent the master from becoming a bottleneck of the system and enable high throughput and performance. Fault tolerance is supported by the replication of the blocks on multiple datanodes, considering intra-rack and inter-rack topology while deciding which nodes will hold which data. For example, if the desired replication factor is 3, the second copy is made on the same rack, and the third copy is made on a different rack. This ensures data availability even in the case of a rack failure. As might be expected, the robustness obtained through replication implies a performance cost, as data must be copied to multiple racks and the client is not given a write acknowledgment until all the copies have been made.

There are some workloads where random reads are required. In HDFS, this entails seeking to the byte offset and reading the file, which can be a costly operation given the large block size. To reduce this cost for sorted data, Hadoop provides a special format, MapFile. It comprises of two separate files: a data file that contains the actual data, and an index file that has the byte offset of a sequence of sorting-key values, separated from each other by a configurable gap. For example, a file with 1k records will have 10 entries in the index file if the gap is defined as 100. When reading, a binary search on the index file is performed and the correct byte offset is located. We use this feature in our migration to store the indices for the re-designed TAPoR.

HBase: A NoSQL Database

HBase is a NoSQL database based on Google's BigTable (Chang, et al., 2008), which was intended to address the requirements of random-read workloads. BigTable is a distributed, column-oriented database, built on top of GFS (Ghemawat, Gobioff, & Leung, 2003) in order to support random access patterns on large data. Apache HBase is an open source Java implementation of BigTable, which stores its contents (i.e. tables) on HDFS.

The results of MapReduce computations can be stored using a variety of methods; for example, the machine native file system, HDFS, HBASE, or a relational database. The choice depends on the access patterns of the target application and the expected latency range. If the computed data is large (in the order of terabytes), storing it in a RDBMS is usually not appropriate. HDFS is best suited to write-once-read-many workloads, not for random read-write operations. Reading a record in HDFS involves a TCP connection to the Namenode (this information can be cached), a TCP connection to the datanode, a seek to reach the specific record of interest, and then the actual reading of the data and transmission to the client. HBase is intended to improve random read-write performance.

HBase belongs to the general class of NoSQL databases. These databases are not a replacement of traditional relational databases; rather, they should be considered their orthogonal counterparts, preferable in use cases where the data is unstructured. This is in contrast to the primary requirement for RDBMs, which is to define and model in the database schema the relations between the stored data entities. They are scalable to big data (petabytes), run in a clustered environment, provide fault tolerance, offer limited transaction support, and usually they do not support specific data types (other than byte arrays). The other main advantage of NoSQL databases is their theoretically unlimited scalability and elasticity; one needs to simply add/remove nodes to scale up/down. On the other hand, they do not support any standard querying language, such as SQL, and they only have custom APIs to access the data, which is stored in de-normalized schemas. This proves good for unstructured data like text, logs, Web pages etc, where meaningful relationships are implicit in the shared words and have to be inferred through processing, rather than explicit in the structure of the text.

There are many databases intended to provide cloud-type data management services, such as HBase[4], Cassandra[5], MongoDB[6], CouchDB[7], etc. Among these, Apache HBase is one of the most popular, having made its mark in academia and industry (Contributors, 2011; Zhang & De Sterck, 2010; Konstantinou, Angelou, Tsoumakos, & Koziris, 2010). Mendeley, an academic social network and a reference manager, has a collection of more than 99 million research papers and uses HBase at its backend (Contributors, 2011; Mendeley, 2011). Facebook, which invented Cassandra (Lakshman & Malik, 2010), the closest HBase competitor in its area, picked HBase as the data store for its recently launched messaging service (Muthukkaruppan, 2011). The official HBase clientele Web page (Contributors, 2011) lists 38 companies that use HBase in their application stack, including Adobe, Facebook, HP, Meetup, Twitter, and Yahoo!.

The HBase Data Model

HBase stores records sorted by a primary key; this is the only key in the entire schema, and the original HBase does not support secondary indices. After defining a table in HBase, and the primary key for each row, one has to define a (set of) column family(ies). As its name suggests, a column family represents a collection of columns, which are accessed in a single transaction, like in one read/write call. Each column family is stored as a separate file on the file system. This helps to limit the number of disk I/O operations in one transaction. Column families are defined at table creation time, although from version 0.20.6 onwards, HBase supports adding column families at a later stage.

For the sake of flexibility, one need not define columns qualifiers before hand; they are appended to the given column family at run time. Each cell can be treated as an independent entity associated with its own row key, column family, column qualifier, data, and creation timestamp.

One can conceptualize HBase data to be stored in a three-dimensional table. Apart from length (number of rows) and breadth (number of column families and columns), the third dimension is the depth of the table (number of distinct cell values over time). One can access the previous value of a given Rowkey:ColumnFamily:ColumnQualifier cell by requesting a specific version number. Cell updates do not alter the cell value; rather, a new value is appended onto the cell's stack of values.

Figure 2 represents a sample schema of a table in HBase. In the figure, the cell value is depicted as Rowkey:ColumnFamily:ColumnQualifier:Data:Timestamp. There are two column families (CF1 and CF2), and three rows. Row1 has two cell values in CF1 and no value in CF2. Row2 has three different values for the CF1:CQ1 combination, the latest one with timestamp t5. Row3 has one cell in CF2 with a qualifier CQ4 (a row can have any qualifier for a given column family). There is no cost incurred by storing empty cells. It is possible to store sparse tables in HBase, expanding to millions of columns to billions of rows. It serves the exact requirement of low latency read and write (random and sequential) with large datasets in a clustered environment.

HBase API

There are no datatypes in HBase; it stores all its data as byte arrays and provides the following API functions for accessing it:

- **get(key):** Fetches a given byte[] row;

- **getScanner(Scan):** Returns a Scanner object that is used to iterate on a subset of a table; the argument Scan defines the start/stop rows, column families, and other filters to be used while scanning the table;
- **put(byte[] row):** Inserts a new row; and
- **delete(byte[] row):** Deletes an existing row.

HBase tables are indexed based on a primary key, which enables fast access to the data when it is queried by row key, through a get. One can also sequentially access a range of table rows by providing the start and end row keys (through the scan function).

HBase Coprocessors

Given the above APIs, the client program requests data through get (one row) or scan (multiple rows) and proceeds to process the collected rows. It is important to note here that the actual processing occurs at the client side, after the selected rows have been fetched from their respective regions, where a region is a subset of a table. HBase originally did not offer any support for deploying code at the nodes where the table regions are stored in order to perform computations local to the data and return results (instead of just table rows) to the client. This limitation makes the cost of several computations prohibitive. Consider, for example, a row-count process. In a very naive implementation, the client has to use the scan API to fetch the

Figure 2. HBase conceptual schema

	CF1		CF2
RK1	RK1:CF1:CQ1:D:t9	RK1:CF1:CQ2:D:t4	
RK2	RK2:CF1:CQ1:D:t3 RK2:CF1:CQ1:D:t4 **RK2:CF1:CQ1:D:t5**		
RK3	RK3:CF1:CQ1:D:t1		RK3:CF2:CQ4:D:t11

entire data and then count it locally. Alternatively, one may implement a MapReduce computation: using the scan API at the node level, the node rows are passed to a mapper process implemented at the node; the results (i.e. counts) are passed to the reducer process to do a global row count.

HBase Coprocessors, inspired by Google's BigTable coprocessors (Dean, 2011) are meant as a means of creating supporting functionalities to simplify the design of the main process and they are used to implement solutions for specific types of frequent workloads. In HBase, they are an arbitrary piece of software deployed per table region and can be used to act as an observer of any operation on the table, or perform a region-level computation.

When coprocessors are used as region observers one can compare them to relational database triggers. They can be used to observe any region activity, invoked either by a client using the APIs (get, put, delete, scan) or by a server-administration process (region split, memstore flush, compactions, etc.).

When coprocessors are used for region-level computation one can compare them to stored-procedure objects in relational databases. They can be used to pre-compute results at the region level and feed these interim results to the client, instead of the raw table rows. This may result in reduced RPC traffic depending on the use case.

Consider for example the use case we described above: computing a row count on a subset of a table. Here, one can use a coprocessor to send the local row count in the target region back to the client, sums the individual results. The client library of coprocessor framework makes sure to execute all the calls to individual regions in parallel. Developers need to define their own coprocessor interface by extending the CoprocessorProtocol interface and instantiating a concrete implementation at the server side. The framework supports the invocation of any arbitrary coprocessor APIs from the client side and the retrieval of the coprocessor results by the client.

LEGACY SYSTEM MIGRATION TO THE HADOOP ECOSYSTEM

The potential advantages of HDFS, MapReduce, Hadoop and HBase have motivated several migration efforts.

Shang, Jiang, Adams, and Hassan (2009) reported the use of MapReduce for software-repository mining. They deployed J-REX, an evolutionary code extractor for Java systems, on a four-machine Hadoop cluster. They reported that the distributed version is four times faster than the single-node version. Moreover, the migration to MapReduce required only a few hundred lines of code and it was easily adaptable to different cluster configurations. Their methodology involves the creation of indices beforehand so that subsequent queries can be answered using the pre-built indices.

Machine learning is an area that commonly involves computationally expensive tasks. MapReduce provides an interface to run such tasks in a clustered environment that hides complexities such as data partitioning, task scheduling, fault tolerance and inter-process communications. Panda, Herbach, Basu, and Bayardo (2009) used MapReduce for classification and regression tree learning on large datasets with their tool called PLANET. They used it to analyze click streams to predict the user experience following the click of a sponsored ad. Chu *et al.* (2006) provide an overview of solving popular machine-learning algorithms (naive Bayes classification, Gaussian discriminant analysis, k-means, neural networks, support vector machines, etc.) in a MapReduce model using a shared-memory multi-processor architecture. Considering the popularity of MapReduce in machine learning, Apache has started Mahout[8], a project for implementing clustering, classification and batch collaborative filtering, on Hadoop.

On the HBase side, applications requiring continuous editing of the data prefer HBase as compared to plain HDFS because the later does not allow random file modifications. One can only append to an existing file in HDFS.

Another interesting family of HBase applications involves those applications requiring high scalability and low latency workload, such as Web applications. The BigTable paper (Chang, et al., 2008) mentions that the BigTable infrastructure is being used for 90 Google products, the list including Google Maps, Gmail, etc. Many more users report their workloads on the Apache HBase site (Contributors, 2011).

In the research community, prior work of using HBase for document analysis has been reported. Konstantinou *et al.* (2010) used HBase for storing document indexes for a real time application. They used the existing APIs, and mentioned that their application has to make client-side merging of two queries before rendering the complete solution. It required two server trips before producing the end result. In a way, this case study underlined the need of an enhanced query support in HBase. Vashishtha and Stroulia (2011) used the coprocessors framework, in particular the endpoints variant, to provide an enhanced query support where the results are computed at the region level, and then all individual results are merged at the client side using the existing coprocessor callback feature.

In another work of creating and storing document indices, Li, Rao, Shekita, and Tata (2009) proposed HIndex, that gets persisted on top of HBase and supports parallel lookup of target indexes. These indexes are fetched and the results are merged at the client side. In the work discussed in this chapter, we did use the coprocessor framework while creating indexes, but designed the schema such that the workload is limited to one row transaction and does not require any client side merging.

Other Cloud Migration Efforts

In addition to Hadoop ecosystem migration, there has also been work on migrating software applications to other cloud platforms. The majority of resources described as being in this space are more accurately about moving an application to a different infrastructure without modifying its architecture; that is, understanding how the behavior of applications will change when working with a virtualization layer or with the limitations imposed by PaaS providers (e.g., Varia, 2010; Ragusa & Puliafito, 2011).

Frey and Hasselbring (2011) describe an approach for identifying the ways existing software would violate the constraints of a cloud service if deployed to it. Constraints include not writing to ephemeral storage, certain operations being disallowed in a PaaS model, etc. A profile of the cloud service constraints is created (they use Google PaaS as an example) and re-used. The OMG-standard Knowledge Discovery Meta-Model[9] is used to model the application. Constraint violations are detected in the model and reported to the developer for repair prior to cloud deployment. They do not consider or address re-architecting an application for deploying to the cloud, nor do they actually discuss an actual application migration.

Li *et al.* (2011) describe a tool to test the performance of an application on a variety of clouds prior to migration. They create a coarse-grained trace of an application's performance and emulate it on the cloud. This work too stops short of actually performing a migration.

REMICS (Mohagheghi & Sæther, 2011) is an EU FP7 research program focused on migrating legacy applications to the cloud. Their heavyweight model-driven approach is based on the OMG standard Architecture Driven Modernization and other existing models. Knowledge is extracted and a model constructed, model-driven engineering is used to produce a new system, and this system is validated against the existing system. At present, they have not reported an implementation or evaluation of their approach. While their models are too comprehensive to reproduce here, we follow similar steps to achieve migration; our demonstration of a successful migration should be very relevant to their ongoing work.

Babar and Chauhan (2011) describe their process for migrating an application to the cloud. Their approach required simpler architectural changes and was performed at the IaaS level. Our PaaS approach offers different insights and tested various levels of re-architecting. While they do not explicitly consider the cost-benefit trade-off, they offer general observations on desirable properties of migrated application.

TEXT ANALYSIS WITH TAPOR

Digital text is growing at an unprecedented rate, because of massive digitization efforts as well as because much of textual production these days is "born digital." A variety of analyses of this data can lead to the discovery of much meaningful knowledge. Such analyses can be done at the lexical level (that entails looking for most frequent words, their distribution across the documents and others) or at the semantic level (finding contextual meaning and relations among various entities in the data itself). In either case, the computation involved is intensive. In this chapter, we concern ourselves with a lexical-analysis tool, TAPoR, developed by Digital Humanists, who are frequently interested in analyzing and comparing different works of same author or works of different authors. This type of analysis can also vary in its scope, ranging from single document to a large corpus. For instance, an interesting use case may involve finding the most popular Latin word in either a single Shakespeare novel, or in all of his collected works. Information

gathered from these analyses can offer interesting insights to literary scholars. The typical workflow involves identifying a text corpus to analyze, then repeatedly executing a variety of queries on that corpus. Each query may require several iterations to adequately tune and filter the results.

The Text Analysis Portal for Research (TAPoR) is a Web-based application that provides a suite of text-analysis tools to scholars and researchers in the Digital-Humanities (Rockwell, 2006). It includes a front-end portal and a back-end Web service called TAPoRware. TAPoR has several deployments across the world and has an increasing number of users.

TAPoRware is a single Web service with 44 operations, implemented in Ruby using the SOAP4R libraries[10]. Each operation runs in O(n), and is bounded by CPU time relative to the size of the input. The tools covered in this chapter are (a) listing the words of a document with their counts, (b) generating word clouds, (c) locating the use of a word in context (concordance), and (d) finding instances of two words located near each other in text (co-occurrence). These operations are described in (Table 1). In addition to accessing the functions via Web services, they may also be accessed via CGI.

A typical TAPoR usage scenario begins with the end user identifying a piece of text to analyze with a given tool. Then, via a Web-services client or the Web front-end, the user selects the relevant parameters for the analysis. Common options include word stemming, excluding stop words, and defining the number of words/sentences/

Table 1. The TAPoR operations (from http://taporware.ualberta.ca)

Operation	Description
List Words	Count, sort and list words of the source text in different orders. It can strip words user specified from the list, or common stop words.
Find Concordance	Find user specified word/pattern anywhere in the text with its context. Display the result in KWIC format.
Find Co-occurrence	Find user specified pattern and co-pattern in a given length of context. Highlight the patterns in the result.
Word Cloud	Using the top k frequent words reported by List Words, generate a visualization of those words and their relative frequency.

paragraphs to display results in-context. In addition, each operation has its own configuration options. The entire text to be analyzed and the configuration options are encoded in a SOAP request and transmitted to the Web service.

The existing TAPoR implementation suffers several limitations that make the flexible experimentation of Digital Humanists with different collections a challenge. One major bottleneck is its lack of scalability to larger documents, due to its design. It was originally built to cater to small documents, processing the document in its entirety for each individual request, though a new request may have only a single different parameter from the previous one. Therefore, if one does a concordance for a word "love" and now wants to do for "blood," it will process the entire document twice. This approach suffices when the document is small, but it is not scalable to larger documents (size over 5-10MB is sufficient to give a response time-out error). This results in a poor end-user experience, as each request takes the same $O(n)$ time, where n is proportional to the document size. An alternative to this approach is the standard way of creating indices of the document, and then using these indices for TAPoR operations. Index creation process is also costly and its cost is proportional to document size; but it pays off in the long run as this cost is incurred only once and the indices are used over and over again. This is expected to be particularly useful for large corpora.

An initial step added the ability for TAPoRware to be load balanced over several processes (cores) or CPUs, or even over multiple physical or virtual machines (Smit, et al., 2009). While this offered some basic scalability benefits, the cap on the size of text corpora still existed, and substantial computation resources were required to scale.

For our TAPoR-migration study, we chose four "recipes," i.e., either individual operations or compositions of operations, to support in the migrated version. We analyzed TAPoR access logs ranging for three years and profiled the workload.

This showed that although TAPoR supports around 44 recipes, the four most popular ones cover 87% of the total requests over the past three years. We prioritized the operations to be implemented in the new service based on the frequency of their use in the old service (Table 2). The migration process benefits (in a way a new implementation would not) from making use of domain knowledge gathered during the lifetime of the original application. We found our decisions and understanding of the domain were heavily informed by the legacy application and its usage patterns.

THE TAPOR MIGRATION

In this section, we describe our experience migrating TAPoR to the cloud. We consider two closely related migrations. For the first case, we describe how we re-architected TAPoR to allow Hadoop to process the text, storing the indices on HDFS. For the second, we use the same architecture and Map-Reduce job for the text processing, but add improved functionality to store the indices in HBase.

Migration to Hadoop and HDFS

In previous work (Vashishtha, Smit, & Stroulia, 2010), TAPoR was migrated to use Hadoop, including a substantial design shift. Hadoop's algorithmic strengths are index building and batch processing; ideally migrated software makes use of these strengths. There is a certain amount of fixed overhead involved with a distributed file system and the map and reduce phases, so the task should warrant increased computing power, a distributed file system, or a robust framework that works around failures.

A key step was to identify the functional requirements of the original and new services, examining what functionality the existing service and new platform offers, and how might it be offered in the new service. In particular, MapReduce

Table 2. Percentage of requests for each operation, based on the original TAPoR deployment

Operation	%
Word Cloud	45.6
List Words	22.0
Concordance	16.3
Collocation	4.6
Co-occurrence	3.1
Pattern Distribution	3.0
Extract Text	3.0
Visual Collocation	1.8
Googlizer	0.6

is designed for offline, batch-processing tasks like index building. It is not intended for on-line processing or request-response style interactions.

For TAPoR, we decided an index-and-query strategy would make best use of MapReduce. Counting every word in a document, for example, necessarily involves reading every word in the document. To achieve the kind of speed-up we needed, we had to begin with an index. We also identified new functional requirements that could not be met by the old implementation but that we could provide during the transition. Our requirements included generating indices of large text corpora that would facilitate querying the collection (or defined sub-collections) in an offline fashion, and querying indices on request.

The next step was to design the new service. One important design consideration is whether to wrap the old service or to re-implement, or something in between. Some applications can be moved to a MapReduce paradigm by applying the thin veneer of a map and a reduce step to existing APIs or functions. For other applications, the map or reduce steps can be implemented such that most of the code is re-used, though integrated into a new application. For yet others, the best way to draw on the power of Hadoop is to re-implement the original application functionality. Regardless of the wrap/re-implement choice, one must determine what happens in the map phase and what happens in the reduce phase.

In our case, the old service processed chunks of text one-time, without maintaining (or persisting) any intermediate state of its computation. Repeated analysis of the same text requires re-uploading and re-analyzing the text from scratch. We chose to re-implement, creating our own indexing algorithms, our own index formats, and new querying algorithms. A substantially similar WSDL is used to maintain syntactic compatibility, though a semantic change was necessary to require uploading the name of an indexed document instead of the document, and two additional operations: one for uploading a document to index and a second one to list the indexed documents.

We designed our indices to allow operations to re-use the same index, to allow us to divide collections into sub-collections easily (e.g., to analyze the collected works of William Shakespeare one day, and only Hamlet the next), and to be quickly sortable and searchable. An index has, for each word, a count of its occurrences in the collection, a list of the files in which that word appears in, and the byte locations for each of those files. For us, a collection consists of a set of files; sub-collections are subsets of this file set.

The need to keep key-value pairs sorted by source file required us to avoid the default Hadoop key (the map operation takes name-value pairs from the documents and distributes them to reduce nodes based on the name). We used a combination of file name and word to keep these keys sorted together by file name. In the map phase, each word is emitted as a key and its byte location and the corresponding file id as values. In the reduce phase, we combine the indices for each word found in the corpus to make a collective index. By default, this index is sorted alphabetically. We created a separate index sorted by frequency of word; one of our functional requirements is to support the common use case of asking for the top k words.

With these design changes, we turned to implementing the new service. A key implementation question is how to get indices/queries/data that live entirely in the Hadoop virtualized environment into the "regular" environment that service requests will arrive from, such as a Tomcat/Axis environment. The HDFS can be queried using the appropriate libraries (available in many programming languages but most reliable in Java); in the index-query methodology, the query algorithms can talk to HDFS without running on MapReduce nodes. Alternatively, indices can be moved out of HDFS and onto a local file system (allowing index-building computation power to be rented on the cloud and a smaller local server to run queries).

The migrated Web service infrastructure is shown in Figure 3. The left side shows the submission of a document, which is processed by the index builder MapReduce task. The index stored in the index store. For this scenario, the index is stored in HDFS. The various implemented operations need to access the indices in different ways. The List-Words and Word-Cloud operations need to access indices in a sequential manner, either sorted by frequency or alphabetically. The Concordance and Co-occurrence operations need to access indices specific to a key word. We use binary search for locating the required index entry. Specifically, we use the MapFileFormat, which provides binary search functionality with lower memory requirements.

The new Web service runs in the Apache Axis SOAP stack[11] on Apache Tomcat 6[12], and is implemented in Java. The majority of the service was generated using the Axis wsdl2java tool. The WSDL for the new service is nearly identical to the old. The main technical change is a new URI for the service. The main semantic change is the "inputText" parameter is now the name of the text collection to query, instead of being the actual text to query. The current operations do not yet support all features of the old service.

Our SOAP server receives incoming SOAP requests and, based on the parameters in these requests, invokes the index-based query algorithms for the requested operations on the specified text collection. This invocation is done using the Java API made available by our index querying implementation. The API could be used by any mechanism, not just a Web services server. The response is wrapped in an appropriate SOAP message and returned to the client.

Finally, we implemented a small front-end client and some command line tools that can be used to test the new service. Regression testing ensures the new service returns the same results as the old service, new functionality is tested, and the performance improvement is measured. A user visits a Web page and selects a text collection to analyze, which operation to use, and the parameters for that operation. The Web page submits via HTTP POST to our client. The form submission is converted into a SOAP message and transmitted to the server. The resulting response is extracted and converted to the appropriate output format before being returned to the user via a standard HTTP response.

Migration to HBase

In the previous section, we discussed the re-architecting and migration of TAPoR to HDFS. As we will see in the experimental results, this improved both scalability and performance. This section describes a further migration to using HBase, which is claimed to be a better alternative for an online querying type of system such as TAPoR because it provides a better random read performance; and since it uses HDFS as its backing file system, it also inherits its advantages.

Schema Design

The first step in using HBase is to create a schema for the data storage. The overall performance of an application using HBase depends on its schema, which should be designed with the expected workload in mind. Our design focused on the four most frequent operations (list words, word cloud, concordance, co-occurrence). We examined all

Figure 3. The architecture of the re-implemented TAPoR: either the HDFS index store (scenario 1) or the HBase index store (scenario 2) is used

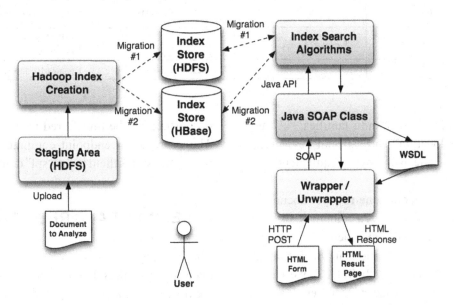

four operations, in particular the expected reads and writes to the files. We considered the same indexing strategy used for the HDFS implementation when estimating reads and writes.

- **List Words:** Is computed from an index that includes a list of all the words in the document and the number of times they occur. This involves reading one index and not reading the source document.
- **Word Cloud:** Is constructed using the output of a List Words operation, so the pattern will be the same.
- **Concordance:** Shows the presence of a target word in a dataset along with a configurable context. It is computed using a position-based inverted index that associates a word with all its byte locations in the document. For a given target word, the byte locations are retrieved from the index, then the document is read around those locations. This requires one read to fetch the index, and then a series of random reads from the byte locations named by the index.

- **Co-occurrence:** Shows how two target words are occurring together in a document. A user can provide a threshold to define the degree of closeness such as "within 10 words" or "within 5 sentences." For a given pair of target words, the algorithm fetches the index for each (as in concordance) and then reads both indices, searching for pairs of byte locations likely to be within the given threshold. The document is read around these locations and the candidate pairs are further filtered based on the threshold (word and sentence distance cannot be determined by byte locations alone). This requires two reads (one per index) and a series of random reads from the selected byte locations of two documents.

We use HBase to improve the performance of the indexing; the actual files are still read from their locations in HDFS. Our goal in designing the schema is to ensure data locality and to limit the number of transactions. Recalling the nature of HBase column families, we created the schema shown in Table 3. The HBase table (named

Table 3. The TAPoR HBase schema

Row Key	bl:foo	bl:bar	bl:sports	spl:Top100
1	3123, 4223, #2	553, 643, 5544, #3		hello:105, world:56, love:45, blood:40
2			434, 423, 545, 646, #4	games:10, soccer:5, sports:4

"docIndex") has two column families, "bl" and "spl" ("byte location" and "special keywords," respectively). The row key is equivalent to a document ID.

This design has only one row per document. Each unique word becomes a column qualifier in the "bl" column family, and each cell value is a list of the byte-offset locations in the document, followed by its frequency. In Table 3, we see the word "foo" occurred twice in Document 1, at byte offsets 3123 and 4223. We store the top K words in the "spl" column family; to read the top K words, one can simply read the "topK" column qualifier in the "spl" family. To read the byte offset of a word, one can retrieve the "bl" family with the target word as the column qualifier: "bl:word." All of these index operations are achieved in a single transaction.

Index Building

The index is created with the same Hadoop job that was used in the HDFS version, to compute the byte offsets for each word. In the reduce phase, these byte offsets are inserted in a table in HBase. Once the reduce phase is complete, a coprocessor endpoint is used to compute the frequency index at the server side, by reading the frequencies of all the words in the document and sorting them in decreasing order. Using a coprocessor for computing the frequency index helped in distributing the computation among the datanodes instead of it all happening at the requesting machine. The inverted index of a document is substantially large, sometimes even larger than the document itself; with a coprocessor, the byte-offset indices

do not need to be transferred to the client side. The coprocessor endpoint computes the top K words and stores them in the "spl" column family.

EXPERIMENT AND RESULTS

The existing legacy TAPoR is not capable of handling large files. In our testing, depending on the timeout settings, it struggled with files above 1MB. Comparing it to the migrated implementations, where we used a 4,000MB file, is not possible. As the scalability benefits are evident, we will primarily focus on the performance gains by the move to HDFS versus the further migration to HBase.

Environment

Where applicable, the original application was tested in a virtual machine that was allocated a single core of a Core2 Duo 1.86 GHz processor with 1GB of memory. It was tested using a 1 MB file from Project Gutenberg, Mary Shelley's The Last Man.

The testing of the migrated versions was conducted on a four-node Hadoop cluster. Each node had 8GB of RAM and two AMD Opteron 800 MHz processors. The nodes shared access to a 4 TB RAID 0 volume. Network latency was negligible. We used Hadoop version 0.20.3 and our modified version of HBase 0.90. The four nodes all served as task nodes and data nodes (running jobs and storing HDFS files), with one additionally assigned to serve as the master and run all of the coordination/dispatch services.

We used a dataset of 54 million tweets from Twitter for our experiments. The file was constructed by pseudo-randomly sampled tweets (chosen by Twitter in response to our API calls) from 46 non-sequential days over a one-year period. Non-English tweets were removed. There are 46 documents in the dataset, one per day, for a total size of 4 GB. (The exact numbers are 53,958,269 tweets, average 11.4 words per tweet, average 71.6 characters per tweet).

Development Effort

Effort estimation is a non-trivial problem (Jorgensen & Shepperd, 2007). We report effort very simply, in terms of a) an objective metric, Source Lines Of Code (SLOC), and b) a subjective description of the conceptual effort required. For each, we excluded UI-related code, focusing on the implementation of the code necessary to answer the questions of the TAPoR users, and not on the formatting or transmission of the answers. We do not quantitatively assess effort.

Both implementations required an understanding of the MapReduce paradigm, as well as domain knowledge. We did approach this problem with an existing level of understanding of MapReduce, which helped when deciding on an indexing strategy capable of leveraging the strengths of MapReduce. Though we had access to the legacy application, several years of logs, and the client, we did not have access to the developer of the legacy application. We went through an informal requirements-elicitation phase where we tried to understand the expected use of TAPoR and tools like it, including several meetings and attending a digital humanities conference.

Our implementation using HDFS required 650 SLOC. Implementing the HDFS version required familiarity with the basic concepts of a file system and the conceptual step to apply these concepts in a distributed fashion.

The HBase-driven version is a mostly independent code base, with only 70 SLOC overlapping (related to reading the context from the files stored in HDFS, which is the same for both). The TAPoR-specific code is 670 SLOC (including the overlap), with an additional 130 SLOC related to modifying the HBase coprocessors. Conceptually, this version required the same knowledge of HDFS, plus the additional understanding of HBase. Designing the schema required a solid understanding of how HBase wrote and retrieved information, and applying the domain knowledge of access patterns. There are additional HBase services (RegionServers, Master, ZooKeeper) that must be run. The changes to coprocessors required not only understanding their use, but also synthesizing an extension to perform text analysis computations locally.

Measured by SLOC alone, the two are fairly close. The domain knowledge required was also similar, and it was available from the legacy application and the client. In terms of conceptual effort, HBase required substantial additional effort to achieve the performance gains. This knowledge is not specific to the application; it is applicable to future migration and maintenance activities within the Hadoop ecosystem.

Methodology

The two variations differ primarily in creating, storing, and accessing the indices. We tested the index building process and two representative operations: List Words (which uses the same indexing strategy as Word Cloud) and Concordance (which uses the same indexing strategy as Co-occurrence).

For List Words, we read the top K words. In the HDFS version, the frequency indices are stored in a file and we simply read the top K lines; in the HBase version, the frequency indices are stored as columns in the "docIndex" table. This presents a comparison between HDFS and HBase read performance.

For Concordance, we read the byte offsets of the target word, and then do a read on the file at the selected byte offsets. We limited our experiments to the first portion of request processing, specifically excluding the step of accessing the original documents on HDFS, which is identical for both variations. As mentioned, we stored the indices in a MapFile in the HDFS version, which supports binary search on its content. The index-reading phase presents a comparison for random reads in HDFS vs. HBase, because the MapFile is a large sorted file, and we are reading the words at random.

We used YCSB (Yahoo! Cloud Serving Benchmark) (Cooper, Silberstein, Tam, Ramakrishnan, & Sears, 2010) to generate load requests similar to List Words and Concordance requests. We created a workload of 500 requests and measure the throughput of both the approaches. The workload consisted of List Words requests for randomly selected documents, and Concordance requests for randomly selected documents and randomly selected words from a common set of the 50 most frequent words. There was only one client for all the 500 requests. This is done to make it more realistic where a client caches the file blocks location (in case of HDFS), or Region location (in case of HBase).

Results

The migrated versions show substantial performance improvements on a per-request basis. In earlier work (Vashishtha, et al., 2010), we showed that on the 1MB test file, the legacy application took 29.75 seconds and 7.27 seconds for List Words and Concordance, respectively. The migrated application (HDFS) indexed the 1MB test file in 60 seconds (mostly overhead) but responded to requests in .4 and .6 seconds, respectively. These numbers include UI processing, network lag, and opening the files in HDFS to obtain context. The cost of indexing is saved within 2-8 requests.

Turning to comparing the two flavors of the Hadoop migration, the HBase version was able

to index the 4GB dataset in half the time of the HDFS version (Figure 4), reducing the time between submitting a dataset and being able to query that dataset by almost 2 hours in this case. This can be attributed to two main reasons. First, in the case of the HDFS version, we needed to run two MapReduce jobs, where the second one was to compute the frequency index. In HBase, the frequency index is computed using a coprocessor endpoint. The Hadoop MapReduce framework has a high starting cost, making the overall cost higher. The second reason is that the write rate of HBase is inherently higher than that of HDFS.

For the List Words service, the HBase approach more than doubled the throughput of the HDFS approach (Figure 5). For Concordance, the HBase throughput was almost 80 times that of the HDFS approach. Though the end-user impact is reduced—the user still has to wait for the HDFS retrieval of context from the original document—the performance improvement of the index process in HBase is substantial. A charitable pro-rating of the original application shows a 4GB file, if it

Figure 4. Time required to construct the index for the two methods

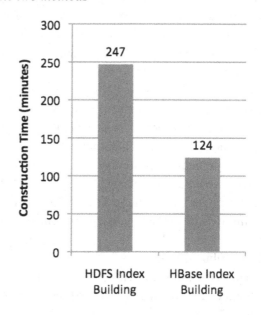

could be processed leveraging the same computing power, would have a throughput of .0002.

Considering scalability, the original application was limited to several megabytes per request. Though we have not explored the limitations of the two approaches, we know that HDFS has been successfully used for similar tasks at the Terabyte scale, and we have demonstrated fast response times at the Gigabyte scale. When comparing the two migrations for scalability, HBase has a more extensible indexing approach, where additional indices can be added as columns to the existing HBase table. We suspect that HBase will support the migration of additional TAPoR services with smaller index size and better scaling than HDFS. We also know we can add additional index information to the HBase table in other column families without increasing the processing time of the existing indices. In the HDFS approach, however, we need to have separate files for each index type, or, possible, design a creative representation to use the same index files for multiple purposes.

Lessons Learned

While migrating TAPoR to index based HDFS/HBase stack greatly reduces the latency as compared to the original implementation, it becomes increasingly difficult to maintain it as the number of users and documents increased. This is because each of the indexes were kept in a separate directory, which resulted in a directory explosion. This is an alarming situation for HDFS because the Namenode keeps the file-system metadata in memory and each directory increases its memory footprint.

Another suboptimal usage of HDFS in the initial design is the TAPoR workload is more about random reads rather than large sequential reads, while the HDFS is specially designed for the later kind of workload. These reasons led us to explore other options such as HBase. With HBase, one can map the one directory per index design to a row(s) in a table. In addition, since HBase stores its data in HFile, one does not need to care about the problem of small documents increasing Namenode memory footprint. HBase also provide much better random reads as compared to plain HDFS as shown by the experiments in the Experiments and Results section.

One key consideration while using HBase is the right schema, which along with meeting the application-specific workload needs, should also be optimized from the HBase perspective. In case of TAPoR, our analysis suggests two levels of indexes, one at the document level (for

Figure 5. The number of operations per minute achieved for each service, for each migration flavor

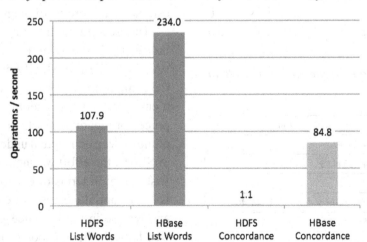

list words and word cloud), and a second one at the document-word level (for concordance and co-occurrence). We initially designed a schema, with each row corresponding to a word, containing as its values the byte-offset locations of the word in the document. To distinguish a word for a document, each such word is prefixed with an auto-generated document ID. Table 4 gives an example of such a schema for a document, with its ID as #1. The row key of a document level index in such a schema will be special keyword, like "Top100" for the top 100 words, as shown in the table. The document with ID 2 also has the word "foo" but it is in a separate row, as shown in the last row of the table.

This schema meets all the requirements for looking up a specific word (one just needs to add the document ID as the prefix), and also for the List-Words functionality where the keyword is given as input. The only drawback with this design is that it results in a tall table, as there is one row for each unique word in the document. This is a drawback because of how HBase stores and reads its data. As mentioned above, HBase stores its data in a special file, called HFile. Within the HFile, the data is arranged in data blocks, followed by an index block at the end of the file. The index block keeps the index of the starting element of each of the data block. While reading a specific record, a binary search on the index block can tell whether that target record is in the HFile or not. For faster look-ups, this index block is kept in memory of the hosting RegionServer. The above

Table 4. An alternative schema for TAPoR on HBase

Row Key	CF:byteLoc
doc#1,foo	3123, 4223, #2
doc#1,bar	553, 643, 5544 #3
doc#1,...	....
doc#1,Top100	hello:105, world:56, love:45, blood:40
doc#2,foo	909, 656, 6786#3

schema results in a large number of rows (a 1 MB document has on average 220,000 words), and it increases the index block size in the HFile. This index block size is directly proportional to the number of rows in the table; as a result, this is not an optimal schema as it increases the memory footprint for the application. Therefore, even though this schema meets all the required functionalities, it is still suboptimal. We believe that this experience with Hadoop and HBase will help others while designing/migrating their application to the Hadoop system.

CONCLUSION

Migrating this legacy application required substantial domain knowledge and knowledge about the target platforms, HDFS, Hadoop, and HBase. We believe that our experience is relevant to the migration of document-manipulating applications in general, since many of those manipulations are bound to refer to words, their locations and their relations. In the first migration phase, the HDFS indices, we achieved substantial improvements over the previous approach in both performance (over time) and scalability. The demonstrated difference in scale is three orders of magnitude, with the limit not established but believed to be at least another 6 orders of magnitude higher. The demonstrated difference in performance is estimated at 4 orders of magnitude.

The second migration phase, moving the indices to HBase, required the additional understanding of HBase. Modifying the source code of the computing platform is a substantial development investment, and adding something like co-processor support to the cloud computing platform requires deep conceptual understanding. In terms of SLOC, the effort was not much more than the first phase; in terms of expertise required, there is a substantial increase. In exchange, there was an increase in performance—the indexing time was halved, the per-lookup index performance improved by about two orders of magnitude, and the bound on index size relative to document size was halved. We do expect that migrating additional TAPoR services along the same path will require substantially less effort now that the modifications are in place, and we believe that the index will be more efficient and more extensible even with these additional services.

The increased effort in migrating did achieve notable performance improvements. The initial move to a scalable, distributed computing platform did achieve the highest gains, for even lower overall cost. However, there was still return on investment for additional changes and optimizations to leverage that platform.

The next step of this work is to measure the bounds of scalability of this approach to see if we can achieve in practice what is promised by theory. We would also like to examine more closely the impact that this has on user experience. Will TAPoR users actually run different analyses if they know repeated requests while fine-tuning parameters will return quickly? At least some of the benefits achieved here were due to the redesign, and we would have improved performance and scalability even in the absence of large-scale computing platforms. The next step in the evaluation is to run the index-based method outside of Hadoop, on a bare-metal machine, and compare the performance and scalability to the versions running on the Hadoop ecosystem. Finally, applying our approach to migrating other applications would show the extent to which our approach and results are generalizable.

ACKNOWLEDGMENT

The authors received funding from AITF (formerly iCore), IBM, and NSERC.

REFERENCES

Babar, M. A., & Chauhan, M. A. (2011). A tale of migration to cloud computing for sharing experiences and observations. In *Proceedings of the 2nd International Workshop on Software Engineering for Cloud Computing,* (pp. 50–56). New York, NY: ACM.

Chang, F., Dean, J., Ghemawat, S., Hsieh, W., Wallach, D., & Burrows, M. (2008). Bigtable: A distributed storage system for structured data. *ACM Transactions on Computer Systems*, *26*(2), 1–26. doi:10.1145/1365815.1365816

Chu, C., Kim, S., Lin, Y., Yu, Y., Bradski, G., Ng, A., & Olukotun, K. (2006). Map-reduce for machine learning on multicore. In *Proceedings of the 2006 Conference on Advances in Neural Information Processing Systems,* (pp. 281-288). Cambridge, MA: The MIT Press.

Cooper, B., Silberstein, A., Tam, E., Ramakrishnan, R., & Sears, R. (2010). Benchmarking cloud serving systems with YCSB. In *Proceedings of the 1st ACM Symposium on Cloud Computing,* (pp. 143–154). New York, NY: ACM.

Dean, J. (2011). *Designs, lessons and advice from building large distributed systems*. Retrieved from http://www.odbms.org/download/dean-keynote-ladis2009.pdf

Dean, J., & Ghemawat, S. (2008). MapReduce: Simplified data processing on large clusters. *Communications of the ACM*, *51*(1), 107–113. doi:10.1145/1327452.1327492

Frey, S., & Hasselbring, W. (2011). An extensible architecture for detecting violations of a cloud environment's constraints during legacy software system migration. In *Proceedings of the 15th Conference on Software Maintenance and Reengineering,* (pp. 269-278). ACM.

Ghemawat, S., Gobioff, H., & Leung, S. (2003). The Google file system. *ACM SIGOPS Operating Systems Review, 37,* 29–43. doi:10.1145/1165389.945450

Gordon, A. W., & Lu, P. (2011). Elastic phoenix: Malleable MapReduce for shared-memory systems. In *Proceedings of the 8th IFIP International Conference on Network and Parallel Computing (NPC).* Springer-Verlag.

Hadoop Wiki Contributors. (2011). *Hbase/poweredby - hadoop wiki.* Retrieved from http://wiki.apache.org/hadoop/ Hbase/PoweredBy

Jorgensen, M., & Shepperd, M. (2007). A systematic review of software development cost estimation studies. *IEEE Transactions on Software Engineering, 33*(1), 33–53. doi:10.1109/TSE.2007.256943

Konstantinou, I., Angelou, E., Tsoumakos, D., & Koziris, N. (2010). Distributed indexing of web scale datasets for the cloud. In *Proceedings of the 2010 Workshop on Massive Data Analytics on the Cloud,* (pp. 1–6). New York, NY: ACM.

Lakshman, A., & Malik, P. (2010). Cassandra: A decentralized structured storage system. *ACM SIGOPS Operating Systems Review, 44*(2), 35–40. doi:10.1145/1773912.1773922

Li, A., Zong, X., Kandula, S., Yang, X., & Zhang, M. (2011). Cloudprophet: Towards application performance prediction in cloud. In *Proceedings of the ACM SIGCOMM 2011 Conference,* (pp. 426–427). New York, NY: ACM.

Li, N., Rao, J., Shekita, E., & Tata, S. (2009). Leveraging a scalable row store to build a distributed text index. In *Proceedings of the First International Workshop on Cloud Data Management,* (pp. 29–36). ACM.

Mendeley, Ltd. (2011). *Free reference manager and PDF organizer.* Retrieved from http://www.mendeley.com/

Mohagheghi, P., & Sæther, T. (2011). Software engineering challenges for migration to the service cloud paradigm: Ongoing work in the REMICS project. In *Proceedings of the 2011 World Congress on Services,* (p. 507-514). IEEE.

Muthukkaruppan, K. (2011). *The underlying technology of messages.* Retrieved from http://www.facebook.com/note.php?note id=454991608919

Panda, B., Herbach, J. S., Basu, S., & Bayardo, R. J. (2009). PLANET: Massively parallel learning of tree ensembles with MapReduce. *Proceedings of the VLDB Endowment, 2*(2), 1426–1437.

Ragusa, C., & Puliafito, A. (2011). Running business applications in the cloud: A use case perspective. *Lecture Notes in Computer Science, 6586,* 595–602. doi:10.1007/978-3-642-21878-1_73

Rockwell, G. (2006). TAPoR: Building a portal for text analysis. In Siemens, R., & Moorman, D. (Eds.), *Mind Technologies: Humanities Computing and the Canadian Academic Community* (pp. 285–299). Calgary, Canada: University of Calgary Press.

Shang, W., Jiang, Z. M., Adams, B., & Hassan, A. E. (2009). MapReduce as a general framework to support research in mining software repositories (MSR). In *Proceedings of the 6th IEEE International Working Conference on Mining Software Repositories,* (pp. 21–30). Washington, DC: IEEE Computer Society.

Smit, M., Nisbet, A., Stroulia, E., Iszlai, G., & Edgar, A. (2009). Toward a simulation-generated knowledge base of service performance. In *Proceedings of the 4th International Workshop on Middleware for Service Oriented Computing.* New York, NY: ACM.

Varia, J. (2010). *Amazon web services - Migrating your existing applications to the AWS cloud.* Retrieved from http://media.amazonwebservices.com/CloudMigration-main.pdf

Vashishtha, H., Smit, M., & Stroulia, E. (2010). Moving text analysis tools to the cloud. In *Proceedings of the IEEE Congress on Services,* (p. 107-114). Los Alamitos, CA: IEEE Computer Society.

Vashishtha, H., & Stroulia, E. (2011). Enhancing query support in HBase via an extended coprocessors framework. In *Proceedings of the 4th European Conference towards a Service-Based Internet,* (pp. 75–87). Berlin, Germany: Springer-Verlag.

Zhang, C., & De Sterck, H. (2010). Supporting multi-row distributed transactions with global snapshot isolation using bare-bones HBase. In *Proceedings of Grid 2010*. Grid. doi:10.1109/GRID.2010.5697970

KEY TERMS AND DEFINITIONS

Cloud Computing: Characterizes the perspective of end users, who are offered a service (which could be in the form of a computing platform or infrastructure) while being agnostic about its underlying technology. The implementation details of the service are abstracted away, and it is consumed on a pay-per-use basis, as opposed to being acquired as an asset.

Column Family: A collection of columns, which are accessed in a single transaction, like in one read/write call. Each column family is stored as a separate file on the file system. HBase stores records sorted by a primary key; however, a (set of) column family(ies) are also defined.

Datanode: The worker nodes in the HDFS architecture; they store and retrieve data blocks (also called data chunks).

Hadoop: An open-source implementation of the MapReduce paradigm.

HBase: A no-SQL database relying on HDFS, an implementation of Google's BigTable.

HBase Coprocessor: An arbitrary piece of software deployed per table region and can be used to act as an observer of any operation on the table, or perform a region-level computation. They offer a means of creating supporting functionalities to simplify the design of the main process.

HDFS: The Hadoop file system.

MapReduce: A scalable and straightforward approach to processing large amounts of data (up to petabyte scale) in parallel, on a cluster of commodity machines. It is conceived to address specifically workloads that are data-parallel in nature. It includes a map function (which consumes raw data as key-value pairs and generates intermediary key-value pairs) and a reduce function which consumes these key-value pairs and somehow ``aggregates'' them to produce the final desired output.

Namenode: The master node in the HDFS architecture; it contains the meta data about mapping files to blocks, and blocks to addresses in datanodes.

ENDNOTES

1. http://aws.amazon.com/
2. http://www.salesforce.com
3. It should be noted here that this approach relied on our own modifications to HBase and that these modifications were sufficiently general to be contributed and accepted to core HBase, and will be generally available in version .92.
4. http://hbase.apache.org/
5. http://cassandra.apache.org/
6. http://www.mongodb.org/
7. http://couchdb.apache.org/
8. http://mahout.apache.org
9. http://www.kdmanalytics.com/kdm/
10. http://rubyforge.org/projects/soap4r/
11. http://ws.apache.org/axis2/
12. http://tomcat.apache.org/

Chapter 11
Geographically Distributed Cloud–Based Collaborative Application

Bogdan Solomon
University of Ottawa, Canada

Cristian Gadea
University of Ottawa, Canada

Dan Ionescu
University of Ottawa, Canada

Marin Litoiu
York University, Canada

ABSTRACT

The amount of multimedia content on the Internet has been growing at a remarkable rate, and users are increasingly looking to share online media with colleagues and friends on social networks. Several commercial and academic solutions have attempted to make it easier to share this large variety of online content with others, but they are generally limited to only sending Web links. At the same time, existing products have not been able to provide a scalable system that synchronizes disparate Web content sources among many users in real-time. Such a goal is especially desired in order to provide the benefits of cloud deployments to collaborative applications. Many Web-based applications cannot predict the number of connections that they may need to handle. As such, applications must either provision a higher number of servers in anticipation of more traffic, or be faced with a degradation of the user experience when a large number of clients connect to the application. Cloud-based deployments can alleviate these issues by allowing the application's server base to auto scale based on the user demand. A cloud deployment can also employ servers in different geographic locations in order to offer better latency and response times to its clients. Moving a collaborative application from using a single server to a cloud and then to a distributed cloud is not a trivial matter, however. This chapter will show our experience with how such a transition can be performed, and will present the architectural changes that had to be implemented at the server and cloud level in order to create a distributed execution that resides in the cloud.

DOI: 10.4018/978-1-4666-2488-7.ch011

Copyright © 2013, IGI Global. Copying or distributing in print or electronic forms without written permission of IGI Global is prohibited.

INTRODUCTION

Web 2.0 has dramatically transformed the way in which information is collected and presented to online users, and the enormous popularity of social networking has created a growing appetite for online multimedia content. Users are no longer satisfied with just viewing simple HTTP pages but expect the ability to share and collaborate with other people, such as friends or colleagues, online and in real-time. This can be seen with services like Google Docs (2011), where multiple users can work on the same document at the same time, and the document is stored on Google's remote servers in the cloud. Other popular websites which offer the ability for online content sharing between users include Facebook and Twitter, yet in both cases, a message posted by a user containing links to photos or videos is later viewed by one or more users separately. In many ways, this is in no way different than sending an e-mail with either links or attachments.

Applications which allow users to collaborate in real-time have been developed by companies like Cisco in the form of WebEx (Cisco, 2011) and Citrix in the form of GoToMeeting (Citrix, 2011). Such applications generally use extra Web browser plugins in order to achieve the collaboration; however, a number of commons characteristics can be seen:

1. Users can communicate via text as well as video/audio.
2. All users view the same shared state of the collaboration.
3. Users can bring external data (documents) into the collaboration.

A similar collaborative application called "Watch Together" was developed and presented in Gadea (2011) by the authors. Watch Together used Adobe Flash on the client side, which connected to an open-source Java based server named Red5.

The server application was responsible for ensuring that the client state remained synchronized across all the clients in a collaborative session. The server application also managed the creation of sessions, the joining of users to existing sessions, and the destruction of sessions. Figure 1 shows the user interface of Watch Together with six collaborative users sharing a YouTube video. Two of the users are streaming video/audio from their Webcams.

While the single-server application performed the desired functionality, a single-server architecture is not scalable. A simple JEE server can be clustered without much difficulty since, from a scalability point-of-view, it will not matter which server the clients connect to. In the case of a collaborative application, data must be passed between servers while collaborative session data has to be replicated across all servers to which clients are connected. This problem becomes even more complicated when the cloud, and therefore the server, is distributed across multiple geographic locations.

This chapter will present an approach to moving the collaborative application from a single server to a cloud, and then to a geographically distributed cloud. The rest of the chapter is structured as follows: Section 2 will present the requirements for the geographically distributed cloud-based application. Section 3 will introduce the architecture of the single-server application. Section 4 will show the changes made to move the application to the cloud, while Section 5 will show the changes which are required to make the application run in a distributed cloud. Finally, Sections 6 and 7 will present future work and conclusions.

REQUIREMENTS AND OVERVIEW OF THE MIGRATION PROCESS

The current application is a Web-based client-server application in which many clients connect

Figure 1. Collaborative application interface

to the same server and collaborate with each other by sending messages to each other via the server connections. This application is to be migrated into a multi-cloud application in which many clients connect to many clouds, with each of the clouds being composed of multiple server instances. From the point-of-view of the clients, the application behaves just as if all clients connect to the same single server. Thus, the application would go from an application such as the one in Figure 2, in which all clients communicate with one server, to an application such as the one in Figure 3. In Figure 3, clients connect to different servers in different clouds, and the servers within a cloud communicate with each other, while the clouds themselves communicate with each other as well.

As mentioned in the previous section, the target application runs in a cloud environment

Figure 2. Single server application

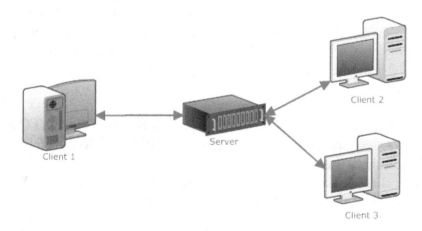

Figure 3. Multiple-cloud-based application

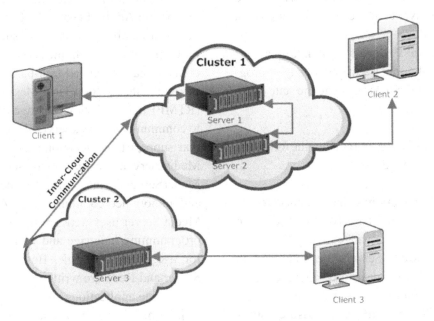

and is a geographically distributed collaborative application. Such an application has a number of important characteristics:

1. **Client-Server Application:** The system uses a client-server architecture in which clients connect to a logical server. Messages sent between clients go through the server. The server is responsible for distributing the messages to the appropriate destination clients.
2. **Cloud-Based Application:** Clients connect to a cluster of virtualized servers. Clients communicating with each other could be connected to different server instances in the cloud.
3. **Collaborative Application:** The system ensures that clients in the same collaborative session view the same state of the shared "workspace."
4. **Geographically Distributed Application:** Clients connect to one of multiple clouds that are distributed throughout various locations. Clients connected to different clouds can still communicate with each other.

The above characteristics result in a number of requirements for the application:

1. **Client Presence:** Clients can see when their contacts come online, go offline, or become busy by joining a collaborative session.
2. **Client Synchronization:** Clients in the same collaborative session must see the same video stream, picture, document, map, etc. in the collaborative part of the application. Network delays can impact this; as such, the synchronization is not meant to be exact to the millisecond.
3. **Client Communication:** Clients in the same session can communicate with each other via text, audio, and video. No restriction is set on how many clients in a session can broadcast video/audio at the same time.
4. **Session Setup:** Any user can invite another available user to a collaborative session (pending restrictions created by the session's controller). Users can participate in only one session at a time.
5. **Session Control:** Any user can choose to see the shared collaboration view. The ses-

sion's controller (typically the creator of a collaborative session) can restrict the control to himself.

6. **Session in Progress Synchronization:** Clients who join a session already in progress must be synchronized to the state of the session.

In addition to these requirements, the following design decisions were taken:

1. **Client Connection:** Clients connect to one of multiple clouds based on a metric which offers good performance to the client.
2. **Server Cloud:** Servers are combined in clouds, which appear to be a single server from the point-of-view of the client.
3. **Server Cloud Location:** Clouds are distributed geographically.
4. **Server Cloud Scaling:** Clouds can scale up and down dynamically.
5. **In-Cloud Communication:** Servers can send messages to other servers within the same cloud. Such messages are distributed via a Group Membership Service (GMS).
6. **Out-of-Cloud Communication:** Servers can send messages to other servers in different clouds. Such messages are distributed via a "gateway," which sends messages to other clouds or receives messages from other clouds.

SINGLE SERVER ARCHITECTURE

This section will present the architecture of a single collaborative server in order to emphasize the types of changes required to move the architecture to a distributed cloud. Later sections will show how the server was modified and what other components were added to the system in order to support the requirements for a cloud-based and geographically distributed deployment.

Since the application is meant to be easily accessible via a Web browser and must support

audio/video communication, the client was developed in Adobe Flash, which is currently the only browser based technology supporting these requirements. As such, the server has to support communication with a Flash-based client. Flash-based clients use Real Time Messaging Protocol (RTMP) and the Action Message Format (AMF) to communicate with a server. Three servers exist that support these technologies: Adobe's Flash Media Server, Wowza Media Server, and Red5 Media Server. All three servers support both RTMP and audio/video communication. Adobe's Flash Media Server uses ActionScript as a server-side programming language and was not considered for use because of this. Both Wowza Media Server and Red5 are written in Java, while their server-side applications are also written in Java. In light of this, Red5 was selected since it is an open source project, therefore making it easier to fix any problems in the server code, while also making it possible to extend the server code to support extra functionality.

In order to achieve better modularity, server functionality is split into four core modules/ services, along with two other modules used for client-side application communication. The four core services are:

1. **UserStateService:** This service is used in order to indicate changes in user presence (coming online, going offline, currently busy), to retrieve the list of connected users, as well as to store the list of contacts for all connected users. The list of contacts is stored in order to decrease the number of messages related to users coming online. When a new user connects to a server, the server simply looks through the lists of already connected users to determine which users are contacts of the newly connected user. These users receive "user online" messages, and the newly connected user receives a list of contacts who are online.
2. **SessionService:** This service manages the various sessions created by users. It stores

a list of currently existing sessions, a hash map of clients to sessions, as well as a hash map of clients which have been invited to a session but have not yet accepted/rejected the invitation. Two other hash maps exist which are mirrors of each other, namely mapping invited clients to clients doing the inviting, and vice-versa. The SessionService is used to create new sessions, join and leave sessions, as well as to broadcast messages in a session. It is also responsible for synchronizing new users to the state of a session. The server, however, does not store the exact state of a session.

3. **WebcamVideoStreamService:** This service is responsible for managing each user's audio/video streams. It allows users to start/stop streaming and notifies the appropriate users that a new stream has been started (using information from the SessionService). Users receiving video/audio streams subscribe to streams published by other users through this WebcamVideoStreamService.

4. **ServerStatsService:** This service generates statistics regarding the server's performance (including CPU usage and memory usage), as well as gathers statistics from the UserStateService, SessionService, and WebcamVideoStreamService (such as bandwidth used for streams, number of users connected, number of active sessions, etc.). The ServerStatsService is therefore used to manage the automatic scaling of the cloud.

In addition to these four core services, two other services are used which support specific client side "apps":

1. **DocumentService:** The DocumentService allows using the Documents app to search for documents by keywords or by the user who uploaded the documents. Files such as spreadsheets, presentations, and PDFs are uploaded by users to the server, where they are converted to SWF files for viewing in the collaborative area of the client application. Uploaded documents can be defined as public or private and the search will ensure correct visibility.

2. **GISSensorService:** The GIS sensor service allows users to receive live data from Geographic Information System (GIS) sensors. Users can discover sensors and subscribe/unsubscribe to/from sensors. Once the user selects a sensor, the service will create the respective server-side subscriber to the GIS data and will forward the data to the user's client as soon as it is available. This data is then displayed by the Maps app and can be shared with other users.

Outside of these six services, the server also contains a main application module called Watch-TogetherServerModule. This module implements a MultiThreadedApplicationAdapter, which is the main entry point in a Red5 application. In addition, a WatchTogetherSession class maintains server-side information regarding the state of a single session, such as the user who is the controller of the session, the session's unique ID, and the list of clients in the session. Figure 4 shows the various classes involved in the server. All services extend a ServiceArchetype class, which injects information about the main server application.

Client-Server Communication

This section will discuss the message types that make up the basic client-server communication: connection setup, session setup, session synchronization, and audio/video communication. It is important to note that user refers to an actual human being, while client refers to the Flash-based software running inside the browser. Numbering is assumed to be consistent between a numbered client and user (i.e. Client 1 is the client used by User 1).

Figure 4. Server side services

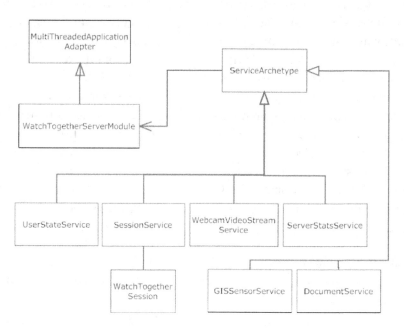

Figure 5. Client-server connection setup

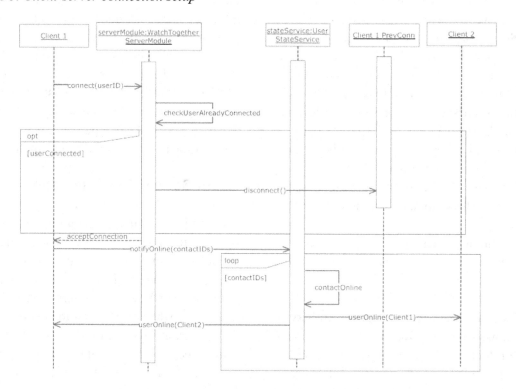

Connection Setup

Figure 5 shows the connection setup process as a sequence diagram. The diagram shows three client connections: Client 1, Client 2, and Client 1 PrevConn. Two of the connections, Client 1 and Client 1 PrevConn, are actually connections associated with the same user (they have the same userID). When the diagram begins, both Client 1 PrevConn and Client 2 are actively connected to the server. In addition, the users represented by Client 1 and by Client 2 are contacts of each other.

The diagram begins with the WatchTogetherServerModule receiving a new connection from Client 1. The connect message contains a field specifying the unique userID of the user which is trying to connect. The WatchTogetherServerModule checks to determine if there is already an active connection for the specified userID. Since a connection by Client 1 PrevConn already exists and uses the same userID, Client 1 PrevConn is sent a disconnect message and the connection information is purged from the server. This is to ensure that each userID can only be connected to the server once. The userID is associated with the new connection to Client 1 and the client is sent an acceptConnection message. Upon reception of acceptConnection, the client sends a message to the UserStateService requiring the server to notify the user's online contacts that Client 1 has come online. The notifyOnline message passes a list of contactIDs to the UserStateService of the server. These contactIDs represent userIDs which are contacts of Client 1 (before attempting a server connection, the list of contacts is obtained by Client 1 through external APIs separate from this server). The UserStateService goes through its internal list of connected userIDs and determines which of these users are also in the contactIDs list received from User 1. Each of these online clients receives a notification regarding the updated status of User 1. At the same time, User 1 receives notifications for each contact which is already online. Since the connection and online notification is done in two steps, it is guaranteed that users will know about each other's status without needing to employ semaphores. Even if two users connect at exactly the same time, by the time the notifyIsOnline message arrives from either client, the server will know that a user with the given userID is already connected.

Session Setup

Figure 6 shows the session setup process as a sequence diagram. The process starts when a user (User 1) invites another user (User 2) to a collaborative session. The inviteUser message is sent to the SessionService, which in turn checks the availability of User 2 via the UserStateService. The reason to check if User 2 is available at this time is due to the fact that User 2 could become "busy" by creating a session or accepting another invitation while User 1's current invitation was in transit. As such, User 1 would be sending an invitation thinking that User 2 was still available. If User 2 is still available, the SessionService checks if User 1 is already in a session. If a session does not already exist for User 1, a new session is created and User 1 is added to a session. The newly created session returns its unique sessionID back to the SessionService, which stores it together with the actual session object. Once the session is created, a message is sent by the SessionService to User 2, notifying User 2 of the invitation. Client 2 therefore displays a dialog with "accept" and "decline" buttons. Once User 2 has decided whether to accept or decline the invitation (or the invitation timeout expires, which also results in a "decline" reply from the client), the respective reply message is sent to the SessionService. The processing of the reply is shown in Figure 7. While User 2 decides if to accept or decline the invitation, the SessionService performs two additional actions which are not shown in Figure 6: if either of the two users (invited or inviter) is available, then the user's availability is changed

Figure 6. Client-server session setup

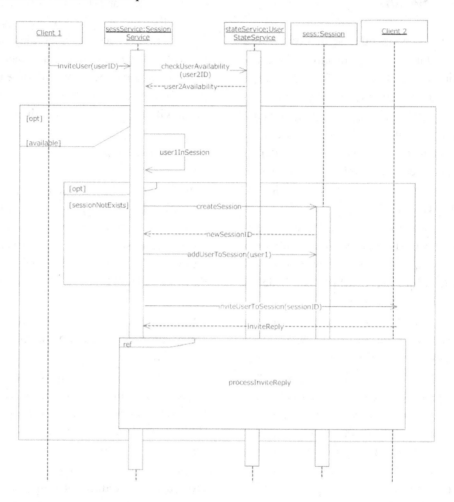

to "busy" and all contacts of the user are notified about the status change.

Once the reply for an invitation is received by the SessionService, the service checks if it is an "accept" or "decline" reply message. If the message is an "accept" message, the user is added to the session, which results in Client 2 receiving a list of all other users in the session. Similarly, any users already in the session (User 1) will receive a message notifying them that User 2 has joined the session. In the first part of Figure 7, User 1 receives a message that the invitation was accepted. Finally, the SessionService asks the Session to synchronize the new user to the session state. The initial synchronization mechanism is shown in Figure 8. If the reply message is a "decline" message, however, User 2's availability is changed to show that the user is available once again to receive invitations and a message is broadcast to all of User 2's contacts to announce the status change. At the same time, User 1 is sent a "decline" message for the invitation. The server then checks to see if the session is empty; a session is defined as empty if there is only one user in the session and there are no invitations that have replies pending. If the session is determined to be empty, the last user in the session has their status changed to "available" and the session is destroyed.

Figure 7. Client-server invitation reply

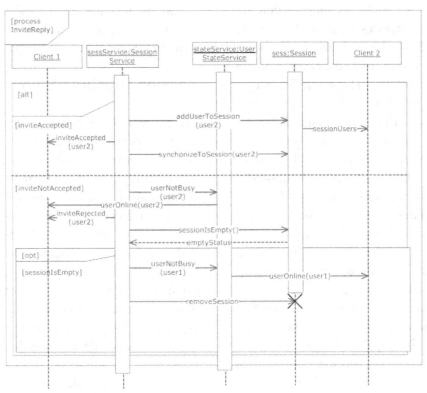

Figure 8. Client-server session initial synchronization

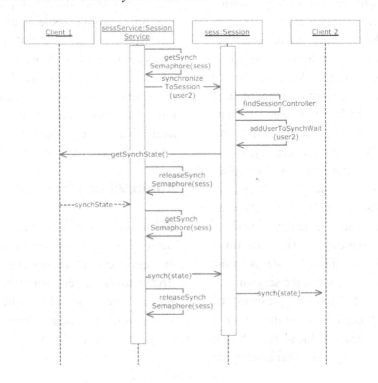

When synchronization is requested, as caused by a new user joining an existing session, the session service obtains a synchronization lock on the session and asks the session to synchronize a new user. The session finds the client, which is the session's controller. The controller is typically the client who initiated the session by inviting another user. If the initial controller leaves the session, a new controller is assigned randomly. Once the controller has been determined, the new user is added to a list of users waiting for synchronization messages. If the list of waiting users only contains one user, a message requesting the synchronized state of the session is sent to the session controller's client, which replies with the current state of the collaborative session. The synchronization lock is released at this point. Upon reception of the current state by the SessionService, the service obtains a synchronization lock on the session and passes the synchronization information to the session, which in turn broadcasts the synchronization state to all clients in the list of clients waiting for synchronization messages. Once all messages have been sent, the lock is released. The reason to use a list of clients waiting for synchronization messages is in order to ensure that the controller does not receive a large number of messages requesting synchronization. Once can imagine a user inviting a large number of contacts to a session, with a large number of these contacts accepting nearly simultaneously. The first "accept" message will generate a synchronization request, while all other accept messages (received by the server before the controller replies with the synced state) will simply wait and not generate extra synchronization requests. Once the synced state reply reaches the server, all waiting users will receive the same state. At the same time, the reason to use a semaphore for access to the two synchronization methods in the session is to ensure consistency in behavior. If, for example, an "accept" reply is received while the server is in the process of broadcasting the synced state to the clients already waiting, it is better to have the

new client wait until all broadcasts have completed and then ask the controller for new synchronization data, rather than trying to add the new client to the broadcast group for the message.

Session Synchronization

The process of maintaining synchronization between users in the same session is relatively easy from the server's point-of-view, as the server only acts as a relay to broadcast the message to all users in the originating user's session. The server does not do any processing of the message and never examines the contents of such a message. Figure 9 shows a sequence diagram of the mechanism used for session synchronization. Initially, the originating client sends a message that is to be sent to all other users in the session. Such a message is generated by the user performing an action in the Flash-based client, where the action is to be reproduced on all clients (for example, if a user pauses a video, the videos of all other users in the session must also pause). Upon receiving such a sendToAll request, the SessionService determines the session which the user is participating in, and then broadcasts the respective message to all other clients in the session. Note that no semaphores or locks are used to block access to broadcast messages. This is due to the fact that even if there are, for example, two users sending synchronization messages to the server at the same time, network delays make it impossible for the server to know which message truly occurred first.

Audio/Video Communication

The audio/video communication setup is an asynchronous setup; upon reception of a new stream, the server cannot simply start sending the new stream to the other clients in the session. The clients have to actually request that the server start sending a certain stream to them. Because of this, the server first notifies the clients that a

Figure 9. Client-server session synchronization

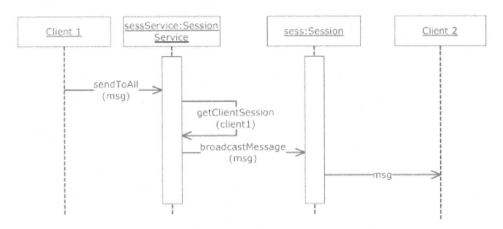

Figure 10. Client-server stream start

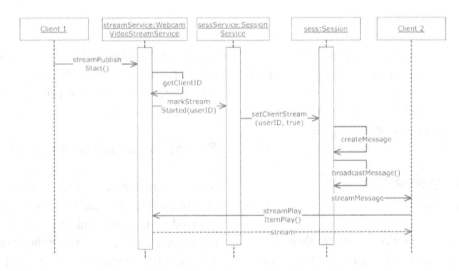

new stream has become available, and the clients then request that the server send them the stream.

The "stream start" and "stream stop" setups are very similar and are show in Figures 10 and 11 respectively. The process starts with the client starting or stopping a stream. This generates a streamPublishStart or streamBroadcastClose event, respectively. Upon receiving the message, the WebcamVideoStreamService retrieves the client's userID from the stream metadata, and then asks the SessionService to mark the respective user's stream as "started" or "stopped." The SessionService finds the user's active session and sets

the user's streaming information in the session as either "started" or "stopped." The SessionService then generates a message to be sent to the other users in the session and broadcasts it. If the message received by the clients is a "stream started" message, the client asks the server to start sending the stream. This generates a streamPlayItemPlay event and the server starts streaming the data to the client. However, if the message received by the clients is a "stream stopped" message, the client asks the server to stop sending the stream. This generates a streamSubscriberClose event and the server stops streaming the data to the client. The

Figure 11. Client-server stream stop

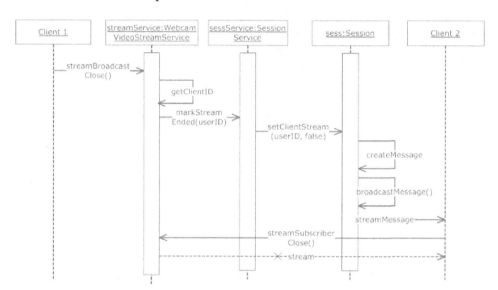

Webcam service also stores the information regarding which clients are streaming at any point in time. This is done in order to let any session-joining client know if it should subscribe to streams from users, which are already streaming their video.

CLUSTERED SERVER ARCHITECTURE

As mentioned in Section 2, the collaborative server must be capable of existing within a cloud deployment in which users connect to any of the cloud's available servers. In addition, a given user can still communicate with any other connected user, even if the users are connected to different servers in the cloud. A number of capabilities therefore had to be developed to allow servers to communicate and understand each other in this fashion. First of all, the cloud based system required a method for servers to discover each other and communicate with each other. Second, the cloud system required a way to replicate user information across the cloud. Finally, the cloud system required a way to proxy a Webcam stream from one server to another such that receiving users

can obtain the stream from whichever server they are connected to. This subsection will describe the architecture that was developed to meet these three requirements.

Server-to-Server Communication

Since a server-based cloud is not static in size and is allowed to scale up and down based on demand, a very important ability of the servers is to discover new servers when they come online, and for servers to broadcast when they leave the cloud. In order to achieve this goal, the cloud architecture uses a Group Membership Service (GMS) (Birman, 1993) to create a group, which the servers can join and leave. The servers then use the group created by the GMS system to communicate with each other. Using a GMS for such communication instead of an approach like broadcasting the messages in the network ensures that multiple clouds can be co-located in the same network and not interfere with each other's inter-server communication. The GMS that was used is the JGroups system (JGroups, 2011), which is the same system used by the JBoss Application Server for clustering. More specifically, the architecture

Figure 12. Server GMS join

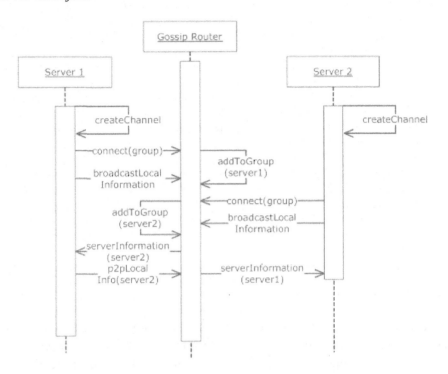

adds an extra component in the form of a Gossip Router, which runs on a specific host and port. The Gossip Router is responsible for registering and deregistering servers from groups, as well as for responding to queries for the members of a group. In order to deal with group members crashing, members periodically send a refresh message to update the status of their group membership. If a long enough amount of time passes without a refresh from a group member, that member is considered dead and is removed from the group. If a group member attempts to join a group with a name that does not exist, then a group with that name is created. One issue with the Gossip Router is that it can be seen as a single point of failure in the architecture. The current cloud deployment assumes that the Gossip Router cannot fail. However, if redundancy is needed, the system could use a backup Gossip Router in case the main router fails.

Upon startup, each server creates a channel through which it communicates with the Gossip Router and with the other servers in the cloud. Communication can be either point-to-point between two servers (if the sender of the message specifies a destination address), or a broadcast inside a group (if no destination address is provided). After a server creates a channel for group communication, the server connects to the predefined group based on its name, and then broadcasts the server's information to the group. This information includes the host address, port on which the server is running, as well as the name of the application. These three values are used to uniquely identify a server application. By depending on all three values, the cloud allows mixed systems in which either a host runs more than one server (each on a different port), or even a single server runs more than one application which joins the group, in which case both the host and port values will match for all applications running on the same server. Figure 12 shows the process of servers joining a group.

Figure 13. Server GMS classes

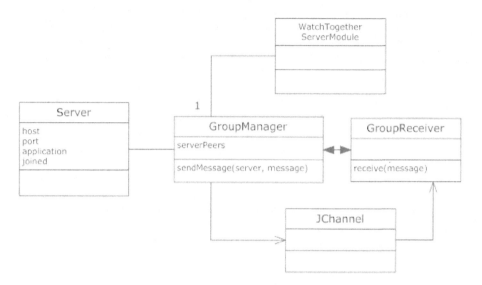

Note that after a server connects to the group, it broadcasts its local information to the group. If other servers already exist in the group, such as in Figure 12 when Server 2 joins, the Gossip Router broadcasts the message to all the existing servers in the group. Upon reception of a new server information broadcast, the receiving server checks if the message has a specific destination, which would mean it was not a broadcast but a point-to-point message. If the message was a broadcast, the receiving server sends a reply with its own information in order for the newly joined server to know the other servers in the cloud. This message is sent as a point-to-point message so as to prevent the newly joined server from also replying to a new server information message and thus creating an infinite loop.

In order to allow for inter-server communication, two components were added to the previously shown modular server architecture: a GroupManager and a GroupReceiver. The GroupManager creates the communication channel and performs the group logic of the server; the GroupReceiver receives messages from other servers, parses them, and passes the message to the corresponding implementation in the GroupManager. On top of these two components, the group system also uses a number of messages for passing data between servers. For the moment, the only important message is the Server message. The other messages will be explained in the following two subsections. Figure 13 shows the components.

The server module creates a GroupManager on startup, which sets up the JChannel and also creates the GroupReceiver. After creation of the receiver, the manager connects to the group and broadcasts a Server message, which contains the local information identifying the server instance (host, port, application) as well as a Boolean which is true if the server is joining the group and false if the server is leaving the group. The GroupManager also stores a list of server peers, which are Server objects representing the other servers in the cloud. New messages sent in the cloud originate from the GroupManager, while all messages from the cloud are received in the GroupReceiver.

Cross-Server User Information Replication

In order for the cloud to allow clients to connect to any of the servers and still allow clients to communicate with each other even if connected to different servers, certain user information has to be replicated across all servers involved. For example, a server has to know which other server a given client is connected to in order to be able to route messages destined for that client. To decrease the number of messages sent between servers, the status of the clients is also stored on all servers, even if the clients are connected to other servers. As such, the replication of user information consists of two parts: data that is being replicated, and messages used to replicate the data to ensure it is synchronized across all servers.

Replicated Data

In order to encapsulate the knowledge of whether a client is local or remote (a local client is connected directly to the server; a remote client is connected to some other server), a GroupClient class was added. This class encapsulates either a client connection, in which case the client is a local client, or a Server object, in which case the client is connected to another server in the same cloud. The remote server's information is represented by this Server object. The GroupClient also contains a sendMessage method, which is agnostic to where the client is actually connected. This method then delegates the actual sending of the message, depending on where the client is connected to. Because of this, servers actually store a list of all GroupClients and not just local clients to the server. Furthermore, all servers store information regarding the activity status of all users (online, busy), and not just local users. As stated previously, the reason to replicate the user status across all servers in the same cloud is that the number of server-to-server messages is reduced. For example, a new user connects to a server and sends the list of contacts to the server. The server then broadcasts a message to all other servers that a new user is online. The server, however, does not need to wait for its peers to reply to the connect message - and in fact no reply is expected - before notifying the newly connected client which of its contacts are online and which are busy. Figure 14 shows the static view of the GroupClient by extending Figure 13. Each server has a list of GroupClients, where each GroupClient has either a localClient object or a remoteServer object. If both objects are set (which should not happen in practice), the client is assumed to be local and the localClient object is used for communication. The figure also shows the ClientConnect message, which is broadcasted by a server in a group whenever a new client connects. The message contains the user's unique ID, the server object where the client has connected, and a Boolean representing if the user has connected or disconnected.

Figure 15 shows the connection sequence diagram and the messages sent between clients and servers. It is an extension of Figure 5. In order to simplify Figure 15, the "Server" entity contains both the actual SystemServerModule and the UserStateService. Upon receiving a new connection from a client, the server asks the GroupManager to broadcast a ClientConnect message using the new userID and at the same time accepts the user connection. The GroupManager creates a new ClientConnect message with the joined Boolean set to true and uses the group channel to broadcast the message. The message is received by Server 2 in the GroupReceiver, which determines if the message was a "connect" or "disconnect" message based on the value of joined in the message. Since this was a "join" message, the GroupReceiver passes the client information to the GroupManager, which stores the client information. At the same time, a second client connects to Server 2 and the process is repeated starting from Server 2. Upon reception of the notifyOnline message from the client,

Figure 14. Server GMS GroupClient classes

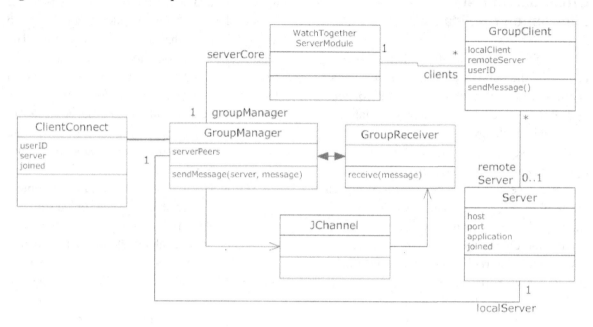

Figure 15. Server group connection setup

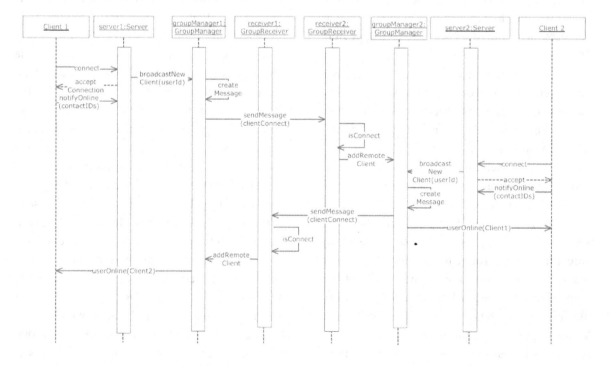

Figure 16. Server GMS group messages

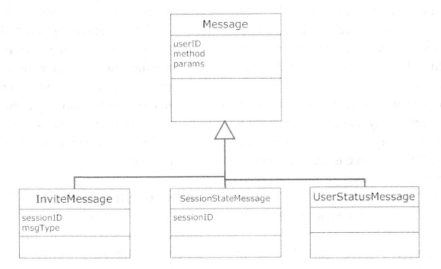

Server 2 already knows that User 1 is online and connected to Server 1, so it sends a message informing User 2 that User 1 is online. On the other side of the server-to-server communication, Server 1 receives the message that User 2 has just come online, and since it knows the list of contacts for User 1, it informs User 1 that User 2 is online.

Figure 15 does not show the process for disconnecting a client which was already connected using the same unique userID, but the process is the same. As soon as a server—either the one to which the new client connects or one of its peers which receives a ClientConnect broadcast—determines that a client with the same unique userID is connected, it sends that client a message, notifying the client that it was disconnected.

Replication Messages

At the same time, a number of messages are used in order to keep session data synchronized across the servers and clients connected to different servers in the same cloud. Figure 16 shows the various possible messages used for maintaining the state across servers. On top of the ClientConnect message previously described, the system uses three types of messages and an abstract class. The

abstract class, named simply Message, defines three properties that all messages will have: userID, which is the unique userID of the destination user for the message; method, which represents the method, which will be called in the destination client; and params, which is an array of parameters to be passed to the method. The first type of message used is InviteMessage, which is used to pass invitation requests to join a collaborative session and invitation replies between users, which are not on the same server. Invitation messages include the sessionID, which the message refers to, as well as a msgType variable, which can be one of "invite," "accept" and "deny." For "invite" messages, the params structure will contain the inviter's unique userID, while for "accept" and "deny," the params structure will contain the ID of the user sending the reply. The SessionStateMessage propagates session synchronization messages and simply contains a sessionID pointing to the session, which the message refers to. All other information is encapsulated in the method and params structures of the Message superclass. Finally, the UserStatusMessage simply extends the Message class without adding any extra property. The reason to actually add this message type is in order to be able to use the GroupReceiver to parse what kind of message has been received. UserStatusMessages have to update the user status in remote servers as well, and, as such, it is not sufficient to simply forward them to the destination client like some of the other Message implementations.

The processing of group replication messages at the receiver is relatively simple. Upon reception of a message, the GroupReceiver determines the message type. If the message is a ClientConnect message, then the server uses the process previously described. Otherwise, the following actions are taken depending on the message type:

1. If the message is a UserStatusMessage or an InviteMessage, then the message is first sent to the destination client, after which the server processes the message to update its internal state.
2. If the message is a UserStatusMessage, then the remote user's status is updated in the server.
3. If the message is an InviteMessage, then the server creates a session if none already exists with the specified ID and performs the actions presented for a single server.
4. If the message is an InviteMessage of type "accept," then the server synchronizes the new client to the session. The server will first try to use a local user to synchronize, even if the local user is not the session controller. If no local users exist in the session, then the server requests that the session controller synchronize the new user through a SessionStateMessage.
5. If the message is an InviteMessage of type "decline," then the server determines if the session is empty (in this case an empty session is defined as one with no local clients, or one local client and no remote clients) and, if not, destroys the session.
6. If the message is a SessionStateMessage, the server broadcasts it to all the clients in the session (including remote clients). If

there is more than one client in a session on a remote server, the server takes care not to send the same message multiple times to the same server. An exception to broadcasting the message exists for the case when the message is a reply to a synchronization request, where only the clients waiting for synchronization and servers with clients waiting for synchronization will receive the message.

Webcam Stream Proxy

A very important consideration is the capability of the cloud architecture to proxy streams such that a client connecting to Server 1 can send a stream to a client connected to Server 2. It is also very important that if, for example, two clients connect to Server 2, only one stream is sent between Server 1 and Server 2. Because of these requirements, audio/video streaming uses two types of messages: StreamMessage and StreamProxyMessage. Figure 17 shows these messages. StreamMessage contains the userID, which the message refers to and the type of stream messages, which can be "stream started" or "stream stopped." This message is generated when a user starts or stops streaming in order to notify other clients that a new stream has started (and allow them to subscribe to the stream). StreamProxyMessages are used to communicate between servers in order to request the creation of proxies. A StreamProxyMessage contains a server object which represents the server towards which the proxy stream should be created, along with a streamName, which is the name of the stream to be proxied. Stream names

Figure 17. Server GMS group stream messages

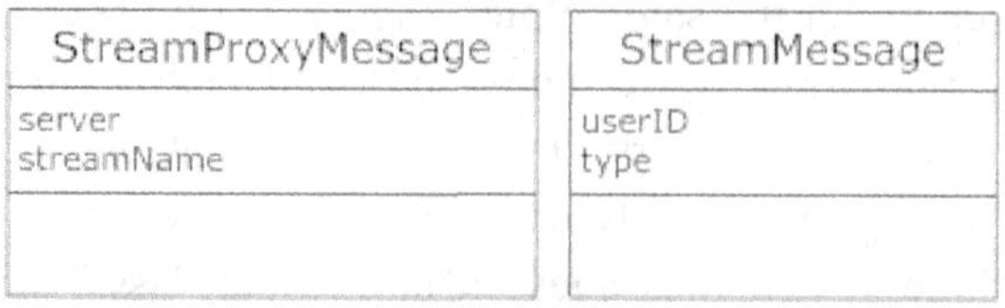

StreamProxyMessage	StreamMessage
server streamName	userID type

Figure 18. Server GMS stream proxy setup

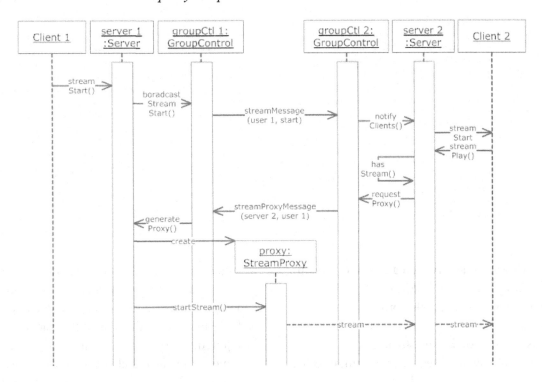

always use the unique userID of the streamer to simplify stream subscriptions.

Figure 18 shows the sequence used in order to set up a stream between two clients connected to two different servers, including the creation of the proxy. This sequence diagram is an extension of Figure 10. In order to simplify the diagram, note that the Server entity contains both the ServerModule and the StreamService components, while the GroupControl entity contains both the GroupManager and the GroupReceiver. The diagram also omits some of the steps already shown in Figure 10, such as obtaining the userID from the streamPublish request and modifying the Session state with regard to the user streaming. The broadcastMessage in Figure 10, which was done locally, becomes a group broadcast which creates a StreamMessage containing the userID and the type of stream message ("start" in this case). Upon receiving the StreamMessage, Server 2 finds the session that User 1 is part of (if any), and notifies the other local clients in the session that a new

stream was started. Upon receiving this message, clients attempt to start playing the stream. Once the play request is received by the server, the server checks if it is already receiving a stream with the given userID. If the server is receiving the stream already (either because the streaming user is also local or because a streaming proxy was already created), the server sends the stream data to the client. If the server is not already receiving the required stream, the server checks to determine if it has already requested the proxy from the other server. If the proxy creation request was already performed, the client is added to a list of clients waiting for the respective stream. If, however, no StreamProxy request has already been created, the server asks the GroupManager to request the creation of a StreamProxy by its server peer. The GroupManager creates a StreamProxyMessage with itself as the server and the ID of the user as the stream name, and sends the message to the server to which the streaming client is connected. Upon reception of the Stream-

Figure 19. Server GMS stream proxy teardown

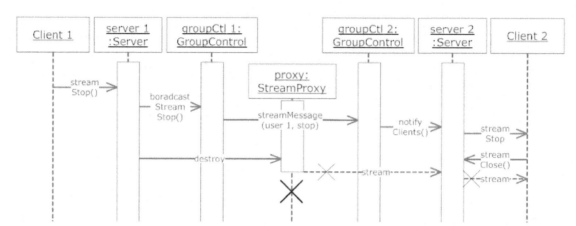

ProxyMessage, the server creates a new Stream-Proxy with the correct destination and source stream, and then starts the proxy. The stream destination server simply passes the data to any clients waiting to play the stream.

The "stop stream" sequence is similar to the "start stream" sequence, with the difference that no StreamProxy message is sent to the streamer client's server. Since the server detects when a client stops streaming, the server automatically destroys the StreamProxy, which also stops the stream and cleans up the stream resources used by the server. Upon detection of a proxy stream being closed, the server, which received the proxy, also cleans up any resources used for the stream. Figure 19 shows the teardown sequence for a stream.

GEOGRAPHICALLY DISTRIBUTED CLOUD BASED ARCHITECTURE

Up to this point, the chapter has introduced an architecture for a cloud of servers which are used to allow users to collaborate in real-time. The assumption is that the cloud will be hosted in a cloud environment that ensures high scalability and availability. When reviewing the requirements presented at the beginning of this chapter, it can

be noted that the architecture is still missing a geographically distributed nature. To deal with the geographical distribution of users and to improve end-to-end latency, a distributed cloud architecture is required. Two components are needed in order to achieve the desired characteristics: a way for servers in different clouds to communicate with each other, and an admission control system which redirects clients to the appropriate cloud based on some form of metric.

Cloud-to-Cloud Communication

While the in-cloud server-to-server communication uses lists composed of the cloud's servers in order to know where the server peers are located, such an approach would be prohibitive for out-of-cloud communications. At the same time, servers inside the same cloud can know the host names and IP addresses of their peers since the servers are on the same network. In a geographically distributed cloud architecture, servers from one cloud cannot know the host names or IP addresses of servers in other clouds. Even if the servers know these values, the values cannot be used since the servers are on different local area networks. Because of this, a tradeoff has to be made between decreasing the number of messages sent between clouds and the global system state stored at each cloud.

To achieve cloud-to-cloud communication, the architecture uses a gateway component placed in each cloud (the possibility of using multiple gateways will also be discussed). The gateway itself is a peer in the GMS group created for the cloud, but instead of processing the messages received like the servers do, the gateway simply broadcasts the messages received to the other clouds. In the case of client-to-client messages, if the destination client is connected to the local cloud (the gateway also stores a list of connected clients), then the message is not sent to other clouds. The gateway is also responsible for receiving messages from other gateways, and broadcasts the messages within the cloud. The following messages must be broadcast by the gateway:

1. **ClientConnect message of type "connect":** Must be sent to all clouds that make up the system since clouds do not know ahead of time where contacts of the newly joined user are located.

2. **ClientConnect message of type "disconnect":** Must be sent to all clouds that make up the system since clouds do not know ahead of time where contacts of the disconnected user are located.

3. **InviteMessage:** If the invited client is in the local cloud, then no action is taken; if the invited client is not in the local cloud, the message is sent to all other clouds.

4. **InviteMessage of type "accept" or "decline":** If the inviter client is in the local cloud, then no action is taken; if the inviter client is not in the local cloud, the message is sent to the originating clouds (a list is kept for invites awaiting reply).

5. **SessionStateMessage:** For each session ID, the gateway stores a list of clouds participating in the session (this is determined by checking the invite "accept" replies received from other clouds or sent to other clouds) and sends the message to the participating clouds. This implies that cleanup also has to be done by the gateway when sessions are destroyed or when another cloud no longer has clients participating in a session; a simple counter can be used to achieve this.

6. **UserStatusMessage:** Must be sent to all clouds that make up the system since clouds do not know ahead of time where contacts of the user whose status changed are located.

7. **StreamMessage:** Must be sent to all clouds forming the system since clouds do not know ahead of time where contacts of the user who started or stopped streaming are located. In the case of "stream start" messages, gateways store the originating cloud address in order to be able to route proxy messages. This data should not be stored as long as a user is streaming at all clouds, which means a new message must be added to notify the gateway that a server is interested in the stream. If all servers reply with "not interested," the data can be deleted from the gateway.

8. **StreamProxyMessage:** Must be sent back to the originating cloud, based on the knowledge from the stream message received previously. Since servers from separate clouds cannot communicate directly, a stream proxy gateway is used which allows a stream to be proxied between two clouds. Figure 20 shows the machines through which the stream is going.

In terms of static structure, the gateway is very similar to the group mechanisms used for each of the servers. The gateway has a GroupManager and a GroupReceiver. The GroupManager creates the communication channel and joins the group using a special ID in order for the servers in the cloud to identify the gateway and not assume it is just another server. The GroupReceiver receives group messages and passes them to appropriate methods in the GroupManager. On top of these two classes, the gateway also uses a CloudManager class, which is responsible for communicating with the other gateways. Since the cloud structure

Figure 20. Geographic cloud streaming

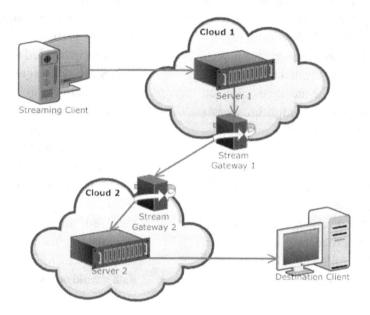

can be assumed to be nearly static (clouds will not be created on the fly), the CloudManager simply uses a list of static IP addresses to know the location of the other gateways. In the case that a new cloud is added to the system, the IP address of the new gateway can simply be added to all the other gateways. This constraint also means that the gateways represent single points of failure. The gateway system uses the same message classes used by the inter-server group communication system.

Note that more reliability can be added to the cloud communication system by using multiple gateways per cloud. Instead of having one gateway for all outward communications, each cloud can have one gateway for communications with each of the other clouds (thus for N clouds, each of the clouds would have N-1 gateways). This approach would also decrease the stress put on the gateways. Instead of using the deployment shown Figure 21, the system would use a deployment such as the one in Figure 22. Stream gateways would use the same approach, with one gateway per communication link. If multiple gateways are used,

the gateways in the same cloud could create their own group to quickly exchange messages without sending the messages to the servers.

The connect and disconnect message sequences are very simple as the gateway simply broadcasts the messages to the other clouds. Figure 23 shows the process used to setup a session across two clouds. The diagram assumes that an invite was sent by a client who is connected to Server 1 in Cloud 1 to Client 2 who is connected to Server 2 in Cloud 2. Server 1 knows that the user is not connected to its cloud since the server has a list of all users connected to that cloud, and, as such, sends the invite request to the gateway. Upon reception, the gateway broadcasts the message to all known external gateways. Gateway 2 receives the broadcast and determines that Client 2 is connected to Server 2 in its local cloud. It therefore saves the invitation information to be able to route the answer back to the originating cloud and routes the message to the appropriate server. Other gateways which receive the message determine that the required client is not connected to the cloud which they manage, and

Figure 21. One gateway per cloud deployment

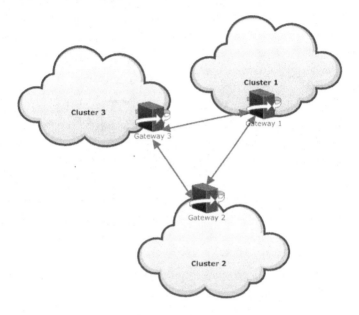

Figure 22. One gateway per cloud communication deployment

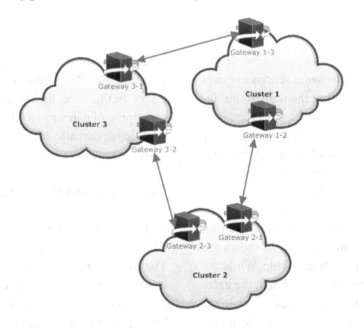

therefore drop the message. Upon reception of the reply from the client, the server determines that the inviter is not in the local cloud and sends the reply to the gateway. The gateway checks if the invite reply is an "accept" or "decline," and if it is an "accept" message, it stores the information that the cloud has one more client in the session the invite was performed in. It also stores the gateway the invitation originated from as being a member in the session and sends the reply

Figure 23. Session setup across clouds

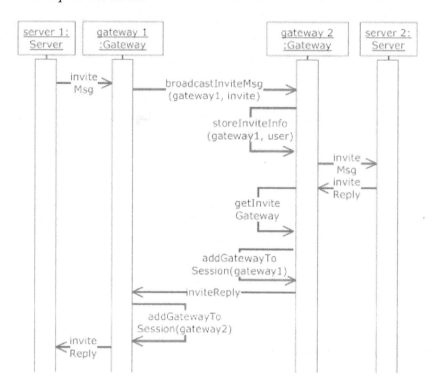

to Gateway 1. Gateway 1 also checks the type of the reply and performs the same actions as Gateway 2 before finally routing the reply to the inviter's server. If multiple gateways per cloud are used, servers broadcast the invite and invite reply to all gateways. In the case of invite replies, gateways which do not have stored data regarding the invite simply drop the message.

The stream setup sequence is more complicated due to the introduction of the streaming proxies in the architecture. Figure 24 shows the sequence diagram for the stream setup. While the "stream started" message goes through the gateways, the proxy request goes back through the stream gateways, which are responsible themselves for creating stream proxies. This ensures that if a user in a cloud already receives a certain stream, no proxy request will go to the originating cloud, since the stream gateway can send the stream itself. It is important to note that the stream gateway checks with the message gateway to see

where the stream originating gateway is, and then uses the equivalent stream gateway to request the proxy. In this case, the stream proxy has to have a mapping of gateways to stream gateways. Such knowledge can also be useful in the case where multiple gateways are used per cloud.

Cloud Admission Control

A single cloud deployment can use a very simple admission control policy such as round robin. The goal of the geographic cloud deployment is to improve the user perceived performance by connecting the user to a cloud, which offers better performance. Because of this requirement, the cloud deployment must use a more complex admission control scheme. A simple way to achieve such admission is to use location-based admission control. Upon receiving a connection request, the admission system determines the user's latitude and longitude by using a Geolocation system,

Figure 24. Stream setup across clouds

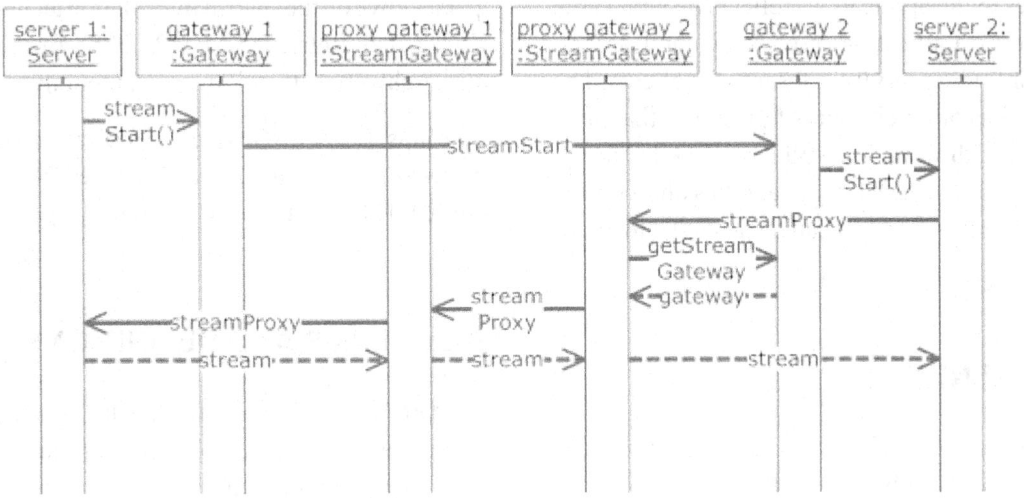

and, based on this information, finds the closest cloud with the service. While very simple to implement, this approach does not guarantee good latency between server and client because short geographic distance does not necessarily mean short Internet route, and also because even if a short route was guaranteed, a short route could be more congested than a longer route.

A second approach to offer admission control is to allow the client to ping a small subset of close clouds and then choose the one with the best ping. This has the advantage of improving the latency between server and client at the expense of a longer startup for the application, which must wait for the reply from the various clouds offered by the admission control system.

FURTHER CHALLENGES

While this chapter has presented the approach to take a single server application and modify the architecture to support initially a cloud deployment followed by a geographically distributed cloud, the chapter did not present any work on how the clouds would determine when and how to scale in an automated fashion. One of the major advantages of cloud deployments is infinite capacity and low cost. However, research in scaling up and down in clouds is still in its infancy and the process is, in general, left to the application.

The first step in scaling the cloud is to introduce an autonomic management system (Horn, 2001), which predicts when the existing system will fail to meet its desired QoS and scales the cloud to maintain the desired QoS.

Secondly, future work must focus on determining the performance of the application in a way similar to Gutwin (2011), which determines the performance hit and overhead introduced by the gateways and server-to-server communication. In cases where the performance would degrade outside desired values, an autonomic system could decide to move users to a common server if they are participating in the same collaborative session, thereby further improving message latencies.

CONCLUSION

This chapter has presented how a real-time collaborative application can be migrated from a deployment that uses only one server to a geographically distributed cloud architecture. The reason for such a modification is to better provide services to the application's clients by being able to scale the application based on demand, as well as by providing services closer to the clients. The chapter has outlined some of the issues that must be dealt with while modifying an architecture to support cloud deployments and has shown how the architecture can be changed to deal with these issues.

REFERENCES

Birman, K. P. (1993). The process group approach to reliable distributed computing. *Communications of the ACM, 36*(12), 37–53. doi:10.1145/163298.163303

Cisco. (2011). *Cisco WebEx web conferencing, online meetings, desktop sharing, video conferencing*. Retrieved November 30, 2011, from http://www.webex.com/

Citrix. (2011). *Web conferencing | GoToMeeting*. Retrieved November 30, 2011, from http://www.gotomeeting.com

Gadea, C., Solomon, B., Ionescu, B., & Ionescu, D. (2011). A collaborative cloud-based multimedia sharing platform for social networking environments. In *2011 Proceedings of 20th International Conference on Computer Communications and Networks (ICCCN),* (pp. 1-6). ICCCN.

Google. (2011). *Google docs - Online documents, spreadsheets, presentations*. Retrieved November 30, 2011, from http://docs.google.com/

Gutwin, C. A., Lippold, M., & Graham, T. C. N. (2011). Real-time groupware in the browser: Testing the performance of web-based networking. In *Proceedings of the ACM 2011 Conference on Computer Supported Cooperative Work,* (pp. 167–176). ACM Press.

Horn, P. (2001). Autonomic computing: IBM's perspective on the state of information technology. *IBM Corp.* Retrieved May 2, 2009, from http://researchweb.watson.ibm.com/autonomic/

JGroups. (2011). *JGroups - A toolkit for reliable multicast communication.* Retrieved November 30, 2011, from http://www.jgroups.org/

KEY TERMS AND DEFINITIONS

Autonomic Computing: Control paradigm for computers in which the computer system becomes 'self-aware' and attempts to self-organize, self-configure, self-heal and self-protect.

Cloud Computing: Distributed architecture where the data and computation are done on a 'cloud' of servers outside the premises of a business.

Collaborative Application: Application which allows multiple users to collaborate with each other via text, audio/video chat, as well as a common shared 'work area' which displays the same information across all users.

Geographically Distributed Cloud: A cloud composed of multiple subclouds which are distributed in different geographic areas and which offers clients better performance by allowing clients to connect to a closer cloud.

GMS: Group Membership Service, a distributed system which allows clients to join or leave a group, and which ensures that other clients receive these join/leave messages with certain guarantees.

Red5: Java-based server for communicating via RTMP/AMF with Adobe Flash-based clients.

Web 2.0: Term used to define the transition towards a webWeb that emphasizes social, interactive and collaborative elements, often through the use of open APIs and technologies.

Section 4
Migrating to Service-Oriented Systems:
Frontier Approaches

Chapter 12
Bridging the SOA and REST Architectural Styles

José C. Delgado
Technical University of Lisbon, Portugal

ABSTRACT

SOA and REST are the most used architectural styles for distributed interoperability solutions. Each is more adequate to a different class of applications and exhibits, advantages and disadvantages. This chapter performs a comparative study between them, after establishing a hierarchical classification of architectural styles and showing how to derive them by progressively introducing architectural constraints. An underlying model, which relates resources, services, and processes, is presented. It is shown that SOA and REST are dual architectural styles, one oriented towards behavior and the other towards state. This raises the question of whether it is possible to combine them to maximize the advantages and to minimize the disadvantages.

This chapter proposes a new architectural style, based on a combination of the best characteristics of SOA and REST, which the authors designate as Structural Services. Unlike REST, resources are able to offer a variable set of operations, and unlike SOA, services are allowed to have structure. This style uses structural interoperability, which includes structural compliance and conformance.

INTRODUCTION

Originally, the Web (Berners-Lee, 1999) was designed as a solution to the problem of browsing remote hypermedia documents, in which text was the main format. This justified the choice of a text markup document description language, HTML (Toshniwal & Agrawal, 2004). Today, the world is rather different. Text is just one among other formats, with binary information (pictures, video, voice) taking a great part of the data bandwidth. Users are no longer satisfied with information browsing and want more value, in the form of services. Organizations are also customers of other organizations, in a value-added chain, and began using the same infrastructure to setup their information systems and integrate them with their partners' (enterprise integration), in which Web services replaced specific application-to-application protocols.

DOI: 10.4018/978-1-4666-2488-7.ch012

Copyright © 2013, IGI Global. Copying or distributing in print or electronic forms without written permission of IGI Global is prohibited.

Fielding (2000, p. 107) contends that, since 1994, the REST style has been used to guide the design of the Web. In fact, most early Web applications were highly scalable, with many clients for each server, and a good match for the REST style. As Web technologies gained generalized acceptance and distributed interoperability became the usual scenario, enterprise class applications transitioned from classical object interoperability, based on RPC (Remote Procedure Call), such as Java-RMI or CORBA (Bolton, 2001), to standard, Web-based technologies. These applications require more flexibility than scalability, since they shifted the client emphasis from quantity (many people for one server) to business functionality. The concept of Web Service appeared as a solution to the interoperability problem, as an extension of the object concept in the distributed realm.

The Web of Documents has evolved into a global Web of Services (Tolk, 2006), in which the interacting parties are both humans and computer applications and content is increasingly dynamic, generated on the fly according to some database and business logic. The underlying logical architecture became less client-server and more peer based, in particular when enterprise applications are involved.

SOA (Earl, 2005), instantiated by Web Services, embodied a major evolution, the transition from the client-server to the service paradigm. Web services required a new protocol (SOAP) and a way to express the interfaces of services (WSDL). HTTP and HTML are technologies that were originally conceived for large-scale applications and human clients. XML, which maintained the text markup style of HTML, made computer based clients easier and, together with HTTP, became the cornerstone of Web Services technologies. This evolutionary transition is perfectly understandable in market and standardization terms, but still constitutes a mismatch towards both humans and applications.

HTTP is an application level protocol, synchronous and committed to the client-server

paradigm. In particular, it does not support full duplex, long running sessions required by general services such as those found at the enterprise level. This has spurred workaround technologies such as AJAX (Holdener, 2008) and Comet (Crane & McCarthy, 2008). Web Sockets, now part of the HTML5 world (Lubbers, Albers, & Salim, 2010), removes this restriction, adds binary support and increases performance.

XML is verbose and complex, has limited support for binary formats, is inefficient in computer terms due to parsing and exhibits symmetric interoperability, based on both sender and receiver using the same schema, which constitutes a relevant coupling problem.

The notion of schema matching (Jeong, Lee, Cho, & Lee, 2008) is used only for service discovery, not for message exchange. This means that Web Services are more a legacy integration and interoperability mechanism than a true and native service oriented solution. Their universal service interoperability came at the price of complexity, with schemas and all the associated standards. Tools automate and simplify a lot, but they just hide the complexity and do not eliminate it. This has spurred a movement towards simpler, more manageable systems, in the form of a resource oriented architectural style, REST (Fielding, 2000), and of a simpler data format, JSON (Zyp, 2010), promoting what is known as RESTful applications (Laitkorpi, Selonen, & Systa, 2009; Li & Chou, 2010).

Whereas SOA emphasizes behavior and rich interfaces, the guiding aspects of REST are state, structure and uniform interfaces. All resources implement the same service, with the same set of operations, albeit with different implementations. These typically exhibit CRUD style (Create, Read, Update, and Delete) and are mapped onto HTTP verbs (GET, PUT, POST, and DELETE). Functionality that in SOA would be modeled as an operation is modeled in REST as a resource.

REST is defined at a lower level than SOA, with a higher semantic gap between the problem and solution spaces. However, it maps directly onto the familiar HTTP protocol and has some interesting scalability properties, which are important for the class of applications in which a server is used by many clients.

In fact, armored with simplicity and scalability, the REST style has become very popular (Pautasso, Zimmermann, & Leymann, 2008), not only among services on the Web but also in cloud computing. All the major providers now offer a REST API to their systems.

Cloud computing is the latest frontier, promising to revolutionize again the way applications work. This is not a mere question of where the software runs. It also affects software development, the architecture of applications, how businesses cooperate, and how people interact with the rest of the world, opening new possibilities. Existing applications and software development methods need to be prepared for all these environments.

This chapter recognizes that both SOA and REST have advantages and disadvantages, best adapted to different classes of applications. Ideally, what we should aim for is an architectural style that could combine these two styles, maximizing the spectrum of applicability while emphasizing the advantages.

To avoid terminology misunderstandings, we consider SOA to refer to its instantiation with Web Services and use the term Service Oriented to designate the more general models based on the service concept.

The main contributions of this chapter are:

- A classification and structuring organization of existing architectural styles, based on constraint refinement;
- A description of how the SOA and REST styles can be combined into a new architectural style, Structural Services.

The chapter is organized as follows:

- The next section establishes the background technologies;
- The following sections establish a hierarchy of architectural styles, by progressively introducing architectural constraints that specialize previous styles. Each style is described and discussed;
- A new architectural style, Structural Services, is proposed as a combination of the constraints of the SOA and REST styles. The basic workhorse is structural interoperability, based on the notions of structural compliance and conformance;
- Finally, we present some information on a preliminary implementation and describe future work.

BACKGROUND

There is currently a continuing debate in the scientific community on which architectural style, SOA or REST, is more adequate for specific classes of applications. The literature comparing these styles is vast (Mulligan & Gracanin, 2009; Becker, Matzner, & Müller, 2010), usually with arguments more on technology issues than on conceptual and modeling arguments. The REST proponents seem to be more active, since this style was rediscovered, or at least became more active, more recently than the standardization of Web Services and their adoption by the market. Besides arguing why REST is better (Pautasso, Zimmermann, & Leymann, 2008), a recurring theme is to try to demonstrate that REST is also adequate for the enterprise class of applications (Pautasso, 2009).

This SOA versus REST debate bears strong similarities with a debate that occurred 30 years ago, in the computer architecture realm. In the beginning of the 80s, in the dawn of the personal computer, complexity was on the rise. The instruction sets of computers were growing and architectures were adding more and more features, with the goal of making them more and more powerful and of better supporting the software. Something that today seems to be happening to WS-* technologies.

Unfortunately, more complex instructions meant more complex hardware and longer circuit delays. Even the simplest instructions began suffering with this and taking proportionately more time to execute. Researchers started to note not only this but also that the complex instructions were actually seldom used, if at all (Patterson & Ditzel, 1980). Due to complexity and semantic gaps, compilers were not able to benefit from complex instructions and were generating, for the most part, only simpler instructions. It should be stressed that computer architects were not programming and programmers were not designing computers.

A new generation of computers appeared, dubbed RISC (for Reduced Set Instruction Computers), with only a handful of simple instructions, architecture completely open to the compiler and, above all, designed together with the compilers. These machines were shown to perform better than CISC (Complex Instruction Set Computers), with emphasis on simplicity and a good match between software and hardware. This bears similarities with the REST-style today (for scalable, Web class of applications).

By the early nineties, it became fashionable to have an instruction set as small as possible and RISC manufacturers flourished. However, RISCs did not win the war and CISCs did not disappear. CISCs learned their lesson from RISCs and, without dogmas, asserted that there is nothing wrong in having complexity in the hardware as long as it is truly useful (performance is always a goal) and does not slow down simple instructions.

The secret lies in balancing and matching the capabilities of technology with the requirements of applications. This is also what should be done today with SOA and REST. It is likely that Web Services and RESTful applications will also follow this path. Big companies, with Web scale applications, have moved towards REST-style APIs, in search of simplicity and a better match to the application style. Researchers have also been looking at how well the REST architectural style can support business and other type of applications (Xu, Zhu, Liu, & Staples, 2008; Li & Chou, 2010; Zou, Mei, & Wang, 2010).

REST itself is not at rest and extensions and new perspectives are being proposed, trying to broaden its spectrum of applicability. Inoue, Asakura, Sato, and Takahashi (2010) note that session state is needed for authentication and propose an extension to deal with this. Kumaran et al. (2008) propose an information centric process model, centering the resource concept on business entities instead of workflow activity instances. Pautasso (2009) shows how a business level language such as BPEL can be used in the REST style. Peng, Ma, and Lee (2009) propose a framework to integrate SOA and RESTful services.

Others propose to represent and transfer not only data but behavior as well. Xu, Zhu, Kannengiesser, and Liu (2010) describe a method to expose process fragments (described declaratively as reusable workflow patterns) as resources and to map business process concepts onto the usual HTTP-style of CRUD operations. Erenkrantz, Gorlick, Suryanarayana and Taylor (2007) go a step further and propose extensions to achieve a Computational REST (CREST), in which the basic entities are computational resources, in the form of continuations (Queinnec, 2003), and provide a base model for code mobility. The client is no longer a mere interface to the user but a computational engine, capable of executing these resources. State transfer is a side effect of this execution. This is in line with the Structural Services style proposed in this chapter.

ARCHITECTURAL STYLES

A Hierarchy of Architectural Styles

Every model needs an underlying vision, which is a description of the fundamental principles, concerns, constraints, characteristics, and properties of the domain of the system under modeling. The vision reflects the basic understanding of the modeler over that domain and constitutes the starting point to elaborate the model, which consists of an abstraction of that system, by refining the concepts and introducing relationships between them. We are interested in the software domain (Gorton, 2006), in particular distributed systems in the Web (Kappel, Pröll, & Retschitzegger, 2006) and cloud (Buyya, Broberg, & Goscinski, 2011) contexts.

That model defines the system's design architecture. Rather than a specific architecture, this chapter tackles the architectural style (Dillon, Wu, & Chang, 2007), which can be seen as a collection of design patterns, guidelines and best practices, in a bottom-up approach, or as a set of constraints on the concepts and on their relationships (Fielding & Taylor, 2002), in a top-down approach. We follow the latter because we believe that a rationale is needed before recognizing design patterns and elaborating on best practices.

Therefore, in this chapter, we describe an architectural style by constraints with respect to another, less detailed, instead of enumerating its characteristics. This allows us to establish a hierarchy of architectural styles, as illustrated by Figure 1.

At the top, we have what Fielding and Taylor (2002) call Null style, which corresponds to stating no restrictions at all or, in other words, to asserting that all the characteristics of this style are shared by all the styles to be considered.

The other architectures styles specialize progressively the Null style by including additional constraints, while reducing the spectrum of entities to which they can apply. For example, the Unified

Resource style considers that a resource is any type of entity, including software applications, people, organizations and other non-computer based entities, but the Software Resource style assumes that all resources are software components. This is further specialized by the Object Oriented and Distributed System styles, which in turn are the basis for the most used architectural styles in the Web and cloud contexts, the Service Oriented, Process, and REST styles.

The Enterprise Architecture style illustrates architecture style composition or, in other words, that an architecture under consideration does not have to be entirely modeled according to a single, pure style. The same happens with the Process style, which is not complete, in the sense that in distributed environments it requires services as the basic units of behavior.

On the other hand, one style can be a specialization of more than one style, as illustrated by the Service Oriented, which combines object oriented, and distribution constraints, and the Structural Service style, to be proposed in this chapter, which specializes both the Service Oriented and REST styles. Multiple inheritance in Figure 1 applies to constraints. If a constraint is required by both architectural styles, the less stringent one is passed on to the Structural Service style. The goal is to obtain the best of both worlds. For example, with respect to the Structural Service style:

- The Service Oriented style allows any number of operations for each resource, whereas REST specifies that all resources must have the same operations. In this case, services win;
- REST depends on structured resources with links, whereas services do not. In this case, REST wins.

The following sections describe these architectural styles in further detail, with the exception of the Enterprise Architecture style, which is outside the scope of this chapter.

Figure 1. A hierarchy of architectural styles

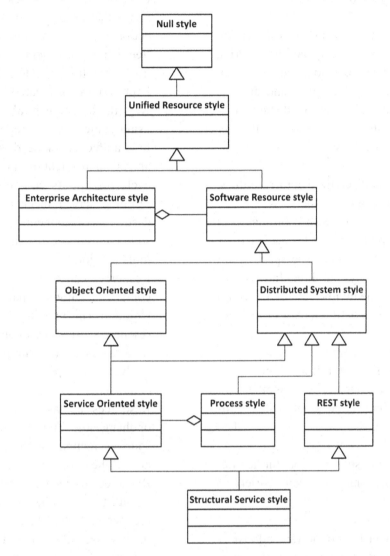

It should be noted that there is no widely accepted, universal definition of the notion of architecture, in particular because it can be defined at various stages in a system's lifecycle, illustrated by Figure 2. Our focus in this chapter is on modeling and design, discussing which type of model may be better suited to design a solution to a given class of problems. Therefore, we deal with architectural styles at the design stage of the system's lifecycle, in a model driven approach. This means analyzing the architecture of the problem and deriving the model of a solution that is a good match for that problem. The architecture of the implementation follows, but is outside the scope of this chapter. The implication is that we have only one architectural component: the resource. The set of resources to use and how they interact constitute the architecture. The set of restrictions we impose on the architecture constitutes the architectural style.

The Unified Resource Style

This is the level at which we introduce the notion of resource, as an entity of any nature (material, virtual, conceptual, noun, action, and so on) that embodies a meaningful, complete and discrete concept, making sense by itself while being distinguishable from, and able to interact with, other entities. We make the following main restrictions:

- The domain is discretized into resources, distinguishable of each other;
- These live in a space with coordinates, in which each point cannot be occupied by more than one resource. The space is not necessarily the physical three-dimensional space. Telephone numbers, vehicle license plate numbers and IP addresses are other examples;
- Each resource has a unique designation that enables to distinguish it from all others;
- A resource can interact with another, but only by sending it a message, which is itself a resource.

This architectural style can be further described by the following additional restrictions and characteristics:

- A resource can be atomic (an indivisible whole) or compound, recursively composed of other resources, its components, with respect to which it performs the role of container. Each component can only have one direct container, yielding a strong composition model, in a tree shaped resource structure;
- The interior of a resource is the set of that resource and all its components. The exterior is the set of all other existing resources;
- Each resource has at least one property that allows to uniquely identifying it (physical coordinates, name, IP address, URI, etc.) among all existing resources. A reference

to a resource X is a resource that implements that property, allowing direct interaction with X, without having to follow the tree shaped container hierarchy. In fact, this transforms the tree into a directed graph;

- Each resource is created in a decentralized way (there is no central resource factory), using some form of replication, and follows a lifecycle that ends by its destruction and is independent of other resources' lifecycle, except its container's. Compound resources have a mechanism to create and destroy its components. Destroying one resource implies destroying all the resources in its interior;
- Resources can migrate (move) from one container to another, changing the system's structure. This may involve a change in the resource's lifecycle, evolving to a migration stage, after which it is moved and then evolved to an operational stage at the new container;
- Resources can have state, either immutable or changeable. The state of a compound resource is recursively the set of the states, if any, of the components in its interior;
- Resources interact exclusively by sending stimuli to each other. There can be no direct access to the state of a resource from its exterior, either to read or to change. A resource X can only send stimuli to its direct components and to its containers (resources accessible by traversing the tree hierarchy upwards, starting at X). However, a direct component can be a reference, in which case a stimulus sent to it is automatically forwarded, routed and delivered to the referenced resource, by means of a suitable mechanism;
- A stimulus is a resource, created in the interior of one resource (the sender) and migrated to the interior of another (the receiver), where it generates a reaction. Reactions can be of any sort, such as changing the

Figure 2. An example of a resource's lifecycle with changeability loops

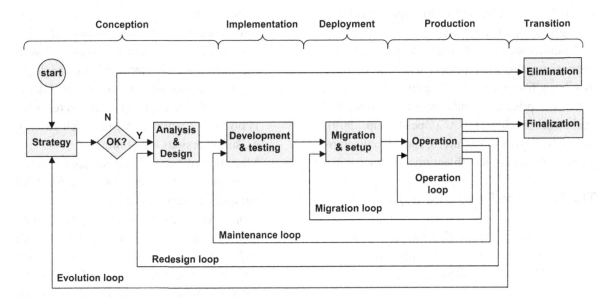

resource's state, creating further resources, deleting existing resources, sending stimuli to other resources (including the sender and the receiver) or just plain ignoring. The concrete reaction does not depend on the sender, only on the stimulus, the receiver, and its state. However, the sender may also be affected, if the receiver reacts back (sends a stimulus back to the sender). The reaction can be classified as:

  ○ Internal, if it affects only the receiver and its interior, with no externally visible effects. However, it may affect the reactions to subsequent stimuli;
  ○ Reflective, if it sends a response stimulus back to the sender;
  ○ Transitive; if it has an effect on other resources in its exterior, besides the sender;
  ○ Mixed, if it consists of a combination of the previous ones.
• If two interacting resources, X and Y, are not in direct contact, they can use an intermediate resource (a channel), with which both are in direct contact and through

which the stimulus migrates (that is the reaction of the channel when it receives the stimulus). The channel can be a compound resource, to cater for routing.

Although we can consider that there is a global resource that contains all others, we do not consider creationist issues, such as whether that global resource is bounded, what lies in its exterior, how was it created or by whom.

This is a very general model that is applicable to any resource, including:

• Computer applications;
• People;
• Other physical resources, such as trucks in a distribution chain, with movements eventually controlled by GPS and/or RFID tags and sensors.

This model poses almost no restrictions on what a resource can be. Namely, stimuli can even be analog and time unbounded. Therefore, this unified resource model, treating all resource types in the same way, naturally supports the integration of computer applications with the physical world, in which structure by composition and movement as migration are the norm.

Complemented with many other aspects and restrictions, this architectural style can be used as a basis for more detailed architectural styles at the enterprise level and enterprise architecture frameworks such as TOGAF (Open Group, 2009), in which all types of resources, and not only computer applications, are object of concern.

The Software Resource Style

Now we restrict the Unified Resource style to the software realm, by constraining the Unified Resource style in the following way:

- Only digital resources of finite size are considered. Analog resources are discretized and humans are represented by human-computer interfaces, such as the browser, and software resources that model their roles in the system. Other types physical of resources (such as trucks) are also modeled by software resources and sensors/actuators;
- A computer application can usually be decomposed into components, or modules, made out of code and/or data and which cooperate to achieve that application's goals. Each component is considered a resource;
- There is a set of predefined resources, atomic and structured. New resources can only be created by replicating and/or composing existing resources, predefined or not;
- The lifecycle of a resource is discretized into a finite number of stages, of which Figure 2 represents a simplified example. This is the sort of lifecycle used by software development methods such as the Rational Unified Process (Kruchten, 2004). In each stage, a resource can have a different digital representation, which can only have a finite number of different states. Whenever a change needs to be made, this lifecycle loops back, to start a new version. The current one is finalized or it can coexist with the new one. The farther back the loop, the more profound the change is. Strategic evaluation can determine that this resource is no longer worthwhile, in which case all existing versions are eliminated;

- Migration of a resource from one container X to another Y, a relevant issue in cloud computing, involves transforming the resource to a passive representation (such as a byte stream), destroying the resource at X, sending the representation to Y and creating a new component in Y from that representation. This corresponds to the migration loop in Figure 2. Cold start migration is usually called deployment;
- Stimuli become messages of finite size. Time unbounded streams can be modeled as a sequence of messages;
- The possible reactions of a resource to messages are discretized and modeled by a finite number of operations. Each operation knows only how to react to a limited set of messages;
- Reception of a message by a resource causes the execution of an operation that knows how to react to it. The mechanism that determines this capability is left unspecified at this level. A policy on what to do, in case a message is received by a resource for which there is no operation that can deal with it, needs to be drawn up;
- Each operation is modeled by a finite number of actions.

Given the recursively-structured nature of resources, Figure 2 can refer to any resource, from the whole application itself down to a small component of that application. No specific programming paradigm is assumed.

The Object Oriented Style

The Object Oriented style appeared as a refinement of the Software Resource style, with the goal of reducing the effort of developing and maintaining applications. This is accomplished by structuring the software according to some principles that tend to limit the impact of a change (affecting fewer resources) and to increase the reusability (allowing resources to be reused and changed, even without the source code). An object is a resource, as defined above.

The main principles (Meyer, 2000) are:

- **P1 – The least semantic gap principle:** The resources in the problem and solution spaces should have a one to one mapping, by modeling each problem resource with a solution resource, with both state and related behavior. This way, a small change in problem requirements translates into a small change in implementation. Prior to the appearance of the Object Oriented style, unorganized functions manipulated global accessible data (structured programming) and one small change in requirements could imply many changes throughout the system;
- **P2 – The information hiding principle:** In each resource, there must be a clear separation between interface (syntax and semantics) and its implementation. This is associated with the least information principle, which states that a resource should expose an interface with only the essential information to enable it to fulfill its obligations towards other resources. This reduces the change propagation effect. A change in one resource affects those that use it only if its interface is affected;
- **P3 – The substitution principle:** By this, a resource X should be able to be used (with its own implementation) wherever a

resource Y is expected, as long as X conforms to Y, a form of polymorphism;
- **P4 – The non-duplication of information principle:** Resources with similar features (state or behavior) should factor them and share a common definition (usually implemented by inheritance) instead of duplicating it. This way, a change in the shared information is only done once and automatically propagated to all the resources that use it;
- **P5 – The open-closed principle:** A resource should be closed (in the Operation stage, in Figure 2) but at the same time open so that it can be changed (usually, up to the Development stage). Actually, this is a corollary of the two previous principles and it means that it is possible to tune up resources by redefining operations, even if the source code is not available. Class libraries use this principle, supported on inheritance and polymorphism.

These are widely accepted principles and most of the software produced today uses the Object Oriented style, which has become widely adopted for the past 20 years. In addition, many legacy applications have been converted to it, with by now classical techniques (De Lucia, et al., 1997).

These principles translate not only to programming best practices (principle P1) but also to the following additional constraints to the Software Resource style:

- Resources must have an encapsulation mechanism (principle P2) that protects some of its components and/or operations from external accesses;
- The lifecycles of resources must be synchronized (compiled and linked together), so that the principles P3, P4, and P5 can be applied. These are design time techniques (second stage in Figure 2) that do not support lifecycle decoupling, since that

would imply distributed inheritance. This is technically feasible, by virtualizing the distribution, and has been done in the past (Gründer & Geihs, 1996), but with low performance and with dependencies that contradict one of the main principles of distributed systems: decoupling. In other words, the application is a whole that cannot be distributed in an easy way. Even resource interoperability middleware based on RPC (Remote Procedure Call), such as Java-RMI and CORBA, was criticized for not being decoupled enough (Waldo, Wyant, Wollrath, & Kendall, 1994; Saif & Greaves, 2001; Vinoski, 2005).

Not all types of applications have embraced this architectural style, though. At the enterprise level, the N-tier class of applications still separates code from (persistent) data. Even if the business logic by itself uses object oriented programming, the fact is that data in the database is global and each problem resource is dispersed by the various tiers, violating the principles described above. This is largely due to the benefits of the relational model, which however do not scale well in the realm of distributed systems. We need distributed resources, not just local ones.

The Distributed System Style

In distributed environments, in which decoupling and interoperability are key factors, we consider as resources only decoupled application components. Two components are decoupled if their lifecycles are not synchronized and each can survive the other. This should not be mixed up with decentralized, which implies lack of central coordination of several resources but not lack of coupling of their lifecycles. Components compiled together and bound to the same application are not decoupled and therefore are considered part of the same resource.

This architectural style implies the following additional constraints:

- Resources must use some communication protocol to exchange messages, using some form of global address, such as a URI;
- Message transmission time must be assumed non-zero, albeit bounded (if a given value is exceeded, a fault may be assumed). This does not preclude start processing an incoming message before fully receiving it;
- Although distribution does not necessarily involve geographical separation, distributed resources must be prepared for unreliable interoperability, temporary or not;
- Data types cannot be assumed valid for the entire application, since decoupled components can evolve independently. Data interoperability mechanisms, with self-describing messages, must be used. This can be achieved by using data description languages such as XML or JSON.

The Service Oriented and Process Styles

We deal with these two styles in the same section, since:

- They are closely related, as explained below;
- Typical SOA instantiations use processes to orchestrate services, thereby using both styles.

By SOA we mean not only what the acronym corresponds to (Service Oriented Architecture), in the abstract sense (Earl, 2007), but also its instantiation by the Web Services technology and associated standards (Earl, 2005). This is the only way to make a concrete comparison with its closest competitor, REST, and corresponds to the actual market context.

SOA uses the service as its main concept, so we could expect SOA to model systems primarily as a set of interacting services. In reality, current SOA systems use services at the bottom architectural layers and processes at higher layers to orchestrate those services. The process is the primary concept and the service a behavior primitive to be invoked by a process.

This means that the SOA style of building applications is a compound architectural style. In fact, Web Services appeared more as an interoperability mechanism (using the self-descriptive features of XML) than as a service oriented modeling solution or even as an architectural style. Service behavior has to be specified by a separate programming language, such as Java, .Net or BPEL, and the most important part is the interface.

The Service Oriented style tries to conjugate the advantages of the Object Oriented and Distributed System styles, which is the reason why Figure 1 depicts it inheriting from these two styles. Objects become distributed resources and pointers become distributed and unreliable references (such as URIs). The Process style entails specifying distributed behavior, supported by services.

The ontology in this domain is far from being established and universally accepted. The service concept, in particular, means different things to different people. Therefore, we give our own definitions:

- A service is a set of logically related reactions by a resource. In other words, it is a facet of that resource that makes sense in terms of the envisaged system. A service is pure behavior (albeit concrete reactions may depend on state) that needs a resource and its components to be implemented. In most cases, only one service will be defined for each resource, but in other cases, usually more complex, it makes sense to organize the full set of the resource's reactions

into several services. Note that a service is defined in terms of reactions to messages (an external view) and not in terms of state or state transitions (an internal view);

- A resource X that sends a message to a resource Y is in fact invoking a service of Y, as long as the reaction to that message belongs to that service, in what constitutes a service transaction between these two resources and in which the resources X and Y perform the role of service consumer and service provider, respectively. A service transaction can entail other service transactions, as part of the chain reaction to the message on part of the service provider;

- A process is a graph of all service transactions that are allowed to occur, orchestrated by control constructs such as decision tests, forks and joins. It starts with a service transaction initiated at some resource X and ends with a final service transaction, which does not react back nor initiates new service transactions. The process corresponds to a use case of resource X and usually involves other resources along the flow of service transactions (including loops, eventually).

Resources entail structure, state, and behavior. Services refer only to behavior, without implying a specific implementation. A service needs a resource to be implemented and different resources can implement the same service in different ways. Processes are a view on the behavior sequencing and flow along services, which resources implement.

We should also note that:

- The entities that communicate are the resources. Services are only abstractions and cater only for a part of the resource, albeit the most important one (behavior). Saying that "a service A sends a message to service B" is an abuse of language, for the sake of simplicity, meaning that "the resource implementing service A sends a message to the resource implementing service B";

- Every system with some sort of activity has both services and processes. The two paradigms are dual of each other and one cannot exist without the other. The difference is what modeling emphasizes. Service oriented systems model problem entities as resources that implement services (much like the object-oriented style, but in a distributed way). Process oriented systems emphasize tasks and activities, in which typically a process corresponds to a system's use case;

- The Service Oriented style is the closest to the object oriented style. The Process style violates almost all the object-oriented principles, but it is popular because we tend to think in terms of how the system performs instead of how it is structured and organized. The problem, inherited from structured programming, is that it difficult the grasp the interactions, dependencies and side effects between processes, which is particularly relevant when changes must be performed.

The main constraints introduced by the Service Oriented style are:

- Resources are divided into two groups, those that are used only as data and those implementing services, offering operations to be invoked. The latter cannot exhibit externally visible structure. In other words, they must be a leave in the resource structure tree;

- Operations need to be invoked explicitly, by name. It is not possible to send a message to a resource that internally chooses the most adequate operation, based on the contents of that message. This should not be mixed up with message based rout-

ing, typically offered by ESB (Enterprise Service Bus) systems, which is a higher level mechanism;

- A service offers a fixed contract. Changing the number, name, arguments, or semantics of operations is not part of normal activities in this style and corresponds to generating a new service version (a new lifecycle iteration of the resource that implements that service).

The main constraints of the Process style are:

- Organize active resources, those implementing behavior, according to the Service Oriented style;

- Orchestrate services according to system wide use cases.

Figure 3 describes a simple example to illustrate these styles. A customer wants to buy a product from a seller company, which delivers it by post. To obtain a cheaper transportation cost, the customer chooses to pick up the parcel with the product at the local post office instead of having it delivered at home. The customer first requests a quotation, then places an order and pays it, with the option of cancelling the order. After that, he polls the mailbox periodically to check for a notification of arrival and, when that happens, he picks up the parcel from the post office.

Figure 4 illustrates how a process can model these interactions. The perspective is that of a case use, in which some higher entity (the modeler) oversees all actions that are occurring, in a global view. This is the Process style.

The Service Oriented style is somewhat different and decouples the processing from each of the services, using the information hiding principle (P2), as discussed above when describing the Object oriented style, but now in a distributed fashion. Each resource deals only with the implementation of its operations and treats others as black boxes. The visibility of flow of activities is

Figure 3. An example of distributed resource interactions

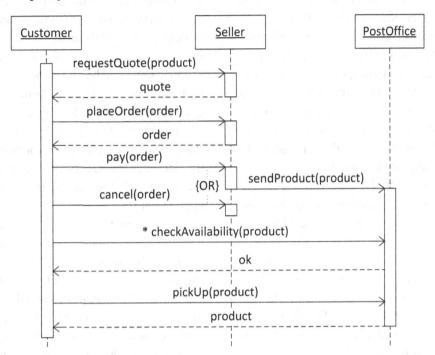

local to each operation, as if we broke the activities in Figure 4 into several processes, each limited to the scope of one of the operations shown in Figure 5.

Overall, the activities executed are the same in both Process and Service Oriented styles. The difference lies in the architecture of the model. The Service Oriented style is less sensitive to changes, in particular if they are local to an operation. In essence, this is the greatest benefit brought by the Object Oriented style.

The REST Style

Fielding (2000) originally proposed this style as recognition of the fact that Web technologies, HTTP in particular, have been conceived for distributed resource access, are enough to implement distributed applications and present significant advantages in terms of performance and scalability.

The main constraints introduced by this style, as proposed by Fielding, are:

- **Client-server:** There is a clear distinction between resources with client and server roles, with the implicit assumptions that clients are the only resources allowed to take the initiative of sending requests and usually greatly outnumber servers;
- **Stateless interactions:** Each request must include all the information needed for the server to process it. Servers do not store session state, which is only maintained by the client, which means that, in each response to a request, the server must return all the information needed for the next request;
- **Explicit cacheability:** All data resources returned as a response by a server must define whether they can be cached or not. If yes, they can be cached at the client to be

reused in future equivalent requests, which improves performance and scalability;

- **Uniform interface:** This means having the same set of operations for all resources, albeit the behavior of operations can differ from resource to resource. This simplifies resource interaction but places a burden on resources, since activities are also modeled as resources, and leads to a processing style based on a state machine;
- **Layered system:** This is a form of encapsulation and information hiding, by controlling visibility across layers. This control is large-grained and not at the resource level;
- **Code-on-demand:** This means that a server can return both data and code representations, enlarging the functionality of the client without preprogramming. This constraint is not mandatory.

The REST style is inspired by Web applications, in which typically there are many clients accessing a Web site and scalability is of paramount importance. This justifies the stateless interaction and cacheability constraints, since the load on the server becomes less dependent on the number of clients.

The rationale for the uniform interface, probably strange for someone with an object oriented mindset, is a logical consequence of the stateless interaction. If the state of the interaction is exchanged between the client and the server in each request-response, what to do next by the client depends on that state, leading to a state machine processing style to model behavior. Each response is equivalent to a closure (Appel & Jim, 1989) that includes the necessary information (including links to other resources) to change to the next application state.

This means that a client should not rely on previous knowledge about the server's resource structure, so that changes in the application can automatically be used by the client without changing it. The client needs only to know how to change state, by pursuing links and using the uniform interface. It is the resource representations retrieved from the server that present the states to which the client can go. But how can the client decide which alternative to pursue without prior knowledge of the resources' representations? The preconized solution is to resort to standardized media types or code-on-demand. The designer of an application needs to decompose it into a dynamic set of resources that fit one of these types and/or to provide the client with the necessary code to provide some state transition.

Figure 4. Process that models the interactions of figure 3

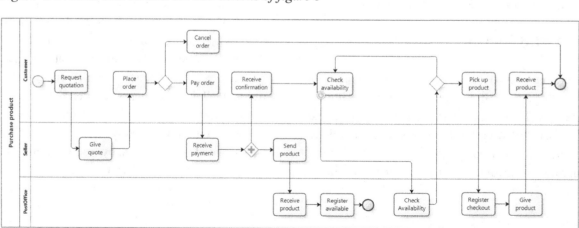

Figure 5. Service oriented style

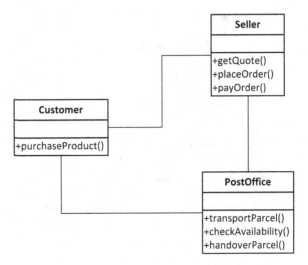

This is what is usually known as HATEOAS (hypermedia as the engine of application state), in which the client analyzes the server's response and typically proceeds by sending a request through one of the links contained in it, leading to a state diagram traversal which overall corresponds to a process.

Figure 6 illustrates another implementation of the example described in Figure 3, now using a state diagram. Implementing it in REST style involves establishing a correspondence between each state and a resource that has a link to change to each possible following state in the diagram. Resources corresponding to actions (such as placing a purchase order) are created at the server and links to them (such as http://company.com/order/item123) returned in a response to the client. Following these links executes the corresponding actions. Such resources are created dynamically, as the state machine progresses.

The use of a fixed set of operations is nothing more than an instantiation of the classical best practices of separating the mechanism of traversing a graph from the processing of individual node graphs (Meyer, 2000). To treat all nodes alike, all nodes must have the same interface.

The principle of Uniform Access, introduced by Meyer (2000), can also be invoked to justify the common interface. According to this principle, an access to a resource with the objective of obtaining some information should be done in just one way, regardless of whether that information is already available as state, needing only to be returned, or computed at the time of the access.

Although conceptually the REST style is not bound to HTTP, the practice shows that this stateless protocol is a perfect match and the only one really used, much as Web Services are the only real instantiation of the SOA style. Usually, the HTTP verbs (operations) used are GET, POST, PUT, and DELETE. Webber, Parastatidis and Robinson (2010) describe this architectural style in detail.

FROM SOA AND REST TO STRUCTURAL SERVICES

Having described the constraints that gave origin to each architectural style, we now compare SOA and REST, with the goal of establishing a rationale to evolve beyond them.

Figure 6. State diagram that models the interactions of figure 3

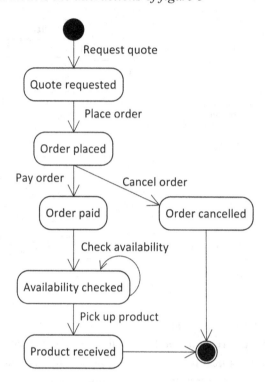

Comparing the SOA and REST Styles

It is useful to compare Figures 4 and 6 and to notice that, apart from process specific details, the flow of activities of the client in one figure is dual of the other's. Figure 4 uses activity based flow, with activities in the nodes and state in between. Figure 6 makes transitions from state to state, implemented by the activities in between.

SOA is guided by behavior and REST by (representation of) state. In UML terminology, SOA uses a static class diagram (Figure 5) as a first approach, to specify which resource types are used and to establish the set of operations provided by each, whereas REST starts with a state diagram (Figure 6), without relevant concern about distinguishing which state belongs to which resource. In the end, they perform the same activities and go through the same states. This should not be a surprise since, after all, the original problem, described by Figure 3, is the same.

REST is more flexible, in the sense that, if the server changes the links it sends in the responses, the client will follow this change automatically by using the new links. This however, is not as general as it may seem, since the client must be able to understand the structure of the responses. It is not merely a question of following all the links in a response. This is why REST favors standardized media types, to reduce the coupling between the client and the server. SOA is more static, since the service contracts are defined beforehand, but benefits from the support provided by tools in detecting errors. This is the classical tradeoff that a programmer has to face when choosing between a dynamic or static typed language.

In REST, there is an interesting side effect of the fact that the client uses a response to perform the next state transition. Only the links corresponding to allowed transitions are there. This is equivalent to dynamically adjusting the interface available to the client, according to the current state of the

Table 1. Comparison of SOA and REST styles in terms of support of the object oriented principles

OO Principles	(Web Services)	REST
P1 – Least semantic gap	Good (services model problem space entities)	Fair (problem space entities do not map as directly onto the REST resources)
P2 – Information hiding	Good (services expose only the WSDL interface)	Fair (resources hide implementation, but expose some structure in the representation's links)
P3 – Substitution	Fair (in simpler cases, the same message can be sent to different services, but it is not a general mechanism if it involves schemas of parameters or results)	Fair (blindly and not model driven, since all resources have the same interface but different semantics)
P4 – Non-duplication of information	Fair (only at design time, with WSDL inheritance)	Poor (No reuse. Each resource must provide its own implementation)
P5 – Open-closed	Fair (no client side substitution, no service-level polymorphism)	Poor (no mechanism to partially reuse and/or redefine links in representations. Server side is in control)

application. This is good protection mechanism, already used in human computer interfaces, with menus that become enabled and disabled, according to context. In SOA, this is not easy to achieve. Once a link to a service is available, all its operations can be invoked.

The flexibility of REST comes at a price, since it lies at a much lower level than SOA and the semantics of the problem do not map as directly onto state diagrams as onto resource class diagrams and processes. Nevertheless, it is simpler than SOA, requiring only basic Web technologies, and scale much better, but only as long as the application complies with the constraints imposed by REST. Complex functionality and bidirectional interactions (requests from server to client) are not a good match for REST.

This means that the ranges of types of applications that are more adequate for SOA and REST are not the same. REST is a better match for Web style applications (many clients, stateless interactions) that provide a simpler interface. This is why all the major Internet application providers, including cloud computing, now have REST interfaces. SOA is a better match for functionally complex, enterprise level distributed applications.

Since the Object Oriented style has long been recognized as a good modeling approach, but unfortunately does not support distributed systems

well, it is relevant to compare SOA and REST at the light of the principles enunciated above in the section describing the Object Oriented style. Table 1 compares the level of support that SOA and REST provide for the five object oriented principles previously enunciated.

From this comparison, SOA seems to look better than REST, which is probably not a big surprise given that SOA is based on services, derived from objects, which is not the case of REST. Therefore, the comparison is not exempt and is somewhat biased, but can nonetheless provide some additional insight.

Problem space entities in Table 1 are the concepts that typically yield classes in the Object Oriented style, such as the Customer, Seller, and Post Office of Figure 3. There is a close correspondence between these entities and application classes, making modeling an easier task and reducing the semantic gap (P1). The actions that these entities are capable of performing are second order concepts that translate to class methods in the Object Oriented style and to service operations in the Service Oriented style.

In REST, this distinction is blurred and both interacting problem entities and their actions are modeled as first order resources. The structure of both data and behavior is converted into resource structure. Although this is essential to promote the uniform interface and to reduce coupling, it lowers the level of the design model and increases the semantic gap and modeling effort. For applications with complex behavior, such as those in the realm of enterprise information systems, this can be a significant disadvantage.

Information hiding (P2) in the Object Oriented style means hiding the implementation of objects, including internal state. This is easy for SOA, which follows the same tenet. In REST, the implementation of resources is also hidden and what the server returns is a representation of a resource and not the resource itself, but the structure of the links in that representation expose some information on how that resource is organized. Before delving into a discussion on how much information is actually exposed, we should acknowledge that this is not the real issue. Hiding as much as possible in the Object Oriented style is crucial to reduce coupling between objects and to facilitate changes to their previously established interaction contracts. However, resources in REST are naturally decoupled, due to the uniform interface and HATEOAS, which means that information hiding is less important in REST. The ability to return alternative representations and even negotiate this with the client, a relevant feature of REST, is not significant with regard to information hiding, since what counts is the information returned, not its representation format.

In distributed contexts, the substitution principle (P3) needs to be decomposed into client and server sides. The latter refers to replacing a SOA service or a REST resource with another, at the server, without its clients (the resources that use it) noticing the change, apart from any side effects resulting from a different implementation. However, all its clients will be affected. The client side substitution refers to the ability of a client, with a link to a service or resource, to replace that link and to use a different service or resource as if it were the original one. In this case, only this client will be affected. Table 1 refers essentially to client side substitution, since at the server it is

always possible to change the implementation of a service or a resource, as long as its interface, which clients use, is not changed.

The non-duplication of information principle (P4), which usually translates to inheritance in the Object Oriented style, is not easy to achieve in distributed systems, in which the lifecycles of resources are independent. SOA is more static and has a glimpse of inheritance in WSDL, but in REST each resource is independent and information sharing is not a part of the model. However, in the same manner as in the case of P2, this is just a consequence of distribution and not as important as in the Object Oriented style.

Finally, the Open-closed principle (P5) says that a service or resource should be able to be changed (opened) from the perspective of a client, while maintaining its normal operation (closed) for other clients. This means client side substitution, not server side. Both SOA and REST present limitations in this respect. In SOA, client side substitution requires maintaining the parameter schemas (instead of mere type conformance, as in the Object Oriented style), although this is not a problem with simple types. In REST, client side substitution is harder or makes no sense, since the client works on resource representations that are dynamically returned from the server and has no control over the links used to transition to the next state.

In spite of the inherent differences between these architectural styles, we think that:

- Object oriented principles are too good not to be satisfied in modeling terms, but need to be adapted to distributed contexts;
- The simplicity, fine-granularity, dynamically adjustable interface and structured resources offered by REST are very desirable.

Therefore, it is our goal to define an architectural style that gathers the best of the Service Oriented and REST styles.

The Structural Services Style

The problems mentioned in P3, and by extension in P5, refer to the ability of the client to invoke transparently another service, without the client noticing it, as it is usual with polymorphism in object oriented programming. These problems stem essentially from the symmetric perspective of data interoperability that XML impose and that contrasts with the asymmetric perspective of services.

With XML, two resources can write and read the same data if they use the same schema. This is valid for all data instances (documents) of that schema. In services, only the client writes the request message and only the service reads it (and vice-versa in the response message). This allows the request message's schema to be decoupled from the schema of the argument of the invoked operation, requiring a weaker form of schema equivalence that increases interoperability and supports polymorphism, as required by the object-oriented principles.

The Structural Services style is derived from both the Service Oriented and REST style, as shown in Figure 1. We define it not by including additional constraints but by combining the constraints inherited from these two styles. The two main ideas are:

- To allow resources implementing services to be structured and have links, as required by REST, but support a variable set of operations, as required by SOA. Now services have both data (components) and behavior (operations) structure;

- Data interoperability between resources, required when exchanging a message, request or response, is based not on a shared schema, XML style, but on structural compliance (Kokash & Arbab, 2009) and structural conformance (Kim & Shen, 2007), as explained below.

In this chapter, we tackle data interoperability only. Semantic interoperability constitutes future work.

Figure 7 depicts an example of a set of structured resources. R_X, R_Y, R_W and R_Z are resources. R_Y exemplifies resource structure. Its interior, with relationships omitted for simplicity, reveals three resources, of which one is also structured, with two resources inside. S_X, S_Y, S_W, and S_Z are services offered by R_X, R_Y, R_W and R_Z, respectively, and their operations are graphically represented by the trapezoid on the left side of each resource. Structured resources, such as R_Y, can offer both behavior, in the form of services, and structure, in the form of internal resources accessible from its exterior. Service S_Y includes the interface of both operations and components of R_Y. Structured access to an internal component is supported by specifying a path that designates that component (in the line of REST).

S_m is the definition that R_X has of S_Y, which needs not include all the features of S_Y. The same

Figure 7. Example scenario of structural services

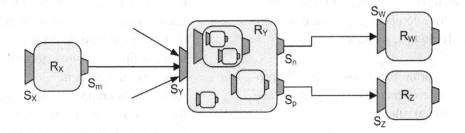

can be said of S_n and S_p with respect to S_W and S_Z, respectively. Resource R_X acts as if it had a reference to a resource offering service S_m. It knows nothing about S_Y and treats it as if it were S_m.

If the resource R_X sends a message to R_Y, which sends a response back, then:

1. The message sent by R_X must be in accordance with what R_Y expects and is able to deal with. We say that S_m must comply with S_Y. This implies satisfying the requirements of S_Y;
2. The response from R_Y to R_X, also a message, must be in accordance with what R_X expects as a response and was designed to expect from R_Y. We say that S_Y must conform to S_m. This implies that S_Y can take the form of S_m without resources that use S_m noticing the difference.

Together, compliance and conformance define interoperability. R_X will be able to interoperate with any resource that implements a service that happens to satisfy these two conditions, even if that resource was not designed to interoperate with R_X. This is the basis for supporting service polymorphism.

This is what already must happen in the invocation of methods of objects, in which compliance and conformance are verified by named typing. However, our environment is distributed and the lifecycles of resources are decoupled, which means that having a name is meaningless in terms of distributed type checking. We need to use structural typing, in which two resources are recursively analyzed, component by component, down to primitive components, to see if they are compatible. To do this, we need:

- A set of primitive resources, with pre-defined interoperability (compliance and conformance) rules;

- A set of resource structuring mechanisms, universally known;
- Algorithms to check structural interoperability (structural compliance and conformance).

Interoperability involves two types of situations:

- Assignment, which happens when:
  ○ A request message arrives at a resource and is assigned to the formal argument of an operation;
  ○ A response arrives at the resource that sent the request message and needs to assigned to some variable for further processing.
- Invocation of a service through a reference, based on a global address such as a URI. However, a reference must be typed by the service of the resource it supposedly references, such as S_m in Figure 7.

Assignments between resources must be made by copy, not by reference as in common object oriented programming languages, since in distributed environments pointers are meaningless. This is consistent with the model of Figure 7 and with the Unified Resource style, in which a resource includes all its components. Distributed references, such as URIs, are in fact primitive resources that have link semantics.

Assignment involves only compliance, which can be informally defined as follows:

- Consider that we have an assignment between two resources, of the form A = B;
- Each resource has a set of mandatory features (components and operations) and a set of optional features, according to some schema that defines it;
- Resource B complies with resource A if, for every feature in the set of mandatory features of A, there is a corresponding fea-

ture in B that complies with it, according to some ordering rules (for example, by matching names or position in the resources). In other words, all the mandatory requirements of A must be contemplated;

- Assignment proceeds by copying each feature in B, mandatory or optional, for which such a correspondence can be found. The remaining ones are ignored. Optional features of A for which there is no such correspondence are maintained unchanged in A.

Invocation of a remote service through a reference is more complex. Consider the case of Figure 7, in which resource R_X has a component k that is a reference to a resource R_m implementing service S_m. Imagine that we perform the assignment k=p, in which p is a reference to resource R_Y, which implements service S_Y. To maintain the contract that R_X expects from the service implemented by the resource referenced by p, this assignment is valid only if:

- For each component c_m of R_m, mandatory or optional, there is a corresponding component in R_Y, which c_m complies with;
- For each operation f_m in R_m, mandatory or optional, there is a corresponding operation f_Y in R_Y, such that the argument of f_m complies with the argument of f_Y and the result of f_Y complies with the result of f_m.

In these circumstances, and after the assignment, k can be used by R_X as if it were a reference to R_m, when in reality it references R_Y. Since this is a runtime assignment, we have reinstated polymorphism and a good support for the P3 and P5 principles of Table 1. Structural compliance and conformance can be checked at compile time or, with degradation in performance, at runtime.

Principle P4 in a distributed environment is best implemented by delegation, in which a resource that does not know how to react to a message forwards that message to a previously assigned delegate (which can be changed at runtime).

Note that structural interoperability is different from trying to structurally compare XML schemas (Formica, 2007; Rajesh & Srivatsa, 2010), which typically is done to find candidate services to invoke, those that have the closest match to specific requirements. This is similarity, not compliance nor conformance.

Structural comparison, to check compliance and conformance according to the rules enunciated in the previous section, can be implemented by using regular expression types (Hosoya & Pierce, 2002), using the method described by Chen and Chen (2008).

ONGOING WORK AND FUTURE RESEARCH DIRECTIONS

It is not easy to implement this style and all its features, only briefly described here, with current technologies, namely Web Services, XML, and HTTP. To reduce mismatches and complexity, we are defining and implementing a language (SIL – Service Implementation Language) to support it, which can be seen as similar to JSON extended with several features, including operations and code, similar to Java. Each resource carries its own schema embedded, valid for that resource only. Data interoperability is structural with static typing, although structural polymorphism can induce a more dynamic environment. SIL has two representations, source and binary, synchronized by a compiler. Messages can be sent in source and compiled at the receiver, just as XML is parsed, but this is slower. This way, we optimize the representation for both humans and computers. Note that the binary representation is not produced by data compression but by true compilation, yielding information optimized for execution.

Both SOA and REST styles are supported. In particular, a service can return, as a response to a request, a structured resource that includes both references (links) and operations, with embedded code, which act as closures and can easily implement state machines.

This is ongoing and unpublished work and space limitations prevent us from presenting and explaining an example here. We have developed a compiler based on ANTLR (Parr, 2007) that is partially implemented and converts source to instructions and data in a binary format (silcodes), in a way similar to Java. The binary code is then interpreted by an interpreter that is implemented in pure Java and that for a simple loop is roughly 100 times slower than a Java Virtual Machine (JVM). However, half of that time is spent just on method dispatch, the mechanism used to execute the various silcodes. A C based interpreter, for example, would be much faster, although harder to develop. We did not use a JVM and bytecodes to maintain flexibility and control of implementation.

Support for distribution is implemented with a Jetty application server. The application level protocol is implemented using only the resource structuring capabilities of the language. For message exchange, we require only a transport level protocol. We use Web Sockets (Lubbers, Albers, & Salim, 2010), with a cache for automatic connection management. This server houses a resource directory for service discovery (still with a basic implementation). The Jetty server maintains normal HTTP capability, which means that it can also deal with SOA and REST based applications, thus promoting compatibility and an evolutionary migration path to the new architectural style, by automatically choosing handlers based on the format of incoming messages.

Cloud applications are one of the envisaged target environments. Resources are not limited to state, as in REST, or to interfaces, as in Web Services. They also include code, which is interpreted, which means that resources under execution can be suspended, serialized with context, migrated to another server and resumed from where they stopped. We have tried this, with two laptop computers interconnected through a VPN connection

to a remote server, with an average ping time of 15 ms and a Web Socket creation time of around 30 ms (created only once). We used a resource with a loop that, after executing a given number of iterations, migrated itself to the server in the other laptop, and then back. The resource was able to perform roughly 200 migrations per second, something hardly achievable with normal HTTP and text based technologies.

Future work will focus mainly on the following activities:

- Completing the implementation. For example, the language supports concurrency and asynchronous communication, based on futures, and delegation, but these features are not implemented yet;
- The current compliance and conformance algorithms work very well, but are executed just at design time, by the compiler. A definition of the interface of the resource to interact with must be used locally, just like a WSDL. Luckily, this is just the public part of the resource specification (just like a Java interface). These algorithms also need to work at the binary level to be checked at message arrival time. An optimization, cache-based mechanism to perform this check only once, for session based interactions between one pair of resources, is foreseen;
- Interfacing to existing programming languages is done as in XML, by generating a stub from the resource description. The way to do this has been devised, based on the set of primitive resources and the general structuring mechanism, but is not implemented yet;
- Carrying out a comparative study on the advantages gained by using a language with the characteristics of SIL for distributed interoperability, instead of others such as XML for data and BPEL for behavior;
- Formalizing the semantics of the language;

- Incorporating semantic information, to tackle semantic interoperability.

CONCLUSION

We have presented a model that integrates resources, services, and processes, and is the basis for a hierarchical classification of architectural styles. The method of describing architectural styles by the constraints they impose on resources and services of the basic model seems to constitute a good way to organize the different architectural styles.

We have shown that the SOA and REST architectural styles are dual of each other, with complementary characteristics. This led to the proposal of a new architectural style, Structural Services, by combining the characteristics of SOA and REST. Services support structure and each resource can offer a different set of operations. An implementation of this style could be conceived with Web Services, for instance including a structural section in WSDL documents, but this would add up to the already very complex Web Services technology. Instead, we opted to use a resource description language that supports both data components and operations, with structural interoperability, supported on structural compliance and conformance, which have been informally introduced.

We have presented some very preliminary results of an implementation of this language, with a compiler that supports a binary resource format and an execution platform connected to an application server. The underlying protocol is supported on Web Sockets because they are full duplex, long-lived, efficient, support binary messages, and we require nothing more than a transport level protocol.

Much work is still needed to have a fully functional system. The goal is not to replace SOA or REST, but rather to evaluate what can be gained by using a technology that natively supports the architectural style that we have proposed, instead of increasing the complexity resulting from the mismatch between this style and classical technologies such as HTTP and XML.

REFERENCES

Appel, A., & Jim, T. (1989). Continuation-passing, closure-passing style. In *Proceedings of the Symposium on Principles of Programming Languages,* (pp. 293-302). ACM Press.

Becker, J., Matzner, M., & Müller, O. (2010). Comparing architectural styles for service-oriented architectures - A REST vs. SOAP case study. In Papadopoulos, G. (Eds.), *Information Systems Development* (pp. 207–215). Springer-Verlag. doi:10.1007/b137171_22

Berners-Lee, T. (1999). *Weaving the web: The original design and ultimate destiny of the world wide web by its inventor*. New York, NY: HarperCollins Publishers.

Bolton, F. (2001). *Pure corba*. Indianapolis, IN: SAMS Publishing.

Buyya, R., Broberg, J., & Goscinski, A. (2011). *Cloud computing: Principles and paradigms*. Hoboken, NJ: John Wiley & Sons. doi:10.1002/9780470940105

Chen, L., & Chen, H. (2008). Efficient type checking for a subclass of regular expression types. In *Proceedings of the International Conference for Young Computer Scientists,* (pp. 1647-1652). IEEE Computer Society Press.

Crane, D., & McCarthy, P. (2008). *Comet and reverse ajax: The next-generation ajax 2.0*. Berkeley, CA: Apress.

De Lucia, A., et al. (1997). Migrating legacy systems towards object-oriented platforms. In *Proceedings of the IEEE International Conference on Software Maintenance*, (pp. 122-129). IEEE Computer Society Press.

Dillon, T., Wu, C., & Chang, E. (2007). Reference architectural styles for service-oriented computing. *Lecture Notes in Computer Science, 4672*, 543–555. doi:10.1007/978-3-540-74784-0_57

Earl, T. (2005). *Service-oriented architecture: Concepts, technology, and design*. Upper Saddle River, NJ: Prentice Hall PTR.

Earl, T. (2007). *SOA: Principles of service design*. Upper Saddle River, NJ: Prentice Hall PTR.

Erenkrantz, J., Gorlick, M., Suryanarayana, G., & Taylor, R. (2007). From representations to computations: The evolution of web architectures. In *Proceedings of the 6th Joint Meeting of the European Software Engineering Conference and the ACM SIGSOFT Symposium on the Foundations of Software Engineering*, (pp. 255-264). ACM Press.

Fielding, R. (2000). *Architectural styles and the design of network-based software architectures*. (Unpublished Doctoral Dissertation). University of California at Irvine. Irvine, CA.

Fielding, R., & Taylor, R. (2002). Principled design of the modern web architecture. *ACM Transactions on Internet Technology, 2*(2), 115–150. doi:10.1145/514183.514185

Formica, A. (2007). Similarity of XML-schema elements: A structural and information content approach. *The Computer Journal, 51*(2), 240–254. doi:10.1093/comjnl/bxm051

Gorton, I. (2006). *Essential software architecture*. Berlin, Germany: Springer-Verlag.

Gründer, H., & Geihs, K. (1996). Reuse and inheritance in distributed object systems. In *International Workshop on Trends in Distributed Systems*, (pp. 191-200). London, UK: Springer-Verlag.

Holdener, A. III. (2008). *Ajax: The definitive guide*. Sebastopol, CA: O'Reilly Media, Inc.

Hosoya, H., & Pierce, B. (2002). Regular expression pattern matching for XML. *Journal of Functional Programming, 13*(6), 961–1004. doi:10.1017/S0956796802004410

Inoue, T., Asakura, H., Sato, H., & Takahashi, N. (2010). Key roles of session state: Not against REST architectural style. In *Proceedings of the 34th Annual Computer Software and Applications Conference*, (pp. 171-178). IEEE Computer Society Press.

Jeong, B., Lee, D., Cho, H., & Lee, J. (2008). A novel method for measuring semantic similarity for XML schema matching. *Expert Systems with Applications, 34*, 1651–1658. doi:10.1016/j.eswa.2007.01.025

Kappel, G., Pröll, B., Reich, S., & Retschitzegger, W. (Eds.). (2006). *Web engineering*. Chichester, UK: John Wiley & Sons.

Kim, D., & Shen, W. (2007). An approach to evaluating structural pattern conformance of UML models. In *Proceedings of the ACM Symposium on Applied Computing*, (pp. 1404-1408). ACM Press.

Kokash, N., & Arbab, F. (2009). Formal behavioral modeling and compliance analysis for service-oriented systems. *Lecture Notes in Computer Science, 5751*, 21–41. doi:10.1007/978-3-642-04167-9_2

Kruchten, P. (2004). *The rational unified process: An introduction*. Boston, MA: Pearson Education Inc.

Kumaran, S., et al. (2008). A RESTful architecture for service-oriented business process execution. In *Proceedings of the International Conference on e-Business Engineering*, (pp. 197-204). IEEE Computer Society Press.

Laitkorpi, M., Selonen, P., & Systa, T. (2009). Towards a model-driven process for designing ReSTful web services. In *Proceedings of the IEEE International Conference on Web Services,* (pp. 173-180). IEEE Computer Society Press.

Li, L., & Chou, W. (2010). Design patterns for RESTful communication. In *Proceedings of the International Conference on Web Services,* (pp. 512-519). IEEE Computer Society Press.

Lubbers, P., Albers, B., & Salim, F. (2010). *Pro HTML5 programming: Powerful APIs for richer internet application development.* New York, NY: Apress.

Meyer, B. (2000). *Object-oriented software construction* (2nd ed.). Upper Saddle River, NJ: Prentice Hall.

Mulligan, G., & Gracanin, D. (2009). A comparison of SOAP and REST implementations of a service based interaction independence middleware framework. In M. Rossetti, et al. (Eds.), *Winter Simulation Conference,* (pp. 1423-1432). IEEE Computer Society Press.

Parr, T. (2007). *The definitive ANTLR reference.* Raleigh, NC: The Pragmatic Bookshelf.

Patterson, D., & Ditzel, D. (1980). The case for the reduced instruction set computer. *ACM SIGARCH Computer Architecture News, 8*(6), 25–33. doi:10.1145/641914.641917

Pautasso, C. (2009). RESTful web service composition with BPEL for REST. *Data & Knowledge Engineering, 68*(9), 851–866. doi:10.1016/j. datak.2009.02.016

Pautasso, C., Zimmermann, O., & Leymann, F. (2008). Restful web services vs. "big"' web services: Making the right architectural decision. In *Proceedings of the International Conference on World Wide Web,* (pp. 805-814). ACM Press.

Peng, Y., Ma, S., & Lee, J. (2009). REST2SOAP: A framework to integrate SOAP services and RESTful services. In *Proceedings of the International Conference on Service-Oriented Computing and Applications,* (pp. 1-4). IEEE Computer Society Press.

Queinnec, C. (2003). Inverting back the inversion of control or, continuations versus page-centric programming. *ACM SIGPLAN Notices, 38*(2), 57–64. doi:10.1145/772970.772977

Rajesh, A., & Srivatsa, S. (2010). XML schema matching – Using structural information. *International Journal of Computers and Applications, 8*(2), 34–41. doi:10.5120/1183-1632

Saif, U., & Greaves, D. (2001). Communication primitives for ubiquitous systems or RPC considered harmful. In *Proceedings of the International Conference Distributed Computing Systems Workshop,* (pp. 240-245). IEEE Computer Society Press. Open Group. (2009). *TOGAF version 9 – The open group architecture framework (TOGAF).* New York, NY: The Open Group.

Tolk, A. (2006). What comes after the semantic web - PADS implications for the dynamic web. In *Proceedings of the 20th Workshop on Principles of Advanced and Distributed Simulation,* (pp. 55-62). IEEE Computer Society Press.

Toshniwal, R., & Agrawal, D. (2004). Tracing the roots of markup languages. *Communications of the ACM, 47*(5), 95–98. doi:10.1145/986213.986218

Vinoski, S. (2005). RPC under fire. *IEEE Internet Computing, 9*(5), 93–95. doi:10.1109/MIC.2005.108

Waldo, J., Wyant, G., Wollrath, A., & Kendall, S. (1994). *A note on distributed computing.* Technical Report SMLI TR-94-29. Mountain View, CA: Sun Microsystems, Inc. Retrieved February 1st, 2012, from https://ftp.uwsg.indiana.edu/kde/devel/smli_tr-94-29.pdf

Webber, J., Parastatidis, S., & Robinson, I. (2010). *REST in practice*. Sebastopol, CA: O'Reilly Media.

Xu, X., Zhu, L., Kannengiesser, U., & Liu, Y. (2010). An architectural style for process-intensive web information systems. *Lecture Notes in Computer Science, 6488*, 534–547. doi:10.1007/978-3-642-17616-6_47

Xu, X., Zhu, L., Liu, Y., & Staples, M. (2008). Resource-oriented architecture for business processes. In *Proceedings of the Software Engineering Conference,* (pp. 395-402). IEEE Computer Society Press.

Zou, J., Mei, J., & Wang, Y. (2010). From representational state transfer to accountable state transfer architecture. In *Proceedings of the International Conference on Web Services,* (pp. 299-306). IEEE Computer Society Press.

Zyp, K. (Ed.). (2010). A JSON media type for describing the structure and meaning of JSON documents. *Internet Engineering Task Force*. Retrieved August 26, 2011, from http://tools.ietf.org/html/draft-zyp-json-schema-03

KEY TERMS AND DEFINITIONS

Architectural Style: Set of constraints imposed on a set of concepts and on their relationships.

Compliance: Property between two services, consumer and provider, which expresses that the consumer fulfills all the requirements to invoke the provider. A consumer must comply with the provider, otherwise an error may occur.

Conformance: Property between service A and another B (A conforms to B) that indicates that A implements all the features of B required to allow it to replace B in its role in some service choreography.

Resource: An entity of any nature (material, virtual, conceptual, noun, action, and so on) that embodies a meaningful, complete and discrete concept, which makes sense by itself and can be distinguished from, although interact with, other entities.

Service: A set of related functionalities that define a meaningful concept in a resource interaction context.

Service Choreography: Contract between several services, which establishes how they cooperate to achieve some common goal.

Structural Interoperability: Property between two resources, which asserts their typed compatibility (conformance and compliance) for interaction, based on their structure and structural interoperability of their components, checked recursively until primitive resources are reached.

Structural Services: Architectural style that combines the SOA and REST architectural styles, by allowing resources that implement services to be structured and have links, as required by REST, and to support a variable set of operations, as required by SOA. Service interaction is based on structural interoperability.

Chapter 13
Considerations of Adapting Service–Offering Components to RESTful Architectures

Michael Athanasopoulos
National Technical University of Athens, Greece

Kostas Kontogiannis
National Technical University of Athens, Greece

Chris Brealey
IBM Canada, Canada

ABSTRACT

Over the past few years, we have witnessed a paradigm shift on the programming models and on architectural styles, which have been used to design and implement large-scale service-oriented systems. More specifically, the classic message-oriented and remote procedure call paradigm has gradually evolved to the resource-oriented architectural style, inspired by concepts pertinent to the World Wide Web. This shift has been primarily driven by multifaceted functional and non-functional requirements of Web enabled large-scale service offering systems. These requirements include enhanced interoperability, lightweight integration, scalability, enhanced performance, even looser coupling, and less dependence on shifting technology standards. As a consequence, several, and sometimes antagonistic, architectures, design patterns, and programming paradigms have emerged on a quest to overcome the constantly expanding enterprise software needs. In the context of resource-oriented architectures, the Representational State Transfer (REST) architectural style has gained considerable attention due to its simplicity, uniformity, and flexibility. More specifically, the potential for scalability and loose coupling, the uniformity of interfaces, and the efficient bridging of enterprise software systems with the Web are significant factors for software architects and engineers to consider REST when designing, implementing, composing, and deploying service-oriented systems. These issues stir discussion among academics and practitioners about how to properly apply REST constraints both with respect to the development of new enterprise systems and to the migration and adaptation of existing service-oriented systems to RESTful architectures. In this chapter, the authors discuss issues and challenges related to the adaptation of existing service-oriented systems to a RESTful architecture. First, they present the motivation

DOI: 10.4018/978-1-4666-2488-7.ch013

Copyright © 2013, IGI Global. Copying or distributing in print or electronic forms without written permission of IGI Global is prohibited.

behind such an adaptation need. Second, the authors discuss related adaptation theory, techniques, and challenges that have been recently presented in the research literature. Third, they identify and present several considerations and dimensions that the adaptation to REST entails, and the authors present frameworks to assess resource-oriented designs with regard to compliance to REST. Fourth, the authors introduce an adaptation framework process model in the context of enterprise computing systems and technologies, such as Model Driven Engineering and Service Component Architecture (SCA). Furthermore, they discuss open challenges and considerations on how such an adaptation process to REST can be extended, in order to yield systems that best conform to the REST architectural style and the corresponding REST constraints. Finally, the chapter is concluded with a summary and a discussion on the points raised and on some emerging trends in this area.

INTRODUCTION

During the past decade, service-orientation has become the dominant computing paradigm in the domain of enterprise software systems. More specifically, it has been argued that Service-Oriented Architectures (SOAs) provide significant benefits to organizations, and generally allow for better alignment of business needs and IT solutions. The fundamental principle is that SOAs organize functionality as collections of interoperable services with standardized interface specification and description methods. Furthermore, service communication is independent of implementation and infrastructure allowing thus, for heterogeneous systems to communicate effectively, and for lowering costs related to integration and interoperation. Even though, SOA as a set of architectural principles is not bound to any specific technology, W3C's Web Services technologies and standards have been the primary choice of architects when implementing SOAs, especially for enterprise and B2B systems. For example, it has emerged as de facto standard that Web Service components are described by specifications written in the Web Service Description Language (WSDL), and invoked by utilizing the SOAP family of protocols. These service components usually follow one of two binding styles: Remote Procedure Call (RPC) and document-based message exchange. The RPC binding style explicitly references the service operation to be invoked, while document-based

binding style promotes the usage of messages that include schema-based elements. These schema-based elements are interpreted by the receiver (i.e. server) in order to dispatch and invoke the appropriate operation. An advantage of this approach is that it is easier to validate the requests since there is a direct reference to a schema to which the message is supposed to conform to. As a result, although RPC was considered to be the dominant style when Web Services were first introduced, tools and frameworks started to support a document-based invocation style. However, in practice has been proven that the inclusion of the operation's name in the message is quite significant for the interoperability and consequently, many document-based Web Service frameworks adopted and implemented a special pattern of document-based style called the "wrapped document" pattern. In the "wrapped document" pattern the message that is sent, is essentially a schema element that is named after the operation's name, and the message that is received is also a schema element whose name follows a similar operation-based convention. In this context, a procedure is known to the service consumer, and it is readily addressable and available to be invoked by service messages, regardless of the particular binding or even technology the service may use to expose its functionality. Services that are published following the procedure-oriented Web Services stack of protocols are integrated over the Web and not through the Web—making the term "Web" included in their name rather unfortunate. Organizations are realizing the need for a more natural integration of their systems with the Web and through the Web in a way that would not have to overcome the challenges that the Web Services stack of protocols sets. Such a development would enable the potential that is raised by exposing existing pieces of software or data as common Web resources so that, the conventional service-providing usage will become easier, and serendipitous re-usage of the resources will be possible, following the example of Web 2.0 technologies such as, mash-ups and widgets.

Resource-orientation, on the other hand, introduces the concept of content-driven decomposition of service capabilities into resources that capture and convey information. Resources are usually defined as "things" that can be named, have state, share a common, uniform interface, are visible, and possibly manipulable through representations of their state. Also, resources are associated with universal identifiers and are addressable by accepting clients' requests that, depending on the communications protocol may include control data (that is, information on how to understand and interpret the client's request), resource metadata, representation data and metadata. Consequently, resources are conceived as information-rich, stateful conceptualizations that not only provide data and functionality but also, link to each other according to specific structural and operational relationships. REST, which stands for Representational State Transfer, is an architectural style containing a set of constraints that can be used to build network-based, resource-oriented architectures. Architectures based on REST demonstrate several significant properties for distributed applications such as scalability, simplicity, reusability and performance, to name a few (Pautasso & Wilde, 2009; Pautasso, Zimmermann, & Leymann, 2008; Vinoski, 2008; Al Shahwan & Moessner, 2010). The largest example of resource-oriented architecture is the Web itself, and its architectural success attracts significant at-

tention from the software engineering community onto how REST could be adopted in the enterprise software domain as well.

Apart from the desired properties and contextual architectural choices, traditional service-oriented systems on the one hand, and REST-based service systems on the other, demonstrate an obvious conceptual mismatch in offering service capabilities. Specifically, the procedure-oriented approach of providing software services differs significantly from the resource-oriented approach due to the distinct methodology of decomposing and publishing service capabilities as addressable units of functionality and data. In the first case, units of functionality are organized into services and service operations, which not only have specific process semantics but also, allow for data retrieval and manipulation. In the latter case, service capabilities are modeled as stateful resources and functionality is published through interaction (retrieval and manipulation) of service consumers with such content-rich resources. Furthermore, an additional diversification between procedure-oriented and resource-oriented services is that the latter makes less out-of-band or a priori assumptions, regarding the client's knowledge of an application's intra-service protocols and conventions and consequently, rely more on the understanding of common and most often standardized processing models and resource relationships. It should be noted that REST's target are Web-scale architectures that span multiple domains and the decisions made regarding the design of such systems should be based on the effect that each decision has in a network-level scale. For example, in an environment like the above, generality is preferred over efficiency in the components' interfaces. Actually this particular choice is formalized by REST with its Uniform Interface constraint. The uniformity of interfaces imposed by this constraint essentially promotes the level of independence between the communicating parts with regard to their internal technological or architectural evolution, reducing the coupling to a minimal set of commonly accepted agreement points. Such interface constraints do not usually restrict architects that employ procedure-oriented approaches, where arbitrary operations are defined to encode custom, component-specific semantics.

It could be noted that during the last few years the community is intensively working on bridging the gap between being able to develop truly conformant large-scale implementations and the currently available methods, models and tooling. More specifically, specialized programming models, development environments, languages, and models along with infrastructure frameworks are required for organizations and businesses to be able to widely adopt RESTful approaches for designing and implementing new resource-oriented service-offering enterprise systems. However, the need for resource-orientation and alignment with the Web goes beyond new systems that are implemented from scratch. Existing service-offering enterprise systems are products of significant investments, and most often provide mission critical, well validated functionality, to a variety of clients. Redeveloping existing functionality in order to follow a more resource-oriented approach and better align service-offering procedural components to RESTful environments would include significant costs of redesigning, re-implementing and re-testing such systems as well as, maintaining duplicate functionality when required. Furthermore, fully migrating already deployed components to REST-based ones would break existing clients, which is usually not acceptable as a choice for large organizations. These issues highlight the need for a methodology to enable an automated or semi-automated adaptation of existing service-offering components in a non-intrusive manner to REST-based exposure of their functionality. In this context, there are interesting questions that arise regarding how someone may map arbitrary, domain, or business-specific procedural interfaces to actions that belong to a uniform interface across a set of resources (which is also unknown beforehand in an adaptation process and should be

also specified), and to whether two paradigms as diverse as the above may converge so that existing components provide their functionalities utilizing both paradigms. In this chapter, we discuss issues and challenges that exist in this domain and we provide a holistic view of a roadmap for adapting procedure-based service-offering components to a resource oriented architecture style. In this respect, we present an adaptation framework along with a process model of how to facilitate and significantly automate the process of providing RESTful expositions of procedural functionality.

This chapter's scope and focus is to provide a baseline and a roadmap for researchers and practitioners to consider, while attempting to address the SOA/WS to REST adaptation problem. Specifically, it aims to provide and discuss the fundamental challenges pertaining to the adaptation problem and present a high-level model as a conceptual guidance for a systematic approach in addressing static, dynamic, and deployment-related adaptation concerns. As a roadmap for the adaptation concepts, that are discussed in detail in Section 3 of this chapter, we first examine the management of quality characteristics that procedure-oriented implementations of service-oriented systems demonstrate in the context of an adaptation/migration process, and how they relate to the proposed adaptation approach. Once the focus of the approach is clarified in the functional and architectural aspect, we proceed discussing issues related to the conformance of a resource-oriented architecture to REST architectural constraints, as these are defined in the REST specification by Fielding. The purpose of such discussion is to present the means by which we can assess the degree of conformance of a migrant/adapted architecture to the REST constraints and to present existing approaches that can assist a software engineer in deciding or evaluating the level of RESTfulness that the adapted view of the system should demonstrate. Since, the adaptation process has to be considered within the context of a practical implementation methodology and deployment scenario, Section 3 discusses the principle of Model-Driven Engineering (MDE) and Service Component Architecture (SCA). MDE allows for the necessary infrastructure to represent software artifacts as MOF-compliant models and the programmatic manipulation of such models for the purposes of adaptation. Similarly, SCA provides a rich framework whereby service-oriented systems can be specified as models and their interactions can be represented in a way that can be customized in the form of different bindings. The interesting implication is that a software architect can include new bindings (such as bindings for supporting RESTful interactions with the service) and the SCA runtime will provide the necessary infrastructure for the new binding to be ubiquitously deployed and used. The interested reader who may want to embark on such an adaptation project can also delve into technical papers presented in various IEEE, ACM, and other venues, conferences, and workshops for obtaining more insights of the various low-level technical challenges involved. A collection of such related approaches is presented and discussed later in the chapter (Section 2.2).

The rest of the chapter is organized as follows. In Section 2, we summarize the background of resource-orientation, the theory of REST and RESTful services in practice, in order to provide to the reader the necessary context and for understanding the basic principles, constraints, and practical considerations of RESTful architectures. Furthermore, Section 2 discusses and presents related work with regard to specific approaches to RESTful service modeling and the adaptation problem, as these are found in the related literature. In Section 3, we present and discuss a set of considerations related to the proposed software adaptation process, as outlined above. In Section 4, we present an adaptation framework as a roadmap to gradually meeting REST's requirements by addressing REST's constraints. Limitations of the approach as well as open issues of the adaptation problem are discussed in Section 5 and a

summarization of the chapter along with future research directions are presented in Section 6.

BACKGROUND AND RELATED WORK

REST in Theory and in Practice

REST in Theory

REST is an architectural style defined by Roy T. Fielding in his dissertation in 2000 (Fielding, 2000). Modern Web's scalability, flexibility, and robustness are often attributed to Web's general conformance to the REST style. However, REST is not tied to any particular standard or protocol and there are no such direct references to Web's technologies or standards for its definition. Fielding's dissertation describes several architectural styles along with the examination of induced properties and he derives REST by combining such styles. Specifically, he describes how each constraint affects architectural elements and what properties are expected to be induced when the constraints are applied in coordination. The specific constraints included in the REST specification are: Client-Server, Stateless, Cache, Uniform Interface, Layered System, and the optional Code-on-Demand constraint. The first three constraints were applied to the Web since its early architecture, while the next three were formalized and applied as the Web architecture evolved. Additionally, the Uniform Interface constraint is regarded as a central feature in REST. Brief descriptions of REST's architectural constraints are provided in Table 1.

RESTful Web Services

For a system's architecture to be fully RESTful it should conform to all of aforementioned REST's constraints. In this respect, utilizing HTTP and URIs to offer services through a Web API does

Table 1. REST architectural constraints

Architectural constraint	Description
Client-Server	The Client-Server constraint models the interactions and separates the role of requesting and the role of providing service.
Stateless (communication)	Stateless constraint refers to client-server communication and requires that every request from the client to the server is independent from previous ones. Consequently, there is no server-side session state kept during such interactions and each request should be descriptive enough to be fully understood on its own.
Cache	The Cache constraint mandates that responses by the server should indicate (probably implicitly) whether they can be cached or not.
Uniform Interface	The Uniform Interface constraint imposes the generality of components' interfaces and requires that these interfaces have system-wide universal semantics. Also, this constraint introduces and describes the resource-oriented modeling of a system's content, realized by its dependence to further architectural constraints, usually referred to as Uniform Interface's subconstraints. Specifically, REST states that the uniformity of interfaces in a RESTful architecture is obtained by its conformance to the four following constraints: identification of resources, manipulation of resources through representations, self-descriptive messages and hypermedia as the engine of application state (usually referred to as HATEOAS or the "hypermedia constraint").
Layered System	The Layered System constraint mandates that the organization of the system follows a hierarchical, layered fashion, where each layer provides services to the layer above and consumes services from the layer below.
Code-On-Demand	Code-On-Demand allows for client agents' logic to be extended by downloadable and executable code. This last constraint is an optional constraint and Fielding argues that it should be supported by an architecture conforming to REST in the general case. However, there may be contexts that this behavior is disabled and that possibility should be acceptable.

not necessarily mean that REST is applied, since HTTP offers a variety of features that may or may not be used in accordance to REST. Additionally, RESTful architectures may be implemented using any communication protocol other than HTTP, as long as it would allow for conforming to REST's constraints. Having said that, the fact that HTTP is inherently REST-enabled and, HTTP's client and server implementations are widely deployed and adopted, make this protocol a very popular and, presumably, a sound choice for implementing systems that are supposed to conform to REST. Figure 1 provides an example of a bookstore service offered through both a procedure-oriented and a resource-oriented API. The left hand side of the picture depicts the use of a procedural service API of a bookstore service where a customer is able to search a catalog, create new orders, add and remove items from orders and submit orders. These operations are directly mapped as "procedures" that pertain to services offered by a service-oriented architecture infrastructure. In this classic

service-oriented paradigm, services are invoked by name using appropriate parameters. On the right hand side of the figure, the same scenario is illustrated but at this time is based on a resource-oriented architecture. In such a context, instead of services there are resources such as "bookstore," "catalog," "order collection," "order item" and "order status." These resources are manipulated using standard HTTP operations such as GET, PUT, POST and DELETE. For example, to create a new order item resource, a POST request can be issued from the client to the server pertaining to the orders collection resource. Similarly, to update the status of a bookstore order a PUT request can be issued to the order status resource.

The subset of Web-based service systems that truly follow REST principles are called RESTful Web services (Richardson & Ruby, 2007). These services utilize HTTP and URI along with common Internet's media types and Web's standards such as XML and JSON for data formatting. Furthermore, during the last few years the com-

Figure 1. Bookstore service example: procedure and resource-oriented alternatives

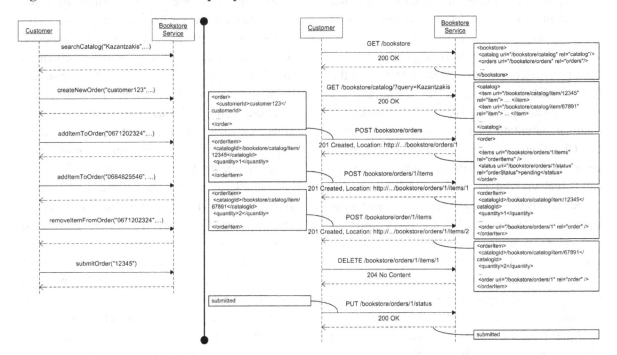

munity has established several conventions into using such Web's protocols and standards to facilitate the systematic development of RESTful Web services. These conventions relate for instance to the mapping of HTTP's methods ("verbs") to CRUD-like semantics (for example, using HTTP's POST method to create a new resource, GET to read a resource, PUT to update an existing resource, and DELETE to delete a resource), restricting the broader semantics that these methods have according to HTTP specification. Similarly, terms like ROA (Resource-Oriented Architecture) (Richardson & Ruby, 2007) and WOA (Web-Oriented Architecture) (Gail, Sholler, & Bradley, 2008) were introduced and defined in order to help the community better organize and communicate the concepts and the variations that REST-based designs demonstrate. Furthermore, several REST-inspired SOA patterns have been proposed (Balasubramanian, 2008), and significant research is also being conducted in the area of RESTful service composition (Pautasso, 2009).

Software Adaptation and Related Work

Software adaptation has been proposed as a discipline over the past few years (Brogi, Canal, & Pimentel, 2006; Canal, Murillo, & Poizat, 2004, 2008); however, the problem of adapting existing software components is an area of long research and discussion (Kell, 2008). Software adaptation relates to the challenges that emerge when reusing existing software artifacts in new applications and which can be addressed by introducing a category of special computational component elements called adaptors. These adaptors are responsible for enabling the communicating components to interact effectively, overcoming mismatches that may exist on both functional and non-functional aspects. These mismatches may relate to any of the four interface levels such as signatures, behaviors, non-functional properties, and semantics. Additionally, adaptation must be non-intrusive and, automatic or at least semi-automatic. In addition, the need for software adaptation is regarded as independent of the point in the life cycle that the system may be in and emerge at any stage of its life cycle.

In order to characterize an adaptation process three parameters can be used: (a) the time that the need for adaptation is detected (requirements, static, dynamic), (b) the adaptation management (manual, automatic), and (c) the adaptation content (functional, non-functional). In this respect, the adaptation approach discussed in this chapter can be categorized as a software adaptation approach that is non-intrusive (existing component implementation is not modified and keeps offering services to existing consumers), the adaptation need is realized at the maintenance stage and the process model demonstrates a high level of automation, limiting user involvement to mostly providing declarative refinement feedback.

Apart from the practitioners' interest in being able to expose existing functionality in a RESTful manner, the challenges and issues that the transition of existing systems to resource-oriented architectures have also attracted significant attention in the academic world. The adaptation approach presented in this chapter was designed and developed by generalizing, abstracting and extending existing methods and techniques in the area of mapping procedure-oriented service-offering systems to resource-oriented ones (Liu, Wang, Zhuang, & Zhu, 2008; Laitkorpi, Koskinen, Systa, 2006, 2009; Athanasopoulos & Kontogiannis, 2010; Upadhyaya, Zou, Xiao, Ng, & Lau, 2011; Kennedy, Stewart, & Jacob, 2011). Although different in several aspects, our framework demonstrates similarities with earlier contributions to the problem, and focuses on a systematic approach of decomposing the adaptation problem into sub-problems pertaining to REST's architectural constraints and to possible architectural decisions that can be taken by the user for driving the adaptation process.

In Laitkorpi et al. (2006) authors introduce a UML-based approach to abstract legacy APIs into a canonical interface model that can be used

to expose REST-like services. Their approach works on the interface level of the legacy system and above. Specifically, they regard as input an API documentation with sufficient information to run the analysis. This information is assumed to involve a set of UML models that describe the structural as well as behavioral aspects of the API. However, such models are not usually available in practice and they would require considerable effort to create them from scratch -probably comparable to writing the adapter code manually. The process proposed in that paper is split into three basic steps: a) API analysis in order to extract an API architecture, which is performed manually, b) canonicalization in order to move from the API architecture to a canonical interface model, and c) operation and structure mapping to generate the adapter code. Similarly, a subsequent work from the same group (Laitkorpi, Selonen, & Systa, 2009) describes a model-driven process for gradually transforming procedure-oriented specification models (e.g. a Sequence Diagram of top-level components) to resource-oriented interfaces. More specifically, the authors describe a process of analyzing and processing functional specifications to create an information model of the service. This model is then mapped to a resource model, which in turn is translated into RESTful service specification artifacts. Both approaches demonstrate how UML can be utilized in a model-driven process to facilitate the process and allow for model-based transitions from procedural conceptualizations of service capabilities to resource-oriented ones.

Furthermore, in Liu et al. (2008), the authors propose a process for reengineering legacy systems to REST. The process starts by analyzing the source code of the system. Informative entities driven methodologies are then used to extract candidate resources. Rules and experts' operations are applied to refine the resource list, and URIs are designed and generated based on mapping strategies. URIs may also carry information with regard to scope, resource representation, and even business rules. Then methods are assigned and representations are designed. Finally, legacy services are wrapped by mappings to REST-based interactions. The starting point of the analysis is the source code as well as models such as ER diagrams, UML diagrams, requirements, and documentation, implying significant human involvement. Furthermore, the process is focused on the design and refinement of URIs in order to map relationship, action and other semantics.

Similarly, in Athanasopoulos and Kontogiannis (2010), a technique for identifying resources from legacy service descriptions is presented. In the adaptation technique presented, WSDL files are analyzed in order to extract REST-like resources. The technique works on the interface level using as input the machine-readable description of the service. Initially a model that captures signature information of the operations is built from the WSDL description. Then the model is extended by categorizing its elements and rules are applied to extract potential resources. Next, a rule-based resource selection is applied and the dependencies between the actual resources are captured in dependency graphs. Finally, resource identifiers are produced based on resources dependencies and operations are assigned according to patterns present on the signature model.

More recently, in Upadhyaya et al. (2011), the authors present an approach and a prototype for migrating Web Services based on SOAP, to REST-based services. The authors describe several steps for the migration process including: the identification of similar operations through clustering, the identification of the resources utilizing operation names as well as input and output parameter names, the identification of resource methods by attempting to map HTTP verbs to existing operations and finally, the message conversion between SOAP-based and HTTP messages. Their prototype also allows the user to review and possibly refine the output of the techniques before deploying the service wrapper.

Finally, viewing the problem from the client-side, the authors in Kennedy, Stewart, and Jacob (2011) discuss a protocol adapter so that SOAP-enabled clients could be used to invoke RESTful services, taking advantage of all of the Web's optimizations and especially caching. The authors provide a discussion around the problem and present a wizard-like prototype that can help the user drive the protocol adapter generation in a user-friendly manner.

Here, in accordance with most of the aforementioned approaches we also propose a model-driven approach for gradual analysis and transformation of software artifacts. Additionally, we extend the collection of the concerns that relate to this type of software adaptation, and pertain to REST constraints and features of RESTful services, and we introduce a clear separation of concerns between structural (static) and behavioral (dynamic) concerns. Then, we propose a process that aims to organize the addressing of these concerns, the capture and description of the required input, as well as, intermediary and output artifacts, and the user's involvement, so that a systematic adaptation can be achieved.

ADAPTATION CONSIDERATIONS

Service Quality Issues

Statelessness and Transactionality

Stateful communication with services is an important issue in service-oriented computing that has to be addressed before applying any adaptation technique. It should be noted that REST's requirement for statelessness affects the communication and not the service itself (resources are inherently stateful entities). Specifically, REST requires that no request should be dependent to a previous one in order to be understood and interpreted. In this respect, server-side volatile session state should not exist in a RESTful system (or at least, should not be observable) and messages should be self-descriptive, completely indicating how they can be understood and interpreted independently for any previous interaction.

Since preserving non-persistent session state is not acceptable in RESTful architectures, a challenge that emerges in the adaptation of SOA/WS systems to REST is how transaction semantics can be modeled effectively in a truly RESTful manner. The general approach that has been proposed in the literature is designing an appropriate resource model that can model transaction semantics persistently when required. Along this lines, a specification for supporting atomicity in REST-based distributed transaction scenarios with coordinated outcomes (such as the two-phase commit protocol) is proposed by the REST-* initiative through defining transaction coordinator and transaction participant resources. Nevertheless, whether REST can accommodate or, whether it is generally suitable as an architectural style for supporting distributed transaction models has been a topic of long debate (Little, 2009; Pardon & Pautasso, 2011). In this respect, several proposals in the literature are exploring transactions and REST through introducing a variety of transaction models and techniques (Marinos, Razavi, Moschoyiannis, & Krause, 2009; Razavi, Marinos, Moschoyiannis, & Krause, 2009; Da Silva Maciel & Hirata, 2009, 2011; Pardon & Pautasso, 2011). The incorporation of such methodologies in an adaptation process may require extensive and probably intrusive reengineering of the adapted system and may fit better in a more generic migration effort—not one leading to encapsulation of existing implementations that this chapter is focused on.

General QoS Features

Most existing Web 2.0 RESTful services have usually relaxed requirements with regard to QoS features when compared to enterprise service scenarios. WS* QoS specifications usually demon-strate a high level of sophistication; however, they are often significantly complex and this is usually why they are not widely adopted. Discussions around RESTful enterprise systems with such requirements advocate a careful analysis of the requirements' rationale and goals and, the utilization of existing Web technologies as means of fulfilling them. To date, the application of standardized QoS frameworks has not been widely examined and only a few such initiatives and respective artifacts exist. This fact may be attributed to a prevailing view in the REST community that the simplicity and generality of RESTful HTTP implementations is a significant advantage that architects should try to preserve, even in complex business scenarios—solutions to business-level problems should not be technical. We consider that an architect should first investigate whether the QoS requirements for the system can be achieved in the context of a RESTful architecture and whether the properties expected to be induced by applying REST, according to its definition, are compatible with the adaptation objectives.

An adaptation approach like the one discussed in this chapter focuses mostly on the functional characteristics of the interfaces and the adaptation process is centered on resource-based exposure of service capabilities. More specifically, the major concern of such an adaptation process is the exposure of source system's functionality as a set of artifacts that define corresponding RESTful interfaces (e.g. collection of resources, media types, universal actions, hypermedia, etc.). Even though QoS requirements for the system are important and should be taken into account in a migration effort, general QoS features can be considered as concerns that go beyond the functional translation of the service interface and could be separately addressed, with the exception probably of statelessness and transactionality as discussed above. In this respect, quality characteristics can be regarded as being configurable in the underlying technology level, similar to SCA's methodological, independent treatment of

QoS aspects. In this way, certain quality features can be achieved by appropriate configuration choices of the underlying run-time component. For example, a configuration point would be whether to utilize HTTP or HTTPS for meeting a security requirement. Having said that, it should be noted that there are other quality characteristics of service-oriented systems, whose preservation is either under question with most of the existing implementation technologies and standardization efforts of RESTful services, or may, in general, require extensive reengineering of the system in order to be supported in the adapted RESTful view of the system. Such issues are still open research challenges in the community.

Levels of RESTful-ness and Induced Properties for the Target System

Evaluating the conformance of REST-claiming systems to REST's constraints is significant in two aspects. First, REST is an architectural style and as such, is used to convey certain architectural properties of interest, facilitating the communication and understanding between software architects, designers, and developers. Characterizing systems as being RESTful while they are not (which is a quite common case on existing Web APIs), may lead to misinterpretations among parties involved in the software development process and, eventually create misconceptions with regard to what REST really means. Second, REST includes a coordinated set of constraints, meaning that when these constraints are applied together, certain properties are expected to appear in the architecture. When one or more constraints are relaxed, probably due to certain, weighted architectural decisions that address specific issues for an application, then this deviation should be able to be captured systematically, so that the trade-offs that are included can be examined with regard to the system-wide desired properties. In this respect, REST is not a good fit for all applications and alternatives or compromises will always be present

in practice. Evaluating RESTful-ness by examining the conformance of an architecture to REST's constraints assists architects in making better decisions with regard to patterns and practices used. Such conformance analysis of a design to REST constraints is important for both developing new systems and adapting existing components to REST. For this purpose, we discuss below a collection of models, approaches and techniques that have been proposed in the literature as means to assist software engineers evaluate the degree of conformance of the target adapted architecture to the REST constraints.

Evaluating Maturity and Constraint Conformance

Since there may be different architectural choices for a system, a collection of levels of maturity (or levels of conformance to REST) have been proposed. These levels of maturity of existing HTTP-based service systems with regard to REST have been empirically organized in a model presented by Leonard Richardson, the so-called Richardson's Maturity Model (RMM) as referred to by Martin Fowler (2010). RMM has four levels, each of which essentially represents different degrees of conformance to REST's constraints, and mainly to the Uniform Interface constraint. Figure 2 presents the RMM levels and depicts respective examples of HTTP-based interactions. The goal of each interaction is to retrieve a list of order items that have been validated that is part of a Shopping service.

Starting from Level 0, the HTTP protocol, although it is an application-layer protocol, is used as a transport mechanism, mainly for invoking remote procedures. At this first level, service systems usually offer a single URI as service end-point which consumers use to send messages to the server that manages the URI to be processed. The Level 0 example in Figure 2 demonstrates a single service endpoint that receives an invocation call for the "listValidOrders" op-

Figure 2. Levels of Richardson maturity model with examples

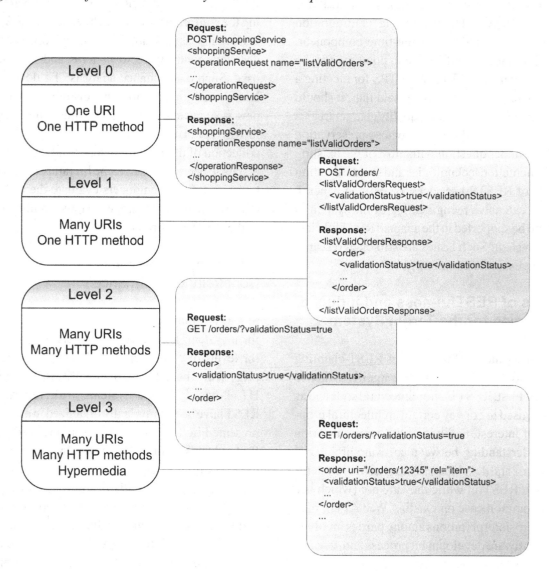

eration using the POST HTTP method and returns a list of order items included in a generic envelop structure. The messages usually contain structured data in formats like XML or JSON, with or without protocols like SOAP encapsulating the data. XML-RPC, XML-JSON and WS* Web Services over HTTP are typical examples of such services.

Level 1 is the first transition to a more RESTful approach by decomposing single endpoints to multiple ones, which provide semantically distinct functionality and data within a service.

These "endpoints" are identified by and accessed through different URIs. In other words, Level 1 introduces the usage of REST-like resources as a way to model and expose service functionality. Up to this level, HTTP methods are not necessarily used according to their semantics and HTTP is mainly used as a medium to tunnel requests rather than as a way to convey the intent of interactions between client and server. In Figure 2, the Level 1 example illustrates that "orders" are assigned a separate URI and the invocation call is targeted

Figure 3. Abstracted view of uniform interface conceptual framework

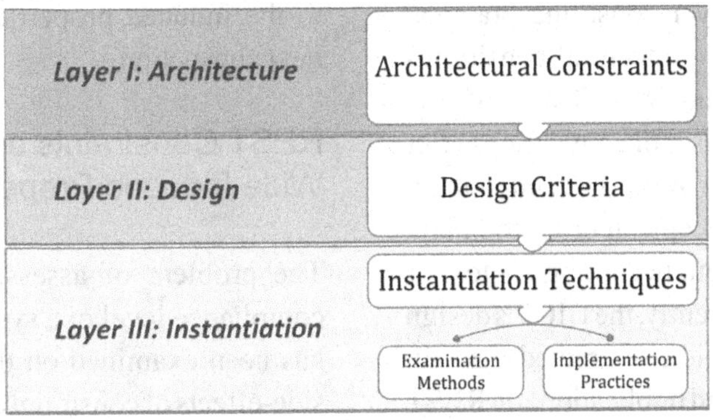

towards that URI (POST is still used as the HTTP method for the interaction). The response includes an indication of the invoked functionality and a list of order items.

Level 2 introduces the usage of HTTP methods (or verbs) according to their semantics in order to convey to the server (and probably intermediaries) the purpose of the request. To generalize this concept, Level 2 includes services that utilize HTTP's control data to indicate the semantics and the properties of the interaction (to the extent that this can be done using a predefined set of control data). For example, GET is used for the retrieval of representations and the safety property (i.e. there should be no server-side side effects because of the interaction) that the HTTP specification requires for GET, is respected. Usually, CRUD-based services are created up until this level for the manipulation of data-rich resources. The Level 2 example illustrates the use of a GET instead of a POST, and the use of a URI to identify the proper collection of resources that the specific interaction operates upon, that is the valid orders. The response contains a representation of the resource, which is a list of valid order items.

Level 3 refers to the hypermedia constraint. Servers provide hypermedia elements to guide clients as to which are the possible future communication interactions, directing thus the transitions of the application state. Level 3 of the maturity model is regarded as a precondition to REST—but

not the only one, since several more constraints must be fulfilled to meet full conformance. Level 3 goes a step further by introducing the usage of hypermedia elements (i.e. links, forms, and controls). In the Level 3 example depicted in Figure 2, in addition to the use of a GET verb and the correct use of a URI to identify the resource, the response from the server also contain hypermedia elements that can be used by the client to correctly interpret the response and plan for the next interaction.

RMM apart from indicating the maturity levels with regard to REST, it also summarizes categories of Web services that are developed under the prism of conflicting forces and essentially represent trade-offs that architects have to make, in order to induce properties to their architectures that may partly differ from the ones induced by REST. With respect to RMM and related discussions on addressing the issue of examining interface uniformity there is work that proposed a conceptual framework for evaluating and assessing a service interface against REST's uniform interface constraint (Athanasopoulos, Kontogiannis, & Brealey, 2011). The Uniform Interface Conceptual Framework (UICF), which was proposed, models a layered approach in constraint conformance evaluation, an abstracted view of which is depicted in Figure 3.

Specifically, architectural constraints in the first layer have direct reference to REST's definition according to Fielding (2000), while design criteria in the second layer constitute practical interpretations of these architectural constraints but in a technology-neutral way. These criteria often represent compromises or conventions after meticulous argumentation over how to implement abstract architectural concepts in order to obtain a uniform interface without becoming context or technology-specific. Currently, the UICF's design layer includes interpretations extracted through reviewing the literature and publications on REST organized in a set of criteria that cover a significant spectrum of issues that a REST designer faces. The major differentiating feature of design criteria at the second layer of the proposed framework, when compared to architectural constraints of the first layer, is that it lowers the level of abstraction by introducing a set of identifiable, concrete practice-oriented conceptual units in order to guide or assess design in a way that is technology-agnostic while not being technology-ignorant. Finally, the design criteria of the second layer are manifested as instantiation techniques in the third layer. In this respect, the instantiation layer is populated with realization-level configurable techniques, which can be used to either examine the conformance of an interface to the REST architectural style, or guide the implementation of systems in order to conform to it.

UICF, RMM and analogous models are of special interest in an adaptation process since such a process should be flexible enough to accommodate architectural compromises based on user input, making deviations from REST constraints' requirements possible. Specifically, the user that drives an adaptation process, should be able to intervene and apply decisions that serve his/her requirements, goals or policies but that may reduce the general conformance to REST. Using assessment models, such deviations can be systematically captured and organized so that they can be further studied in terms of their effects on desired and induced properties. Two such conformance assessment approaches that help assess the effects of a reduced constraint conformance to the induced properties, are discussed in the next subsection.

REST Constraints and Architecture-Wide Induced Properties

The problem of assessing and evaluating the compliance level of a system to REST principles has been examined on the basis of the possible side-effects of constraint deviations to the induced properties of an architecture (Navon & Fernandez, 2011). The analysis is performed by utilizing influence diagrams that reflect positive and negative effects between architectural constraints/styles and properties. Such diagrams can be constructed and used, to systematically study how each level of conformance may affect the properties, and to highlight the trade-offs included in such architectural decisions.

HTTP-based APIs have been also empirically examined with regard to Uniform Interface constraint and its subconstraints by Jan Algermissen (2010), where a discussion is also provided regarding how each expected architecture-wide property is affected, given the level of conformance to Uniform Interface constraint (which essentially defines a categorization of HTTP-based URIs). The examination is performed with regard to properties such as performance (network performance, network efficiency), visibility, modifiability (evolvability, extensibility), simplicity, scalability, as well as different costs pertaining to the architecture's lifecycle (initial, maintenance, and evolution costs).

We consider that in the adaptation process, the level of RESTful-ness for the target system results from the choices that the user guiding the process, makes. We regard the above frameworks as complementary methodologies and we do not explicitly use predefined compliance levels since the adaptation framework should be able to cover a wide range of requirements. However, the architect driving the adaptation process should be aware to the above concepts and trade-offs, and should be able to recognize the probable side effects of the choices he or she makes during the process.

Practical Considerations: Model-Driven Engineering and Service Component Architecture

Model-Driven Engineering (MDE) (Schmidt, 2006; Kent, 2002) has been proposed as a methodology that is based on creating, processing and using models to describe, develop and document software. Software models are abstractions that represent knowledge about the domain and the application, and they are used to design, develop and even to automatically generate system artifacts, such as source code. MDE technologies are regarded as an effective way to address the complexity related to the design of software systems with complex requirements. We view the SOA/WS to REST adaptation process as being "model-driven," significantly utilizing respective Model-Driven Engineering standards and technologies. Specifically, throughout the process, models that capture system, application, technology, or adaptation-specific information can be extracted, analyzed, processed, and generated.

A model-based approach in building service-oriented systems and applications is proposed by Service Component Architecture (SCA). SCA is a set of specifications that uses open standards and significantly separates the concerns of non-functional requirements and service implementation assembly. SCA specifications are a product of wide collaboration in the software engineering community (Open SOA Collaboration), and since 2007, the specifications are in the process of formal standardization through OASIS (Open CSA member section). In addition, SCA provides a domain of research and several contributions on service-oriented computing research are based on or are extending SCA notions (Chu, Shen, & Jiang, 2009; Li, Zhang, & Jin, 2009). In the context of SCA and model-based assembly of service-oriented architectures, the need for converging procedure-oriented and resource-oriented components on the interface level becomes critical. In a typical SCA assembly scenario, an SCA composite is created by connecting together SCA components that provide and consume services. These SCA composites can be also used as SCA component implementations in other assemblies. Each component provides services whose interfaces are restricted in that they should be translatable into WSDL (although the actual translation may never occur in practice) with respect to the exposed functionality. The access mechanisms for the exposed services are separately handled by the definition and usage of different bindings (e.g. SOAP Web Service, JMS, EJB Session Bean, JCA, JSON-RPC, etc.).

Due to the SCA's dependency on the concept of operation, the introduction and usage of RESTful Web services in SCA assemblies is not as easy as it would be expected for such an assembly model. Similarly, the usage of procedure-oriented service systems through RESTful exposition and bindings becomes quite cumbersome. Workarounds that have been proposed include the implementation of additional source code, to manually encapsulate capabilities or the annotation of existing implementations with REST-specific tags. Both cases require considerable effort from the analyst, whose primary focus should be the composition of business functionality instead of technical issues such as infrastructure code or implementation annotations. Implementations in an SCA assembly may be based on a variety of technologies, written in different languages, and supported by different frameworks, which make intrusive workarounds less efficient. Our approach aims to enable SCA infrastructure and its runtime so that REST bindings can be added in a more flexible way, achieving thus the goals and objectives of the adaptation process. More specifically, SCA brings significant flexibility in building service-oriented architectures, and for reusing existing services (e.g. legacy services implemented in COBOL) by assembling them together with new services that utilize modern technologies and programming paradigms. In this respect, RESTful exposition of procedural systems would provide additional benefits to organizations reusing and exposing their well-validated, value-proven systems to wider audiences, and even the Web, in a Web-friendly manner. We consider that SCA and SCA runtime environments can provide an important role in automating the adaptation process and deploying the RESTful adapted services in a unified and transparent way. For example, by utilizing a model-based framework such as SCA and by adding a new REST binding, one could access back-end system and services in a RESTful way, without losing, through the SCA runtime, the capability of accessing the same services with all the other bindings defined for this component/service.

Figure 4 depicts MDE's and SCA's roles in the adaptation framework we are proposing. In this figure, we borrow the idea of the "horseshoe" model from the area of software reengineering (Byrne, 1992; Bergey, Smith, Weiderman, & Woods, 1999) and adapt it to abstract and simplify the adaptation process we discuss in detail in the following sections, and also to highlight MDE's and SCA's involvement. In a nutshell, the left part of the horseshoe model relates to the analysis of the original procedurally-invoked service components and the extraction of possible domain models from service descriptions and data schemas. The top part of the model deals with the identification of resource descriptions and actions (i.e. create, read, update, delete) to the identified resources, given the existing functionality. The right part of the model relates to the generation of SCA infrastructure aiming to add REST bindings to existing SCA service components and SCA assemblies so that, service related resources that have been identified can be accessed in a RESTful manner.

Figure 4. MDE's and SCA's roles in the adaptation framework

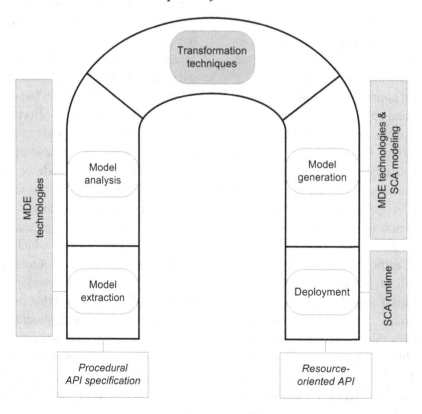

ADAPTATION PROCESS AND FRAMEWORK

As discussed above, the non-intrusive adaptation of procedure-oriented service systems to REST-based ones requires a methodology and a corresponding process model that addresses the complete set of the required constraints included in REST. In this respect, we propose an adaptation framework working on the interface level and above, having as general target the ability to restrict the description of the system according to each constraint, in a systematic manner. Consequently, the framework entails components, which implement adaptation steps that are part of the overall adaptation process, and each of which addresses specific concerns regarding the set of REST's constraints. First of all, the adaptation process is divided into two phases based on the "time" of the application of the adaptation task: design-time phase and run-time phase. The design-time phase attempts to adapt the facets and align the views of the system's data and functionality to most of the principles of the Uniform Interface constraint (referred to as static/structural concerns), and also caching, hypermedia and certain additional interface rendering issues (referred to as dynamic/behavioral concerns). Run-time phase addresses Client-Server, Layered-System, and Stateless communication constraints. The goal of the adaptation is that the external view of the system may eventually conform to REST by respecting the restrictions each REST constraint imposes to the architecture. However, whenever this is not possible or there are trade-offs related to a full conformance to REST, the adaptation process should allow for user refinement and tuning. In this respect, the adaptation outcome should transparently allow for RESTful interactions with the service-offering component (at least to the extent that the architect decided to go). In this section, we present a model for the adaptation process along with the intermediate artifacts, to serve as

a roadmap for further research to automate the vertical architectural adaptation of "RESTifing" a procedural service system. Figure 5 demonstrates the process model of the adaptation framework.

Process Model: General Description

As discussed above, the adaptation process is split into two phases: the design-time phase and run-time phase. During the design-time phase a set of techniques are applied to the specification and description artifacts of the system along with adaptation configuration metadata. User involvement is modeled in the form of output inspection and review, which essentially depends on the sophistication of the employed techniques as well as, on user's interest in applying specific architectural decisions (e.g. relaxing a certain constraint in the context of an identified architectural trade-off). The run-time phase consumes the outcome of the design-time phase and does not require user involvement other than the configuration of the run-time context (e.g. artifacts required for an SCA runtime environment). During the run-time automated mapping and management of interactions take place, which can be tuned to different levels of "smartness" given the adaptation goals (for example, managing virtual resources that represent process instance semantics and do not exist in the back-end).

The design-time phase is conceptually further split into sub-phases based on a separation between static/structural concerns of API modeling and dynamic/behavioral ones. In the first sub-phase, the process takes as input the existing API description and adaptation configuration metadata, it then applies several specialized techniques, and finally, renders a RESTful service model as an output, along with feedback data that can be edited by the user to refine the techniques' application. Specifically, during this step, resources are extracted from existing interface description artifacts and they are organized into a model based on their properties

Figure 5. Adaptation framework process model

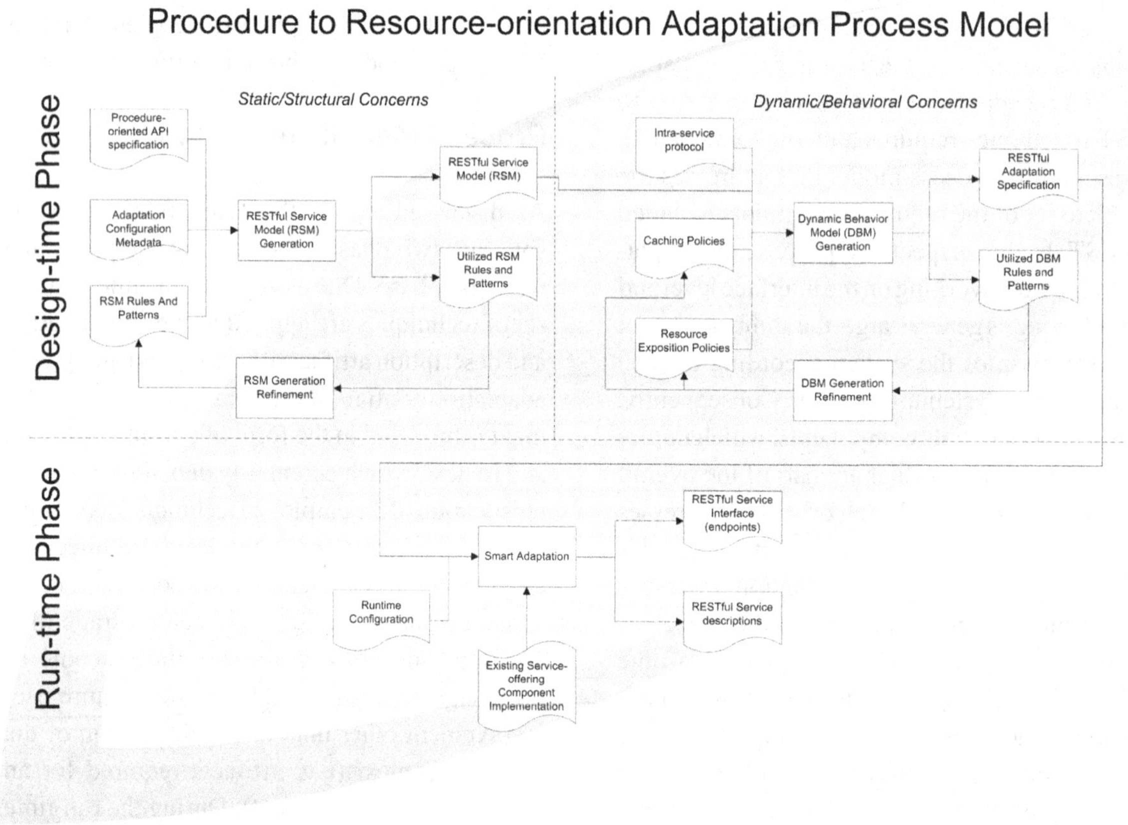

Procedure to Resource-orientation Adaptation Process Model

and relationships. Next, the second sub-phase takes place, where the RESTful service model along with a dependency model of the service operations and user-defined policies about caching and resource exposition is submitted to a process that creates the final adaptation specification. This output incorporates instructions about several dynamic aspects of a RESTful service.

The RESTful adaptation specification is then used as input in the run-time phase to render an adapter that will handle requests, map them to invocations to the existing component and provide responses in a way that is compliant to REST (or to some chosen compromise). In the next section, the adaptation phases, components, and artifacts are further discussed and descriptions of each adaptation component and input/output artifacts are provided.

Adaptation Framework Components

In this section, we discuss in more detail the adaptation process as this is depicted in Figure 5.

Procedure-Oriented API Specification

We regard the adaptation process as taking place on a per service level where the term "service" represents a set of one or more operations (also referred to as procedures or functions), offered by the service-providing component in order to accomplish one or more specified tasks, and/or to provide functionality and data to service consumers. In this respect, a procedure-oriented API specification can be any programmatic application interface description that inherently follows the procedural paradigm for functionality and data description, according to which a server-side operation should be invoked to process the specified input, and provide computed output in predefined forms (that is input and output parameters and their types are defined, described and known before the invocation). For example, interface description languages (e.g. WSDL) and generally any formalized language for expressing operation signatures and parameter types, would qualify for such an API specification. Going a step further, different syntaxes are acceptable as long as they are WSDL portType translatable, meaning that their expressiveness could be mapped concisely to the W3C language for Web Service description.

Adaptation Configuration Metadata

- The selection of the communication protocol that should be used and possibly the RESTful usage conventions of that protocol should be employed (control metadata, resource metadata, etc.) for representational state transfer.
- The selection of the identifier mechanism that should be utilized in order to assign identifiers to the extracted resources and of the predefined rules or templates that should be followed in order to meet identifier design requirements.
- The design of the format of the exchanged messages and the representation type negotiation that should take place during interactions.

RESTful Service Model (RSM) and RSM Generation Process

The RSM generation process takes as input the aforementioned artifacts and produces a service model that ideally (with the exception of alternate, less RESTful, configurations) conforms to the Uniform Interface constraint and especially to the subconstraints: identification of resources,

manipulation of resources through representations and self-descriptiveness. The generated RESTful Service Model (RSM) contains a set of extracted resources, a set of identifiers that map to each extracted resource, a set of possible manipulation actions that belong to a predefined fixed set of actions, as well as, a set of representations for these resources. For each resource, identifier and representation that are extracted, explicit mappings that trace back to the original procedural service are also captured and included in the model. RSM also contains certain structural relationships between the extracted resources. More specifically, the hypermedia constraint is not fully addressed at this point; however certain resource relationships (such as containment relationships or construction dependencies) that are extracted during the generation process in conjunction with the values of respective RSM rules would also supply enough information to inject certain hypermedia information during interactions as metadata.

As discussed above, during the generation process a set of REST-like resources is extracted. This set may also be extended with virtual resources to accommodate specific modeling and mapping patterns (e.g. model non-canonicalized procedure invocations as resources with full life cycle). Furthermore, the resource relationships are discovered based on structural and naming conventions identified at the API specification. Operations are characterized with respect to their potential semantics and properties, and the interactions are "canonicalized" to the predefined choices of the selected communication protocol and possibly the subset of these choices indicated by the conventions that the user chose to be used (e.g. HTTP CRUD-like, HTTP GET-POST-only conventions). The RESTful service model should also internally preserve the appropriate mapping information that is required to eventually construct valid invocation messages to the existing back-end component.

RSM Rules and Patterns

Aside from the configuration metadata, the generation of the RESTful service model requires the application of certain transformation rules and mapping patterns. Such rules and patterns guide and configure the resource model extraction process, the assignment of resource relationships, the mapping between operation semantics, the properties and communication protocol's control metadata and, the creation of virtual resources to accommodate for different levels of conformance to REST's constraints. These rules and patterns are selected and populated with values during the RESTful Service Model (RSM) generation process. After that, the end user should be able to edit these values and reinitiate the RSM generation process which when executed again should render a RESTful service model that is compliant to the rules and values that the user chose. Some of the challenges that this set of rules and patterns aim to answer pertain to:

- The resource modeling patterns that should be used when possible, the selection of mapping patterns that are of highest priority, and the selection of the generic/static resource relationships that are of interest and of heuristics that should be utilized to extract such relationships.
- The selection of the specific rules to utilize for characterizing operations' properties (e.g. safety, idempotency, etc.), and the heuristics that should be used for the "canonicalization" of the interaction intents as identified during the RSM generation process.

RSM Generation Refinement Process

The RSM generation process is regarded as the most significant and difficult process part to fully automate, due to the fact that interface-level information does not provide all the required information to extract significant resources and to characterize operations. Also, the apparent deflection of procedure-oriented and resource-oriented application modeling would sometimes make such a generation process ineffective, especially when working with purely command-like interfaces (e.g. one-word operations with generically typed input/output). In this respect, we assume user involvement as a way to refine the generation process by providing values to a set of rules and patterns. In this way, an effective output of the RESTful service model (mainly the set of resources, a subset of their relationships, and mappings between intents and back-end invocations) is generated, which is consequently inspected before examining further aspects, especially those of prescribing the dynamic behavior of a RESTful system. However, we regard user refinement as optional, meaning that the RSM generation process should be sophisticated enough to be able to identify a set of rules and patterns to utilize. The user would declaratively participate in the process to improve the output by refining these rules and patterns and the values of their points of variability. In this respect, the initial set of rules and patterns to be utilized by the process may as well be empty.

Above we described the steps and artifacts that are parts of the design-time phase of the adaptation. Specifically, these elements are included in the first sub-phase during which mostly static/structural modeling concerns of the RESTful service interface are addressed. During the second sub-phase of the design-time phase, the RESTful service model that was generated is being enriched in order to model and prescribe several aspects of the dynamic behavior of the system that is being adapted to the REST architectural style. The dynamic aspects we consider are: caching policies about the exposed resources, exposition choices of the generated resource set (e.g. filtering) and the effective enablement of the hypermedia mechanism to guide the application state. Caching and exposition policies are imposed by user choices, which may be supported and validated by respective mechanisms (for example, filtering policies should be validated so that there are no conflicts between the back-end functionality that is expected to be mapped and the filtering options).

Intra-Service Protocol

IDLs and generally machine-readable procedural interface descriptions like WSDL descriptions do not usually provide information with regard to the order and the conditions that each operation of the service should or could be invoked. Consequently, WSDL-translatable interface descriptions are not adequate by themselves in order to indicate how state transitions of the extracted resource set may take place through their possible manipulations. The intra-service protocol is usually implicit or described in human-readable documentation that accompanies the service. However, the problem has been identified in several research areas (for example, automated Web Service composition, automated testing of Web Services and Web Service behavioral modeling and adaptation), and several techniques to extract such ordering or dependency models between operations have been proposed (Gu, Li, Xu, 2008; Bai, Dong, Tsai, & Chen, 2005; Bertolino, Inverardi, Pelliccione, & Tivoli, 2009). In the adaptation roadmap, we regard such information either being provided by the user or extracted through employing such techniques. The intra-service protocol is rendered in terms of the existing procedural operations. The protocol's implied dependencies are mapped to resource dependencies and links which essentially create the "engine" of application state, allowing for the injection of hypermedia elements during interactions at runtime. An indication of the expressiveness of the formalism used to describe the intra-service protocol, is its equivalence to UML 2.0 Sequence Diagrams.

Caching Policies

Cache-ability is a central concept in REST and resource-oriented architectures, both in theory and in practice. REST includes it as a constraint since responses should indicate the cache-ability of the representation they are conveying. By caching representations of resources the efficiency of the communication is improved as well as, the performance as this is perceived by the requesting end. In this respect, cache-ability is a central aspect of RESTful architectures and improves scalability by allowing system-wide caching optimizations to be applied. It is generally accepted that such optimizations are critical for network-based distributed systems, in order to be able to scale. Usually service-offering procedural components do not indicate whether the responses they provide or which parts of them may be cached and for how long, and even if they do, they usually provide such information following their own patterns or techniques. However, for a system to be REST-adapted effectively, providing a process to handle such application of caching policies is regarded as mandatory in the context of an adaptation framework reference architecture. In our conceptualization of the adaptation process, caching information in the form of policies can be explicitly supplied by the user. An alternative would be to utilize techniques that analyze dynamically generated usage data. Once caching policies are defined, they are validated and then they are attached to the final output of the RESTful service model. Caching policies may also include constraints and conditions over what can be cached and how based on run-time information (e.g. based on a particular value of an exchanged representation of another resource), remaining however protocol-agnostic.

Resource Exposition Policies

The adaptation process may have as a goal a partial description of the system in terms of REST-like resources based on contextual conditions formed at runtime. Furthermore, additional links between the extracted resources may have to be present under specific circumstances. For example, an architect guiding the process may want to restrict the granularity of the extracted resources for a particular subset of clients and provide explicit links between particular resources under state-related conditions, aligning the system to externally imposed standards or processes. In the adaptation process model discussed here, we also consider the processing and the application of such policies by explicitly providing respective information to the dynamic model generation process. In this way, the user is able to address business or technical concerns by allowing conditional exposition and linking of specific parts of the resource set in a context-aware manner.

Dynamic Behavior Model (DBM) and DBM Generation Process

In our approach, we identify and distinguish a subset of the dynamic behaviors that may occur in a RESTful system which we recognized as critical for the adaptation process and which can be prescribed during the design-time phase. The analysis that takes place is centered on processing the application's protocol and on taking into account contextual and state-specific policies that control parts of the run-time behavior of the adapter (such as hypermedia injection, caching information, etc.). The dynamic behavior model that is generated includes information about these dynamic aspects of the system in the form of consumable prescriptions by a "smart" adapter. Being able to denote and enact dynamic behavior system models as these can be achieved by the smart adapter, essentially addresses the HATEOAS or hypermedia constraint which appears to be central when the goal of the adaptation is a truly RESTful system, as well as the REST's cache-ability constraint. In addition, the dynamic behavior model of the system is constructed taking into account

resource exposition policies, which provide flexibility and better alignment of the final output of the system to the adaptation goals.

DBM Rules and Patterns

The way that the particular dynamic aspects of the behavior of the service system are modeled, is guided by respective rules and patterns. These rules and patterns follow the same paradigm with RSM rules and patterns where the user can review and adapt and customize in order to render the final model. User involvement is again modeled via a refinement loop and is optional. However, the initial set of caching and exposure policies should not be empty (unless the architect is not interested in applying caching and exposition policies). Examples of such choices are, expressions regarding what sets of resources should be cached, conditions that should be met in order for the caching information to be injected, what relationships between the resources should become visible to the client/agent at runtime and under what conditions, expressions setting the resources that should be filtered, etc.

DBM Refinement Process

At this step, the user inspects the output of the DBM generation process along with the set of rules and patterns that were utilized in order to yield the dynamic behavior model of the system. He/she is then able to modify this set by either changing the values of the variation points of the rules, or to rearrange the predefined patterns available for each aspect. These actions essentially reflect to the caching and resource exposition policies. Presumably, after the refinement the generation process should automatically render a possibly different DBM in order to meet user's expectations.

RESTful Adaptation Specification

As discussed above, the dynamic behavior model is part of the final output of the design-time phase. Essentially, RSM and DBM constitute the RESTful adaptation specification. The meta-model for this specification should be expressive enough to cover both categories of concerns (static/structural and dynamic/behavioral). The adaptation specification provides all the essential information for the runtime phase of the adaptation to take place. In other words, whatever was extracted, mapped, modeled and probably refined during the design-time phase should be included or described in the final specification, which will be used as input at the deployment of the adapting component.

Following the design-time phase, the run-time adaptation phase consumes the specification as a prescription of yielding appropriate adaptation logic for a procedure-oriented service-offering component to provide a RESTful or REST-like interface. This phase is considered fully automated, given the RESTful adaptation specification from the design-time phase, and an initial configuration of the runtime/infrastructure which is the environment into which the adapter will exist.

Runtime Configuration

The adaptation process is based on the assumption that whatever adapter may exist, there is a layer of infrastructural components that are capable of dealing with a variety of technical issues, such as providing implementations and bindings for the communication protocols to be used for the RESTful adaptation of the system. We model the run-time adaptation phase as being dependent to a configuration description that essentially addresses the issues related to integrating the adapter's deployment to the available infrastructure environment. Ideally, the infrastructure should allow for the adapter to be invisible to a potential service composition process. For instance, in SCA's environment the adapter should be working on the

level of the domain runtime providing a RESTful binding in a way that is transparent to anyone that assembles a service composition. However, the runtime may have to model the adapter as a separate component, with or without indicating the component's relationship or its interaction with the existing service-offering component.

Smart Adaption Process

At this point, the RESTful adaptation specification is processed and a smart adaptation component is produced, capable of accepting and processing RESTful requests, managing resources, mapping the requests to back-end service invocations, receiving the responses from the invoked services and yielding RESTful responses that include information, hypermedia and representation meta-data (e.g. caching information). Furthermore, depending on the extracted resource model, the smart adapter may also serve as origin-server for virtual resources. In terms of REST's constraints, the smart adapter preserves the Client-Server style of interaction that a RESTful architecture requires. In addition, it should be noted that the smart adapter's architecture should conform to the Layered System constraint. Consequently, the client should not be able to distinguish whether it interacts with the origin-server or with an intermediary such as the adapter.

The "smartness" of the adapter relates to the sophistication of the mediation. For example, in an ideal scenario, the client-server interactions initiate via certain entry-points that map to an initial set of resource identifiers (usually mentioned as "bookmarks"). The client-server interaction beyond the entry-point identifiers should deliver the service's functionality through client's enactment to hypermedia provided by the smart container at runtime. Consequently, the resources described by the extracted resource model should become visible and probably addressable through identifiers (or identifier construction regimens) contained into smart adapter's responses. Additionally, the adapter is responsible for applying conditional caching and exposure policies that may include state-based, request value-based or context-based conditions.

The smart adaptation process is regarded as being fully automated with respect to the production and the configuration of the adapter, since all the required information regarding the adaptation should be already provided.

RESTful Service Interface (Entry Points) and Descriptions

The smart adaptation output is the set of RESTful entry-points available for interaction and one or more descriptions of the RESTful interface (human and/or machine-readable). A description should contain the resource model, the representation types used, and probably standardized or custom relationship semantics between resources that guide the transitions between states.

The adaptation process presented in Figure 5 depicts a more detailed view of the proposed activities and tasks to transform a procedural service-oriented API to a RESTful architecture. Even though the horseshoe model (Figure 4) aims to depict a high-level abstraction and simplification of the overall adaptation in order to highlight the relationship to existing methodologies (MDE) and frameworks (SCA), it still associates to the proposed adaptation process model. More specifically, the mapping between the proposed process model and the horseshoe model can be summarized in the following points. First, the design-phase, as depicted in Figure 5, associates to the model extraction, model analysis and the application of the transformation techniques (Figure 4) as these pertain to both structural and behavioral adaptation aspects of the API. Second, the run-time phase as depicted in Figure 5 associates to the model generation and deployment phase (Figure 4) for the target adapted system.

DISCUSSION: OPEN CHALLENGES AND LIMITATIONS

This chapter has discussed a process model for adapting procedural interfaces of service-oriented systems to RESTful architectures. However, there is a number of open research issues and challenges that need be addressed.

First, not all service-offering components, and not every service, are suitable for being adapted to offer their functionality through resources and their uniform manipulation. The uniform interface that RESTful architectures require generally reduces efficiency when compared to custom procedural interfaces (Fielding, 2000). Such efficiency may be vital for a system, and a careful examination of the problem should take place before offering a RESTful version of the system's capabilities. In this respect, an interesting, open problem is how to systematically assess which procedural interfaces are good candidates to undergo RESTful adaptation, how to identify the ones that might be in conflict with RESTful exposure of the functionality, and how to capture and evaluate such incompatibilities. It is noted that the approach discussed in this chapter can be applied once the procedural interface has been empirically evaluated as a good candidate for RESTful adaptation. Additionally, the adaptation roadmap we propose does not generally address QoS and non-functional requirements that may exist for large-scale or critical software systems. As discussed above, we regard such concerns as being treated separately and we focus on an adaptation process for the functional part of the interfaces. In this respect, a systematic process and framework for assessing API suitability for REST adaptation should also take into account QoS-related concerns, especially with regard to complex security policies (e.g. authentication, non-repudiation) that the service system should support, since currently the major technologies and frameworks that are used to implement RESTful service systems do not provide such capabilities in a standardized fashion.

Furthermore, resource extraction is a fundamentally heuristic process. In most methods that were reviewed in the literature pertaining to the extraction of resources using existing artifacts, fundamentally depended on the active involvement of an expert/user to either manually extract or modify the extracted resource collections. We restrict user involvement on refining the output of such an extraction process. However, such restriction requires the user to be familiar with the effects of the variation points that are provided for refinement. Generally speaking, the heuristic nature of the problem is linked to the fact that REST resources lack a strict formal definition and long discussions and debates take place over what should constitute a proper resource and what should not, given the definition in Fielding's dissertation.

Intra-service protocols should essentially be reflected to hypermedia mechanisms that eventually guide state transitions in a RESTful exposure of the system. However, such protocols are not usually provided, and techniques that are used to extract them do not guarantee providing all the acceptable use cases for a service. An interesting approach in the hypermedia-enablement of existing services is proposed in Liskin, Singer, and Schneider (2011). However, further research is needed in order to minimize the required informational input.

Finally, the presented adaptation process can be semi-automated during its design-time phase, requiring user involvement for refining certain aspects of the adaptation outputs as well as explicitly imposing caching and exposition policies. Further automation may be achieved though formalizing empirical knowledge into the respective issues, both during the generation of the resource model as well as during the modeling of the dynamic aspects of the interface. In addition, service usage data may play an interesting role in configuring certain aspects of the RESTful layout of the API.

Such knowledge and data could be acquired by observing and analyzing system execution as well as actual user adaptation tactics when refining rules and patterns.

SUMMARY AND FUTURE DIRECTIONS

In this chapter, we discussed the problem and challenges associated to adapting procedure-oriented service-offering components in order to yield resource-oriented interfaces through appropriate runtime encapsulation. Related work in the area was presented along with considerations regarding to the application of a systematic adaptation process. Consequently, we introduced an adaptation framework along with a process model and discussed the components, the steps, and the artifacts included in the model as well as, the context in which the framework would operate. The roadmap describes a methodology framework for adapting existing services into RESTful or REST-based APIs and assists in the direction of the convergence and interoperability of two distinct paradigms in service interface design namely, procedure-orientation, and resource-orientation. Additionally, we constraint the framework on being implementation-agnostic and focus our analysis on machine-readable interface descriptions, user-provided metadata and specific interface-level information.

The proposed adaptation process model has been applied in a case study pertaining to a variety of service descriptions obtained from the Programmable Web. More specifically, we have designed and implemented a methodology and supporting prototype tools first, for the representation of mappings between procedural and resource-oriented paradigm, second, for the automatic resource model extraction, and third for the modeling of user refinement feedback. In addition, we are currently experimenting with techniques that related to the dynamic concerns described above and we plan to build an extension to an open source SCA runtime domain that would better serve as infrastructure for our smart adaptor component. Through our experience with implementing the steps of the process model discussed above, an interesting challenge is to maintain a balance between trade-offs that related to, from one hand, the a wide spectrum and structural variety of different service descriptions (e.g. diverse possible WSDL descriptions, data schemas), and on the other hand, restricting user involvement to a simple, declarative, and easy to perform sequence of tasks.

To our knowledge, there is limited work on addressing in an end-to-end, automated or semi-automated manner, the problem of RESTful exposure of existing procedural services. Nevertheless, the area of REST and resource-oriented architectures will ever grow larger, as the need for efficient lightweight integration of components and data considered as Web resources, increases. In this context, interesting new emerging trends in the area include the specification of various QoS properties in REST as these are pertinent to WS* protocols (e.g. WS-Security), the handling of stateful systems in a stateless architecture such as REST, the denotation of transactions and transaction semantics as these are well understood in procedural systems to REST systems, and the consistent evolution/co-evolution of REST and SOA/WS models and APIs once the adaptation process is completed.

REFERENCES

Al Shahwan, F., & Moessner, K. (2010). Providing SOAP web services and RESTful web services from mobile hosts. In *Proceedings of the Fifth International Conference on Internet and Web Applications and Services,* (pp. 174-179). IEEE.

Algermissen, J. (2010). *Classification of HTTP-based APIs*. Retrieved October 10, 2011, from http://www.nordsc.com/ext/classification_of_http_based_apis.html

Athanasopoulos, M., & Kontogiannis, K. (2010). Identification of REST-like resources from legacy service descriptions. In *Proceedings of the 17th Working Conference on Reverse Engineering,* (pp. 215-219). IEEE.

Athanasopoulos, M., Kontogiannis, K., & Brealey, C. (2011). Towards an interpretation framework for assessing interface uniformity in REST. In *Proceedings of the Second International Workshop on RESTful Design,* (pp. 47–50). ACM.

Bai, X., Dong, W., Tsai, W., & Chen, Y. (2005). WSDL-based automatic test case generation for web services testing. In *Proceedings of the 2005 IEEE International Workshop on Service Oriented System Engineering,* (pp. 215-220). IEEE.

Balasubramanian, R. (2008). *REST-inspired SOA design patterns*. Retrieved October 10, 2011, from http://www.soamag.com/I24/1208-3.php

Bergey, J., Smith, D., Weiderman, N., & Woods, S. G. (1999). *Options analysis for reengineering (OAR): Issues and conceptual approach*. Technical Report CMUSEI1999TN014. Pittsburgh, PA: Carnegie Mellon University.

Bertolino, A., Inverardi, P., Pelliccione, P., & Tivoli, M. (2009). Automatic synthesis of behavior protocols for composable web-services. In H. Van Vliet & V. Issarny (Eds.), *Proceedings of the 7th Joint Meeting of the European Software Engineering Conference ESEC and the ACM SIGSOFT Symposium on the Foundations of Software Engineering,* (pp. 141-150). ACM.

Brogi, A., Canal, C., & Pimentel, E. (2006). On the semantics of software adaptation. *Science of Computer Programming, 61*(2), 136–151. doi:10.1016/j.scico.2005.10.009

Canal, C., Murillo, J. M., & Poizat, P. (2004). First international workshop on coordination and adaptation techniques for software entities. In C. Canal, J. M. Murillo, & P. Poizat (Eds.), *First International Workshop on Coordination and Adaptation Techniques for Software Entities,* (pp. 133-147). Berlin, Germany: Springer.

Canal, C., Murillo, J. M., & Poizat, P. (Eds.). (2008). Practical approaches to software adaptation. *Journal of Universal Computer Science, 14*(13).

Chu, Q., Shen, Y., & Jiang, Z. (2009). A transaction middleware model for SCA programming. In *Proceedings of the First International Workshop on Education Technology and Computer Science,* (pp. 568-571). IEEE.

Da Silva Maciel, L. A. H., & Hirata, C. M. (2009). An optimistic technique for transactions control using REST architectural style. In *Proceedings of the 2009 ACM Symposium on Applied Computing,* (pp. 664-669). ACM Press.

Da Silva Maciel, L. A. H., & Hirata, C. M. (2011). Extending timestamp-based two phase commit protocol for RESTful services to meet business rules. In *Proceedings of the 2011 ACM Symposium on Applied Computing,* (pp. 778–785). ACM.

Fielding, R. T. (2000). *Architectural styles and the design of network-based software architectures.* (Doctoral Dissertation). University of California. Irvine, CA.

Fowler, M. (2010). *Richardson maturity model.* Retrieved October 10, 2011, from http://martinfowler.com/articles/richardsonMaturityModel.html

Gail, N., Sholler, D., & Bradley, A. (2008). *Tutorial: Web-oriented architecture: Putting the web back in web service.* Retrieved October 10, 2011, from http://www.gartner.com/id=797713

Gu, Z., Li, J., & Xu, B. (2008). Automatic service composition based on enhanced service dependency graph. In *Proceedings of the 2008 IEEE International Conference on Web Services,* (pp. 246-253). IEEE.

Kell, S. (2008). A survey of practical software adaptation techniques. *Journal of Universal Computer Science, 14*(13), 2110–2157.

Kennedy, S., Stewart, R., Jacob, P., & Molloy, O. (2011). StoRHm: A protocol adapter for mapping SOAP based web services to RESTful HTTP format. *Electronic Commerce Research, 11*(3), 245–269. doi:10.1007/s10660-011-9075-3

Kent, S. (2002). Model driven engineering. In M. Butler, L. Petre, & K. Sere (Eds.), *Proceedings of the Third International Conference on Integrated Formal Methods,* (vol 2335, pp. 286-298). Springer-Verlag.

Laitkorpi, M., Koskinen, J., & Systa, T. (2006). A UML-based approach for abstracting application interfaces to REST-like services. In *Proceedings of the 13th Working Conference on Reverse Engineering,* (pp. 134-146). IEEE.

Laitkorpi, M., Selonen, P., & Systa, T. (2009). Towards a model-driven process for designing ReSTful web services. In *Proceedings of the 2009 IEEE International Conference on Web Services,* (pp. 173-180). IEEE.

Li, W., Zhang, Y., & Jin, J. (2009). Research of the service design approach based on SCA_OSGi. In *Proceedings of the 2009 International Conference on Services Science Management and Engineering,* (pp. 392–395). IEEE.

Liskin, O., Singer, L., & Schneider, K. (2011). Teaching old services new tricks: Adding HATEOAS support as an afterthought. In *Proceedings of the Second International Workshop on RESTful Design,* (pp. 3–10). ACM.

Little, M. (2009). *REST and transactions?* Retrieved October 10, 2011, from http://www.infoq.com/news/2009/06/rest-ts

Liu, Y., Wang, Q., Zhuang, M., & Zhu, Y. (2008). Reengineering legacy systems with RESTful web service. In *Proceedings of the 32nd Annual IEEE International Computer Software and Applications Conference,* (pp. 785-790). IEEE.

Marinos, A., Razavi, A., Moschoyiannis, S., & Krause, P. (2009). RETRO: A consistent and recoverable RESTful transaction model. In *Proceedings of the 2009 IEEE International Conference on Web Services,* (pp. 181-188). IEEE.

Navon, J., & Fernandez, F. (2011). The essence of REST architectural style. In Wilde, E., & Pautasso, C. (Eds.), *REST from Research to Practice.* Berlin, Germany: Springer. doi:10.1007/978-1-4419-8303-9_1

Pardon, G., & Pautasso, C. (2011). Towards distributed atomic transactions over RESTful services. In Wilde, E., & Pautasso, C. (Eds.), *REST from Research to Practice.* Berlin, Germany: Springer. doi:10.1007/978-1-4419-8303-9_23

Pautasso, C. (2009). RESTful web service composition with BPEL for REST. *Data & Knowledge Engineering, 68*(9), 851–866. doi:10.1016/j.datak.2009.02.016

Pautasso, C., & Wilde, E. (2009). Why is the web loosely coupled? A multi-faceted metric for service design. In *Proceedings of the 18th World Wide Web Conference,* (pp. 911-920). ACM.

Pautasso, C., Zimmermann, O., & Leymann, F. (2008). Restful web services vs. "big" web services: Making the right architectural decision. In *Proceeding of the 17th international conference on World Wide Web,* (pp. 805-814). ACM.

Razavi, A., Marinos, A., Moschoyiannis, S., & Krause, P. (2009). RESTful transactions supported by the isolation theorems. In *Proceedings of the 2009 International Conference on Web Engineering,* (pp. 394-409). Springer-Verlag.

Richardson, L., & Ruby, S. (2007). *RESTful web services.* New York, NY: O'Reilly.

Schmidt, D. C. (2006). Guest editor's introduction: Model-driven engineering. *Computer, 39*(2), 25-31.

Upadhyaya, B., Zou, Y., Xiao, H., Ng, J., & Lau, A. (2011). Migration of SOAP-based services to RESTful services. In *Proceedings of the 13th IEEE International Symposium on Web Systems Evolution,* (pp. 105–114). IEEE.

Vinoski, S. (2008). Serendipitous reuse. *IEEE Internet Computing, 12*(1), 84–87. doi:10.1109/MIC.2008.20

KEY TERMS AND DEFINITIONS

Architectural Style: A set of constraints on architectural elements (component, connectors, data elements), their features, their roles and their relationships applied in coordination to induce certain system-wide properties to the conforming architectures.

Model-Driven Engineering (MDE): Is a methodology based on creating, processing and using models to describe, develop and document software.

Representational State Transfer (REST): An architectural style for designing network-based hypermedia applications. REST includes six architectural constraints and was invented by Roy Fielding while developing HTTP.

RESTful Web Services: Is a collection of technologies and practices that utilize existing Web standards and protocols to develop and provide services over the Web.

Service Component Architecture (SCA): A collection of specifications that uses open standards and separates the concerns of non-functional requirements and service implementation assembly.

Software Adaptation: The actions related to producing a category of special computational component elements called adaptors in order to be able to reuse existing software artifacts in new applications without altering their implementation.

Web Services: A collection of standards and technologies to implement SOAs. Web Services use the SOAP family of protocols to exchange XML-based messages to access service functionality and return service results. Service interfaces usually include operations whose signatures and invocation mechanisms are described by WSDL documents. Web Services are centered on procedural conceptualizations of service capabilities.

Chapter 14
Model Driven Integration of Heterogeneous Software Artifacts in Service Oriented Computing

Eric Simon
Laboratoire Informatique de Grenoble, France

Jacky Estublier
Laboratoire Informatique de Grenoble, France

ABSTRACT

Systems evolutivity requires complex operations on services, including migration, duplication, updating, and a number of administration-related actions. However, current environments are heterogeneous and require integration to manage services. It is a complex problem, because it implies a transformation of life cycle related concepts. This integration does not fit very well in the service-oriented approach: indeed this approach is consumer-centered and considers that services are hosted by third parties, while administration is a provider view. Therefore, there is a gap between technologies used to compose applications and technologies that provide them. In the context of system adaptability, this gap becomes a major challenge to be solved. The authors propose an execution environment, which provides a homogeneous service representation used to integrate: their functionalities, their life-cycle and management operations, and lifecycle related concerns, like deployment. Their approach includes two integration mechanisms: the technologies integration supported by wrappers and concerns integration supported by the run-times.

INTRODUCTION

Current trend in software engineering aims to integrate a patchwork of artifacts like devices or software components in a global and common universe. We observe this trend for example in

DOI: 10.4018/978-1-4666-2488-7.ch014

the Ubiquitous Computing and Cloud Computing domains. It is interesting to observe that, despite of their opposite administration logic, these domains share a number of requirements related to distribution, dynamic discovery, composition and interoperability. On one hand, the Ubiquitous Computing domain aims to interconnect computing devices to provide added-value services to

Copyright © 2013, IGI Global. Copying or distributing in print or electronic forms without written permission of IGI Global is prohibited.

people. In this domain, the interaction between a consumer and devices has to be transparent. On the other hand, the Cloud Computing domain aims to virtualize the infrastructure and to modularize the framework, in order to execute a distributed application according to technical and financial requirements. The localization of the artifacts, presented as services, is not relevant. In these domains, the purpose is to focus on Quality of Service (QoS) like availability for instances. Here, it is the topology of the infrastructure, which is transparent.

Both domains require the integration of data and functions and use Service-Oriented Computing (SOC) to implement them. Data integration is related to data acquisition and transmission from a source system to a target system. Devices in the Ubiquitous Computing, and software components in the Cloud, are both developed to be reused. Consequently, they are not directly compatible and require some sort of alignment. In Service-Oriented Computing, this integration is generally made possible through abstraction (common format) or on the fly transformation. Functionalities integration aims to reuse the functionalities of an existing system. Similarly to data integration, being in the Cloud Computing or in the Ubiquitous Computing, functionalities are presented as Services to be shared and reused between systems. Indeed the Service-Oriented approach allows this integration type because it allows abstracting a legacy system to focus on its functionalities; it is the goal of the Enterprise Service Bus (ESB) technologies (Chappell, 2004). In this type of integration, the syntax, and the grammar of a description is transformed upon operation calls.

However, the administration logic of these two domains is really different. Indeed, in the Ubiquitous Computing domain, the adaptation and the administration of applications are driven by the changes of the devices availability. In the Ubiquitous Computing, the administration is made in a bottom-up way. In the Cloud Computing, the administration of the application is driven by the requirements of the application Quality of Service. In the Cloud, the administration is made in a top-down way. In both cases, devices and services in the Cloud are often implemented using different technologies. The multiplication of technologies in a same system involves the integration of the administration operations to automatize the administration or to be understandable and usable by a human administrator. However, administration integration is much more a complex problem than data and functionalities integration. It is no longer a data transformation or operation alignment issue but the transformation of life-cycle related concepts. Furthermore, contrarily to data and functionalities integration, administration integration does not fit very well in the Service-Oriented approach: indeed this approach is consumer-centered and considers that services are hosted by third parties, while the administration is based on a provider view. So there is a gap between the technologies used to compose applications (e.g.: BPEL [IBM, 2003]) and service consumers, and technologies that provide them.

However, the current needs in terms of adaptability and evolutivity of systems require the services migration, their duplication, updating, and a set of actions related to administration. Therefore, in the context of adaptability, this gap becomes a major challenge to be solved.

In the first section, we present the Cloud and Ubiquitous domains according to the administration needs for adaptation. This section extracts the essential information characterizing our problem.

In the second section, we propose an approach to design a platform for the Model Driven Integration of Heterogeneous Software Artifacts in Service Oriented Computing. This platform can be used as well for the Cloud Computing and the Ubiquitous Computing; indeed the underlying goal is to interconnect these two worlds.

The next section addresses the experimentations in a concrete use case on a platform named the Service Abstract Machine (SAM).

Finally, the last section concludes this chapter with the lessons learned.

CLOUD AND UBIQUITOUS: ADMINISTRATION PROBLEM

An essential characteristic of Cloud Computing and Ubiquitous Computing domains is the flexibility and the dynamicity of the execution environment. It is why most frameworks and approaches are based on the Service-Oriented approach. Briefly, the principle of the Service-Oriented approach (Service-Oriented Computing or simply SOC) is based on the separation between functionalities providers and consumers. The interaction between the provider and the consumer goes through abstract functionalities. This separation comes from the needs to separate the dynamism management from the implementation. These mechanisms provide theoretically dynamic features; for example, a consumer chooses a service based on its specification and it can potentially substitute it by another. This capacity allows the composition dynamic Service-Oriented applications. In summary, a Service:

- Is independent from the technology used to implement it;
- Has an abstract description which allows its discovery, binding, and invocation by a consumer;
- Has no dependency toward other services (Web).

Ironically, the main advantage of SOC which is the separation between the consumer/provider interaction protocol and the implementation becomes the main problem for the dynamically reconfigurable runtime architectures. Indeed, architectures are defined in term of interface, i.e. from the service point of view, while actual architectures are seem as composition of implementations, i.e. from a component point of view. However, the reconfigurability and the adaptability are central aspects of flexible system as the Cloud Computing or the Ubiquitous Computing.

In the remainder of this section, we detail the philosophies of the Cloud Computing and the Ubiquitous Computing, and their needs of administration to compose flexible applications.

Clouds

The concept of Cloud Computing is primarily commercial. The business model is to externalize servers park to third party companies allocating resources on-demand. These companies provide computing power and storage and they charge the resources actually used. These resource providers ensure the availability of resources as well as the isolation with other applications. Consequently, a company does not necessarily need to buy a dedicated servers park to ensure the availability of their applications. In consequence, a company has an illusion of infinite computing resources and does not need to set up plans for resource provisioning (Armbrust, 2009). Cloud Computing avoids an up-front commitment allowing a flexible development functions on the resources required (Armbrust, 2009). And finally, the ability to pay for use of computing resources allows reducing the application execution costs because the company does not maintain a dedicated servers park (Armbrust, 2009).

In summary, Cloud Computing can be viewed as the maintenance of resource pools with on-demand resource allocation.

For that, Cloud Computing implies to virtualize the hardware and to support the dynamically resize resource allocation or moving customers from one physical server to another transparently (Geelan, 2009).

In practice, the flexibility proposed by cloud provider is limited.

Take the example of Amazon EC 2 (Amazon, 2009), who virtualizes physical hardware, but not the platforms. A user must install a set of stack from the kernel to upwards. Consequently, scalability is limited because it is only possible to clone the stack on one or more servers. The software stack can be viewed as a unique instance.

Nevertheless in the case of AppEngine (Google) and AppScale (Chohan, 2010) (Open source implementation of AppEngine), flexibility is better because granularity is reduced in introducing a separation between the stateless computation tier and the storage tier. Each tier can be scaled on-demand.

However, the real challenge is not to clone one or two instances to support the scalability, but reduce the granularity of the service order to increase the application flexibility and try to guarantee better Quality of Service (QoS).

Application and Adaptation

In the case of Cloud Computing, the application is well defined and adaptation occurs in well-defined scenarios. Figure 1 shows an adaptation example. In the initial case, the running application is conformed to its definition but the CPU load exceeds the criteria defined by the QoS; consequently, a component is moved to reduce the CPU load.

In this example, the application is conformed to its definition. Theoretically in a top-down approach, applications are already conformed to their definition because they are been obtained by instantiation from their definition. Indeed a component does not arbitrarily disappear as a reevaluation of a binding. In Cloud Computing, as in other top-down approach, the application architecture is imposed, and we adapt the execution environment driven by the application definition and its QoS. Dynamism is limited and the set of possible scenarios is closed. Note that in Cloud, some services are provided by third-party companies like Utility Services. Consequently, these services are not be managed by application administrator and so they can be suddenly unavailable; application can become non-conforming to its definition.

In summary, in Cloud Computing, there are two adaptation types:

- Adapt the execution environment to respect some non-functional aspects;
- Repair the application to respect the functional definition.

Figure 1. Adaptation example from cloud computing

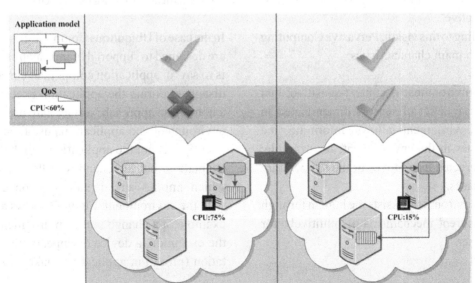

Figure 2. Adaptation example from ubiquitous computing

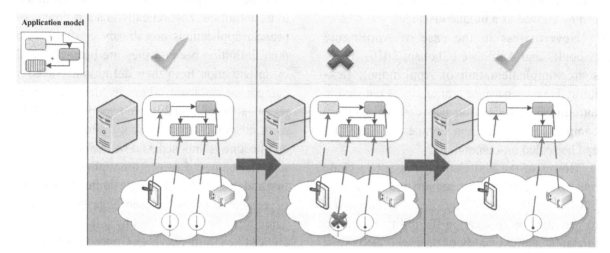

Ubiquitous Computing

Although the terms of Ubiquitous Computing and Pervasive Computing are generally used by people in an interchangeable way; these are two different concepts.

The aim of Pervasive Computing is to promote a physical environment, which assists humans in their daily tasks through computing devices (Lyytinen, 2002; Satyanarayanan, 2002; Lyytinen, 2010). The interactions between the user (human) and his environment (including computing devices) must be "transparent" or the least possible disruptive.

According to this vision, Pervasive Computing defines two main characteristics:

- The environment is context-sensitive; that is to say a set of sensors disseminated in the environment allows informing the changes in the environment; for example: the targeted user moves or the temperature increases.
- The environment assists the human through transparent mechanisms or intuitively for the user.

Both characteristics imply first that the interaction and the perception are restricted in space; and secondly that, devices must be self-configuring and could self-adapt according to users.

The Ubiquitous Computing introduces in Pervasive Computing the large-scale mobility aspect. "In its ultimate form, Ubiquitous Computing means any computing device, while moving with us, can build incrementally dynamic models of its various environments and configure its services accordingly" (Lyytinen, 2002).

Applications and Adaptation

In the case of Ubiquitous Computing, applications are designed to support dynamic availability; that is to say an application component can appear or disappear during the application execution. It is a bottom-up approach: services are present in the environment and applications use them. Consequently it is not the application which drives the adaptation, but the changes in the environment which implies an adaptation to be consistent with the environment. Figure 2 shows a reaction example of a change in the environment: during the execution, a device disappears; its representation (proxy) in application makes no sense to exist. Consequently, its representation is removed from the application.

Ubiquitous Computing is context-sensitive and it can have an infinite of scenarios for the application. In such context, we do not define an application but we try to constraint the execution environment to be consistent with a desired state. Note that some Ubiquitous approaches (Saha, 2010; Ferry, 2009) use both third-party services and proprietary services (and so manageable).

In summary, applications in Ubiquitous Computing are designed bottom-up and the adaptation is a reaction to changes in the execution environment.

Artifacts Administration

Although Pervasive Computing and Ubiquitous Computing have an interaction restricted in space, it does not mean that services are near users. Ubiquitous Computing can need to be coupled with a large-scale distributed system to provide some services to users. We argue the couple Cloud Computing (in the meaning of a private cloud where it is possible to act on a service function with QoS rules) and Ubiquitous Computing seems a realistic approach to make applications self-adapting according to the "Context." This approach is also adopted by the Minalogic national project: iDeviceCloud, where sensors are supported by local "smart" gateways interconnected thanks a global cloud (Minalogic, 2011).

We are aware that it is a very large problem. It is why, in this chapter we focus on the capability to move and adapt an application; more precisely on a set of administration properties must have the application's artifacts. Now, in Cloud like in Ubiquitous we can distinguish three types of artifacts:

- Service (consumer view), e.g. Web-Service;
- Embedded-Service, e.g. UPnP and DPWS;

- Service provider, e.g. Component approach (WS-Spring, EJB…) or Service-Oriented Component (iPOJO, SCA, Blueprint…).

Service (Consumer View)

A Service element like Web-Service is a view of functionalities. A Service is software resource that provides a standard functionality and which is independent of the state or context of other services (Papazoglou, 2007). A service is described by an external service description. The description is available for searching, binding, and invoking (Arsanjani, 2004). In summary, service is an architectural style to expose functionalities independently from implementation. Consequently, a service has natively not administration operations as create of destroy instances, because it is simply an invocation façade.

As defined by Papazoglou (2007), services are independent of context of other services. An application is built with the preexisting services. It is a bottom-up approach where the only choice for adaptation is to replace a service by existing one another.

Embedded Service

As defined in the Ubiquitous Computing section, the devices or the software functionalities in the environment are presented as services. Contrary to usual services, an embedded-service has a dynamic availability: an embedded-service can appear or disappear during the execution.

However, a device can have states and this is generally the case like in UPnP (UPnP Forum). Second point, generally the life cycle of device services is associated to the device; indeed, it has no sense to create, destroy, or move a service which is a representation of a physical object: temperature or humidity sensors. However, we currently see appear ubiquitous devices (e.g. smartphone, smart sensors…) where it is possible to deploy proprietary services. Consequently, as well as proprietary service is manageable, the service has a dynamic availability too; in consequence, we have a merger between the top-down and the bottom-up approaches for the administration. In summary, embedded-services have dynamic availability and might have administration operations.

Service Provider

Service is an architectural style of communication hiding the functionalities implementation. The service provider is the implementation of service. In the case where the service is provided by a third party then this element is not available. In the other case, that is a proprietary service, this element is the implementation, which provides the service. This implementation like component should provide administration operations. Consequently, in the case of a Service-based application where the services are proprietary then the adaptations possibilities are numerous; for example: create, destroy, or migrate a service. Since it is a proprietary service, its life cycle is mastered and it does not evolve independently of the administrator.

Service-Oriented Component Approach

Currently, some approaches based on the Service-Oriented Component are used in the Ubiquitous Computing, like iPOJO (Escoffier, 2007) or Blueprint (OSGi Alliance, 2009), and in large-scale distributed systems (including Grid and Cloud) with SCA (OSOA).

The Service-Oriented Component approach appeared for the first time with Cervantes and Hall (2004). They define that the approach "introduces concept from service orientation into a component model. The motivation for such a combination emerges from the need to introduce explicit support for dynamic availability into a component model" (p. 3) (Cervantes & Hall, 2004). According to this approach, loose coupling is introduced between components of an application. It allows supporting dynamic availability and offers con-

sequently more facilities to adapt application. However, the application is built following a bottom-up approach where each component tries to resolve its dependencies at execution; there is no application model. In the case of SCA, the use of Service-Oriented Component approach offers a better flexibility for the applications. However, application is defined with an assembly model following a top-down approach. Variability and dynamic availability are not defined and so not supported natively.

In summary, Service-Oriented Component approach:

- Provides service administration operations from Component approach;
- Supports generally the dynamic availability.

Characterizations and Challenges

In this chapter, we address only the capability to act on the application's artifacts. This problem can seem simple but Cloud Computing and Ubiquitous Computing suffer from the same problem: services heterogeneity regarding to both technological and behavioral.

Consequently, we propose an execution environment, which integrates the wider services from different technologies in characterizing their behavior. This characterization is necessary to build a reliable application. Indeed, for example, we do not bind a component with an embedded-service if the component does not support a dynamic availability of the dependency.

For the services integration, we are mainly interested on the following administration operations: create, destroy, and link instances. In the case of the service characterization, we focus on both dynamic availability (behavior) and their supported administration operations (nature).

In summary, we target the following application:

Table 1. Characterization artifacts according to their nature

	Only Usable	*Usable and Manageable*
Static availability	• In practice Service (WS…)	• Service provider (Component…) • Service-Oriented Component (SCA)
Dynamic availability	• Embedded-Service (UPnP, DPWS…)	• Service-Oriented Component (iPOJO, Blueprint)

Figure 3. Software artifacts classification

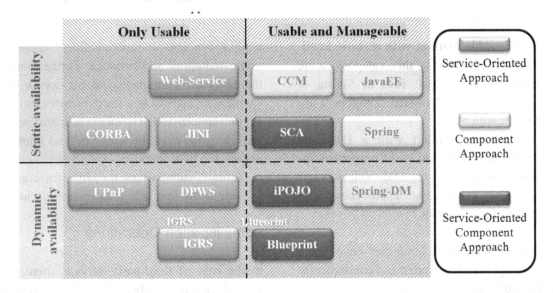

- Built using a mix of top-down and bottom-up approaches;
- With artifacts from heterogeneous technologies;
- With artifacts having different natures, summarized in the Table 1.

A HOMOGENEOUS REPRESENTATION OF THE EXECUTION ENVIRONMENT FOR THE ADMINISTRATION

Ubiquitous Computing domain aims to interconnect computing devices to provide a service for users. Cloud Computing domain aims to virtualize the infrastructure and to granulize the framework, in order to execute a distributed application according to requirements, technical aspects or financial aspects. These two approaches are different on a number of aspects: application definition: top-down versus bottom-up; adaptation needs: QoS optimization versus application consistence with the physical world. In spite of their differences, these two domains share a same need: dynamic and automatic adaptation. In this chapter, we focus on the administration of application's artifacts.

As shown by Figure 3, the artifacts, which compose the applications, can be put into four categories:

- **Artifact only usable with a static availability:** Service-Oriented Architecture such as Web-Service;
- **Artifact only usable with a dynamic availability:** Embedded-Services technologies such as DPWS or UPnP;

Table 2. Concepts existing in the different approaches

	Service-Oriented Architecture	Embedded-Services	Component	Service-Oriented Component
Functionalities description	Yes	Yes	Yes	Yes
Implementation	No	No	Yes	Yes
Instance	~Endpoint	~Endpoint	Yes	Yes
Dependency	No	No	Yes	Yes

- **Manageable artifact with a static availability:** We find in this category some Component approach such as Spring or CCM as Service-Oriented Component approach with SCA;
- **Manageable artifact with a Dynamic availability:** We find still Component approaches with Spring-DM and Service-Oriented Component approaches with iPOJO and Blueprint.

These approaches/technologies have goals and challenges really different and consequently they have not all:

- The same concepts;
- Administration operations;
- A dynamic behavior.

We will see in the next sections these three points according to different technologies/approaches, which are: the Service-Oriented Architectures, the Embedded-Services Technologies, the Component Approaches and the Service-Oriented Component Approaches.

Concepts

Among the four types of artifacts, we can classify them between third-party services and service providers. In the case of third-party service, only the functionalities description containing the addresses of invocation points (Endpoint) is available; while the service providers have the explicit concepts of functionalities description, implementation, and instance. Furthermore, in the cases of Component and Service-Oriented Component approaches, the dependencies are an explicit concept too. It is not the case of all service providers; for example, OSGi defines implicitly in code the dependencies.

Table 2 summarizes the different concepts existing in the four technologies/approaches.

Administration Operations

In the case of third-party service, there is no administration operation; indeed, it is complex to administrate a service instance if there is no access to the service implementation or the instance. Note that extensions exist for any Service-Oriented Architecture to manage service like WS-Management (DMTF, 2010); however, they allow only modifying functional parameters, but not act on the service life cycle.

In the case of service providers, it is possible to deploy a service implementation and instantiates a service instance. Nevertheless all service providers do not explicitly provide the administration operations to instantiate or dispose a service instance. For example, it is the case for OSGi, where service instances life cycle is implemented in the deployment units.

Although the link modification is permitted, it does not make of the same way. Indeed, in the case of Component approaches and of SCA for the Service-Oriented Component, the link modification is made by the administrator or

Table 3. Basic administration operations existing in the different approaches

	Service-Oriented Architecture	Embedded-Services	Component	Service-Oriented Component
Install/Uninstall	No	No	Yes	Yes
Instantiate/Dispose	No	No	Yes	Yes
Link modifications	No	No	Yes (top-down)	Yes (top-down or bottom-up)

by the middleware according to the application model (top-down way); whereas in the case of Service-Oriented Component approaches such as iPOJO, this modification is made by the service instance or by the service instance container itself (bottom-up way).

Table 3 summarizes the different administration operations authorized in the four technologies/approaches.

Dynamic Behavior

Finally, we focus on the artifacts behavior on their availability. Indeed, what is important in architecture is whether an artifact used can appear or disappear unexpectedly. In most Service-Oriented Architectures (SOA), services are, in practice, supposed to be always here or have a QoS guarantying a good availability. Indeed, generally the services from classic SOAs (WS, CORBA…) do not appear and do not disappear every minute! It is not necessarily the case of embedded service, where their availability depends on the context changes. It is little more complicate in the case of components and Service-Oriented Components. Some approaches do not support dependencies on services, which have a dynamic availability; while others do. However, in the technologies, which support it, artifacts have not necessarily a dynamic behavior. For example, the availability of a temperature service, which requires a temperature sensor, depends of the dynamic behavior of the sensor: if the sensor is always here then the temperature service has a static availability,

whereas if the sensor can appear or disappear then the temperature service has a dynamic behavior.

In simplifying, the dynamic availability can be resumed at the simple question: Does the technology supports dynamic availability? Can the service appear and disappear without anyone explicitly acting on it?

Note the following three points:

- The behavior of an artifact is under control of the administrator and is consequently considered as static;
- The behavior is not under control and consequently it is considered as dynamic;
- A dependency support or not the dynamic availability of required services.

Table 4 summarizes the different availabilities for the artifacts of the four technologies/approaches.

ABSTRACTION APPROACH

We want to be able to administrate the life cycle of the different artifacts of an application. However, on one hand these artifacts can be a third-party service, embedded service or proprietary service where only proprietary service is manageable. On the other hand, these services do not use from the same technology; consequently, it is necessary to integrate both the service functionalities and their life cycle operations for the proprietary service.

For that, we propose an execution environment which provides a homogeneous representation of

Table 4. Dynamic behavior from the administrator view

	Service-Oriented Architecture	Embedded-Services	Component	Service-Oriented Component
Dynamic availability of the artifact	According to the QoS, in practice: No	Yes	According to: the technology, the component implementation and its dependencies	
Dynamic availability supported by the dependencies	The dependency concept does not exist		According to the dependency	

Figure 4. The execution environment

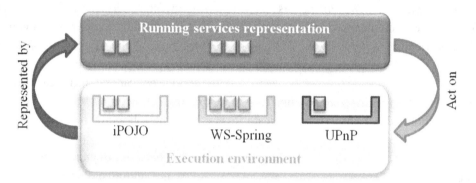

services and which integrates their available life cycle operations. Consequently, this representation describes the execution state of running heterogeneous services and it is possible to act on them through the representation (see Figure 4).

Furthermore, to adapt an application, the information and the life cycle on the running service are not generally sufficient. Consequently, the execution environment contains extension mechanisms to integrate new concerns.

In the remainder of this section, we will first discuss on the integration mechanisms of heterogeneous services. In a second step, we will address the integration mechanisms of other concerns. And finally, we will introduce some results of our experimentations.

Vertical Integration: Abstraction of Services in a Homogeneous Model

Our execution environment is structural into three parts:

- The set of existing service technologies;
- The wrappers which translate the concepts and the life-cycle operations;
- The homogeneous environment which allows manipulating the concepts translated into a model.

As shown in Figure 5, the principle is that each technology is subsumed by a specific wrapper. The wrappers make the translation of concepts and life-cycle operations from the specific technology to the homogeneous model layer and reciprocally.

Homogeneous Model Layer

Our homogeneous model layer allows accessing to an existing service from a specific technology and to manipulate this life cycle if the operations are reachable and authorized. For that, we have defined, in a first step, a service meta-model based on the Service-Oriented Component ap-

Figure 5. Integration mechanism of services

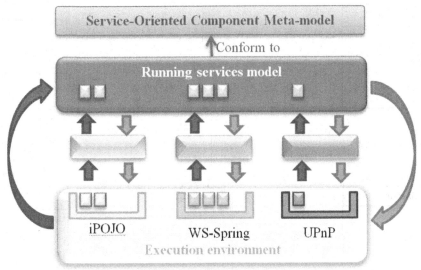

proach. Indeed, this paradigm presents three main advantages:

1. An homogeneous model that can represent a service, an embedded service, a component or a Service-Oriented Component;
2. A sufficient granularity close to the execution;
3. A permissive model for the dynamic aspects.

A Service is thus a software artifact providing functionalities, but not necessarily invocation interfaces or invocation endpoints. This definition includes components, which do not provide functionalities. An artifact (Service) has several aspects: specification, implementation, and instance, which are different materializations of the concept. Consequently, Specification, Implementation, and Instance are subclasses of the artifact abstract class.

The Figure 6 defines the concept of service as artifact during the execution. The three materializations of a service are required to analyze and adapt the execution. Consequently this meta-model defines the following concepts:

*   A Specification is the abstract definition of a service. A Service is a consistent set of functionalities described by zero or more interfaces. A Specification contains a set of explicit dependencies, through relationships references, towards others Service Specifications. Furthermore, it has a set of properties characterizing a part of this behavior according to a specific concern. For the third-party service and the embedded service, specifications are a translation of their abstract description like WSDL or SCPD. For the Service-Oriented Component like Component, specification is abstract description for an equivalence component set; in this case, specification contains both the functional interfaces and the dependencies. Consequently, it is possible to substitute an implementation by another sharing the same specification without changing the dependency relationships. It is possible with our specification concept to represent the conceptual architecture independently of implementations.
*   An Implementation is the code realizing a specification. This code can be, for ex-

Figure 6. Meta-model of the homogeneous model

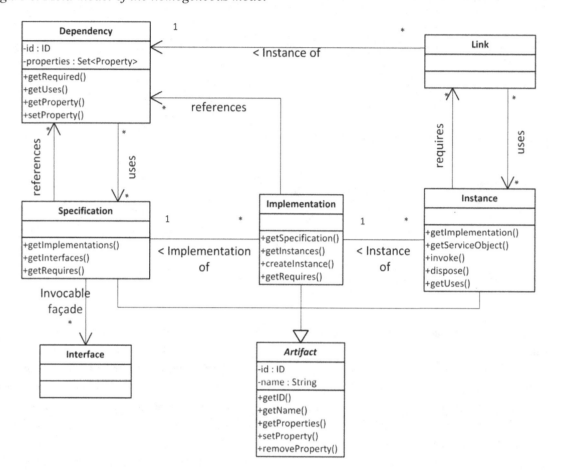

ample, an instance factory, a simple class, or the component container. In all cases, it must be the functional code of the artifact. Conversely, a specification may be provided by a number of implementations, and can be considered as equivalent. The provides relationship has a strong semantics: the implementation object inherits all the properties values, relationships and interfaces of its specifications. An implementation can add dependencies, through relationship references, toward other specifications. For the Service-Oriented Component and the Component approaches, the implementation concept is the component implementation. If the implementation allows, the representation provides

the administration operation to create an instance. However, for the third-party service or the embedded-service, we considered the proxy implementation as the implementation of the service; however in this case it is not possible instantiate ourselves an instance, because it correspond to a remote and unique service which is not manageable.

• Instances are runtime entities corresponding to the execution of an implementation. An instance inherits all the properties and relationships of its associated implementation; and for that reason, it provides and requires specifications of their implementation. For the Service-Oriented Component and the Component approaches, the translation of the instance concept is trivial: it is the component instance. For the third-party service and the embedded-service, the instance concept is the corresponding proxy. Note that, only component-based approaches (including Service-Oriented Component) have dependencies; and consequently only they may have instance dependencies relationship (link). A client can invoke the running service either in using the link on the instance concept to the real service, or with the invoke reflective operation on the instance.

- A Dependency is the definition of dependency to a specification. More simply, it is an explicit declaration of a link, which could be existed during the execution between two instances.
- A Link is a dependency instance. It links two instances during the execution. A Link has the property of this dependency.

Each concept has predefined properties:

- Specification, Implementation and Instance can have dynamic or static property (exclusive); for dynamic, it means that their life cycle is not totally under-control and they can appear or disappear during the execution. Static means their life cycle is under control of the administrator and they are theoretically already available. If a static materialization of service disappears then it will be treated as an error.
- Implementation can have the Instantiable=true property. It means that it is possible to instantiate a service instance from the implementation.
- Instance can have the Disposable property. If true then the dispose administration operation is available.
- Dependency can have the Dynamic property. It means that the dependency support the dynamic availability required services.

For example, it can dynamically select another service instance implementing the same specification.

The meta-model that we propose allows representing applications composed with heterogeneous artifacts and acting on them. However, the runtime model changes during the execution, consequently we continually reconstruct it and we emit events for each change in the architecture: apparition, disappearing and modification on the three materialization of an artifact. Consequently, the runtime model of services is supported by our platform, which provides:

- A register for each materialization;
- An event mechanism for the change notification.

Platform must guarantee the consistency between the representation and the execution reality.

Wrappers

Third-party service, embedded-service and service provider (component-based approach) have very different concepts. However, even for each approach, each technology has differences for the syntax, the semantics or, more bothering, for the artifacts administration. Consequently, although the artifacts can be classified into four main categories, it is necessary that each technology is supported by a specific wrapper which makes the translation from the target technology to our model and reciprocally: from our model to the technology.

From a Specific Technology to the Homogeneous Model

The Figure 7 shows the mechanisms to integrate the iPOJO service in our homogeneous model. There are two main mechanisms: mechanism for the representation and mechanism to act on the

Figure 7. Mechanism for a descriptive model of iPOJO

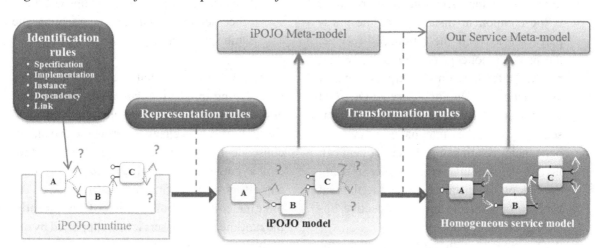

Table 5. Identification example of concepts for the AXIS2, UPnP, and iPOJO technologies

	AXIS 2	UPnP	iPOJO
Functionalities description	Java interface generated from the WSDL	Java interface generated from the SCPD[1]	The Java interfaces of the component provided as service
Implementation	Implementation of the Java proxy	Implementation of the Java proxy	Component (Factory at the runtime)
Instance	The proxy	The proxy	The instance registered in the OSGi registry
Dependency	\	\	Dependency Handler

running service. In a first time, a wrapper identifies elements required for the three materializations. In a second step, it uses these elements to build the runtime model conforming to the meta-model of the technology. Finally, we make a transformation from the specific runtime model to our model. Information from the specific technology is used to characterize the services: dynamic, instatiable…

Identification is the most difficult part. For the component-based approach, the semantic discrepancy is low, and is not a real problem. In the case of third-party service and the embedded service, the concepts of implementations and instances do not generally exist; but a simple solution is to consider the implementation and the instance of proxy as respectively the concepts of implementation and instance.

The Table 5 shows an identification example of concepts for technologies.

However, service providers are difficult to integrate; typically: OSGi. In OSGi, the principle is that a module (deployment unit) can be deployed and activated. The module can provide services and require other services; but this information is implicit, there is no declaration. Everything is entangled in the module, the life cycle of services is coded in the module and does not necessarily correspond to the life cycle of the module. It is very difficult to identify finely, during the execution, the specification, implementation, and dependency concepts. In the case of OSGi, several strategies can be applied:

- Consider the bundle as the implementation of services which allows integrating

Figure 8. Mechanism for a prescriptive model of iPOJO

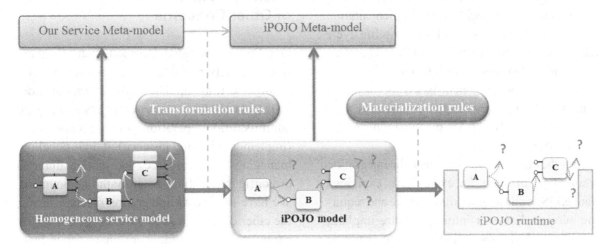

coarsely the OSGi services in our homogeneous model;

- Migrate the OSGi bundle in a technology easily supported; that is to say: migrate the OSGi code to a technology providing a finer granularity like the component-based approaches;
- An intermediate solution is to add missing metadata in the module that will be supported by the corresponding wrapper; thus preventing the code migration.

From the Homogeneous Model to a Specific Technology

The obtained model can be used to manage the "real" services. For that, the rules of translation are coded in the specific element and when an administration operation is called, this code is called to act on the elements of the specific technology.

Conceptually, the principle is to define the transformation rules from our Service-Oriented Component meta-model to the specific meta-model, in the Figure 8: iPOJO, and then wrappers are used to materialize the action on the "real" services. For the third-party service and the embedded-service, the life cycle administration operations are not available and this mechanism

is useless. For the service providers, it depends on the technology and the artifact. For example, it is easy to instantiate from an implementation but it is not already authorized. For OSGi, the creation of a specific instance is not possible because the implementation concept and so its life-cycle administration operations are not defined.

Synthesis and Limitations

The aim of a wrapper is to subsume a specific technology. A wrapper defines a meta-model of the technology for the service concern and knows our meta-model. It defines the transformation rules:

- For the bottom-up way (technology to our model), the rules are used to instantiate and characterize the different materializations in the homogeneous model from the targeted elements of the technology;
- For the top-down way (homogeneous model to the technology), the rules allow to generate the code in the materialization to translate the operations to a set of technology dependent operations.

In the case of third-party services and embedded-services, the semantic alignment is relatively easy: only the specification is translated, proxy is used to materialize the implementation and instance concepts; and finally, no life cycle administration operation is available. The characterization depends on each service.

In the case of component-based approach, the semantic discrepancy for the concepts is very low, and generally, the life cycle administration operations are defined.

For the other service providers, the integration can be very difficult; for example, as explained above, OSGi allows providing service and requiring service; however information are implicit, the life cycle is not defined and the semantic discrepancy is a real gap. It is always possible to integrate services; however, their administration may not be possible. Therefore, if the administration of an artifact with a strong semantic gap is required, it is necessary to migrate to a technology that allows its administration.

In summary, a major part of our approach for the integration of the life-cycle administration operations is supported by the wrappers. Although some artifacts can be integrated, any technologies are too complicated to integrate them properly. We think that this approach is interesting for the application including legacy artifacts where the code migration can be too expensive or simply not necessary; because it allows providing a "best effort" representation of technologies; that is to say that the representation can do at least that the targeted technology allows doing.

We are aware that for adaptation need exposed above, on the one hand, these three materializations are not enough to represent the system and on the other hand the life-cycle operations: create, dispose and rebind, are not enough too. It is why our approach defines integration mechanisms of other concerns.

Integration Mechanisms of Other Concerns

Our Service-Oriented Component meta-model is deliberately restricted. This meta-model is a minimal set to manipulate the running application. This meta-model alone provides basic life-cycle administration operations on the component (implementation and instance). It does not allow managing other resources like native libraries or configuration file or simply the deployment. We have defined an integration mechanism for the other concerns to add new concept, add new administration operations, or characterize for a given view concepts from other concerns. We have identified three extension types for the concerns:

- The extensions which are designed to integrate the execution state of concerns of the underlying technologies such as deployment (see Figure 8). For this extension type, we have generalized our approach for services for the other concerns, that we named: integration runtime;
- The extensions which aim to add a specific concern at the homogeneous model independently technologies, such as a deployment unit repository based on the deployment concerns (see Figure 8). This extension type does not require integration mechanism for the technologies. We named this type: runtime;
- The extensions are intended to act on the homogeneous state models to manage or guaranteed an aspects as running an application; named: manager. This chapter does not address this extension type.

Nevertheless, in the Service-Oriented Computing, there are a number of concerns that may overlap. Natively, we do not seek to resolve the competition between two extensions. However, we define an execution environment specialized for a given execution context. As for the

Figure 9. Generalization of the reflexive model for other concerns

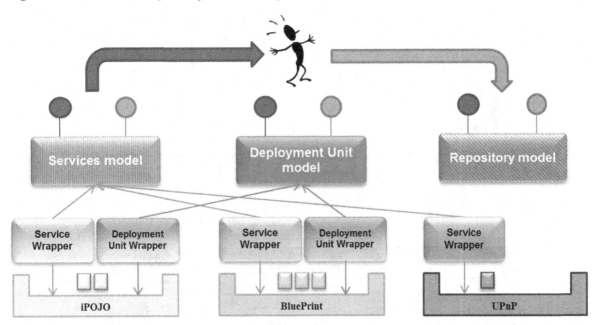

Service-Oriented technologies, we never add random concerns; it is the administrator (human or machine) to support the composition of the execution environment and to resolve conflicts related to recovery.

Figure 9 shows an execution environment with two extensions: an integration runtime for the deployment-unit concept and a runtime for the repositories of deployment-unit. In this example, the deployment-unit integrates the underlying technologies in a homogeneous execution state model. Indeed the deployment-unit administration: install, uninstall, activate, and deactivate depends on the artifact framework. In this case too, it is necessary to integrate the concept and its administration operations. The repository concept can be built over the deployment-unit concept; that is to say, it uses the concept of deployment-unit from the homogeneous model and delegates the administration to the concerning extension: deployment-unit runtime.

Figure 10 is an example of an extended meta-model according to the Deployment-Unit and Repository concepts. In this example the Deploy-ment-Unit meta-model references and reuses some concepts from the Service-Oriented Component meta-model. A Deployment-Unit is "tangible" unit, which will be copied and transferred, where it uses to package the classes that can be shared, loaded, and used. In our case, the Deployment-Unit extension represents the deployment-units existing in the execution environment; consequently, the deployment-units are already installed. The administration operations for this concept are limited to uninstall, activate (load), and deactivate (unload). A deployment-unit contains resources such as Class, Package, or Artifact. Furthermore it can require—requires relationship—other deployment-units and these links—uses relationship—are derived from the links between instances.

The Repository extension allows finding a Deployment-Unit according to a query and installing it.

These two extensions provide more administration operations and increase the number of possible adaptation scenarios. However, this example shows an implicit problem: the notion of

Figure 10. Service-oriented component meta-model extended

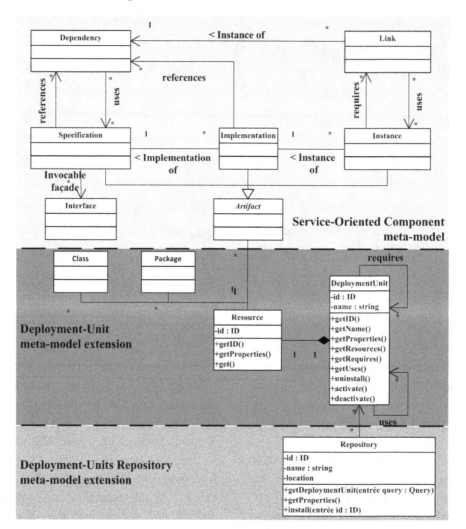

state. If a Deployment-Unit is only in the repository then it is not reachable through the execution state model of deployment-units. If it is installed but not activated then the artifacts will not be reachable through the service execution state model. Consequently, depending on the state of a concept instance, it could be reference or used in other extensions as shows in Figure 11. The semantic of concept is invariant, but it can be enriched by other concerns and the manipulation context changes too.

Last point, this architecture type is a problem at the implementation phase. Indeed, if a client finds a deployment-unit in a repository, he keeps the reference during the installation. However, implement a transparent mechanism to move from an execution state model to another to guarantee the continuity of an instance concept is complicated.

Synthesis and Limitations

In summary, our extensions mechanism allows supporting other concerns of technologies and providing new features: new concepts, new properties (such as state property), and new administrations operations. This approach modularizes concerns

Figure 11. Reusability of concepts between extensions

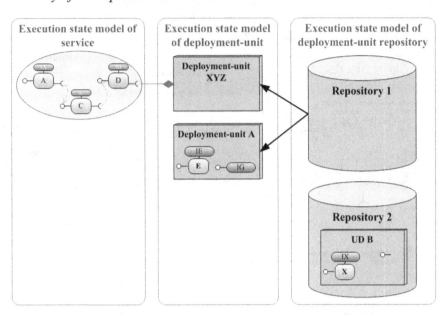

and allows composing easily an execution environment for given needs on the demand. However, the implementation of such extensions is complicated; indeed to keep continuity of a concept instance during the execution.

Conclusion of the Approach

The targeted problem is the capability to act on the artifacts of a service-based application. This problem is not simple, so Cloud Computing, Ubiquitous Computing, and other software approaches suffer of a same problem: the services used to compose applications can be very heterogeneous regarding both technology and behavior.

The approach, allows integrating both heterogeneous services and their life-cycle administration operations. Establishing that these administration operations on services are not sufficient to adapt application for the Cloud and the Pervasive Computing needs, we have define some mechanism to integrate other concerns such as the deployment. This approach provides representations can be at least that the targeted technology allows doing. However, it delegates

some difficulties either on the wrappers either on the extensions. Indeed any technologies are too complicated to integrate their artifacts and any concerns seem too complicated to integrate them such as security.

However, we still believe that this approach is interesting for the application including legacy artifacts, which is one of the problems of the Cloud Computing and the Ubiquitous Computing.

IMPLEMENTATION AND EXPERIMENTATIONS

We have implemented much of the approach proposed above; that we named: Service Abstract Machine or simply SAM (Adele, 2007). This implementation has been used in three projects. In the remainder of this section, we will introduce briefly the implementation; then its use in the three projects and finally we will evaluate the cost of the integration overhead.

Figure 12. SAM architecture

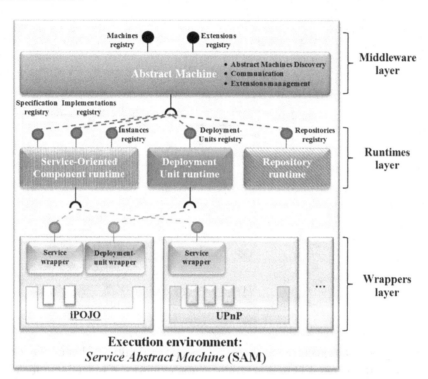

Implementation

SAM is implemented over the OSGi and iPOJO technologies following the Service-Oriented approach. SAM can be decomposed in three layers:

- The middleware layer, named Abstract Machine (AM), provides the discovery, communication and notifications protocols, as well a registry containing the different standardized extensions, and another registry containing the representation of the different discovered machines.
- The runtimes layer is the set of the different runtimes: in our case the Service-Oriented Component, Deployment-Units and Repository runtimes. Each extension exposes as extension services its functionalities. Extension services are required by the Abstract Machine.

- The wrappers layer is the set of wrappers, which allow integrating the different concerns of a technology. We have implemented Services wrappers for iPOJO, UPnP, DPWS, and partially for the Web-Services (AXIS 2); and a Deployment-Unit wrapper for iPOJO. The way to integrate the wrappers is specific to each runtime.

The Figure 12 exhibits the SAM architecture.

Experimentations

SAM has been implemented and experimented partially for the SEMbySEM (2007) European project (ITEA2), but it has been reused in two internal projects of our team: FOCAS (Pedaraza, 2008; Pedaraza, 2009) and Selecta (Estublier, 2009; Estublier, 2010). These three projects have test and validate different mechanisms of our approach. In the remainder of this section, we will describe the SEMbySEM project and briefly the FOCAS and Selecta projects.

SEMbySEM

SEMbySEM is a research project funded by the European Commission within the ITEA2 programme. It aims to provide a software system dedicated to the monitoring and management of systems of all sizes. It uses semantic representations of the components from which systems are made up (SEMbySEM, 2007).

The Abstract Machine has been used to constitute the distributed execution environment of the infrastructure and SAM for the sensors integration exposed as services. In the project, SAM has been mainly used for managing the dynamism; precisely for the apparition and the disappearing of sensors and Abstract Machines. The application used by the demonstrator, explained on "SEMbySEM Demonstrator" site (Adele, 2010), has been implemented programmatically.

FOCAS

The FOCAS project (Framework for Orchestration, Composition, and Aggregation of Services) (Pedaraza, 2008, 2009) is an internal project of our team which uses:

- The process model of workflow technology as a central and structuring;
- The technology of service-oriented approach for the implementation of its processes in order to obtain the flexibility provided by the properties of loose coupling and late binding;
- The model-driven engineering to provide a framework for the effective implementation of the project.

FOCAS has used SAM in the one of its implementation to use heterogeneous services: iPOJO,

UPnP, DPWS and partially the Web-Services with Axis2. In summary, the FOCAS orchestrator uses SAM such as an abstraction layer hiding the underlying technologies. It does not seek to deploy or manage services; it uses it for the services integration in its execution space.

Selecta

The Selecta project (Estublier, 2009, 2010) is an internal project too. It is a selection language, which uses to define a high enough level of abstraction, the concepts of composite applications. One of use of the Selecta language was to implement a composer for the service-based application from an abstract application model. This composer has been implemented over SAM using the Service-Oriented Component and the Deployment-Unit extensions to deploy and initialize iPOJO service-based applications defined by models. In summary, Selecta uses SAM to integrate services functionalities and the administration operations on the services and the deployment-units.

Integration Overhead

The three previous projects validate the functionalities but not to evaluate the overhead of the integration. Consequently, we have defined a test protocol to evaluate the integration overhead between SAM and the iPOJO technology. We have compared the performance of an application running on a bare iPOJO platform with respect to the same application running on SAM. The test "application" is made of a large number of instances; each instance is connected to two other similar instances forming therefore a binary tree of service instances. The principle of the test is:

- A recursive instantiation of a binary tree: the memory used and the time are observed before and after the instantiation.

Figure 13. Overhead test on a binary tree

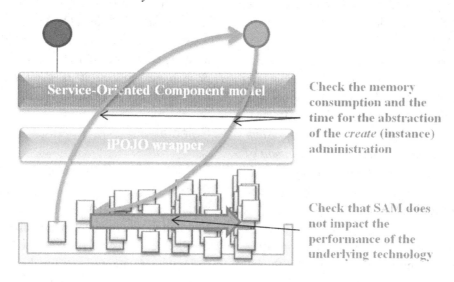

Figure 14. Instantiation: 1) used memory and 2) time

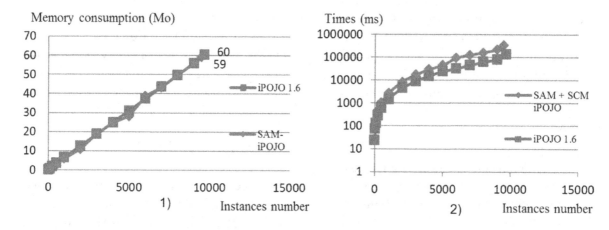

- A recursive invocation on the first node of the tree: the time is observed at the beginning and at the end of the invocation.

In first step, we perform this test on the iPOJO technology. Then we redirect the instantiation operation of iPOJO on the operation of the implementation concept instance of our service execution sate model. And finally we perform again the test. As shown in the Figure 13, the first step allows evaluating the integration overhead of the instantiation operation; the second step

allows checking that SAM does not impact the performance of the underlying technology.

Evaluation has been performed on the SAM implementation (version 1.3.0) based on the iPOJO technology (version 1.6.0) with the following configuration: Intel Core Duo E8600 3.33GHz, 4GB of RAM, running over Windows XP and JDK 1.6.0 18. Figure 14 shows the results.

In this evaluation, the number of created objects for the translation of the instantiation from SAM to iPOJO is insignificant. The second diagram shows that the SAM progression curve of the instantiation time follows the iPOJO progression curve. On average, the gap between iPOJO and SAM for the invocation is less than 1%; consequently we consider that the invocation time is not impacted. Indeed SAM does not act on the service calls between a consumer and a provider coming from the same SOA. Note that the overhead is specific for each technologies according to mechanisms used to integrate it.

Experimentations Synthesis and Limitations

The three projects have used SAM to build applications in three different ways: programmatic (SEMbySEM), orchestration (FOCAS) and structural composition driven by models (Selecta); consequently, SAM can be used in a number of domains.

The integration of the services functionalities has been checked by the FOCAS project for the iPOJO, UPnP, DPWS and partially for Web-Services; and by SEMbySEM and Selecta for iPOJO too.

The integration of the administration operations for the services and the deployment-units has been checked by the Selecta project.

The extensibility mechanism has been checked by Selecta with the Deployment-Unit extension.

Finally, the notification mechanism for the dynamism has been checked by the SEMbySEM project for the different materialization (Specification, Implementation and Instance) of services and for the Abstract Machines layer.

The experimentations show that the SAM goal to hide heterogeneity providing a homogeneous execution state model has been reached, but "low level" legacy services cannot support high level operations like semantic of structural composites. The full capability of the approach can only be obtained when developing SAM service using a specific software engineering environment. Consequently a native SAM Service-oriented Component framework is currently developed; on the one hand, to use the full capability for

adaptation; and to the other hand, to provide a reference framework when the migration of an artifact is required. This experimentation is partially developed for the SEMbySEM European project, which has used SAM functionalities to implement a distributed and dynamic application.

During the different experimentations, the mainly difficulties came from the semantic discrepancies between the meta-models used in traditional SOC technologies and our meta-model. When using legacy services, it is not possible to get, from the underlying platform, all the information that can appear in SAM meta-model. Nevertheless, the wrappers having a deep knowledge of the underlying technology can infer some of the missing information. This is the case for the dynamic behavior attributes, but also for other attributes as well. In this point of view, the SAM execution state models are the best possible approximation of the reality.

A second difficulty is that SOC technologies do not provide the same features (e.g.: distribution, management, security, etc.), which may require extensive development for specific technologies to support a particular activity such as the package management. SAM does not try to address all the concerns of SOA platforms in Service-Oriented Component model, those missing concerns are simply out of the scope of the Service-Oriented Component meta-model. We rely instead on the SAM extension mechanism to address them.

FUTURE RESEARCH DIRECTIONS

From the conceptual point of view, there are two interesting directions. The first is to define an environment from the design to the execution of an application; that is to say, treats the design, implementation, configuration, deployment, and execution phases in a homogeneous environment to be able to bridge the semantic discrepancies in providing the missing or implicit information from target technologies. The second direction is to explore other concerns much more complex such as the security or the transaction aspect.

From the technical point of view, there is an interesting direction: the experimentations in FOCAS and SEMbySEM have shown a limitation for the embedded-services and third-party services whose are the generic proxy dependent of a specific technology. In these projects, we have predeployed specific proxies to support the generic proxy. Consequently, it will be interesting to automatize the deployment of the specific proxy to improve the dynamism and the services integration such as the ROSE project (Bardin, 2010).

CONCLUSION

Currently software trend to require capabilities of dynamicity and adaptability during the execution such as in Cloud Computing or in Ubiquitous Computing. For that, it is necessary to have an execution environment, which first defines mechanisms to support the dynamicity in the running application and second provides probes and actuators on the running application needed by the adaptation. However, the current applications are composed of various artifacts. For example for the Cloud or the Ubiquitous, we find third-party services, embedded-services and proprietary services provided by service-providers. Alas, these different artifacts do not provide probes and actuators, and when they provide them, they are not necessarily from the same technology.

In summary, artifacts can have different behaviors, syntaxes and semantics, but to adapt applications it is necessary both to integrate the services functionalities and to act on their life cycle.

It is why, we propose an execution environment which provides a homogeneous representation of services to integrate their functionalities and which integrates their available life cycle operations to act on their life cycle. Establishing that these administration operations on services

are not sufficient to adapt application needs, we have defined some mechanisms to integrate other concerns such as the deployment.

Our approach includes two integration mechanisms: the technologies integration supported by the wrappers and the concerns integration supported by the runtimes. Wrappers aim to integrate a point of view for a specific technology in a model representing the execution state of this point of view; our main example is the services point of view that we integrate in our Service-Oriented Component models. Runtimes are points of view defined by concepts, properties, and administration operations on the concept instances. They can potentially use wrappers if they depend of underlying technologies. Our main example for the concerns integration, other than services, is the deployment concern.

A major part of our approach has been implemented by the Service Abstract Machine (SAM) prototype. SAM has been used in three projects and provides conclusive results for the integration mechanisms and for the dynamic aspect. These experimentations show that the execution state models can be at least that the targeted technology allows doing.

During the different experimentations, the mainly difficulties came from the semantic discrepancies between the meta-models used in traditional SOC technologies and our meta-model. Nevertheless, the wrappers having a deep knowledge of the underlying technology can infer some of the missing information. This is the case for the dynamic behavior attributes, but also for other attributes. In this point of view, the SAM execution state models are the best possible approximation of the reality.

A second difficulty is that SOC technologies do not provide the same features (e.g. distribution, management, security, etc.), which may require extensive development for specific technologies to support a particular activity such as the package management. SAM does not try to address all the concerns of SOA platforms in Service-Oriented Component model, those missing concerns are simply out of the scope of the Service-Oriented Component meta-model. We rely instead on the SAM extension mechanism to address them.

We are aware that some difficulties are delegated either on the wrappers either on the extensions, whose can be or can seem too complicated to integrate the artifact type (e.g. OSGi) or the concern (e.g. security). It is almost already possible to integrate a functionality of an artifact through a proxy or an adaptor. However, it is not the case for the management of its life cycle or its dependencies which is not the same from a technology to another. In summary, as long as we only want to use the functionalities of an artifact; it is often possible to integrate it as a service. Nevertheless, in the case of the life cycle management of artifacts required by Cloud Computing, integration can become very problematic not to say impossible. In this case, according to need and cost, migration of the legacy code to a supported technology may be required. However, we still believe that this approach is interesting for the application including legacy artifacts, which is one of the significant problems of the Cloud Computing and the Ubiquitous Computing.

REFERENCES

Adele. (2007). *Service abstract machine*. Retrieved from http://sam.imag.fr

Adele. (2010). *SEMbySEM demonstrator*. Retrieved from http://sam.imag.fr/index.php/sbs-demoarticle.html

Amazon. (2009). *Amazon elastic compute cloud (amazon EC2)*. Retrieved from http://aws.amazon.com/ec2

Armbrust, M., Fox, A., Griffith, R., Joseph, A. D., Katz, R. H., & Konwinski, A. … Zaharia, M. (2009). *Above the clouds: A Berkeley view of cloud computing*. Berkeley, CA: University of California.

Arsanjani, A. (2004). *Service-oriented modeling and architecture: How to identify, specify, and realize services for your SOA*. Retrieved from https://www.ibm.com/developerworks/webservices/library/ws-soa-design1/

Bardin, J., Lalanda, P., & Escoffier, C. (2010). Towards an automatic integration of heterogeneous services and devices. In *Proceedings IEEE 2010*. Hangzhou, China: Asia-Pacific Services Computing Conference. doi:10.1109/APSCC.2010.89

Cervantes, H., & Hall, R. (2004). Autonomous adaptation to dynamic availability using a service-oriented component model. In *Proceedings of the ICSE, IEEE Computer Society*, (pp. 614-623). IEEE Press.

Chappell, D. A. (2004). *Enterprise service bus*. New York, NY: O'Reilly Media.

Chohan, N., Bunch, C., Pang, S., Krintz, C., Mostafa, N., & Soman, S. … Dekel, E. (2010). AppScale: Scalable and open AppEngine application development and deployment 4 cloud computing. In *Proceedings of Cloud Computing*, (Vol. 34, pp. 57-70). Berlin, Germany: Springer.

DMTF. (2010). *Web-service for management*. Retrieved from http://www.dmtf.org/sites/default/files/standards/documents/DSP0226_1.1.pdf

Escoffier, C., Hall, R. S., & Lalanda, P. (2007). iPOJO: An extensible service-oriented component framework. In *Proceedings of the IEEE International Conference on Services Computing (SCC 2007)*, (pp. 474-481). IEEE Press.

Estublier, J., Dieng, I., & Lévêque, T. (2010). Software product line evolution: The selecta system. In *Proceedings of the 2010 ICSE Workshop on Product Line Approaches in Software Engineering (PLEASE 2010)*, (pp. 32-39). ACM.

Estublier, J., Dieng, I., Simon, E., & Vega, G. (2009). Flexible composites and automatic component selection for service-based applications. In *Proceedings of the 4th International Conference on Evaluation of Novel Approaches to Software Engineering (ENASE)*. Milan, Italy: ENASE.

Ferry, N., Hourdin, V., Lavirotte, S., Rey, G., Tigli, J.-Y., & Riveill, M. (2009). Models at runtime: Service for device composition and adaptation. In *Proceedings of the 4th International Workshop Models@run.time at Models 2009*, (pp. 51-60). Models.

Geelan, J., Klems, M., Cohen, R., Kaplan, J., Gourlay, D., & Gaw, P. … Berger, I. W. (2009). *Twenty-one experts define cloud computing*. Retrieved from http://cloudcomputing.sys-con.com/node/612375

Google. (2012). *Google AppEngine*. Retrieved from http://code.google.com/appengine/

IBM. (2003). *Business process execution language (BPEL) for web services*. Retrieved from http://www.ibm.com/developerworks/library/specification/ws-bpel/

Lyytinen, K., & Yoo, Y. (2002). Issues and challenges in ubiquitous computing. *Communications of the ACM, 45*(12), 62–65.

Minalogic. (2011). *iDeviceCloud*. Retrieved from http://idevicecloud.minalogic.net

OSGi Alliance. (2009). *OSGi service platform core specification release 4.2*. Retrieved from http://www.osgi.org/download/r4v42/r4.core.pdf

OSOA. (2012). *Service component architecture*. Retrieved from http://www.osoa.org/display/Main/Service+Component+Architecture+Home

Papazoglou, M. P., & Heuvel, W.-J. (2007). Service oriented architectures: Approaches, technologies and research issues. *The VLDB Journal, 16*, 389–415. doi:10.1007/s00778-007-0044-3

Pedraza, G., Dieng, I., & Estublier, J. (2009). *FOCAS: An enginering environment for service-based applications*. Paper presented at the 4th International Conference on Evaluation of Novel Approaches to Software Engineering (ENASE). Milan, Italy

Pedraza, G., & Estublier, J. (2008). An extensible services orchestration framework through concern composition. In *Proceedings of the 1st International Workshop on Non-functional System Properties in Domain Specific Modeling Languages (NFPDSML)*. NFPDSML.

Saha, D., & Mukherjee, A. (2003). Pervasive computing: A paradigm for the 21st century. *IEEE Computer, 36*, 25–31. doi:10.1109/MC.2003.1185214

Satyanarayanan, M. (2002). Pervasive computing: Vision and challenges. *IEEE Personal Communications, 8*, 10–17. doi:10.1109/98.943998

SEMbySEM. (2007). *Service management by semantics*. Retrieved from http://www.sembysem.org/

UPnP Forum. (2012). *Universal plug'n play specifications*. Retrieved from http://upnp.org/sdcps-and-certification/standards/

ADDITIONAL READING

Abowd, G. D., Dey, A. K., Brown, P. J., Davies, N., Smith, M., & Steggles, P. (1999). Towards a better understanding of context and context-awareness. In *Proceedings of the 1st International Symposium on Handheld and Ubiquitous Computing (HUC 1999)*, (pp. 304-307). Springer-Verlag.

Arsanjani, A., Ghosh, S., Allam, A., Abdollah, T., Gariapathy, S., & Holley, K. (2008). SOMA: A method for developing service-oriented solutions. *IBM Systems Journal, 47*, 377–396. doi:10.1147/sj.473.0377

Blair, G., Bencomo, N., & France, R. B. (2009). Models@ run.time. *IEEE Computer*, *42*, 22–27. doi:10.1109/MC.2009.326

Cervantes, H., & Hall, R. S. (2004). A framework for constructing adaptive component-based applications: Concepts and experiences. In *Proceedings of CBSE*, (pp. 130-137). Springer.

Endrei, M., Ang, J., Arsanjani, A., Chua, S., Comte, P., & Krogdahl, P. … Newling, T. (2004). *Patterns: Service-oriented architecture and web services*. New York, NY: IBM Redbooks.

Floch, J., Hallsteinsen, S., Stav, E., Eliassen, F., Lund, K., & Gjorven, E. (2006). Using architecture models for runtime adaptability. *IEEE Software*, *23*, 62–70. doi:10.1109/MS.2006.61

Foster, I., Zhao, Y., Raicu, I., & Lu, S. (2008). Cloud computing and grid computing 360-degree compared. In *Proceedings of the Grid Computing Environments Workshop (GCE 2008)*, (pp. 1-10). GCE.

France, R., & Rumpe, B. (2007). Model-driven development of complex software: A research roadmap. In Proceedings of the Future of Software Engineering (FOSE 2007), (pp. 37-54). IEEE Press.

Ganek, A. G., & Corbi, T. A. (2003). The dawning of the autonomic computing era. *IBM Systems Journal*, *42*, 5–18. doi:10.1147/sj.421.0005

Grace, P., Blair, G. S., & Samuel, S. (2005). A reflective framework for discovery and interaction in heterogeneous mobile environments. In *ACM SIGMOBILE Mobile. Computer Communication Review*, *9*(1), 2–14. doi:10.1145/1055959.1055962

Hall, R. S. (1999). *Agent-based software configuration and deployment*. (Doctoral Dissertation). University of Colorado. Boulder, CO.

Hall, R. S., Pauls, K., McCulloch, S., & Savage, D. (2011). *OSGi in action: Creating modular applications in Java*. New York, NY: Manning Publications.

Horn, P. (2001). *Autonomic computing: IBM's perspective on the state of information technology*. New York, NY: IBM.

Kephart, J. O. (2005). Research challenges of autonomic computing. In *Proceedings of the 27th International Conference on Software Engineering (ICSE 2005)*, (pp. 15-22). ICSE.

Kephart, J. O., & Chess, D. M. (2003). The vision of autonomic computing. *IEEE Computer*, *36*, 41–50. doi:10.1109/MC.2003.1160055

Kramer, J., & Magee, J. (2007). Self-managed systems: An architectural challenge. In *Proceedings of the Future of Software Engineering (FOSE 2007)*, (pp. 259-268). IEEE Press.

Lehmann, G., Blumendorf, M., Trollman, F., & Albayrak, S. (2010). Meta-modeling runtime models. In *Proceedings of the 5th Workshop on Models@run.time*, (vol 641, pp. 1-12). Models.

Papazoglou, M. P., Traverso, P., Dustdar, S., & Leymann, F. (2007). Service-oriented computing: State of the art and research challenges. *Computer*, *40*, 38–45. doi:10.1109/MC.2007.400

Vogel, T., Seibel, A., & Giese, H. (2010). Toward megamodels at runtime. In Proceedings of the 5th International Workshop on Models@run.time at the 13th IEEE/ACM International Conference on Model Driven Engineering Languages and Systems (MoDELS 2010), (pp. 13-24). Oslo, Norway: IEEE/ACM.

Wen Cheng, S., Cheng Huang, A., Garlan, D., Schmerl, B., & Steenkiste, P. (2004). Rainbow: Architecture-based self-adaptation with reusable infrastructure. *IEEE Computer*, *37*, 46–54. doi:10.1109/MC.2004.175

Yang, J. (2003). Web service componentization. *Communications of the ACM, 46*, 35–40. doi:10.1145/944217.944235

Yang, J., & Papazoglou, M. P. (2004). Service components for managing the life-cycle of service compositions. *Information Systems, 29*, 97–125. doi:10.1016/S0306-4379(03)00051-6

KEY TERMS AND DEFINITIONS

Administration Operation: In this chapter, the administration operation designates an operation whichoperation, which acts on a non-functional aspect of an artifact. For example: create an instance from an implementation, destroy an instance or install a deployment-unit.

Artifact: An artifact is a consistent software element such as the components.

Component-Based Approach: This approach type is based on software components whose can be defined as a unit of composition. These components are designed as a black box. This term includes both the classical component models and the service-oriented component approaches.

Embedded -Service: An embedded -service is a service-provider embedded in a device, where only the service part is available.

Service -Provider: A service -provider is an artifact which provides its functionalities through the service concept from the service-oriented approach.

Third-Party Service: A third-party service is a service where the service-provider belongs to a third-party and consequently it is not available.

ENDNOTES

[1] Service Control Protocol Description.

Compilation of References

Adele. (2007). *Service abstract machine*. Retrieved from http://sam.imag.fr

Adele. (2010). *SEMbySEM demonstrator*. Retrieved from http://sam.imag.fr/index.php/sbsdemoarticle.html

ADM. (2010). *Architecture-driven modernization*. Retrieved March 26, 2012, from http://adm.omg.org/

Ahmad, A., & Pohl, K. (2010). Pattern-based customizable transformations for style-based service architecture evolution. In *Proceedings of the 2010 International Conference on Computer Information Systems and Industrial Management Applications (CISIM)*, (pp. 371–376). Washington, DC: IEEE Computer Society Press.

Al Shahwan, F., & Moessner, K. (2010). Providing SOAP web services and RESTful web services from mobile hosts. In *Proceedings of the Fifth International Conference on Internet and Web Applications and Services*, (pp. 174-179). IEEE.

Alahmari, S., Roure, D. D., & Zaluska, E. (2010). A model-driven architecture approach to the efficient identification of services on service-oriented enterprise architecture. In *Proceedings of the 2010 14th IEEE International Enterprise Distributed Object Computing Conference Workshops*. IEEE Press.

Alahmari, S., Zaluska, E., & Roure, D. D. (2010). A service identification framework for legacy system migration into SOA. In *Proceedings of the IEEE International Conference on Services Computing*, (pp. 614–617). IEEE Computer Society.

Algermissen, J. (2010). *Classification of HTTP-based APIs*. Retrieved October 10, 2011, from http://www.nordsc.com/ext/classification_of_http_based_apis.html

Almonaies, A., Cordy, J., & Dean, T. (2010). Legacy system evolution towards service-oriented architecture. In *Proceedings of the International Workshop on SOA Migration and Evolution (SOME)*, (pp. 53-62). Madrid, Spain: OFFIS.

Amazon. (2009). *Amazon elastic compute cloud (amazon EC2)*. Retrieved from http://aws.amazon.com/ec2

Amsden, J. (2010). Modeling with SoaML, the service-oriented architecture modeling language: Part 1 service identification. *IBM DeveloperWorks*, Retrieved September 28, 2011, from http://www.ibm.com/developerworks/rational/library/09/modelingwithsoaml-1/index.html

Apache Software Foundation. (2009). *Apache Axis2*. Retrieved October 6, 2011, from http://ws.apache.org/axis2

Appel, A., & Jim, T. (1989). Continuation-passing, closure-passing style. In *Proceedings of the Symposium on Principles of Programming Languages*, (pp. 293-302). ACM Press.

Arcelli, F., Tosi, C., & Zanoni, M. (2008). Can design pattern detection be useful for legacy system migration towards SOA? In K. Kontogiannis, G. A. Lewis, D. B. Smith, & M. Litoiu (Eds.), *SDSOA 2008: Proceedings of the 2nd International Workshop on Systems Development in SOA Environments*, (pp. 63–68). Washington, DC: IEEE Computer Society Press.

Armbrust, M., Fox, A., Griffith, R., Joseph, A. D., Katz, R. H., & Konwinski, A. ... Zaharia, M. (2009). *Above the clouds: A Berkeley view of cloud computing.* Berkeley, CA: University of California.

Arsanjani, A. (2004). *Service-oriented modeling and architecture: How to identify, specify, and realize services for your SOA.* Retrieved from https://www.ibm.com/developerworks/webservices/library/ws-soa-design1/

Arsanjani, A., & Allam, A. (2006). Service-oriented modeling and architecture for realization of an SOA. In *Proceedings of the 2006 IEEE International Conference on Services Computing (SCC) 2006,* (p. 521). IEEE Press.

Arsanjani, A., Ghosh, S., Allam, A., Abdollah, T., Ganapathy, S., & Holley, K. (2004). SOMA: A method for developing service-oriented solutions. *IBM Systems Journal, 47*(3), 377–396. doi:10.1147/sj.473.0377

Arsanjani, A., Ghosh, S., Allam, A., Abdollah, T., Ganapathy, S., & Holley, K. (2008). SOMA: A method for developing service-oriented solutions. *IBM Systems Journal, 47,* 377–396. doi:10.1147/sj.473.0377

Artefactual. (2010). *AABC data migration toolkit.* Retrieved on December 2010, from http://www.artefactual.com/wiki/index.php

Athanasopoulos, M., & Kontogiannis, K. (2010). Identification of REST-like resources from legacy service descriptions. In *Proceedings of the 17th Working Conference on Reverse Engineering,* (pp. 215-219). IEEE.

Athanasopoulos, M., Kontogiannis, K., & Brealey, C. (2011). Towards an interpretation framework for assessing interface uniformity in REST. In *Proceedings of the Second International Workshop on RESTful Design,* (pp. 47–50). ACM.

Auer, S., et al. (2010). *Use cases and requirements for mapping relational databases to RDF.* Retrieved from http://www.w3c.org

Aversano, L., Canfora, G., & Cimitile, A. (2001). *Migrating legacy systems to the web – An experience report.* Paper presented at 5th European Conference on Software Maintenance and Reengineering (CSMR 2001). Lisbon, Portugal.

Aversano, L., Cerulo, L., & Palumbo, C. (2008). Mining candidate web services from legacy code. In *Proceedings of the 10th International Symposium on Web Site Evolution, 2008 (WSE 2008).* WSE.

Aversano, L., Di Penta, M., & Palumbo, C. (2007). *Identifying services from legacy code: An integrated approach.* Paper presented at the Working Session on Maintenance and Evolution of SOA-Based Systems (MESOA 2007), ICSM 2007: 23rd IEEE International Conference on Software Maintenance. Paris, France.

Babar, M. A., & Chauhan, M. A. (2011). A tale of migration to cloud computing for sharing experiences and observations. In *Proceedings of the 2nd International Workshop on Software Engineering for Cloud Computing,* (pp. 50–56). New York, NY: ACM.

Bai, X., Dong, W., Tsai, W., & Chen, Y. (2005). WSDL-based automatic test case generation for web services testing. In *Proceedings of the 2005 IEEE International Workshop on Service Oriented System Engineering,* (pp. 215-220). IEEE.

Balasubramaniam, S., Lewis, G. A., Morris, E., Simanta, S., & Smith, D. (2008). *SMART: Application of a method for migration of legacy systems to SOA environments.* Paper presented at the 6th International Conference on Service-Oriented Computing. Berlin, Heidelberg.

Balasubramanian, R. (2008). *REST-inspired SOA design patterns.* Retrieved October 10, 2011, from http://www.soamag.com/I24/1208-3.php

Bao, L., Yin, C., He, W., Ge, J., & Chen, P. (2010). Extracting reusable services from legacy object-oriented systems. In *Proceedings of the IEEE International Conference on Software Maintenance (ICSM 2010).* IEEE Press.

Bardin, J., Lalanda, P., & Escoffier, C. (2010). Towards an automatic integration of heterogeneous services and devices. In *Proceedings IEEE 2010.* Hangzhou, China: Asia-Pacific Services Computing Conference. doi:10.1109/APSCC.2010.89

Basili, V., Rombach, H.-D., & Caldiera, C. (1994). Goal question metric paradigm. In *Encyclopedia of Software Engineering* (*Vol. 1,* pp. 528–551). New York, NY: John Wiley.

Battaglia, M., Savoia, G., & Favaro, J. (1998). Renaissance: A method to migrate from legacy to immortal software systems. In *Proceedings of the 2nd Euromicro Conference on Software Maintenance and Reengineering (CSMR 1998),* (p. 197). Washington, DC: IEEE Computer Society.

Beaton, J., Jeong, S. Y., Xie, Y., Jack, J., & Myers, B. A. (2008). Usability challenges for enterprise service-oriented architecture APIs. In *Proceedings of the IEEE Symposium on Visual Languages and Human-Centric Computing (VL/HCC),* (pp. 193–196): IEEE Computer Society.

Bechara, G. (2008). *Web services versioning.* Retrieved October 6, 2011, from http://www.oracle.com/technetwork/articles/web-services-versioning-094384.html

Becker, J., Matzner, M., & Müller, O. (2010). Comparing architectural styles for service-oriented architectures - A REST vs. SOAP case study. In Papadopoulos, G. (Eds.), *Information Systems Development* (pp. 207–215). Springer-Verlag. doi:10.1007/b137171_22

Becker, K., Pruyne, J., Singhal, S., Milojicic, D., & Lopes, A. (2011). Automatic determination of compatibility in evolving services. *International Journal of Web Services Research, 8*(1), 21–40. doi:10.4018/jwsr.2011010102

Beck, K., & Andres, C. (2004). *Extreme programming explained: Embrace change* (2nd ed.). Reading, MA: Addison-Wesley.

Beier, A., & Uhlig, D. (2009). Flow graph manipulator (FGM) - Reverse engineering tool für komplexe software-systeme. *Softwaretechnik-Trends, 29*(2), 39–40.

Belady, L., & Lehman, M. (1975). The evolution dynamics of large programs. *IBM Systems Journal, 3,* 11.

Bender, M., Lörnker, A., & van der Vekens, A. (2008). Evolution of a PL/I application towards SOA. *Object-Spectrum, 18*(5), 54–63.

Bennett, K. H., & Rajlich, V. T. (2000). Software maintenance and evolution: A roadmap. In A. Finkelstein (Ed.), *Proceedings of the Conference on the Future of Software Engineering,* (pp. 3-22). ACM Press.

Bennett, K. (1995). Legacy systems: Coping with success. *IEEE Software, 12*(1), 19–23. doi:10.1109/52.363157

Bergey, J., Smith, D., Weiderman, N., & Woods, S. G. (1999). *Options analysis for reengineering (OAR): Issues and conceptual approach.* Technical Report CMUSEI1999TN014. Pittsburgh, PA: Carnegie Mellon University.

Bergey, J. (2001). *Options analysis for reengineering (OAR): A method for mining legacy assets.* DTIC.

Bergey, J., Smith, D., Weiderman, N., & Woods, S. (1999). *Options analysis for reengineering (OAR): Issues and conceptual approach. No. CMU/SEI-99-TN-014.* SEI.

Berners-Lee, T. (1999). *Weaving the web: The original design and ultimate destiny of the world wide web by its inventor.* New York, NY: HarperCollins Publishers.

Berry, D. (2009). *Avoid disaster, embrace people-processes like change management.* Retrieved October 6, 2011, from http://blogs.oracle.com/governance/2009/06/avoid_disaster_embrace_peoplep_1.html

Bertolino, A., Inverardi, P., Pelliccione, P., & Tivoli, M. (2009). Automatic synthesis of behavior protocols for composable web-services. In H. Van Vliet & V. Issarny (Eds.), *Proceedings of the 7th Joint Meeting of the European Software Engineering Conference ESEC and the ACM SIGSOFT Symposium on the Foundations of Software Engineering,* (pp. 141-150). ACM.

Bhallamudi, P., & Tilley, S. (2011). SOA migration case studies and lessons learned. In *Proceedings of the IEEE International Systems Conference (SysCon 2011).* IEEE Press.

Bhat, U., & Jadhav, S. (2010). Moving towards non-relational databases. *International Journal of Computers and Applications, 1,* 40–46. doi:10.5120/284-446

Bianculli, D., Ghezzi, C., & Pautasso, C. (2009). Embedding continuous lifelong verification in service life cycles. In E. Di Nitto & S. Dustdar (Eds.), *PESOS '09: Proceedings of the 2009 ICSE Workshop on Principles of Engineering Service Oriented Systems,* (pp. 99–102). New York, NY: Association for Computing Machinery.

Bichler, M., & Lin, K.-J. (2006). Service-oriented computing. *Computer, 39*(3), 99–101. doi:10.1109/MC.2006.102

Birman, K. P. (1993). The process group approach to reliable distributed computing. *Communications of the ACM, 36*(12), 37–53. doi:10.1145/163298.163303

Bisbal, J., Lawless, D., Wu, B., & Grimson, J. (1999). Legacy information systems: Issues and directions. *IEEE Software, 16*(5), 103–111. doi:10.1109/52.795108

Bizer, C. (2003). D2R MAP – A database to RDF mapping language. In *Proceedings of Twelfth International World Wide Web Conference,* (pp. 2-3). IEEE.

Blain, M. (2010). Data migration in app engine. *Google I/O 2010*. Retrieved November 2010 from http://www.google.com/events/io/2010/

Blake, M. B., & Nowlan, M. F. (2008). Taming web services from the wild. *IEEE Internet Computing, 12*(5), 62–69. doi:10.1109/MIC.2008.112

Boehm, B., Huang, L., Apurva, J., & Madachy, R. (2004). The ROI of software dependability. *IEEE Software Magazine, 21*(3), 54–61.

Boldyreff, C., Lavery, J., & Allison, C. (2004). Modelling the evolution of legacy systems to web-based systems. *International Journal of Software Maintenance and Evolution, 16*(2), 5–22. doi:10.1002/smr.282

Bolton, F. (2001). *Pure corba*. Indianapolis, IN: SAMS Publishing.

Borchers, J. (1997). Erfahrungen mit dem einsatz einer reengineering factory in einem großen umstellungsprojekt. *HMD - Praxis der Wirtschaftsinformatik, 34*(194), 77–94.

Box, D., Ehnebuske, D., Kakivaya, G., Layman, A., Mendelsohn, N., Nielsen, H. F., et al. (2000). *Simple object access protocol (SOAP) 1.1*. Paper presented at the World Wide Web Consortium. New York, NY.

Brinkkemper, S. (1996). Method engineering: Engineering of information systems development methods and tools. *Information and Software Technology, 38*(4), 275–280. doi:10.1016/0950-5849(95)01059-9

Brockmans, S., Volz, R., Eberhart, A., & Löffler, P. (2004). Visual modeling of OWL DL ontologies using UML. In S. A. McIlraith, D. Plexousakis, & F. van Harmelen (Eds.), *Proceedings of the Third International Semantic Web Conference (ISWC) 2004,* (pp. 198-213). ISWC.

Brodie, M. L., & Stonebrake, M. (1993). *DARWIN: On the incremental migration of legacy information system. Technical Report*. Berkeley, CA: University of California.

Brodie, M. L., & Stonebraker, M. (1995). *Migrating legacy systems: Gateways, interfaces and the incremental approach*. San Francisco, CA: Morgan Kaufmann.

Brodie, M. L., & Stonebraker, M. (1998). *Migrating legacy systems: Gateways, interfaces & the incremental approach*. San Francisco, CA: Morgan Kaufmann Publishers Inc.

Brogi, A., Canal, C., & Pimentel, E. (2006). On the semantics of software adaptation. *Science of Computer Programming, 61*(2), 136–151. doi:10.1016/j.scico.2005.10.009

Brown, K., & Ellis, M. (2004). Best practices for web services versioning: Keep your web services current with WSDL and UDDI. *IBM DeveloperWorks*. Retrieved October 6, 2011, from http://www-128.ibm.com/developerworks/webservices/library/ws-version

Bucchiarone, A., Kazhamiakin, R., Cappiello, C., Di Nitto, E., & Mazza, V. (2010). A context-driven adaptation process for service-based applications. *PESOS '10: Proceedings of the Second International Workshop on Principles of Engineering Service-Oriented Systems,* (pp. 50–56). New York, NY: Association for Computing Machinery.

Buse, R., & Weimer, W. (2010). Learning a metric for readability. *IEEE Transactions on Software Engineering, 36*(4), 546–558. doi:10.1109/TSE.2009.70

Buyya, R., Broberg, J., & Goscinski, A. (2011). *Cloud computing: Principles and paradigms*. Hoboken, NJ: John Wiley & Sons. doi:10.1002/9780470940105

Canal, C., Murillo, J. M., & Poizat, P. (2004). First international workshop on coordination and adaptation techniques for software entities. In C. Canal, J. M. Murillo, & P. Poizat (Eds.), *First International Workshop on Coordination and Adaptation Techniques for Software Entities,* (pp. 133-147). Berlin, Germany: Springer.

Canal, C., Murillo, J. M., & Poizat, P. (Eds.). (2008). Practical approaches to software adaptation. *Journal of Universal Computer Science, 14*(13).

Canfora, G., Fasolino, A. R., Frattolillo, G., & Tramontana, P. (2006). Migrating interactive legacy systems to web services. In *Proceedings of the 10th European Conference on Software Maintenance and Reengineering (CSMR) 2006,* (pp. 27-36). CSMR.

Canfora, G., & Di Penta, M. (2006). Testing services and service-centric systems: Challenges and opportunities. *IT Professional, 8*(2), 10–17. doi:10.1109/MITP.2006.51

Canfora, G., Fasolino, A., Frattolillo, G., & Tramontana, P. (2008). A wrapping approach for migrating legacy system interactive functionalities to service oriented architectures. *Journal of Systems and Software, 81,* 463–480. doi:10.1016/j.jss.2007.06.006

Card, D., & Agresti, W. (1988). Measuring software design complexity. *Journal of Systems and Software, 8,* 185. doi:10.1016/0164-1212(88)90021-0

Card, D., & Glass, R. (1991). *Measuring software design quality.* Englewood Cliffs, NJ: Prentice-Hall.

Cardoso, J., Voigt, K., & Winkler, M. (2009). Service engineering for the internet of services. *Lecture Notes in Business Information Processing, 19,* 15–27. doi:10.1007/978-3-642-00670-8_2

Carriere, J., Kazman, R., & Woods, S. (1998). Requirements for integrating software architecture and reengineering models: CORUM II. In M. Blaha, A. Quilici, & C. F'erhoef(Eds.), *WCRE 1998: Proceedings of the Working Conference on Reverse Engineering,* (pp. 154–163). New York, NY: Association for Computing Machinery.

Cervantes, H., & Hall, R. (2004). Autonomous adaptation to dynamic availability using a service-oriented component model. In *Proceedings of the 26th International Conference on Software Engineering,* (pp. 614-623). Washington, DC: IEEE Computer Society Press.

Cetin, S., Altintas, N. I., Oguztuzun, H., Dogru, A., Tufekci, O., & Suloglu, S. (2007). Legacy migration to service-oriented computing with mashups. In S. Dascalu, P. Dini, S. Morasca, T. Ohta, & A. Oboler (Eds.), *ICSEA 2007: Proceedings of the Second International Conference on Software Engineering Advances.* Washington, DC: IEEE Computer Society Press.

Chang, F. (2008). Bigtable: A distributed storage system for structured data. *ACM Transactions on Computer Systems, 26*(2), 1–26. doi:10.1145/1365815.1365816

Chang, F., Dean, J., Ghemawat, S., Hsieh, W., Wallach, D., & Burrows, M. (2008). Bigtable: A distributed storage system for structured data. *ACM Transactions on Computer Systems, 26*(2), 1–26. doi:10.1145/1365815.1365816

Chang, W. Y., Abu-Amara, H., & Sanford, J. (2010). *Transforming enterprise cloud services.* Dordrecht, The Netherlands: Springer. doi:10.1007/978-90-481-9846-7

Channabasavaiah, K., Holley, K., & Tuggle, E. M. (2004). *Migrating to a service-oriented architecture.* Retrieved from ftp://service.boulder.ibm.com/s390/audio/pdfs/G224-7298-00_FinalMigratetoSOA.pdf

Chapin, N. (1977). *A measure of software complexity.* Paper presented at 3rd National Computing Conference. Dallas, TX.

Chappell, D. A. (2004). *Enterprise service bus.* New York, NY: O'Reilly Media.

Chauhan, T., Chaudhary, S., Kumar, V., & Bhise, M. (2011). Service level agreement parameter matching in cloud computing. In *Proceedings of the World Congress on Information and Communication Technologies (WICT),* (pp. 564-570). WICT.

Chawla, M., & Peddinti, V. (2007). Exposing SOA enabled C apps as web services. *SOA World Magazine.* Retrieved October 6, 2011, from http://webservices.sys-con.com/read/314105.htm

Chen, F., Li, S., Yang, H., Wang, C. H., & Chu, C.-C. W. (2005). Feature analysis for service-oriented reengineering. In *Proceedings of the 12th Asia-Pacific Software Engineering Conference.* IEEE.

Chen, F., Yang, H., Qiao, B., & Chu, W. C. (2006). A formal model driven approach to dependable software evolution. In *Proceedings of the 30th Annual International Computer Software and Applications Conference.* IEEE.

Chen, F., Zhang, Z., Li, J., Kang, J., & Yang, H. (2009). *Service identification via ontology mapping.* Paper presented at the 33rd Annual IEEE International Computer Software and Applications Conference (COMPSAC 2009). Seattle. WA.

Chen, L., & Chen, H. (2008). Efficient type checking for a subclass of regular expression types. In *Proceedings of the International Conference for Young Computer Scientists,* (pp. 1647-1652). IEEE Computer Society Press.

Chohan, N., Bunch, C., Pang, S., Krintz, C., Mostafa, N., & Soman, S. ... Dekel, E. (2010). AppScale: Scalable and open AppEngine application development and deployment 4 cloud computing. In *Proceedings of Cloud Computing,* (Vol. 34, pp. 57-70). Berlin, Germany: Springer.

Chu, C., Kim, S., Lin, Y., Yu, Y., Bradski, G., Ng, A., & Olukotun, K. (2006). Map-reduce for machine learning on multicore. In *Proceedings of the 2006 Conference on Advances in Neural Information Processing Systems,* (pp. 281-288). Cambridge, MA: The MIT Press.

Chu, Q., Shen, Y., & Jiang, Z. (2009). A transaction middleware model for SCA programming. In *Proceedings of the First International Workshop on Education Technology and Computer Science,* (pp. 568-571). IEEE.

Cisco. (2011). *Cisco WebEx web conferencing, online meetings, desktop sharing, video conferencing.* Retrieved November 30, 2011, from http://www.webex.com/

Citrix. (2011). *Web conferencing | GoToMeeting.* Retrieved November 30, 2011, from http://www.gotomeeting.com

Cobug.com. (2011). *COBOL user groups.* Retrieved March 19, 2012, from http://www.cobug.com/

Comuzzi, M., & Pernici, B. (2009). A framework for QoS-based web service contracting. *ACM Transactions on the Web, 3*(3).

Cooper, B., Silberstein, A., Tam, E., Ramakrishnan, R., & Sears, R. (2010). Benchmarking cloud serving systems with YCSB. In *Proceedings of the 1st ACM Symposium on Cloud Computing,* (pp. 143–154). New York, NY: ACM.

Corbi, T. A. (1989). Program understanding: Challenge for the 1990s. *IBM Systems Journal, 28*(2), 294–306. doi:10.1147/sj.282.0294

Cornelissen, B., Zaidman, A., van Deursen, A., Moonen, L., & Koschke, R. (2009). A systematic survey of program comprehension through dynamic analysis. *IEEE Transactions on Software Engineering, 35*(5), 684–702. doi:10.1109/TSE.2009.28

Crane, D., & McCarthy, P. (2008). *Comet and reverse ajax: The next-generation ajax 2.0.* Berkeley, CA: Apress.

Crasso, M., Rodriguez, J. M., Zunino, A., & Campo, M. (2010). Revising WSDL documents: Why and how. *IEEE Internet Computing, 14*(5), 30–38. doi:10.1109/MIC.2010.81

Cuadrado, F., García, B., Duenas, J., & Parada, H. A. (2008). A case study on software evolution towards service-oriented architecture. In *Proceedings of the 22nd International Conference on Advanced Information Networking and Applications - Workshops.* IEEE.

Da Silva Maciel, L. A. H., & Hirata, C. M. (2009). An optimistic technique for transactions control using REST architectural style. In *Proceedings of the 2009 ACM Symposium on Applied Computing,* (pp. 664-669). ACM Press.

Da Silva Maciel, L. A. H., & Hirata, C. M. (2011). Extending timestamp-based two phase commit protocol for RESTful services to meet business rules. In *Proceedings of the 2011 ACM Symposium on Applied Computing,* (pp. 778–785). ACM.

Davies, J., Shaffer, D., & Demed, L. (2009). *Oracle SOA suite 11g.* Retrieved from http://www.oracle.com/technetwork/middleware/soasuite/overview/wp-soa-suite-11gr1-2-129551.pdf

De Lucia, A., et al. (1997). Migrating legacy systems towards object-oriented platforms. In *Proceedings of the IEEE International Conference on Software Maintenance,* (pp. 122-129). IEEE Computer Society Press.

De Lucia, A., Francese, R., Scanniello, G., & Tortora, G. (2008). Developing legacy system migration methods and tools for technology transfer. *Software, Practice & Experience, 38*(13), 1333–1364. doi:10.1002/spe.870

de Lucia, A., & Tortora, G. (2010). *Metamorphos: Methods and tools for migrating software systems towards web and service oriented architectures: Experimental evaluation, usability and technology transfer.* Catanzaro, Italy: Rubbettino.

Dean, J. (2011). *Designs, lessons and advice from building large distributed systems.* Retrieved from http://www.odbms.org/download/dean-keynote-ladis2009.pdf

Dean, J., & Ghemawat, S. (2008). MapReduce: Simplified data processing on large clusters. *Communications of the ACM*, *51*(1), 107–113. doi:10.1145/1327452.1327492

Del Castillo, R. P., García-Rodríguez, I., & Caballero, I. (2009). PRECISO: A reengineering process and a tool for database modernisation through web services. In *Proceedings of the 2009 ACM Symposium on Applied Computing*. ACM Press.

Den Haan, J. (2009). *A framework for model-driven SOA*. Retrieved October 6, 2011, from http://www.theenterprisearchitect.eu/archive/2009/06/03/a-framework-for-model-driven-soa

Deruelle, L., Melab, N., Boune, M., & Basson, H. (2001). Analysis and manipulation of distributed multi-language software code. In *Proceedings of the First IEEE International Workshop on Source Code Analysis and Manipulation*, (pp. 43–54). Washington, DC: IEEE Computer Society Press.

Di Nitto, E., Ghezzi, C., Metzger, A., Papazoglou, M., & Pohl, K. (2008). A journey to highly dynamic, self-adaptive service-based applications. *Automated Software Engineering*, *15*, 313–341. doi:10.1007/s10515-008-0032-x

Dillon, T., Wu, C., & Chang, E. (2007). Reference architectural styles for service-oriented computing. *Lecture Notes in Computer Science*, *4672*, 543–555. doi:10.1007/978-3-540-74784-0_57

DMTF. (2010). *Web-service for management*. Retrieved from http://www.dmtf.org/sites/default/files/standards/documents/DSP0226_1.1.pdf

Donofrio, N., Sanchez, C., & Spohrer, J. (2010). Collaborative innovation and service systems: Implications for institutions and disciplines. In Grasso, D., & Burkins, M. (Eds.), *Holistic Engineering Education*. Berlin, Germany: Springer.

Drake, T. (1996). Measuring software quality – A case study. *IEEE Computer Magazine*, *29*(11), 78–87.

Dushin, F., & Newcomer, E. (2007). Handling multiple credentials in a heterogeneous SOA environment. *Security and Privacy*, *5*(5), 80–82. doi:10.1109/MSP.2007.110

Earl, T. (2005). *Service-oriented architecture: Concepts, technology, and design*. Upper Saddle River, NJ: Prentice Hall PTR.

Earl, T. (2007). *SOA: Principles of service design*. Upper Saddle River, NJ: Prentice Hall PTR.

Ebert, J., Riediger, V., & Winter, A. (2008). Graph technology in reverse engineering: The TGraph approach. In R. Gimnich, U. Kaiser, J. Quante, & A. Winter (Eds.), *Proceedings of the 10th Workshop Software Reengineering (WSR)*, (pp. 67–81). Bonn, Germany: Gesellschaft für Informatik.

Ebert, J., & Bildhauer, D. (2010). Reverse engineering using graph queries. *Lecture Notes in Computer Science*, *5765*.

Eclipse Foundation. (2009). *Web tools platform (WTP) project*. Retrieved October 6, 2011, from http://www.eclipse.org/webtools

Elshof, J. (1976). An analysis of commercial PL/I programs. *IEEE Transactions on Software Engineering*, *2*(1), 306.

Enterprise Service-Oriented Architecture. (2012). *SAP enterprise service-oriented architecture: Adoption program*. Retrieved from http://www.sap.com/platform/soa/adoptionprogram.epx

Erdmenger, U. (2009). Der parsergenerator BTRACC2. *Softwaretechnik-Trends*, *29*(2), 34–35.

Erdmenger, U., & Uhlig, D. (2011). Ein translator für die COBOL-java-migration. *Softwaretechnik-Trends*, *31*(2), 10–11.

Erdogmus, H. (2008). The infamous ratio measure. *IEEE Software*, *25*(3), 4–7. doi:10.1109/MS.2008.81

Erenkrantz, J., Gorlick, M., Suryanarayana, G., & Taylor, R. (2007). From representations to computations: The evolution of web architectures. In *Proceedings of the 6th Joint Meeting of the European Software Engineering Conference and the ACM SIGSOFT Symposium on the Foundations of Software Engineering*, (pp. 255-264). ACM Press.

Erickson, J., & Siau, K. (2008). Web service, service-oriented computing, and service-oriented architecture: Separating hype from reality. *Journal of Database Management*, *19*(3), 42–54. doi:10.4018/jdm.2008070103

Erl, T. (2006). *Service-oriented architecture – Concepts, technology, and design*. Boston, MA: Prentice Hall.

Erl, T. (2008). *SOA – Principles of service design*. Boston, MA: Prentice Hall.

Erl, T. (2009). *SOA design patterns*. Upper Saddle River, NJ: Prentice Hall.

Erl, T. (2009). *Web service contract design and versioning for SOA*. Boston, MA: Prentice Hall.

Erl, T., Karmarkar, A., Walmsley, P., Haas, H., Umit, Y., & Liu, C. K. (2009). *Web service contract design and versioning for SOA*. Upper Saddle River, NJ: Prentice Hall.

Erradi, A., Anand, S., & Kulkarni, N. (2006). Evaluation of strategies for integrating legacy applications as services in a service oriented architecture. In *Proceedings of the IEEE International Conference on Services Computing (SCC 2006)*. IEEE Press.

Escoffier, C., Hall, R. S., & Lalanda, P. (2007). iPOJO: An extensible service-oriented component framework. In *Proceedings of the IEEE International Conference on Services Computing (SCC 2007)*, (pp. 474-481). IEEE Press.

Espinha, E. (2011). Understanding service-oriented systems using dynamic analysis. In D. Smith & G. Lewis (Eds.), *Proceedings of the 2011 International Workshop on the Maintenance and Evolution of Service-Oriented and Cloud-Based Systems (MESOCA)*. Washington, DC: IEEE Computer Society Press.

Estublier, J., Dieng, I., & Lévêque, T. (2010). Software product line evolution: The selecta system. In *Proceedings of the 2010 ICSE Workshop on Product Line Approaches in Software Engineering (PLEASE 2010)*, (pp. 32-39). ACM.

Estublier, J., Dieng, I., Simon, E., & Vega, G. (2009). Flexible composites and automatic component selection for service-based applications. In *Proceedings of the 4th International Conference on Evaluation of Novel Approaches to Software Engineering (ENASE)*. Milan, Italy: ENASE.

Evans, E. (2004). *Domain-driven design: Tackling complexity in the heart of software*. Boston, MA: Addison-Wesley Professional.

Evdemon, J. (2005). *Principles of service design: Service versioning*. Redmond, WA: Microsoft Corporation. Retrieved October 6, 2011, from http://msdn2.microsoft.com/en-us/library/ms954726.aspx

Fang, R., Lam, L., Fong, L., Frank, D., Vignola, C., Chen, Y., et al. (2007). A version-aware approach for web service directory. In F. Leymann & M.-C. Shan (Eds.), *Proceedings of 2007 IEEE International Conference on Web Services*, (pp. 406–413). Washington, DC: IEEE Computer Society Press.

Fan, J., & Kambhampati, S. (2005). A snapshot of public web services. *SIGMOD Record*, *34*(1), 24–32. doi:10.1145/1058150.1058156

Fareghzadeh, N. (2008). Service identification approach to SOA development. *World Academy of Science. Engineering and Technology*, *21*, 258–266.

Ferry, N., Hourdin, V., Lavirotte, S., Rey, G., Tigli, J.-Y., & Riveill, M. (2009). Models at runtime: Service for device composition and adaptation. In *Proceedings of the 4th International Workshop Models@run.time at Models 2009*, (pp. 51-60). Models.

Fielding, R. T. (2000). *Architectural styles and the design of network-based software architectures*. (Ph.D. Dissertation). University of California. Irvine, CA.

Fielding, R., & Taylor, R. (2002). Principled design of the modern web architecture. *ACM Transactions on Internet Technology*, *2*(2), 115–150. doi:10.1145/514183.514185

Fleurey, F., Breton, E., Baudry, B., Nicolas, A., & Jézéquel, J.-M. (2007). Model-driven engineering for software migration in a large industrial context. In Engels, G., Opdyke, B., Schmidt, D., & Weil, F. (Eds.), *Model Driven Engineering Languages and Systems* (Vol. 4735, pp. 482–497). Berlin, Germany: Springer. doi:10.1007/978-3-540-75209-7_33

Fleurey, F., Breton, E., Baudry, B., Nicolas, A., & Jézéquel, J.-M. (2007). Model-driven engineering for software migration in a large industrial context. *Lecture Notes in Computer Science*, *4735*, 482–497. doi:10.1007/978-3-540-75209-7_33

Flurry, G. (2008). Service versioning in SOA. *IBM DeveloperWorks*. Retrieved October 6, 2011, from http://www.ibm.com/developerworks/websphere/techjournal/0810_col_flurry/0810_col_flurry.html

Formica, A. (2007). Similarity of XML-schema elements: A structural and information content approach. *The Computer Journal*, *51*(2), 240–254. doi:10.1093/comjnl/bxm051

Fowler, M. (1999). *Refactorings in alphabetical order*. Retrieved March 23, 2012, from http://www.refactoring.com/catalog/index.html

Fowler, M. (2010). *Richardson maturity model*. Retrieved October 10, 2011, from http://martinfowler.com/articles/richardsonMaturityModel.html

Frey, S., & Hasselbring, W. (2011). An extensible architecture for detecting violations of a cloud environment's constraints during legacy software system migration. In *Proceedings of the 15th Conference on Software Maintenance and Reengineering*, (pp. 269-278). ACM.

Fuhr, A., Gimnich, R., Horn, T., & Winter, A. (2009). Extending SOMA for model-driven software migration into SOA. *Softwaretechnik-Trends, 29*(2).

Fuhr, A., Horn, T., & Riediger, V. (2011). Using dynamic analysis and clustering for implementing services by reusing legacy code. In M. Pinzger, D. Poshyvanyk, & J. Buckley (Eds.), *Proceedings of the 18th Working Conference on Reverse Engineering (WCRE)*, (pp. 275–279). Washington, DC: IEEE Computer Society Press.

Fuhr, A., Horn, T., Riediger, V., & Winter, A. (2011). Model-driven software migration into service-oriented architectures. *Computer Science - Research and Development*. Retrieved from http://www.se.uni-oldenburg.de/documents/fuhr+2011.pdf

Fuhr, A., Horn, T., & Riediger, V. (2011). An integrated tool suite for model-driven software migration towards service-oriented architectures. *Softwaretechnik-Trends, 31*(2), 8–9.

Gadea, C., Solomon, B., Ionescu, B., & Ionescu, D. (2011). A collaborative cloud-based multimedia sharing platform for social networking environments. In *2011 Proceedings of 20th International Conference on Computer Communications and Networks (ICCCN)*, (pp. 1-6). ICCCN.

Gail, N., Sholler, D., & Bradley, A. (2008). *Tutorial: Web-oriented architecture: Putting the web back in web service*. Retrieved October 10, 2011, from http://www.gartner.com/id=797713

Gannon, G., Zhu, H., & Mudian, S. (2010). *On-the-fly wrapping of web services to support dynamic integration*. Paper presented at 17ᵗʰ Working Conference on Reverse Engineering (WCRE 2010). Boston, MA.

Gebhart, M. Baumgartner, & Abeck, S. (2010). Supporting service design decisions. In J. Hall, H. Kaindl, L. Lavazza, G. Buchgeher, & O. Takaki (Eds.), *Proceedings of the Fifth International Conference on Software Engineering Advances (ICSEA) 2010*, (pp. 76-81). ICSEA.

Gebhart, M., & Abeck, S. (2009). Rule-based service modeling. In K. Boness, J. M. Fernandes, J. G. Hall, R. J. Machado, & R. Oberhauser (Eds.), *Proceedings of the Fourth International Conference on Software Engineering Advances (ICSEA) 2009*, (pp. 271-276). ICSEA.

Gebhart, M., Baumgartner, M., Oehlert, S., Blersch, M., & Abeck, S. (2010). Evaluation of service designs based on SoaML. In J. Hall, H. Kaindl, L. Lavazza, G. Buchgeher, & O. Takaki (Eds.), *Proceedings of the Fifth International Conference on Software Engineering Advances (ICSEA) 2010*, (pp. 7-13). ICSEA.

Gebhart, M., Sejdovic, S., & Abeck, S. (2011). Case study for a quality-oriented service design process. In L. Lavazza, L. Fernandez-Sanz, O. Panchenko, & T. Kanstrén (Eds.), *Proceedings of the Sixth International Conference on Software Engineering Advances (ICSEA) 2011*, (pp. 92-97). ICSEA. Retrieved from http://www.thinkmind.org/

Gebhart, M. (2011). *Qualitätsorientierter entwurf von anwndungsdiensten*. Karlsruhe, Germany: KIT Scientific Publishing.

Gebhart, M., & Abeck, S. (2011). Metrics for evaluating service designs based on SoaML. *International Journal on Advances in Software, 4*(1-2), 61–75.

Gebhart, M., & Abeck, S. (2011). Quality-oriented design of services. *International Journal on Advances in Software, 4*(1-2), 144–157.

Geelan, J., Klems, M., Cohen, R., Kaplan, J., Gourlay, D., & Gaw, P. … Berger, I. W. (2009). *Twenty-one experts define cloud computing*. Retrieved from http://cloudcomputing.sys-con.com/node/612375

Ghemawat, S., Gobioff, H., & Leung, S. (2003). The Google file system. *ACM SIGOPS Operating Systems Review, 37*, 29–43. doi:10.1145/1165389.945450

Gimnich, R., & Winter, A. (2005). Workflows der software-migration. *Softwaretechnik-Trends, 25*(2), 22–24.

Gipp, T., & Winter, A. (2007). Applying the ReMiP to web site migration. In S. Huang & M. Di Penta (Eds.), *Proceedings of the Ninth IEEE International Symposium on Web Site Evolution (WSE),* (pp. 9–13). Washington, DC: IEEE Computer Society Press.

Giunchiglia, F., & Svaiko, P. (2003). Semantic matching. *The Knowledge Engineering Review Journal, 18*(3).

Gold, N., Knight, C., Mohan, A., & Munro, M. (2004). Understanding service-oriented software. *IEEE Software, 21*(2), 71–77. doi:10.1109/MS.2004.1270766

Google. (2011). *Google docs - Online documents, spreadsheets, presentations.* Retrieved November 30, 2011, from http://docs.google.com/

Google. (2012). *Google AppEngine.* Retrieved from http://code.google.com/appengine/

Gordon, A. W., & Lu, P. (2011). Elastic phoenix: Malleable MapReduce for shared-memory systems. In *Proceedings of the 8th IFIP International Conference on Network and Parallel Computing (NPC).* Springer-Verlag.

Gorton, I., & Zhu, L. (2005). Tool support for just-in-time architecture reconstruction and evaluation: An experience report. In G.-C. Roman, W. Griswold, & B. Nuseibeh (Eds.), *ICSE 2005: Proceedings of the 27th International Conference on Software Engineering,* (pp. 514–523). New York, NY: Association for Computing Machinery.

Gorton, I. (2006). *Essential software architecture.* Berlin, Germany: Springer-Verlag.

Grace, A., Lewis, G. A., Morris, E. J., Smith, D. B., & Simanta, S. (2008). *SMART: Analyzing the reuse potential of legacy components in a service-oriented architecture environment.* Technical Note: CMU/SEI 2208-TN-008. Retrieved from http://www.sei.cmu.edu/reports/08tn008.pdf

Greenfield, J., & Short, K. (2004). *Software factories: Assembling applications with pattern, models, frameworks, and tools.* New York, NY: Wiley Publishing.

Grønmo, R., Jaeger, M. C., & Hoff, H. (2005). Transformations between UML and OWL-S. In A. Hartman & D. Kreische (Eds.), *Proceedings of the First European Conference on Model Driven Architecture – Foundations and Applications (ECMDA-FA) 2005,* (pp. 269-283). ECMDA-FA.

Grønmo, R., Skogan, D., Solheim, I., & Oldevik, J. (2004). Model-driven web services development. In S. Yuan & J. Li (Eds.), *Proceedings of the 2004 IEEE International Conference on e-Technology, e-Commerce and e-Service (EEE) 2004,* (pp. 42-45). IEEE Press.

Gründer, H., & Geihs, K. (1996). Reuse and inheritance in distributed object systems. In *International Workshop on Trends in Distributed Systems,* (pp. 191-200). London, UK: Springer-Verlag.

Gu, Z., Li, J., & Xu, B. (2008). Automatic service composition based on enhanced service dependency graph. In *Proceedings of the 2008 IEEE International Conference on Web Services,* (pp. 246-253). IEEE.

Gui, G., & Scott, P. D. (2006). Coupling and cohesion measures for evaluation of component reusability. In *Proceedings of the 2006 International Workshop on Mining Software Repositories.* IEEE.

Gupta, P. (2010). *Characterizing policies that govern service-oriented systems.* (Unpublished Master's Thesis). University of Victoria. Victoria, Canada.

Gutwin, C. A., Lippold, M., & Graham, T. C. N. (2011). Real-time groupware in the browser: Testing the performance of web-based networking. In *Proceedings of the ACM 2011 Conference on Computer Supported Cooperative Work,* (pp. 167–176). ACM Press.

Guzman, I., Polo, M., & Piattini, M. (2007). An ADM approach to reengineer relational databases towards web services. In *Proceedings of the 14th Working Conference on Reverse Engineering (WCRE 2007).* WCRE.

Haase, P., Math, T., Schmidt, M., Eberhart, A., & Walther, U. (2010). Semantic technologies for enterprise cloud management. In *Proceeding of the Ninth International Conference on Web Services.* Shanghai, China: IEEE.

Hadoop Wiki Contributors. (2011). *Hbase/poweredby - hadoop wiki.* Retrieved from http://wiki.apache.org/hadoop/ Hbase/PoweredBy

Halstead, M. (1977). *Elements of software science.* Amsterdam, The Netherlands: North-Holland.

Hielscher, J., Kazhamiakin, R., Metzger, A., & Pistore, M. A. (2008). A framework for proactive self-adaptation of service-based applications based on online testing. *Lecture Notes in Computer Science, 5377,* 10–13. doi:10.1007/978-3-540-89897-9_11

High, R., Kinder, S., & Graham, S. (2005). *IBM's SOA foundation: An architectural introduction and overview*. Retrieved October 6, 2011, from http://download.boulder.ibm.com/ibmdl/pub/software/dw/webservices/ws-soa-whitepaper.pdf

Holdener, A. III. (2008). *Ajax: The definitive guide*. Sebastopol, CA: O'Reilly Media, Inc.

Horn, P. (2001). Autonomic computing: IBM's perspective on the state of information technology. *IBM Corp*. Retrieved May 2, 2009, from http://researchweb.watson.ibm.com/autonomic/

Horn, T. (2011). Program understanding: A reengineering case for the transformation tool contest. In P. van Gorp, S. Mazanek, & L. Rose (Eds.), *Electronic Proceedings in Theoretical Computer Science: Proceedings of the Fifth Transformation Tool Contest (TTC),* (pp. 17–21). Open Publishing Association.

Horn, T. (2011). Solving the TTC 2011 reengineering case with GReTL. In P. van Gorp, S. Mazanek, & L. Rose (Eds.), *Electronic Proceedings in Theoretical Computer Science: Proceedings of the Fifth Transformation Tool Contest (TTC),* (pp. 131–135). Open Publishing Association.

Horn, T., & Ebert, J. (2011). The GReTL transformation language. *Lecture Notes in Computer Science, 6707*, 183–197. doi:10.1007/978-3-642-21732-6_13

Horridge, M. (2011). A practical guide to building OWL ontologies using Protégé 4 and CO-ODE tools. Retrieved September 28, 2011, from http://owl.cs.manchester.ac.uk/tutorials/protegeowltutorial/resources/ProtegeOWLTutorialP4_v1_3.pdf

Hosoya, H., & Pierce, B. (2002). Regular expression pattern matching for XML. *Journal of Functional Programming, 13*(6), 961–1004. doi:10.1017/S0956796802004410

Hoyer, P., Gebhart, M., Pansa, I., Link, S., Dikanski, A., & Abeck, S. (2009). A model-driven development approach for service-oriented integration scenarios. In *Proceedings of the 2009 Computation World: Future Computing, Service Computation, Cognitive, Adaptive, Content, Patterns*. IEEE.

Hoyer, P., Gebhart, M., Pansa, I., Dikanski, A., & Abeck, S. (2010). Service-oriented integration using a model-driven approach. *International Journal on Advances in Software, 3*(1-2), 304–317.

Hutcheson, M. (2003). *Software testing fundamentals – Fundamental metrics for software testing*. New York, NY: John Wiley & Sons.

IABG. (2009). *V-model XT, version 1.3*. Retrieved March 19, 2012, from http://v-modell.iabg.de/dmdocuments/V-Modell-XT-Gesamt-Englisch-V1.3.pdf

IBM. (2003). *Business process execution language (BPEL) for web services*. Retrieved from http://www.ibm.com/developerworks/library/specification/ws-bpel/

IBM. (2006). IBM RUP for service-oriented modeling and architecture V2.4. *IBM DeveloperWorks*. Retrieved September 28, 2011, from http://www.ibm.com/developerworks/rational/downloads/06/rmc_soma/

IBM. (2012). *Interpretation of UML elements by UML-to-BPEL transformations*. Retrieved September 28, 2011, from http://publib.boulder.ibm.com/infocenter/rsahelp/v7r0m0/index.jsp?topic=/com.ibm.xtools.transform.uml2.bpel.doc/topics/rubpelmap.html

Idu, A., Khadka, R., Saeidi, A., Jansen, S., & Hage, J. (2012). *Technical report on performing a systematic literature review*. Retrieved March 26, 2012, from http://servicifi.files.wordpress.com/2012/01/technical_report_drft.pdf

Indika. (2011). *Differences between SaaS and SOA*. Retrieved from http://www.differencebetween.com/difference-between-saas-and-vs-soa/

Inoue, T., Asakura, H., Sato, H., & Takahashi, N. (2010). Key roles of session state: Not against REST architectural style. In *Proceedings of the 34th Annual Computer Software and Applications Conference,* (pp. 171-178). IEEE Computer Society Press.

Institute for Software Technology. (2012). *JGraLab*. Retrieved March 19, 2012, from http://jgralab.uni-koblenz.de

Ionita, A. D., Catapano, A., Giuroiu, S., & Florea, M. (2008). Service oriented system for business cooperation. In *Proceedings of the 2nd International Workshop on Systems Development in SOA Environments, SDSOA 2008,* (pp. 13–18). New York, NY: ACM Press.

ISO. (1993). *Software product evaluation*. Geneva, Switzerland: ISO/IEC Standards Office.

Java.net. (2011). *JAXB reference implementation*. Retrieved March 19, 2012, from http://jaxb.java.net/

Java.net. (2011). *JAX-WS reference implementation.* Retrieved March 19, 2012, from http://jax-ws.java.net/

Jboss.org. (2011). *RichFaces project page.* Retrieved March 19, 2012, from http://www.jboss.org/richfaces

Jeffery, K., & Neidecker-Lutz, B. (2010). *The future of cloud computing: Opportunities for European cloud computing beyond 2010.* Geneva, Switzerland: European Commission, Information Society and Media.

Jeong, B., Lee, D., Cho, H., & Lee, J. (2008). A novel method for measuring semantic similarity for XML schema matching. *Expert Systems with Applications, 34,* 1651–1658. doi:10.1016/j.eswa.2007.01.025

JGroups. (2011). *JGroups - A toolkit for reliable multicast communication.* Retrieved November 30, 2011, from http://www.jgroups.org/

Jiang, Y., & Stroulia, E. (2004). Towards reengineering web sites to web-services providers. In *Proceedings of the 8th European Conference on Software Maintenance and Reengineering (CSMR 2004).* CSMR.

Johnston, S. (2004). Rational UML profile for business modeling. *IBM DeveloperWorks.* Retrieved September 28, 2011, from http://www.ibm.com/developerworks/rational/library/5167.html

Johnston, S. (2005). UML 2.0 profile for software services. *IBM DeveloperWorks.* Retrieved September 28, 2011, from http://www.ibm.com/developerworks/rational/library/05/419_soa/

Jorgensen, M., & Shepperd, M. (2007). A systematic review of software development cost estimation studies. *IEEE Transactions on Software Engineering, 33*(1), 33–53. doi:10.1109/TSE.2007.256943

Juric, M. B., & Šaša, A. (2010). Version management of BPEL processes in SOA. In *Proceedings of the 2010 IEEE Sixth World Congress on Services,* (pp. 146-147). New York, NY: Association for Computing Machinery.

Kajko-Mattsson, M., Lewis, G., & Smith, D. (2007). A framework for roles for development, evolution and maintenance of SOA-based systems. In *Proceedings of the International Workshop on Systems Development in SOA Environments.* New York, NY: Association for Computing Machinery.

Kajko-Mattsson, M., Lewis, G., & Smith, D. (2008). Evolution and maintenance of SOA-based systems at SAS. In *Proceedings of the 41st Hawaii International Conference on System Sciences.* New York, NY: Association for Computing Machinery.

Kappel, G., Pröll, B., Reich, S., & Retschitzegger, W. (Eds.). (2006). *Web engineering.* Chichester, UK: John Wiley & Sons.

Kazman, R., Woods, S., & Carrière, J. (1998). Requirements for integrating software architecture and reengineering models: CORUM II. In *Proceedings of the Firth Working Conference on Reverse En-gineering (WCRE),* (pp. 154–163). Washington, DC: IEEE Computer Society Press.

Kazman, R., & Carriere, J. (1999). Playing detective: Reconstructing software architecture from available evidence. *Automated Software Engineering, 6*(2), 106–138. doi:10.1023/A:1008781513258

Kazman, R., O'Brien, L., & Verhoef, C. (2001). *Architecture reconstruction guidelines.* DTIC.

Kell, S. (2008). A survey of practical software adaptation techniques. *Journal of Universal Computer Science, 14*(13), 2110–2157.

Kemmerer, C., & Paulk, M. (2009). The impact of design and code reviews on software quality. *IEEE Transactions on Software Engineering, 35*(4), 534–550. doi:10.1109/TSE.2009.27

Kennedy, S., Stewart, R., Jacob, P., & Molloy, O. (2011). StoRHm: A protocol adapter for mapping SOAP based web services to RESTful HTTP format. *Electronic Commerce Research, 11*(3), 245–269. doi:10.1007/s10660-011-9075-3

Kent, S. (2002). Model driven engineering. In M. Butler, L. Petre, & K. Sere (Eds.), *Proceedings of the Third International Conference on Integrated Formal Methods,* (vol 2335, pp. 286-298). Springer-Verlag.

Khadka, R. (2011). Service identification strategies in legacy-to-SOA migration. In *Proceedings of the Doctoral Consortium of the 26th International Conference on Software Maintenance (ICSM 2011).* ICSM.

Khadka, R., & Sapkota, B. (2010). An evaluation of dynamic web service composition approaches. In *Proceedings of the 4th International Workshop on Architectures, Concepts and Technologies for Service Oriented Computing (ACT4SOC 2010)*. ACT4SOC.

Khadka, R., Reijnders, G., Saeidi, A., Jansen, S., & Hage, J. (2011). A method engineering based legacy to SOA migration method. In *Proceedings of the 27th IEEE International Conference on Software Maintenance (ICSM)*, (pp. 163–172). Washington, DC: IEEE Computer Society Press.

Khadka, R., Saeidi, A., Jansen, S., Hage, J., & Helms, R. (2011). *An evaluation of service frameworks for the manangement of service ecosystems*. Paper presented at the 15th Pacific Asia Conference on Information System (PACIS 2011). Brisbane, Australia.

Khadka, R., Sapkota, B., Pires, L. F., Sinderen, M., & Jansen, S. (2011). *Model-driven development of service compositions for enterprise interoperability*. Paper presented at the 3rd International IFIP Working Conference on Enterprise Interoperability (IWEI 2011). Retrieved from http://dx.doi.org/10.1007/978-3-642-19680-5_15

Khadka, R., Saeidi, A., Idu, A., Hage, J., & Jansen, S. (2012). *Legacy to SOA evolution: Evaluation results. No. UU-CS-2012-006*. Utrecht, The Netherlands: Utrecht University.

Khusidman, V., & Ulrich, W. (2007). *Architecture-driven modernization: Transforming the enterprise draft* (*Vol. 5*). OMG.

Kim, D., & Shen, W. (2007). An approach to evaluating structural pattern conformance of UML models. In *Proceedings of the ACM Symposium on Applied Computing*, (pp. 1404-1408). ACM Press.

Kim, S., Kim, M., & Park, S. (2008). Service identification using goal and scenario in service oriented architecture. In *Proceedings of the 15th Asia-Pacific Software Engineering Conference (APSEC)*, (pp. 419–426). Washington, DC: IEEE Computer Society Press.

Kitchenham, B. (2004). *Procedures for performing systematic reviews*. NICTA Tech. Rep. 0400011T.1. Keele, UK: Keele University and National ICT Australia.

Kokash, N., & Arbab, F. (2009). Formal behavioral modeling and compliance analysis for service-oriented systems. *Lecture Notes in Computer Science, 5751*, 21–41. doi:10.1007/978-3-642-04167-9_2

Konstantinou, I., Angelou, E., Tsoumakos, D., & Koziris, N. (2010). Distributed indexing of web scale datasets for the cloud. In *Proceedings of the 2010 Workshop on Massive Data Analytics on the Cloud*, (pp. 1–6). New York, NY: ACM.

Kontogiannis, K., Lewis, G. A., & Smith, D. B. (2008). A research agenda for service-oriented architecture. In *Proceedings of the Second International Workshop on Systems Development in SOA Environments*, (pp. 1–6). New York, NY: Association for Computing Machinery.

Kontogiannis, K., Lewis, G. A., Smith, D. B., Litoiu, M., Muller, H., Schuster, S., et al. (2007). *The landscape of service-oriented systems: A research perspective*. Paper presented at the International workshop on Systems Development in SOA Environments (SDSOA 2007). Minneapolis, MN.

Krafzig, D., Banke, K., & Slama, D. (2005). *Enterprise SOA: Service oriented architecture best practices*. Boston, MA: Prentice Hall.

Krishna, B., Reddy, E., Jagadamba, K., Krishnamoorthy, S., & Krishna, P. (2009). A unified and scalable data migration service for the cloud environments. In *Proceedings of COMAD*. COMAD.

Kruchten, P. (2003). *The rational unified process: An introduction* (3rd ed.). Reading, MA: Addison-Wesley.

Kruchten, P. (2004). *The rational unified process: An introduction*. Boston, MA: Pearson Education Inc.

Kumaran, S., et al. (2008). A RESTful architecture for service-oriented business process execution. In *Proceedings of the International Conference on e-Business Engineering*, (pp. 197-204). IEEE Computer Society Press.

Laird, B., & Brennan, C. (2006). *Software measurement and estimation – A practical approach*. New York, NY: John Wiley & Sons. doi:10.1002/0471792535

Laitkorpi, M., Koskinen, J., & Systa, T. (2006). A UML-based approach for abstracting application interfaces to REST-like services. In *Proceedings of the 13th Working Conference on Reverse Engineering*, (pp. 134-146). IEEE.

Laitkorpi, M., Selonen, P., & Systa, T. (2009). Towards a model-driven process for designing ReSTful web services. In *Proceedings of the IEEE International Conference on Web Services,* (pp. 173-180). IEEE Computer Society Press.

Lakshman, A., & Malik, P. (2010). Cassandra: A decentralized structured storage system. *ACM SIGOPS Operating Systems Review, 44*(2), 35–40. doi:10.1145/1773912.1773922

Laskey, K. (2008). Considerations for SOA versioning. In *Proceedings of 12th Enterprise Distributed Object Computing Conference Workshops,*(pp. 333–337). New York, NY: Association for Computing Machinery.

Lee, S. P., Chan, L. P., & Lee, E. W. (2006). Web services implementation methodology for SOA application. In *Proceedings of the IEEE International Conference on Industrial Informatics.* IEEE Press.

Lehman, M. M. (1996). Laws of software evolution revisited. In C. Montangero (Ed.), *Proceedings of the 5th European Workshop on Software Process Technology (EWSPT 1996),* (pp. 108-124). London, UK: Springer-Verlag.

Leinecker, R. C. (2000). *Com+ unleashed.* Sams.

Lewis, G. A., & Smith, D. B. (2008). SMART tool demonstration. In K. Kontogiannis, C. Tjortjis, & A. Winter (Eds.), *Proceedings of the 12th European Conference on Software Maintenance and Reengineering,* (pp. 332–334). Washington, DC: IEEE Computer Society Press.

Lewis, G. A., Chapin, N., Kontogiannis, K., & Smith, D. B. (Eds.). (2010). *Proceedings of the third international workshop on a research agenda for maintenance and evolution of service-oriented systems (MESOA 2009).* Pittsburgh, PA: Carnegie Mellon University.

Lewis, G. A., Kontogiannis, K., & Smith, D. B. (Eds.). (2011). *Proceedings of the Fourth International Workshop on a Research Agenda for Maintenance and Evolution of Service-Oriented Systems (MESOA 2010).* Pittsburgh, PA: Carnegie Mellon University.

Lewis, G. A., Morris, E. J., & Smith, D. B. (2006). Analyzing the reuse potential of migrating legacy components to a service-oriented architecture. In G. Visaggio, G. A. Di Lucca, & N. Gold (Eds.), *Proceedings of the 10th European Conference on Software Maintenance and Reengineering (CSMR 2006),* (pp. 15–23). Washington, DC: IEEE Computer Society Press.

Lewis, G., Morris, E., Simanta, S., & Smith, D. (2008). *SMART: Analyzing the reuse potential of legacy components in a service-oriented architecture environment.* Technical Note CMU/SEI-2008-TN-008. Retrieved from http://www.sei.cmu.edu/library/abstracts/reports/08tn008.cfm

Lewis, G., Morris, E., Smith, D., & O'Brien, L. (2005). Service-oriented migration and reuse technique (SMART). In *Proceedings of the 13th IEEE International Workshop on Software Technology and Engineering Practice.* IEEE Press.

Lewis, G., Smith, D., Chapin, N., & Kontogiannis, K. (2009). *MESOA 2009: 3rd International workshop on maintenance and evolution of service-oriented systems.* No. 1424448972. SEI.

Lewis, G. A., Smith, D. B., & Kontogiannis, K. (2010). *A research agenda for service-oriented architecture (SOA): Maintenance and evolution of service-oriented systems.* Pittsburgh, PA: Carnegie Mellon University.

Lewis, G., Morris, E. J., Smith, D. B., & Simanta, S. (2008). *SMART: Analyzing the reuse potential of legacy components in a service-oriented architecture environment.* Pittsburgh, PA: Carnegie Mellon University.

Lewis, G., Morris, E., O'Brien, L., Smith, D., & Wrage, L. (2005). *SMART: The service-oriented migration and reuse technique. No. CMU/SEI-2005-TN-029.* Software Engineering Institute.

Lewis, G., Morris, E., Simanta, S., & Smith, D. (2011). Service orientation and systems of systems. *IEEE Software, 28*(1), 58–63. doi:10.1109/MS.2011.15

Lewis, G., Morris, E., & Smith, D. (2005). Migration of legacy components to service-oriented architectures. *Journal of Software Technology, 8,* 14–23.

Lhotka, R. A. (2005). SOA versioning covenant. *Search-WinDevelopment.com*. Retrieved October 6, 2011, from http://searchwindevelopment.techtarget.com/tip/0,289483,sid8_gci1277472,00.html

Li, A., Zong, X., Kandula, S., Yang, X., & Zhang, M. (2011). Cloudprophet: Towards application performance prediction in cloud. In *Proceedings of the ACM SIGCOMM 2011 Conference,* (pp. 426–427). New York, NY: ACM.

Li, L., & Chou, W. (2010). Design patterns for RESTful communication. In *Proceedings of the International Conference on Web Services,* (pp. 512-519). IEEE Computer Society Press.

Li, N., Rao, J., Shekita, E., & Tata, S. (2009). Leveraging a scalable row store to build a distributed text index. In *Proceedings of the First International Workshop on Cloud Data Management,* (pp. 29–36). ACM.

Li, S., & Tahvildari, L. (2008). E-BUS: A toolkit for extracting business services from java software systems. In *Proceedings of the Companion of the 30th International Conference on Software Engineering*. IEEE Press.

Li, W., Zhang, Y., & Jin, J. (2009). Research of the service design approach based on SCA_OSGi. In *Proceedings of the 2009 International Conference on Services Science Management and Engineering,* (pp. 392–395). IEEE.

Li, Z., Anming, X., Naiyue, Z., Jianbin, H., & Zhong, C. (2009). A SOA modernization method based on toll-gate model. In *Proceedings of the 2009 International Symposium on Information Engineering and Electronic Commerce*. IEEE.

Lientz, B. P., & Swanson, E. B. (1980). *Software maintenance management: A study of the maintenance of computer application software in 487 data processing organizations*. Reading, MA: Addison-Wesley.

Li, S.-H., Huang, S.-M., Yen, D. C., & Chang, C.-C. (2007). Migrating legacy information systems to web services architecture. *Journal of Database Management, 18*(4), 1–25. doi:10.4018/jdm.2007100101

Liskin, O., Singer, L., & Schneider, K. (2011). Teaching old services new tricks: Adding HATEOAS support as an afterthought. In *Proceedings of the Second International Workshop on RESTful Design,* (pp. 3–10). ACM.

Litoiu, M. (2004). Migrating to web services: A performance engineering approach. *Journal of Software Maintenance and Evolution: Research and Practice, 16*(1-2), 51–70. doi:10.1002/smr.285

Little, M. (2009). *REST and transactions?* Retrieved October 10, 2011, from http://www.infoq.com/news/2009/06/rest-ts

Liu, Y., Wang, Q., Zhuang, M., & Zhu, Y. (2008). Re-engineering legacy systems with RESTful web service. In *Proceedings of the 32nd Annual IEEE International Computer Software and Applications Conference,* (pp. 785-790). IEEE.

Li, W. (1997). An empirical study of software reuse in reconstructive maintenance. *Journal of Software Maintenance, 9*(2), 69. doi:10.1002/(SICI)1096-908X(199703)9:2<69::AID-SMR147>3.0.CO;2-5

Lu, X., Zou, Y., Xiong, F., Lin, J., & Zha, L. (2009). ICOMC: Invocation complexity of multi-language clients for classified Web services and its impact on large scale SOA applications. In K. Nakano & S. Olariu (Eds.), *Proceedings of the 2009 International Conference on Parallel and Distributed Computing, Applications and Technologies,* (pp. 186–194). Washington, DC: IEEE Computer Society Press.

Lubbers, P., Albers, B., & Salim, F. (2010). *Pro HTML5 programming: Powerful APIs for richer internet application development*. New York, NY: Apress.

Lublinsky, B. (2007). Versioning in SOA. *Architect Journal, 11*. Retrieved October 6, 2011, from http://msdn2.microsoft.com/en-us/arcjournal/bb491124.aspx

Lyytinen, K., & Yoo, Y. (2002). Issues and challenges in ubiquitous computing. *Communications of the ACM, 45*(12), 62–65.

Maedche, A., & Staab, S. (2002). Measuring similarity between ontologies. In *Proceedings of the International Conference on Knowledge Engineering and Knowledge Management (EKAW),* (pp. 251–263). EKAW.

Mahbub, K., & Zisman, A. (2009). Replacement policies for service-based systems. In A. Dan, F. Gittler, & F. Toumani (Eds.), *ICSOC/ServiceWave 2009: Proceedings of the 2009 International Conference on Service Oriented Computing,* (pp. 345–357). New York, NY: Association for Computing Machinery.

Mahmood, Z. (2007). The promise and limitations of service oriented architecture. *International Journal of Computers*, *1*(3), 74–78.

Marchetto, A., & Ricca, F. (2008). Transforming a java application in an equivalent web-services based application: Toward a tool supported stepwise approach. In *Proceedings of the 10th International Symposium on Web Site Evolution (WSE 2008)*. WSE.

Marchetto, A., & Ricca, F. (2009). From objects to services: Toward a tool supported stepwise approach. *International Journal on Software Tools for Technology Transfer*, *11*, 427–440. doi:10.1007/s10009-009-0123-4

Marinos, A., Razavi, A., Moschoyiannis, S., & Krause, P. (2009). RETRO: A consistent and recoverable RESTful transaction model. In *Proceedings of the 2009 IEEE International Conference on Web Services*, (pp. 181-188). IEEE.

Martin, E., & Xie, T. (2006). Understanding software application interfaces via string analysis. In L. J. Osterweil, D. Rombach, & M. L. Soffa (Eds.), *ICSE 2006: Proceedings of the 28th International Conference on Software Engineering*, (pp. 901–904). New York, NY: Association for Computing Machinery.

Mateos, C., Crasso, M., Zunino, A., & Campo, M. (2010). Separation of concerns in service-oriented applications based on pervasive design patterns. In *Proceedings of Web Technology Track (WT) - 25th ACM Symposium on Applied Computing (SAC 2010)*, (pp. 2509-2513). Sierre, Switzerland: ACM Press.

McCabe, T. (1976). A complexity measure. *IEEE Transactions on Software Engineering*, *2*(4), 308–319. doi:10.1109/TSE.1976.233837

McClure, C. (1981). *Managing software development and maintenance*. New York, NY: Van Nostrand.

Mell, P., & Grance, T. (2011). *The NIST definition of cloud computing*. Retrieved from http://www.nist.gov/itl/cloud/index.cfm

Mendeley, Ltd. (2011). *Free reference manager and PDF organizer*. Retrieved from http://www.mendeley.com/

Metzger, A., Sammodi, O., Pohl, K., & Rzepka, M. (2010). Towards proactive adaptation with confidence: Augmenting service monitoring with online testing. In R. de Lemos & M. Pezzè (Eds.), *Proceedings of the 2010 ICSE Workshop on Software Engineering for Self-Adaptive and Self-Monitoring Systems*, (pp. 20–28). New York, NY: Association for Computing Machinery.

Meyer, B. (2000). *Object-oriented software construction* (2nd ed.). Upper Saddle River, NJ: Prentice Hall.

Microsoft Corporation. (2007). *Real world SOA at the edge*. Retrieved from http://download.microsoft.com/download/d/d/e/ddeb427d-dc05-4ab0-b47e-74f0a936d892/Real-World-SOA-At-The-Edge.pdf

Microsoft Corporation. (2009). *Windows communication foundation*. Retrieved October 6, 2011, from http://msdn.microsoft.com/en-us/netframework/aa663324.aspx

Mietzner, R., Metzger, A., Leymann, F., & Pohl, K. (2009). Variability modeling to support customization and deployment of multi-tenant-aware software as a service applications. In *Proceedings of the ICSE Workshop on Principles of Engineering Service Oriented Systems (PESOS)*, (pp. 18-25). Washington, DC: IEEE Computer Society Press.

Millham, R. (2010). Migration of a legacy procedural system to service-oriented computing using feature analysis. In *Proceedings of the 2010 International Conference on Complex, Intelligent and Software Intensive Systems*. IEEE.

Minalogic. (2011). *iDeviceCloud*. Retrieved from http://idevicecloud.minalogic.net

Mittal, K. (2005). Build your SOA, part 1: Maturity and methodology. *IBM DeveloperWorks*. Retrieved October 6, 2011, from http://www-128.ibm.com/developerworks/webservices/library/ws-soa-method1.html

Mohagheghi, P., & Sæther, T. (2011). Software engineering challenges for migration to the service cloud paradigm: Ongoing work in the REMICS project. In *Proceedings of the 2011 World Congress on Services*, (p. 507-514). IEEE.

Müller, H. (2010). *Perspectives on SOA control science.* Paper presented at the Fourth International Workshop on a Research Agenda for Maintenance and Evolution of Service-Oriented Systems (MESOA 2010). Timisoara, Romania.

Müller, H. A., Pezzè, M., & Shaw, M. (2008). Visibility of control in adaptive systems. In K. Sullivan & R. Kazman (Eds.), *ULSSIS 2008: Proceedings of the Second International Workshop on Ultra-Large-Scale Software-Intensive Systems,* (pp. 23–26). New York, NY: Association for Computing Machinery.

Mulligan, G., & Gracanin, D. (2009). A comparison of SOAP and REST implementations of a service based interaction independence middleware framework. In M. Rossetti, et al. (Eds.), *Winter Simulation Conference,* (pp. 1423-1432). IEEE Computer Society Press.

Muthukkaruppan, K. (2011). *The underlying technology of messages.* Retrieved from http://www.facebook.com/note.php?note id=454991608919

Mynampati, P. (2008). SOA governance: Examples of service life cycle management processes. *IBM DeveloperWorks.* Retrieved October 6, 2011, from http://www.ibm.com/developerworks/webservices/library/ws-soa-governance/index.html

MySQL. (2010). *Sakila database for MySql.* Retrieved on December 2010, from http://dev.mysql.com/doc/sakila/en/sakila.html

Nadico, O. (2007). SOA transformation of legacy applications. *ObjectSpectrum, 17*(5), 18–21.

Nagarajan, M., Verma, K., Sheth, A., Miller, J., & Lathem, J. (2006). Semantic interoperability of web services-challenges and experiences. In *Proceeding of the Fourth IEEE International Conference on Web Services,* (pp. 3-4). Chicago, IL: IEEE Press.

Nakamura, M., Igaki, H., Kimura, T., & Matsumoto, K.-I. (2009). Extracting service candidates from procedural programs based on process dependency analysis. In *Proceedings of the IEEE Asia-Pacific Services Computing Conference.* IEEE Press.

Nasr, K. A., Gross, H.-G., & Deursen, A. V. (2010). Adopting and evaluating service oriented architecture in industry. In *Proceedings of the 2010 14th European Conference on Software Maintenance and Reengineering.* IEEE.

Nasr, K., Gross, H., & Van Deursen, A. (2011). Realizing service migration in industry—Lessons learned. *Journal of Software Maintenance and Evolution, 21*(2), 113–141.

Natis, Y. (2003). *Service-oriented architecture scenario.* Stamford, CT: Gartner Group.

Navon, J., & Fernandez, F. (2011). The essence of REST architectural style. In Wilde, E., & Pautasso, C. (Eds.), *REST from Research to Practice.* Berlin, Germany: Springer. doi:10.1007/978-1-4419-8303-9_1

O'Brian, J. A., & Marakas, G. M. (2008). *Management information systems.* Columbus, OH: McGraw-Hill.

OASIS. (2007). *Web services business process execution language (BPEL), version 2.0.* Retrieved September 28, 2011, from http://docs.oasis-open.org/wsbpel/2.0/wsbpel-v2.0.html

Obofoundry. (2011). *Obofoundary relationship ontology.* Retrieved on January 2011 from http://www.obofoundry.org/ro/

O'Brien, L., Smith, D., & Lewis, G. (2005). *Supporting migration to services using software architecture reconstruction.* Paper presented at the 13th IEEE International Workshop on Software Technology and Engineering Practice (STEP 2005). Budapest, Hungary.

O'Brien, L., Smith, D. B., & Lewis, G. A. (2005). Supporting migration to services using software architecture reconstruction. In Kontogiannis, K., Zou, Y., & Di Penta, M. (Eds.), *Proceedings of Software Technology and Engineering Practice 2005* (pp. 81–91). Washington, DC: IEEE Computer Society Press. doi:10.1109/STEP.2005.29

Oldevik, J., Olsen, G. K., Brönner, U., & Bodsberg, N. R. (2011). Model-driven migration of scientific legacy systems to service-oriented architectures. In A. Fuhr, V. Riediger, W. Hasselbring, M. Bruntink, & K. Kontogiannis (Eds.), *CEUR Workshop Proceedings: Joint Proceedings of the First International Workshop on Model-Driven Software Migration (MDSM 2011) and Fifth International Workshop on Software Quality and Maintainability (SQM 2011),* (pp. 4–7). CEUR-WS.org.

Oman, P., Coleman, D., Ash, D., & Lowther, B. (1994). Using metrics to evaluate software system maintainability. *IEEE Computer Magazine, 27*(8), 44.

OMG. (2006). *UML profile and metamodel for services (UPMS), request for proposal.* Retrieved September 28, 2011, from http://www.omg.org/cgi-bin/doc?soa/06-09-09.pdf

OMG. (2009). *Service oriented architecture modeling language (SoaML) – Specification for the UML profile and metamodel for services (UPMS), version 1.0 beta2.* Retrieved September 28, 2011, from http://www.omg.org/spec/SoaML/1.0/Beta2/PDF

OMG. (2010). *OMG unified modeling language (OMG UML), superstructure, version 2.3.* Retrieved September 28, 2011, from http://www.omg.org/spec/UML/2.3/Superstructure/PDF/

OMG. (2011). *Business process model and notation (BPMN), version 2.0.* Retrieved September 28, 2011, from http://www.omg.org/spec/BPMN/2.0/PDF

Oracle. (2011). *JavaServer faces technology.* Retrieved March 19, 2012, from http://java.sun.com/j2ee/javaserverfaces/

Ordiales Coscia, J. L., Mateos, C., Crasso, M., & Zunino, A. (2011). Avoiding wsdl bad practices in code-first web services. In *Proceedings of the 12th Argentine Symposium on Software Engineering (ASSE2011)*, (pp. 1–12). ASSE.

OSGi Alliance. (2009). *OSGi service platform core specification release 4.2.* Retrieved from http://www.osgi.org/download/r4v42/r4.core.pdf

OSOA. (2009). *Service component architecture (SCA), SCA assembly model specification, version 1.0.* Retrieved September 28, 2011, from http://www.osoa.org/download/attachments/35/SCA_AssemblyModel_V100.pdf?version=1

OSOA. (2012). *Service component architecture.* Retrieved from http://www.osoa.org/display/Main/Service+Component+Architecture+Home

Panda, B., Herbach, J. S., Basu, S., & Bayardo, R. J. (2009). PLANET: Massively parallel learning of tree ensembles with MapReduce. *Proceedings of the VLDB Endowment, 2*(2), 1426–1437.

Papazoglou, M. P. (2003). Service-oriented computing – Concepts, characteristics and directions. In T. Catarci, M. Mecella, J. Mylopoulos, & M. E. Orlowsk (Eds.), *Proceedings of the Fourth International Conference on Web Information Systems Engineering (WISE) 2003,* (pp. 3-12). WISE.

Papazoglou, M., Traverso, P., Dustdar, S., Leyman, F., & Kramer, B. (2006). Service-oriented computing: Research roadmap. In F. Curbera, B. J. Kramer, & M. P. Papazoglou (Eds.), *Dagstuhl Seminar Proceedings: Vol. 5462: Service Oriented Computing (SOC).* Schloss Dagstuhl, Germany: Internationales Begegnungs und Forschungszentrum für Informatik. Retrieved October 6, 2011 from http://drops.dagstuhl.de/volltexte/2006/524/pdf/05462.SWM.Paper.524.pdf

Papazoglou, M. (2008). *Web services: Principles and technology.* Reading, MA: Addison-Wesley.

Papazoglou, M. P., & Heuvel, W.-J. (2007). Service oriented architectures: Approaches, technologies and research issues. *The VLDB Journal, 16*, 389–415. doi:10.1007/s00778-007-0044-3

Papazoglou, M. P., Traverso, P., Dustdar, S., & Leymann, F. (2008). Service-oriented computing: A research roadmap. *International Journal of Cooperative Information Systems, 17*(2), 223–255. doi:10.1142/S0218843008001816

Papazoglou, M., Pohl, K., Parkin, M., & Metzger, A. (2010). *Service research challenges and solutions for the future Internet: Towards mechanisms and methods for engineering, managing, and adapting service-based systems.* New York, NY: Springer.

Papazoglou, M., Pohl, K., Parkin, M., Metzger, A., & van den Heuvel, W.-J. (2010). The s-cube research vision. In Papazoglou, M., Pohl, K., Parkin, M., & Metzger, A. (Eds.), *Service Research Challenges and Solutions for the Future Internet: Towards Mechanisms and Methods for Engineering, Managing, and Adapting Service-Based Systems* (pp. 1–26). New York, NY: Springer.

Papazoglou, M., Traverso, P., Dustdar, S., & Leymann, F. (2007). Service-oriented computing: State of the art and research challenges. *Computer, 40*(11), 38–45. doi:10.1109/MC.2007.400

Papazoglou, M., & Van Den Heuvel, W. J. (2006). Service-oriented design and development methodology. *International Journal of Web Engineering and Technology, 2*(4), 412–442. doi:10.1504/IJWET.2006.010423

Pardon, G., & Pautasso, C. (2011). Towards distributed atomic transactions over RESTful services. In Wilde, E., & Pautasso, C. (Eds.), *REST from Research to Practice*. Berlin, Germany: Springer. doi:10.1007/978-1-4419-8303-9_23

Parr, T. (2007). *The definitive ANTLR reference*. Raleigh, NC: The Pragmatic Bookshelf.

Patterson, D., & Ditzel, D. (1980). The case for the reduced instruction set computer. *ACM SIGARCH Computer Architecture News, 8*(6), 25–33. doi:10.1145/641914.641917

Pautasso, C., & Wilde, E. (2009). Why is the web loosely coupled? A multi-faceted metric for service design. In *Proceedings of the 18th World Wide Web Conference,* (pp. 911-920). ACM.

Pautasso, C., Zimmermann, O., & Leymann, F. (2008). Restful web services vs. "big'" web services: Making the right architectural decision. In *Proceedings of the International Conference on World Wide Web,* (pp. 805-814). ACM Press.

Pautasso, C. (2009). RESTful web service composition with BPEL for REST. *Data & Knowledge Engineering, 68*(9), 851–866. doi:10.1016/j.datak.2009.02.016

Pedraza, G., & Estublier, J. (2008). An extensible services orchestration framework through concern composition. In *Proceedings of the 1st International Workshop on Non-functional System Properties in Domain Specific Modeling Languages (NFPDSML)*. NFPDSML.

Pedraza, G., Dieng, I., & Estublier, J. (2009). *FOCAS: An enginering environment for service-based applications*. Paper presented at the 4th International Conference on Evaluation of Novel Approaches to Software Engineering (ENASE). Milan, Italy

Peltz, C. (2003). Web services orchestration: A review of emerging technologies, tools, and standards. *Hewlett Packard, Co*. Retrieved March 23, 2012, from http://itee.uq.edu.au/~infs3204/interesting_websites/WSOrchestration.pdf

Peltz, C., & Anagol-Subbarao, A. (2004). Design strategies for web services versioning: Adapting to the needs of the business. *Web Services Journal, 4*. Retrieved October 6, 2011, from http://webservices.sys-con.com/read/44356.htm

Peng, Y., Ma, S., & Lee, J. (2009). REST2SOAP: A framework to integrate SOAP services and RESTful services. In *Proceedings of the International Conference on Service-Oriented Computing and Applications,* (pp. 1-4). IEEE Computer Society Press.

Perepletchikov, M., Ryan, C., Frampton, K., & Tari, Z. (2007). Coupling metrics for predicting maintainability in service-oriented designs. In *Proceedings of the 18th Australian Software Engineering Conference (ASWEC 2007)*. ASWEC.

Petcu, D., Craciun, C., Neagul, M., Rak, M., & Lazcano-tegui Larrarte, I. (2011). Building an Interoperability API for sky computing. In *Proceedings of the International Conference on High Performance Computing and Simulation (HPCS),* (pp. 405-411). HPCS.

Pinker, E., Seidmann, A., & Foster, R. (2002). Strategies for transitioning old economy firms to e-business. *Communications of the ACM, 45*(5), 77–90. doi:10.1145/506218.506219

Puhr, P., & Sneed, H. (1989). *Code stripping as a means of instrumenting embedded systems. EU ESPRIT Project 1258 – Report-1258-3*. Liverpool, UK: EU ESPRIT.

Queinnec, C. (2003). Inverting back the inversion of control or, continuations versus page-centric programming. *ACM SIGPLAN Notices, 38*(2), 57–64. doi:10.1145/772970.772977

Ragusa, C., & Puliafito, A. (2011). Running business applications in the cloud: A use case perspective. *Lecture Notes in Computer Science, 6586*, 595–602. doi:10.1007/978-3-642-21878-1_73

Rajesh, A., & Srivatsa, S. (2010). XML schema matching – Using structural information. *International Journal of Computers and Applications, 8*(2), 34–41. doi:10.5120/1183-1632

Rajlich, V. T., & Bennett, K. H. (2000). A staged model for the software life cycle. *IEEE Computer, 33*(7), 66–71. doi:10.1109/2.869374

Ramanujam, S., Gupta, A., Khan, L., Seida, S., & Thuraisingham, B. (2009). R2D: A bridge between the semantic web and relational visualization tools. In *Proceedings of the Third International Conference on Semantic Computing,* (pp. 303–311). Berkeley, CA: IEEE.

Ravichandar, R., Nanjangud, C., Narendra, K., & Ponnalagu, D. (2008). Morpheus: Semantics-based incremental change propagation in SOA-based solutions. In W. Chou, P. Hofmann, & M. Devarakonda (Eds.), *Proceedings of the IEEE International Conference on Services Computing,* (pp. 193–201). Washington, DC: IEEE Computer Society Press.

Razavi, A., Marinos, A., Moschoyiannis, S., & Krause, P. (2009). RESTful transactions supported by the isolation theorems. In *Proceedings of the 2009 International Conference on Web Engineering,* (pp. 394-409). Springer-Verlag.

Razavian, M., & Lago, P. (2010). *Towards a conceptual framework for legacy to SOA migration.* Paper presented at the Fifth International Workshop on Engineering Service-Oriented Applications (WESOA 2009). Stockholm, Sweden.

Razavian, M., Nguyen, D. K., Lago, P., & van den Heuvel, W.-J. (2010). The SAPIENSA approach for service-enabling pre-existing legacy assets. In G. A. Lewis, F. Ricca, M. Postina, U. Steffens, & A. Winter (Eds.), *Proceedings of the International Workshop on SOA Migration and Evolution (SOAME),* (pp. 21–30). Oldenburg, Germany: OFFIS.

Razavian, M., & Lago, P. (2010). A frame of reference for SOA migration. In Di Nitto, E., & Yahyapour, R. (Eds.), *Towards a Service-Based Internet* (*Vol. 6481*, pp. 150–162). Berlin, Germany: Springer. doi:10.1007/978-3-642-17694-4_13

Razavian, M., & Lago, P. (2010). Towards a conceptual framework for legacy to SOA migration. *Lecture Notes in Computer Science, 6275,* 445–455. doi:10.1007/978-3-642-16132-2_42

Razavian, M., & Lago, P. (2010). A frame of reference for SOA migration. *Lecture Notes in Computer Science, 6481,* 150–162. doi:10.1007/978-3-642-17694-4_13

Reddy, V. K., Dubey, A., Lakshmanan, S., Sukumaran, S., & Sisodia, R. (2009). Evaluating legacy assets in the context of migration to SOA. *Software Quality Journal, 17*(1), 51–63. doi:10.1007/s11219-008-9055-6

Reijnders, G., Khadka, R., Jansen, S., & Hage, J. (2011). *Developing a legacy to SOA migration method. No. UU-CS-2011-008.* Utrecht, The Netherlands: Utrecht University.

Reiss, S. P. (2009). Semantics-based code search. In *Proceedings of the 31st International Conference on Software Engineering (ICSE) 2009,* (pp. 243-253). ICSE.

Reiss, S. (2006). Incremental maintenance of software artifacts. *IEEE Transactions on Software Engineering, 32*(9), 682. doi:10.1109/TSE.2006.91

REMICS. (2012). *Reuse and migration of legacy applications to interoperable cloud services.* Retrieved from http://www.remics.eu/

Ricca, F., & Marchetto, A. (2009). A quick and dirty meet-in-the-middle approach for migrating to SOA. In *Proceedings of the Joint International and Annual ERCIM Workshops on Principles of Software Evolution (IWPSE) and Software Evolution (Evol) Workshops.* IWPSE.

Richardson, L., & Ruby, S. (2007). *RESTful web services.* New York, NY: O'Reilly.

Robinson, I. (2006). Consumer-driven contracts: A service evolution pattern. *MartinFowler.com.* Retrieved October 6, 2011, from http://www.martinfowler.com/articles/consumerDrivenContracts.html

Rockwell, G. (2006). TAPoR: Building a portal for text analysis. In Siemens, R., & Moorman, D. (Eds.), *Mind Technologies: Humanities Computing and the Canadian Academic Community* (pp. 285–299). Calgary, Canada: University of Calgary Press.

Rodriguez, J. M., Crasso, M., Zunino, A., & Campo, M. (2010). Automatically detecting opportunities for web service descriptions improvement. In *Proceedings of the 10th IFIP WG 6.11 Conference on e-Business, e-Services, and e-Society (I3E 2010),* (vol 432, pp. 139-150). Buenos Aires, Argentina: Springer.

Rodriguez, J. M., Crasso, M., Mateos, C., Zunino, A., & Campo, M. (2010). The EasySOC project: A rich catalog of best practices for developing web service applications. In *Proceedings of Jornadas Chilenas de Computación (JCC) - INFONOR 2010* (pp. 33–42). Antofagasta, Chile: SCC. doi:10.1109/SCCC.2010.12

Rodriguez, J. M., Crasso, M., Zunino, A., & Campo, M. (2010). Improving web service descriptions for effective service discovery. *Science of Computer Programming, 75*(11), 1001–1021. doi:10.1016/j.scico.2010.01.002

Saha, D., & Mukherjee, A. (2003). Pervasive computing: A paradigm for the 21st century. *IEEE Computer, 36,* 25–31. doi:10.1109/MC.2003.1185214

Saif, U., & Greaves, D. (2001). Communication primitives for ubiquitous systems or RPC considered harmful. In *Proceedings of the International Conference Distributed Computing Systems Workshop,* (pp. 240-245). IEEE Computer Society Press. Open Group. (2009). *TOGAF version 9 – The open group architecture framework (TOGAF)*. New York, NY: The Open Group.

Salama, R., & Aly, S. G. (2008). *A decision making tool for the selection of service oriented-based legacy systems modernization strategies.* Paper presented at the The International Conference on Software Engineering Research and Practice. Las Vegas, NV.

Salehie, M., & Tahvildari, L. (2009). Self-adaptive software: Landscape and research challenges. *ACM Transactions on Autonomous and Adaptive Systems, 4*(2).

Sarkar, S., & Rama, G. (2007). API-based and information: Theoretic metrics for measuring the quality of software modularization. *IEEE Transactions on Software Engineering, 33*(1), 14–32. doi:10.1109/TSE.2007.256942

Šaša, A., & Juric, M. (2010). Version management of service interfaces in SOA. In S. S. Yau, E. Geig, M.-C. Shan, & P. Hung (Eds.), *Proceedings of the 2010 Sixth World Congress on Services,* (pp. 150–151). Washington, DC: IEEE Computer Society Press.

Satyanarayanan, M. (2002). Pervasive computing: Vision and challenges. *IEEE Personal Communications, 8,* 10–17. doi:10.1109/98.943998

Schelp, J., & Aier, S. (2009). SOA and EA-sustainable contributions for increasing corporate agility. In *Proceedings of the 42nd Hawaii International Conference on System Sciences*. IEEE.

Schmidt, D. C. (2006). Guest editor's introduction: Model-driven engineering. *Computer, 39*(2), 25-31.

Schwaber, K. (2004). *Agile project management with scrum*. Redmond, WA: Microsoft Press.

Seacord, R. C., Plakosh, D., & Lewis, G. A. (2003). *Modernizing legacy systems*. Boston, MA: Addison-Wesley.

Seacord, R. C., Plakosh, D., & Lewis, G. A. (2003). *Modernizing legacy systems: Software technologies, engineering processes, and business practices*. Reading, MA: Addison-Wesley Professional.

SEMbySEM. (2007). *Service management by semantics.* Retrieved from http://www.sembysem.org/

Servicifi. (2010). *ServiciFi: Decomposing monolithic software systems in the finiancial domain.* Retrieved March 26, 2012, from http://servicifi.org/

Shang, W., Jiang, Z. M., Adams, B., & Hassan, A. E. (2009). MapReduce as a general framework to support research in mining software repositories (MSR). In *Proceedings of the 6th IEEE International Working Conference on Mining Software Repositories,* (pp. 21–30). Washington, DC: IEEE Computer Society.

Simon, F., Seng, O., & Mohaut, T. (2006). *Code-quality-management*. Heidelberg, Germany: Dpunkt.

Slatkin, B. (2009). Building scalable, complex apps on app engine. *Google IO 2009*. Retrieved on January 2011 from http://www.google.com/events/io/2009/sessions/BuildingScalableComplexApps.html

Smit, M., Nisbet, A., Stroulia, E., Iszlai, G., & Edgar, A. (2009). Toward a simulation-generated knowledge base of service performance. In *Proceedings of the 4th International Workshop on Middleware for Service Oriented Computing*. New York, NY: ACM.

Smith, D., & Lewis, G. (2007). *Standards for service-oriented systems.* Paper presented at the 11th European Conference on Software Maintenance and Reengineering (CSMR 2010). Amsterdam, The Netherlands.

Smith, D., O'Brien, L., & Bergey, J. (2002). Using the options analysis for reengineering (OAR) method for mining components for a product line. In *Proceedings of the Software Product Lines.* Software Product Lines.

Sneed, H. (1996). *Encapsulating legacy software for re-use in client/server systems.* Paper presented at Working Conference on Software Reverse Engineering (WCRE 1996). Monterey, CA.

Sneed, H. (2000). Encapsulation of legacy software – A technique for reusing legacy software components. In Verhoef (Ed.), *Annals of Software Engineering,* (vol 9, pp. 113-132). Amsterdam, The Netherlands: Baltzer.

Sneed, H. (2005). *An incremental approach to system re-placement and integration.* Paper presented at 9th European Conference on Software Maintenance and Reengineering (CSMR 2005). Manchester, UK.

Sneed, H. (2006). Integrating legacy software into a service oriented architecture. In G. Visaggio, G. A. Di Lucca, & N. Gold (Eds.), *Proceedings of the 10th European Conference on Software Maintenance and Reengineering (CSMR 2006),* (pp. 3–14). Washington, DC: IEEE Computer Society Press.

Sneed, H. (2007). *Migrating to web services: A research framework.* Paper presented at the International Workshop on SOA Maintenance Evolution (SOAM 2007), 11th European Conference on Software Maintenance and Re-engineering (CSMR 2007). Amsterdam, The Netherlands.

Sneed, H. (2010). Measuring web service interfaces. In *Proceedings of the 12th IEEE International Symposium on Web Systems Evolution,* (pp. 111–115). IEEE Press.

Sneed, H. (2010). *SOA integration as an alternative to source migration.* Paper presented at SOAME Workshop. Timisoara, Romania.

Sneed, H. (2011). SOA integration as an alternative to source migration. In G. A. Lewis, D. B. Smith, & K. Kontogiannis (Eds.), *Proceedings of the Fourth International Workshop on a Research Agenda for Maintenance and Evolution of Service-Oriented Systems (MESOA 2010),* (pp. 41–48). Pittsburgh, PA: Carnegie Mellon University.

Sneed, H. M. (2006). Integrating legacy software into a service oriented architecture. In *Proceedings of the 10th European Conference on Software Maintenance and Reengineering (CSMR) 2006,* (pp. 4-14). CSMR.

Sneed, H. M. (2008). COB2WEB: A toolset for migrating to web services. In *Proceedings of the 10th International Symposium on Web Site Evolution (WSE 2008).* WSE.

Sneed, H., & Majnar, R. (1998). *A case study in software wrapping.* Paper presented at International Conference on Software Maintenance (ICSM 1998). Washington, DC.

Sneed, H., & Nyary, E. (1999). *Salvaging an ancient legacy system at the German foreign office.* Paper presented at the International Conference on Software Maintenance (ICSM 1999). Oxford, UK.

Sneed, H. (1991). Economics of software re-engineering. *International Journal of Software Maintenance, 3*(3), 129.

Sneed, H. (1995). Understanding software through numbers. *International Journal of Software Maintenance, 7*(6), 405–427. doi:10.1002/smr.4360070604

Sneed, H. (1998). Measuring reusability of legacy software systems. *International Journal of Software Process, 4*(1), 43–54.

Sneed, H. (2009). A pilot project for migrating COBOL code to web services. *International Journal on Software Tools for Technology Transfer, 11,* 441–451. doi:10.1007/s10009-009-0128-z

Sneed, H. M. (1995). Planning the reengineering of legacy systems. *IEEE Software, 12*(1), 24–34. doi:10.1109/52.363168

Sneed, H. M. (1995). Understanding software through numbers: A metric based approach to program comprehension. *Journal of Software Maintenance: Research and Practice, 7*(6), 405–419. doi:10.1002/smr.4360070604

Sneed, H. M. (2009). A pilot project for migrating COBOL code to web services. *International Journal on Software Tools for Technology Transfer, 11*(6), 441–451. doi:10.1007/s10009-009-0128-z

Sneed, H. M., Wolf, E., & Heilmann, H. (2010). *Softwaremigration in der praxis: Übertragung alter softwaresysteme in eine moderne umgebung.* Heidelberg, Germany: Dpunkt.

Sneed, H., & Merey, A. (1985). Automated software quality assurance. *IEEE Transactions on Software Engineering, 11*(9), 909–916. doi:10.1109/TSE.1985.232548

Sneed, H., & Sneed, S. (2003). *Web-basierte systemintegration*. Wiesbaden, Germany: Vieweg Verlag. doi:10.1007/978-3-322-89822-7

Solomon, A., & Litoiu, M. (2011). Using simulation models to evolve business processes. In G. A. Lewis, D. B. Smith, & K. Kontogiannis (Eds.), *Proceedings of the Fourth International Workshop on a Research Agenda for Maintenance and Evolution of Service-Oriented Systems (MESOA 2010)*, (pp. 9–21). Pittsburgh, PA: Carnegie Mellon University.

Sommerville, J. (2006). *Software engineering* (8th ed.). Reading, MA: Addison-Wesley.

Spanoudakis, G., & Zisman, A. (2010). Discovering services during service-based system design using UML. *IEEE Transactions on Software Engineering, 36*(3), 371–389. doi:10.1109/TSE.2009.88

Sparx Systems. (2010). *XML schema generation*. Retrieved September 28, 2011, from http://www.sparxsystems.com.au/resources/xml_schema_generation.html

Spohrer, J., Maglio, P. P., Bailey, J., & Gruhl, D. (2007). Steps toward a science of service systems. *IEEE Computer, 40*(1), 71–77. doi:10.1109/MC.2007.33

Springsource.org. (2011). *Spring web flow 2*. Retrieved March 19, 2012, from http://www.springsource.org/webflow

Stahl, T., Voelter, M., Bettin, J., & Stockfleth, B. (2006). *Model-driven software development: Technology, engineering, management*. Hoboken, NJ: John Wiley & Sons.

Stein, R., & Zacharias, V. (2010). RDF on cloud number nine. In Proceedings of the Workshop on NeFoRS: New Forms of Reasoning for the Semantic Web: Scalable and Dynamic. IEEE.

Stevens, W., Myers, G., & Constantine, L. (1974). Structured design complexity. *IBM Systems Journal, 13*(2), 115–138. doi:10.1147/sj.132.0115

Stroulia, E., & Wang, Y. (2005). Structural and semantic matching for assessing web service similarity. *International Journal of Cooperative Information Systems, 14*(4), 407–438. doi:10.1142/S0218843005001213

Sward, R. E., & Whitacre, K. J. (2008). A multi-language service-oriented architecture using an enterprise service bus. In M. B. Feldman & L. C. Baird (Eds.), *SIGAda 2008: Proceedings of the 2008 ACM Annual International Conference on SIGAda,* (pp. 85–90). New York, NY: Association for Computing Machinery.

Swissql. (2010). *SwiSQL migration solution – Database migration tools*. Retrieved December 2010 from www.swissql.com/dbmigration-tool-ds.pdf

Teppe, W. (2010). Wiedergewinnung von informationen über legacy-systeme in reengineeringprojekten. *Softwaretechnik-Trends, 30*(2), 68–69.

Tolk, A. (2006). What comes after the semantic web - PADS implications for the dynamic web. In *Proceedings of the 20th Workshop on Principles of Advanced and Distributed Simulation,* (pp. 55-62). IEEE Computer Society Press.

Toshniwal, R., & Agrawal, D. (2004). Tracing the roots of markup languages. *Communications of the ACM, 47*(5), 95–98. doi:10.1145/986213.986218

Tran, H., Zdun, U., & Dustdar, S. (2011). VbTrace: Using view-based and model-driven development to support traceability in process-driven SOAs. *Software & Systems Modeling, 10*(1), 5–29. doi:10.1007/s10270-009-0137-0

Umar, A., & Zordan, A. (2009). Reengineering for service oriented architectures: A strategic decision model for integration versus migration. *Journal of Systems and Software, 82*, 448–462. doi:10.1016/j.jss.2008.07.047

University of Limerick. (2011). *CSIS - Department of computer science and information systems*. Retrieved March 19, 2012, from http://www.csis.ul.ie/

Upadhyaya, B., Zou, Y., Xiao, H., Ng, J., & Lau, A. (2011). Migration of SOAP-based services to RESTful services. In *Proceedings of the 13th IEEE International Symposium on Web Systems Evolution,* (pp. 105–114). IEEE.

UPnP Forum. (2012). *Universal plug 'n play specifications*. Retrieved from http://upnp.org/sdcps-and-certification/standards/

Van den Bos, G., Knapp, S., & Doe, J. (2001). Role of reference elements in the selection of resources by psychology undergraduates. [from http://jbr.org/articles.html]. *Journal of Bibliographic Research, 5*, 117–123. Retrieved October 13, 2001

Van den Heuvel, W., Zimmermann, O., Leymann, F., Lago, P., Schieferdecker, I., Zdun, U., & Avgeriou, P. (2009). Software service engineering: Tenets and challenges. In *Proceedings of the 2009 ICSE Workshop on Principles of Engineering Service Oriented Systems (PESOS) 2009,* (pp. 26-33). ICSE.

Van Geet, J., & Demeyer, S. (2007). Lightweight visualizations of COBOL code for supporting migration to SOA. *Electronic Communications of the EASST, 8.*

van Geet, J., & Demeyer, S. (2010). Reverse engineering on the mainframe: Lessons learned from in vivo research. *IEEE Software, 27*(4), 30–36. doi:10.1109/MS.2010.65

van Sinderen, M. (2008). Challenges and solutions in enterprise computing. *Enterprise Information System, 2*(4), 341–346. doi:10.1080/17517570802442063

Varia, J. (2010). *Amazon web services - Migrating your existing applications to the AWS cloud.* Retrieved March 23, 2012, from http://media.amazonwebservices.com/CloudMigration-main.pdf

Vashishtha, H., & Stroulia, E. (2011). Enhancing query support in HBase via an extended coprocessors framework. In *Proceedings of the 4th European Conference towards a Service-Based Internet,* (pp. 75–87). Berlin, Germany: Springer-Verlag.

Vashishtha, H., Smit, M., & Stroulia, E. (2010). Moving text analysis tools to the cloud. In *Proceedings of the IEEE Congress on Services,* (p. 107-114). Los Alamitos, CA: IEEE Computer Society.

Vemuri, P. (2008). IEEE TENCON - 2008 Modernizing a legacy system to SOA - Feature analysis approach. In *Proceedings of the TENCON 2008 - 2008 IEEE Region 10 Conference.* IEEE Press.

Villegas, N. M., & Müller, H. A. (2011). Context-driven adaptive monitoring for supporting SOA governance. In G. A. Lewis, D. B. Smith, & K. Kontogiannis (Eds.), *Proceedings of the Fourth International Workshop on a Research Agenda for Maintenance and Evolution of Service-Oriented Systems (MESOA 2010),* (pp. 111–133). Pittsburgh, PA: Carnegie Mellon University.

Vinoski, S. (2005). RPC under fire. *IEEE Internet Computing, 9*(5), 93–95. doi:10.1109/MIC.2005.108

Vinoski, S. (2008). Serendipitous reuse. *IEEE Internet Computing, 12*(1), 84–87. doi:10.1109/MIC.2008.20

W3C RDB2RDF Incubator Group. (2009). *A survey of current approaches for mapping relational database to RDF.* Retrieved from http://www.w3c.org

W3C. (2007). *Semantic annotations for WSDL and XML schema.* Retrieved September 28, 2011, from http://www.w3.org/TR/sawsdl/

W3C. (2007). *Web services description language (WSDL) version 2.0 part 1: Core language.* Retrieved September 28, 2011, from http://www.w3.org/TR/wsdl20/

W3C. (2009). *OWL 2 web ontology language.* Retrieved September 28, 2011, from http://www.w3.org/TR/2009/REC-owl2-overview-20091027/

Wahli, U., Ackerman, L., Di Bari, A., Hodgkinson, G., Kesterton, A., Olson, L., & Portier, B. (2007). *Building SOA solutions using the rational SDP. IBM Redbooks: SG24-7356-00.* Armonk, NY: IBM International Technical Support Organization.

Waldo, J., Wyant, G., Wollrath, A., & Kendall, S. (1994). *A note on distributed computing.* Technical Report SMLI TR-94-29. Mountain View, CA: Sun Microsystems, Inc. Retrieved February 1st, 2012, from https://ftp.uwsg.indiana.edu/kde/devel/smli_tr-94-29.pdf

Wang, Y., & Stroulia, E. (2003). Semantic structure matching for assessing web-service similarity. In *Proceedings of the 1st International Conference on Service Oriented Computing (ICSOC) 2003,* (pp. 194-207). ICSOC.

Warren, I., & Ransom, J. (2002). Renaissance: A method to support software system evolution. In *Proceedings of the 26th Annual International Computer Software and Applications Conference.* IEEE.

Webber, J., Parastatidis, S., & Robinson, I. (2010). *REST in practice.* Sebastopol, CA: O'Reilly Media.

Wikipedia. (2011). *Mashup (web application hybrid).* Retrieved October 6, 2011, from http://en.wikipedia.org/wiki/Mashup_%28web_application_hybrid%29

Winter, A., & Ziemann, J. (2007). Model-based migration to service-oriented architectures: A project outline. In H. M. Sneed (Ed.), *CSMR 2007 Workshop on a "Research Agenda for Service-Oriented Architecture Maintenance"*, (pp. 107–110). Amsterdam, The Netherlands: Vrije Universiteit Amsterdam.

Winter, A., & Zillmann, C. (2011). *The SOAMIG process model in industrial applications*. Paper presented at 15th European Conference on Software Maintenance and Reengineering. Oldenburg, Germany.

Winter, A., Zillmann, C., Fuhr, A., Horn, T., Riediger, V., Herget, A., et al. (2011). The SOAMIG process model in industrial applications. In T. Mens, Y. Kanellopoulos, & A. Winter (Eds.), *Proceedings of the 15th European Conference on Software Maintenance and Reengineering,* (pp. 339-342). Washington, DC: IEEE Computer Society Press.

Worms, K. (2011). *Challenges for maintenance and evolution of service-oriented systems at credit Suisse.* Paper presented at the Fourth International Workshop on a Research Agenda for Maintenance and Evolution of Service-Oriented Systems (MESOA 2010). Timisoara, Romania.

Wu, B., Lawless, D., Bisbal, J., Grimson, J., Wade, V., O'Sullivan, D., et al. (1997). Legacy systems migration - A method and its tool-kit framework. In *Proceedings of the Joint 1997 Asia Pacific Software Engineering Conference and International Computer Science Conference*. IEEE.

Wu, B., Lawless, D., Bisbal, J., Richardson, R., Grimson, J., Wade, V., & O'Sullivan, D. (1997). The butterfly methodology: A gateway-free approach for migrating legacy information systems. In *Proceedings of the Third IEEE International Conference on Engineering of Complex Computer Systems (ICECCS),* (pp. 200–205). Washington, DC: IEEE Computer Society Press.

Wurms, K. (2010). *Experience of a Swiss bank in migrating to SOA*. Paper presented at 25th International Conference on Software Maintenance (ICSM 2010). Timisoara, Romania.

Xiao, H., Guo, J., & Zou, Y. (2007). Supporting change impact analysis for service oriented business applications. In *Proceedings of the International Workshop on Systems Development in SOA Environments (SDSOA 2007), ICSE Workshops 2007*. Washington, DC: IEEE Computer Society Press.

Xu, X., Zhu, L., Liu, Y., & Staples, M. (2008). Resource-oriented architecture for business processes. In *Proceedings of the Software Engineering Conference,* (pp. 395-402). IEEE Computer Society Press.

Xu, X., Zhu, L., Kannengiesser, U., & Liu, Y. (2010). An architectural style for process-intensive web information systems. *Lecture Notes in Computer Science, 6488,* 534–547. doi:10.1007/978-3-642-17616-6_47

Yourdon, E., & Constantine, L. L. (1979). *Structured design: Fundamentals of a discipline of computer program and systems design.* Upper Saddle River, NJ: Prentice-Hall, Inc.

Zachos, K., Maiden, N. A. M., & Howells-Morris, R. (2008). Discovering web services to improve requirements specifications: Does it help? In B. Paech & C. Rolland (Eds.), *Proceedings of the 14th International Working Conference on Requirements Engineering: Foundation for Software Quality (REFSQ) 2008,* (pp. 168-182). REFSQ.

Zachos, K., Maiden, N. A. M., Zhu, X., & Jones, S. (2007). Discovering web services to specify more complete system requirements. In J. Krogstie, A. L. Opdahl, & G. Sindre (Eds.), *Proceedings of the 19th International Conference on Advanced Information Systems Engineering (CAiSE) 2007,* (pp. 142-157). CAiSE.

Zawawy, H., Mylopoulos, J., & Mankovski, S. (2011). Requirements-driven framework for root cause analysis in SOA environments. In G. A. Lewis, D. B. Smith, & K. Kontogiannis (Eds.), *Proceedings of the Fourth International Workshop on a Research Agenda for Maintenance and Evolution of Service-Oriented Systems (MESOA 2010),* (pp. 22–40). Pittsburgh, PA: Carnegie Mellon University.

Zdun, U. (2002). *Reengineering to the web – A reference architecture*. Paper presented at 6th European Conference on Software Maintenance and Reengineering (CSMR 2002). Budapest, Hungary.

Zhang, L., Arsanjani, A., Allam, A., Lu, D., & Chee, Y. (2007). Variation-oriented analysis for SOA solution design. In E. Feig & H. T. Kung (Eds.), *Proceedings of the 2007 IEEE International Conference on Services Computing (SCC 2007),* (pp. 560–568). Washington, DC: IEEE Computer Society Press.

Zhang, Z., & Yang, H. (2004). Incubating services in legacy systems for architectural migration. In *Proceedings of the 11th Asia-Pacific Software Engineering Conference (APSEC) 2004,* (pp. 196-203). APSEC.

Zhang, Z., Liu, R., & Yang, H. (2005). Service identification and packaging in service oriented reengineering. In *Proceedings of the 7th International Conference on Software Engineering and Knowledge Engineering (SEKE)*. SEKE.

Zhang, Z., Liu, R., & Yang, H. (2005). Service identification and packaging in service oriented reengineering. In W. C. Chu, N. J. Juzgado, & W. E. Wong (Eds.), *Proceedings of the 7th International Conference on Software Engineering and Knowledge Engineering (SEKE),* (pp. 241-249). Skokie, IL: Knowledge Systems Institute.

Zhang, Z., Yang, H., & Chu, W. C. (2006). Extracting reusable object-oriented legacy code segments with combined formal concept analysis and slicing techniques for service integration. In *Proceedings of the 6th International Conference on Quality Software*. IEEE.

Zhang, Z., Yang, H., Zhou, D., & Zhong, S. (2010). A SOA based approach to user-oriented system migration. In G. Min & T. El-Ghazawi (Eds.), *Proceedings of the 2010 IEEE 10th International Conference on Computer and Information Technology (CIT),* (pp. 1486–1491). Washington, DC: IEEE Computer Society Press.

Zhang, Z., Yang, H., Zhou, D., & Zhong, S. (2010). A SOA based approach to user-oriented system migration. In *Proceedings of the 2010 10th IEEE International Conference on Computer and Information Technology (CIT 2010)*. IEEE Press.

Zhang, C., & De Sterck, H. (2010). Supporting multi-row distributed transactions with global snapshot isolation using bare-bones HBase. In *Proceedings of Grid 2010*. Grid. doi:10.1109/GRID.2010.5697970

Zhang, Z., Zhou, D.-D., Yang, H.-J., & Zhong, S.-C. (2010). A service composition approach based on sequence mining for migrating e-learning legacy system to SOA. *International Journal of Automatic Computing, 7,* 584–595. doi:10.1007/s11633-010-0544-2

Ziemann, J., Leyking, K., Kahl, T., & Dirk, W. (2006). *Enterprise model driven migration from legacy to SOA.* Paper presented at the Software Reengineering and Services Workshop. Passau, Germany.

Ziemann, J., Leyking, K., Kahl, T., & Werth, D. (2006). SOA development based on enterprise models and existing IT systems. In Cunningham, P. (Ed.), *Exploiting the Knowledge Economy: Issues, Applications and Case Studies*. Amesterdam, The Netherlands: IOS Press.

Zillmann, C., Winter, A., Herget, A., Teppe, W., Theurer, M., Fuhr, A., et al. (2011). The SOAMIG process model in industrial applications. In *Proceedings of the 15th European Conference on Software Maintenance and Reengineering (CSMR 2011)*. CSMR.

Zillmann, C., Gringel, P., & Winter, A. (2010). Iterative zielarchitekturdefinition in SOAMIG. *Softwaretechnik-Trends, 30*(2), 72–73.

Zimmermann, Y., Uhlig, D., & Kaiser, U. (2010). Tool- und schnittstellenarchitektur für eine SOA-migration. *Softwaretechnik-Trends, 30*(2), 66–67.

Zou, J., Mei, J., & Wang, Y. (2010). From representational state transfer to accountable state transfer architecture. In *Proceedings of the International Conference on Web Services,* (pp. 299-306). IEEE Computer Society Press.

Zyp, K. (Ed.). (2010). A JSON media type for describing the structure and meaning of JSON documents. *Internet Engineering Task Force*. Retrieved August 26, 2011, from http://tools.ietf.org/html/draft-zyp-json-schema-03

About the Contributors

Anca Daniela Ionita is Professor at University "Politehnica" of Bucharest, Automatic Control and Computers Faculty, where she has worked since 1990, soon after obtaining her MSc. Degree. In 1994, she obtained a Ph.D. degree in "Automated Systems" at the same university. Between 2004 and 2006, Dr. Ionita was Researcher at University Joseph Fourier, Grenoble, with a Marie Curie Individually-Driven Fellowship. Then, she returned to Romania as Professor at University "Politehnica" of Bucharest, and collaborator of SIVECO Romania, playing major roles in national and European research projects. She teaches Software Engineering and Model Driven Engineering, in Romanian, English, and French, and is responsible of the educational work package in a Romanian strategic project that promotes service innovation through open and continuous education. She serves in several editorial advisory boards, programme, and organization committees of international conferences and workshops. Her current research is focused on service engineering and management, business process modeling, and model driven engineering.

Marin Litoiu is a Professor and the Director of Adaptive Systems Research Lab, York University, Toronto, Canada. He holds Doctoral degrees from University Politehnica of Bucharest and Carleton University of Ottawa. Prior to joining York, he was a Senior Research Staff Member with Centre for Advanced Studies, IBM Toronto Lab, where he led the research programs in Software Engineering, System Management, and Autonomic Computing. He was the Director of Research for Centre of Excellence for Research in Advanced Systems (CERAS) and Chair of the Board of Directors for Consortium for Software Engineering Research (CSER). Dr. Litoiu's current research interests include adaptive and autonomic systems, cloud computing and Web technologies, performance modeling and evaluation, and software engineering.

Grace Lewis is a Senior Member of the Technical Staff at the Software Engineering Institute (SEI) at Carnegie Mellon University (CMU), in the Research, Technology, and Systems Solutions (RTSS) Program. She is part the deputy for the Advanced Mobile Systems (AMS) initiative and the technical lead for the Edge-Enabled Tactical Systems Project. Her current interests and projects are in mobile computing, cloud computing, and Service-Oriented Architecture (SOA). Her latest publications include multiple reports and articles on these subjects and a book in the SEI Software Engineering Series. She is also a member of the technical faculty for the Master in Software Engineering program at CMU. Grace holds a B.Sc. in Systems Engineering and an Executive MBA from Icesi University in Cali, Colombia, and a Master in Software Engineering from CMU.

* * *

Juncal Alonso, Master Engineer in Telecommunications from the University of the Basque Country, is a R&D Engineer working at the ICT Division/European Software Institute projects area of TEC-NALIA. She has a two-year experience as ICT Consultant for private telecommunication companies. After this, she joined ESI in 2007, where she has worked as researcher in several projects (both national and international) such as COIN (FP7), DiYSE (ITEA2), mCloud (Spanish Government). Her area of research includes information systems for interoperability and collaboration, business process management, new organizational forms and Future Internet applications in the Web. Currently, she is part of the "Migration to Cloud" team in TECNALIA, where she is developing research activities in areas such as: feasibility analysis for the software modernization process, architectures for multi-tenant applications and databases, and software modernization methodologies.

Michael Athanasopoulos is a Ph.D. candidate at the Department of Electrical and Computer Engineering at the National Technical University of Athens, Greece. His research interests include software architectures for network-centric computing systems, service-oriented computing, model-driven engineering, and SOA programming models, and he is currently working on his dissertation on the adaptation of procedural service-oriented systems to architectures that conform to the REST architectural style. Michael is also a PhD Fellowship student at Center of Advanced Studies, IBM Canada. Previously, he worked in the banking sector as a Software Engineer. He graduated from the School of Electrical and Computer Engineering at the National Technical University of Athens.

Gorka Benguria, Computer Engineer (BSc) from the University of Deusto (Bilbao, Spain), is a R&D Engineer working at the ICT Division/European Software Institute projects area of TECNALIA. He has a twelve-year experience in consultancy and research projects in the IT. He has worked in consultancy and tooling of SPI methodologies and models such as EFQM, SPICE, and CMMi. He has also worked in methodologies, tools, and languages for SOA, being involved in the development of the OMG SoaML specification. Currently, he is part of the "Migration to Cloud" team in TECNALIA. He is involved in the European REMICS Project that investigates tools, methodologies, and languages to support the migration of the legacy systems in diverse languages (i.e. COBOL, PLSQL, or Java) to the Cloud. He is also involved in the FACIT project that deals with the SaaS supported application of software methodologies and models in SMEs.

Shreyansh Bhatt obtained his Masters of Technology from Dhirubhai Ambani Institute of Information and Communication Technology, Gandhinagar. He is working in a protocol development team at Stoke Networks, Bangalore. His research interests includes Semantic Web, cloud computing, large scale distributed cloud datastores.

Minal Bhise obtained her Masters of Engineering and PhD in Computer Science from Birla Institute of Technology and Science, Pilani. She has been working in distributed databases, Semantic Web, and cloud databases. She is a faculty at DA-IICT, Gandhinagar, India.

Chris Brealey is a Senior Technical Staff Member with IBM Software, Rational Enterprise Architecture, Design, and Construction. Chris is based at the IBM Toronto Canada Lab. He is a Chief Architect for Rational Application Developer, with focus on SOA and SCA, cloud computing, mobile computing, and application lifecycle management. He is a regular mentor on fellowship projects in the Centers for Advanced Studies (CAS). Chris previously led the architecture and delivery of the RAD Web services tools. Chris joined IBM in 1989 after his graduation from the University of Victoria with a BSc in Computer Science.

Marcelo Campo (http://www.exa.unicen.edu.ar/~mcampo) received a Ph.D. degree in Computer Science from the Universidade Federal do Rio Grande do Sul, Brazil, in 1997. He is a full Associate Professor at the UNICEN, Head of the ISISTAN, and member of the CONICET. His research interests include intelligent aided software engineering, software architecture, and frameworks.

Sanjay Chaudhary obtained his PhD in Computer Science from Gujarat Vidyapeeth. His research areas are distributed computing, service-oriented computing, and information, and Communication Technology (ICT) applications in agriculture. He is a Professor and Dean (Academic Programs) at Dhirubhai Ambani Institute of Information and Communication Technology (DA-IICT), Gandhinagar, India.

Marco Crasso (http://www.exa.unicen.edu.ar/~mcrasso) received a Ph.D. degree in Computer Science from the UNICEN in 2010. He is a member of the ISISTAN and the CONICET. His research interests include Web service discovery and programming models for SOA.

José C. Delgado is an Associate Professor at the Computer Science and Engineering Department of the Instituto Superior Técnico (Lisbon Technical University), Lisbon, Portugal, where he earned the Ph.D. degree in 1988. He lectures courses in the areas of Computer Architecture, Information Technology, and Service Engineering. He has performed several management roles in his faculty, namely Director of the Taguspark campus, near Lisbon, and Coordinator of the B.Sc. and M.Sc. in Computer Science and Engineering at that campus. He has been the coordinator of and researcher in several research projects, both national and European. As an author, his publications include one book, several book chapters, and more than 40 papers in international refereed conferences and journals.

Uwe Erdmenger studied Computer Science at the Chemnitz University of Technology (Germany). In his diploma thesis, he analyzed the possibilities of modeling geometric data in a declarative manner. Since September 1996, he works as a Software Developer and Project Manager for pro et con, a company specialized in software migration, program analysis, and reverse engineering. In the last ten years, he has worked in various large migration projects for several companies and has developed tools for automation the migration process. His main interests are meta-tools for syntax graph modeling, declarative description of model-to-model transformation rules, and tools to process this transformation.

Marisa Escalante graduated as Computer Engineer (BSc) from the University of Deusto (Bilbao, Spain). In the first few years, Marisa worked in projects concerning the implementation of software process improvement programmes with a focus on the SME sector in the Spanish market. She worked mostly with SW-CMM®, SPICE (ISO/IEC 15504), and ISO 9001. In 1999, she joined the ESI Training Service Unit to work on the development of PEPIT. From 2002, she is working in the R&D department in EC funded projects and in national projects. Her main research focus is ICTs, software engineering, service engineering, and ambient intelligence. Currently, she is part of the "Migration to Cloud" team in TECNALIA, where she is working in several R&D projects in this area.

Jacky Estublier leads a research group on Software Engineering at Grenoble University, with a focus on large industrial applications. His research interest was originally on software configuration management, with the development of the Adèle configuration manager. Since the 2000, he focuses on process support, interoperability, development environments, and service technology. This trend of work contributes to model driven software engineering and dynamic systems fields. Recently, he was leading the design and development of the SAM and APAM service platforms. Dr. Estublier was a program committee member of all the major conferences in the field of software engineering and responsible of many European funded research projects.

Andreas Fuhr studied Computer Science (B.Sc.) at the Johannes-Gutenberg University of Mainz (Germany) and Computer Science (M.Sc.) at the University of Koblenz-Landau (Germany). In his Bachelor's thesis, he analyzed the potential of extending IBM's SOMA method by model-driven migration techniques. In his Master's thesis, he explored the identification of legacy code able to implement services by dynamic analysis and data mining techniques. Since April 2011, he is working as a Scientific Staff Member and PhD student at the Institute for Software Technology at the University of Koblenz-Landau. His main research interests are software engineering, model-driven software development, and data mining.

Cristian Gadea is an Electrical and Computer Engineering PhD student at the School of Information Technology and Engineering at the University of Ottawa, Canada, where he also obtained his undergraduate degree in Software Engineering (2007) and Master's degree in Computer Science (2010). Under the supervision of Professor Dan Ionescu, his Master's work resulted in the creation of an open and reusable architecture based on the publisher/subscriber messaging model that uses a collaborative Web-based environment to monitor and display data from multiple real-time sensor networks. His interests include Web 2.0, distributed systems, GIS, mobile computing, human-computer interaction, virtual environments, and video game technologies.

Michael Gebhart studied Computer Science at the University of Karlsruhe in Germany from 2003 to 2008. From 2008 to 2011, he did his PhD at the Faculty of Informatics at the Karlsruhe Institute of Technology (KIT). His research work focuses on software engineering and the design of distributed systems. He investigates the quality-oriented design of services in service-oriented architectures and the application of these methods on the design of cloud solutions. The motivation of this effort is to provide guidelines and metrics that help to design services with certain quality attributes, such as high flexibility and maintainability. The developed methodologies help to verify the fulfillment of these quality attributes based on formalized service design models. Today, Dr. Michael Gebhart continues his research and works as author, visiting lecturer, and consultant in the context of service-oriented architectures and the design of services.

Jurriaan Hage is an Assistant Professor at the Department of Information and Computing Sciences at Utrecht University, The Netherlands. His research focuses on static analysis including type and effect systems for (lazy) functional languages, feedback-oriented static analysis, and plagiarism detection. He is currently involved in three research projects on higher-ranked polyvariance, future internet testing, and software system evolution through servicification.

Tassilo Horn studied Computer Science at the University of Koblenz-Landau. In his diploma thesis, he developed an optimizer for the graph query language GReQL, which performs transformations on the syntax graph of the query. Some transformations, such as "selection as soon as possible" are also well known in other domains like databases, while others are special to the domain of GReQL and TGraphs. Since June 2008, he works as a Scientific Staff Member and PhD student at the Institute for Software Technology. His main research interests are graph querying and transformation techniques including their application in software reengineering and maintenance.

Andrei Idu is a Master's student in Business Informatics (MBI) at the Department of Information and Computing Sciences at Utrecht University, The Netherlands. Currently, he is working on his Master's thesis titled "A Method for ERP Software Product Data Reorganization and Migration" at AFAS Software B.V., The Netherlands.

Dan Ionescu, Professor and Director of the Network Computing and Control (NCCT) Research Laboratory of the University of Ottawa, received Dipl. Ing. and Dr. Ing. degrees from the Polytechnic Institute of Bucharest, Romania, and a Diploma in Mathematics from the University of Timisoara, Romania. He has been with the University of Ottawa since 1985, where he is currently Professor in Computer Engineering and the Director of the Network Computing and Control Technologies (NCCT) Laboratory. Dr. Dan Ionescu is a member of various IEEE, IFIP, and IFAC groups. His recent research works are oriented towards the control plane architectures for cloud applications, as well as application of control theory in the assurance of QoS-based services, formal methods for real-time and distributed systems, as well as towards distributed software technologies.

Slinger Jansen is an Assistant Professor at the Department of Information and Computing Sciences at Utrecht University, The Netherlands. His research focuses on software product management and software ecosystems, with a strong entrepreneurial component. He currently leads two research projects into the domains of variability in multi-tenancy architectures and software system evolution through servicification.

Uwe Kaiser studied Computer Science at the Technical University Dresden from 1973 until 1978. From 1978 until 1994, he worked in different positions at the Faculty for Computer Science at the Technical University Karl-Marx-Stadt/Chemnitz, among others as leader of the Department Programming Languages and Compiler. The topics of his doctorate and habilitation contain the design and the implementation of meta-tools for the development of compilers and reengineering tools from the engineering viewpoint. In 1994, he founded the company pro et con Innovative Informatikanwendungen GmbH, the Managing Director of which he is to this day. The company content is the development of tools for automated software migration based on scientific compiler building methods. The company pro et con GmbH realizes complex, commercial migration projects by using these tools.

Ravi Khadka is a PhD Researcher at the Department of Information and Computing Sciences at Utrecht University, The Netherlands. His main research focuses in Model-Driven Engineering (MDE), SOA, and service composition, and legacy to SOA migration. He completed his Master's in Computer Science from University of Twente, The Netherlands.

Kostas Kontogiannis is an Associate Professor at the Department of Electrical and Computer Engineering at the National Technical University of Athens, Greece. Previously, he was an Associate Professor at the Department of Electrical and Computer Engineering at the University of Waterloo, Canada, where he led for more than ten years the Software Re-Engineering Group. His current research interests focus on the design and development of tools for software re-engineering with particular emphasis on software transformations, and legacy software migration to network-centric computing platforms. Specific topics of interest and current work include techniques and tools for source code representation, recognition of programming patterns and idioms, system partitioning and clustering, quality preserving source code transformations, component-based software engineering, distributed objects, markup languages, and techniques for the integration of systems and services. Dr. Kontogiannis is also Visiting Scientist and Principal Investigator, at the Center for Advanced Studies, IBM Canada. He holds a B.Sc from the University of Patras, Greece, in Mathematics, a M.Sc from the Katholieke Universiteit Leuven, Belgium, in Computer Science, and a Ph.D from McGill University, Canada, also in Computer Science.

Cristian Mateos (http://www.exa.unicen.edu.ar/~cmateos) received a Ph.D. degree in Computer Science from the UNICEN, in 2008, and his M.Sc. in Systems Engineering in 2005. He is a full time Teacher Assistant at the UNICEN and member of the ISISTAN and the CONICET. He is interested in parallel/distributed programming, grid middlewares, and service-oriented computing.

Leire Orue-Echevarria graduated as Computer Engineer (BSc) from the University of Deusto (Bilbao, Spain) and Politecnico di Milano (Milan, Italy) in 1998. Her professional experience ranges from different sectors such as safety critical V&V or development of turnkey Web content management systems covering the whole software lifecycle from requirements to validation in different companies all over Europe (i.e. Spain, Germany, Austria). She started working at TECNALIA in 2008, where her main roles are as Senior CMMI Consultant and R&D Project Leader of projects at regional (SMART-WORK), national (mCloud), and European level (COIN). She is now leading the team "Migration to Cloud," and is focusing her research on software modernization techniques and tools, cloud architectural implications, and business models.

Volker Riediger is Senior Researcher and Lecturer at the Institute for Software Technology of the University of Koblenz, Germany. He holds a diploma in Computer Science and Linguistics. After 8 years in industry-development of scientific measurement and control systems, and software systems for the German public forestry administration, he received his PhD in Reverse Engineering of Preprocessor Languages at the University of Koblenz. Currently, his activities cover research on graph technology, application of scientific results in industry cooperation, and teaching in graduate and undergraduate classes. Volker Riediger is member of the GI (Gesellschaft für Informatik), Spokesman of the GI section SRE (Software Reengineering), and Lecturer at VWA (Verwaltungs- und Wirtschaftsakademie Koblenz).

Juan Manuel Rodriguez (http://www.exa.unicen.edu.ar/~jmrodri) is working on his Ph.D. Thesis about quality of Web services APIs at the UNICEN, being founded by the Argentinean National Council for Scientific and Technical Research (CONICET) and working under the supervision of Alejandro Zunino and Marcelo Campo. He holds a Systems Engineer degree from the UNICEN. He is a member of ISISTAN Research Institute.

Amir Saeidi is a PhD Researcher at the Department of Information and Computing Sciences at Utrecht University, The Netherlands. His main research focuses in program analysis and verification. He completed his Master's in Computer Science from Indian Institute of Technology, Delhi (IITD).

Gonzalo Salvatierra is currently working on his M.Sc. thesis about legacy COBOL system migration to service oriented platforms at UNICEN. He is working under the supervision of Marco Crasso and Cristian Mateos. He holds a Systems Engineer degree from the UNICEN.

Eric Simon holds a PhD from Grenoble University entitled "SAM: An Execution Environment for Dynamic and Heterogeneous Service-Oriented Applications," under the direction of Dr. Jacky Estublier, in which he designed and developed the Service Abstract Machine (SAM) platform. His research applies a model driven engineering approach to solve a number of issues arising in service technologies and more specifically, heterogeneity, distributed and dynamic execution, and run-time software engineering.

Michael Smit is a Province of Ontario Postdoctoral Fellow at York University in Toronto, Canada, and a member of the Adaptive Systems Research Lab led by Marin Litoiu. He completed his PhD with Eleni Stroulia at the University of Alberta in 2011. His research interests include autonomic/adaptive computing, cloud technologies, and service-oriented applications.

Dennis Smith recently retired from the Software Engineering Institute (SEI) at Carnegie Mellon University (CMU). He was the lead for System of Systems Practice (SoSP) initiative in the Research, Technology, and Systems Solutions (RTSS) Program, where he directed and conducted research related to engineering and organizational challenges in Systems of Systems (SoS) environments. Dennis co-organized the development a SOA research agenda and co-developed SMART, a method for migration of legacy systems to SOA environments. He holds an M.A. and PhD from Princeton University, and a B.A. from Columbia University.

Harry Sneed was born in Gulfport Mississippi in 1940, graduated from Sewanee Military Academy in 1958, served in the Army until 1965, and attended the University of Maryland, where he graduated with a Masters Degree in Public Administration and Information Sciences in 1969. He started his work in the IT field as a Programmer/Analyst with the U.S. Navy Dept. Later, he went to Germany and worked for Siemens as a Systems Programmer and Test Manager. From there he went to Budapest, Hungary, to lead a software lab and has been there ever since. In 2005, he chaired the International Conference on Software Maintenance. He has written 21 books in German language and published more than 400 articles and papers. He is a senior member of the IEEE from which he was given an award in 1996 for his contributions to Software Reverse- and Reengineering. In 2009, he received the Stevens Award for Outstanding Achievement.

Bogdan Solomon graduated with his Bachelor and Master's degrees in Software Engineering at University of Ottawa and is currently a PhD. student at University of Ottawa. His research in the Network Computing and Control Technologies Research Laboratory (NCCT Lab) at University of Ottawa under Professor Dan Ionescu is related to the area of Autonomic Computing with respect to the self-management of cloud-based applications. Previous work in the area of autonomic computing resulted in a pattern-based architecture and framework for autonomic systems, which controlled an application running on a cluster of IBM WebSphere servers. The architecture used Web service standards in order to decouple the various components of the framework.

Eleni Stroulia is a Professor and NSERC/AITF Industrial Research Chair on Service Systems Management (w/ support from IBM) with the Department of Computing Science at the University of Alberta. Her research addresses industrially relevant software engineering problems with automated methods, based on artificial intelligence techniques. Her team has produced automated methods for migrating legacy interfaces to Web-based front ends, and for analyzing and supporting the design evolution of object-oriented software. She has more recently been working on the development, composition, run-time monitoring, and adaptation of service-oriented applications, and on examining the role of Web 2.0 tools and virtual worlds for innovative service delivery.

Werner Teppe is Head of General Services and Projects at Development of Amadeus, Germany, in Bad Homburg. He is responsible for software engineering and large technical infrastructure projects. He holds a diploma in Computer Science from Technical University of Darmstadt. After university, he became a member of the core team at START Datentechnik, which built the first online reservation system (START System) for the entire travel industry in Germany. Later on, he was responsible for hardware, system software planning, databases, and data communication systems for the START data centers in Frankfurt. After this, he was responsible for large migration projects, which migrated the START system from a mainframe to a UNIX environment at the end. Within this project (ARNO), the operating system, the programming language, the data communication system, and the file system have been changed. In 2009, he chaired the Industrial Track of CSMR in Kaiserslautern. Werner is member of the GI special interest group on Software Reengineering (SRE). His main interests are transferring research results on software engineering into the industrial practice.

Himanshu Vashishtha is a Software Engineer at Cloudera. He completed his Masters in Computing Science at the University of Alberta in 2011, where he focused on cloud computing, particularly Hadoop and its related projects. His interests include distributed and parallel computing and software engineering. His future projects fall in the overlap of those two areas, continuing to build or migrate applications to distributed environments in order to increase their scalability and availability. He completed his undergraduate work at the Institute of Technology, Banaras Hindu University. He is an active open source contributor to the Apache HBase project.

Andreas Winter chairs the Software Engineering Group at Carl von Ossietzky University, Oldenburg. Current researches include software engineering foundations, modeling and meta-modeling, interoperability, and software evolution. He was involved in the development of the GUPRO meta-model-based framework for program comprehension, in the design of the graph interchange language GXL, and the development of the SOAMIG software migration methodology. He served as program- and general-chair of the European Conference on Software Maintenance and Reengineering (CSMR), and currently chairs the CSMR steering committee. He is a founding member of the GI Group on Software Reengineering and Member at Large of the IEEE-CS Technical Activities Committee.

Alejandro Zunino (http://www.exa.unicen.edu.ar/~azunino) received a Ph.D. degree in Computer Science from the UNICEN, in 2003, and his M.Sc. in Systems Engineering in 2000. He is a full Adjunct Professor at UNICEN and member of the ISISTAN and the CONICET. His research areas are Grid computing, service-oriented computing, Semantic Web services, and mobile agents.

Index

W